EARLY MODERN
EUROPEAN WITCHCRAFT

Early Modern European Witchcraft

Centres and Peripheries

EDITED BY
Bengt Ankarloo
AND
Gustav Henningsen

CLARENDON PRESS · OXFORD

Oxford University Press, Walton Street, Oxford OX2 6DP

Oxford New York Toronto
Delhi Bombay Calcutta Madras Karachi
Kuala Lumpur Singapore Hong Kong Tokyo
Nairobi Dar es Salaam Cape Town
Melbourne Auckland Madrid
and associated companies in
Berlin Ibadan

Oxford is a trade mark of Oxford University Press

Published in the United States
by Oxford University Press Inc., New York

British Library Cataloguing in Publication Data
Early modern European witchcraft: centres and
peripheries.
1. Europe. Witchcraft, History
I. Ankarloo, Bengt   II. Henningsen, Gustav
III. Haxornas Europa 1400–1700.   English
133.4'3'094
ISBN 0–19–820388–8

Library of Congress Cataloging in Publication Data
Haxornas Europa 1400–1700.   English.
Early modern European witchcraft.
Translation of: Haxornas Europa 1400–1700.
Bibliography: p.
Includes index.
1. Witchcraft—Europe—History. 2. Witchcraft—
Scandinavia—History. I. Ankarloo, Bengt, 1935–
II. Henningsen, Gustav. III. Title.
BF1584.E9H3913 1989 133.4'3'09409024 89–8540
ISBN 0–19–820388–8

3 5 7 9 10 8 6 4 2

Printed in Great Britain
on acid-free paper by
Biddles Ltd,
Guildford and King's Lynn

PREFACE

THE idea behind this volume began to take shape at meetings in Schleswig and in Paris in the autumn of 1980. In that year the University of Kiel arranged within its *Sonderforschungsgebiet Skandinavien und der Ostseeraum* a colloquium about 'Hexenprozesse in Norddeutschland und in Skandinavien'; and a few months later the small organization of scholars with the grand name 'The International Association for the History of Crime and Criminal Justice' met in Fernand Braudel's Maison des Sciences de l'Homme. In these two international settings Gustav Henningsen and I began discussing the possibility of collecting and publishing the Scandinavian contributions on a topic which had played such an important role in the historiography of the seventies: the great European witch persecutions. Two aims were set. First, the Scandinavian reports should be compared with those from other European peripheries; second, the new trends within historical anthropology and the history of *mentalités*, which were discernible around 1980, should be cross-fertilized with the regional surveys.

With these plans we turned to the major sponsors of humanistic research in Scandinavia, the Nordic Cultural Endowment and the national research councils of Denmark, Norway, and Sweden. With the exception of the Danish Council, which immediately gave a positive response, these scientific policy-makers coolly declined to co-operate. Now, in retrospect, we are thankful for this reverse, because it made us turn to a private foundation, the *Institutet för rättshistorisk forskning grundat av Gustav och Carin Olin*, which generously accepted our proposal. This enabled us to carry out our plans with the greatest possible freedom, both scholastic and financial. We were able to engage some of the most prominent scholars in the field, even though they were living far from our periphery.

In 1984 the Olin Foundation arranged an international witchcraft symposium in Stockholm. Most of the contributors to this volume took part on that occasion. Important additions have, however, been made in the form of articles about the Catholic and Protestant demonologists, and about the regional history of witchcraft in Portugal and Iceland. A conference report was published in Swedish in 1987. Peter Burke encouraged this English version.

Now that the work is complete, I must first of all thank Gustav Henningsen, my co-editor and friend over many years. Without his extensive international network of scholarly contacts, and his indefatigable energy, this project would certainly have assumed a much more modest shape. The two of us would like to express our profound appreciation of the support given us by the Olin Foundation. We also want to thank our own respective institutions—the Department of History in Lund and the Danish Folklore Archives in Copenhagen— for allowing us to use our time and their technical resources to finish the well-nigh impossible task first outlined on the back of the *Carte du Jour* in a cellar restaurant on boulevard Raspail.

Bengt Ankarloo

Lund
August 1988

ACKNOWLEDGEMENTS

THIS collection of essays was first published by the Olin Foundation in Swedish: Bengt Ankarloo and Gustav Henningsen (eds.), *Häxornas Europa 1400–1700: Historiska och antropologiska studier* (Rättshistoriska studier, 13; Lund, 1987).

Maia Madar's contribution was translated from Estonian by Rita Ilisson; Gustav Henningsen's and Jens Chr. V. Johansen's from Danish by Anne Born; Carlo Ginzburg's from Italian; Robert Muchembled's from French; and Julio Caro Baroja's from Spanish by Paul Falla.

The Bibliography was compiled by Peter Burke and the Index by Peter Rea.

CONTENTS

FIGURES

MAPS

TABLES

Introduction

GUSTAV HENNINGSEN AND
BENGT ANKARLOO

THE study of early modern European witchcraft has to a great extent been the domain of English and American scholars, and this has affected our general understanding and formulation of problems. Some of the questions in the current debate are simply wrong or have to be redefined because they were raised from an oblique, Anglo-Saxon angle. To take an example, the cross-cultural approach launched by the two English historians Alan Macfarlane and Keith Thomas has provoked a discussion of whether historical European witchcraft was comparable to African witchcraft today. As Robert Rowland demonstrates below, the real problem is that Macfarlane and Thomas drew on African anthropological studies for keys to interpret village-level witchcraft in sixteenth- and seventeenth-century Essex. 'Both authors appear to have been led astray by the undoubted similarities between what is the general situation in African witch-believing societies and what is, in the European context, a problematic special case', observes Rowland. English witches did not fly, did not go to the sabbath, copulate with devils, or feast on the flesh of murdered infants. What made the comparison easy, he concludes, was that 'most of the features which distinguished European from African witchcraft were absent in England'.

This leads directly to another question: the so-called 'peculiarities' of English witchcraft. That it greatly differed from Continental tradition is obvious, but England was not a special case. Most of what has so far been identified as peculiar to English witchcraft should from now on be considered as characteristic for large parts of northern Europe, as becomes clear from the contributions to Part III of this volume. In other words, while studying the case of England, several generations of Anglo-Saxon historians have unwittingly been engaged in a comparison between central and peripheral variants of a phenomenon common to most of Europe. The English 'peculiarities' could furthermore be extended to many lower-court trials on the Continent, where the accused were simply tried for *maleficium* and not asked demonological questions by their local judges.[1]

The Anglo-Saxon monopoly of witchcraft studies has probably also delayed the exploration of such an important question as the origin of the European witch persecution. Owing to linguistic barriers, international scholarship has concentrated on France and Germany. The inconvenience of such an arbitrary limitation has clearly been demonstrated during the last few years with the discovery that persecution of witches was initiated in Renaissance Italy, and not in medieval France as previously accepted. Over a decade ago two historians, an Englishman and an American, came independently to the conclusion that the few sources as we have about French witch-trials in the thirteenth and fourteenth centuries were nothing but forgeries.[2] The exposure has left us with a new chronology of the witch persecution beginning in the fifteenth century and thus coinciding with the early modern period of which it—as demonstrated by Robert Muchembled below—becomes highly symptomatic. How new the phenomenon was may be illustrated by the trial of Joan of Arc in Normandy in 1431. She was tried by an ecclesiastical court for heresy and sorcery; not for witchcraft. Several points in her confession could have been used for accusing her of this crime as well, but her judges apparently lacked any experience whatsoever in this matter. Only twenty years later this new kind of prosecution was introduced in Normandy, when the Inquisition conducted a series of witch-trials, including a famous one against Guillaume Adeline, professor of theology at the Sorbonne, for preaching that there were no such things as witches.[3] Thus during the last decade the study of European witch-persecution has experienced two revolutions: a chronological one, which has already obliged us to withdraw the phenomenon from medieval history and redefine it as a Renaissance problem, and a geographical one, where northern Italy becomes the centre for an innovation in criminal justice, the diffusion of which we shall comment upon later.

[1] Cf. for France, Robert Muchembled, *La Sorcière au village (XVIᵉ au XVIIᵉ siècle)* (Paris, 1979), ch. 3, 'La Sorcellerie dans la société paysanne', and Robin Briggs, 'Witchcraft and Popular Mentality in Lorraine, 1580–1630', in Brian Vickers (ed.), *Occult and Scientific Mentalities in the Renaissance* (Cambridge, 1984), 337–49; for Denmark and Spain, Gustav Henningsen, *The European Witch-persecution* (Copenhagen, 1973).

[2] Norman Cohn, *Europe's Inner Demons* (London, 1975; 2nd edn. St Albans, 1976), ch. 7, 'Three Forgeries and Another Wrong Track'; and Richard Kieckhefer, *European Witch Trials: Their Foundation in Popular and Learned Culture, 1300–1500* (Berkeley, 1976), ch. 2.

[3] Cohn, *Europe's Inner Demons* (1976 edn.), 230.

A third major change in the historiography of witchcraft had already occurred in the late sixties, thanks to a successful combination of historical and social-anthropological method. For Rossell Hope Robbins, the synthesizer of witchcraft studies until 1959, the whole phenomenon remained incomprehensible: 'the shocking nightmare, the foulest crime and deepest shame of western civilization, the blackout of everything that *homo sapiens*, the reasoning man, has ever upheld.'[4] A great advance was made in 1967 when Hugh Trevor-Roper published his famous essay entitled 'The European Witch-craze', where he attempted to situate the phenomenon in a broad historical context, and for the first time in historical scholarship pointed out that 'witch-craze' had its own rationality. Trevor-Roper was concerned only with the mass persecution of witches, which he explained as camouflaged hunts of heretics; the single trials of village witches remained out of his purview.[5] Yet it was precisely here that a paradigmatic shift in the historiography of witchcraft took place. The pioneering studies of Macfarlane and Thomas[6] demonstrated how witch-trials fulfilled a function in the popular belief system at village level. In the event the two English scholars proved the functionality of witchcraft accusation to such an extent that they raised a new question, which so far had not occurred to anyone: why witch prosecution came to an end—and as a matter of fact this problem continues to intrigue modern scholars in this field.

The question, however, belongs to a whole series of problems which cannot be solved by explaining the social, structural circumstances in which witchcraft accusations and prosecutions occurred; that is one of the reasons for the recent change from a functionalist to an acculturation model in witchcraft historiography. 'There is', notes Stuart Clark (below), 'a revival of interest in the mentalities involved and, in particular, in the interaction, at the level of beliefs and attitudes, between the concerns of the professionals and literate classes and those of the social groups from which the accused by and large came.'

[4] Rossell Hope Robbins, *The Encyclopedia of Witchcraft and Demonology* (London, 1959), 3.
[5] Hugh R. Trevor-Roper, 'The European Witch-craze of the Sixteenth and Seventeenth Centuries', in his *Religion, the Reformation, and Other Essays* (London, 1967), 90–192; cf. Pelican edn. (Harmondsworth, 1969), esp. the foreword, where the author explains that his critics are 'barking up the wrong tree' when they refer to his essay as dealing with the European witch-persecution in general.
[6] Alan Macfarlane, *Witchcraft in Tudor and Stuart England* (London, 1970); Keith Thomas, *Religion and the Decline of Magic* (London, 1971).

The mentality of the professional and literate classes is the main theme of the three essays in Part I of the volume. Julio Caro Baroja, who already in 1961[7] anticipated the anthropological approach, outlines the long and complicated theological process by which pagan and popular beliefs were 'diabolized' at the same time as the reality of the diabolic acts was called into question. The 'Augustinian doctrine' was subsequently replaced by a 'doctrine of the absolute reality of diabolic acts', which Caro Baroja finds expressed in a text by Thomas Aquinas. The zenith of the diabolization process was reached in the sixteenth century, when the *démonomanie* turned into *démonolatrie*. Our grand old man of witchcraft studies takes his point of departure from Classical Antiquity and analyses Catholic demonological literature and folk religion throughout the whole period.

Stuart Clark deals similarly with the Protestant demonologists, whose literary work is surveyed here for the first time. 'Protestant witchcraft writings', he observes, 'were . . . dominated by the pastorate . . . not by jurists or philosophers.' They are more concerned with popular magical techniques and less with witchcraft in the proper sense of the word. Indeed, there was 'clearly an important strand of doubt built into Protestant demonology itself', maintains Clark, since most pastors were opposed to witch-hunting if it meant the neglect of the teachings regarding affliction which they derived from the book of Job.

The third essay is written by John Tedeschi, an expert on the Roman Inquisition and its judicial manuals. In contrast to Caro Baroja he stresses 'the theoretical safeguards enforced in practice by the Roman Congregation and imposed upon the provincial tribunals where procedural abuses were most likely to occur'. This contribution puts an end to much of the nonsense still prevalent about inquisitorial practice in witch-trials. In fact, there is a startling contrast between the procedures described here and the judicial practices of civil courts elsewhere in Europe and in Italy itself, observes Tedeschi:

Physicians were consulted to establish . . . whether an illness or death might have had a natural cause, before jumping to the assumption that a *maleficium* had been perpetrated. The search for the devil's mark was unknown . . . and the failure on the part of the accused to . . . shed tears . . . was considered

---

[7] Julio Caro Baroja, *Las brujas y su mundo* (Madrid, 1961; English trans., *The World of the Witches*, Chicago and London, 1964—also in French, German, and Italian translations).

unimportant. Alleged participants at sabbaths were not allowed to name their accomplices . . . No witch was ever sent to the stake as a first offender if she showed the signs of repentance.

On reading Tedeschi's essay, which concentrates on Italy, we should bear in mind two important facts: (1) that the procedure described in *Malleus maleficarum* was incompatible with the practice prescribed for the Holy Office and was in the event intended for secular and ecclesiastical courts only. Historians tend to overlook the fact that this is clearly expressed in the very title of *Malleus*, part III: 'Relating to the judicial proceedings in both the ecclesiastical and civil courts against witches.'[8] Modern historians tend to classify the Inquisition as a kind of ecclesiastical court, but to the mind of an inquisitor there existed *three* categories of jurisdiction: the secular, the ecclesiastical, and the inquisitorial courts; (2) that from about 1530 the Holy Office did not conduct witch-trials anywhere outside Italy, Spain, and Portugal together with their overseas colonies. After that date the Holy Office had ceased to function in all other countries.[9] Any mention of witches 'tried by the Inquisition' in sixteenth- and seventeenth-century Germany, France, or elsewhere in Central Europe should therefore be handled with the greatest scepticism, as they probably always on closer examination will turn out to refer to secular or ecclesiastical judges using inquisitorial procedure.[10]

Another problem which could not be solved with the functionalist approach of the seventies was the origin of the witches' sabbath. Margaret Murray's tenacious theory of a western European witch cult[11] had been dismissed over and over again, and it had eventually become a dogma that the sabbath was a learned construct, the popular origins of which it was useless to seek. The authors of the four essays

[8] Jakob Sprenger and Heinrich Kramer [Institor], *Malleus maleficarum* (1486 or 1487?), trans. with introductions, bibliography, and notes by Montague Summers (London, 1928; 1971 edn.), 194.
[9] Cf. Gustav Henningsen and John Tedeschi, with Charles Amiel (eds.), *The Inquisition in Early Modern Europe: Studies on Sources and Methods* (Dekalb, 1986).
[10] Examples of this misunderstanding may be found throughout Robbins's *Encyclopedia of Witchcraft*, and even in H. C. Erik Midelfort, *Witch Hunting in Southwestern Germany, 1562–1684* (Stanford, 1972), e.g. p. 21.
[11] Margaret Alice Murray, *The Witch-cult in Western Europe* (London, 1921). Much of Murray's theory was anticipated by Jules Michelet in *La Sorcière* (Paris, 1862), and by the Spanish humanist Pedro de Valencia (1555–1620)—see Gustav Henningsen, *The Witches' Advocate: Basque Witchcraft and the Spanish Inquisition* (Reno, 1980), 6–9. For other predecessors to Murray, see Cohn, *Europe's Inner Demons*, pp. 103 ff.

in Part II deal with this problem each in his own way. Robert Muchembled is in line with the position of the seventies, when he regards the sabbath as 'simply and solely a figment created by theologians, whose ideas governed the imagination of the élite classes of Europe in the late Middle Ages'. But he parts with the dogma of learned origins when he states that the demonologists' description of the sabbath 'was a diabolized version of practices, customs and beliefs which really existed among peasant folk ... with the difference that every one of its features is given a negative coefficient'. Both he and Robert Rowland look upon the witch persecutions as an effect of the acculturation of rural areas by the religious and political élite, but Rowland tries to give this process a more specific explanation using the analytical tools developed during the social-anthropological study of witchcraft. The similarities and differences between African and European witch-beliefs, which played such a prominent role in the debate during the seventies, are here given an explanation which appears to be final. As opposed to African village communities, Early Modern Europe was already a complex society. In this fact Rowland finds not only the main reason for the differences in witch-beliefs, but also the very origin of the European myth about the sabbath, for, as he puts it,

in the context of the institutionalized repression of witchcraft, only a confession to being a night-witch could establish the necessary link between the cultural levels of the witch-hunters and the suspected witches, between the accusations of malefice brought by fellow villagers and the demonological significance that the witch-hunters attached to such accusations.

While Muchembled and Rowland are concerned with explaining the social interaction in the process, of acculturation, Carlo Ginzburg and Gustav Henningsen are more interested in the content of this process. According to Ginzburg, 'the stereotype of the sabbath represents a fusion of two distinct images. The first, a product of the learned culture, ... centred on the supposed existence of a hostile sect, inspired by the devil ... The second image, rooted in folk-culture, was based on belief in the extraordinary powers of particular men and women who—in a state of trance, and often in animal form or riding upon animals—travelled to the realm of the dead in order to bring prosperity to the community.' The fusion of the two traditions took place shortly after 1350 in the Western Alps. And 'after fusion, diffusion'. In the trials of the next two and a half centuries all over Europe, Ginzburg sees repetitions of the sabbath stereotype born in the Western Alps, 'though often embellished with the details from local tradition'. A step further in this direction goes Gustav Henningsen. He wants to explain the sabbath myth as a diabolization of a tradition exemplified by the Sicilian fairy cult, the members of which regularly had orgiastic meetings with the fairies in a state of dreamlike trance. Henningsen shows that the black sabbath of the witches is a negative version—element by element—of this white sabbath of the fairies and their followers. Similar spirit cults can be traced over large parts of the Mediterranean world, where, significantly enough, witch-beliefs were long absent. Further discussion of the sabbath beliefs may be found in the third part of our volume, where the authors discuss witchcraft in Hungary, Portugal, and other European peripheries, which are here introduced into the comparative study of what remains a confusing phenomenon.

Part III deals with the great witch persecutions in northern and eastern Europe, their character and chronology. Regional comparisons become in this context an important theme. It has long been known that the pace and intensity of the European witch-hunt varied widely in different countries and regions. Several explanations have been given. Fernand Braudel, in his first major work, *La Méditerranée*, opposed an urban lowland to the mountainous wilderness primarily in cultural terms:

The mountains are as a rule a world apart from civilizations, which are urban and lowland achievements. . . . Everywhere in the sixteenth century, the hilltop world was very little influenced by the dominant religion at sea level; mountain life persistently lagged behind the plain. . . . A separate religious geography seems then to emerge for the mountain world, which constantly had to be taken, conquered and reconquered.[12]

This explains, in Braudel's mind, why magic practices and superstitions abounded in the everyday life of mountain areas. The outbreaks of 'diabolism' occurred more strongly in the uplands, 'whose primitive isolation maintained them in backwardness'.

In his essay on the European 'witch-craze', Trevor-Roper took up the theme with explicit reference to Braudel:

The mountains, then, are the home not only of sorcery and witchcraft, but also of primitive religious forms and resistance to new orthodoxies. Again and

[12] Fernand Braudel, *The Mediterranean and the Mediterranean World in the Age of Philip II* (1949; English trans. 2 vols., London, 1972–3; 1976 edn.), i. 34–8.

again they have to be won back to sound religion. . . . The old rural superstition, which had seemed harmless enough in the interstices of known society, assumed a more dangerous character when it was discovered, in strange, exaggerated form, among the barely subdued 'heretics' of the highlands. Thanks to that social gulf, that social unassimilability, witchcraft became heresy.[13]

Social and geographical distance made the élite more antagonistic to cultural deviation, which previously might have been frowned upon but generally tolerated at home.

Most theories about relationships between centre and periphery have in common that they describe it in holistic terms as an interaction between economies, nations, regions, classes, or, as here, between cultures and subcultures. The Norwegian sociologist Johan Galtung has suggested another, more individualistic, approach. Pointing out that the relation is best described as a network interaction between individuals, he has tried to operationalize it in a number of personal characteristics such as age, sex, habitat (urban–rural and regional), income, education, and profession. His description of two extremes in a matrix with these indices is very suggestive: 'On the one hand an old woman in a very distant rural district, with low income, almost no education, working as a paid or unpaid farm hand; on the other hand a middle aged man ("in his best years") living in a metropolitan area, with high income and education, as for instance a banker.'[14] With only minor changes this juxtaposition could be applied to describe the relationship between witch and inquisitor in a Braudelean sixteenth-century Europe. An analytical framework of this kind clearly makes us much more sensitive to the richness and complexities of such networks of cultural interaction, especially if we add a historically dynamic dimension. On the other hand, by reducing the analysis to the individual level we may lose sight of the strange regularities that emerge from a more holistic perspective. A structuralist, for instance, would take an immediate interest in the asymmetrical dichotomies in Galtung's description of the old hag and the banker. It may be useful to have both levels in mind when discussing the European witch persecutions. They express both interpersonal action on the local

---

[13] Trevor-Roper, 'The European Witch-craze', p. 107.

[14] Johan Galtung, 'Sosial posisjon og sosial adferd: Sentrum—periferi, begreber og teorier', in *Periferi og sentrum i historien* (Studier i historisk metode, 1; Oslo, 1975), 13.

level and major shifts in the relationship between centre and periphery as part of a historical transition encompassing world economies, national states, and pre-capitalist class relations in Early Modern Europe.

The method of identifying cultural differences in geographical terms as practised by Braudel and Trevor-Roper can obviously be supplemented. The religious differences between a Greek-Orthodox, a Roman-Catholic, a Calvinist, and a Lutheran Europe must be seriously considered in the study of a crime which was defined mainly in religious and theological terms. Similarly, in penal law there is an important dividing line between on the one hand an inquisitorial procedure influenced by Roman and Canon law as practised in southern and central Europe, and on the other hand the legal system of Britain and Scandinavia with strong accusatorial elements. In his survey of Scandinavian witchcraft as seen from an Anglo-Saxon point of view, William Monter (in Part IV) emphasizes the uniformity associated with the Lutheran churches and a relatively autonomous Germanic legal tradition in all the Nordic countries. At the same time, we must admit that the European witch persecutions had so many traits in common that they must be regarded as a single, unified phenomenon. Their foundations in theology and law were everywhere the same. Their victims were mostly women. They occurred in the period 1450 to 1750, and their history is coincident with that of the growth and consolidation of the modern power-state, the Reformation and Counter-Reformation, and the introduction of a new paradigm in natural science and of Cartesian scepticism as a mental attitude among the educated élites. The details in this picture of a uniform phenomenon should be studied in a supra-national perspective: the whole European region must be the basis of analysis and conclusions. The traditional history of witchcraft was, as we have seen, built on observations from a nucleus area encompassing the British Isles, France, Germany, and northern Italy with the Alps. Future research must aim at a synthesis including the geographical peripheries of Europe: the Mediterranean region, the Balkans, the Danube Basin, eastern Europe, and Scandinavia. From this wider perspective it should be possible to assess more clearly what in the end was the common European basis of witchcraft and witch persecutions. At the same time, the picture emerging from the new regional studies gets more varied and complex. Are these differences emerging from the regional studies to be explained as variations on a single theme; and on the other hand, are the remaining similarities genuine affinities rather than the results of independent but converging lines of development?

In recent scholarship there seems to be a great deal of consensus about a picture of the European witch persecutions as resulting from a dynamic situation, in which the centre gradually imposes its values on the periphery. According to this view the *maleficium* conflict between neighbours at village level was reinterpreted and 'diabolized' by the Catholic inquisitors, the Protestant pastors, and the bureaucratic élite created everywhere by the emerging national states. It is probably an expression of such basic assumptions when some of our contributors identify the clergy and the judiciary as the main actors behind the repression. It becomes a point of interest to find out what education they had had at some foreign or indigenous university, or to what extent they had been influenced by the major demonologies such as *Malleus* or Carpzov's *Practica*. But in such cases we are not dealing with the spread of culture perceived as a free flow of ideas, but with a violent and painful innovation process. In the discussion during the last few years diffusion as a theoretical concept has been replaced by terms like acculturation and hegemony. A social dimension has been added to the asymmetrical relations between a cultural centre and its more or less backward periphery. An élite with an international network of communications and control over churches, courts of law, and schools, make use of this control to persuade the peasants to change their superstitious or otherwise offensive behaviour and to learn reason and order. This point is strongly emphasized by Robert Muchembled: 'We must not mistake the part for the whole,' he warns us, 'witch-hunting is fundamentally not a religious but a political phenomenon, and it is only one aspect of the penetration and opening-up of the countryside.' This statement, which reminds us of Foucault, directly links cultural homogenization with the extension of power. The concept of cultural influence from the centre towards the periphery and down the social ladder is frequently reflected in the terminology: the ideas which made the persecutions possible (like those which later put an end to them) had to 'penetrate' to the peasantry before history could take its course.

Several contributors draw our attention to the spatial and social aspects of this penetration. A process of diffusion on a comparatively low regional level, like that in central and northern Sweden in the 1670s, exhibits according to Bengt Ankarloo such obvious regularities that it can easily be mapped in a very real sense. A comparison with the spread of innovations or epidemics is not far-fetched in this case. The visualization of a spatial diffusion also directs one's attention to the local and regional chronologies. The further out in the peripheries, the later the beginnings (and the end) of the great hunt. Maybe, with the single exception of Portugal, most regions in southern and western Europe were the first both to adopt and to dismiss the diabolized image of a maleficent witch, whereas the east-central and northern parts lagged behind. Gábor Klaniczay makes some reflections concerning such observations:

... the rhythm of the diffusion of these waves of witch-hunting is consistent with a more general model of how in European history forms of social organization and cultural patterns have spread to the 'periphery' from the more developed parts of Europe.... I think it can be accepted, even without a more detailed analysis of this 'periphery-effect' of European social and cultural evolution, that the belatedness of the witch persecutions fits well into the general cultural position of these northern, central, and eastern regions within Europe.

The late participation of Hungary in the mass persecutions is a sign that innovation was also late here; and the same phenomenon might well account for the peak of witchcraft and sorcery trials in eighteenth-century Portugal which Francisco Bethencourt finds it difficult to explain. Thus the witchcraft chronology becomes an index among others of regional differences in the historical and cultural development of Europe.

To shed more light on this problem, we can, albeit with some difficulty, collect evidence from our contributors to compile a rough timetable of the beginnings, culmination, and cessation of persecutions in the northern and eastern peripheries of Europe. In Denmark, as presented by Jens Christian V. Johansen, the intensity was highest around 1620, followed by a relatively long period with few processes, coming to an almost complete stop at the end of the seventeenth century. In Norway under similar legal conditions Hans Eyvind Naess notes a clear if somewhat belated intensification after 1617, when a new, more repressive law was enacted. But there was no drastic reduction in the number of trials during the following decades, as in Denmark. On the other hand, we witness a last increase in the 1660s. In Sweden and Finland a low but stable incidence during most of the seventeenth century was broken by a sudden and violent outburst during the great craze of the seventies. In fact, it is possible to discern a culmination in the period 1660–80 encompassing the whole of northern Scandinavia, including Norway and Iceland. This coincided, as Klaniczay points out, with the last great trials in the German area from Salzburg to Mecklenburg, but compared to western Europe it was late. In the Netherlands, France, England, and Spain, the persecution (apart from a few late scandals) had begun to cease after 1610. This early decriminalization, which has only recently received proper attention, was mainly based on purely legal considerations and had little to do with the 'enlightenment' of later decades.[15] The legal handling of witchcraft cases by the Inquisition in Rome and Portugal, as analysed here by Tedeschi and Bethencourt, was equally cautious. Turning towards the eastern periphery, we find a Baltic chronology which is hard to assess. In Estonia there was a characteristically late outburst in the 1690s, but according to Maia Mader the majority of the trials belonged to the first half of the century. Hungary and Poland, which were the principal cases in Klaniczay's argument, are clear-cut examples of the peripheral delay predicted by the diffusion theory. Denmark appears in this context to be an anomaly. As pointed out by Johansen, there were hardly any traces in the seventeenth century of a legal doctrine similar to that of the Inquisition or the Paris *parlement*. So the Danish chronology, which seems to be of a western type, must have a different explanation. The diffusionist theory we have discussed so far actually presupposes two successive ideological movements: the advent of a demonology, which made the persecution possible; and the emergence of a rationalist and sceptical counter-ideology, which put an end to witch-trials. The former seems to be well documented all over the Nordic region. The latter was not obviously different in Denmark. Naess emphasizes the moderating influence of the professional jurists in Norway from the 1650s onwards. In Sweden several members of the aristocratic and enlightened circles around Queen Christina gave voice to serious doubts about the great craze in the early seventies. Were these counter-currents in Norway and Sweden weaker than those in Denmark? We do not know. Perhaps the whole diffusionist theory is flawed in its over-simplicity. It seems necessary, to put it mildly, to assess the structural pre-conditions for the break-

---

[15] Alfred Soman, 'La Décriminalisation de la sorcellerie en France', *Histoire, économie et société*, 4 (1985), 179–223.

through and effect of the demonologist and rationalistic ideas, respectively. The north Scandinavian and Baltic witch-beliefs have interesting and possibly ancient traits in common. Some of them remind us of the observations by Ginzburg and Klaniczay of a pre-Christian, shamanistic substratum in quite diferent parts of Europe. Kirsten Hastrup points out that 'in Iceland there was always an element of shamanism present in popular belief'. Persons could change shape (they were *hamrammr*), or practise *utiseti* ('sitting out'), a meditative-ecstatic withdrawal from the ordinary social sphere. Iceland was also similar to Finland and Estonia in another respect: a majority of the magical operators were men. According to Antero Heikkinen and Timo Kervinen, the supernatural in Finnish popular beliefs was more often associated with men. It was only under the influence of the European witch stereotype that 'people in Finland finally accepted the idea that witches were women. ... In Karelia, however, the female witch never replaced the male sorcerer.' In Maia Madar's witchcraft statistics from Estonia, the men are in a clear majority among the suspects, and Juhan Kahk tells about the more or less unsuccessful efforts of the Swedish authorities to eradicate what was perceived of as idolatry. Thus it was not uncommon for the peasants of Estonia 'openly' to make 'caustic remarks about the Christian faith and about the local clergy ... Intimidations alone could not destroy the spirit of Estonian religion.' An interpretation of this missionary repression (including the witch persecution) as an aspect of the powerful expansion of the modern state is in line with the idea of the cultural periphery in the mountains, those 'vertical norths' which Braudel and Trevor-Roper were talking about. Jean Delumeau and Peter Burke date the final Christianization of the European countryside to the centuries of the witch persecution,[16] and consequently Stuart Clark sees 'the history of Early Modern witchcraft at the very heart of the reforming process'. The demonology is the 'other side of' the missionary message.

In the end it therefore becomes important to deal with the complex question of what was really diffused according to the geographical and chronological pattern we have observed so far. Is it in fact the same phenomenon that we witness in western Europe in the 1610s, in

---

[16] Cf. Jean Delumeau, *Catholicism between Luther and Voltaire* (1971; English trans. London, 1977), and Peter Burke, *Popular Culture in Early Modern Europe* (London, 1978).

Sweden and Finland around 1670, and in Hungary and Portugal another half-century later? As we have seen, European witchcraft had two main components: the popular beliefs in a malevolent and harmful magic (*maleficium*), and the idea entertained by the learned élite of a diabolical conspiracy against Christendom. Only when the latter was applied to the elements of popular lore could persecution on a large scale begin.[17] A necessary pre-condition for the spread of witch persecution (and later of its decline) was that some élite ideas penetrated into the lower strata. This process of acculturation gained a further dimension when the élite had a different ethnic background from the peasantry, as in Finland and Hungary, or in the Baltic areas under Swedish rule. Juhan Kahk bluntly declares that the witch persecution in Estonia was an expression of Swedish imperialism.

Robert Rowland's contribution deals with important aspects of this problem. He, too, has been struck by the uniformity of the confessions made in court by witches all over Europe. But rather than trying to explain the similarities in terms of external factors such as the diffusion of ideas or the unrestrained use of torture, he turns to the discourse itself, and makes it the object of a rigorous, structuralist analysis. According to Rowland the European witch-figure has emerged from the fusion of two distinct but metaphorically related elements of belief, which in other cultures, as in Africa, are kept strictly apart: the well-known, everyday witch of the village, and the mysterious, night-flying creature associated with the nightmare counter-world. Other scholars, too, have, as we have seen, been close to this realization, when observing how the traditional maleficent magic was gradually reinterpreted within the confines of a Christian cosmology: *maleficium* became diabolized. Sixteenth-century Europe was not an African village. The process by which *maleficium* was transformed and reinterpreted took place on a continental scale and involved several socio-cultural levels. A large and complex social system like Early Modern Europe was held together by many different integrative forces and processes, which continually brought different social levels and geographical regions into contact with each other. It was precisely in such a process of integration that the sabbath was related to malefice in 'the model underlying witchcraft confessions'.

To describe in detail how this process of change came about is one of the major tasks of future research. Some of our contributors have

---

[17] Cf. Henningsen, *The Witches' Advocate*, pp. 391ff.

already started on this. The Protestant clergymen in Stuart Clark's essay developed their demonological ideas as a direct extension of their everyday pastoral duty of explaining both fortune and adversity as the work of divine providence. Their tracts contain 'a litany of questions which accurately express popular incomprehension of pastoral aims: how can magical practitioners be evil when they help their clients?' The problems of day-to-day acculturation at village level could not be expressed more clearly. The process of acculturation is also a major theme in the essays of Klaniczay and Bethencourt on, respectively, Hungary and Portugal. We shall not, however, go into details here about their conclusions, which complement each other in an interesting way, thanks to the authors' very different fields of observation.

Social integration was an important pre-condition for the state-building process in early modern Europe. Seen from a legal and cultural point of view, it took two forms: standardization and participation.[18] The emergence of a national literature and of literacy on a national scale obviously had highly integrative consequences. Everywhere princes tried to introduce more uniform legal and fiscal systems with techniques borrowed from the *Corpus Iuris* and the book-keeping of the merchant capitalists. The imposition of new legal and bureaucratic measures was considerably mitigated by the participation in power-play of locally appointed groups. Tax collectors and jurymen became important mediators between centre and periphery: they came to have values and elements of a self-image which had been formed higher up. At the same time, they could from their intermediary position influence and even change the signals from the centre. The varying degree of success of the local élites is emphasized by several of our authors. Muchembled makes an interesting distinction between 'open' and 'closed' communities. In a 'closed' village, people made no use of the courts set up by princes and lords, but went on settling their differences with the use of direct violence or a kind of mob justice. In the 'open' areas, where the process of acculturation had been successful, the civil administration, including the courts, was used for conflict-resolution and other local purposes. That the witch was brought to official trial can be seen as an expression, as it were, of integration and progress, and this is probably the greatest paradox of the European witch persecution.

[18] Stein Rokkan, 'Dimensions of State Formation and Nation-building', in Charles Tilly (ed.), *The Formation of National States in Western Europe* (Princeton, 1975), 562–600.

I
WITCHCRAFT, LAW, AND THEOLOGY

I

Witchcraft and Catholic Theology

JULIO CARO BAROJA

PRELIMINARY NOTE

At a time when so many works of great learning and discernment have been written concerning the history of magic in general and witchcraft in particular, it may appear foolhardy to seek to add to them. However, the present author would point out by way of excuse that he merely wishes to throw light on a specific subject, namely, how the figure of the witch, already known in pagan antiquity, took on different characteristics in subsequent periods, after the triumph of Christianity. Finally, as will be seen, the witch-figure became the basis of an immense theological and juridical construction, superimposed on far more ancient and simple facts; and this construction was the work of intellectuals, although their culture was of a very special type. As has been said, the theme is a limited one; but it is of particular theoretical interest, and may be relevant to a revision of the basic concepts of modern anthropology: functionalism on the one hand, structuralism on the other, and, finally, historicism.

I

The historical figure with which this book is mainly concerned is denoted by different words in the European countries of Romance language and Catholic tradition: in France *sorcière*, in Italy *strega*, in Spain *bruja*. The French word derives from a particular meaning of Latin *sors*, like the obsolete Spanish *sortero* and *sortiario*;[1] the Italian from *striga*, which, like *strix*, is used either for a bird or for a witch-woman.[2] The Spanish term is clearly of different origin; but the long

---

[1] The Basque word *sorguin* or *sorguín* contains the same element. Spanish *sortilegio* or *sortílego* seem to be learned forms or Latinisms.

[2] *Strigae* in Petronius, *Sat.* lxiii. 4: a real 'witches' tale'.

article by Juan Corominas on its etymology is inconclusive,[3] and García de Diego merely says that its derivation is uncertain.[4] The same author indicates that *brujo* (skin, peel) and *borujo* (pack, bundle) come from Latin *voluculum* (bundle, wrapping).[5] This might lead us to suppose that *bruja* is derived from an unattested *volucula*, signifying one who flies: the forms *volucra* and *volucres* were used for sirens, witches, and flying creatures in general.[6] The Spanish word, in both its masculine and its feminine form, is occasionally found from early times with an *o* instead of a *u*: *broxa* occurs in Aragonese and Catalan texts and in a Latin work by Martin of Arles on the witches of Navarre.[7] But the form *bruxa* became generalized and is progressively documented in literary and theological texts of the fifteenth and sixteenth centuries; also in dictionaries and lexicons giving its equivalent in other languages and proposing etymologies, which, however, have not found acceptance.

The best-known reference in an early literary text is in the prose drama *La Celestina* (*c*.1500), where the old woman speaks to Pármeno of the excellent qualities of his mother, and relates how 'they accused her of being a witch' because she was discovered by night at a crossroads, carrying candles and digging up handfuls of earth.[8] Other texts of that date or somewhat later use terms that are regarded as synonyms. For example, Fray Juan de los Angeles in his *Consideraciones sobre el Cantar de los Cantares* says that 'Jeremiah compares the world and the flesh to lamiae, which, as many believe, are what we call *brujas* or *hechiceras* [sorceresses] (*latine striges vel sagas*), who at night seek out children at the breast to suck their blood and kill them with their cursed arts.'[9] Thus an author writing at the end of the sixteenth century (his book was published in Madrid in 1607) not only introduced classical terms for comparison, but also referred to biblical texts, whose relevance here is doubtful.[10]

---

[3] Juan Corominas, *Diccionario crítico etimológico de la lengua castellana* (4 vols.; Madrid, 1954–7), i. 530*a*–532*a*, with numerous examples. Corominas believes the word to be pre-Roman.

[4] Vicente García de Diego, *Diccionario etimológico español e hispánico* (Madrid, 1974), 127*b*.   [5] García de Diego, *Diccionario*, pp. 127*b* and 1055 (no. 7262).

[6] Ovid, *Fast*. vi. 131: 'sunt avidae volucres'. His description of the striga is very clear.

[7] Corominas, *Diccionario*, i. 530*a* and 531*a*.

[8] Fernando de Rojas, *La Celestina*, act vii: ed. Julio Cejador, i (Madrid, 1913), 243.

[9] *Obras místicas del M.R.P. Fr. Juan de los Angeles*, pt. ii (Nueva biblioteca de autores españoles, 24; Madrid, 1917), 56*a*.

[10] Jeremiah, Lam. 4: 3, speaks of *lamiae* [in the Vulgate; AV 'sea monsters'—translator's note]: these are sometimes confused with witches, but, according to various

The word *bruja* continued to be written with an *x* until late in the eighteenth century. It is significant that at one time it also denoted a species of owl, a night-bird.[11] The witch-figure is familiar to Spanish classical writers of the Golden Age; but Cervantes, Lope de Vega, and Francisco de Quevedo all refer to it with a touch of irony or scepticism as to the witch's powers. Other less-known authors also emphasize the aspect of falsity or spuriousness. For example, in *La Mosquea*, by the comico-epic poet José de Villaviciosa (1589–1658), a terrifying figure is addressed with the words:

> Art thou perchance a vile phantasm,
> Or some *lying* witch and sorceress,
> That by force of nature or cataplasm
> Drainest the living substance?[12]

In Lope de Vega's *La Dorotea* the belief in erotic witchcraft plays a considerable part, but Julio, an educated man, is made to say that 'It is with lovers as with witches, who believe that they are carried bodily to the place whither their imagination takes them.'[13] This short text introduces a point that, as we shall see, theologians were to debate for centuries; while other texts again reflect the belief that witches sucked the blood of children and grown persons.[14] Returning to the aspect of deceit, we may notice that the so-called *Diccionario de autoridades* stated in 1726 that the word *brujerías* was used by transference for 'feminine intrigue, deception and childish jokes'.[15] But the author who wrote more extensively and in a more richly comic vein concerning witches and beliefs about them, not only in Andalucia and Castille but also in

---

authors, were fabulous beings of a special kind. Dion Chrysostomos in *Or.* lv. 10 (ed. H. Lamar Crosby, iv (London and Cambridge, Mass., 1962), 388–9) says that nurses used to frighten children with tales of *lamiae*.

[11] *Diccionario de la lengua castellana*, known as '*de Autoridades*' (6 vols.; Madrid, 1726–39), i. 692*a*, gives this as an obsolete sense. The modern dictionaries that give most information, apart from Corominas, are: *Diccionario histórico de la lengua española* (2 vols.; Madrid, 1936), ii. 375*b*–376*b*, and Samuel Gili Gaya, *Tesoro lexicográfico, 1492–1726* (fasc. 1–3 (A–Ch); Madrid, 1947–52), fasc. ii, pp. 378*c*–379*a*.

[12] Canto 5: *Poetas épicos*, i (Biblioteca de autores españoles, 16), 593*a*: an allusion to witches' alleged practice of anointing and sucking.

[13] *La Dorotea*, act i. v: ed. Américo Castro (Madrid, n.d. (1913?)), 36.

[14] e.g. Quevedo: 'Que chupais sangre de niños/como bruxas infernales', in a ballad on old women, *musa* 6, no. 32: *Obras*, iii (Biblioteca de autores españoles, 69), 176*b*. Also other refs., ibid., to old women's magic practices.

[15] *Diccionario de la lengua castellana*, i. 692*b*, s.v.

Navarre, was Cervantes in *El coloquio de los perros*, on which valuable and learned comments were made a considerable time ago.[16]

With more or less knowledge and in a more or less cursory manner, Spanish novelists and comic dramatists refer to witches and witchcraft, and even to memorable witch-hunting episodes.[17] In a world in which freedom of conscience was not recognized as in the Protestant countries—though the expression and its meaning were known, as we may see from *Don Quixote*[18]—the subject, which caused agitation for centuries among European peoples, gave rise to doubts, and more than doubts, deriving from two contrary attitudes represented by different Catholic theologians, beginning with a Father of the Church.

II

Greek and Latin texts from pagan antiquity are sufficient to show that the image of the witch or sorceress that we find in them was transmitted to Christian society. Among the Romans it was commonly thought that men were by nature prone to thieving, while women, no less naturally, were inclined to witchcraft and poisoning. According to Quintilian, 'latrocinium facilius in viro, veneficium in femina credas'.[19] Pliny the Elder likewise believed in propensities due to sex.[20] Greek antiquity, on the other hand, has left us real archetypes of witches, each reflecting a particular form of their activity. Circe and Calypso are figures who work their will upon men by amorous means, the type of the *femme fatale*; while Medea is a tragic heroine prompted by despair to magic acts.[21] Throughout the Classical world, the female figure of antiquity appears at various levels of dignity: at the highest, when she might be taken for a demi-goddess; at the middle level, that of lovers depicted by lyric and erotic poets; and at the lowest, that of country women casting malicious spells, or aged crones of grotesque,

---

[16] The fullest edn. is still that of Agustín G. de Amezúa, *'El casamiento engañoso' y 'El coloquio de los perros'* (Madrid, 1912), 265–365, with notes and introduction.

[17] Thus in Moreto's comedy *De fuera vendrá* . . ., II. ix, the comic servant Chichón says: 'I would have you know I'm a nobleman, and it isn't my fault if my mother was a witch; they cooked her goose for it in Logroño.' (An allusion to the famous trial, see below). See *Comedias escogidas de Don Agustín Moreto Cabaña* (Biblioteca de autores españoles, 39), 68*c*.

[18] The Moor Ricote uses the phrase with ref. to Germany in *Don Quijote*, pt ii, ch. 54.

[19] Quintilian, *Inst. or.* v. 10. 25.   [20] Plinius, *Historia naturalis*, xxv. 5. 10–11.

[21] Julio Caro Baroja, 'Arquetipos y modelos en la historia de la brujería', in *Ritos y mitos equívocos* (Madrid, 1974), 215–58.

sordid appearance.[22] Often, however, the female figure is represented as protected by, associated, or allied with feminine, nocturnal divinities: the moon, Selene, Diana, or the terrifying crossroads figure of Hecate. In relation to these deities, witches possessed a power of coercion and, as it were, conjuration.[23] In the Middle Ages, it can be seen from penitential canons that witches were believed to fly through the air on particular occasions under the auspices of Diana or Herodias;[24] and in the recent folklore of some countries we find a belief in female spirits inhabiting mountains or caves and presiding over witches' actions.[25]

Officially, the triumph of Christianity left little room for any conception other than that inherited from Hebrew monotheism, according to which there are only two spheres of action in human life: the Good, pursued by those who submit to the law of God, and the Evil, inhabited by followers of the devil and demons. In Christian ethics, all that is morally wrong—beliefs, vices, violent passions—is of diabolical origin, and the ancient divinities are nothing but representations of the devil, by whom, according to Christian belief, the whole of humanity was plunged into error until the advent of the Messiah. In consequence of this view, to which we may give the name of 'diabolization', devilish powers were attributed to witches and sorcerers, male and female, and, in fact, to all those involved in the grand catalogue of 'magic arts', of which we shall speak presently.[26] But this far-reaching 'diabolization' is combined with a different tendency which consists in belittling the reality of the supposedly diabolical acts of witchcraft. The devil *deceives* his adepts, making them believe in acts which are false and imaginary. We have seen, for instance, how in seventeenth-century Spain people spoke of the 'falsity' of witches' acts, and this is an inheritance from the doctrine of the early Church: there are things which are evil, being of diabolical origin, and which are at the same time false. There is an apparent contradiction here, which will be found to emerge as the subject is treated historically.

---

[22] My early work *Las brujas y su mundo* (Madrid, 1961; English trans., *The World of the Witches*, Chicago and London, 1964) contains a chapter (pp. 17–40, in English edn.) on the characterization of witches and sorceresses in Greek and Latin texts, to which others could be added.

[23] On these divinities see *The World of the Witches*, pp. 24–7.

[24] Ibid., pp. 60–1.

[25] e.g. in the Basque Country: ibid., pp. 237–8.

[26] On this process of diabolization see ibid., pp. 41–4.

The Christian theologian inherited from some rationalist writers, Greek and Latin, arguments for making fun of pagan myths and beliefs which, ever since the time of pre-Socratic philosophers, had been judged unseemly and contrary to the majesty of the Olympian gods. But there is a difference between the jesting of Lucian and the mockery of certain Christian authors who insist on the absurdity and, above all, the immorality of paganism. The same writer who proclaims the value of absurdity in relation to his own creed insists on the inadmissible absurdity of other beliefs and on giving double versions of them, in a way that was also practised in the ancient world. There is a huge difference between the figure of Dionysus in Euripides' *Bacchae* and in the *Frogs* of Aristophanes. The same thing happened as regards the devil. Popular anecdote transforms the embodiment of ultimate terror into a figure of fun, a small-time liar and deceiver seeking to entrap men and women who are in search of Christian perfection. Those who follow the devil are taken in by him, and witches and wizards are the victims of private fantasies.

This brings us to a fundamental point in the history of Christian, especially Catholic, theology with reference to the acts attributed to witches. The relevant text is one in which St Augustine, relating a personal experience, says:

When I was in Italy I heard of certain women, innkeepers by trade, and practitioners of these evil arts, who (it was said) gave travellers cheese to eat and thereby transformed them into beasts of burden. When they had performed the task they reverted to their proper form. Their minds did not turn to those of beasts, but remained human and rational.

St Augustine is well aware that this is more or less the same story as that related by Apuleius in his best-known work, *The Golden Ass*, but he does not believe that it happens in reality. Demons do not have power to affect the soul or to transform the body. But he passes on what he has heard in Italy and compares it with the tale of a certain Praestantius concerning an incident that happened to his father. The latter had consumed some kind of poisonous drug, also in a cheese, but this time in his own house. He remained apparently asleep in bed, but could not be awakened. In a few days' time he returned to his senses and related what had happened during his long dream or trance. He had turned into a horse, one of several that were carrying loads of grain to the army in Rhaetia. It was later found that this transport of grain did in fact take place during the man's trance. St

Augustine relates other cases of dreams with strange effects, on the authority of trustworthy persons, and explains in this way such poetic 'facts' as Circe's use of spells (*carmina*) to transform Odysseus' companions into swine.[27] By divine permission, the demons of paganism might succeed in other deceptions also.[28]

For a long time, throughout the Middle Ages, St Augustine's thesis was adopted by Catholic theologians (less so, however, by lawyers and lay magistrates, who dealt with the crime of witchcraft from a civil point of view). There is diabolical action, yes; there are substances which serve to carry it out; but the basic reality is lacking. The tendency to limit the power of the devil also led to the invention, in medieval times, of burlesque accounts of his relations with old sorceresses.[29] But, on the other hand, little by little, artists went on creating images of the devil that were intended to inspire terror, though grotesque ones were invented as well. Thus there came to be new ways of representing the 'Fallen Angel', dissimilar from those of, say, the sixth century, in which he has no particularly terrifying features. It was in the period of Romanesque and still more of Gothic art—in capitals, portals, miniatures, paintings, and so on—that the devil took on forms that were frightening as well as grotesque; these continued down to the time of the Renaissance, and later still in the illustrations to popular books.[30] Such representations were not only authorized by the Church, but reflected the intention to educate or guide the populace by means of images. The devil has power over men; but in relation to God he is an imitator, a skilful charlatan, as Tertullian says, especially where magic acts are concerned. His 'miracles' are illusory.[31]

As the centuries passed, the Church became ever stronger; but she could not prevent people continuing to believe in the absolute reality of almost all the acts attributed to witches and wizards. There is a famous text of doubtful origin, but which exercised great authority, setting out the criterion observed by canon lawyers since, at latest, the

---

[27] He expressly cites Virgil, *Ecl.* viii. 70.

[28] Augustin, *De civitate Dei*, lviii. 18.

[29] Texts by Vincent of Beauvais and others in *The World of the Witches*, pp. 63–4. The practice of ridicule came later.

[30] Jacques Levron in *Le Diable dans l'art* (Paris, 1935) gives an idea of this, using classic works such as those by E. Mâle and others.

[31] Tert. *Apol.* xxii–xxiii. These 'demons', with which may be included the *daimones* of Socrates and the Platonists, are invisible and insensible. But there is always a basic illusion: 'Quid ergo de caeteris ingeniis, vel etiam viribus fallacia spiritualis edisseram?'

tenth century. This is the *Canon episcopi*, supposed to have been promulgated by a council at Ancyra in the year 314, which in fact did not take place. The canon appears in a work entitled *De ecclesiasticis disciplinis* or *De disciplinis ecclesiasticis* by Regino, abbot of Prüm in Germany, who died in 915. It reads:

Bishops and their auxiliaries shall endeavour as far as possible to uproot from parishes all kinds of sorcery and magic, which are pernicious inventions of the Devil. They shall expel with ignominy men and women guilty of this vice. Holy Church must be purged from such a plague. Nor should any credence be given to what follows: viz. that certain women, perverted and dedicated to Satan, seduced by diabolical fantasies and deceits, believe and profess that they ride at night-time with Diana, goddess of the pagans, and with Herodias, astride certain beasts, in a company of innumerable other women, traversing immense spaces and obeying Diana's orders like those of a mistress who convokes them on certain nights. It would not be so bad if they were the only ones who die in such impiety, but they attract many others. Great throngs, deceived by this false persuasion, believe in all these lies and thus fall back into pagan error. Therefore priests should preach wherever it may be necessary to point out the falsity of these errors and make it known that such tricks are produced by the Evil One who seduces the mind by vain imaginations. It is Satan who ... having gained possession of the soul of an unfortunate woman ... takes on the appearance of divers persons and deceives the spirit of the one in his power, by showing her unknown persons or guiding her on strange voyages. The soul that has abandoned itself to him imagines that it is accomplishing in the body things that take place only in the mind. Does it not happen to all of us in dreams to be transported a long way off, and to see during that dream things we have never seen while waking? But no one is so mad as to believe that such scenes, which are only in the mind, have taken place in the body. So it must be loudly proclaimed that those who believe such things have lost the faith and no longer belong to God, but only to him in whom they believe, that is the Devil.[32]

This is the doctrine followed by the canonist Burchard of Worms, and later by Yves of Chartres and Gratianus,[33] as well as by doctors with especial doctrinal interests, such as John of Salisbury in *Policraticus*.[34] It remained in effect from the tenth to the thirteenth century, and

---

[32] Regino of Prüm, *De disciplinis ecclesiasticis et religione christianae*, ed. Baluze (Paris, 1671), vol. ii, col. 364. The text has been transcribed many times, both in old treatises on witchcraft and books on the devil, and in modern histories: cf. *The World of the Witches*, pp. 268–9 nn. 7–9.

[33] *The World of the Witches* p. 269 nn. 11–12. Burchard, *Decret*. x. 1; xix. 5; Ivon or Ives of Chartres, *Decret*. xi. 30; Gratianus, *Decret*. ii. 26; v. 12.

[34] Johan of Sailisbury, *Policraticus*, ii. (Leiden, 1639), 83.

at the beginning of the fourteenth it was still repeated in the texts of certain councils. It may be called an Augustinian doctrine of an essentially psychological or spiritual character.

It is not easy to describe the process whereby, at a certain time, a different criterion came to be adopted by many Catholic theologians, and eventually by the Church itself as director of social and spiritual life. There was, however, a philosophical element which united with more commonplace ideas, with the result that judicial practice, in conformity with Scholastic teaching, came to accept the *absolute reality* of the deeds attributed to witches: not only those described above, but others as well. During the same centuries in which the old thesis was maintained, a number of ideas became widespread as to the existence of real devil-worshippers or learned men who made a pact with the devil. Rightly or wrongly, persecution was meted out to certain groups at odds with the Papacy, on the ground that they were not what they claimed to be, but practised horrible rites and committed misdeeds without number. In papal documents and trials the influence of the devil was described as constant, and a body of doctrine was evolved according to which his followers actually *invert* the practices of divine worship and all normal and agreeable customs, living in a state of unmixed horror. Many studies have been devoted to the groups accused of such perversions, which remain incomprehensible, and the charges have often been considered huge falsifications. Historians have approached them from opposite angles according to their different religious tendencies. There is, for instance, the trial of the Templars, an action already condemned by Dante, with trumped-up charges and confessions extracted by torture; other, less well-known persecuted groups include the 'Stedingers', accused of still more improbable acts and beliefs and the Cathars and Albigensians, who were also misrepresented as diabolists.[35] In all these cases the actual intervention of the devil was taken for granted, with a multiplicity of appropriate images. Finally, an absolute doctrine was expressed in the terms of a passage from St Thomas Aquinas (*c*.1225–74): 'The Catholic faith declares that demons are able to do harm by their operations, and to impede sexual congress.'[36] Thus the reality of

---

[35] Dante defends the Templars in *Purg.* xx. 93–102, ascribing their trial to royal avarice. On the charges against the Cathars (sodomy, satanism, etc.) see René Nelli, *Le Phénomène cathare* (Paris, 1964), 82.

[36] Aquinas, *Quaestiones quodlibetales*, xi. 10, in *Comment. in Job*, i. Quoted in many works on witchcraft.

diabolical action was maintained, not only as affecting the mind.[37] This goes far to explain the increased violence of persecution and the categorical return to the doctrine laid down in Exodus 22: 18: 'Thou shalt not suffer a witch to live.'[38]

III

There is no doubt that the principles elaborated and applied in the thirteenth century acquired full authority in the fourteenth and fifteenth. It is also clear that the dramatis personae, as we may call them, were to a certain extent associated with new qualities. It can no longer be imagined that churchmen limited the devil's power to the sphere of mental life. That power appeared ever stronger; it included the propagation of doctrines contrary to the Faith, such as that of the Albigensians or the Jewish minorities. The Church also strove to banish the last residue of pagan ideas as to the role of 'Noctiluca', Diana, or what were thought to be the equivalent Germanic deities.[39] The master of witches and wizards, who clearly carry out his orders, is the devil, appearing at covens in the form of a he-goat. The doctrine crystallized and was applied everywhere; it was international, like the Church itself, and was intended to eradicate whatever might today come under the heading of local folklore or particularism. This was a second phase of the process of diabolization, with vast consequences for European communities at the end of the Middle Ages and the beginning of the modern age. The 'crime of witchcraft' was rooted in a body of doctrine with effects undreamt-of in those communities, and produced a veritable state of terror. It is not our concern here to describe the course of trials for collective witchcraft (which have a lengthy history in the Pyrenean area), but to emphasize that the Church systematically modified its judgement and the legal procedures relating to persons charged with witchcraft in particular or magic in general. This modification may also correspond to an increased belief in magic, and more extensive practice of its various manifestations.

[37] On the character of demons: *Summa theol.* i, *quaestio* 63, in 9 articles.

[38] Women who practised necromancy are mentioned in the Old Testament, e.g. the Witch of En-dor (1 Sam. 28: 7–20).

[39] The connection between witches and Germanic divinities is fully discussed by Jacob Grimm in *Deutsche Mythologie* (4 vols.; Berlin and Vienna, 1981), i. 221–6 and iii. 87–9.

The key document in this respect is the bull *Super illius specula* (1326) of John XXII, referring to the many Christians

who ally themselves with Death and make a covenant with Hell; who sacrifice to demons, making and causing to be made images, rings, mirrors, phials and similar objects intended as magic bonds to hold fast the demons whom they interrogate and from whom they obtain answers, having recourse to the same demons to satisfy their depraved desires.[40]

Without doubt there were persons of all social classes who practised what was much later called 'satanism'. But it is also certain that the practice and theory of papal inquisitors did much to foster beliefs that were afterwards ridiculed in such phrases, current in Spain, as 'to believe in witches' or 'tales of witches'. From the eighteenth century onwards, writers mistakenly ascribed to 'popular ignorance' the attitude of those who were in fact far from ignorant. Thus, in the *Encyclopédie* by Diderot and d'Alembert, 'Sorcellerie' is defined as an 'opération magique, honteuse et ridicule, attribuée stupidement par la superstition à l'invocation et au pouvoir des démons'; and the article continues: 'On n'entendit jamais parler de sortilèges et de maléfices que dans les pays et les tems d'ignorance.'[41] This reflects a certain optimism as to the power of civilization in general. But in the fourteenth and fifteenth centuries the subject was codified not by the ignorant, but by educated people such as canon lawyers, jurists, and inquisitors. A much more telling attack has been levelled against the Church by those who accuse it of seeking to enlarge its power by fostering belief in the existence of true satanism.[42] From the time of the publication of the first writings designed to facilitate inquisitorial practice (many more of which were to follow in the fourteenth and fifteenth centuries), witches and wizards were depicted far more specifically as devil-worshippers, and methods of persecution were prescribed accordingly.[43] This was true not only of juridical but of

---

[40] Bulls in chronological order in the *Magnum bullarium romanum* (1857-) and earlier editions such as the *Bullarium privilegiorum ac diplomatum romanum pontificum usque ad Clementem XII amplissima collectio*... (28 folio vols.; Rome, 1738-45).

[41] *Encyclopédie, ou dictionnaire raisonné des sciences, des arts et des métiers*, xv (Neuchâtel, 1765), 115b.

[42] Thus the canon Johann Döllinger, *El Pontificado* (1861), Spanish trans. by Demetrio Zorrilla (Madrid, n.d.), 171-80.

[43] Before the invention of printing there were texts like that of Bernard Gui, known for his zeal and brutality, at the beginning of the 14th c., but also others that were much copied. The inquisitor's propensity for using torture, overriding medical statements, and, in general, adopting attitudes most calculated to facilitate sentencing, persisted

more theological writings: for instance, the *Formicarium* of Johannes
Nider in the fifteenth century.[44]

Other works, developing ideas that have aroused horror and
repulsion in later times, bear titles indicating that they were intended
to serve as guides or manuals, or 'directories' like the work of
Eymerich[45] and others. It is usually supposed that codifications and
subsequent compilations of laws have always signified an advance in
legal science; but actually they have sometimes had no effect, or a
negative one, as Renan observed.[46] It must be admitted, on the other
hand, that the most brutal code of witch-hunting that has ever existed
was written, printed, and put into effect during the Renaissance; and
that its authors, contemporaries of Leonardo da Vinci, were men of
genius, or at any rate intelligence, free from any prejudice imposed by
authority or tradition. In December 1484 Pope Innocent VIII, himself
a loose-liver, issued the bull *Summis desiderantes effectibus*, describing
the activities of witches and wizards in the dioceses of Mainz,
Cologne, Trier, Salzburg, and Bremen. They are accused of carnal
relations with demons, and of using enchantments, spells, and
sorceries to bring about the death of children and domestic animals,
the failure of harvests, diseases without number, impotence, and
sterility. The Pope, as we know, derived his information from a report
by the two Dominicans Heinrich Kraemer (Institor) and Jakob
Sprenger, who obtained full powers to persecute those charged with
such offences. The worst consequence of the papal zeal was the
publication of the sadly famous *Malleus maleficarum* ('Hammer of
witches'); in later editions this was combined with Nider's work and

---

very late, as may be seen from C. Carena of Cremona, *Tractatus Sanctissimae Inquisitionis,
de modo procedendi in causis Fidei, in tres partes divisus* (Lyons, 1649), 214*a*, 262*b* (pt. ii, title
12, 'De Sortilegis', in 321 paras.).

[44] Johannes Nider, *Formicarium seu dialogus ad vitam christianam exemplo formicae
incitativus* (1st edn. Augsburg, 1475; 2nd edn. Strasburg, 1517—the author, however,
lived from 1380 to 1438). Frequently published with the *Malleus* (see below).

[45] An extremely rare impression: Nicolaus Eymerich, *Directorium inquisitorum.
Sequuntur decretales tituli de summa trinitate et fide catholica*. At the end appears the statement: 'Explicit totum directorium inquisitorum haereticae pravitatis compilatum Avi-
nione per fratrem Nicolaum Eymerici, ordinis fratrum predicatorum sacre theologie
magistrum ac inquisitorem Aragonie haereticae pravitatis. Impressum Barchinonae per
Joannem Luschner Alemanum. Sub factis et expensis . . . Didaci de Deça episcopi Pal-
entini . . . anno M.D. III' (Barcelona, 1503). The work was reprinted in Rome (1578) and
in later editions, also an abridged translation (Lisbon [= Paris], 1762), contrary to
Church authority.

[46] Esp. in his commentary on 'L'Histoire secrète de Procope' in *Essais de morale et
critique* (Paris, 1859), 283–5.

others to form a corpus entitled *Malleus maleficorum*. The two friars evidently thought that far more women than men were given to sorcery; in this they followed ancient ideas, as we have seen. In any case, they expounded systematically the belief that sorcerers formed a sect with its own rites of initiation, abjuration, and so on, and in Part III of the work they described methodically the legal procedure to be followed in cases of witchcraft. The *Malleus* has given rise to different kinds of commentary in different times: in our own day it has been reprinted by, among others, supposed satanists, while on the other hand it has been described as a 'stupid book'.[47] Books that are merely stupid, however, do not have the unusual destiny of this one, which inspired the publication of others as late as the seventeenth century, and witch-hunts that continued in Protestant countries after the Reformation. In this paper, however, we are concerned only with Catholic Europe.

As to Spain, there were trials of witches and wizards in Vizcaya at the beginning of the sixteenth century; but differing views were held by theologians before, during, and after the period of Institor and Sprenger. Fray Lope de Barrientos, bishop of Cuenca (1382–1469), in a treatise on divination, adhered firmly to the position of the *Canon episcopi*.[48] Alonso de Madrigal (1409–55), bishop of Ávila, known by the nickname *El Tostado*, expounds two opposite theses in different places, but essentially follows St Augustine.[49] Much later, the famous Francisco de Vitoria (1486–1546) accepted the possibility of illusion, but also thought that 'sometimes' there might be real cases of

---

[47] The work, with the title indicated, was published at Cologne in 1486, prefaced by the papal document. Later editions also include this document, and contain Nider's work following the *Malleus*. Thus, for instance, a *Mallei maleficorum, ex plurimis authoribus* [sic] *coaceruatus, ac in duos tomos distinctus* (Lyons, 1584): in vol. i, the *Malleus*, with index, occupies pp. 1–464; Nider's treatise, pp. 465–540. Vol. ii contains more modern treatises, mentioned below. The *Malleus* has appeared in several modern editions and translations.

[48] Lope de Barrientos, *Tratado de la adivinanza*, published by Fray Luis G. A. Cetrino, *Anales salmantinos*, i (Salamanca, 1927), 177–9.

[49] H. C. Lea uses Hansen's edition of Tostado's text in *A History of the Inquisition of Spain* (4 vols.; New York, 1907), iv. 209. Late in the 17th c. there appeared *El Tostado sobre Eusebio: Mineral de letras divinas y humanas, en la Historia general de todos los Tiempos y Reynos del Mundo . . .*, compiled by Fray Joseph de Almonazid (Madrid, 1677), 671–2 (pt. iii, ch. 197): 'De las bruxas, y de las cosas que dellas se cuenten, como se deben entender.' This is an interpretation already used by St Augustine, illustrated by a Spanish case of a witch who anointed herself, fell to the ground, and, when she recovered consciousness, related things that had happened to her.

metamorphosis, nocturnal flight, etc.[50] This explains certain fluctuations that are found in inquisitorial practice.

In Italy, attitudes were perhaps still more varied; sometimes they reflect group loyalties. We have seen how the Dominicans, first and foremost, were associated with inquisitorial persecutions, and naturally they were the primary defenders of the *Malleus* against its opponents. As we shall see later, the well-known rivalry between Dominicans and Jesuits affected the views on witchcraft held by the two Orders. The principal Italian critics of the *Malleus* and, in general, of works affirming the reality of sorcery and magic were men of varying educational background: firstly philosophers and pure theoreticians, secondly lawyers, thirdly theologians, and finally scientists and physicians. The complex situation in Renaissance Italy cannot be fully described here; but, limiting ourselves to the theme of popular sorcery, we may note the attack on the *Malleus* by Gian Francesco Ponzinibio of Florence, who published a *Tractatus de Lamiis* in 1520; he was answered by a Dominican with inquisitorial functions, Fra Bartolommeo de Spina, in a treatise usually published with the *Malleus* and Nider's and other similar works.[51] Before Ponzinibio, a churchman defended the ancient doctrine and was opposed by another Dominican.[52] But, independently of polemics, books were published expressing complete credulity, such as that by Paulus Grillandus. This author is of especial interest for his knowledge of the origins of traditions and beliefs that have prevailed in southern Italy until modern times; some of these are pure inventions that have been repeated from place to place according to well-known principles of localization and actualization.[53] Grillandus is particularly interesting on the South and the Benevento region.

It should be noted also that great Italian theologians of the fifteenth century unhesitatingly followed what may be called the 'old' doctrine.

---

[50] Francisco de Vitoria, 'Relección del arte mágica', in *Relecciones teológicas*, Spanish trans. by Jaime Torrubiano y Ripoll, iii (Madrid, 1917), 152–3.

[51] De Spina wrote several treatises. The first, *Questio de strigibus*, in 32 chs., was published in the collections mentioned: e.g *Mallei maleficarum, ex plurimis auctoribus coadunati*, ii (Lyons, 1614), 147–259. The second, entitled *R.P.F. Bart. Spin. In Ponzinibium de Lamiis, apologia prima*, was followed by three more: published in the same compilation, pp. 260–317, the first and second in 12 chs. each, the third in 5 chs., the fourth in 1. The method is scholastic, and the refutation of the *Canon episcopi* furnishes a fundamental basis to both works.

[52] Thus Samuel de Cassinis *vis-à-vis* the Dominican Vincente Dodo.

[53] Paulus Grillandus, *Tractatus de hereticis, et sortilegiis omnifarium coitu* . . . (Lyons, 1536 and 1545); much quoted by subsequent writers.

Just as in Spain, the literary world made considerable use of the theme of magic; perhaps even more so in Italy, but in a way that could imply doubt or even satire.

The other Catholic country that produced an abundant theological and legal literature on the subject of witchcraft was France. There, from the second half of the sixteenth century, there was a tendency towards systematization that came to exercise great influence; it was represented largely by layfolk, but belongs to a later period than the one we are concerned with at present. Within the group connected with the works published together with the *Malleus*, two other authors must be considered. Firstly Bernard Basin, a noted preacher and a doctor of Paris University who became a canon of Saragossa, author of *De artibus magicis et magorum maleficiis*, published in 1483 and later editions (Paris, 1506). Basin interpreted the sources very much in his own way, invoking the authority of the pagan classics. His position, like Vitoria's, was eclectic: he accepted the reality of certain facts, and also the power of demons to control the imagination. Like others, he believed women to be more given to magic arts than men; he explained this in part by their physical make-up, greater impressionability, and a kind of erotic malice. The work consists of nine propositions and an equal number of conclusions.[54] Another text of the *Malleus* group is by the Swiss Ulrich Molitor, advocate to the bishop of Constance, who died in 1492. Besides works in German he wrote *De lamiis et pythonicis mulieribus*, published in 1489 in his native city and in Cologne. The Constance edition presents a new feature, namely, woodcuts representing the acts attributed to witches and wizards, no doubt as an awful example to readers. This, as we shall see, was also done in sixteenth-century works. Molitor's learned treatise, in ten chapters, is dedicated to Archduke Sigismund of Austria, and is in the form of a colloquy between the author, the archduke, and one Conrad Schatz. It refers to the popular belief (of that day and this) that witches fly by night on broomsticks, as depicted by painters around that time, and discusses the nature of covens. The most familiar traditions of Germanic folklore are also noted, as are hagiographic episodes that provided inspiration to artists, such as the Temptations of St Anthony.[55] Molitor's work is certainly more entertaining than others

[54] Bernard Basin, *De artibus magicis et magorum maleficiis* (Paris, 1483; 2nd edn., 1506). The author is briefly mentioned by Nicolás Antonio in *Bibliotheca Hispana Nova*, i (Madrid, 1783), 222a. The work is in *Mallei maleficarum, ex plurimis auctoribus*, ii. 9–31.

[55] Ulrich Molitor, *De lamiis et pythonicis mulieribus* (n.p., 1489), repr. *Tractatus utiliss. et necessarius, per viam dialogi, de Pythonicis mulieribus*, in *Mallei maleficarum*, ii. 32–70.

of the same intention, including two more in the *Malleus* group: Jean
Gerson's *Tractatus de probatione spirituum*,[56] and, by Thomas Murner,
OFM, *Libellus de Pythonico contractu*.[57] The former is of no concern to
our study, and the latter is also not quite of our period; it is mainly an
attack on astrology and divinatory practices.

IV

But we must now move forward in time, to the second half of the
sixteenth century.

In France there are two facts that seem to me significant. First, the
authors of the best-known works on popular belief in the reality of the
acts attributed to male and female sorcerers are laymen; and secondly,
these laymen introduce concepts of wide range and significance.
Leaving secondary authors aside, we come to the figure of Jean Bodin
(*c*.1530–96). Bodin, a lawyer from Angers, is doubtless better known as
a founder of political science than as the author of *De la Démonomanie
des Sorciers*, which was published in 1580 and put on the Index not long
afterwards.[58] But, however suspect his ideas from the point of view of
Catholic orthodoxy, this 'black sheep' evinces a strong belief in the
power of the devil; as a good lawyer, he also displays a tendency to
codification and systematization. The word 'démonomanie' that
occurs in his title (no acute accent in old editions) actually becomes
'daemonolatria' in the work of a later author. We thus reach the
culmination of the process of the 'diabolization' of witchcraft. Later
this process was to give rise to such conceptions as 'satanic',
'satanism', and 'satanology', which were unfamiliar in Spain till well
into the eighteenth century, unlike the name *Satán* or *Satanás*. To this
phase belongs, as will be seen, the widespread idea that witches and
wizards, in their worship of Satan, do no more than invert Catholic

[56] *Docti et acutissimi sacra pagina Doctoris Ioannis de Gersono, Cancellarii Parisiensis,
Tractatus perutilis de probatione Spirituum incipit foeliciter*, in *Mallei maleficarum*, ii. 71–80.

[57] *Tractatus perutiles de Pythonico contractu, fratris Thomas Murner, liberalium artium
Magistri, ordinis Minorum. Ad instantiam generosi domini Ioannis Mohrner der Mersperg
compilatus*, in *Mallei maleficarum*, ii. 81–146.

[58] *De la Démonomanie des Sorciers. A Monseigneur M. Chrestofle de Thou Chevalier Seigneur
de Coeli, premier Président en la Cour de Parlement, et Conseiller du Roy en son priué Conseil. Par I.
Bodin angevin* (Paris, 1580). Later edns. were published in 1582, 1586, 1587, 1604, etc.; and
there were translations into Latin, German, and Italian. However, *De magorum
Daemonomania* was placed on the Index by a decree of 1594: cf. *Indice general de los libros
prohibidos* (Madrid, 1844), 45*a*.

practices; hence the 'black Mass' and other rites that have come down to our time in decadent societies, being regarded as perverse and exploited by certain writers in the late nineteenth and early twentieth century. Bodin deals with almost all aspects of the 'magic arts'—not only traditional witchcraft, but also divination—and after the fourth book he undertakes to refute the famous work by Jean Wier.[59] Wier (1515–88), physician to the Duke of Cleves, had applied rational methods to the analysis of what was reported of witches and wizards, and had concluded that their punishment was not fully justified. In the face of legal codifications, displays of sacred and profane erudition, and the constant invocation of authority, Wier and others like him discussed the issue freely and expressed their doubts and experiences, though as yet with circumspection. During the first half of the sixteenth century other attempts were made to explain by natural causes such facts as the trances of sorcerers; a famous passage by Dr Laguna relates to this subject.[60] But the opposite doctrinal tendency produced new and famous fruits: for instance, the work of the Lorraine magistrate Nicolas Remi or Remy (Remigius; 1554–1600), known as 'le Torquémada lorrain', whose *Daemonolatria*, published at Lyons in 1595, attracted severe criticism.[61] The most significant aspect of this book, based on terrible experiences and on principles established by the *Malleus*, etc., is that 'mania' turns into 'latria': the supreme worship that is due only to God is given to the Evil One, in a sacrilegious and abominable manner, and is given to him directly, unequivocally. Remi is to Lorraine what Henri Boguet is to the Jura or Pierre de Lancre to the Labourd district, somewhat later on. It has never been easy to fathom the mentality of these lay judges, some of whom were men of great learning, or to understand their activity in countries which, at least in theory, disapproved of inquisitorial tribunals; but we have their books, attesting what they thought and what they did. Nowadays some believe that their persecutions and others like them were undertaken for political reasons, to establish

---

[59] *De la Démonomanie*, ed. cit., fos. 218–52. Johan Weyer's work *De praestigiis daemonum et incantationibus ac veneficiis lib. VI* was published at Basle in 1564 and went through several edns., including French translations. The French version of 1579 was reprinted in Paris in 2 vols. in 1885 under the title *Histoires, disputes et discours . . .*, in the series Bibliothèque diabolique.

[60] Text reproduced in Andrés Laguna, *Materia medica*, iv. 75 (Antwerp, 1555), 421–2.

[61] *Nic. Remigii Daemonolatria lib. III, ex judiciis capitalibus noningentorum plus minus hominum, qui sortilegii crimen intra annos quindecim in Lotharingis capti fuerunt* (Lyons, 1595; also later edns.).

control over unreliable regions. Certainly for a long time the civil laws and authorities were at least as strict on the subject of witchcraft as were the ecclesiastical courts.

However, before moving on in time, we should note how, independently of judicial practice, Catholic theologians went on elaborating the body of doctrine concerning all forms of magic, in ways that confront us with both sociological and psychological problems.

A number of theoretical works of interest were written at times when a revival of witchcraft took place in a particular area. One of these was a treatise by Martín de Arles y Andosilla, canon of Pamplona, who wrote in the fifteenth century of the witches of Navarre—whom he believed to be numerous among the common people, but concerning whom he adopted a cautious position.[62] As regards persecutions and trials in the first half of the sixteenth century, there is another treatise in Spanish by Fray Martín de Castañega, published at Logroño in 1529,[63] which describes clearly the opposition between the sacraments of the Church and what he calls the 'execraments' of sorcerers: that is, the inversion we have spoken of, creating a kind of diabolical Church. Castañega also knows and comments on the different opinions as to why there are more witches than wizards, and adduces names that have a Basque appearance, such as 'Xorguinos'. Other general treatises of about this date give less space to witchcraft as such, but reflect the interest aroused especially by recent trials in Navarre;[64] this interest is also seen in some works of literature and secular history. In a literary work, inspired by familiar classical Latin texts, it is curious to note that Navarrese witches are credited with the same activities as those of ancient Thessaly, being regarded as from the same stock.[65] But it is clear that the centuries have not elapsed in vain.

[62] Martín de Arles y Andosilla, *Tractatus de supersticionibus* (Lyons, 1510; 2nd edn. Paris, 1517).

[63] Martín de Castañega, *Tratado muy sotil y bien fundado de las supersticiones y hechizerías, y varios conjuros y abusiones y otras cosas al caso tocantes y de la possibilidad y remedio dellas* (Logroño, 1529); a very rare work.

[64] e.g. that of Pedro Ciruelo, *Reprouacion de las supersticiones y hechicerias* (Salamanca, 1556), fo. xix[v]. There are earlier edns. of 1529, 1539, and 1551.

[65] *El Crotalón* (Buenos Aires, 1945), 77 (canto 5).

V

Greco-Latin culture still played a dominant role in sixteenth-century Europe, both in Catholic and in Protestant countries—perhaps with more vital continuity in the former, especially in Italy. It may also be said that that culture exercised a powerful influence on authors concerned with magic in general and witchcraft in particular, from a theoretical point of view. The most striking example is Martín del Rio (1551–1609), a Spanish Jesuit born in Antwerp. He was distinguished for his studies of classical literature, but still more for a voluminous work, both learned and credulous, written shortly before 1600, the *Disquisitionum magicarum libri sex*.[66] The first book treats of the generally accepted types of magic: the 'natural', the 'artificial', and the 'deceitful'; the second, of 'demoniac magic' and its efficacy; the third, of 'spells' and 'vain observances'. The fourth book deals with 'prophecy', 'divination', and 'conjecture'; the fifth discusses the function of judges and the order of criminal proceedings; the sixth treats of the office of confessors and of licit and illicit remedies. In book ii more especially, and throughout the work, witches are dealt with under *quaestio 16*, which speaks of nocturnal covens and the question whether witches are transported from place to place. Del Rio is familiar with almost all the authorities we have mentioned and with some others: both those who, unlike him, accept the theory of a trance or illusion, and those (including a Calvinist writer) who believe that the occurrences are real. He cites numerous cases and witnesses in favour of the second view: some very recent, from the 1580s and even from 1590. His views are close to those of Remi and far from those of Jean Wier.[67] His immense erudition goes some way to disprove the eighteenth-century idea that belief in witchcraft was founded in 'ignorance': a theologian like del Rio, or a magistrate like Bodin, were anything but ignorant. In del Rio's case, one may rather speak of a 'world-view' decisively influenced by ideas of authority and by literary erudition, as opposed to the view of those authors—including some of much earlier date—who believed that right ideas must be founded on experiment and direct observation of the real world.

[66] Cf. my essay 'Martín del Rio y sus Disquisiciones mágicas', in *El señor Inquisidor y otras vidas por oficio* (Madrid, 1968), 171–96. The *Disquisitiones* were published at Louvain in 1599–1600; other edns. followed at intervals until at least 1747.

[67] Martín del Rio, *Disquisitionum magicarum libri sex* (Venice, 1616), 154*a*–171*a* (bk ii, *quaestio* 16).

There is no doubt that at the end of the sixteenth and the beginning of the seventeenth century there was a positive obsession with the devil's physical presence in the world. Following Molitor's example, some authors accompanied their texts with hair-raising illustrations of alleged events. An example is the *Compendium maleficarum* of F. M. Guazzo (Guaccius) of Milan, which shows witches and wizards on their way to covens, abjuring the Faith, receiving the devil's baptism, writing their names in the book of death (being erased from that of life), vowing to sacrifice children, kissing the rump of the horned and winged Satan, worshipping him on his throne, dancing, feasting, raising storms, seeking out corpses with which to make magic spells, and turning themselves into animals for the same purpose.[68] This book was published in the author's native city in 1608, a date of importance in the history of witchcraft, as we shall see.

It must be confessed that these woodcuts, like others of the same period depicting infernal and diabolic scenes, are less frightening than those of Goya, although he, as a child of the Enlightenment, was concerned to satirize popular beliefs and their reflection in Spanish works of Guazzo's day. The latter's work appeared immediately before a trial of witches and sorcerers in the far north of the kingdom of Navarre, the accused being condemned at an *auto da fé* held at Logroño on 7–8 November 1610. The proceedings were described in Spanish in a far from theoretical *Relación*,[69] the publication of which produced scandal and surprise. For a considerable time afterwards more or less burlesque allusions were made to it, in the style of the passage quoted from Moreto (note 17, above). After 1800, during a period of criticism of inquisitorial excesses, the *Relación* was reprinted with notes by Leandro Fernández de Moratín, a friend of Goya's,[70] and there is no doubt that it provided the artist with inspiration for his terrifying etchings. In fact it gives a fairly free account of the trial: while two of the judges accepted the absolute truth of all the testimony and confessions, a third dissented. Together with details of time and place, and references to particular individuals, the *Relación* comprised

---

[68] The twelve engravings are reproduced in the 1st edn. of *Las brujas y su mundo*, figs. 2–13 following p. 304.

[69] *Relación de las personas que salieron al Auto de la Fee que los señores Doctor Alonso Bezerra Holguin del ábito de Alcántara; licenciado Juan de Valle Alvarado y licenciado Alonso de Salazar Frias . . ., celebraron en la cuidad de Logroño, en siete y en ocho dias del mes de Noviembre de 1610 Años. Y de las cosas y delitos porque fueron castigados* (Logroño, 1611). Full text published by the present author in *Brujería vasca* (San Sebastiàn, 1975), 71–121.

[70] Edns. of 1812, 1820, 1836, etc.

a systematic account of all that had been alleged against witches and wizards since the fifteenth century. The principal events in the case were stated to have taken place in a mysterious spot, the cave of Zugarramurri: a natural tunnel in a calcareous mass, worn away by a river still known in Basque as 'hell-stream' (*infernuko erreka*). The cave served both as a temple and as a court. A secret society with a hierarchy of degrees carried out wicked acts under the direction of the devil in the form of a he-goat, and struck terror into the surrounding villages. As in many other such cases, evidence was furnished by women, children, and infirm old people. The affair had important consequences which have only become known in modern times. The third, dissenting judge at Logroño—*licenciado* Alonso Salazar y Frias, a man well grounded in the law—asked for and obtained a revision of the case. The detailed investigations which resulted are described in full by Gustav Henningsen in an excellent book;[71] they made it possible to establish, by purely judicial procedure, the falsity of most of the evidence that had been taken as certain. Salazar y Frias did not discuss the matter like a doctor, a natural scientist, or a critical philosopher (such as Montaigne or Charron), but in the style of a lawyer examining the procedure followed in the particular case before him. As a result he obtained an edict of pardon, and from that date onwards scarcely any trials for collective witchcraft were brought by the Spanish Inquisition. This suspension did not apply to cases of individual witchcraft and other magic practices.[72]

The action of the other two judges at Logroño is paralleled by that of Pierre de Lancre, the famous magistrate of the *parlement* of Bordeaux, who presided over a terrible persecution in the Labourd country (bordering on Navarre), which he described in a work entitled *Tableau de l'inconstance des mauvais anges et démons*, published in Paris in 1612 and illustrated by a curious engraving showing what was alleged against witches and wizards in the affidavits endorsed by the author.[73]

[71] Gustav Henningsen, *The Witches' Advocate: Basque Witchcraft and the Spanish Inquisition* (Reno, 1980).

[72] For subsequent cases see Julio Caro Baroja, *Vidas mágicas e Inquisición* (2 vols.; Madrid, 1967).

[73] The full title is significant: *Tableau de l'inconstance des mauvais anges et démons. Où il est amplement traicté de la Sorcelerie et Sorciers. Livre tres curieux et tres utile, non seulement aux juges, mais à tous ceux qui vivent soubs les loix Chrestiennes. Avec un discours contenant le procédure faicte par les Inquisitions d'Espagne et de Navarre, à 53 Magiciens, Apostats, Juifs, Sorciers, en la ville de Logrogne en Castille, le 9 de Novembre 1610. En laquelle on voit combien l'exercise de la justice en France est plus juridiquement traicté, et avec de plus belles formes qu'en tous autres Empires, Royaumes, Republiques et Estats* (Paris, 1612). A later work by De Lancre contains some

Here again we have a man of great learning and some literary talent, who, unlike Salazar y Frias, represents the 'realist' view initiated by the authors of the *Malleus*. Much has been written about Pierre de Lancre, not all of it sensible; but it can be said that he is the last systematic author on this subject who possessed judicial authority and himself carried out violent repression. He magnifies the alleged offences of witches and wizards in a small, economically backward region, as though a diabolical court might have existed there, and as if the unfortunate, accused villagers were steeped in satanic lore.[74] This of course is contrary to the idea of the ignorance and simplicity of country folk in general that emerges from many French and Spanish texts of his time, in which the contrast between rural life and court life is a constant theme.[75] Pierre de Lancre, in fact, stands for an ultimate degree of 'sophistication' with regard to so widespread a phenomenon as belief in witches—a phenomenon whose recurrent characteristics have little to do with such fabulous constructions.

VI

It cannot be said without qualification that theologians and theorists of the kind described in the foregoing pages were no longer numerous after the first two decades of the seventeenth century, but they certainly had less influence than before. In Spain, for instance, there appeared the very systematic treatise of Francisco Torreblanca, a lawyer from Cordoba.[76] In Portugal, Valle de Moura published a work consisting of several 'monographs' that are not without interest.[77]

supplementary material: *L'Incrédulité et mescreance du sortilège plainement convancue* . . . (Paris, 1622).

[74] Much confusion is still caused by the practice of attributing the ideas of the persecutors to the persecuted, and confusing the world of the populace with that of the controversialists.

[75] On the attitude towards country folk see Julio Caro Baroja, *Las formas complejas de la vida religiosa: Religión, sociedad y carácter en la España de los siglos XVI y XVII* (Madrid, 1978), 325–61.

[76] *D. Francisci Torreblanca Villalpando Cordubensis juris consulti Juris Spiritualis practicabilium libri* xv. *Ex lege Domini sive revelatis a Deo, per Sacram Scripturam, vel in Communi Ecclesiae, vel in particulari hominum* (Cordoba, 1635). There are less complete earlier edns. A large part of this work is devoted to witchcraft.

[77] *De incantationibus seu ensalmis. Opusculum primum, auctore Emanuele de Valle de Moura Doctore Theologo, ac Sanctae Inquisitionis Deputato Lusitano Patria Calantica* (Evora, 1620). The book consists of a series of themes treated monographically.

But it is also the case that, within the bounds of Catholic orthodoxy, a number of authors expressed reservations or open disapproval of the credulity and severity of judges and inquisitors. It is noteworthy, for instance, that among the Jesuits, in contrast to such as del Rio, there were those who adopted a critical attitude for one reason or another,[78] and eventually others whose direct experience led them to much more radical conclusions. The most famous case is that of Friedrich von Spee, a German Jesuit who died in 1635 at the age of 44, and who in 1631 published anonymously at Rinteln a work entitled *Cautio criminalis seu de processibus contra sagas liber. Authore incerto theologo orthodoxo.*[79] A French translation was published twenty-nine years later by F. Bouvet, a doctor at Besançon; this was used in 1868 by J. Tissot, professor of philosophy at Dijon, in a work on the imagination.[80]

Von Spee's work was based on his own experience of courts and prisons, primarily as a confessor. He examines the circumstances in which people were accused of sorcery, and the variety of accusations supported by more than doubtful testimony. He refers to the influence of preachers, and to the fact that lawyers and inquisitors were remunerated in proportion to the number of convictions. He describes the forms of detention, interrogation, and inspection; the obtaining of confessions by torture, the passing of sentence, accusations of complicity, and retractation *in extremis.* The whole system was permeated by deception and prejudice. Men and women were inexorably condemned to death in accordance with a stereotyped image of their crime or crimes. The most difficult aspect for the free imagination to accept was the accepted notion of the nature of witchcraft. Von Spee's work was chiefly appreciated by intellectuals years after his death, and was the subject of a commentary by Leibniz.[81] It is

---

[78] e.g. Adam Tanner, SJ, who had the honour of being himself mentioned as a sorcerer in the *Dictionnaire infernal* by J. Collin de Plancy (Paris, 1863), 650*a*–651*a*. This work, as is known, contains a great many fables.

[79] Spee (or Spé) is also noted as a German religious poet; his lyric works, published posthumously, combine Christian faith with pagan erudition.

[80] Friedrich von Spee, *Advis aux criminalistes sur les abus qui se glissent dans les procès de sorcellerie, dediés aux magistrats d'Allemagne. Livre tres nécessaire en ce temps icy à tous juges, conceillers, confesseurs (tant des juges que des criminels), inquisiteurs, prédicateurs, advocats, et même aux medecins par le P. N. S. J., theologien romain* (Lyons, 1660). Bouvet's French translation was extensively used by J. Tissot in *L'Imagination, ses bienfaits et ses égarements surtout dans le domaine du merveilleux* (Paris, 1868), 372–437.

[81] G. W. Leibnitz (1646–1716), *Die Theodizee*, pt i, paras 96–7: ed. Arthur Buchanan (Hamburg, 1968), 159–60.

interesting to note how some Catholic theologians in later years took up Spee's ideas and forgot those that had directly preceded them. The most striking case is that of Nicolas-Sylvestre Bergier (1718–90) in an article 'Sorcellerie' in the theological dictionary that forms part of the *Encyclopédie méthodique*.[82] He gives three definitions of 'sorcery', and says as regards the third:

The common people understand by 'sorcerers' those who have the power to fly through the air at night-time to remote places where they worship the Devil and abandon themselves to intemperance and lust. This is in fact a baseless illusion: the so-called 'witches' sabbath' is a disease of the imagination caused by certain drugs used by the wretches who seek after it. This is proved by unquestionable experience.

As his authority, Bergier cites Malebranche.[83] Very well; but in laying the whole responsibility on unlearned people he forgets the works of theologians, inquisitors, judges, and civil magistrates, who, as we have seen, make great play of their erudition and describe the 'sabbath' (also called *aquelarre* in Spanish) in lurid detail.

Bergier's view is similar to that of other Catholic theologians and philosophers in the eighteenth century. But it does not reflect what actually occurred from the end of the fifteenth to the beginning of the seventeenth century: namely, the process of 'diabolization' that we have described and that came to affect the ideas of the common people. It is also true, however, that the investigation of popular traditions sometimes shows that earlier ideas concerning persons in direct relations with witches, dictating their conduct and other matters, were at variance with the theologians' interpretation postulating constant dependence on a demon in bodily shape, possessing special attributes and so on.

I thus come to the end of my purpose, which was to show how, starting from a group of pre-Christian concepts and beliefs which were further developed among the nations of classical civilization, new concepts and beliefs were created under the influence of a Christian theological interpretation which went through at least two phases and

---

[82] *Encyclypédie méthodique: théologie par M. l'Abbé Bergier, Chanoine de l'Eglise de Paris, et Confesseur de Monsier Frère du Roi*, iii (Paris, 1790), 522*b*–524*a*.

[83] Bergier, *Encyclopédie méthodique*, iii. 522*b*–523*a*. This author believed that there was no question of an artifice of the devil, which was an idea that had originated among the northern barbarians and penetrated to '*nos climats*'. He refers to the testimony of Leibnitz, saying that according to von Spee there was no single case of a convicted person who could say with certainty that he had attended a sabbath.

which, in course of time, became attenuated and disavowed its own previous principles.

It is certain that in the mid-nineteenth century there were memorable cases of rural communities dominated by fear of witches and wizards, even in western Europe.[84] It is also known that the legitimacy of belief in the power of certain persons to work evil in the devil's name was defended and illustrated by men of good faith,[85] and also by all kinds of occultists, satanists, and so on. But the subject we are concerned with from the historico-cultural point of view has little or nothing to do with the theme of demonological literature. It is a question of seeing how the function of the witch existed independently of its pagan or Christian interpretation, in societies of different types; how a set of ideas and supposed facts came to centre around it; how these changed in such a way as to alter the general picture of the witch's personality in a given society; and how, finally, 'collective representations' were sometimes created by authorities concerned with their own techniques, who in the present case were theologians on the one hand and jurists on the other.

---

[84] See Dr A. Constant, *Relation sur une épidémie d'hystéro-démonopathie en 1861* (2nd edn. Paris, 1863). This describes how the ills afflicting children at Morzines (Haute-Savoie) were attributed to an unpopular *curé* who was said to be the chief of a group of sorcerers (pp. 40–1). Tissot (*L'Imagination*, pp. 544–89) gave much attention to the case, considered as primarily one of demoniac possession.

[85] There are popular accounts of a fairly misleading nature, e.g. I. Bertand, 'La Sorcellerie', in a collection entitled *Religions et sciences occultes* (Paris, 1912).

2

Protestant Demonology: Sin, Superstition, and Society (c.1520–c.1630)

STUART CLARK

I

IN 1584 the Elizabethan sceptic Reginald Scot claimed that only the Catholic Church really took witchcraft seriously. Witchmongers and massmongers were one and the same thing, whereas the religion of the gospel could stand 'without such peevish trumperie'. It was, he said, 'incomprehensible to the wise, learned or faithfull; a probable matter to children, fooles, melancholike persons and papists'. All the same, he was obliged to acknowledge the demonologies of leading European Protestant theologians like Lambert Daneau and Niels Hemmingsen, and he deplored the way in which the ordinary English clergy lent credibility to popular witchcraft beliefs by recognizing the existence of healers and conjurors in their parishes and making allegations against local witches.[1] In 1653, after nearly seventy more years of active Protestant publishing on the subject, another English sceptic, Robert Filmer, was in no doubt about the essential consensus across denominational lines: 'for both those of the reformed Churches, as well as these of the Roman in a manner, agree in their Definition of the sinne of Witch-craft.'[2] This change of emphasis has been mirrored in modern times. Like Scot, Georg Längin and Wilhelm Gottlieb Soldan (anti-Catholic) and Johann Diefenbach and Nikolaus Paulus (anti-Protestant) blamed witch-hunting on their religious opponents.[3]

---

[1] Reginald Scot, *The discoverie of witchcraft* (London, 1584), quotations at sig. Biv^r, p. 472; cf. sig. Bii^v, pp. 4–6.

[2] [Robert Filmer], *An advertisement to the jury-men of England, touching witches* (London, 1653), 3.

[3] Georg Längin, *Religion und Hexenprozess* (Leipzig, 1888); Wilhelm Gottlieb Soldan, *Geschichte der Hexenprozesse*, ed. Max Bauer (2 vols.; Munich, 1912); Johann Diefenbach, *Der Hexenwahn vor und nach der Glaubensspaltung in Deutschland* (Mainz, 1886); Nikolaus Paulus, *Hexenwahn und Hexenprozess vornehmlich im 16. Jahrhundert* (Freiburg im Breisgau, 1910).

More recently, historians have tended to concur with Filmer. H. R. Trevor-Roper argued that the evangelists of all the major churches were equally involved, both at the level of actual prosecutions and in the elaboration of theory, a view in which he has been followed by Jean Delumeau.[4]

But in any case, these questions are now seen to rest on outmoded assumptions. It no longer seems appropriate to apportion responsibility, if this is to have moralistic overtones. The very idea of drawing confessional correlations across the history of witchcraft has also been overtaken by fresh inquiries into local patterns of witch-hunting. It has become clear that the incidence and severity of the campaigns actually mounted against witches depended on a complex interplay of social, institutional, and ideological circumstances, which could cut across religious affiliation. This is well illustrated in William Monter's recent sketch of what he calls the 'map of social controls' for the period. Here, striking regional differences emerge in the witch-hunting profiles of Calvinist and Catholic Europe. The Scottish and Dutch experiences were at opposite ends of the spectrum of severity; Mediterranean and Northern Catholic reactions to witchcraft were also strongly divergent.[5]

Above all, there is considerable sympathy for the view that what is reflected in these episodes is not so much differences between the religions of the churches involved (or any inter-sectarian strife) as their common missionary determination to impose the fundamentals of Christian belief and practice on ordinary people. One component of this new evangelism was a campaign—again, in an important, if paradoxical, sense, jointly mounted—to discredit and eradicate a wide range of popular cultural forms as 'superstitions'. Delumeau's celebrated proposal that the Protestant and Catholic Reformations, despite their theological and liturgical rivalries, were jointly attempting to 'Christianize' the average Westerner has the merit of embracing the widest possible considerations of cultural change—even if it betrays a degree of cultural condescension.[6] But it also allows us to locate the history of early modern witchcraft at the very heart of the

---

[4] Hugh R. Trevor-Roper, *The European Witch-craze of the 16th and 17th Centuries* (Harmondsworth, 1969; repr. 1985), 64–7, 72–3; Jean Delumeau, *La Peur en Occident (XIVe–XVIIIe siècles): Une cité assiégée* (Paris, 1978), 359–60.

[5] E. William Monter, *Ritual, Myth and Magic in Early Modern Europe* (Brighton, 1983), *passim*, esp. 43–97.

[6] Jean Delumeau, *Catholicism between Luther and Voltaire*, trans. J. Moiser (London, 1977), 154–74.

reforming process. In a further important essay, Delumeau has himself shown how natural it was (for Protestants at least) to move between the categories of superstition and demonism: 'Le comportement protestant est en effet inintelligible sans la restitution de l'univers diabolique familier aux hommes de la Renaissance.'[7] And if demonology sheds crucial light on the impetus to reform, so evangelism helps to make much better sense of witch-hunting. This is a principle that has been put to work successfully in the cases of Calvinist Scotland,[8] the Catholic north of France,[9] and the Duchy of Luxembourg,[10] and although relatively untried in Germany, it applies well to the circumstances of the witch-trials in the Catholic ecclesiastical territory of Bamberg.[11]

Does this mean that early modern demonology, whatever the faiths of its authors, was simply the uniform expression of a new form of social control—what Christina Larner has called 'Christian political ideology'? If we take only its fundamental ingredients, there does seem to be little to distinguish the Protestant from the Catholic versions. Concerning the mechanics of demonism, the limitations on the powers of devils to effect changes in the natural world, and their consequent resort to illusion, there is total agreement, based on a shared intellectual indebtedness to Augustine and Aquinas. On the general causation of witchcraft phenomena, Jerome Zanchi, Otto Casmann, and Pietro Martire Vermigli spoke with the same voice as Francesco Torreblanca, Peter Binsfeld, or Martín del Rio.[12] The eschatological view that witchcraft flourished because the world was in a state of terminal decline was as common among French Catholic

---

[7] Jean Delumeau, 'Les Réformateurs et la superstition', in *Actes du colloque sur l'Amiral de Coligny et son temps* (Société de l'Histoire du Protestantisme Français, Paris, 1974), 460.

[8] Christina Larner, *Enemies of God: The Witch-hunt in Scotland* (London, 1981), 25, 157–60.

[9] Robert Muchembled, 'Sorcières du Cambrésis: L'Acculturation du monde rural aux XVIᵉ et XVIIᵉ siècles', in Marie-Sylvie Dupont-Bouchat, Willem Frijhoff, and Robert Muchembled, *Prophètes et sorciers dans les Pays-Bas: XVIᵉ–XVIIIᵉ siècle* (Paris, 1978), 155–261; cf. Robert Muchembled, 'Witchcraft, Popular Culture, and Christianity in the Sixteenth Century with Emphasis upon Flanders and Artois', in Robert Forster and Patricia Ranum (eds.), *Ritual, Religion, and the Sacred* (London, 1982), 213–36.

[10] Marie-Sylvie Dupont-Bouchat, 'La Répression de la sorcellerie dans le duché de Luxembourg aux XVIᵉ et XVIIᵉ siècles', in Dupont-Bouchat, Frijhoff, and Muchembled, *Prophètes et sorciers*, pp. 41–154.

[11] Robert Walinski-Kiehl, 'Catholicism, Cultural Conflict and Witch-hunting in Seventeenth-century Bamberg' (unpublished conference paper, May 1985).

[12] I have attempted a discussion of this point in 'The Scientific Status of Demonology', in Brian Vickers (ed.), *Occult and Scientific Mentalities in the Renaissance* (Cambridge, 1984), 351–74.

authors such as Sébastien Michaëlis, Pierre Nodé, and Jean le
Normant, as among the writers of Lutheran Germany and Calvinist
England—in this case reflecting the popularity of apocalyptic history
in both Reformations. And when the proper judicial response to
witchcraft was debated, Protestant and Catholic authors were alike
prompt to call down the authority of the secular magistrate and to
defend it with a mixture of Old Testament precedents, Pauline
political theory, and (what Max Weber would later call) 'charismatic
legitimation'. On none of these matters was there a characteristically
'Protestant' or 'Catholic' view, a fact amply illustrated by the
frequency with which the demonological authorities of one religion
were cited by the exegetes of the other. What were important here, as
John Teall has perceptively noted, were not 'specific confessional
peculiarities but problems general to the period'.[13]

All the same, it would be odd to find in the literature of demonism
and witchcraft no reflection whatsoever of theological preferences.
Unity on essentials does not rule out differences of accent; nor can the
common evangelism hide disagreements about tactics and priorities.
While allowing that there was no essentially Protestant doctrine of
witchcraft, Monter suggests that nearly all Protestant writers on the
subject 'insisted on a few common elements', above all, the extent of
divine power and providence.[14] Larner, too, while arguing that 'the
different types of theological position prevalent in seventeenth-
century Scotland are less important than the introduction of Christianity itself', provides for a theological emphasis on God's rewarding
of sin with earthly punishments.[15]

With these various pointers in mind, what fresh questions ought to
be asked of the Protestant literature on demonology and witchcraft?
Its possible relationship to the campaign to reform popular religiosity,
and hence its relevance to recent accounts of 'reformation' as a social
and cultural phenomenon, become crucially important. To think of it
as integral to the aims of reformers would add weight to a version of
the 'acculturation thesis', so very different were its perceptions of
misfortune and redress from those of the audience at which it was
directed. At the same time this would further help to rescue the whole

---

[13] John Teall, 'Witchcraft and Calvinism in Elizabethan England: Divine Power and
Human Agency', *Journal of the History of Ideas*, 23 (1962), 22; cf. p. 34. I give a full account
of the historical and political opinions of early modern demonologists in a forthcoming
study, *Witchcraft in Early Modern Thought*, pts. iii and v.

[14] Monter, *Ritual*, p. 31.

[15] Larner, *Enemies of God*, p. 201.

2. *Protestant Demonology* 49

subject of demonology from the realm of the peripheral, the irrational, and the dysfunctional in early modern affairs. In the process it seems reasonable to look at those matters, never entirely foreign to Catholic discussions, on which Protestant authors nevertheless concentrated. This will certainly involve tracing, in an attenuated sense, a 'Protestant view' of witchcraft; but my aim will be to preserve the sense in which this was only one possible expression of a shared model of acculturation.

Finally, there is the straightforward question of just what sort of opinions accompanied the hunting of witches in Protestant cultures. Historians have long been concerned with the social structural circumstances in which witchcraft accusations and prosecutions occurred. Now there is a revival of interest in the mentalities involved and, in particular, in the interaction, at the level of beliefs and attitudes, between the concerns of the professional and literate classes and those of the social groups from which the accused by and large came.[16] No one could doubt for a moment the potential influence of the clergy in this respect, both as general moulders of opinion and as participants in particular investigations and trials. The literature teems with instances of the involvement of individual pastors—from John Ferrall of Brenchley in the Kent of Reginald Scot, to Thomas Naogeorgus in the imperial city of Esslingen in south-western Germany in the 1560s; from the Lutheran church superintendents Peder Palladius and Jørgen Erikssøn in sixteenth-century Denmark and Norway, to the Calvinist kirk minister James Hutchison in Paisley in Scotland in 1697.[17] It was usual for Protestant authorities to ask local clergymen for theological advice on the subject of witchcraft—as happened, for instance, in Strasburg in 1538 and Nuremberg in 1590.[18]

[16] The classic study remains Carlo Ginzburg, *The Night Battles: Witchcraft and Agrarian Cults in the Sixteenth and Seventeenth Centuries*, trans. J. and A. Tedeschi (London, 1983). See also Clive Holmes, 'Popular Culture? Witches, Magistrates, and Divines in Early Modern England', in Steven L. Kaplan (ed.), *Understanding Popular Culture: Europe from the Middle Ages to the Nineteenth Century* (Berlin, 1984), 85–111.

[17] Scot, *Discoverie*, pp. 4–5; H. C. Erik Midelfort, *Witch-hunting in Southwestern Germany, 1562–1684* (Stanford, 1972), 88–90; for Palladius and Erikson, see Hans Eyvind Naess, ch. 14, below; Larner, *Enemies of God*, pp. 163–7. Naess's essay reveals a considerable degree of general pastoral involvement in witchcraft examinations in Norway, and, in particular, pastoral responsibility for the questions actually put to suspects.

[18] Johannes Janssen, *History of the German People at the Close of the Middle Ages*, trans. A. M. Christie and M. A. Mitchell (17 vols.; London, 1896–1910), xvi. 275–6; Harmut H. Kunstmann, *Zauberwahn und Hexenprozess in der Reichsstadt Nürnberg* (Nuremberg, 1970), 177–84. Cf. Bengt Ankarloo, *Trolldomsprocesserna i Sverige* (Lund, 1971), 328 (English summary).

The Scandinavian materials in this volume alone would justify the claim that the Protestant pastorate played a vital role in witch-hunting; as would the contrasting evidence from the Dutch Republic, where its influence was decisively curbed. It seems reasonable, therefore, to re-examine a literature which reflected its views and which, as we shall see, was dominated by its evangelical and pastoral priorities. What, then, could be read (and heard) on the topic of witchcraft in the first century or so of European Protestantism?[19]

II

An immediate complexity is the subject's potentially very wide diffusion.[20] It was an academic commonplace of the period that witchcraft had three essential components: divine permission, demonic potency, and human ill-will. Thinking and writing about it were therefore allied naturally to general theology and casuistry, as well as to the specialisms of demonology (properly so called) and pneumatology. This explains why it is found deeply embedded in a work of dogmatics like Jesper Brochmand's *Systema universae theologiae* (1633),[21] or summarized in the collections of theological *loci communes* by Johann Manlius[22] and Andreas Gerhard (Hyperius),[23] or integrated with the account of the evil angels in Jerome Zanchi's *De operibus Dei intra spacium sex dierum creatis*.[24] Discussions of angels and devils, spectral

---

[19] I have concentrated on the period down to *c*.1630 on the grounds that by then a distinctive tradition among Protestant writers had been established. Those who sustained it through the 17th c. did not significantly alter it.

[20] A convenient starting-point is the lists of (*a*) *hexenpredigten*, and (*b*) other miscellaneous discussions of witchcraft, in Diefenbach, *Der Hexenwahn*, pp. 204–5 (I have not traced all of the latter).

[21] Jesper (or Caspar) Brochmand, *Systema universae theologiae* (Copenhagen, 1633); I have used the 5th edn. of 1658 (Ulm and Frankfurt am Main), where the witchcraft section is at vol. ii, ch. xix, pp. 68–9. For Brochmand (who was Bishop of Sealand) and the relevance of his views both to Danish witch-trials and the theological faculty at Copenhagen, see Jens Christian V. Johansen, ch. 13, below, and also his 'Witchcraft in Elsinore, 1625–6', *Mentalities*, 3 (1985), 7–8.

[22] Joannes Manlius, *Locorum communium collectanea* (Basle, 1563), pt. i, pp. 33–48 ('De malis spiritibus seu diabolis, et ipsorum operibus', in the section 'De Creatione').

[23] Andreas Gerhard (Hyperius), 'Whether that the devils have bene the shewers of magicall artes', in *Two commonplaces taken out of Andreas Hyperius*, trans. R. V. (London, 1581), 47–81.

[24] Jerome Zanchi, *Operum theologicorum* (8 vols. in 3; Heidelberg, 1605), iii (in i), cols. 167–216. Zanchi was Prof. of Theology at Strasbourg and Heidelberg. Of his demonology, Richard Baxter wrote: 'no Man hath given us a more full Testimony in general of

phenomena and hell, could obviously provide occasions for treating of demonism and witchcraft,[25] but so too could the guidebooks of the analysts of conscience.[26] However, this is just a beginning. Biblical commentary also frequently gave rise to excursions into demonology, magic, and witchcraft, as was the case, for example, with Pietro Martire Vermigli's study of 1 Samuel 28 (Saul and the witch of Endor).[27] Questions concerning the efficacy of demonic operations and the nature of magical actions were dealt with by Protestant physicians and natural philosophers such as Wilhelm Adolf Schreiber (Scribonius), John Cotta, and (later) Heinrich Nicolai.[28] They were also the subject of dissertations and theses defended in the faculties of philosophy, theology, and medicine in the Protestant universities.[29] The forty-five theses *Adversus magiam et magos* were part of a series which the Lutheran

Diabolical Operations', *The certainty of the world of spirits* (London, 1691), 134; cf. 108. Zanchi also wrote a work on divination: *De divinatione tam artificiosa, quam artis experte, et utriusque variis speciebus tractatus* (Hanover, 1610).

[25] Examples of Protestant works in these areas are Andreas Althamer, *Eyn predig von dem Teüffel, das er alles Unglück in der Welt anrichte* (Nuremberg, 1532); Sebastian Fröschel, *Von dem heiligen engeln. Vom Teuffel und des Menschen Seele* (Wittenberg, 1563), sigs. Hii^r–Lv^v; Otto Casmann, *Angelographia* (Frankfurt, 1597), pt. ii ('De malis angelis'); Marcus Scultetus, *Praesidium angelicum. Ein nützlich Handbüchlein. Von guten und bösen Engeln* (Wittenberg, 1616), 343–637; Abraham Seidel, *[Pneumatologia] Πνευματολογια, oder Kurtzer Bericht von denen Geistern* . . . (Erfurt, 1648); Ludwig Lavater, *De spectris, lemuribus et magnis atque insolitis fragoribus* . . (Zurich, 1570); Christopher Irenaeus, *Spiegel der Hellen und Zustand der Verdampten* (Ursel, 1579).

[26] Heinrich Decimator, *Gewissens Teuffel: Das ist:* . . . *Bericht von dem aller erschrecklichsten, Grewlichsten und grossen Teuffel, des Gewissens Teufel* (Magdeburg, 1604) (Decimator was a theologian at Mühlhausen in Thuringia); Friedrich Balduin, *Tractatus de casibus conscientiae* (Wittenberg, 1628); Ludvig Dunte, *Decesiones mille et sex casuum* . . .: *Das ist, Kurz und richtige Erörterung ein tausend und sechs Gewissens Fragen* (Lübeck, 1636). For Dunte and his influence on the witch-hunter Nils Psilander, see Juhan Kahk, ch. 10, below; cf. the influence of practical theology in Sweden, Ankarloo, *Trolldomsprocesserna*, p. 339.

[27] Pietro Martire Vermigli, *In duos libros Samuelis prophetae* . . . *commentarii doctissimi* (Zurich, 1575), fos. 155^v–168^v. A good indication of the range of biblical commentaries dealing with demonological themes is given by Jodocus Hocker's extensive citations from such sources throughout his *Der teufel selbs* (see below, n. 89).

[28] Wilhelm Adolf Schreiber (Scribonius), *De sagarum natura et potestate* (Marburg, 1588), fos. 1–92; John Cotta, *The triall of witch-craft* (London, 1616); Heinrich Nicolai, *De magicis actionibus tractatus singularis philosophico–theologicus et historicus* (Danzig, 1649). Schreiber was a physician and Prof. of Philosophy at the universities of Marburg and Korbach; Cotta was an English physician; and Nicolai was Lutheran Prof. of Philosophy at Danzig.

[29] This is very much a neglected area, but a beginning may be made with Lynn Thorndike, *A History of Magic and Experimental Science* (8 vols.; New York, 1934–58), vii, ch. 12, 'Interest in the Occult at German Universities', 338–71.

divine Georg Sohn disputed at Marburg and Heidelberg; in 1570 the
Tübingen theologian Jacob Heerbrand presided at a disputation on
magic and witchcraft, with Nicolaus Falco as respondent; and in 1606
the academic Tobias Tandler brought together a number of Wittenberg and Helmstadt dissertations and published them with his own
Dissertatio de fascino et incantatione.[30] During the seventeenth century the
Swedish and Finnish universities were also producing dissertations
on witchcraft and allied subjects.[31] In addition, throughout Protestant
Europe there was an extensive literature devoted to what might be
called the narrative and exemplary aspects of the subject. This
included a very great number of popular pamphlet accounts of
individual cases, the wide circulation of *Teufelserzählungen*,[32] the
specialist collections of stories culled from general accounts of magic
and witchcraft—like the publisher Henning Gross's *Magica, seu
mirabilium historiarum de spectris et apparitionibus spirituum . . . Libri II*
(1597),[33] the inclusion of witchcraft episodes in the principal hand-

[30] Georg Sohn, 'Theses de plerisque locis theologicis, in academiis Marpurgensi et
Heidelbergensi ad disputandum propositae, XVI', in *Operum Georgii Sohnii sacrae
theologiae doctori tomus primus* (Heidelberg, 1609), 154–7; Jacob Heerbrand (*praeses*.), *De
magia disputatio ex cap. 7. Exo*. (Tübingen, 1570); Tobias Tandler, *Dissertatio de fascino et
incantatione* (Wittenberg, 1606). On Heerbrand, see Midelfort, *Witch-hunting*, pp. 40–2;
on Tandler, see Thorndike, *History of Magic*, vii. 340–5. Thorndike speaks of a 'lively
interest in magic' at Wittenberg. As examples of disputations at Utrecht and of the
orthodox academic demonology of Dutch Calvinism in the 1630s, see the collection by
the Professor and Rector of the university, Gijsbert Voet, *Selectarum disputationum
theologicarum* (5 vols.; Utrecht, 1648–69), i. 906–84 ('De natura et operatione
daemonum'), iii. 539–632 ('De magia'), and cf. iii. 91–226 ('De superstitione').

[31] See e.g. Johannes Rudbeckius, *Propositiones de angelis* (Vesterås, 1624); Georg
Alanus, *De magia naturali* (Abo, 1645); S. L. Vigelius, *De angelographia* (Åbo, 1650);
Samuel Skunk, *De superstitiosa divinatione* (Upsala, 1668); Petrus Ljung, *De praestigiis
daemonum fraudibusque affinibus* (Upsala, 1672); Andreas Norcopensis, *De oraculis* (Stock-
holm, 1674); Andreas Wanochius, *Dissertatio pneumatica de potentia malorum spirituum*
(Åbo, 1688). I am grateful to Bengt Ankarloo for these details. For the dissertations at
Finland's Turku Academy, see Antero Heikkinen and Timo Kervinen, ch. 12, below,
and Heikkinen's *Paholaisen Littolaiset* (Helsinki, 1969), 367–9 (Bibliography).

[32] R. Alsheimer, 'Katalog protestantischer Teufelserzählungen des 16. Jhts', in
Wolfgang Brückner (ed.), *Volkserzählung und Reformation: Ein Handbuch zur Tradierung und
Funktion von Erzählstoffen und Erzählliteratur in Protestantismus* (Berlin, 1974), 417–519.
Brückner's whole volume is an essential guide to the narrative traditions which
impinged on Protestant demonology; but see esp. pp. 239–42, 393–416, 609–10, 673–8,
726–8.

[33] The work appeared first at Eisleben in 1597, and was republished at Leyden in
1656 with the different title: *Magica de Spectris et apparitionibus spiritum, de vaticiniis, divina-
tionibus, . . .* It was published in a German trans. at Eisleben in 1600, and edited and
trans. into English by Thomas Bromhall with the title *A treatise of specters; or, An history of
apparitions, oracles, prophecies and predictions, with dreams, visions and revelations . . .* (London,
1658).

books of cautionary tales and moral *exempla*,[34] and the citing of
especially striking instances by the authors of prodigy books and
wonder-sermons.[35] Finally, there was the contribution of the lawyers
and jurists—the Marburg attorney Abraham Saur, the Calvinist
Melchior Goldast (whose *Rechtliches Bedencken, von Confiscation der
Zauberer und Hexen-Güther* was not published until 1661), and the two
great Lutheran authorities, Johann Georg Godelmann and Benedikt
Carpzov. Godelmann's *Tractatus de magis, veneficis et lamiis* (1591) was
the work of an expert jurist, and it originated in the lectures on the
Carolina which he gave at the university of Rostock in 1584. It deals
exhaustively and learnedly with the magic arts and demonic witchcraft,
but concentrates on the proper judicial procedures for investigating
and punishing them. Carpzov was professor of law at Leipzig, and his
well-known, almost notorious, treatise of 1635 was likewise a manual
for magistrates. It sought to codify procedures in the German courts in
much the same way as the *Malleus maleficarum*—one of Carpzov's
principal sources—had done one and a half centuries before.[36]

To range so superficially over so much material may seem cavalier.
And yet much of it remains contextual to the main body of Protestant
witchcraft writings—its intellectual, moral, and juridical surroundings, as it were, rather than the central territory itself. Several of these
items include specialist discussion of witchcraft, but few betray the
priorities of a church. The theological account of demonism is not
particularly distinctive. The academics occupied themselves with the
epistemology of magic, the narrators and compilers with telling a good
story, and the lawyers with disputes about procedure. This is not
to say that mere polemic made any difference. James VI and I's
Daemonologie (1597) is certainly a very Protestant work, but only in the
sense that the author, rather predictably, makes polemical capital out
of the subject at the expense of Catholicism—an association born of

[34] See e.g. Andreas Hondorff, *Promptuarium exemplorum. Historienn und Exempel buch*
(n.p. [Leipzig], 1568), fos. 73–90ᵛ, 167–8ᵛ, 267–72ᵛ.
[35] See e.g. Caspar Goldwurm, *Wunderzeichen buch: Das ist, warhafftige beschreibunge aller
furnemen, Seltzamen, ungewonlichen, Gottlichen und Teuffelischen, guten und bosen, heilsamen
und verführischen zeichen, gesichte unnd missgeburt ...* (Frankfurt am Main, 1567), fos.
cxxivᵛ–cxliiᵛ; Georg Zaemann, *Wunderspiegel* (Stralsund, 1625), 33–71.
[36] Abraham Saur, *Ein Kurtze, trewe warnung, anzeige und underricht: ob auch zu dieser unser
zeit unter uns Christen, Hexen, Zäuberer und Unholden vorhanden ...* (Frankfurt am Main,
1582); Melchior Goldast, *Rechtliches Bedencken, von Confiscation der Zauberer und Hexen-
Güther* (Bremen, 1661)—written in 1629; Johann Georg Godelmann, *Tractatus de magis,
veneficis et lamiis recte cognoscendis et puniendis libri tres* (Frankfurt, 1591); Benedikt Carpzov,
Practica nova Imperialis Saxonica rerum criminalium (Wittenberg, 1635).

the universal Protestant claim that Catholicism was itself a kind of witchcraft. Otherwise, the book is indistinguishable from the general run of European demonologies.[37] Much the same is true of the extensive Protestant literature dealing with demonic possession. Many of the German cases seem to have aroused interest of the sort which bordered on sectarian propaganda.[38] The most substantial treatment of all, the Swiss Calvinist Pierre Viret's *Le monde à l'empire et le monde demoniacle* (1561), is also the most contentious, treating possession as a series of metaphors for the global decline wrought by Catholic failings.[39] The technique of 'demonologizing' a moral target was also adopted by a further group of writers, the authors of the *Teufelbücher*, in order to discredit particular social evils (e.g. 'Faulteufel', 'Spielteufel', 'Fluchteufel'). But these works were part of a flourishing Protestant literature of the reformation of manners and, with one or two exceptions, were not in fact concerned with demonism and witchcraft at all.[40]

While it is, therefore, important to appreciate the depth of Protestant demonological interests and the variety of contexts in which they could be discussed, there is still a core of specialist texts, numbering about forty items, to be considered. And what is immediately striking about this group is that nearly all of them were written by pastors or those in a position to influence strongly the education and training of the Protestant ministry. This gives them much more uniformity, and at

[37] James VI (and I), *Daemonologie, in forme of a dialogue* (Edinburgh, 1597). For accounts of its contents, see Stuart Clark, 'King James's *Daemonologie*: Witchcraft and Kingship', in Sydney Anglo (ed.), *The Damnèd Art: Essays in the Literature of Witchcraft* (London, 1977), 167–73; and Christina Larner, 'James VI and I and Witchcraft', in Alan G. R. Smith (ed.), *The Reign of James VI and I* (London, 1973), 85–6, repr. in Larner, *Witchcraft and Religion: The Politics of Popular Belief* (London, 1984).

[38] For an introduction to this subject, see H. C. Erik Midelfort, 'Sin, Melancholy, Obsession: Insanity and Culture in 16th-Century Germany', in Kaplan (ed.), *Understanding Popular Culture*, pp. 134–42. For a typical example, see the possession tract by the Württemberg preacher Samuel Huber, *Erklärung des grossen Abentheurlichen Abentheurs, Welches die Wurtzburgische Jesuiter, ob und mit einer Legion Teuffels, in einem besessnen Schmidknecht, zu Heidingsfeld in Bistumb Würtzburg, getriben, unnd für ein Wunderwerck aussgeben haben* (Tübingen, 1590).

[39] Pierre Viret, *Le monde à l'empire et le monde demoniacle fait par dialogues* (Geneva, 1561); for an account of this work, see Claude Dubois, *La Conception de l'histoire en France au XVIe siècle* [1560–1610] (Paris, 1977), 443–65.

[40] The most convenient source is *Theatrum diabolorum, das ist: Warhaffte eigentliche und kurtze Beschreibung allerley grewlicher, schrecklicher und abschewlicher Laster* (Frankfurt am Main, 1569, 1575, 1587). For a representative sample in modern edition, see Ria Stambaugh (ed.), *Teufelbücher in Auswahl* (5 vols.; Berlin, 1970–80). Essential commentary and bibliography, is in Heinrich Grimm, 'Die deutschen Teufelbücher des 16. Jhts', *Archiv für Geschichte des Buchwesens*, 16 (1959), 513–70.

the same time makes them a truer expression of the Protestant version of religious reform. In the latter class were Lambert Daneau, who published his *Dialogus de veneficiis* in 1574 (in French as well as Latin) while he was professor of theology at the Genevan Academy (following thirteen years as a pastor), Niels Hemmingsen, who had himself studied at Wittenberg under Melanchthon and whose *Admonitio de superstitionibus magicis vitandis* was published in Copenhagen in 1575 when he was vice-chancellor of the university,[41] and Caspar Peucer, another Wittenberg student of Melanchthon, who wrote his highly successful *Commentarius de praecipuis divinationum generibus* while holding that university's chairs of medicine and mathematics (he replaced Melanchthon as Rector in 1560). It is to be expected that Wittenberg, as well as Tübingen, should have been prominent sources of the ideas on which Protestant demonology, both in Germany and Scandinavia, came to depend. But the formative period of witchcraft theory in England should also be seen against a university background. Henry and Robert Holland, George Gifford, and, above all, William Perkins were all trying to translate into practical, pastoral terms the Calvinism of Elizabethan Cambridge, and their views about witchcraft are inseparable from this wider campaign. The comparable influence of Turku and Tarto Universities on the history of witchcraft in Finland and Estonia is dealt with in essays elsewhere in this volume.

As for the pastors themselves, they included several who were *Hofprediger* or superintendents—for example, Hermann Hamelman (Gandersheim in Brunswick), Arnold Mengering (Dresden, Altenburg, Halle), Andreas Musculus (Frankfurt an der Oder, Brandenburg), Hinrich Rimphoff (Verden), Hermann Samson (Riga, Livonia), and Joachim Zehner (Henneberg). Heinrich Bullinger, Abraham Scultetus, and William Perkins were major figures in their respective territorial reform movements; Matthäus Alber and Johann Brenz both had important roles in the reformation in the Duchy of Württemberg. These men were often the drafters of the new church ordinances and the conductors of visitations, as well as the general propagandists of Protestantism; some of them were prolific writers on a wide range of other issues. The only French Calvinist to write substantially on the subject, other than Daneau, was another clergyman, Francois Perrault

---

[41] For the general influence of Hemmingsen, see Poul G. Lindhardt, 'Til belysning af Niels Hemmingsens inflydelse på dansk prædiken omkring 1600 (For the Elucidation of Niels Hemmingsen's Influence on Danish Preaching about 1600)', in *Festskrift til Jens Nørregaard* (Copenhagen, 1947), 131–45; Johansen, ch. 13, below.

(or Perreaud), the Huguenot pastor at Thoiry in the Pays de Gex
(Vaud).[42] Most of the Protestant experts were in fact German
Lutherans, with English Calvinists, some of them of 'Puritan' persuasion, occupying the second place numerically. On the whole they
were utterly representative of the new styles of ministry.

Protestant witchcraft writings were thus dominated by the pastorate
and its concerns—not by jurists or philosophers—and their tone is not
so much intellectual as evangelical and homiletic. Several texts had
been given as individual sermons or series of sermons, and retained
this form in print. Samson's *Neun ausserlesen und wolgegründete Hexen
Predigt* (1626) were delivered first in Riga Cathedral as part of an
intensive campaign to evangelize the region. The minister at Nebra in
Thuringia, David Meder, introduced his *Acht Hexenpredigten* (1615) by
citing 2 Timothy 4 on the duties of pastors ('. . . thue das Werk eines
evangelischen Predigers, richte dein Amt redlich aus'), and explained
that he had originally preached them to the people of Hohenlohe,
where he had been general inspector of churches and schools and
pastor of Öhringen. Daniel Schaller's *Zauber Händel* (1611) was likewise the printed version of eight sermons which he had devised for his
parishioners at the *Marienkirche* in Stendal and which formed part of
his ordinary weekly programme there. Zehner's *Fünff Predigten von den
Hexen* (1613) and Johannes Rüdinger's substantial *De Magia illicita,
decas concionum* (1630) fall into the same category; Zehner was pastor of
Schleusingen, and Rüdinger of Ober-Oppurg in Saxony. Even when
they did not end up in sermon form, Protestant demonologies turn out
to have originated in this way. The title-page of William Perkins's *The
damned art of witchcraft* (1608) said that its contents had been 'framed
and delivered . . . in his ordinarie course of preaching';[43] Bernhard
Albrecht had already given eighteen different sermons on witchcraft in
Augsburg before he published his *Magia; das ist Christlicher Bericht von
der Zauberey und Hexerey* in 1628. With pastors so dominant, this is
likely to have been the pattern in many other cases.

In its power to alter the opinions and behaviour of ordinary people,
the sermon was selective and partial. But its influence on the structure
and content of Protestant witchcraft writings shows that these too

[42] Francois Perrault, *Demonologie* (Geneva, 1653). On Perrault, see Elisabeth
Labrousse, 'Le Démon de Maçon', in Paola Zambelli (ed.), *Scienze, credenze occulte, livelli
di cultura* (Florence, 1982), 249–75.
[43] William Perkins, *A discourse of the damned art of witchcraft* (Cambridge, 1610), title-
page.

were aimed at a general lay audience (as well as at the pastorate as a whole) rather than at academic specialists. The dialogue was another favoured form and, while this could easily lend itself to intellectualism (James VI and I's interlocutors are called Philomathes and Epistemon), it was also employed to give freer rein to the questions and reservations concerning witchcraft which pastors must have encountered on a daily basis, and to suggest techniques for settling them. In Adrian Rheynmann's *Ein christlich und nothwendig gesprach, von den bösen abtrünnigen Engeln*, 'Theophilus' is given the opportunity of expressing the sort of 'Manicheistic' doubts concerning the presence of evil in the scheme of Providence which Rheynmann, like so many others, must have heard from his parishioners (he was pastor of Meiden in the Upper Palatinate). And in two remarkable cases, those of George Gifford's *A dialogue concerning witches and witchcraftes* (1593) and Robert Holland's *Tudor and Gronow* (*c*.1595), attempts were made actually to capture the sort of conversation that would have occurred when peasant villagers debated magic and witchcraft with their clerical mentors. There is a strong sense of the authentic about these depictions of Calvinists arguing their way through a barrage of popular objections to the new divinity and its ideals of piety. But the didactic element in demonology is still uppermost. Gifford, preacher at Maldon in Essex, chose the dialogue form as 'fitter for the capacity of the simpler sort'. With Gifford as his model, Holland placed his imaginary conversation among the Welsh-speaking inhabitants of parishes like his own in Pembrokeshire and Carmarthenshire.[44]

Throughout this 'evangelical demonology' it was, above all, the Bible on which authors relied for support—often to the exclusion of all other authorities. There was also much less resort to Catholic witchcraft texts at this level than among the Protestant philosophers and jurists. This Biblicism, together with their focus on pastoral work, also led the clerics to stress the spiritual and moral implications of magic and witchcraft rather than their concrete manifestations. It was, of course, consistent with their soteriology that they should concentrate

---

[44] George Gifford, *A dialogue concerning witches and witchcraftes* (London, 1593), sig. A3^r. Gifford's general evangelical aims as a local pastor are well captured in D. Wallace, 'George Gifford, Puritan Propaganda and Popular Religion in Elizabethan England', *Sixteenth-century Journal*, 9 (1978), 27–49. For Robert Holland, see Stuart Clark and Prys Morgan, 'Religion and Magic in Elizabethan Wales: Robert Holland's Dialogue on Witchcraft', *Journal of Ecclesiastical History*, 27 (1976), 31–46. The text of Holland's dialogue (in Welsh) is repr. in Thomas Jones, *Rhyddiaith Gymraeg, 1547–1618* (Cardiff, 1956), 161–73.

more on what these activities meant than on sensationalism or technical detail. While they did not entirely neglect traditional demonological topics like transvection, metamorphosis, and sexuality, they showed little enthusiasm for them. The Bible provided little or no help in these areas, whereas its influence on interpretations of the spiritual and moral significance of witchcraft was total. At the heart of the crime was the demonic pact, but not so much for the feats which it subsequently enabled individuals to achieve, as for the act of apostasy itself—a kind of allegiance which Henry Holland in his *A treatise against witchcraft* (1590) likened to treason and rebellion against 'the kingdome and Citie of God'.[45] The sabbath in particular received few discussions in these texts and was often ignored altogether. A typical example is the treatise *Gründlicher Bericht von Zauberey und Zauberern*, which the Calvinist preacher at Oppenheim, Dittelsheim, and Offenbach, Anton Praetorius (Schultze), published first in 1598 under the pseudonym Johann Scultetus. He certainly deals with the causation of magical actions and the reality of night-flying, banqueting, demonic procreation, and metamorphosis (as well as offering lengthy advice on procedure to magistrates), but each chapter of the work is dominated by a very substantial *Erinnerung*, in which the spiritual lessons to be learned by the attentive Christian reader are analysed.[46] The English divine Thomas Cooper considered the ceremonies of the witches sabbath in some detail, but mainly in order to unravel the symbolism of what was done in terms of Calvinist doctrines of affliction and the godly life. Thus, one of the errors highlighted by the devil's insistence that witches undergo fresh baptism is the presumption that salvation is certain once the seal of baptism is made, 'as if outward Baptisme made a Christian, and nothing else'. One of the subtitles of his *The mystery of witch-craft* (1617) indicates the order of priorities in much of Protestant demonology: 'As also the severall stratagems of Sathan, ensnaring the poore Soule by his desperate practize of annoying the bodie.'[47] Even when the devil actually seized the bodies of demoniacs, the assault was deemed to have greater significance as a moral index of the sins of the last times than as a literal reality. This is the position

---

[45] Henry Holland, *A treatise against witchcraft* (Cambridge, 1590), sig. A2ʳ. Henry Holland was minister of Orwell (Cambridgeshire) from 1580 and of St Bride's, London, from 1594.

[46] There is an account of the work in Paulus, *Hexenwahn*, pp. 183–94.

[47] Thomas Cooper, *The mystery of witch-craft* (London, 1617), 88–124, quotation at p. 115.

taken by the church superintendent of Mecklenburg, Andreas Celichius, in his *Notwendige Erinnerrung*. *Von des Sathans letzten zornsturm* (1595), a work stimulated by the rash of cases of demonic possession in Mecklenburg, Friedburg, and Spandau in Brandenburg in the 1590s. And eschatology also made spiritual sense of demonism for the *Hofprediger* and theology professor at Frankfurt an der Oder, Andreas Musculus. For him the devil's 'tyranny' suggested both immediate chastisement for immorality and unheedfulness, and God's forewarnings of more terrible judgements to come.[48]

In Zehner's sermons witchcraft often seems only a vehicle for the author's homiletic reflections on temptation, sin, repentance, and forgiveness, a sequence to which demonic assaults on men, their magical counteractions, and the divine rewards for these could easily be assimilated. In much the same way, Jacob Graeter, preacher and dean of the imperial city of Schwäbisch Hall, devoted his two *Hexen oder Unholden Predigten* of 1589 to moral issues arising from demonic deception and the nature and powers of fiends and witches. His chosen texts (from Luke 6: 36–42 and Luke 1: 39–45) show that these are as much exercises in casuistry as in demonology. Rheynmann too approached devils and demonism in the context of the spiritual well-being to be derived even from physical attack. A history of the devil and an account of demonic powers to know and to effect are used to focus the themes of sin, punishment, and redemption—there is no mention of sabbaths or even, in this case, witches.[49]

Yet this brings us, somewhat paradoxically, to the heart of Protestant attitudes to witchcraft. For one matter forced itself on the attention of the pastor-demonologists to an overwhelming extent—the origin, nature, and significance of everyday misfortunes. So important were these issues that they may almost be said to underlie the whole of Protestant demonology. The aim in most of the discussions we have been considering was to correct popular misapprehensions about the basic causation of unpleasant events. But what this entailed was an emphasis *away* from the layman's view of witchcraft. It was constantly urged that to blame these afflictions only on witches was at least a kind of hypocrisy, and probably outright atheism; while to apply one's own

---

[48] Andreas Musculus, *Von des teufels tyranney Macht und Gewalt, sonderlich in diesen letzten tagen, unterrichtung* (Erfurt, 1561), repr. in *Theatrum diabolorum*, and in Stambaugh (ed.), *Teufelbücher*, iv. 189–270.

[49] See also the even more elementary, homiletic account of the history of the devil in Fröschel, n. 25, above.

counter-witchcraft or to seek it from specialists in beneficent magic was a species of idolatry. The first response undervalued the spiritual function of misfortune as a retribution for sin and a test of faith, and questioned God's providential control over affairs; it even implied Manicheism, since it suggested a source of evil independent of God. The second ignored the need for repentance or the benefits of 'bearing the cross', and attributed specious powers to the supposedly protective or curative properties of persons, places, times, and things.

The remedy was to transfer attention not merely from the devil to God, but from witch to victim, throwing the burden of responsibility on the latter's individual conscience. Gifford's formulation is a model: 'Looke then to the causes, if wee will remoove the effects. As if thou feare God, and Satan afflict thee, stand fast in faith and patience, and waite upon God for thy deliverance ... looke not upon the witch, lay not the cause where it is not, seeke not helpe at the hands of devils, be not a disciple of witches, ...'[50] The real significance of the events attributed to witchcraft was that, like all cases of affliction, they offered an opportunity for introspection and spiritual betterment; sin, not sorcery, was the cause of misfortune.

Erik Midelfort traced one version of these arguments to a sermon on hailstorms preached by Johann Brenz in 1539 and, later, closely followed by other Lutherans like Matthäus Alber and Wilhelm Bidembach of Stuttgart.[51] Alan Macfarlane found another in Gifford's *A dialogue concerning witches and witchcraftes*.[52] But these arguments were in fact invariably used or implied throughout the evangelical demonology of Protestant Europe. In England, for example, Richard Bernard, who called himself a 'plaine Countrey Minister' (he was preacher at Batcombe in Somerset), opened his witchcraft tract *A guide to grand jury men* (1627) with a chapter entitled: 'God's hand is first to bee considered in all crosses, whatsoever the meanes be, and whosoever the instruments: for he ruleth overall.' All afflictions (he argued) were necessarily providential, and demonic afflictions merely a special case. The appropriate response was a patient 'searching of our waies, ... to the acknowledgement of our sinnes'. Some misfortunes blamed on witches were (while still providential) only natural contingencies to be met with natural resources; the others were only

---

[50] Gifford, *A dialogue*, sig. H3ᵛ.
[51] Midelfort, *Witch-hunting*, pp. 36 ff.
[52] Alan Macfarlane, 'A Tudor Anthropologist: George Gifford's *Discourse* and *Dialogue*', in Anglo (ed.), *The Damnéd Art*, pp. 140–55.

demonic, for witches themselves were completely powerless (unless they too used natural means), however strong the proofs of their involvement.[53] Such views were commonplace in Germany itself, quite apart from their appearance in the hailstorm sermons, and acted as the framework for most of the extended discussions. Heinrich Bullinger, for example, argued that witchcraft was only achieved with demonic powers, and that these were only granted in order to see how the faithful would react to *maleficium*. Echoing Calvin's harsh view that (for example) loss of children pre-empted parental complacency, Bullinger finished not with an attack on the vehicles of affliction, but with a statement of God's absolute 'lordship' over the affairs of men.[54] Zehner's second sermon is likewise typical in using the story of Job in order to attribute the disasters wrought by witches to a demonic agency working well within divine limits and for divine purposes: 'we should not then be so dispondent, if we perceive how the devil through his intermediaries works such great mischief to man and beast.' God only intends to punish the irreligious or try the faithful, and in both cases the spiritual challenge is infinitely more significant than the physical hurt.[55] As Johann Ellinger succinctly put it: 'where God allows evil, it is certain that a greater good follows from it.' This was the fundamental moral principle at work in his *Hexen Coppel*,[56] as well as in the witchcraft writings of David Meder, Daniel Schaller, and Bernhard Albrecht.

The fact that the pastors of the Protestant Reformation returned to these arguments again and again sets them off from their Catholic counterparts. They were derived naturally from Protestant theology itself, notably its providentialism and both its heightened sensitivity to any hint of dualism and its intense fideism. They were also more readily supportable from the Bible than the scholastic demonology favoured by many of the great Catholic experts. A combination of the Mosaic injunctions and prophetic warnings against wizards, the story

[53] Richard Bernard, *A guide to grand jury men* (London, 1627), 1–81, quotations at p. 9, sigs. A5ᵛ–A6ʳ.

[54] Heinrich Bullinger, *Von hexen und unholden wider der Schwartzen Künst, aberglaubigs segnen, unwarhafftigs Warsagen, und andere dergleichen von Gott verbottne Künst*, in *Theatrum de veneficis* (Frankfurt am Main, 1586), 304–5.

[55] Joachim Zehner, *Fünff Predigten von den Hexen, ihren anfang, Mittel und End in sich haltend und erklärend* (Leipzig, 1613), 17–35, quotation at p. 31.

[56] Johann Ellinger, *Hexen Coppel; das ist, Uhralte Ankunfft und grosse Zunfft des unholdseligen Unholden oder Hexen, welche in einer Coppel von einem gantzen Dutzet auff die Schaw und Musterund geführet* (Frankfurt am Main, 1629), 49 (cf. pp. 49–52). Diefenbach gives an earlier edn. at Darmstadt, 1623.

of Job, and the doctrines of grace derived from the New Testament
gave perfectly adequate scriptural backing; indeed, there is a sense in
which these sources could comfortably sustain only the kind of witchcraft beliefs Protestants came to hold. They were in fact very frequently the direct inspiration for particular writings or were the
subject of repeated and extensive commentary. Job's response to
tribulation was so crucial to the whole enterprise that the Book of Job
in particular must be regarded as its scriptural cornerstone. But above
all, perhaps, these views on witchcraft reflected the circumstances
which confronted pastors whenever they tried to instil Protestant
theology and its corresponding piety into ordinary parishioners. In
this sense, Protestant demonology arose at the intersection of clerical
and popular culture, with the result that 'witchcraft' came to include a
very wide range of proscribed behaviour, most of it far removed from
the classic stereotype of devil-worship.

III

Nothing distinguishes Protestant demonology more than its preoccupation with popular magical technique—that is, with the enormous repertoire of rituals for good health, healing, and fertility, for
preventing misfortune, and for divination which existed outside or
along the borders of official religion and yet was constitutive of much
of early modern popular culture. These are practices which to the
modern view look tangential to demonic witchcraft and to *maleficium*,
but the authors we are considering often saw things the other way
round. Pastors could not fail to see that they were more prominent in
the lives of those they wished to reform than any element of *maleficium*;
and they also felt that (as a New England divine was later to say) 'these
divinations and operations are the Witchcraft more condemned in
Scripture than the other'.[57] The Mosaic law thought to be aimed
specifically at malevolent witches was seen as only one ingredient
in a code of behaviour directed at all the forbidden arts, however
benevolent they might seem. More representative than Exodus 22: 18
('Thou shalt not suffer a witch to live') was Deuteronomy 18: 10–11:

---

[57] John Hale, *A modest enquiry into the nature of witchcraft* . . . (Boston, 1702), repr. in
G. L. Burr (ed.), *Narratives of the Witchcraft Cases, 1648–1706* (New York, 1914), 426.

There shall not be found among you any one that maketh his sonne or his daughter to passe thorow the fire, or that useth divination, or an observer of times, or an inchanter, or a witch.

Or a charmer, or a consulter with familiar spirits, or a wyzard, or a Necromancer.

This was the text which furnished the pastors with their demonological categories; or, if we prefer, into which they 'translated' their own vocabulary of terms. It was continuously relied on for inspiration and support. Whole demonologies were organized according to the types of magic it distinguished—notably, the two very substantial treatises by Bernhard Albrecht and Niels Hemmingsen. Hermann Hamelman, leading reformer of Westphalia and *Generalsuperintendent* of Gandersheim in Brunswick at the time, delivered a sermon there in October 1570 which is drawn entirely from the list of practices in Deuteronomy. Hamelman denounced those who resorted to them in the Germany of his day, and pleaded with his fellow pastors to make their eradication an evangelical priority.[58] Henry Holland's *A treatise against witchcraft* opens with a long analysis of the eight types of 'witches which are mentioned in scripture'; all of them are taken from this same text.[59] And in 1612, another Englishman, James Mason, drew together a discussion of exorcists, healers, blessers, and conjurors (itself inspired by Acts 19: 11–16) by also assimilating them to the Mosaic typology.[60]

Unambiguously malevolent witchcraft, with its explicit demonic allegiance and acts of *maleficium*, was in fact rarely considered outside this framework. Holland sandwiches it between his exegesis of Deuteronomy and a chapter dealing with those who 'are wont to seeke after these wise men, and cunning women . . . in sickenesse, in losses, and in all extremities'.[61] Bullinger places it at the end of his tract *Von hexen und unholden*, having already considered the private use of

[58] Hermann Hamelman, *Eine Predigt zu Gandersheim . . . Wider die Beschwerer, Wicker, Christallenkücher, Zeuberer, Nachweiser, und Seegner . . .* (n.p., 1572). Hamelman's contribution to Hocker's *Der teuffel selbs* consists not only of seven additional chapters on the traditional activities of devils, but a commentary entitled *Folget der Segen und Wicker-teuffel, Item, der Chrystallen Teuffel, das ist, Ein bericht von dem Segen, Büssen, Wickern, Nachweysern, Teuffelsbeschwerer, Chrystallensehers und Schwartzkünstlern*, repr. in *Theatrum diabolorum* (1569 edn.), fos. cxxxv^v–cxlii^r; cf. Grimm, 'Die deutschen Teufelbücher', pp. 528, 551–2, for a bibliography of this work.

[59] Holland, *A treatise*, sigs. B3^v–D4^r.

[60] James Mason, *The anatomie of sorcerie: Wherein the wicked impietie of charmers, inchanters, and such like, is discovered and confuted* (London, 1612), 85–8.

[61] Holland, *A treatise*, sig. F4r.

blessings, conjurations, and exorcisms ('Segnungen', 'ßeschwörungen'), the various professions of astrology ('Sternseher', 'Tagweiler', 'Planetenprediger'), and the arts of necromancy and divination ('Abgestorbenen seelen fragen', 'Wahrsagen').

Rüdinger's massive demonology *De Magia illicita* includes ten sermons on demonic magic and witchcraft, but ten more on soothsaying, 'the observation of days', augury, conjurations, astrology, necromancy, and the interpretation of dreams.

Two other works which begin with traditional demonology and end by 'demonologizing' popular magic are *Der Zauber-Teufel* (1563) by Ludwig Milichius, who taught at the Marburg Academy and was preacher at Seelheim, then Homberg, and, finally, Corbach, and Hermann Samson's witchcraft sermons. Separated by over sixty years they each confront the standard nexus of problems—the nature of affliction, the resort to magical instead of spiritual remedies, and the affront to Providence in any practice which claims to provide foreknowledge. Samson voices the underlying evangelical principle at work: of all the causes of sorcery, he says, superstition is the first.[62] Nor should it be forgotten that a substantial portion of Johann Weyer's *De praestigiis daemonum* (1563), usually regarded as important for other reasons, is devoted to 'superstitious' cures for bewitchment. Here, as elsewhere, Weyer wrote as a typical Lutheran demonologist.[63] Even a single sermon on *maleficium*, like Alber and Bidembach's of 1562, ends up as a denunciation of the practitioners of popular magic ('Wahrsager', 'Teufelsbeschwörer', 'Christalseher', 'Zeichendeuter', 'Tagweiler').[64]

Very often classic, devil-worshipping witchcraft is quite over-

---

[62] Ludwig Milichius, *Der Zauber-Teuffel: Das ist, von Zauberei, Warsagung, Beschwehren, Segen, Aberglauben, Hexerey, und mancherley Wercken des Teufels* . . . (Frankfurt am Main, 1563), repr. in *Theatrum diabolorum*, and in Stambaugh (ed.), *Teufelbücher*, i. 1–185; Hermann Samson, *Neun ausserlesen und wolgegründete Hexen-Predigt* . . . (Riga, 1626), sigs. Pii^v–Tii^v, Oiv^r. In this context, see also Paulus Einhorn, *Wiederlegung der Abgötterey und nichtigen Aberglaubens, so vorzeiten auss der Heydnischen Abgötterey in diesen Lande* (Riga, 1627), extracts in *Scriptores rerum Livonicarum*, ii (Riga and Leipzig, 1853), 639–52; Einhorn was a Livonian preacher and, later, superintendent of Kurland.

[63] See esp. book v; and for a brief account, see Christopher Baxter, 'Johann Weyer's *De praestigiis daemonum*: Unsystematic Psychopathology', in Anglo (ed.), *The Damnèd Art*, pp. 64–6.

[64] Matthaeus Alber and Wilhelm Bidembach, *Ein summa etlicher predigen vom Hagel und Unholden* (Tübingen, 1562), sigs. Ci^v–Cii^r. I have not been able to consult the following, cited in this connection by Hamelman: Nicolaus Erbenius, *Confutatio magicae ac idolatricae consecrationis creaturarum, aliarumque horrendarum superstitionum, simplicibus utilis* (Erfurt, 1564). Erbenius was successively pastor of Sondershausen and Hörter in Thuringia, *Generalsuperintendent* of Alfeld, and preacher at Erfurt.

shadowed by its (apparently) beneficent counterparts. This is very much the case with the tract *Hexen Coppel; das ist, Uhralte Ankunfft und grosse Zunfft des unholdseligen Unholden oder Hexen* (1623) by the Lutheran deacon, Johann Ellinger. Ellinger admits that devil-worshippers are the essential witches, but he recognizes them in only one of twelve categories of magical art. Amongst the rest are some learned varieties—pyromantics, aeromantics, hydromantics, and geomantics—but also the familiar blessers, soothsayers, crystalgazers, *Schatzgräber*, diviners, and exorcists.[65] George Gifford's *Dialogue* is also taken up very largely with the methods of what he revealingly called the 'other sort of Witches, whome the people call cunning men and wise women'—that is, the unofficial agencies for healing, divination, detection, and counter-witchcraft.[66] Throughout the Protestant literature on witchcraft in England it is on these practices and their moral and cultural significance that demonologists concentrate their attention. William Perkins even thought that the injuries of the maleficent witch functioned merely to drive victims to the wise man or woman for a remedy. The latter did 'a thousandfold more harme then the former' and was 'the more horrible and detestable Monster'.[67] In some European contributions to the genre, witchcraft as traditionally understood virtually disappears altogether. Abraham Scultetus's *Warnung für der Warsagerey der Zauberer und sterngücker* (1608) is a commentary on the last four verses of Isaiah 47, with their references to 'inchantments', 'sorceries', 'astrologers', 'starre-gazers' and 'monethly prognosticators'.[68] The Lutheran pastor of Trossingen in Württemberg, Johann Spreter, only found space in his *Eyn Kurtzer Bericht, was von den Abgotterischen Sagen und Beschweren zuhalten* ... (1543) to deal with divination.[69]

---

[65] Ellinger, *Hexen Coppel*, p. 45, and *passim*.

[66] Gifford, *A dialogue*, sig. A3ʳ.

[67] Perkins, *Discourse*, pp. 174–8; cf. Johann Brenz, *Ein Predig von dem Hagel und Ungewitter*, trans. in H. C. Erik Midelfort, 'Were there really Witches?', in Robert Kingdon (ed.), *Transition and Revolution* (Minneapolis, 1974), 217.

[68] These are the terms from the King James trans.; the equivalents in the German are 'Beschwörern', 'Zauberer', 'die Meister des Himmelslauss', 'die Sternkucker', and 'die nach den Monaten rechnen'.

[69] Cf. the attack on divination and the prophetic arts in Francis Coxe, *A short treatise declaringe the detestable wickednesse of magicall sciences, as necromancie, conjurations of spirites, curiouse astrologie and such lyke* ... (London, 1561). The Englishman Richard Argentine's *De praestigiis et incantationibus daemonum et necromaticorum* (Basel, 1568), is also largely concerned with divination by demonic means, but the author's religious affiliations are uncertain; he willingly conformed to Edwardian Calvinism, Marian Catholicism, and Elizabethan Anglicanism.

But whatever the precise target, the popular culture of fortune and misfortune was always offensive for the same two reasons. It proffered what Keith Thomas called the 'rival therapy' of practical magic as a way of dealing with those contingencies (including *maleficium*) which reformers called 'Providence', and was thus antithetic to the whole thrust of Protestant belief. And in doing so it adopted techniques which seemed indistinguishable from demonic witchcraft itself. To use any of the forbidden arts and rituals or to consult with those who did with expectations of success was at least implicit witchcraft, for they had no efficacy in nature and no warrant in Scripture. If they did work, the devil must be held to have co-operated. There were thus no differences in kind between any of the categories of Deuteronomy 18. As Perkins said:

> by Witches we understand not those onely which kill and torment: but all Diviners, Charmers, Juglers, all Wizzards, commonly called wise men and wise women; yea, whosoever doe any thing (knowing what they doe) which cannot be effected by nature or art; and in the same number we reckon all good Witches, which doe no hurt, but good, which doe not spoile and destroy, but save and deliver.[70]

Three final illustrations will show why this was the common view. In 1565 the pastor of Biberach in Württemberg, Conrad Platz, published a virulent denunciation of popular blessers and conjurors (*Segensprecher, Beschwörer*) which exactly paralleled those of the English 'Puritan' demonologists. Bemoaning the inconstancy which led men to abandon God in serious illness, Platz focused on their recourse to those who claimed to heal by the power of words—for him (as, necessarily, for all Protestant demonologists) the very worst kind of superstition. For the sick to turn their backs on Providence and on the legitimate human skills of the physicians was bad enough, for it showed lack of patience, lack of trust, and lack of belief. But to put faith in the promises of blessers—a prerequisite for the success of their charms—was also a hideous travesty of the doctrine of salvation. And to claim that holy words in particular had an inherent efficacy was an outright rejection of the second commandment. If success was obtained, if children and livestock in fact recovered, this was by demonic intervention and should not be taken as a gain but as a loss— as a *punishment* for lack of steadfastness in affliction. The pious

[70] Perkins, *Discourse*, p. 255.

'should prefer a thousand times to be ill and miserable in God, than to be bright and healthy with the devil, to die in God, than to survive with the devil, to have sick horses, oxen and sheep or to have none at all, than to have strong, healthy, well-made horses and other beasts with the devil's help and by means of devilish conjurations and blessings'.[71] It was one thing to say the words of blessing over the baptized child as part of a formal ceremony, and quite another to bless adults and cows in the home and in the fields; it was one thing to speak of the 'power' of prayers and sermons, but quite another to attribute to utterances a material efficacy. Christ had healed and exorcised by pronouncing words, but the modern charmers and exorcists fell short of this 'not by a peasant's shoe but by more than a hundred well-measured German miles'. He was, after all, said Platz, the Son of God.

Niels Hemmingsen published the single most important Danish contribution to the witchcraft debate in Copenhagen in 1575. His *Admonitio de superstitionibus magicis vitandis* opened by defining magic as a belief in the physical power of symbols: 'A magical superstition is therefore anything that comes from the Devil, through the medium of human beings, by whatever is imagined to be in words, signs, figures and characters, whether an express agreement with the Devil occurs or not.' Since the devil wished to subvert the pure religion of the Word, his first task was to corrupt the sense in which words were efficacious. The response of the Protestant demonologist was equally clear. Because the power of the Word was only semantic, the efficacy of magic must be totally specious, its results depending on purely natural interventions by those demons with whom, expressly or implicitly, magicians were in league. Hemmingsen's reference to the *anicula saga* and his ridiculing of popular divination techniques shows that he was not thinking of intellectual magic.[72] Like Platz, he argued that the same degree of impiety resided in all magical effects, whether helpful or harmful; if the body was indeed healed, then a 'leprosy' was placed in the soul instead. Those who resort to the diabolical arts in ill-health 'shake off faith, lay aside the choice of God, leave the fear of God, disregard God's ordinances, call into doubt His divine promises,

---

[71] Conrad Wolffgang Platz, *Kurtzer, Nottwendiger, unnd Wollgegrundter bericht, Auch Christentliche vermanung, von der Grewlichen, in aller Welt gebreuchlichen Zauberey, Sünd dem Zauberischen Beschwören und Segensprechen* . . . (n.p., 1565), sigs. Fiii^v–Fiv^r.

[72] Niels Hemmingsen, *Admonitio de superstitionibus magicis vitandis* (Copenhagen, 1575), sigs. B1^v, B7^r–B8^v: 'Magica ergo superstitio est, quiquid sit a Diabolo mediante homine, quibusvis conceptis verbis, signis, figuris, characteribus, sive intercedit pactum expressum cum Diabole, sive non.'

and cast off the patience which belongs to Christians'.[73] Hemmingsen considers these spiritual crimes in turn before arguing that mental responses to sickness ought to begin with reflection on sin, move on to the therapy of repentance, and conclude with requests for divine assistance. Only then may the physical remedies which God has placed in nature and the hands of doctors be applied. Following this initial discussion of magic and affliction, Hemmingsen devotes the bulk of his treatise to a detailed analysis of six of the types of arts condemned in Deuteronomy 18: divination, prestigiation, augury, *maleficium* (including harmful weather), incantation (by words or gestures), and beneficent magic.[74] Usually it is their popular applications he has in mind. In this context, his concluding advice to pastors is significant. Above all, he argues, they must destroy the common belief that the sin of those who practise magic with good intent (*ut opem afflictus ferant*) is less than that of those who resort to outright witchcraft: 'For faith in the divine promises chokes in the hearts not only of those who practice *magia* but also of those others who seem to heal by the magicians' art.'[75]

Bernhard Albrecht's *Magia* of 1628 was something of a summation of the Lutheran tradition of witchcraft studies. He himself traced it to the views he had heard in Wittenberg and Jena well over thirty years before, and he cited many other Lutheran pastors and theologians as supporting authorities. To some degree, it seems to balance a traditional concern for the devil-worship of the 'black' witch (*Hexe*) with the newer hostility to the 'white' equivalents. Albrecht devotes a substantial chapter to the usual agenda of questions regarding flying, the sabbath, copulation with devils, metamorphosis, and, of course, *maleficium*.[76] But 'magic' is again defined to include *any* use of an object, gesture, or form of words which assumes that it has a power other than that with which it was created. Since such a use could plainly not be either godly or natural it must be demonic; and this embraced benevolent as well as malevolent intentions.[77] Once again, however, it is the former which dominate the discussion. Taking his categories from Deuteronomy 18, Albrecht spends most of a substantial treatise analysing the individual practitioners of popular techniques for procuring good fortune—*Beschwörer, Segensprecher,*

---

[73] Ibid. sig. D3ᵛ.   [74] Ibid. sigs. G3ᵛ–M3ʳ.   [75] Ibid. sig. N1ʳ.
[76] Bernhard Albrecht, *Magia; das ist, Christlicher Bericht von der Zauberey und Hexerey ins gemein, und dero zwölfferley Sorten und Arten insonderheit* . . . (Leipzig, 1628), 186–235.
[77] Ibid. 10–11, 21–4, 130, 137–8.

Zeichendeuter, Warsager, and so on. In each case the task is to separate out the residue of licit practices from the mass of 'superstitions'. Blessings are appropriate between pastor and flock, or before meals, or at the deathbed; they should not be hung round the necks of livestock or buried under thresholds. Days are in some sense special if marked by notable spiritual events, but not in the sense of the *Tagwähler*, who plots the daily co-ordinates of propitiousness.[78] Albrecht's knowledge of the usages he condemns is circumstantial; his section on 'the superstitious' reads like an ethnography of Ascension Day, Good Friday, and baptism rituals. He also writes in the usual way about the real nature of affliction and the proper responses to it. But what is remarkable in his book is the sheer weight of the attention given to the everyday practices of those who understood affliction and redress in very different terms.

IV

Speaking of the German Lutheran version of the general view of witchcraft we have been considering, Erik Midelfort labelled it 'providential'. For him its *locus classicus* was Johann Brenz's hailstorm sermon of 1539, and its theological home was the university of Tübingen. It was taken up by Spreter, Alber, Bidembach, Heerbrand, Platz, and eventually by so many other Württemberg theologians, pastors, and jurists that it became an orthodoxy in the Duchy and the foundation of Tübingen legal opinion. It also influenced men like Jacob Graeter in Schwäbisch Hall and David Meder in neighbouring Hohenlohe. For Midelfort it was marked essentially by moderation. Because it emphasized the moral implications of misfortune and its providential origin, it played down the direct, physical threat of witchcraft. In particular, it tried to divert the moral energies of the victims of affliction away from vengeance against witches towards self-scrutiny and repentance—away from the model of Moses and towards the model of Job. This helped accordingly to mollify the tenor of witch-hunting in the German south-west.[79]

Two modifications may now be suggested to this account of a demonological tradition. The first, prompted simply by a wider angle

---

[78] Ibid. 40–1, 70–4.
[79] Midelfort, *Witch-hunting*, pp. 36–56.

of vision, is that a 'providential' account of witchcraft and a tendency to spiritualize its meaning were general features of Protestant pastoral demonology, wherever it was found in Europe. For none of the writers in this genre failed to emphasize the power of God and the powerlessness of witches. If the latter used natural means they would, after all, be no different from other criminals, a point which Johann Weyer turned astutely to his advantage: it was the very fact that they attributed spurious powers to created things (powers that God had not given them) that made them 'witches' in the first place. This attribution was fundamentally repulsive to Protestants everywhere, especially when it also involved ingredients 'transferred' from religious worship. The devil's role (with divine permission) was to sustain the illusion of power by providing the necessary efficacy. His presence was therefore implied even in the simplest forms of magic or the most trivial superstitions. As we have seen, this widened the category of 'witchcraft' enormously, but not at the expense of the doctrine of Providence or by making the crime anything else but a spiritual affront. Hence the popularity, throughout Protestant Europe, of the story of Job, who short-circuited the whole network of assumptions surrounding the magic of affliction by acknowledging no source of his ills other than divine and no remedies other than patience and faith. The 'providential' tradition was therefore at work in Albrecht's Augsburg, Zehner's Henneberg, and Musculus's Brandenburg, as well as in Württemberg. It was found in many of the Protestant demonologies brought together by the Frankfurt am Main printer Nicholas Basse in the very popular compendium *Theatrum de veneficis* of 1586. It influenced Hemmingsen's *Admonitio* and the pastors of Denmark, as well as the demonologists within the Swedish spheres of influence in the Baltic and eastern Europe. Neither Daneau nor Perrault, it is true, were particularly clear contributors, but their colleagues among the English Calvinists were all pure 'providentialists'. Richard Bernard was only drawing together a line of thought to which Gifford, the Holland brothers, Perkins, Mason, Alexander Roberts, and Thomas Cooper had already contributed. All were exponents of the views which Midelfort found in Württemberg, and all saw the task of combating popular misapprehensions about the nature of misfortune and the powers of witches as more important than simply driving home the dangers of satanism pure and simple. It looks very much as though the Württemberg pastors were exponents of a general north-European view rather than of a southwest German speciality.

A reasonably constant theology was one explanation for this wider uniformity; but so too were the demands of a common evangelism. A second modification to Midelfort's account is needed to take account of recent work on the actual carrying of the Reformation to the populations of later sixteenth-century Europe. His view was that the witchcraft beliefs of the Württemberg orthodoxy were derived essentially from intellectual reformulations of an earlier tradition, notably that associated with the medieval *Canon episcopi*, rather than from the pastoral aims of clergymen or the practical problems they faced when confronting their flocks. But we now know far more about the challenges faced by reformers, who wished not merely for better doctrine or even improved morals, but for fundamental changes in popular culture. Keith Thomas's pioneering research on the extraordinary density and range of the magical practices to which ordinary English people turned when faced with material needs has been followed by studies which reveal comparable patterns of belief and behaviour in early modern France and Germany. The evidence for the use of para-liturgical and even pre-liturgical rituals in every conceivable situation of practical need is now overwhelming.[80] So too is the evidence for their continued professionalization at the hands of specialists. Of course, witch-trials themselves yield many examples of both. But the protocols of clerical visitations also suggest a remarkable degree of resilience in the personal use of aids like blessings and conjurations and the resort to experts in magical healing, protection, and divination—so great as to lead Gerald Strauss to the view that the Lutherans actually failed to reform the religious beliefs and behaviour of ordinary Germans.[81] It is clear that at the end of the sixteenth century ordinary people still had ideas about misfortune, about magic and witchcraft, and (ultimately) about the sources of good and evil in

---

[80] Keith Thomas, *Religion and the Decline of Magic* (Harmondsworth, 1973), 27–300; his chapter 'Magic and Religion' (pp. 301–332) is a seminal discussion of several of the themes I explore in this essay. See also Robert Muchembled, *Culture populaire et culture des élites dans la France moderne* (Paris, 1978), 57–135; R. W. Scribner, 'Ritual and Popular Religion in Catholic Germany at the time of the Reformation', *Journal of Ecclesiastical History*, 35 (1984), 47–77; cf. R. W. Scribner, 'Cosmic Order and Daily Life: Sacred and Secular in Pre-industrial German Society', in Kaspar von Greyerz (ed.), *Religion and Society in Early Modern Europe, 1500–1800* (London, 1984), 17–32. In the present volume, see Robert Muchembled, ch. 5, below.

[81] Gerald Strauss, 'Success and Failure in the German Reformation', *Past and Present*, 67 (1975), 30–63; and by the same author, *Luther's House of Learning: Indoctrination of the Young in the German Reformation* (London, 1978), 249–308. For a contrasting viewpoint, see James M. Kittelson, 'Successes and Failures in the German Reformation: The Report from Strasbourg', *Archive for Reformation History*, 73 (1982), 153–75.

the world which could be radically at odds with those of their reformers.

What emerges from this collision of belief structures is not only forms of witch-hunting but the pastoral demonology of European Protestantism—its context being less one of intellectual theorizing, than the process historians have come to call 'acculturation'. Given the known patterns of popular culture and the intentions of evangelists, Protestant demonologies contain exactly the arguments and materials one would expect to find in them. It has been a claim of this essay that their genesis lay typically in first-hand clerical experiences in which local clergymen, visitation officials, and church governors shared. Ethnographically they exactly complement what we know about popular culture from the records of such experiences. Hemmingsen's list of divination techniques (with sieves, keys laid in the Bible, etc.), Platz's sample invocations to the sun and moon, Milichius's account of the rituals of St John's Eve, the descriptions of popular blessings in Samson and Bullinger are each familiar in this sense.[82] Albrecht's detailed account of the blessings and spells used to protect animals and crops and to ward off inclement weather and diseases ought to be set alongside Strauss's discoveries in the visitation records for Nassau-Wiesbaden (Hesse); or his chapter on 'The Superstitious' alongside the great Catholic collection of superstitions by Jean-Baptiste Thiers.[83]

Important and valid criticisms have been made concerning the use of the idea of acculturation in studies of cultural change in Early Modern Europe. In particular, historians are justifiably wary of any global application of the concept.[84] Yet even taking this into account, it has to be admitted that in Protestant demonology the perceptions of an educated minority with regard to the 'failings' of popular culture

---

[82] Hemmingsen, *Admonitio*, sig. Ci^r; Platz, *Kurtzer ... bericht*, sigs. Bvi^r–Bvi^v; Milichius, *Zauber-Teuffel*, pp. 16–17; Samson, *Neun...Hexen Predigt*, sig. Ti^v; Bullinger, *Von hexen und unholden*, pp. 300–1. For a good example of a demonologist encountering such beliefs and practices at first hand, see Kahk, ch. 10, below, on Herman Samson.

[83] Albrecht, *Magia*, pp. 39–48, 130–9, and esp. 183; cf. Strauss, *Luther's House of Learning*, p. 304. For an earlier specialist tract on the subject, see Christoph Vischer, *Einfeltiger Bericht wider den ... Segen, damit man Menschen und Viehe zu helffen vertmeinet* (Schmalkalden, 1571); Vischer was *Generalsuperintendent* of Meiningen at the time and had held the same position in Schmalkalden. For a collection of 'zaubersegen', see Ulrich Jahn, *Hexenwesen und Zauberei in Pommern* (Breslau, 1886), 40–196.

[84] Two recent examples are Peter Burke, 'A Question of Acculturation?', in Zambelli (ed.), *Scienze, credenze occulte, livelli di cultura*, pp. 197–204; Jean Wirth, 'Against the Acculturation Thesis', in Greyerz (ed.), *Religion and Society*, pp. 66–78. See also Greyerz's own introduction to *Religion and Society*, pp. 1–14.

are recorded in an especially vivid and revealing form. The result may very well be a cultural caricature and it certainly hides the degree of both uniformity and interchange between 'élite' and 'popular' cultures. But the texts as they stand still have to be interpreted; and there remains a case for seeing them, in *intention* at least, as among the purest examples of early modern cultural proscription.[85] In this respect, it is important to notice that Protestant demonologies were not virulently anti-Catholic, their hostility being directed more at popular irreligion than at the enemy sect.

The degree of change in attitudes and behaviour which reformers required in the sphere of witchcraft beliefs falls little short of total; a complete conceptual 'translation' was aimed at. The texts place clerical and popular beliefs about misfortune at opposite ends of the spectrum of accountability. A wide gulf also opened up between a spiritualized and a this-worldly reading of everyday experience. Moral absolutism replaced the variable, contingent morality which George Gifford condemned as 'country divinity'. Witches traditionally assumed to be harmful in matter-of-fact physical ways (*maleficium*) were now said to be, in some higher theological sense, vehicles of the spiritual benefits brought by a true understanding of Providence; those healers and diviners who brought much-needed physical relief to villagers were now said to be the real agents of the devil, and those who consulted them not Christians but 'pagans' or 'heathens'. A very wide range of everyday recipes and rituals was denounced as having no efficacy and no value. Above all, there was continual repetition of the idea that it was better to die in piety than to be healed by magic, a particularly pure example of the way the moral preferences of ordinary people were reversed.

So great is the distance which a text like Gifford's *Dialogue* opens up between its participants that one often has the sensation that they are talking at conceptual cross-purposes.[86] It is also striking to find the demonologists returning again and again to a litany of questions which

---

[85] Clive Holmes speaks of a 'vigorous attempt by some of the Protestant clergy not merely to police but to transform popular belief and action': 'Popular Culture? Witches, Magistrates and Divines in Early Modern England', in Kaplan, *Understanding Popular Culture*, p. 86. See also Günther Lottes, 'Popular Culture and the Early Modern State in 16th Century Germany', in Kaplan (ed.), *Understanding Popular Culture*, pp. 173–9.

[86] At the end of a long dialogue in which the Calvinist 'Daniel' has sought to convince the villager 'Samuel' that the practices of the rural cunning men and women were just as much a matter of witchcraft as *maleficium* itself, Gifford allows Samuel to remain confused on the issue, and a local healer, 'Goodwife R', to re-state the claims for a beneficent magic; see *A dialogue*, sigs. M3^r–M4^v.

accurately express popular incomprehension of pastoral aims
(Albrecht answered them on three occasions in one text[87]): how can
magical practitioners be evil when they help their clients; how can
they be evil if the means they use are derived from religious sources or
inspire a kind of faith; how can it be evil to resort to them for successful remedies when all others have failed? To this stubborn utilitarian-
ism it was common to reply that the criterion should not be what
worked but what was permitted. This was a further difference of kind
between the categories which shaped ordinary experience and the
ambitions of the Protestant agents of acculturation—a difference
which helps to explain the latter's limited success.

However distorted or distanced the perception of the target culture
may have been, it could still be vital in inspiring actions. An active
pastorate, committed to a programme of sermons on the themes we
have considered, was surely not an inconsiderable element in the
circumstances surrounding witch-hunting—especially if we set aside
for a moment variable local conditions and influences, and concentrate on more constant international ingredients. At this level of
analysis, William Monter has recently suggested that the states with
Erastian Protestant churches (Lutheran Scandinavia, the Lutheran
principalities in Germany, 'Anglican' England) did in fact have closely
comparable witch-hunting profiles. It therefore seems reasonable to
infer that one at least of the reasons for the uniformity itself might be
the ideological constancy of pastoral views across national frontiers.
But Monter also argues that its substance was a less severe attitude to
witchcraft than that taken elsewhere in Europe. And this raises the
question of whether the moderation of the Württemberg Lutherans
was likewise part of a more general Protestant phenomenon.[88]

Certainly the doubts and hesitations of Brenz, Alber, and Bidembach were widely shared. It was fundamental to pastoral demonology
as a whole that victims of misfortune exaggerated or otherwise mis-
understood its supposed origin in the malevolence of individuals, and
that they were foolish to think of eradicating it by eradicating witches;
religious rather than punitive remedies were to be sought. With some
help from the universal assumption that witches wielded no independent powers of their own, this must have made for a kind of

---

[87] Albrecht, *Magia*, pp. 44–8, 178–81, 257.
[88] Monter, *Ritual*, pp. 28–9. On the close cultural ties which linked the Baltic and
German pastors see Ankarloo, *Trolldomsprocesserna*, p. 339; Heikkinen, *Paholaisen
Littolaiset*, p. 375; and Naess, ch. 14, below.

moderation in apportioning guilt. Jodocus Hocker stated the general view that it was superstitious to attribute every illness to bewitchment;[89] the Calvinist Anton Praetorius followed the Lutheran Brenz in saying that witches were totally powerless over the weather;[90] Johann Ellinger complained of the haste with which people wished to get anyone suspected of using sorcery to the stake.[91] In England, Gifford in Essex and Bernard in Somerset condemned the same popular excesses. Gifford spoke of 'a broyle against old women, which can any wayes be suspected to be witches, as if they were the very plagues of the world, and as if all would be well, and safe from such harmes, if they were rooted out, and thus they fall a rooting out without all care';[92] Bernard talked of the raging hostility towards witches as 'vaine, dissolute, and irreligious', and even asked for 'patience' towards them.[93]

Everywhere there were fears that innocent blood was being shed, and demands for more rigorous proofs of faith. In their advice to magistrates, Protestant pastors repeatedly asked for the use of the regular legal procedures and questioned the role of rumour, the use of ordeals, and the application of torture.[94] It is also highly significant that these cautions were repeated by the greatest of the early Protestant legal experts on witchcraft, Johann Georg Godelmann, the third book of whose *Tractatus de magis, veneficis et lamiis* is marked by discrimination and restraint (it was dedicated to the Duke of Mecklenburg). He insisted that witchcraft be treated as an ordinary offence, not a *crimen exceptum*; he refused to admit as evidence confessions concerning impossibilities (including the sabbath); and he defended a rigorous separation between the perpetration of real harm (*veneficium*) and the imaginary deeds of deluded women (*lamiae*). Like the pastors he lamented the readiness to accuse and to punish; just as the Romans once clamoured for the blood of Christians with cries of

---

[89] Jodocus Hocker, *Der teufel selbs das ist Warhafftiger . . . bericht von den Teufeln, Was sie sein, Woher sie gekommen. Und was sie teglich wircken . . .*, in *Theatrum diabolorum* (Frankfurt am Main, 1569), fo. cvxᵛ. For the complicated bibliography of Hocker's tract, see Grimm, 'Die Deutschen Teufelbücher des 16. Jhts', pp. 528, 551–2.

[90] Praetorius, *Gründlicher Bericht von Zauberey und Zauberern*, pp. 97–109.

[91] Ellinger, *Hexen Coppel*, 'Dedicatio'.

[92] Gifford, *A dialogue*, sig. Diʳ.

[93] Bernard, *A guide to grand jury men*, pp. 8–9; cf. pp. 10, 54, 73–4.

[94] Hocker's sceptical analysis of these matters and his close agreement with Weyer's views is a good example, *Der teufel selbs*, fos. cxiiiiᵛ–cxxiiʳ. In his additions to Hocker's tract, Hamelman said he was in agreement with its cautionary tone; see *Theatrum diabolorum*, fos. cxxxiiiiʳ–cxxxvᵛ.

'To the beasts', so now the populace shouted 'To the stake' whenever a woman was suspected of witchcraft. Godelmann suggested a three-fold distinction between those who made a demonic pact and committed real *maleficium*, those who made the pact without committing *maleficium*, and those whose 'crimes' were in fact impossibilities and self-delusions.[95] According to his published sermons of 1626, Hermann Samson was advocating the same policy as a Lutheran orthodoxy in early seventeenth-century Riga. Witches in the first category deserved death, those in the second, non-capital punishment, and those in the third, medical treatment.[96]

Historians interested in tracing demonological scepticism and opposition to witch-hunting have tended to look no further (amongst Protestant authors) than Johann Weyer and Reginald Scot, adding perhaps Weyer's supporter Johann Ewich and the other German moderates Witekind and (later) Johann Matthäus Meyfart. But there was clearly an important strand of doubt in-built in Protestant demonology itself. Indeed, it would not be too paradoxical to say that *most* Protestant pastors were opponents of witch-hunting if it meant the neglect of those spiritual and moral truths regarding affliction which they derived from the Book of Job. No doubt this was why Weyer's ideas (though not the demonological pyrrhonism of Scot) found so much support.[97] The influences may well have operated in the other direction too, with Weyer and Scot repeating many of the 'Brenzian' cautions. What is certainly true is that 'belief' and 'scepticism' in witchcraft matters were not fixed or separable, but relative categories which operated along a continuum of reactions to the crime.

In any case, we should not exaggerate pastoral moderation; most

---

[95] Godelmann, *Tractatus de magis*, book iii. sig. A4ᵛ, pp. 1–7, 59–60, 142–5; it should be noted that the German trans. of this work (1592) was undertaken by the Hessian Superintendent, Georg Schwartze (Nigrinus). For a reappraisal of these aspects of Godelmann's *Tractatus*, see Sönke Lorenz, 'Johann Georg Godelmann—Ein Gegner des Hexenwahns?', in Roderich Schmidt (ed.), *Beiträge zur pommerschen und mecklenburgischen Geschichte* (Marburg, 1981), 61–105.

[96] Samson, *Neun . . . Hexen Predigt*, sigs. Xiiᵛ–Xiiiᵛ. Samson contrasted Lutheran willingness to discriminate between types of witchcraft with the views of the Jesuits and Calvinists, whose greater severity (he argued) stemmed from their view that the crime was essentially one of heresy. Samson said he was reflecting the views of Johann Brenz (in a letter to Jacob Heerbrand), Praetorius, and Witekind, as well as those of Godelmann.

[97] Midelfort, *Witch-hunting*, pp. 26, 235 n. 77. On Witekind, see Carl Binz (ed.), *Augustin Lercheimer und seine Schrift wider den Hexenwahn* (Strasbourg, 1888). On Meyfart, see Christian Hallier, *Johann Matthaüs Meyfart* (Neumünster, 1982), 66–71.

did not go as far as Weyer, as his own correspondence with Brenz makes clear. The general view was that there were in fact plenty of real witches who, despite their utter powerlessness, should be punished—(as Brenz again put it), 'because they are without fear of God, lead a godless and un-Christian life, give themselves entirely to the devil to corrupt and harm mankind, and not because they actually cause any harm, as they think they do; for they cannot harm'.[98] Their guilt was thus partly one of intention and mainly one of allegiance. In England, Gifford and other Elizabethan divines demanded greater not less severity in the laws. It was precisely because the 1563 statute dealt mainly with the actual harms wrought by witches that it missed the heinousness of their demonic allegiance, an omission only partly remedied in the legislation of 1604.[99] Even on the issue of powerlessness itself, pastors could be intractable. Paulus Frisius of Nagold, in the heart of moderate Württemberg, wrote that even though witches could not actually effect any non-natural *maleficium* and relied on the devil to achieve this, yet 'one takes the intention for the deed and action . . . and punishes them as if they had even themselves done it'.[100] In moderate England, too, we find Richard Bernard arguing that the devil's actions could be imputed to witches 'and they may bee said to doe, what the spirits doe, though their own words and deedes have no force in themselves to effect their wills . . .'.[101] Above all, the pastor demonologists made up for any caution regarding malevolent witchcraft by their sustained and bitter attacks on its 'benevolent' equivalent—popular magic. Not only did they try to extend capital criminality to its practitioners; they even thought their clients were culpable too—in the case of James Mason, of the *same* sin.[102] In this respect, the penalty incurred by the most famous client of all—King Saul—provided them with a standard.

There is now also a considerable body of evidence which indicates that a significant proportion of those who appeared as defendants in

[98] Brenz, *Ein Predig von dem Hagel*, ed. cit., p. 217. The correspondence with Weyer follows in Midelfort's edn. at pp. 219–26.

[99] Holmes, 'Popular Culture?', p. 87; Gifford, *A dialogue*, sigs. K3ʳ-K3ᵛ; Perkins, *Discourse*, pp. 251–6.

[100] Paulus Frisius, *Von dess Teuffels nebelkappen; das ist: Ein Kurtzer begriff den gantzen handel von der Zäuberey, belangend, zusammen gelesen* (?Frankfurt am Main, 1583), in *Theatrum de veneficis*, p. 223.

[101] Bernard, *A guide to grand jury men*, p. 160.

[102] Mason, *The anatomie of sorcerie*, p. 92; cf. Bernard, *A guide to grand jury men*, pp. 254–8; Platz, *Kurtzer . . . Bericht*, sigs. Gviiʳ-Hiiᵛ; Alber and Bidembach, *Ein summa etlicher predigen*, sigs. Ciᵛ-Ciiʳ.

early modern witchcraft trials were practitioners of 'white' magic—precisely those healers, diviners, and blessers who feature so prominently in the demonologies. It may be true that this was partly the result of their ambiguous position within their own communities, but the pastoral hostility we have traced in texts must surely have been at work.[103] Did Reformation Europe turn on its countryside magicians as it became clear that the first phase of evangelism had not removed the need to consult them and that men and women were returning to their 'superstitions' (as Hemmingsen sourly put it) like dogs returning to old vomit?[104] Until much more is known about these aspects of witch-hunting it would be rash to conclude that demonological opinion had a calming and mollifying effect in Protestant cultures. To offset Godelmann there is always the figure of Benedikt Carpzov . . .

V

As for the question of what was denominationally unique to Protestant demonology, it is necessary to insist again that we are left not with a clear dichotomy of views but with a matter of emphasis. For whether one speaks of 'the reform of popular culture',[105] 'the attack on popular magic',[106] or simply of 'acculturation', these were evidently as much

---

[103] Individual examples, like those of Ursula Kemp who said that 'though she could unwitch, she could not witch' (*A true and just recorde, of . . . all the witches, taken at S. Oses, in the countie of Essex* (London, 1582), sig. A2) or Joan Peterson, whose clients came to her trial to give evidence of her cures (*The Witch of Wapping . . .* (London, 1652), p. 3), are found in cases from all over Protestant Europe. For general treatments of the subject, see Richard Horsley, 'Who Were the Witches? The Social Roles of the Accused in the European Witch Trials', *Journal of Interdisciplinary History*, 9 (1979), 689–715; id., 'Further Reflections on Witchcraft and European Folk Religion', *History of Religions*, 19 (1979), 71–95; Clarke Garrett, 'Witches and Cunning Folk in the Old Regime', in Jacques Beauroy *et al.* (eds.), *The Wolf and the Lamb* (Saratoga, Calif., 1976), 53–64; Tekla Dömötör, 'The Cunning Folk in English and Hungarian Witch Trials', in Venetia Newall (ed.), *Folklore Studies in the Twentieth Century* (Woodbridge, 1980), 183–7. The essays in the present volume again illustrate this point; see esp. Naess, ch. 14, below, and his discussion of how easily the cases of wise women could turn into witch trials, pp. 372–5.

[104] Hemmingsen, *Admonitio*, sig. F2ʳ: 'Incipiunt homines fastidiri panem illum suavissimum Evangelii, et cupiunt iterum satiari carnibus superstitionum, quas olim prae nausea eiecerant . . .'.

[105] Peter Burke, *Popular Culture in Early Modern Europe* (London, 1978), 207 and, more generally, 207–43.

[106] Robert Evans, *The Making of the Habsburg Monarchy, 1550–1700* (Oxford, 1979), 381–418.

Catholic as Protestant phenomena. Catholic priests were just as assuredly involved in Catholic witch-hunting as were Protestant pastors in their own lands. No faith had a monopoly of definitions of superstition. It is from one of the great Catholic treatments of the subject, the *Traité des superstitions* by Jean-Baptiste Thiers, that historians have derived much of their ethnography of early modern popular culture in France.[107] In the earlier period the German Catholics Jodocus Lorichius and Peter Binsfeld both linked superstition to witchcraft via the practices of popular magicians and the expectations of their clients—in Binsfeld's case, in a guide for priests.[108] The Spaniard Francisco Peña's annotations to Nicolas Eymerich's fourteenth-century inquisitors' manual indicate that diviners and soothsayers (*sortilegii, divinatores*) could trouble Counter-Reformation clerics as much as their Protestant enemies.[109] But Pedro Ciruelo's *Reprobación de las supersticiones y hechicerías* (?1530) shows that Catholic theologians did not need Trent to tell them that the entire range of popular magical practices was offensive to the faith—and for the same reasons as it became offensive to Lutherans and Calvinists.[110]

Even the doctrine that the individual was ultimately responsible for the misfortunes which afflicted him (in the sense that they always signified aspects of his personal relationship with the God who brought them) has been found in the faith of Catholic urban élites and the pastoral efforts of the Counter-Reformation.[111] In one remarkable case, Jacob Vallick's *Von Zäuberern, Hexen, und Unholden*, we even have

---

[107] On Thiers, see François Lebrun, '*Le Traité des superstitions* de Jean-Baptiste Thiers', *Annales de Bretagne*, 83 (1976), 443–65; Monter, *Ritual*, pp. 114–29, cf. (on Jansenism) p. 89.

[108] Jodocus Lorichius, *Aberglaub Das ist, Kurtzlicher bericht, Von Verbottenen Segen, Artzneyen, Künsten, vermeintem Gottsdienst, und andern spöttlichen beredungen* . . . (Freiburg im Breisgau, 1593); this tract considers all the detailed 'superstitious' and 'magical' practices on which Protestant writers concentrated their attacks—the passage on witches is at pp. 98–102. I have used the French edn. of Binsfeld's treatise: Peter Binsfeld, *La théologie des pasteurs et autres prestres ayant charge des ames*, trans. P. Bermyer (Rouen, 1640), 314–27. Binsfeld was, of course, a major contributor to Catholic demonology in his *Tractatus de confessionibus maleficorum et sagarum* (Trier, 1589).

[109] Nicolas Eymerich, *Directorium inquisitorum . . . cum scholiis seu annotationibus eruditissimis D. Francisci Pegnae Hispani* . . . (Rome, 1578), 88–9 (2nd pagination).

[110] Pedro Ciruelo, *A Treatise Reproving all Superstitions and Forms of Witchcraft*, trans. E. A. Maio and D'Orsay W. Pearson (London, 1977), esp. 113–359.

[111] Robin Briggs, 'Witchcraft and Popular Mentality in Lorraine, 1580–1630', in Vickers (ed.), *Occult and Scientific Mentalities*, p. 340. For an early 16th-c. Catholic whose views on witchcraft were comparable to those found later in Württemberg, see the remarks concerning Martin Plantsch in Midelfort, *Witch-hunting*, pp. 34–6, and Heiko Oberman, *Masters of the Reformation* (Cambridge, 1981), 158–83.

a fictional dialogue which depicts in simple, everyday terms the typical experiences of the village pastor when confronting popular attitudes to affliction and witchcraft. It opens when 'Elyzabeth' complains to her neighbour 'Mechtilt' that her horses are sick, her butter will not come, and her husband is incapacitated (*unvermugen*). She fears bewitchment, naming both the suspected witch and the occasion when the troubles began. Vallick's response, through Mechtilt and the priest who later joins the conversation, is already summarized in his opening address, 'To the Reader'. It is a sign of spiritual fickleness to welcome God's good fortune while ascribing ill fortune to witches and devils, since, in effect, the latter was only a version of the former. Bearing the cross had positive spiritual benefit by purging complacency, whereas absence of adversity could be a sign of divine indifference. Besides, facile suspicion and false accusation might easily threaten innocent lives. There is an extraordinarily close resemblance between this tract (it was originally published in Dutch sometime before 1576) and Gifford's homespun *Dialogue*, which opens with just such a village confrontation, follows identical arguments, and ends with precisely the same cautions. Indeed, the identity with Protestant views is so uncannily close that one has to keep reminding oneself that Vallick was the Catholic priest of Groesen (or Groessen) in Gelderland, a remote region otherwise little touched by either Reformation.[112] As long as there are texts like this in the canon of early modern demonology the view that Protestants and Catholics shared exactly comparable evangelistic aims will command attention.

It is not the case, therefore, that the Protestant demonologists dealt with themes which found no place in Catholic literature—only that they dealt with them very much to the exclusion of other elements in witchcraft beliefs. Their views about witchcraft, as Teall remarked, 'rested on narrower foundations' than did those of the Catholics.[113] I have argued that this preoccupation may be traced partly to the characteristic stresses in Protestant theology and in particular to attempts to colonize popular minds. The topic of witchcraft was important in Reformation thought because of its natural, essentially

---

[112] Jacob Vallick, *Von Zäuberern, Hexen, und Unholden. Fürnemlich aber was Zäuberen für ein Werck seye, was Kranckheit, Schade, und Hindernuss darauss erstehe. Auch was Gegen Artzney darwider zu gebrauchen seye*, in *Theatrum de veneficis* (1586), pp. 54–69. The work was first published in German in Cologne, 1576, 'auss Niderlandsicher sprach in hochteutsch ubergesetzt'. I am grateful to Dr Alastair Duke of the University of Southampton for biographical information concerning Vallick.

[113] Teall, 'Witchcraft and Calvinism', pp. 28–9.

unforced relevance both to new demands for doctrinal purity and to the problems of clerical practice, and not because of any mere sensationalism or obscurantism. It was already an integral element in the culture of those at whom reform was aimed; transmuted by the demands of acculturation into a somewhat different entity, it became integral to the idea of reform itself. There is an important sense in which the subject 'dissolves' into this larger frame of reference.[114] The concepts, the arguments, and the very language of Protestant demonology (including its tone of voice) ought to be seen as continuous with those found in the records of church commissions, *Kirchenordnungen*, visitation protocols and reports, the findings of church courts, and other manifestations of the reforming impulse. The result should be a two-way traffic in better understanding—with the history of witchcraft placed reassuringly at the heart of major changes attempted in European culture, and the themes of the recent historiography of the Protestant Reformation viewed from a fresh but confirming perspective.

---

[114] The idea of the analytical 'dissolution' of witchcraft derives from a suggestion by Malcolm Crick, *Explorations in Language and Meaning* (London, 1976), 112–13.

3
Inquisitorial Law and the Witch *
JOHN TEDESCHI

BY approaching the subject of the present volume from the point of view of the legal historian rather than that of the ethnologist or the social historian, I have attempted in this paper to provide a general legal and bureaucratic background against which the witchcraft question may be studied. My intention is to investigate the organization and procedures of a court system, rather than pursue the socio-economic or folkloristic implications of the witch persecutions. The following thesis regarding the type of legal justice administered by the Congregation of the Holy Office in Rome may appear novel to some readers. In fact, the contrast between the procedures described here and the judicial practices of civil courts elsewhere in Europe and in Italy itself is startling.

In trials conducted under Roman jurisdiction loose allegations were not permitted and witnesses made their depositions under oath. To forestall charges stemming from personal animosities, the accused were asked in advance to provide the names of individuals whom they considered their enemies. So that they might prepare a proper defence, the records of the trial proceedings were provided to the prisoner and to his lawyer in writing (with the names of the prosecution witnesses deleted). Judicial torture, which was carefully circumscribed, might only be applied after the defence had made its case and where the *indicia*, the evidence, was compelling. No properly conducted inquisitorial trial commenced with torture.

Specifically, in witchcraft proceedings, all the above and other safeguards as well were in effect. Physicians were consulted to establish

* Much of the research on the present paper was conducted while I was a Fellow at the Institute for Research in the Humanities, University of Wisconsin, Madison, during the academic year 1976–7. An abridged Spanish translation of this paper, 'Organización y procedimientos penales de la Inquisición Romana: Un bosquejo', has appeared in Angel Alcalá (ed.), *Inquisición española y mentalidad inquisitorial* (Barcelona, 1984).

The following abbreviations have been used: BA (Bologna, Biblioteca Comunale dell'Archiginnasio); BAV (Biblioteca Apostolica Vaticana); Bodl. (Bodleian Library, Oxford University); BRB (Bibliothéque Royale, Brussels; documents subsequently transferred to State Archives); TCD (Trinity College Library, Dublin).

the *corpus delicti*, namely to verify whether an illness or death might have had a natural cause, before jumping to the assumption that a *maleficium* had been perpetrated. The search for the devil's mark was unknown in the inquisitorial process, and the failure on the part of the accused to evince emotion or shed tears during the interrogation was considered unimportant. Alleged participants at sabbaths were not allowed to name their accomplices, and the testimony of witnesses who suffered from poor reputations could not lead to the torture of the defendant. In serious cases, sentences pronounced by provincial tribunals were scrutinized by the Congregation of the Holy Office in Rome and implausible confessions were deemed invalid. No witch was ever sent to the stake as a first offender if she showed the signs of repentance. Even in the extreme case of witches convicted of having caused a fatal injury, it was only Gregory XV, in 1623, in opposition to the prevailing inquisitorial tradition, who attempted to have the death sentence invoked.

I suggest further that many aspects of modern criminal law were already in place in rudimentary form or were being introduced in the tribunals of the Roman Inquisition in the sixteenth century. The arraigned had the benefit of a defence attorney; confessions obtained extrajudicially were invalid; appeals could be made to a higher court; first offenders were dealt with infinitely more leniently than recidivists. Imprisonment as a punishment, rather than merely for the purpose of custody during the trial, was practised by the Inquisition long before it was adopted by civil authorities at the close of the sixteenth century. Before that time, when pronouncing sentence, secular courts could only choose from among several extreme alternatives: the stake, mutilation, banishment. A sentence to life imprisonment by the Holy Office meant, as it does today, parole after a few years, subject to good behaviour; and house arrest, joined to work-release programmes, tentatively being considered at present by some of our more progressive communities, was a common form of penal service practised by the Inquisition in its day.[1]

The evidence adduced in the course of this paper is drawn from theory and practice—from the legal manuals prepared for the use of

---

[1] Carlo Reviglio della Veneria compares inquisitorial judicial procedures with their modern counterparts in the Italian penal code (*Codice italiano di procedura penale*) in his *L'Inquisizione medioevale ed il processo inquisitorio* (2nd rev. and expanded edn. Turin, 1951), Appendix i, 'L'Inquisizione medioevale e la legislazione penale moderna', 163–98. The piece first appeared in the *Revue internationale de doctrine et de législation pénale comparée* (1940).

inquisitors and from the actual records produced by the Inquisition at work. But it must be pointed out that most of this documentation is relatively late, primarily from the last quarter of the sixteenth century onwards. Because there are so few surviving records for the early years of the century, the comparison of witchcraft trials at the two poles of the *Cinquecento* will be difficult to accomplish, but ought to be a crucial area of future research. There are compelling questions to answer raised by the picture of mass executions occurring in the early decades of the century.[2]

And more study must be devoted to secular trials for witchcraft in Italy in states where the jurisdiction of the Inquisition was curbed. No statistics for Spanish and Italian witchcraft will be complete until even the trials performed by civil courts are studied and counted. How many were held, what procedures did they follow, what was their chronology? The precise influence of the notorious *Malleus malefi-carum* on these proceedings, ecclesiastical and secular alike, also needs to be investigated.

Our records inform us that in the 1580s, roughly, the preoccupation of inquisitors turned heavily from the pursuit of Protestantism in Italy to crimes of sortilege and magic, which came to account for over 40 per cent of their activity. The largest number of these cases did not involve the perpetration of a *maleficium* with harmful effects. It was not witchcraft that was involved, then, but rather magical arts to accomplish desired ends—healing, the recovery of lost treasures, the conquest of a loved one's favours. And the practitioners were not exclusively old women. Among them were ecclesiastics in large numbers employing and abusing sacramental paraphernalia and liturgical rites and prayers, sometimes with, but often without, formal apostasy to the devil.

While moral justice was impossible, given the presupposition of the Church that it had the right, even the duty, to persecute those who differed in their religious beliefs, legal justice in sixteenth-century terms *was* indeed dispensed by the Roman Inquisition. It is clear that the provisions for proper procedure contained in the manuals for the use of inquisitors were scrupulously enforced by Rome. And in

---

[2] For a recent excellent discussion of one early 16th-c. witch hunt, see Albano Biondi, 'Gianfrancesco Pico e la repressione della stregoneria', in *Mirandola e le terre del basso corso del Secchia della Deputazione di storia patria per le antiche provincie modenesi: Biblioteca*, NS 76 (1984), 331–49.

penetrating to the sources behind the sources, the correspondence, memoranda, and appeals which passed between Rome and the provincial courts, the austere picture of inquisitorial justice which we derive from trial dossiers and sentences is notably altered.

Our subject here is the judicial and penal system of the Roman Inquisition, the institution which was established on ancient foundations in mid-sixteenth-century Italy as a response to the Protestant challenge in that country.[3] It is not to be confused with the medieval inquisition which came into being early in the thirteenth century (and of which it was a continuation), or with the Spanish tribunal founded in 1478, which had a separate history.[4]

With the bull *Licet ab initio*, July 1542, the Pope was not creating a brand-new institution *ex nihilo*, for inquisitors had, of course, operated in the Middle Ages.[5] Like other sixteenth-century monarchs, he re-shaped a previously existing governmental function as part of a

---

[3] For a general orientation, see J. Tedeschi, 'Preliminary Observations on Writing a History of the Roman Inquisition', in F. Forrester Church and Timothy George (eds.), *Continuity and Discontinuity in Church History* (Leiden, 1979), 232–49. For the external history of this institution, see Ludwig von Pastor, *The History of the Popes from the Close of the Middle Ages*, (English trans. 40 vols.; St Louis, 1898–1953), xii. 503–13; xiii. 210–24; xiv. 259–318; xvi. 305–52, 478–82; xvii. 288–343, 400–4; xix. 296–322; xxi. 192–7; xxiv. 198–219. An excellent thumbnail sketch of the Inquisition, from its medieval origins, is in Niccolò del Re, *La curia romana*, (3rd edn. Rome, 1970), 89–101. For the bibliography (still lacunous, even in the 2nd much expanded edn.), see Emil van der Vekene, *Bibliotheca bibliographica historiae Sanctae Inquisitionis* (2 vols.; Vaduz, 1982–3).

[4] The first step in comparing the two institutions (Spanish and Roman) has already been taken by Agostino Borromeo, 'Spanische und römische Inquisition', forthcoming in the *Vorträge* of the Institut für Europäische Geschichte, Mainz. See also the correspondence preserved in the Archivo Histórico Nacional, Madrid, exchanged between the *Suprema* and its agent in Rome: Pilar Huerga Criado, 'Los agentes de la Inquisición Española en Roma durante el siglo XVII', in Joaquin Pérez Villanueva, *La Inquisición Española: Nueva visión, nuevos horizontes* (Madrid, 1980), 243–56. The distinguished Spanish jurist Francisco Peña, who spent much of his career in Holy Office circles in Rome, remarked on differences between Spanish and Roman procedures in his extensive commentary to Nicolas Eymerich's *Directorium Inquisitorum* (Rome, 1570) and in his 'Instructio, seu Praxis Inquisitorum', published in Cesare Carena's *Tractatus de Officio Sanctissimae Inquisitionis* (Bologna, 1668), 348–434 (1st edn. 1636). The *Tractatus* itself is an important source because it is based on Carena's long service as *consultore* and Fiscal Advocate in the tribunal of Cremona, in Spanish Lombardy. Descriptions of the workings of the Spanish Inquisition began to be compiled in Rome itself. Among the handbooks drawn up at the order of the Congregation of the Holy Office containing sections 'De S.to Officio Hispaniarum,' see BAV, Borg. lat. 558. The extent to which the several Spanish inquisitorial manuals published in Italy throughout the 16th c. actually saw service in Italian courts should also be investigated.

[5] Pastor, *Popes*, xii. 503. The Bull, dated 21 July 1542, is published in Carolus Cocquelines, *Bullarum, privilegiorum ac diplomatum pontificum amplissima collectio* (14 vols. in 28; Rome, 1733–62), iv¹. 211–12.

programme to centralize authority.[6] The defence of the faith was placed in the hands of a commission of cardinals whose assignment it became to appoint provincial inquisitors (generally members of the Dominican and Franciscan Orders), and co-ordinate and supervise their efforts. Responsibility for the uprooting of heresy, previously vested in both bishops and inquisitors, now became principally the burden of the inquisitorial courts.[7] Problems which had been caused by overlapping spheres of activity were greatly reduced, if not totally eliminated. The authority of the inquisitorial tribunals gained precedence over all other tribunals, lay and ecclesiastical alike.[8] Privileges exempting clergy and laity from prosecution were annulled.[9] A local inquisitor, beset by an aggressive bishop or by an uncooperative magistrate, could be certain that the most powerful ecclesiastics in Rome stood behind him and his cause. Two future popes were among the first six cardinals appointed to the Holy Office in 1542.[10] And in the reorganization of the Curia achieved in 1588 by

[6] Jean Delumeau, 'Les Progrès de la centralisation dans l'état pontifical au XVIᵉ siècle', *Revue historique*, 226 (1961), 399–410; Paolo Prodi, *La crisi religiosa del XVI secolo* (Bologna, 1964), 112ff.; id., *Il sovrano pontefice* (Bologna, 1982).

[7] For a discussion of the respective roles of the bishop and inquisitor, see the influential manual by Umberto Locati, *Opus quod iudiciale inquisitorum dicitur ex diversis theologis et I.U.D. . . . nuper extractum . . . nunc auctum et correctum* (Rome, 1570), 168f. Locati (d. 1587) had served as Commissioner General of the Holy Office in Rome. The precedence of the inquisitor over the bishop in the pursuit of heresy stemmed from the fact that the former was delegated to his office by the Pope and could cite witnesses and pursue suspects even outside his area of jurisdiction. In hierarchical terms a bishop outranked an inquisitor.

[8] For an actual example, see the case of Rainero Manzella, a Neapolitan, who in 1564 had been in the prison of the governor of Rome, the Torre di Nona, but was transferred to the Holy Office for trial when heretical activity on his part came to light. This information is contained in his sentence, dated 8 Feb. 1567, now preserved in TCD, MS 1224, fo. 116. The principle is reaffirmed in a decree of the Roman Congregation dated 24 Oct. 1584: Ludwig von Pastor, 'Allgemeine Dekrete der Römischen Inquisition', *Historisches Jahrbuch der Görres-Gesellschaft*, 33 (1912), 479–549, at p. 517. Naturally, the priority of ecclesiastical over secular proceedings was only observed in the states of the Church. Everywhere else the Holy Office conducted its affairs at the pleasure of the lay authorities.

[9] The lifting of exemptions from inquisitorial prosecution for members of Orders was accomplished by Paul III and renewed by successive pontiffs with the Bull, *In Apostolici culminis*, dated 14 Jan. 1542 (Cocquelines, *Bullarum*, iv¹. 194–5). Before this a religious member was under the exclusive jurisdiction of his superior. This was emphasized, e.g., in various decrees concerning Franciscans: Bartolomeo Fontana, 'Documenti vaticani contro l'eresia luterana in Italia', *Archivio della società romana di storia patria*, 15 (1892), 71–165, 365–474, at pp. 140, 158 (memorials dated 23 June 1534 and 15 Dec. 1537).

[10] Marcello Cervini (Marcellus II, 1555); Gianpietro Carafa (Paul IV, 1555–9). Other popes who served as inquisitors were Michele Ghislieri (Pius V, 1566–72); Felice Peretti (Sixtus V, 1585–90); Giovanni Battista Castagna (Urban VI, 1590); Giovanni

Sixtus V, the Holy Office was ranked in the place of honour among the fifteen departments or Congregations into which papal government was divided.[11] The seats of the local inquisitions were usually Dominican convents.[12] The fact that the inquisitor was an agent of the central papal government and not to be interfered with by the superior of the house is repeated in numerous official communications from the cardinals of the Roman Congregation. On the other hand, inquisitors were reminded that they were bound by the rules of their order and that they were expected to participate in the regular routines of their house, seeking no special dispensation from the communal discipline beyond what was strictly necessary (see Endnote A).

The evidence is drawn from a wide assortment of printed and manuscript sources. Despite the inaccessibility of the archives in the Palace of the Holy Office in Rome, we do not suffer from a shortage of original inquisitorial documents. Among our most important printed materials are legal manuals composed between the early fourteenth and the mid-seventeenth centuries by such lawyers or practising inquisitors as Nicolas Eymerich, Zanchino Ugolini, Iacobo de Simancas, Juan de Rohas, Umberto Locati, Eliseo Masini, Francisco Peña, Prospero Farinacci, and Cesare Carena.[13] A significant number of these authorities used in the Italian courts were Spaniards and several of their works were published in Italy in the sixteenth and seventeenth centuries.[14]

Antonio Facchinetti (Innocent IX, 1591); Camillo Borghese (Paul V, 1605–21): Pastor, *Popes, passim.*

[11] By virtue of the Bull *Immensa Aeterna Dei*, dated 22 Jan. 1588. See Cocquelines, *Bullarum*, iv[4]. 393.

[12] Descriptions of the Milanese, Bolognese, and Modenese establishments are contained respectively in Luigi Fumi, 'L'inquisizione romana e lo stato di Milano', *Archivio storico lombardo*, ser. 4, 13 (1910), 5–124, 285–414; 14. 145–220, esp. 8ff. m; Antonio Battistella, *Il S. Officio e la riforma religiosa in Bologna* (Bologna, 1905), *passim*; Albano Biondi, 'Lunga durata e microarticolazione . . .: Il sacro tribunale a Modena (1292–1785)', *Annali dell'istituto storico italo-germanico in Trento*, 8 (1982), 73–90, esp. pp. 81f.

[13] The origin and historical development of these legal handbooks is carefully analysed by Antoine Dondaine, 'Le Manuel de l'Inquisiteur (1230–1330)', *Archivum Fratrum Praedicatorum*, 17 (1947), 85–194. An incomplete list of the printed editions can be found in Emil van der Vekene, *Bibliotheca bibliographica historiae Sanctae Inquisitionis, ad indicem*. Brief bio-bibliographical sketches of the principal authors are contained in J. Friedrich von Schulte, *Die Geschichte der Quellen und Literatur des canonischen Rechts* (3 vols.; Stuttgart, 1875; repr. Graz, 1956), *ad indicem*.

[14] e.g. N. Eymerich's *Directorium Inquisitorum*, ed. F. Peña (Rome, 1570, etc.; in the notes that follow I cite from the Rome, 1587 edn.); the anonymous *Repertorium*

Surprisingly large quantities of manuscript records are also available. Thousands of trials have survived intact in Italian public or ecclesiastical archives and libraries—in Udine, Venice, Modena, Rovigo, Naples, and elsewhere; extensive series of correspondence between the supreme Congregation of the Holy Office in Rome and some of its provincial tribunals are preserved in Bologna and Modena; a large body of sentences spanning a century and a half (1556–1700) found their way in the mid-nineteenth century to Trinity College, Dublin (a part of the Napoleonic loot that was never returned to Rome after the collapse of his empire).[15] And in the Vatican Library one encounters manuscript inquisitorial manuals, handbooks, and memoranda, materials which had been copied for the use of cardinals who sat on the Holy Office and which were transferred to this repository along with their other papers at their deaths.[16]

Granted that such documents are available, what about their trustworthiness as historical sources? Could not inquisitors have attempted to suppress or distort information so that their activity would remain hidden from contemporaries and posterity alike? On the contrary, it was strict Holy Office practice to preserve detailed records of all its proceedings from the first summons to the final sentencing. The insistence on the meticulous recording of every word uttered during a trial was intended to discourage the inclination of inquisitors to ask leading questions which would suggest to the accused how they should reply. A permanent member of every inquisitorial court was the notary, who took down in writing every question and every answer, including the exclamations of pain emitted by the victims of torture.[17] If even this was recorded, what could have

Inquisitorum (Venice, 1575, etc.); Joannes a Rojas, . . . *Tractatus de Haereticis* (Venice, 1583); Iacobo de Simancas, *Praxis Haereseos, sive Enchiridion Iudicum violatae religionis* (Venice, 1568) and *De Catholicis Institutionibus Liber* (Rome, 1575). This list could be expanded.

[15] See J. Tedeschi, 'La dispersione degli archivi della Inquisizione Romana', *Rivista di storia e letteratura religiosa*, 9 (1973), 298–312; and in an expanded English version in Gustav Henningsen and John Tedeschi, in association with Charles Amiel (eds.), *The Inquisition in Early Modern Europe: Studies on Sources and Methods* (Dekalb, 1986), pp. 3–32.

[16] See Patricia H. Jobe, 'Inquisitorial Manuscripts in the Biblioteca Apostolica Vaticana: A Preliminary Handlist', in G. Henningsen and J. Tedeschi, *The Inquisition in Early Modern Europe*, pp. 33–53.

[17] See BRB, MS II. 290, vol. ii, fo. 172, letter of the senior member of the Roman Congregation, Giulio Antonio Santorio, Cardinal of Santa Severina, to the Florentine inquisitor, dated Rome, 18 Nov. 1600: 'Per ordine della S.ta di N.ro S.re, Vra R.tia per l'avvenire nello essamine de' testimonii, et costituti de' rei nel Santo Officio faccia scrivere per extensum tutti gli interrogatorii, et repliche per ovviare à pregiudicii che si

been concealed? By bringing renegade Christians to punishment—but above all to reconciliation with the Church—inquisitors were redeeming offences committed against God and saving souls for eternal life. A frequent preamble to final sentencing is the Biblical story of the prodigal son, a popular paradigm for the inquisitors, who compared themselves to the loving and forgiving father. And every manual emphasized that since the inquisitor's authority was delegated directly by the Pope he was considered incapable of error in the commission of the duties of his office.[18]

Inquisitors thus did not feel that they had anything to hide. What little modern scholarly discussion exists concerning the trustworthiness of inquisitorial sources has focused on the possible distortions in the evidence ensuing from the cultural and linguistic gaps that often separated judges and defendants.[19] The scrupulous recording of every word and gesture transpiring in the trial chamber has never been questioned.

This is not to say that inquisitors worked in public; far from it. Each official took a solemn vow of secrecy, conducted interrogations in strict privacy, and jealously guarded the records of trial proceedings.[20] There were several reasons for this. Witnesses for the prosecution remained anonymous, since they had to be protected from possible retaliation by the family and friends of the accused. Moreover, once a defendant named his accomplices, the Holy Office might have to

fanno in non scriversi gl'interrogatorii, et per vedere se siano suggestivi o no ...' Cf. Eliseo Masini, *Sacro Arsenale ovvero prattica dell' officio della Santa Inquisitione* (1st edn. Genoa, 1621), 123: 'Et procuraranno i giudici, che il notaro scriva non solamente tutte le risposte del reo, ma anco tutti i ragionamenti che farà, e tutte le parole ch'egli proferirà ne' tormenti, anzi tutti i sospiri, tutte le grida, tutti i lamenti e le lagrime che manderà.' Unless I indicate otherwise, all refs. to Masini are to this edn. of the *Arsenale*. I cite later expanded edns. only for material not contained in the 1st. Masini served as inquisitor of Genoa, 1609–27.

[18] The infallibility of the office of inquisitor is plainly stated, among others, by the Dominican Silvestro Mazzolini da Prierio, *Modus Solennis et Authenticus ad inquirendum ... Lutheranos* (Rome, 1553), Tertia Regula: 'Necesse est summe, ut inquisitor ipse quoque certus sit, se non posse errare in hoc actu.' See also Masini, *Sacro Arsenale*, p. 9, where God, by virtue of his punishment of Adam and Eve, is hailed as the first in the long line of inquisitors.

[19] This is the burden of Carlo Ginzburg's *I benandanti: Stregoneria e culti agrari tra Cinquecento e Seicento* (2nd edn. Turin, 1974), now in English: *The Night Battles: Witchcraft and Agrarian Cults Between the Sixteenth and Seventeenth Centuries* (Baltimore and London, 1983), *passim*.

[20] For the vow of absolute secrecy which even the cardinals of the Roman Congregation had to take, see their decree dated 25 Jan. 1560: Pastor, 'Allgemeine Dekrete', p. 502.

move swiftly to bring them into custody. Its effectiveness would have been seriously impaired if word of their incrimination leaked out to them before they could be apprehended. And finally, a reason which may seem unexpected, the reputation of the accused had to be protected.

It was an often reiterated principle that inquisitors should exercise caution before making an arrest. 'Great prudence must be exercised in the jailing of suspects,' wrote Eliseo Masini in his authoritative manual, the *Sacro Arsenale*, 'because the mere fact of incarceration for the crime of heresy brings notable infamy to the person. Thus it will be necessary to study carefully the nature of the evidence, the quality of the witnesses, and the condition of the accused.'[21] And in a letter written in 1573 by an official of the Roman Congregation to the Bolognese inquisitor: 'Let not your reverence be hasty in proceeding to make an arrest because the mere capture, or even the rumour of it causes serious harm.'[22] Again, in a letter dated 4 March of the same year from Antonio Balduzzi, Commissioner General of the Roman Inquisition, to the Bolognese official: 'Concerning that Carmelite friar . . . they [meaning the Cardinals of the Holy Office] have ordered that, unless your reverence possesses more evidence against him than what has been sent to us, he is not to be disturbed in any way, and he is to be left in peace and to his prayers.'[23] The case of a suspected witch arrested by the Bolognese inquisitor in violation of accepted procedure elicited the following reprimand from the Cardinal of Santa Severina, writing on 18 May 1591: 'And even if Antonia [a principal accuser of the defendant] was indisposed and anguished by the death of her son and for this reason you did not question her, I have been asked to remind you that in the future you must cross-examine witnesses under oath before making an arrest.'[24] Unsworn testimony was not acceptable.

There was little fear of prosecution for the *sponte comparente*, the offender who freely presented himself unsummoned to the Inquisition before the tribunal had received evidence against him. All the manuals unfailingly prescribe that he was to be treated benignly. Salutary penances, a private abjuration, and perhaps a fine customarily would be the extent of the punishment.[25]

---

[21] Masini, *Sacro Arsenale*, p. 277.
[22] BA, MS B. 1860, fo. clx, letter from Fra Paolo da Ferrara, dated 7 Nov. 1573.
[23] Ibid., fo. cxix.   [24] BA, MS B. 1861, fo. 133.
[25] Masini, *Sacro Arsenale*, p. 79: '. . . non dovrà esser dal giudice fuorche benigna-mente ricevuto et piacevolmente trattato, e paternamente spedito, senza alcun rigor di

The rules prescribed by Masini for the investigation of witchcraft show a high regard for due process.

In prosecuting suspected witches the inquisitor must not reach the point of incarceration, inquisition or torture until the *corpus delicti* is judicially established. The presence of sickness in a man or the presence of a corpse in themselves do not constitute adequate evidence, since infirmity and death do not need to be connected to acts of witchcraft but can result from a large number of natural causes. The first step, therefore, is to question the physician who attended the patient.

In examining the house of the suspected witch the notary was to list everything—items which would serve the prosecution as well as such things as religious icons, devotional books, etc., which would be to the advantage of the defendant. If such dubious objects as powders and ointments were discovered, they were to be examined by experts 'to determine if they could have been used for ends other than sorcery'. Inquisitors were not to permit themselves to be troubled over the discovery of large quantities of pins and needles, natural items for women to possess.[26]

We have abundant evidence that these theoretical safeguards were actually enforced in practice by the Roman Congregation and imposed upon the provincial tribunals where procedural abuses were most likely to occur. In a series of letters to the nuncio, archbishop, and inquisitor of Florence written in March 1626 the Holy Office in

carceri, e senza spese, tormenti, ò pene di qual si voglia sorte. E spontaneo comparente s'intende esser solamente quello, che non prevenuto d'indicii, nè citato, ò ammonito in particolare, viene ad accusar se stesso'; Carena, *Tractatus*, p. 235: 'Haeretici sponte comparentes, mitissime sunt tractandi.' The benevolent treatment afforded to this class of individual is confirmed by such a hostile critic as Hieromino Piazza, an apostate from the Roman Church, who had once served as vicar of the inquisitor in Osimo (Ancona): '. . . for the Inquisition (as it is true) never punishes nor treats them with severity, that go and voluntarily accuse themselves of what sins soever they have committed . . . on the contrary, they are kindly receiv'd, and privately and secretly dispatch'd only with some salutary penance . . .' Hieron. Bartholomew Piazza, *A Short and True Account of the Inquisition and its Proceedings . . . in Italy . . .* (London, 1722), 54.

[26] There is virtually no discussion of witchcraft in the 1st edn. of the *Sacro Arsenale*. The safeguards discussed here made their first appearance in print beginning with the Genoa, 1625 edn., pp. 175–82. The text borrows heavily from a Roman *Instructio* which circulated in MS among the provincial tribunals of the Holy Office. See J. Tedeschi, 'The Roman Inquisition and Witchcraft: An Early Seventeenth-century "Instruction" on Correct Trial Procedure', *Revue de l'histoire des religions*, 200 (1983), 163–88, repr. in a rev. and corrected Italian version as 'Appunti sulla "Instructio pro formandis processibus in causis strigum, sortilegiorum & maleficiorum"', *Annuario dell'istituto storico italiano per l'età moderna e contemporanea*, 37–8 (1985–6), 219–41.

Rome attempted to quell a witch panic in that city which had led secular authorities to intervene, resulting in gross miscarriages of justice. Summing up the evidence that it had received, the Roman Congregation wrote, 'these matters are extremely fallacious, and, as daily experience demonstrates, much more real in the imagination of men than in the reality of events; too often every illness whose cause is not immediately discernible, or whose remedy is not readily available is attributed to malefice.' The nuncio was then asked to inform 'cotesti principi' that the voice suggesting the presence of many witches in Florence and the *contado* had no basis in fact.[27]

In addition to such growing scepticism in Roman legal circles in regard to witchcraft, two crucial procedural points spared Italy the epidemics of bloody witch persecutions that ravaged northern Europe from the late sixteenth to the end of the seventeenth century. The first was the insistence by the Inquisition that the testimony of a suspected witch was of extremely limited validity as a basis for prosecution against others. Judges were instructed, for example, to discount the testimony of a witch against persons whom she named as participants at sabbaths, since witches were frequently transported to these nocturnal reunions not physically but only in their fancy and in illusions inspired by the devil.[28]

The second point consists in the fact that the notorious devil's mark, which if discovered on the body of the defendant in secular trials was treated as a piece of evidence almost as conclusive as a confession, played no part in inquisitorial procedure.[29] Unlike lay

---

[27] BAV, Barb. lat., 6334, fo. 67ᵛ: '. . . dalli processi fatti dal canonico non consta cosa concludente de' maleficii, se bene egli vi habbi usato isquisita diligenza, che simili materie sono fallacissime, et come l'esperienza cotidiana mostra assai maggiori nell' apprensione degli huomini che nella realtà de' successi, riducendosi troppo facilmente a maleficio ogni malattia della quale non sia conosciuta subito la causa, o trovato efficace il rimedio . . . la voce levata, che in Fiorenza et nel contado sieno molte streghe non ha fondamento reale . . .'.

[28] See, among other authorities, Bernardo da Como, 'Tractatus de strigibus', in his *Lucerna Inquisitorum Haereticae Pravitatis* (Venice, 1596), 151; I. de Simancas, *De Catholicis Institutionibus*, tit. xxxvii, nos. 14, 15. For an instance of this doctrine in practice, see the letter from Cardinal Camillo Borghese of the Holy Office in Rome to the inquisitor of Florence (16 Oct. 1604): BRB, MS II. 290, vol. ii, fo. 4: 'Inoltre le dico, che nelle cose che la detta donna depone di haver visto nè giuochi diabolici non se le crede contra di altre persone . . .' For late 17th-c. evidence that co-participants at sabbaths were still being named in secular trials in Poschiavo (Valtellina), see Olimpia Aureggi, 'La stregoneria nelle Alpi Centrali', *Bollettino della società storica valtellinese*, 15 (1961), 114–58, at pp. 132f.

[29] In the Valtellina, municipal statutes considered the discovery of the presumed devil's mark sufficient evidence to convict for witchcraft. A special officer of the court expert in such matters, the *ravetta*, usually the executioner's assistant, was assigned to

courts, which invariably administered the death penalty for witchcraft when the offender confessed participation in the sabbath, apostasy to the devil, or perpetration of a *maleficium*,[30] the Inquisition treated witchcraft as any other heresy, and the first offender who expressed a desire to repent was reconciled to the Church.[31]

Various legal safeguards for the rights of the accused were part of the trial procedure. If, after the completion of the interrogation and the presentation of evidence by the prosecution, he had neither cleared himself nor confessed to the charges, he was permitted to prepare his defence, receiving a notarized copy of the entire trial record conducted up to that point (with the names of the prosecution witnesses deleted). He was then allowed several days to study the evidence against him, and he was permitted to call friendly witnesses to testify on his behalf.[32] In the case of the indigent, the inquisitor was

make the necessary identification: Olimpia Aureggi, 'La stregoneria nelle Alpi Centrali', p. 135. See also the account in the celebrated and widely diffused legal manual, Joost Damhouder, *Praxis rerum criminalium* (Antwerp, 1570), 146: 'Mulieres autem maleficae, quae iam voluntate depravata, et consensu in consortium daemonum per pacta transierunt, notas quasdam et signa symbolica ab ipsis recipiunt, quibus exciti daemones mox prosiliunt.' Damhouder was a doctor of both laws and an imperial councillor who practised in Bruges.

[30] For 16th-c. restatements of the attitude towards witchcraft in the civil law, see Paolo Grillando, 'Tractatus de sortilegiis' (1st edn. 1536) in the miscellaneous volume, *Tractatus universi iuris* (Venice, 1584), vol. xi, pt. 2, fo. 394ʳ: 'De iure autem civili haec sortilegia gravius puniuntur, quia iura ipsa multum abhorrent artem maleficam ... & ideo omnes isti malefici puniuntur ultimo supplicio ...'; J. Damhouder, *Praxis rerum criminalium*, pp. 130f.: 'Gravissimum et omnium criminum maximum est, crimen laesae maiestatis divinae, cum longe gravius sit aeternam, quam temporalem offendere maiestatem ... blasphemia in Deum, de iure civili, poena mortis punitur.'

[31] See e.g. Prospero Farinacci, *Tractatus de Haeresi. Editio novissima* (Lyon, 1650), q. 181, n. 48 (p. 61): 'Bene verum est, quod si lamiae poenitentes veniam petunt, et ad Ecclesiam ex corde redire volunt, sunt admittendae ad poenitentiam, ac etiam reconciliandae, nec ullo pacto Curiae seculari tradendae; etiam quod infantes occiderint, seu alia atrociora et nefanda crimina perpetraverint'; I. Simancas, *De Catholicis Institutionibus*, tit. xxxvii, no. 16 (p. 282): 'Posthaec, de poenis lamiarum videndum est, quas si constiterit haereticas fuisse, punire debent inquisitores, perinde atque alios quoscunque haereticos ... si veram poenitentiam agere voluerint, recipiendae sunt benigne iuxta canonicas sanctiones ...' Francesco Albizzi, a cardinal who served a long term in the Congregation of the Holy Office, in his *De Inconstantia in Iure* (Amsterdam, 1683), p. 349, provides a long list of authorities who argued that penitent witches in their first fall were not to be handed over to the secular arm, even where death or injury had ensued from an alleged *maleficium*. Gregory XV attempted to legislate against this position with a Bull, *Omnipotentis Dei* (20 Mar. 1623) which imposed the death sentence even for a first offence when the act of witchcraft had resulted in a fatal injury: Cocquelines, *Bullarum*, vol. v, pt. 5, pp. 97–8.

[32] On the defence phase of the trial (the *processo ripetitivo*), as opposed to the prosecution phase (the *processo informativo*), see Masini, *Sacro Arsenale*, pp. 85–108. The right of

obliged to provide travel expenses for defence witnesses who might have to be summoned from distant parts.[33] If the accused failed to take advantage of his right to legal defence, the prosecution testimony was considered as *ipso facto* accepted by him, and he threw himself on the mercy of the court.[34]

Despite such provisions, it would have been difficult for anyone unpractised in the law to mount an effective defence, a fact recognized by the Inquisition.[35] When the defendant declared that he lacked experience in such matters and would like the help of a lawyer, this information had to be duly entered in the trial records, and his wishes heeded.[36] It appears to have been the preferred usage of the Holy Office, at least in the seventeenth century, to allow the prisoner to suggest the names of three lawyers, of whom one was assigned to serve him by the court.[37] The defendant's right to counsel was an ancient feature of inquisitorial procedure (see Endnote B). But by modern standards of jurisprudence their relationship was a curious one: if the lawyer became convinced that his client was indeed a heretic who could not be persuaded to abandon his error, he was obliged to discontinue the defence or fall under suspicion himself. In other words, the fall into error could be defended, but pertinacity in adhering to it could not. In a real sense, much more so than today, defence attorneys

---

the accused to see and to rebut the testimony of the prosecution witnesses was emphasized in a decree of the Roman Congregation dated 20 Oct. 1562. Pastor, 'Allgemeine Dekrete', p. 503.

[33] Masini, *Sacro Arsenale*, p. 268: 'Se un reo nel Santo Officio allegarà per sua difesa qualche cosa da provarsi, anco in parti assai lontane, e non porrà egli per la sua povertà farla provare, è obligato il giudice in ogni miglior modo a ricercarla, & investigarla, acciò senza difese non si rimanga alcuno in cosi santo tribunale, & in cosa di tanta importanza.'

[34] Ibid (1665 edn.), p. 129.

[35] Masini, *Sacro Arsenale*, p. 85: 'E perchè tal repetitione è molto difficile, dee con somma isquisitezza & diligenza maneggiarsi, perciochè da essa pende l'honore, la vita, & i beni de' rei. La onde convien si faccia dall'inquisitore istesso & con gran cautela, e sollecitudine, per impedire ogni fraude, e schifare ogni cavillatione ...'

[36] Ibid., p. 86: 'Et dicendo il reo, di non intendersi di tal cosa, e non saper quello che si habbia a fare, & che volentieri parlarà col Signor Procuratore, ò avvocato, & poi si risolverà intorno alla detta repetitione, dovrà cotal sua risposta registrarsi ...' The selection of the defence attorney seems to have been a joint responsibility of defendant and tribunal. See the letter from the Roman Congregation to the inquisitor of Modena, dated 7 Mar. 1626: '... il solito del tribunale è che gli rei nominino tre avvocati almeno, et uno di essi sia poi eletto dall' Inquisitore' (BAV, Barb. lat. 6334, fo. 56ᵛ).

[37] BAV, Barb. lat. 6334, fo. 56ᵛ, letter from the Roman Congregation of the Holy Office to the inquisitor of Modena, 7 Mar. 1626: '... il solito del tribunale è che gli rei nominino tre avvocati almeno, et uno di essi sia poi eletto dall'inquisitore.'

were officers of the court.[38] Nevertheless, even with this limitation, the discovery of inconsistencies in the arguments of the prosecution and the strategic use of friendly witnesses were obviously enhanced by the attorney's presence. He could frequently present extenuating circumstances and persuade the courts to milder sentencing.

Nor was legal aid reserved for those who could afford it, as we learn from a letter dated 16 August 1603 from a cardinal of the Roman Congregation to the inquisitor of Florence: 'If due to their poverty they [the defendants in a given case] do not have funds for a lawyer . . . your reverence must provide one so that they do not remain undefended.'[39] It is interesting to note, for purposes of comparison, that the defence attorney was excluded from the great Imperial law code, the *Carolina* (named after Charles V), published in 1532;[40] that in France the legal reforms introduced in 1539 by the Ordinance of Villers-Cotterets specified that 'in criminal matters the parties shall in no wise be heard through counsel or the agency of anyone else';[41] and that in England, until the Prisoners Counsel Bill of 1836, felons, except in treason trials, were denied the services of a defence lawyer.[42] Illogically, counsel had been permitted in less serious crimes, misdemeanours, from a much earlier date.

The right to counsel and other safeguards in the inquisitorial system of law were impaired, but by no means rendered ineffectual, by the anonymity of informers or prosecution witnesses. The defendant could know the evidence against him, but not the names of his accusers (see Endnote C). The Inquisition acknowledged that this provision, established centuries before to preserve witnesses from possible reprisals, placed the defendant at a disadvantage. 'Because', wrote Masini, 'the capacity for defending himself which we grant to the accused is somewhat deficient, since we do not inform him who

[38] Masini, *Sacro Arsenale* (1653 edn.), p. 416: 'Quell'avvocato, il quale, conoscendo apertamente il reo esser veramente heretico, ad ogni modo lo difende, è infame, e degno di grave punitione . . .' And if, in the course of his duties, the attorney learned the names of the defendant's accomplices he was to reveal them to the court: Pastor, 'Dekrete', p. 504: '. . . et si in prosecutione causae alicuius complicis vel alterius culpabilis notitiam habere continget, quam citius revelare teneatur sub poena arbitrio cardinalium' (decree of the Congregation of the Holy Office, Rome (18 June 1564)).

[39] BRB, MS ii. 290, vol. i, fo. 118. Cf. Masini, *Sacro Arsenale*, p. 268.

[40] See John Langbein, *Prosecuting Crime in the Renaissance: England, Germany, France* (Cambridge, Mass., 1974), 189.

[41] Ibid., p. 313, Article 163 of the Ordinance.

[42] David Melinkoff, 'Right to Counsel: The Message from America', in Fredi Chiappelli (ed.), *First Images of America* (2 vols.; Berkeley, 1976), i. 405–13, at p. 406. Until 1695 the same rule had applied to indictments for high treason.

the accusers are, it is necessary that the evidence for conviction be absolutely clear and beyond doubt.'[43] At the commencement of his defence the accused was required to name any persons whom he suspected bore him malice. If these coincided with the prosecution witnesses, the inquisitor was obliged to investigate their motives and credibility. If the results were positive, their testimony was examined for possible perjury. The sentences delivered against false witnesses indicate that this duty was taken seriously.[44]

Judicial torture began to be adopted by secular courts as an extreme measure for obtaining confessions early in the thirteenth century, and it was introduced into the inquisitorial process in the Bull 'Ad Extirpandam' issued by Innocent IV on 15 May 1252. The Bull expressed the view that if it was proper to employ torture in cases involving the simple theft of earthly goods, how much more justification was there in applying it against heretics, whose offence, the theft of souls, was so much greater.[45] Masini, in his *Sacro Arsenale*, did not consider torture an unfitting instrument in the hands of the Church, because its chief beneficiaries were the victims of torture themselves: 'heretics,' he wrote, 'by confessing their crimes become converted to God, and through reconciliation save their souls.'[46]

Interrogation with torture might be employed in two general situations: first, where the burden of evidence against the defendant clearly indicated a guilt which he or she denied but had been incapable of disproving, and second, where it was suspected on reasonable grounds

---

[43] *Sacro Arsenale*, p. 283.

[44] Ibid., p. 41. Cf. TCD, MS 1224, fo. 74. Sentence emitted 6 June 1566 against eight Neapolitans who had falsely accused of heresy a Dr Marco di Rosa of Acerno. Each of the perjurers was condemned to the galleys. In the case of Hettore Bussone, who had recruited the others, the sentence stated '... ti condemniamo ad essere frustato publicamente per Roma nelli lochi soliti ... et poi che sii mandato in galera per dieci anni a servire per un remigante.' In addition, all the false witnesses were condemned to pay the expenses and damages suffered by the innocent victim.

[45] Piero Fiorelli, *La tortura giudiziaria nel diritto comune* (2 vols.; Milan, 1953), i. 79 and John Langbein, *Torture and the Law of Proof: Europe and England in the Ancien Régime* (Chicago and London, 1977), 5 ff. On the latter see the critical comments by Mirjan Damaska, 'The Death of Legal Torture', *Yale Law Journal*, 87 (1978), 860–84. Raoul Charles van Caenegem, 'La Preuve dans le droit du Moyen Âge occidental', *Recueils de la société Jean Bodin*, 17 (1965), 691–753. On the torture applied in witchcraft cases by secular magistrates, see Olimpia Aureggi, 'Stregoneria retica e tortura giudiziaria', *Bollettino della società storica valtellinese*, 17 (1963–4), 46–90. For a survey of the position of the Catholic Church, see Antonio Reyes, 'La confesión y la tortura en la historia de la iglesia', *Revista española del derecho canonico*, 24 (1968), 595–624.

[46] *Sacro Arsenale*, p. 120.

that the confession had not been full and sincere and all the accomplices had not been named.[47] Torture was rigidly controlled and various safeguards were enforced in Roman practice. In the first place, the judge could not proceed to the *rigoroso esamine*, interrogation under torture, unless the evidence against the accused was compelling and until the defence had presented its case. 'Never commence with the torture but with the evidence', was Masini's formula. 'It would be iniquitous and against all human and divine law to expose anyone to torment without weighty evidence.'[48] Nor did the inquisitor alone determine whether torture was justified in a given case. He was clearly obliged to seek the opinion of the *consultori*, the half-dozen lawyers and theologians who formed a permanent advisory committee for every inquisitorial court;[49] and when the question was especially difficult, it was laid before the supreme tribunal in Rome, with the testimony of the defendants and witnesses reported in their own words, in the

[47] Iacobi Simancas, *Enchiridion Iudicum Violatae Religionis* (Antwerp, 1573), 245: 'Cum reus negat obiecta crimina, & plene probata non sunt, plerunque ad quaestionem pervenire oportet. Est autem quaestio invita conscii hominis confessio, ut Aristoteles, tradit'; Masini, *Sacro Arsenale*, p. 120: 'Havendo il reo negato i delitti oppostili, & non essendosi essi pienamente provati, è necessario per haverne la verità venir contro di lui al rigoroso essame, essendo stato à punto ritrovata la tortura per supplire al difetto de'testimonii quando non possono intera prova apportare contro del reo.' Torture was frequently ordered 'pro ulteriore veritate et super complicibus', even when the defendant had confessed. See e.g. the decree of Paul IV, confirmed by Pius V, July 1569 in BAV, Barb. lat. 1370, p. 248 and published in Locati, *Opus quod iudiciale inquisitorum dicitur*, p. 477: 'In haerendo decretis alias per se record. Paulum papam quartum Sanctissimus D. N. Pius Papa Quintus decrevit omnes et quoscunque reos convictos et confessos de haeresi pro ulteriori veritate habenda, et super complicibus, fore torquendos arbitrio dominorum iudicum.'

[48] Masini, *Sacro Arsenale* (1653 edn.), p. 147: 'Bene sconverrebbe da dovero, anzi sarebbe cosa iniquissima, e contro alle leggi humane e divine, l'esporre à i tormenti chi che sia, non precedendo alcun legitimo e provato indicio; e oltre a ciò la confessione, ch'indi seguisse, sarebbe invalida, e di niun momento, ancorche il reo persistesse costantissimamente in essa, *non dovendosi mai cominciare dalla tortura, ma dagl'indicii*' (my italics).

[49] Masini, *Sacro Arsenale*, p. 120: '... fa di bisogno [where the application of torture is in question] per caminar sicuramente, che l'Inquisitore proponga prima nella Congregatione de'Consultori del Santo Officio il processo offensivo e difensivo, & col dotto e maturo conseglio di essi (ancorche il lor voto non sia decisivo ma solamente consultivo) si governi, & operi sempre. O pure essendo la causa grave e difficoltosa, ne dia parte al Sacro e Supremo Tribunale della Santa e Universale Inquisitione Romana, & di là n'attenda la risolutione.' BA, MS B. 1859 is composed entirely of 'Consilia et vota in Materia S. Officii', Bolognese documents of the 15th and 16th c. See Locati, *Opus quod iudiciale inquisitorum dicitur*, p. 482 for the text of the usual 'Forma sententiae interlocutoriae ad supponendum aliquem quaestionibus, seu tormentis.'

vernacular, not in Latin translations prepared by the court.[50] In the course of the sixteenth century it became increasingly the practice for Rome, minutely informed on the progress of all trials conducted in the provincial courts, to issue the instructions for torture, instructions which even the cardinal inquisitors felt needed the sanction of their own advisers and legal experts. Correspondence reveals that generally it was the Pope himself, who personally presided over the meetings of the Congregation of the Holy Office in Rome, where the disposition of cases was discussed, who gave the order for torture.[51]

Deviations from accepted procedure were not tolerated, as we observe in the letter written on 18 November 1589 from the Cardinal of Santa Severina to the inquisitor of Florence because his vicar and the episcopal court of Pistoia had mistreated three women suspected of sorcery and sacrilegious acts. The confessions which had been obtained from them under torture were to be thrown out of court on the following grounds: first, the evidence against them had not been of sufficient weight to justify torture, since it was based primarily on the testimony of a witness who enjoyed a poor reputation in the town; and second, the torments had been administered before the women had been given an opportunity to respond to the charges. The Florentine inquisitor was then ordered to proceed immediately to Pistoia and assume personal direction of the trial.[52]

Another important provision serving to inhibit the use of torture

---

[50] BAV, Barb. lat. 6334, fo. 56ᵛ, letter from the Roman Congregation to the inquisitor of Saluzzo, 7 Mar. 1626: 'In tanto avverto a V.R. che non deve venire, come ha fatto, alla tortura de' rei in quelle cause nelle quali vuole consultare la S. Congregazione prima di haverne l'ordine di qui, et insieme che li sommarii che manda, sieno non latini, ma volgari, et con le parole stesse nelle cose sostantiali de' testimonii et del reo . . .'

[51] See e.g., from the many cases which could be cited, the letter of the Cardinal of Pisa, a member of the Roman Holy Office, to the inquisitor of Bologna, 26 July 1572: BA, MS B. 1860, fo. 79: 'Si è proposto in Congregatione et fatto vedere da consultori il caso di M.ro Pavolo Vasellaro, et di comun parere si è concluso che se gli habbia a dare di buona corda per chiarirsi se è veramente relapso, et se le cose che se li oppongono sono state dette da lui con mala intentione . . .' On papal participation in the decision-making process, see e.g. the case of a Neapolitan bigamist, Antonio Frezza, whose trial was transferred to Rome. On 20 Sept. 1607, 'S.mus decrevit ut torqueatur supra intentione et si nihil superveniat, abiuret de vehementi, et damnetur ad triremes per vᵐ (quinquennium)' (BAV, Borg. lat. 558, fo. 162ʳ). The pope in question would have been Paul V. The composition and routines of the Congregation of the Holy Office in Rome is described in an early 17th-c. MS published by Luigi Firpo, 'Una relazione inedita su l'inquisizione romana', *Rinascimento*, 9 (1958), 97–102.

[52] BRB, MS II. 290, vol. ii, fo. 6.

was the requirement that both inquisitor and bishop (or their representatives) agree to and be present during its application.[53] A further restriction was the physical condition and age of the defendant. There are numerous instances where Rome is informed, after it has instructed the provincial inquisitor to proceed to interrogation under torture, that the examining physician has declared the defendant incapable of supporting it.[54] During the sixteenth century more than one jurist resurrected the ancient teaching of the Roman legist Ulpian that 'torture is a fragile and dangerous thing and the truth frequently is not obtained by it. For, many defendants because of their patience and strength are able to spurn the torments, while others would rather lie than bear them, unfairly incriminating themselves and also others.'[55] Nevertheless, well into the seventeenth century the Inquisition, as well as every other European court system, continued to rely on this device to reach

---

[53] This regulation dates to the reign of Clement V (1305–14). See Fiorelli, *Tortura*, ii. 54; Bernardo da Como, *Lucerna Inquisitorum Haereticae Pravitatis* (Venice, 1596), p. 124; Masini, *Sacro Arsenale* (1653 edn.), p. 405. Failure to observe this provision by the inquisitor of Siena evoked a reprimand from Cardinal Giovanni Ricci of the Roman Congregation (letter of 12 Feb. 1568): 'Si lamentano anchora quelli del vescovo che voi non lasciate essere presente al dare della corda il vicario di esso monsignore, il che noi non credemo che voi usiate di fare, et però datici aviso come passa questo facto': Paolo Piccolomini, 'Documenti fiorentini sull'eresia in Siena durante il secolo XVI (1559–1570)', *Bullettino senese di storia patria*, 17 (1910), 175.

[54] See e.g. the letter of the Cardinal of Santa Severina to the inquisitor of Bologna, 1 May 1593, BA, MS B. 1861, fo. 175: 'Ho data parte à questi Ill.mi et Rev.mi SS.ri Cardinali Generali Inquisitori miei colleghi di quanto V.R.tia scriveva circa Fabio Locatelli, al quale secondo l'attestatione dei medici mandatemi con la sua de'XVII ricevuta à 30 di Marzo non si poteva dar corda ne stanghetta, et le loro Ill.me et R.me Signorie hanno ordinato che s'el detto Fabio è capace di qualche altra sorte di tormento, V.R.tia glielo facci dare ad arbitrio di lei, havendo rigguardo a tutte le debite circonstanze. Et quando non sia habile a sostenere alcuna sorte di tormento, proceda all'espeditione della sua causa con consiglio di theologi et canonisti della sua congregatione per giustitia'; also the sentence against Francesco Vidua of Verona, 25 Apr. 1580: '... non si potendo per via dei tormenti levare le presuntioni et suspitioni le quali sono contra di te, et questo per la indispositione del tuo corpo, habbiamo determinato di venire alla ... sententia' (TCD, MS 1225, fo. 184).

[55] Locati, *Opus quod iudiciale inquisitorum dicitur*, p. 377: 'Nota tamen quod tormentis et quaestionibus non semper est fides adhibenda. Nam plerique patientia, sive duritia tormentorum, ita tormenta contemnunt, ut veritas ab eis exprimi nullo modo possit. Alii autem tanta sunt impatientia, ut in quovis mentiri quam pati tormenta velint, et ita fit, ut etiam vario modo fateantur, et non tantum se, verumetiam alios criminentur ...' Cf. Iacobo Simancas, 'De Catholicis Institutionibus', in *Tractatus illustrium in utraque tum pontificii, tum Caesarei juris facultate iurisconsultorum, de iudiciis criminalibus S. Inquisitionis*, xi[2] (Venice, 1584), fo. 203ᵛ; Ioannis à Royas, 'De haereticis', ibid., fo. 229ᵛ; Conradi Bruni, 'De haereticis', ibid., fo. 313ᵛ.

its decisions in situations where it was felt that essential evidence was being held back.[56]

For inquisitors, the most crucial information that they required consisted in determining the intention behind the offender's criminal act. Heresy, in the eyes of the Church, was a sin of the intellect, and a heretic was a person who consciously espoused a doctrinal error. Following St Augustine, the Spanish jurist Simancas declared: 'A heretic is not one who lives badly, but who believes badly' (*non est hereticus, qui male vivit, sed qui male credit*).[57] Thus, for example, in the case of a convicted bigamist it would have to be determined whether the bigamy presupposed conscious disbelief in the sacrament of marriage. A person who had been apprehended in the act of hurling excrement against a statuette of the Virgin would be interrogated to determine whether he had acted in a fit of anger or whether he indeed did not believe in the Virginity of the Mother of God. The manner in which these questions were answered had serious implications. If the court deemed that heretical intent could not be proven, the offender was sentenced as one 'suspect' of heresy. If the intent was proven, then the condemnation was for formal heresy. All first offenders who wished to be reconciled to the Church were usually spared regardless of the category of their guilt. However, in the event of a second fall, if the offender had abjured as a formal heretic at the conclusion of his first trial, he would be liable to the extreme penalties reserved for the relapsed.[58]

When torture was employed in inquisitorial tribunals, it customarily consisted in the elevation of the victim by means of a cord and

---

[56] For instances where the defendant's ability to adhere to his original testimony under torture influenced the court's decision, see the following letters of the Roman Congregation: to the inquisitor of Alessandria, dated 29 Aug. 1626: '. . . havendo Fra Pompeo Bianco Carmelita purgati con la tortura quasi del tutto gli inditii che contra di lui resultano . . .' (BAV, Borg. lat. 6334, fo. 247ᵛ); to inquisitor of Perugia, dated 9 Oct. 1626: 'Questi miei SS.ri Ill.mi hanno approvato il parere di V.R. di spedire il sud.o Fra Gio. Salice giachè ha sostenuto la corda con relegarlo in un convento della sua Religione . . .' (ibid., fo. 280ᵛ).

[57] Iacobo de Simancas, *De Catholicis Institutionibus Liber* (Rome, 1575), 228. For a discussion of the appropriation by Nicolas Eymerich in his *Directorium Inquisitorum* of the Thomistic doctrine that heresy consists of the intellectual choice of a mistaken doctrine and attachment with one's heart to that doctrine, see Louis Sala-Molins, 'Utilisation d'Aristote en droit inquisitorial', in *XVI Colloque International de Tours: Platon et Aristote à la Renaissance* (Paris, 1976), 191–9.

[58] Masini, *Sacro Arsenale* (1665 edn.), pp. 229 and esp. 160ff. 'Modo di esaminare il Reo ne' tormenti pro ulteriori veritate, et super intentione.'

pulley, his arms bound behind his back.[59] In this position, after the room had been cleared of even the gaolers, and only the inquisitor, the episcopal delegate, and the notary remained, the accused was interrogated.[60] The ordeal generally did not go beyond thirty minutes, and an hour was the maximum permitted. According to Masini, the addition of weights to the feet of the defendant, and dropping him in sudden jerks stopping just short of the floor, universally practised in secular courts, had become strictly prohibited in his day.[61] 'Torture', he prescribed, 'should be moderate in such a way that the victim is preserved, if innocent, to enjoy his freedom, and if guilty to receive his just punishment.'[62]

It is hard to imagine more than one conclusion to any case in which torture was used. And yet, in an astonishing number of cases involving both men and women, it did not produce admissions of guilt or

[59] This was the most common form of torment practised in both secular and ecclesiastical courts. See e.g. Jacob Döpler (*Theatrum poenarum, suppliciorum et executionum criminalium* (Sondershausen, 1693), 295–301), who provides a graphic description of the cord being applied to a robust victim whose dislocated limbs had to be readjusted at the conclusion of his ordeal. When the *strappado* was inapplicable, other methods of torture were available. See Masini, *Sacro Arsenale*, p. 131: 'Et perchè il reo alle volte, ò per notorii difetti del corpo, ò per minorità evidente degli anni, si rende incapace del tormento della corda, & convien perciò dargli altro tormento, ò di fuoco (se ben questo, per esser molto pericoloso, hormai poco si usa), ò di stanghetta, ò di cannette, che altri chiamano suffoli, ò di bacchetta ...' Torture by fire was accomplished 'nudatis pedibus, illisque lardo porcino inunctis & in cippis iuxta ignem validum retentis' (p. 131); by the *stanghetta*, 'in terra prostratus, talo pedis dextri denudato inter duos ferreos taxillos concavos posito, & ministro eos stanghetta comprimente ...' (p. 133); by the *cannette*, '... manibus ante iunctis, & inter binos earum singulos digitos sibilis accommodatis, & ministro fortiter praemente ...' (p. 133).

[60] The provision that the chamber of torture should be cleared of all superfluous officials, including gaolers, is contained in a letter directed to the inquisitor of Bologna (13 June 1573) from Antonio Balduzzi, *Commissario* of the Roman Congregation (BA, MS B. 1860, fo. cxxxix), which prescribes interrogation under torture for a certain Constanza Guaina: '... gli facci dar la corda, et nel processo si scriva il tempo che vi sarà stata. L'avertirò ancho che non lassi stare i sbirri ne altri in loco tormentorum per più secretezza, che così s'usa in questo Sant'Officio, che quando hanno ligati et alzati i rei si fanno partire. Però di questo mi rimetto alla prudenza vostra.'

[61] Masini, *Sacro Arsenale* (1653 edn.), p. 182.

[62] Ibid., p. 409. Masini was simply echoing a doctrine already being enunciated a century earlier by Bernardo da Como (d. 1510?), *Lucerna Inquisitorum*, p. 127: 'Tortura debet esse moderata, & debet iudex animadverte ad indicia & ad qualitatem personae, an sit fortis in resistendo, an ne; et debet ita torquere, ut tortum servet incolumem innocentiae vel supplicio, ut sic si deliquit possit pati supplicium debitum, si vero est innocens, non patiatur corporis defectum.' The first posthumous edn. of this work was published in 1566. On the author, see J. Quetif and J. Echard, *Scriptores Ordinis Praedicatorum* (2 vols.; Paris, 1719–23; repr. New York, 1959), ii, pt. 1, pp. 22–3.

revision of the original testimony.[63] The effect of torture might depend on such factors as the thickness of the rope, the physique and stamina of the victim, and perhaps even his or her access to amulets or other presumed magical devices thought capable of dulling the sensations of pain either because they possessed narcotic properties or, even if innocuous, for their psychological effects as placebos.[64]

Confessions obtained by this means were not considered valid until their ratification twenty-four hours later outside the chamber of torments.[65] Sentences were ordinarily reviewed in Rome before they were pronounced, and the circumstances surrounding confessions

[63] e.g. TCD, MS 1226, fo. 184, sentence emitted at Novara, 2 June 1581, against Margarita 'dicta la Mora de Casale', who had been denounced to the inquisitor as a 'lamia': 'Quae in carceribus detenta et examinata, omnia semper negavit, quare de consilio peritorum sufficienter torta, nihil amplius confessa est sed semper in negatione persistit, et de eodem consilio relevata fuit et dimissa.' A recent study conducted on a thorough examination of the criminal law proceedings of the *Parlement* of Paris for the late 16th and early 17th c. reveals that torture produced a confession rate of only 1%: Alfred Soman, 'Deviance and Criminal Justice in Western Europe, 1300–1800: An Essay in Structure', *Criminal Justice History*, 1 (1980), 1–28, at p. 24. See also Langbein, *Torture*, p. 185: 'We must bear in mind that no aspect of the human condition has changed so greatly in the twentieth century as our tolerance of pain. The common pain-killers and anesthesia have largely eliminated the experience of pain from our lives. In disease, childbirth, surgery, and dentistry, our ancestors were acclimated to levels of suffering we find incomprehensible.'

[64] How to withstand torture was naturally a great concern for the accused, and special preparations which were thought to give strength to the victim might circulate among the prisoners, as mentioned in the sentence emitted at Mantua, 24 Feb. 1581 against Don Nicolò Zani, a parish priest (TCD, MS 1226, fo. 57): '. . . mentre ch'eri qui carcerato doppo la confessione delle sopradette cose fosti deposto avanti di noi qualmente havevi scritte con le tue proprie mani sopra tre bolettini la forma del Santis- simo Sacramento della Eucarestia e che n'havessi dato duoi de quelli a un tuo compagno mentre eri prigione e, ritenuto l'altro per te stesso, et ch'havevi insegnato a detto compagno che ingiotessi uno de quelli bolettini quando era condotto ai tormenti perchè per virtù di quello non haveria confessato cosa alcuna.' The phenomenon is treated in detail in the unpublished 'La Prattica di procedere con forma giudiciale nelle cause appartenenti alla S.ta fede', by Deodato Scaglia, OP, Bishop of Melfi: BAV, Barb. lat., 4615. Ch. 28 of this treatise, dated 1637, deals with the question 'De i Maleficii di taciturnità in tortura'. On the physical characteristics which strengthened resistance to torture, see Fiorelli, *La tortura giudiziara*, i. 215. Cf. Io. Bapt. Scanaroli, *De Visitatione Carceratorum, Libri Tres* (Rome, 1655), p. 292, where he declares that women have much greater resistance than men 'quia habent maiorem pectoris latitudinem', and because 'carent certis partibus quae maxime dolorem augent'.

[65] Masini, *Sacro Arsenale*, p. 144. The Congregation of the Inquisition in Rome scrutinized trial records sent to it by the provincial tribunals for fulfilment of this provision. See e.g. the letter of the Cardinal of Pisa to the Bolognese inquisitor, 27 Oct. 1571, BA, MS B. 1860, fo. liii: 'Si sono havute le due vostre di XIII et XVII del presente . . . et l'essamine che ci havete mandato, fatto da voi a quel Mro Agostino nella tortura. Si aspettarà che lo facciate ratificare extra tormenta, dandoci poi aviso di tutto quello che haverà detto.'

obtained under duress, especially if retracted during the twenty-four hour interval, received special scrutiny. I can cite, among others, the case of a certain Maria de Gentili, a Bolognese woman suspected of being a witch, who had confessed to a homicide. After a thorough review of the proceedings by the Roman Congregation, the Cardinal of Santa Severina wrote to the inquisitor of Bologna on 18 May 1591: 'there are too many contradictory elements in her confession which do not agree with the evidence presented in the trial.' Her punishment was temporary banishment from the city of Bologna.[66] Finally, there are numerous examples of requests to Rome appealing against the decisions of the provincial tribunals, cases in which both trial records and defendants were transferred to the higher court and the investigation reopened. Thus in 1593 a certain Giovanni Paolo delle Agocchie, who had been sentenced by the Bolognese court to five years of service on the papal galleys, had his sentence commuted by the Holy Office in Rome to a fine of 200 scudi.[67] And when, at the conclusion of his trial, a priest of Verona, similarly condemned to a harsh galley sentence, claimed that he had not been permitted a full defence, his case was reopened and he was assigned an attorney.[68]

In the area of penal practices as well, a close examination of the sources may dispel some lingering misconceptions. The solemn words pronounced in countless sentences have misled modern scholars to form an incorrect impression of inquisitorial justice. Condemnation to a *carcere perpetuo* (perpetual prison) was actually intended by the canonists to suggest a confinement of roughly three years, provided, of course, that the accused demonstrated sincere signs of contrition;[69] *carcere perpetuo irremissible* indicated eight years;[70]

---

[66] BA, MS B. 1861, fo. 133: '... non sopravenendo altro, essendosi venuto in parere ch'ella non si debba rilasciar alla corte secolare ... perchè le sue confessioni quanto all'homicidio sono parse assai inverisimili per molte circonstanze che si raccogliono dal suo processo.'

[67] Ibid., fo. 171, letter from the Cardinal of Santa Severina to the inquisitor of Bologna, 13 Mar. 1593. Agocchie had already begun to serve his term. The fine was to be applied 'per sovvenire alli poveri carcerati'.

[68] BAV, Barb. lat. 6334, fo. 66ʳ, letter dated 21 Mar. 1626, from the Roman Congregation of the Holy Office to the inquisitor of Verona: 'Se don Bernardino Anderlini condannato alla galera per 10 anni non ha potuto, com'egli suppone intieramente difendersi, gli miei SS.ri Ill.mi ordinano, che se gli dia di nuovo le difese, et si proceda anco ex officio d'avvocato che lo difenda, et però trattandosi di pena molto grave, et di persona per il sacerdotio qualificata, V.R. non mancherà di darli ogni giusta commodità di giustificarsi ...'

[69] Simancas, *Enchiridion*, p. 293: '... haec poena perpetui carceris post lapsum triennii remitti solet' (following Plato, *Laws*, bk. x); id., *De Catholicis Institutionibus*

[*See opposite page for n. 69 cont. and n. 70*].

and true imprisonment for life, *immuratio* (which itself might be commuted to a lesser term), denoted confinement in a cell surrounded by four walls, and not literally a walling in, as some writers have supposed.[71] I have encountered instances of pardons granted even within six months of sentencing to individuals destined to so-called perpetual imprisonment, although it was more customary to allow a few years to elapse. Let us look at two examples. Antonio de Ludovisi and Hieronimo Guastavillani were among a group of Bolognese gentlemen found guilty of heretical activities and sentenced on 20 September 1567—Ludovisi to *carcere perpetuo* and Guastavillani to *immuratio*. During the years 1573–4 a number of letters were exchanged between the Roman Congregation and the inquisitor of Bologna concerning their conduct in confinement. It was concluded that they had earned a reduction of their sentences. Both men were granted permission to doff that mark of shame, the *habitello*, the penitential garment worn by the convicted heretic, and to leave their monastic prisons. Guastavillani, however, was limited in his movements to the *contado* of Bologna and prohibited from entering the city proper.[72]

In the sixteenth century, outside Rome, the Church possessed very

---

(Rome, 1575), 113: 'Solet poena perpetui carceris post lapsum triennii plerumque remitti, si eo tempore vincti humiles et veri poenitentes fuerint.' Francisco Peña's commentary on Eymerich (*Directorium*, p. 590) follows this opinion. See also T. Delbene, *De Officio S. Inquisitionis circa Haeresim* (Lyons, 1666), 467: 'Regulariter cum condemnato ad carcerem perpetuum dispensatur post annos tres' (cited from Nikolaus Paulus, *Hexenwahn und Hexenprozess vornehmlich im 16. Jahrhundert* (Freiburg im Breisgau, 1910), 252).

[70] Simancas, *De Catholicis Institutionibus*, p. 113: 'Ubi autem poenitentia imposita est poena carceris irremissibilis, remitti solet post octo annos.'

[71] Antonio Battistella (*Il S. Officio e la riforma religiosa in Bologna*, p. 77) fell into this error. Paulus, *Hexenwahn*, demonstrated conclusively that in inquisitorial speech *muros* designated the walls of a prison. See ch. 12, 'Die Einmauerung der Hexen in Rom'. The first trial of Domenico Scandella, 'Menocchio', had concluded with the following judgement: 'Te sententialiter condemnamus ut inter duos parietes immureris, ut ibi sibi semper et toto tempore vitae tuae maneas.' Within two years (18 Jan. 1586) he presented a supplication to be released and was granted his village of Montereale as a *carcere perpetuo*: Ginzburg, *The Cheese and the Worms*, pp. 93, 165.

[72] Their sentences are in TCD, MS 1224, fos. 201, 203. For the correspondence between Rome and Bologna, see BA, MS B. 1860, fos. cxxxii, clxlv, clxxxviiii. For a case where release from prison occurred only a few months after sentencing, see the letter of Cardinal Arigoni of the Holy Office to the inquisitor of Bologna, 22 Oct. 1611, granting 'gratia della pena del carcere' to a certain Baldassar Soprani, 'abiurato costì a mesi passati a ciò possa haver cura de suoi figlioli piccioli, et della moglie ben spesso inferma' (BA, MS B. 1864, fo. 38).

few actual prisons.[73] Thus, monastic imprisonment,[74] house arrest,[75] or confinement to a geographical area which might range in size from one's village to an entire city or *contado*[76] were the possibilities generally available to the sentencing judges. The elderly, modest wage-earners with large families and nubile daughters, and witches whose husbands would take them back, were frequently assigned to their homes and to their shops,[77] especially since monks tended to view prisoners in their midst as unwelcome burdens on their usually poor and overcrowded monasteries.[78] In secular practice, imprison-

[73] The fullest account of the Roman prison system (together with the apposite legislation) is in the monumental work by G. B. Scanaroli, *De Visitatione Carceratorum Libri Tres*. On aspects of this system, see the recent studies by Vincenzo Paglia, 'La pietà dei carcerati': Confraternite e società a Roma nei secoli XVI–XVIII (Rome, 1980), and Giovanni Scarabello, 'La pena del carcere: Asnetti della condizione carceraria a Venezia nei secoli XVI–XVIII', in Gaetano Cozzi (ed.), *Stato, società e giustizia nella repubblica veneta (sec. XV–XVIII)* (Rome, 1980), 317–76. For the best recent discussion of the development of the legal doctrine of incarceration, see Nicoletta Sarti, 'Appunti su carcere-custodia e carcere-pena nella dottrina civilistica dei secoli XII–XVI', *Rivista di storia del diritto italiano*, 53–4 (1980–1), 67–110.

[74] This could be of two kinds, varying in severity, as we see from the case of Don Flavio Uberti, a Celestine, who was condemned to spend one year 'in carcere formali' in a monastery, followed by four more years in a house of his order 'in loco di prigione' (TCD, MS 1228, fo. 111, sentence pronounced 24 Mar. 1603). The first form of imprisonment involved formal confinement in a cell. The second permitted circulation about the grounds of the monastery, subject, however, to the performance of salutary penances as prescribed by the inquisitors. Thus, in the case of Fra Angelo da Casale sentenced at Mantua c.30 June 1581 as a necromancer, he was condemned '. . . tre volte in pubblico refettorio dove mangiano i frati tuoi sedere in terra con acqua e pane della famiglia e fare le prostrationi' (TCD, MS 1226, fo. 178).

[75] See n. 77, below.

[76] TCD, MS 1225, fo. 224, sentence dated 16 June 1580 against Giannina Caravello, suspected of witchcraft: confinement 'in la tua terra di Croda'; TCD, MS 1224, fo. 139, sentence dated 29 Mar. 1567 against Jacobum Aemilium Laodicensem Germanum: 'Tibi pro carcere assignamus urbem, quam non exitis sine nostri licentia . . .'; TCD, MS 1224, fo. 142, sentence dated 1 Apr. 1567 against Hugo Villeti: 'Ti assignamo la città di Roma ed li suoi borghi e distretto per priggione . . .'

[77] TCD, MS 1226, fo. 314, sentence pronounced at Vicenza, 13 Oct. 1581, against Antonio Bonente di Cittadella: 'Te condaniamo al carcere perpetuo et usando con te misericordia et compatendo alla tua senile età, et havendo riguardo al stretto carcere qual hai patito, et alla tua povertà con la gravezza de'molti tuoi figlioli, ti assignamo al presente pro carcere la casa tua in Cittadella'; TCD, MS 1225, fo. 118, sentence pronounced at Bergamo on 26 Feb. 1580 against Ludovicus de Moianonibus. The term of his *carcere perpetuo* was to be served 'in domum et apothecam propriam'.

[78] BA, MS B. 1860, fo. lxix, letter of the Cardinal of Pisa to the inquisitor of Bologna, 12 Mar. 1572: 'Fu ragionato in questa ultima congregatione intorno il fatto di quel cieco a chi fu dato per carcere da cotesto S.to Ufficio il Monasterio di S. Proculo; et perchè fu fatta relatione ch'egli haveva il modo di vivere del suo, et che ritornandosene a casa saria stato governato da la moglie assai meglio che non era da quei padri, li quali dall'altro canto si aggravavano di farli più le spese, allegando oltra il danno ancho

3. Inquisitorial Law and the Witch

ment *ad poenam* (as punishment) rather than simply *ad custodiam* (for the purpose of custody during the trial phase of the judicial process) did not make its appearance until late in the sixteenth century.[79] Based on the records connected with the trial of Giordano Bruno, and a personal visit, Luigi Firpo has reconstructed conditions in the Roman prisons of the Holy Office housed in the Palazzo Pucci, debunking legendary assertions made by older writers: cells were commodious and well lit, furnished with a bed, table, sheets, and towels. The prisoners had access to a barber, bathing facilities, laundry service, and mending, and were permitted a change of clothing twice weekly. They appeared periodically before the Congregation to testify concerning their material needs; and the cardinals, in turn, were obliged to inspect conditions in the prisons. As for the disabilities, prisoners could not converse with their fellows in other cells; they could not attempt to read or write about matters that did not immediately concern their cases; nor could they converse privately with their gaolers or use them to communicate with the outside world.[80] These optimum conditions were clearly not met in the provincial tribunals. There facilities were frequently inferior, as we

l'incomodità che causava ad essi loro . . .' A subsequent letter from Rome to Bologna (ibid., fo. cv, 19 Dec. 1572) improved the prisoner's lot once again: he was to be assigned the entire city of Bologna as a prison and freed from the obligation of wearing the penitential garment, the *habitello*, 'acciò possi procurare da vivere'.

[79] Locati, *Opus quod iudiciale inquisitorum dicitur*, p. 37: 'Carcer regulariter est ad custodiam, non autem ad poenam . . . sed hoc intellige de iure civili, non de iure canonico.' See also Langbein, *Prosecuting Crime in the Renaissance*, p. 195: 'It must be remembered that the Carolina [1532] dates from half a century before the advent in Europe of the sentence of imprisonment as a regular mode of punishment.' Cf. also by the same author, 'The Historical Origins of the Sanction of Imprisonment for Serious Crime', *Journal of Legal Studies*, 5 (1976), 35–60. Natalie Z. Davis, *The Return of Martin Guerre* (Cambridge, Mass., 1983), 87.

[80] See Luigi Firpo, 'Il processo di Giordano Bruno', *Rivista storica italiana*, 60 (1948), 542–97; 61 (1949), 5–59, at 60. 577. The provision for the regular inspection of prisons by inquisitors was an ancient one (Eymerich, *Directorium*, p. 590) and was reinforced by numerous decrees issued by the Roman Congregation during the 16th c. See e.g. decree of 18 June 1564 in Pastor, 'Dekrete', p. 504. On the change of laundry for inmates, see the decree of 14 Mar. 1595, ibid., p. 533. On the expenses incurred by the Holy Office for the maintenance of its prisoners in Rome during a single month (Nov. 1596), see Angelo Mercati, *Il sommario del processo di Giordano Bruno*, (Vatican City, 1942), 121–6. For a more general discussion, see Antonino Bertolotti, *Le prigioni di Roma nei Secoli XVI, XVII e XVIII* (Rome, 1890), and esp. Scanaroli, *De Visitatione Carceratorum, passim*. For Philip Camerarius's own first-hand account of his Roman incarceration, see his 'Relatio de Captivitate sua Romana et liberatione fere miraculosa', in J. G. Schelhorn, *De vita, fatis ac meritis Philippi Camerarii* (Nuremberg, 1740), 104 p., and the long study and edn. of the text by Lech Szczucki, *Philippus Camerarius: Prawdziwa i wierna relacja o uwięzieniu w Rzymie* (Warsaw, 1984).

learn from prisoners' appeals and from the repeated attempts by Rome to remedy the situations.[81]

There is little that one can say in mitigation of that living hell that was the world of the galleys. The Church, together with every other Mediterranean sea power, reserved this fate for many of its offenders (see Endnote D). The evidence suggests that the galleys were considered appropriate punishment for individuals convicted of especially serious and perverse crimes: gross blasphemers who had vilified the cardinal dogmas of the Church, arch-heretics, abusive judges, necromancers who had grossly defiled the altar and sacraments, prison breakers, false witnesses and perjurers, and defendants who had been obstructive and evasive during their trials (see Endnote E). The Church claimed a higher standard of behaviour from ecclesiastics than from laymen. Consequently, the former incurred heavier penalties, which frequently took the form of galley sentences.[82] The hardships endured by the convict at sea were well-known, and officials pondered the proper uses of this form of penal servitude. This concern even touched that unflinching persecutor of heretics, Michele Ghislieri (the future Pius V), while he served in Rome as Commissioner General of the Holy Office. Replying on 20 June 1556 to an enquiry from the inquisitor of Genoa, he described the reluctance of the Roman Congregation to assign its prisoners to the galleys, which they considered a form of penance fit only for the desperate and the damned.[83] Again, writing on 29 September 1563, Ghislieri reassured the Jesuit Cristoforo Rodriguez (on a mission to the Waldensians in the Puglie and Calabria) in regard to the fate of the local inhabitants. 'Concerning those that have been sent to the galleys, your Reverence should give us an account of each one individually, mentioning if they are burdened by families, because if they should persevere in their repentance—and if it is not feigned—their sentences

---

[81] BAV, Barb. lat. 6334, fo. 38ʳ, letter of the Roman Congregation to the inquisitor of Rimini, 14 Feb. 1626: 'Gasparo Giurza [?] già fiscale di cotesto S.to Officio si duole della lunga prigionia in carcere humido et cattivo con evidente pericolo della salute sua in età già grave et valetudinaria, facendo istanzá di essere quantoprima spedito et in tanto habilitato. Questi miei SS.ri Ill.mi mi hanno commesso di scrivere a V.R. che subito mandi quello che ha contra di lui ... et in tanto con sicurtà de tutto carcere lo habiliti a miglior stanza'; ibid., fo. 42ᵛ, letter from Roman Congregation to Bishop of Lucca, 21 Feb. 1626, ordering more comfortable prisons for two women 'sortileghe' accused of attempted murder: '... si sono dolute [the women] di essere già molti mesi ritenute in pessime prigioni con evidente pericolo della vita ...'

[82] See the sentence against the priest Hieronymo del Pozzo, Endnote E, below.

[83] Letter printed in Pastor, *Popes*, xiv. 459, in which Ghislieri referred to galley service as 'penitentia da disperati o da dimonii et di poco frutto'.

will be certainly commuted.'[84] Members of the nobility and academics (but not ecclesiastics) were generally spared galley service, but the question of eligibility seems not to have been settled juridically if it could still be raised by the inquisitor of Malta early in the seventeenth century. In this, as in other instances, Rome advised that a general rule could not be formulated and that each case should be settled on its merits.[85] Expiration dates of sentences were observed, and many among the condemned survived and returned to their former lives.[86] Those who became physically unfit for the oar had their sentences commuted to a lesser punishment.[87] There are shreds of evidence that the way was open for prisoners to purchase the services of substitutes more apt for the life than themselves;[88] and that some individuals

[84] Mario Scaduto, 'Tra inquisitori e riformati', *Archivum historicum Societatis Iesu*, 15 (1946), 47.

[85] The inquiry of the Holy Office of Malta (12 May 1604) is preserved in BAV, Borg. lat. 558, fo. 52. The same advice was also received by the inquisitor of Milan: Fumi, 'L'inquisizione romana', p. 31. According to Doepler (*Theatrum Poenarum*, p. 793), practices in Italy varied: 'Nobiles et minores in Regno Neapolitano loco ejusdem poenae triremium relegantur in aliquam insulam . . . sed in statu ecclesiastico hoc male servatur, quia etiam nobiles transmittuntur ad triremes . . . sed doctores ad triremes de facili condemnari non debent . . .'

[86] But justice might be thwarted when prisoners were not on papal vessels. See e.g. the strenuous efforts made by the nuncio to Naples, Antonio Sauli, to free several convicts, citizens of the states of the church, sentenced during the reign of Pius IV. The galleys on which they were serving had subsequently been sold to Spain and their officers refused to recognize that their terms had expired. The Pope himself (Gregory XIII) was taking a keen interest in the affair, as we learn from a letter dated 1 Mar. 1572 to Sauli from the Cardinal Secretary of State, Tolomeo Galli: 'De li forzati vedo che V.S. si piglia quel travaglio et usa quella diligenza che conviene per obedir al commandamento di N.S. et meritar insieme col far opera di charità tanto degna. Così son certo che lei supererà tutte le difficultà et subterfugii di quelli che li hanno in potere.' Pasquale Villani (ed.), *Nunziature di Napoli, i, 26 Luglio 1570–24 Maggio 1577* (Rome, 1962), 397.

[87] In two sentences to the galleys pronounced by the inquisition of Verona in Aug. and Sept. 1580 (TCD, MS 1225, fos. 265 and 294), it was specified that if the prisoners at any time became *inhabili* their sentences were to be commuted to banishment.

[88] TCD, MS 1226 fo. 10ff., dossier containing the case of Carlo Chiavello of Savona, 'speciaro', sentenced to twenty years in the galleys by the inquisitor of Genoa (8 Jan. 1581). An appeal had been addressed to the Pope on his behalf which alleged that 'il povero huomo si ritrova vecchio, infermo, crepato dalle parti da basso, inutile a essercitare tal pena . . . trovandosi carrico di sette figlioli . . . tra quali quattro femmine, che senza l'aiuto paterno andaranno in ruina con pericolo anco dell'anime loro . . .' In a letter to Cardinal Savello of the Roman Congregation (9 June 1581) the inquisitor of Genoa disputed many of these facts: '. . . ha [Chiavello] molti figlioli costui ma è molto accomodato di robba perchè trafica bene et adesso in galera fa mercantia di vino et non si lascia mancar. È molto industrioso, vecchio non è, nel che ha supplicato il falso. È huomo d'anni 40 in circa più et meno . . . et a questo v'è il rimedio, compri un schiavo Mahumettano et lo facci vogar per lui. Ha il modo di poter farlo.'

sentenced to the galleys actually may never have set foot aboard one, although their alternative duties ashore were probably no less harsh.[89] The stake, incarceration, and the triremes are those dramatic forms of penal procedure which are generally associated with inquisitorial practice. But a survey of the thousands of surviving sentences suggests that in actual fact milder forms of punishment prevailed. Most frequently encountered are public humiliation, in the form of abjurations read on the cathedral steps on Sundays and feast days before the throngs of churchgoers, and secondly, salutary penances, fines to be paid for the benefit of charitable establishments, and a seemingly endless cycle of prayers and devotions to be performed over many months or years.[90] Despite popular notions to the contrary, only a small percentage of cases concluded with capital punishment. The death penalty was reserved for three principal categories of offenders: the obstinate and unrepentant who refused to be reconciled to the Church, those who had suffered a previous sentence for formal heresy,[91] and individuals convicted of attempting to overturn such central doctrines of the Church as the Virgin Birth and the full divinity of Christ.[92] We possess

[89] See Giacinto Gigli, *Diario Romano, 1608–1670* (Rome, 1958), 191, which describes the reading of a sentence in St Peter's in Rome (19 Mar. 1640) against a Capuchin who had apostatized from his order and married: '. . . questo fu condannato in galera, o per dir meglio, nel loco destinato per i Religiosi delinquenti a Civitavecchia'; and ibid., p. 481, where Gigli reports services performed in the city during a plague in July 1656: 'Li ammalati erano portati al Lazzaretto dentro una bara coperta da doi schiavi, cioè huomini condannati alla galera . . .'

[90] This conclusion is based on a close analysis of the sentences preserved in Trinity College, Dublin.

[91] Mandatory execution of the *relapsus* dated to the decretal 'Ad Abolendam' issued by Pope Lucius III, 4 Nov. 1184: Henri Maisonneuve, *Études sur les origines de l'inquisition* (2nd edn. Paris, 1960), 153. On the pertinacious heretic who, even though convicted, tenaciously clung to his error, see, among many other authorities, the discussion in C. Carena, *Tractatus*, p. 65.

[92] Paul IV established a class of crimes against the central doctrines of the Church which called for the death penalty even when the accused was neither relapsed nor impenitent. The two Bulls, *Cum quorundam hominum* (22 July 1556) and *Cum ex apostolatus officio* (15 Feb. 1558), are printed in the appendix to Eymerich's *Directorium*, pp. 121–5. Cf. also the unpublished 'Pratica per procedere nelle cause del S. Officio', attributed to Cardinal Desiderio Scaglia, ch. 16, 'Di quelli che negano la Trinità, la Divinità di Christo, la sua Concettione di Spirito Santo, la sua morte per nostra Redentione, o la Verginità di Maria Nostra Signora': Bodl., MS Mendham 36. An example of the pertinent offences is contained in a letter from the Cardinal of Santa Severina to the inquisitor of Florence, dated 2 Mar. 1591. BRB, MS II. 290, vol. ii, fo. 18: 'V. R.^tia. avvertisca, che per la Bolla di Papa Paolo 4 di felice memoria promulgata contra quelli che negano, ò non credano la S.ma Trinità, la perpetua Virginità della Beatissima

fragmentary figures on the numbers of those handed over by the Italian inquisitions to the secular arm. Only five of the first thousand defendants who appeared before the tribunal of Aquileia-Concordia in the Friuli between 1551 and 1647 were put to death.[93] A tentative calculation for Venice has counted fourteen executions between 1553 and 1588, and four extraditions to the same fate in Rome between 1555 and 1593.[94] Only seven executions for heresy have been counted in Milan during the seventy years, 1560–1630;[95] and of more than two hundred sentences contained in the documents preserved in Trinity College, Dublin for the years 1580–2, only three called for condemnations to the stake.[96] In the witchcraft trials in the Friuli studied by Carlo Ginzburg, he did not encounter a single execution.[97] As for Rome itself, the names of ninety-seven ascertained victims of the Holy Office have been extracted from the records for the period 1542 to 1761.[98] If this is still not a pleasant picture, it is also not the unfettered violence which we have been led to imagine.

The final act in the inquisitorial process, the *auto-da-fé*, the public

sempre Vergine Maria, ò la Divinità di Christo N.ro Sig.^re, ancorche siano nel primo lapso, et siano penitenti, nondimeno si rilasciano al braccio secolare.' In actual practice, however, I have encountered an extraordinary number of cases of individuals convicted of the heresies specified in the Pauline decrees who were spared the death penalty. A long sentence to the galleys was frequently substituted. See e.g. the case of Don Ottavio Piamontesi, who was sentenced at Reggio on 21 Apr. 1581 to ten years in the galleys for blasphemies in which he had denied the Virgin Birth, etc.: TCD, MS 1226, fo. 126. Relaxation to the secular arm was also prescribed by Paul IV for individuals not in holy orders who celebrated mass or heard confessions. The decree, dated 17 Feb. 1559, is published in Locati, *Opus quod iudiciale inquisitorum dicitur*, p. 476.

[93] See [Luigi DeBiasio and Maria Rosa Facile], *1000 Processi dell'inquisizione in Friuli* (Quaderni del Centro Regionale di Catalogazione dei Beni Culturali, 4; Udine, 1976).

[94] Paul F. Grendler, *The Roman Inquisition and the Venetian Press, 1540–1605* (Princeton, 1977), 57.

[95] Mario Bendiscioli, 'Penetrazione protestante e repressione controriformistica in Lombardia all' epoca di Carlo e Federico Borromeo', in E. Iserloh and P. Manns (eds.), *Festgabe Joseph Lortz* (2 vols.; Baden-Baden, 1958), 404.

[96] TCD, MS 1225, fo. 344; MS 1226, fos. 297, 377.

[97] *The Night Battles, passim.*

[98] I allude to the records of the *Venerabile Arciconfraternità di San Giovanni Decollato*, whose function it was to accompany the condemned to their death: Domenico Orano, *Liberi pensatori bruciati in Roma dal XVI al XVIII secolo* (Rome, 1904; rep. Livorno, 1971). To these, Orano suspected, should be added fifteen others whose names are found in the *Archivio del Governatore* (p. xiv), and thirty others whose names are found in the lists of the confraternity but whose certificates of execution could not be located among the books of the *Provveditore* (pp. 118–19). The figures for executions by the Holy Office for heresy are not seriously affected by Luigi Firpo, 'Esecuzioni capitali in Roma (1567–1671)', in *Eresia e riforma nell'Italia del Cinquecento. Miscellanea*, i (Florence and Chicago, 1974), 307–42.

ceremony where, after sentencing, penitent heretics abjured[99] and were reconciled to the Church, and the obdurate and relapsed went to their fate, took place in an atmosphere which evoked visions of the Last Judgement in at least one spectator (see Endnote F). These 'acts of faith' were held in the presence of great throngs and before assembled dignitaries of church and state ensconced on specially erected platforms. In Rome, the scenes of these macabre affairs were generally the misnamed Campo dei Fiori or the bridge by the Castel Sant'Angelo. The condemned were accompanied by official comforters belonging to the charitable confraternity assigned to this purpose.[100] Before being burned, gentlemen were beheaded, lesser mortals hung. And even those who were condemned to the agony of being burned alive because they refused to the bitter end to recant their errors and be reconciled to the Church, might have, in later usage at least, the moment of final release hastened.[101]

[99] All writers distinguished between abjurations performed *de levi* and *de vehementi* and *de formali*. The former took place privately in the episcopal residence or in the seats of the various Inquisitions, the two latter publicly on Cathedral steps and during the *autos*. Because of the stigma attached to the ceremony, before ordering a public abjuration inquisitors were expected to consider whether an offender was a family head 'habens filias nubiles': Carena, *Tractatus*, p. 317. The second category of abjuration was infinitely more serious, because '. . . qui de vehementi abiurat, si relabatur in haeresim, relapsorum poena punitur, et curiae seculari traditur . . .'. Cf. F. Peña, commentary to N. Eymerich's *Directorium*, p. 488. Minors (under 25 years old) who abjured as formal heretics were exempted from the punishment of the relapsed in case of a second conviction. See the letter from the Roman Congregation to the inquisitor of Milan, dated 21 Mar. 1626: '. . . se egli [a certain Albertino accused of sortilege] ha col cuore apostatato abiuri de formali, essendo l'età sua d'anni 16 molto bene capace d'abiura, nella quale però attesa la minorità dovrà mettersi la clausola, "citra poenam relapsi"' (BAV, Barb. lat. 6334, fo. 69ᵛ). The moment of abjuring might be transformed into a last desperate attempt to proselytize and exhort the assembled throngs. Two such cases are reported by Andrea Del Col, 'L'abiura trasformata in propaganda ereticale nel duomo di Udine', *Metodi e ricerche*, 2 (1981), 57–72. The second instance of a fraudulent abjuration occurred in 1567 (see n. 24 of Del Col's article).

[100] The surviving records of the *Venerabile Arciconfraternità di San Giovanni Decollato* have been published by Domenico Orano, *Liberi pensatori bruciati in Roma dal XVI al XVIII secolo*. On the confraternity, see Vincenzo Paglia, *La morte confortata:Riti della paura e mentalità religiosa a Roma nell'età moderna* (Rome, 1982). Cf. Adriano Prosperi, 'Il sangue e l'anima: Ricerche sulle compagnie di giustizia in Italia', *Quaderni storici*, 17 (1982), 959–99.

[101] For instances of burnings where small sacks of gunpowder were hung around the victims' necks, see Henry Charles Lea, *Materials Toward a History of Witchcraft*, arranged and ed. Arthur C. Howland (3 vols.; Philadelphia, 1939; repr. New York, 1957), ii. 674, 808, and Aureggi, 'La stregoneria nelle Alpi Centrali', p. 128n. Cf. also Deodato Scaglia's unpublished 'La Theorica di procedere tanto in generale, quanto in particolare ne' casi appartenenti alla Santa Fede', p. 78: 'La prattica però, che per certa equità hoggidi [the work is dated 1637] s'usa è di far prima stroncar questi rei innanzi che si accenda il fuoco'; I have used the version of this text preserved in Bodl., MS Add. C. 31.

In conclusion, capricious and arbitrary decisions, misuse of authority, and wanton abuse of human rights were not an integral part of inquisitorial procedure, and they were not tolerated. There is a scrupulous, almost pedantic reverence for tradition, which Fra Paolo da Ferrara, a high functionary in the Roman Congregation, sums up in a letter dated 7 November 1573 to the Bolognese inquisitor: 'Your reverence should not allow himself to be persuaded by anyone to innovate or give unusual penances and punishments, regardless who is involved, but should follow common practice, and the sound teachings of Simancas.'[102] And when the same inquisitor of Bologna, who had suspected Protestant sympathies behind a simple failure to observe a day of fasting, exceeded proper limits of investigation, Antonio Balduzzi, Commissioner of the Roman Inquisition, wrote a sad letter of reproach:

Concerning that poor man who ate meat it seems to me that you acted much too harshly against him. I know well that I [and Balduzzi had himself once served as inquisitor of Bologna] would not have done half of what was done by you. A man who, as soon as he was corrected, admitted his mistake and explained that he had forgotten that it was a fast day and a Saturday, a man almost unknown to other men, to have put him in prison and tortured him to me seems too much.[103]

And Cesare Carena, who discussed the question of forbidden foods at length, would have agreed. Unless the act was consciously and admittedly committed in contempt of the Church, it did not in itself render the offender suspect of heresy; and torture *super intentione* was never to be applied in any case before the tribunal, unless the suspicion against the accused was of a vehement or serious nature.[104]

As we have seen, the central tribunal's quest for uniformity resulted in a series of measures which assigned the final disposition of all but the most ordinary cases to Rome.[105] There are many letters, almost

---

[102] BA, MS B. 1860, fo. clx.

[103] Ibid., fo. clxliii (21 August 1574).

[104] *Tractatus*, pp. 214, 216: 'Ex quibus colligitur, quod comedens carnes in die Ieiunij, etiam sine licentia superioris, si id non faciat in Ecclesiae contemptum, sed ex iusta causa, maxime per medicum approbata non est de haeresi suspectus ...'; 'Quo ad torturam super intentione, illa non videtur danda regulariter, nisi vehementer suspectus.'

[105] Pastor, 'Dekrete', p. 515, decree of 18 Sept. 1581: '... quod Inquisitores sententias omnes transmittant ad hoc Sanctum Officium, non autem processus, nisi in arduis causis; sed bene ante expeditionem summarium transmittant et responsum expectent'. This provision is reaffirmed in the decree of 7 Sept. 1594 (p. 532).

sarcastic in tone, in which the cardinal inquisitors attempt to distinguish for the benefit of the local officials what is ordinary business from what is not.[106] It became the custom for the latter to send a detailed summary of most trials to the Roman Congregation itself, and then await instructions before pronouncing sentence— which was not done until the cardinal inquisitors were genuinely convinced that they were in full possession of all the facts in a case, including extenuating circumstances.[107] Thus, in the case of a grocer of Legnago who had denied the immortality of the soul, they determined that he had come to his erroneous opinion 'through ignorance and passion and that he had not learned it consciously from others';[108] and before proceeding to a decision against a monk of the Order of San Salvador who had run away from his monastery, they wanted to know at what age he had entered his religious vocation.[109] Finally, in the case of a blasphemer from Bologna who had desecrated a crucifix, they needed to be informed whether his sacrilege had been committed while in a state of reason or during a fit of anger, and whether he had been an offender before.[110]

[106] BA, MS B. 1860, fo. cxx, letter of the Commissioner of the Holy Office in Rome, Antonio Balduzzi, to the inquisitor of Bologna, 11 Mar. 1573: '. . . non mi pare d'havere a dirvi cosa particolare se non sodisfare a due dimande vostre, l'una quello ch'io intendo per le cose piccole ch'havete a trattare da voi senza altrimenti molestarne questi SS.ri Ill.mi, a che vi dico, prima ch'io non voglio ch'in cosa alcuna ch'io vi scriva da me come frate Antonio habbiate come decisione e leggi, ma come avvisi e pareri amichevoli e fraterni. Appresso vi dico, che le cose che vi passarano per le mani da se si mostraranno se sono piccole o grandi, e se sono degne d'avisarne questo S.to Tribonale, ò no, e che quà io non vi saprei dare regola certa, ma il vostro giudicio v'ha da regolare. Certo è che non ogni minutia, ne d'ogni depositione s'ha da scrivere. Ma quando le cause sono fondate ò volete venire à qualche atto importante come di sentenza, ò simile, è bene d'avisarne, e dire ancho il parere delli vostri consultori e sempre date aviso delli complici che fossero nominati.' Provincial inquisitors generally possessed authority to pronounce judgement 'nelle cause ordinarie, et che non sono gravi per la qualità delle persone et delli delitti', according to the advice sent to the Florentine official by the Cardinal of Santa Severina on 21 May 1594. Copies of sentences had to be sent to Rome in all cases. Brussels MS II. 290, vol. ii, fo. 170.
[107] BA, MS B. 1860, fo. clxv, letter of Antonio Balduzzi to the inquisitor of Bologna, 26 Dec. 1573: 'Il sfrattato ch'ha preso moglie desiderarei mandassi il caso in forma continente, e quello che s'ha contra di lui, e quello che confessa perchè di queste materie che tanto importano, non è bene parlarne cosi in aere ma con la verità ben fondata.'
[108] TCD, MS 1225, fo. 194, sentence pronounced 26 Apr. 1580 against Giovanni Francesco Pegorari da Legnago, 'speciale'.
[109] BA, MS B. 1860, fo. clxxi, Balduzzi to the inquisitor of Bologna, 23 Jan. 1574.
[110] Ibid., fo. clxiii, Balduzzi to the inquisitor of Bologna, 3 Dec. 1573: 'Quanto al fatto di quello ch'ha ferito e mal trattato l'imagine del crocifisso, a volere buona rissolutione bisogna che V.R. mi scriva se l'ha fatto in disprezzo, et ad animo quieto vel calore

It is impossible to condone coercion, the stake, and the other horrors perpetrated in the name of religion during the Reformation era. They were employed both by the Inquisition and by almost all other judicial bodies in Europe. In the sixteenth century they were an unquestioned part of legal proceedings. But I believe that future research will show that they were used less frequently, with greater moderation, and with a higher regard for human rights and life in the tribunals of the Holy Office than elsewhere. Scepticism and incredulity in regard to witchcraft invaded Roman legal circles early in the seventeenth century, at a time when the lands north of the Pyrenees and the Alps remained in the grip of a witch-hunting mania. It was a modest step towards sanity, and a glimmer of hope at the end of a dark tunnel.

ENDNOTES

A. Both sides of the question are discussed in a letter from the Roman Congregation of the Holy Office to the General of the Dominicans, dated 4 Sept. 1580: Pastor, 'Allgemeine Dekrete', p. 546: 'Nostro Signore havendo inteso che gl'inquisitori della religione di s. Domenico, sotto il manto del s^{to} Offizio, pretendono del tutto essere immuni dall' obbedienza de' suoi superiori, non vogliono come gl'altri obedire nè servare la regola, uscendo anco a posta loro da' monasteri, senza sapersi dove vadano, e facendo anco lo stesso li loro compagni, vicarii, notari et altri ministri, donde ne nasce molta rilassazione di obedienza regolare con disservizio di Dio e scandalo del prossimo, e che dall' altra parte gl'inquisitori si dolgono che, non solamente non possono per le straniezze de loro superiori regolari o per dubio di non dispiacere a principi e gentiluomini e generar odio al convento, far l'ufficio suo, ma spesse volte sono impediti e li sono generate di molte difficoltà da suoi superiori stessi . . .'. See also the *Ordini da Osservarsi da gl'Inquisitori, per Decreto della Sacra Congregatione del Sant'Officio di Roma*, dated 1611. A copy of a 1656 reprint is among the remains of the Holy Office of Florence formerly preserved in BRB, MS II. 290, vol. iv, fo. 1 (recently transferred to the State Archives). This document is one of the most comprehensive single statements I have seen on the regulation of convents housing inquisitorial establishments: '. . . che [inquisitors] esercitino l'officio loro con diligenza, ma con manco incommodo della disciplina Regolare che sia possibile, particolarmente nell'osservanza della clausura, che possano stare le porte de' conventi serrate, & gl'altri luoghi consueti, & che sotto ombra del Santo Officio

iracundiae, et s'ha altri indicii di mala vita di questo tale circa la santa fede perché queste circostanze sgravano assai il delitto . . .' Madness and anger were admissible as extenuating circumstances, but only after thorough investigation. See Carena, *Tractatus*, p. 281 '. . . Inquisitor non debet esse admodum facilis ad credendum excusationem desumptam ex ira . . .' On the release of a certain Antonio da Bassano 'in preda d'humor melanconico' by the Venetian inquisitor, see the letter of the nuncio, F. G. A. Facchinetti to M. Bonelli, dated 8 June 1566. *Nunziature di Venezia*, ed. Aldo Stella (Rome, 1963), viii. 59.

non si trasgredisca ogni ordine, & ogni legge, che si suol fare da superiori nell' haver tanti che gli servono, & si esentono dal Choro, da gli studii & da ogni obedientia, nel voler mantenere, o mantellare sotto l'ombra del Santo Officio ciascuno che pare. Però ogn'uno starà sotto l'obedienza de i Superiori, i quali ne potranno disporre come de gl'altri Frati, nel tempo che non saranno occupati nel servitio del Sant' Officio.'

B. Eymerich, *Directorium*, p. 446 (a 14th-c. compilation): 'Et sic concedentur sibi [to the suspect] advocatus, probus tamen, & de legalitate non suspectus, vir utriusque iuris peritus, & fidei zelator . . .' It is difficult to say how frequently defendants availed themselves of legal aid, since the majority of trials are no longer extant and I have not attempted a systematic search among the surviving records. There is evidence of its use in the famous trials of Pietro Carnesecchi. See Giacomo Manzoni (ed.), 'Estratto del Processo di Pietro Carnesecchi', *Miscellanea di storia italiana*, 10 (1870), 187–573, at p. 569, which mentions that several lawyers had been chosen by the defendant. More than one attorney, including Marc' Antonio Borghese, served Cardinal Giovanni Morone during his trial in the reign of Paul IV: Pastor, *Popes*, xiv. 305. A defence counsel was offered to the Frenchman Jean Dupuy at his trial in Turin in 1595: Bibliothèque nationale, Paris, Cod. Latinus 8994, fo. 389. The defence counsel assigned to Lisia Fileno, Ludovicus de Silvestris, doctor in both laws, during his Ferrarese trial (1540) curiously also served as one of the *consultori* pronouncing judgement in his case. See Antonio Rotondò (ed.), *Camillo Renato, opere, documenti e testimonianze* (Florence and Chicago, 1968), 188. And for an instance of legal aid to the indigent or lower classes in society, see n. 39, and the case of the celebrated Domenico Scandella, 'Menocchio', who enjoyed the services of an attorney at his first trial (1584): Carlo Ginzburg, *The Cheese and the Worms: The Cosmos of a Sixteenth-century Miller* (Baltimore, 1980), 7f. Even these bits of scattered evidence taken from printed sources disprove the modern scholars who continue to state that defence counsels did not operate in inquisitorial courts. With a Bull issued on 27 Aug. 1561, Pius IV reaffirmed the election of lawyers and notaries to defend cases before the tribunal of the Inquisition, *Regesti di bandi, editti, notificazioni e provvedimenti diversi relativi alla città di Roma ed allo Stato Pontificio, i (Anni 1234–1605)* (Rome, 1920), 32.

C. Albert C. Shannon, 'The Secrecy of Witnesses in Inquisitorial Tribunals and in Contemporary Secular Trials', in John Mundy (ed.), *Essays in Medieval Life and Thought Presented in Honor of Austin Patterson Evans* (New York, 1955), 59–69. The provision for the anonymity of witnesses, dating to 1254, was founded on the need to shield them from possible retaliation on the part of friends and family of the accused. This was not an idle pretext. See e.g. the violence worked by a powerful landholder of Imola, Roderico Alidosio, upon a vassal who had testified against him. The information is contained in a letter from Cardinal Millino of the Roman Congregation to the inquisitor of Florence, 7 Nov. 1609 (BRB, MS II. 290, vol. i, fo. 183: 'È venuto a notitia di questa Sacra Congregatione che detto Alidosio sotto vari pretesti ha fatto ritener carcerato per cinque mesi Anibale delle Vigne da Castel del Dio in vendetta di essersi essaminato contro di lui nel Sant'Officio, et che hora l'astringe a pagare 155 lire . . . per le spese mentre è stato ritenuto prigione . . .' For other cases of this type see Fumi, 'L'inquisizione Romana', p. 37. Jean-Pierre Dedieu, 'The Archives of the Holy Office of Toledo as a Source for Historical Ethnology', in G. Henningsen and J. Tedeschi, in association with Charles Amiel (eds.), *The Inquisition in Early Modern Europe*, questions the extent to which the names of prosecution witnesses remained concealed. This is an important question which calls for detailed study. The repeated reminders to provincial inquisitors that 'testium nomina publicari non debent' indicates that it must indeed have been difficult to observe the required anonymity. For a case where, contrary to correct procedure, the names of accusers and witnesses were communicated to the defendant—a priest charged with solicitation of sexual favours in the confessional— see the letter from the Roman Congregation of the Holy Office to the inquisitor of Verona, 23 May 1626 (BAV, Barb. lat. 6334, fo. 133): 'Non lascerò d'avvisarla che si sono maravigliati questi miei SS. ri Ill. mi che contra lo stile del Tribunale si siano manifestati al reo li nomi delle denuntianti et di testimonii, interrogandolo se conosce Francesca, Achillina, Agnes et se mai in confessione ha trattato con loro di cose dishoneste . . .' It would have been practically impossible to preserve the anonymity of the accusers when they and the accused belonged to the same family. A letter from the Holy Office in Rome to the inquisitor of Cremona (22 Aug. 1626) discusses the case of a certain Giovanni Paolo Resta who had aggravated his case by threatening the life of his father-in-law, who had denounced him as a blasphemer to the court (ibid., fo. 240ᵛ).

D. Unfortunately, there is nothing for Italy comparable to Paul W. Bamford's *Fighting Ships and Prisons: The Mediterranean Galleys of France in the Age of Louis XIV* (Minneapolis, 1973) or Ruth Pike's *Penal Servitude in Early Modern Spain* (Madison, 1983). Cf. Pike's 'Penal Servitude in Early Modern Spain: The Galleys', *Journal of European Economic History*, 2 (1982), 197–217. One can consult with great profit, however, the numerous studies on 16th-c. seafaring by Alberto Tenenti, e.g. his 'Gli schiavi di venezia alla fine del Cinquecento', *Rivista storica italiana*, 67 (1955), 52–69. An extremely important source for galley life in the 16th c. is Cristoforo Canale's *Della milizia marittima*, ed. Mario Nanni Mocenigo (Rome, 1930), written *c.*1540, a year or two before Venice changed from voluntary to largely convict labour on its galleys. This departure was conceived by Canale, *Provveditore Generale dell'Armata*, who died in combat with Barbary corsairs on 18 June 1562. On this brilliant naval theoretician, see A. Tenenti's *Cristoforo da Canal: La Marine vénitienne avant Lépante* (Paris, 1972). For the papal navy see Alberto Guglielmotti's *Storia della marina pontificia* (10 vols.; Rome, 1886), esp. vii. 195 ff. for regulation of convict life on the galleys, wardrobe, alimentation, dockside duties, etc. On the Turkish slaves who comprised a large percentage of the crews of the Christian vessels in the 16th and 17th c. and on the possibilities open to them of purchasing their freedom see Antonino Bertolotti, 'La schiavitù in Roma dal secolo XVI al XIX', *Rivista di discipline carcerarie*, 17 (1887), 3–41; Jean Mathieux, 'Trafic et prix de l'homme en Méditerranée aux XVIIe et XVIIIe siècles', *Annales ESC*, 9 (1954), 157–64. The best recent treatment is Andrea Viario, 'La pena della galera', in G. Cozzi (ed.), *Stato, società e giustizia nella repubblica veneta (sec. XV–XVIII)*, pp. 377–480.

E. TCD, MS 1226, fo. 316, sentence to three years in the galleys pronounced in Milan (13 Oct. 1581) against Giovanni Francesco Castiglione for blasphemy and sacrilege: '. . . che biastemando hai tagliato li piedi a una imagine d'uno crocifixo depinto . . . che hai gettato delli danari in faccia di detto crocifixo depinto, dicendo "piglia traditore" . . . che hai detto che non volevi più Iddio dalla tua parte, ma il demonio.' Individuals liable to the death penalty for heresies proscribed in the special decrees of Paul IV (see n. 92) frequently had their sentences reduced to terms of service on the galleys or imprisonment. See also TCD, MS 1228, fo. 218, sentence to seven years in the galleys ('remigando nel pane del dolore') pronounced in Rome against Guido Ricci da Monte Alcino for bigamy and the use of false witnesses. TCD, MS 1224, fo. 217, sentence against Jammone de Mina of Faenza, 'hortulano' (20 Sept. 1567)—he had repeatedly denied his heresies and finally confessed under torture; so that he might be an 'essempio alli ostinati et renitenti al confessare la verità, ti condenniamo alla galera per cinque anni'. TCD, MS 1224, fo. 211, sentence against Don Hieronymo del Pozzo, priest of Faenza (20 Sept. 1567), who escaped the galleys because of a physical disability: '. . . meritando tu grandissima pena per essere sacerdote . . . attesa l'infirmità tua ti condenniamo ad essere immurato perpetuamente'. TCD, MS 1225, fo. 294, sentence to seven years in the Venetian galleys pronounced at Verona on 11 Sept. 1580 against Giacomo dell'Amingella da Brenzon, a bigamist, who 'più volte hai tentato di fugire rompendo le carcere'; the fact that the accused had attempted flight on one occasion or another is mentioned in many galley sentences. TCD, MS 1227, fo. 139, sentence dated 31 May 1582 against Joannes Pilutius de Castro Julianelli, condemned to seven years of galley service for the unjust prosecution of four women 'sub praetextu quod essent striges'. Pastor, 'Dekrete', p. 531, decree of the Roman Congregation, dated 25 May 1593: 'Illmi etc. decreverunt et declaraverunt quod decretum alias die 19 septembris 1591 habitum quod fratres ordinis Minorum de Observantia reperti culpabiles in materia nicromantiae condemnentur ad triremes per decennium, stare et intelligi debeat ita, ut usque ad talem poenam inclusive damnari possint plus et minus iuxta delictorum, personarum, locorum et temporum scandalique resultantis et aliarum circumstantiarum qualitatem, dummodo talis poena non excedatur.'

F.   '. . . licet enim cum ita res haec celebratur in Hispania, videre, horrendum, ac tremendum spectaculum, & quasi imaginem futuri iudicii, quo nihil esse potest ad terrorem incutiendum in hac causa aptius et accomodatius . . .': F. Peña's account in N. Eymerich, *Directorium*, p. 512. See also Bodl. MS Mendham 36, fos. 235–6, an undated description of a Madrid *auto* carried out among the screams of a frenzied crowd ('burn them alive'), the rolling of drums, the crack of musket fire, the clashing of metal, the barking of dogs, themselves hurled on the flames with a woman accused of bestiality. For an Italian description, where the platform intended to seat the members of the Holy Office collapsed under their weight, inspiring the victim to shout 'Behold God's judgement', see esp. the vivid contemporary account in the *Avvisi di Roma* cited by Pio Paschini, 'Episodi dell'inquisizione a Roma nei suoi primi decenni', *Studi romani*, 5 (1957), 292 f.: 'È stato brusciato questi di un gentil-huomo piemontese di Cunio, il quale è stato lungamente in Calabria, ove ha seminato la heresia lutherana, et è stato fatt'ogni possibile per farlo rivocare, d'un suo fratello ed d'altri suoi parenti venuti a posta di Piemonte per questo, ma non ha mai voluto moversi della sua opinione, et cosi è morto costantissimamente, et inanti la morte sua essendosi fatto un palco, sopra il quale erano i R. mi Alessandrino, Carpi, Araceli, Reumano, et volendovi anche montare il R. mo di Queva [all Cardinals of the Inquisition], cadette il palco, pur nisuno si fece male, et allora vedendo quello il condannato, cominciò a cridar che questo era giudicio di Idio.' Numerous accounts of these events, both published and unpublished, have survived. For a partial listing, see van der Vekene, *Bibliotheca bibliographica historiae Sanctae Inquisitionis* i. 151–253.

II
ORIGINS OF THE WITCHES' SABBATH

4

Deciphering the Sabbath *

CARLO GINZBURG

THE theme of witchcraft in Europe, formerly considered marginal and even frivolous, has in the last fifteen years become a subject of international discussion among historians. However, few of the numerous studies have devoted much attention to the sabbath—the nocturnal meeting of witches and sorcerers—although it is clearly of decisive importance in the history of witchcraft and witch-hunting. The principal exception is Norman Cohn's work *Europe's Inner Demons* (1975), which makes two main points: (1) The picture of the sabbath which took shape in the first decades of the fifteenth century was a modern elaboration, by lay and ecclesiastical judges and demonologists, of an aggressive stereotype that had been applied in former times to Jews, the early Christians, and medieval heretical sects; (2) There was no ritual reality corresponding to this image. The nocturnal assemblies described with so much macabre and picturesque detail in the trials and treatises of demonology were—like the sect of witches and wizards who supposedly took part in them—a projection of the fears and obsessions of judges and inquisitors.

I shall revert presently to the second point, based on an examination of the old theses of Margaret Murray (*The Witch-cult in Western Europe* (1921)). The first point seems to me unacceptable, since it postulates the continuity and homogeneity of a stereotype which in fact underwent radical modification at a particular time owing to the introduction of different elements belonging either to the world of scholarship or to that of folklore. All this suggests that the sabbath is to be regarded as a culturally mixed phenomenon rather than a mere projection of the dominant culture.

The main components of the stereotype as described by Cohn are sexual orgies, cannibalism, and the worship of a bestial divinity. But

* This paper is a summary, provisional in some respects, of the conclusions of several years' research: see now Carlo Ginzburg, *Storia notturna: Una decifrazione del sabba* (Torino, 1989).

apart from the chronological hiatus between the beginning of the eighth century and the end of the eleventh,[1] the documentary evidence on which this interpretation is founded presents a still more glaring discontinuity as regards content. The anthropophagy attributed to medieval heretical sects was a sort of endo-cannibalistic ritual wherein the children of incestuous unions were devoured at nocturnal meetings.[2] The image of the witch pursuing the children or adults of a community in order to eat them or make them fall sick is very different and much more directly aggressive. To discover how it can have come into being, I propose to analyse a body of evidence differing from that presented by Cohn.

We may begin with the rumour which spread in France during the summer of 1321, that lepers had conspired to poison wells and rivers. This charge was almost immediately extended to the Jews, who were accused of having instigated the lepers, sometimes at the behest of the Muslim rulers of Granada and Tunis. In this way the pre-existing notion·of an enemy within, the accomplice and instrument of an external enemy, led to a ferocious persecution which was the first of its kind in European history. An examination of chronicles, confessions extracted by torture, and deliberately fabricated evidence leads to the certain conclusion that two plots were brewed in France at that time by the lay and ecclesiastical authorities: one against the lepers, and the other, immediately afterwards, against the Jews. After burnings at the stake and other massacres, lepers were segregated and Jews expelled. Both measures were advocated, some months before the discovery of the alleged plot, in a letter addressed to Philip V of France by the consuls of the seneschalsy of Carcassonne.[3]

---

[1] Viz. from John of Ojun's sermon against the Paulicians of Armenia to the charges against the heretics of Orleans collected to Adhémar de Chabannes (cf. Norman Cohn, *Europe's Inner Demons* (London, 1975), 18 ff.). The proof that the dialogue *On the Operation of Demons*, attributed to Michael Psellus, was in fact written at least two centuries later (cf. Philippe Gautier, 'Le "De daemonibus" du Pseudo-Psellos', *Revue des études byzantines*, 38 (1980), 105–94, esp. 131) implies, if I am not mistaken, the possibility that it was also influenced by anti-heretical Western stereotypes, rather than the other way round.

[2] The charge levelled by John of Ojun (*Domini Johannis Philosophi Ozniensis Armeniorum Catholici Opera*, ed. G. B. Aucher (Venice, 1834), 85 ff.) is repeated more or less literally by Flavio Biondo in a celebrated passage against the Fraticelli (*Italia illustrata* (Verona, 1482), fo. E^{r–v}).

[3] Malcolm Barber, 'The Plot to overthrow Christendom in 1321', *History*, 66 (1981), 1–17; also the documents analysed by Robert Anchel, *Les Juifs en France* (Paris, 1946), 79–91, and V. R. Rivière-Chalan, *La Marque infâme des lépreux et des christians sous l'Ancien Régime* (Paris, 1978).

In 1347, at a time when the Black Death was raging in Europe, an accusation similar to that of 1321 again emanated from Carcassonne. This time, according to the authorities, it was only the Jews who had poisoned the waters to spread the plague. Once again, the conspiracy was discovered by torture and as a result of persecuting the Jewish communities of the Dauphiné and regions around Lake Geneva.[4] But in the same area, some decades later, in 1409, the Inquisition accused Jewish and Christian groups of jointly practising rites that were 'contrary to Christian faith'. This enigmatic description probably referred to the notion of the diabolical sabbath that begins to take shape in the *Formicarius*, a treatise by the Dominican Johannes Nider, written in 1437 during the Council of Basle, and based on facts concerning witch-trials that he had been informed of by the inquisitor at Evian and a judge from Berne. Nider stated that in the past sixty years or so a new form of sorcery had arisen: a sect in the full sense, with a ritual involving devil-worship and profanation of the Cross and the sacraments. This chronological evidence is corroborated from the other side of the Alps: at the beginning of the sixteenth century, the Dominican inquisitor Bernardo da Como writes that it appears from the record of trials in the archives of the local Inquisition that the sect of witches had originated some 150 years earlier.[5]

Thus the picture of the sabbath took shape in the Western Alps about the middle of the fourteenth century, half a century earlier than the date traditionally accepted by scholars. More important than the earlier dating, however, is the 'lepers–Jews–witches' gradation that emerges from our reconstruction. The creation of the image of a sect of witchcraft, additional to that of isolated witches and warlocks, must be regarded as a separate chapter—destined to be a most important one—of the segregation or expulsion of marginal groups which characterized European society from the fourteenth

---

[4] Jacob Twinges von Königshoven, *Die alteste Teutsche so wol Allgemeine als insonderheit Elsassische und Strassburgische Chronicke*... (Strasburg, 1698), 1029–48. On the beginnings of the persecutions, cf. J. Shatzmiller, 'Les Juifs en Provence pendant la peste noire', *Revue des études juives*, 133 (1974), 457–80. For their cultural background, cf. S. Guerchberg, 'La Controverse sur les prétendus semeurs de la peste noire d'après les traités de peste de l'époque', ibid. 108 (1948), 3–40.

[5] L. Wadding, *Annales Minorum*, 9 (Rome, 1734), 327–9; J. Nider, *Formicarius*, i. 5, ch. 4 (repr. in *Malleus quorundam maleficarum*..., vol. ii, pt. ii (Frankfurt, 1582). For the date of the work, cf. K. Schieler, *Magister Johannes Nider*... (Mainz, 1885), 379 n. 5. Cohn (*Europe's Inner Demons*, p. 145) rejects the statement by Bernardo da Como, overlooking the fact that it agrees with Nider's indications.

century onwards. It is also an instructive event from the theoretical point of view. Initially it stemmed from a deliberate political intention, or even a plot (cf. those of 1321), which was assured of success by a prompt popular response. But the successive links in this chain make it impossible to speak of a plot. The schema of a hostile group conspiring against society was progressively renewed at all levels, but directed against targets that could not have been foreseen. The prodigious trauma of the great pestilences intensified the search for a scapegoat on which fears, hatred, and tension of all kinds could be discharged. The supposed nocturnal meetings of witches and wizards, who came flying from far away to brew their diabolical schemes, embodied the image of an organized, omnipresent enemy with superhuman powers.

As we know, witches and wizards flew to the sabbath, sometimes in animal form or riding on animals. These two elements of flight and metamorphosis were not part of the aggressive stereotype concerning the sect of well-poisoners. They are first heard of in 1428, in certain witch-trials at Sion in the Valais and at Todi (we shall come back to this synchronism later). That these themes originated in folklore has long been known, but scholars have never gone beyond this evident fact. Certain popular beliefs, antedating the sabbath proper but linked to it in many respects, provide us with a clue.

The best-documented case is that of the Friulian *benandanti*. These persons, denounced by their fellow-villagers in about 1570, told the inquisitors that during the year, when the Ember Days came round, they fell into a sort of trance. Some of them, mostly men, said that they then went fighting in far-off places, 'in the spirit' or in a dream, armed with stalks of fennel; their adversaries were witches and wizards, armed with sorghum stalks, and they were fighting for the fertility of the fields. Others, mostly women, said that, either 'in the spirit' or in a dream, they witnessed processions of the dead. All those questioned attributed their extraordinary powers to the fact that they were born with a caul. The inquisitors, having overcome their first astonishment, tried to make the *benandanti* confess that they were sorcerers and had taken part in a witches' sabbath. Under this pressure the *benandanti* altered their story by degrees so that eventually—but more than fifty years later—it conformed to the stereotype of the sabbath, which had not previously figured in the proceedings of the Friulian Inquisition.

The inquisitors' reaction is very understandable. The nocturnal excursions of the *benandanti* were preceded by a kind of trance which left the body as if dead, after which the spirit left it in the form of an animal (a mouse or butterfly) or riding on an animal (a hare, dog, pig, or the like). This clearly suggested the animal metamorphoses attributed to witches on their way to the sabbath. The evident analogy can be interpreted from a different point of view than the inquisitors'. In *I benandanti* (1966) I pointed out that in the case of witches as well as of *benandanti*, 'that state of lethargy—provoked by the use of sleep-inducing ointments or by a catalepsis of an unknown nature—was sought after as the ideal way to reach the mysterious and otherwise unattainable world of the dead, of those spirits that wandered over the face of the earth without hope of peace.' In my opinion it is here that we should seek the underlying unity of the myth of the *benandanti*, looking beyond the agrarian and the funeral versions. The sorcerers who are enemies of the fertility of the fields reflect the ancient notion of the unappeased dead; the processions of the dead are already a partially Christian image, similar to that of the souls in Purgatory. In either case the *benandanti*, men or women, appear as professional intermediaries between the community and the realm of the dead. My conclusion was that:

Such phenomena as trances, journeys into the beyond astride animals or in the form of animals . . . to recover seed grain or to assure the fertility of the land, and . . . participation in processions of the dead (which procured prophetic and visionary powers for the *benandanti*) form a coherent pattern which immediately evokes the rites of the shamans.[6]

When writing the above words I confined myself to suggesting, without elaborating, the analogy between *benandanti* and shamans:[7] the distance between Friuli and Siberia seemed altogether too great. But I now believe that the disconcerting heterogeneity of culture, space, and time between these realities can be offset by morphological research, the results of which may in the future serve as a guide to historical reconstruction.

Wittgenstein, when proposing the idea of 'perspicuous presentation' (*übersichtliche Darstellung*) as an alternative to Frazer's genetic explanations, emphasized the need to find 'intermediate links'.[8] In our case this implies the adoption of a firmly comparativist point of view.

---

[6] Carlo Ginzburg, *I benandanti: Stregoneria e culti agrari tra Cinquecento e Seicento* (Turin, 1966), 91 and 51–2; Engl. trans. *The Night Battles: Witchcraft and Agrarian Cults in the Sixteenth and Seventeenth Centuries* (London, 1983), 59 and 32.

[7] Ginzburg, *I benandanti*, p. xiii; *The Night Battles*, p. xxi n. 14.

[8] Ludwig Wittgenstein, *Remarks on Frazer's 'Golden Bough'* (London, 1979), 9.

As regards the 'funeral' *benandanti* who, in a dream, witness the processions of the dead, two similarities or connections immediately suggest themselves. Firstly, with evidence concerning the myth of the 'furious horde' or 'wild hunt' (*wütischend Heer, wilde Jagd, mesnie sauvage*, etc.), or the spirits of the dead, usually conducted by a male deity such as Herlechinus, Odin, Herod, or Arthur. Secondly, with stories (especially the famous *Canon episcopi*) of women dreaming of flying by night, mounted on animals, in the train of Diana, 'paganorum dea', or other female divinities (Holda, Perchta, Herodias, etc.). All this adds up to a fairly substantial dossier, essentially Franco-German, but with an important extension to the Po valley. Originally the material I was able to collect on the theme of battles for fertility was meagre and more dispersed. As a parallel to the *benandanti* I was able to find only the Dalmatian *kersniki* and the case, which appears to be exceptional, of an old werewolf brought to justice in Livonia at the end of the seventeenth century. But the second dossier expands in its turn to include a number of characters well-rooted in European folklore: the Balkan *zduhači*, the Hungarian *táltos*, the Corsican *mazzeri*, the Ossetian *burkudzäutä*, Baltic werewolves, shamans of Lapland (*noai'di*) and of Siberia.[9] What is the common feature of these beings (who are deliberately mentioned here in no particular order)?

To begin with, they are certainly intermediaries between the world of the living and that of the dead, to which they are given access in an ecstatic trance. But an answer of this kind may be misleading, especially in view of the inclusion of shamans in this variegated list. It might be thought that the connecting link between all these figures is

[9] On *zduhači* and *táltosok* see the excellent essay by Gábor Klaniczay, 'Benandante-kresnik–zduhač–táltos', *Ethnographia*, 94 (1983), 116–33; thanks to the author's kindness I have been able to read an English trans. of the Hungarian text (now published as 'Shamanistic Elements in Central European Witchcraft', in Mihály Hoppal (ed.), *Shamanism in Eurasia* (Göttingen, 1984), 404–22). On the *mazzeri*, cf. Georges Ravis-Giordani, 'Signes, figures et conduites de l'entre-vie et mort: *Finzione, mazzeri, et streie corses*', *Études corses*, 12–13 (1979), 361ff. (where the analogy with the *benandanti* is discussed). On the *burkudzäutä*, cf. Georges Dumézil, *Le Problème des centaures* (Paris, 1929), pp. 91–3. There is a large bibliography on werewolves; as to the link with persons born with a caul (like the *benandanti*), see the excellent essay by Roman Jakobson and Marc Szeftel, 'The Vseslav Epos', *Memoirs of the American Folklore Society*, 42 (1947), 13–86, and Roman Jakobson and G. Ružičić, 'The Serbian *Zmaj Ognjeni Vuk* and the Russian Vseslav Epos', *Annuaire de l'institut de philologie et d'histoire orientale et slave*, 10 (1950), 343–55. On the *noai'di*, see esp. T. I. Itkonen, 'Der "Zweikampf" der lappischen Zauberer', *Journal de la société finno-ougrienne*, 62 (1960), fasc. 3, pp. 3–73. On the mythical battles of shamans, cf. László Vajda, 'Zur phaseologischen Stellung des Schamanismus', *Ural-Altaische Jahrbücher*, 31 (1959), 456–85, esp. 471–3.

purely (and generically) a typological one: after all, mediators between this world and the next, or 'shamans' in the vague sense, have been found in the most various cultures.[10] The resemblance that I have pointed out, on the other hand, is a specific one, as is the reference to the shamans of Eurasia—which, it may be remarked, has already been proposed for several of these figures, in particular the *táltos*.[11] It is a resemblance which does not even exclude real and precise superpositions, but is not based on them. For instance, the fact that in Friuli individuals born with a caul were regarded as future *benandanti*, and that among the Yurak Samoyeds of Siberia they are regarded as future shamans,[12] might be interpreted as a superficial coincidence. But it takes on its full value within a profound isomorphism embracing phenomena scattered over a huge geographical area, of which we have information dating from remote antiquity (Herodotus already mentions belief in werewolves among the Neuri). (See Endnote A.)

We cannot here go into the detail of this isomorphism, but it will suffice for the moment to point out that the existence of a deep-seated connection makes it possible to consider variants that are apparently diverse. Thus persons who are destined to undertake the ecstatic voyage are those born with some physical peculiarity (with a caul, like the *benandanti*, or with teeth, like the *táltos*), or at a particular time of year (the twelve days during which the dead were thought most likely to roam); or again, persons who have passed certain initiatory tests. They usually make the journey riding on animals or in animal form, but also sometimes on broomsticks (of course), or other modes of conveyance such as ears of corn, benches, or stools (among the Ossetes, or at Mirandola near Modena). During their ecstasy they fight against beings with diverse names (nearly always sorcerers or spirits of the dead) for various purposes: to ensure a good harvest, to conquer disease, or to scan the future. Their powers are known to their fellow-humans, but—except in the case of the shamans—the ecstatic journey is made in private rather than in public.[13]

---

[10] e.g. in certain African cultures: cf. Marc Augé, *Génie du paganisme* (Paris, 1982), 253.

[11] Cf. in particular the research by G. Róheim and V. Diószegi, cited and commented on by Klaniczay in 'Benandante–kresnik . . .', *passim*. My hypothesis on the relation between *benandanti* and shamans was subsequently confirmed by Mircea Éliade, 'Some Observations on European Witchcraft', *History of Religions*, 14 (1975), 149–72, esp. 153–8.

[12] Toivo Lehtisalo, *Entwurf einer Mythologie der Jurak-Samojeden* (Helsinki, 1924), 114. On persons born with a caul, cf., from a different view, Nicole Belmont, *Les Signes de la naissance* (Paris, 1971).

[13] G. Klaniczay rightly emphasizes this last point in 'Benandante–kresnik . . .'. The

These distinctive traits form a mythic combination that is clearly recognizable. We can discern fragments of it in trials for witchcraft, even at a late date, when we encounter what appear to be extravagant details alien to the demonological stereotypes—as when a Scottish witch in 1662 speaks of flying to the sabbath mounted on a straw or a beanstalk.[14] Conversely, even in fairly early evidence, we can perceive, grafted on to the substratum of popular belief, elements belonging to the stereotype of the sabbath: the presence of the devil, the profanation of the sacraments, or the negative transformation of beneficent or neutral figures such as werewolves. It is indeed clear that in this field the absolute dating of the sources (penitentials, annals, trials, etc.) is not necessarily identical with the relative dating of the phenomena they mention or describe. The consequences for research are evident. Chronology (one of the eyes of history, to use an antique metaphor) proves to be more or less unusable; so we must have recourse to the other eye, geography, reinforced by morphology. In other words, as far as this mythical, pre-sabbath level is concerned, historical research much endeavour to place in a temporal sequence the spatial dispersion of data, having first collated them according to morphological affinity.

Given a mythical complex that has left traces from Scotland to the Caucasus and from the Mediterranean to Siberia, any attempt at interpretation seems extremely hazardous. We may begin by citing the alternatives that are theoretically possible. The analogies that exist may be attributed (1) to chance; (2) to the necessity imposed by mental structures common to the human species; (3) to diffusion; or (4) to a common genetic source. This corresponds to the enumeration used by Dumézil over thirty years ago when presenting his research on the tripartite Indo-European ideology.[15] After discussing and rejecting the first three possibilities, Dumézil opted for the last. We may follow his conclusions, but only up to a certain point, since, as we shall soon see, the data of our problem are very different from his.

reference to Mirandola is from G. F. Pico, *Strix sive de ludificatione daemonum* (Bologna, 1523), fo. D V[r].

[14] R. Pitcairn, *Ancient Criminal Trials in Scotland* (Edinburgh, 1833), iii. II. 603–4 ('Confessions of Issobell Gowdie'). The author remarks with understandable emphasis (p. 604 n. 7): 'The above details are, perhaps, in all respects, the most extraordinary in the history of witchcraft of this or of any other country. Any comment would only weaken the effect of such very remarkable descriptions.'

[15] Georges Dumézil, *Leçon inaugurale*, delivered on Thur. 1 Dec. 1949 at the Collège de France, chair of Indo-European civilization (Nogent-le-Rotrou, 1950).

Hypothesis (1) can in any case be ruled out: the convergences are too many and too complex to be put down to chance. I would also firmly exclude hypothesis (2), in all its possible formulations. 'Mental structures' may be taken as meaning either psychological archetypes, possibly conceived as a reflection of ontological structures, or dispositions of a formal character. But the mythical complex we are speaking of presents too many variants to be identified with supposed but unprovable archetypes, and too many specific coincidences to be identified in terms of a formal disposition. We are thus left with the third and fourth possibilities: diffusion or a common genetic source.

Dumézil's choice of the latter option was clearly based on the parallelism with the proved derivation of European languages from a previously existing language (which may have first divided into dialects). This parallelism would fall to the ground if the tripartite ideology were also met with outside the Indo-European area. Dumézil sharply opposed any contention that this was so, using arguments that I am unfortunately not able to judge.[16] But in our case the area involved is not only very large but is linguistically heterogeneous, as it includes speakers not only of Indo-European languages but also of Uralian (Lappish, Hungarian) and Altaic ones (Tunguz, etc.). This being so, how plausible are the hypotheses of diffusion and of a common source?

We may say at once that neither can be summarily dismissed. The theory of diffusion no doubt rests on linguistic parallelism, that is to say the fact of borrowings, in both directions, between Indo-European and non-Indo-European languages. Such borrowings, either in the historical or the proto-historical period, might well have been accompanied by the transmission of mythical complexes such as that we are concerned with. The very close resemblance between Friulian *benandanti* and Ossetian *burkudzäutä* is surprising in view of the geographical and cultural distance, even though both belong to the Indo-European language area. But the existence of Ossetian loan-words in Hungarian may suggest a chain extending from the Caucasus to Friuli and comprising similar morphological phenomena such as the Friulian *benandanti*, the Balklan *zduhači*, the Hungarian *táltos*, and the Ossetian *burkudzäutä*. On the basis of such reasoning and the valuable evidence provided by linguistic borrowings we might seek to

[16] John Brough, 'The Tripartite Ideology of the Indo-Europeans: An Experiment in Method', *Bulletin of the School of Oriental and African Studies*, 23 (1959), 69–85; Georges Dumézil, *Mythe et épopée* (3 vols.; Paris, 1973), iii, app. 3.

link, one after the other, all the points on the globe that we have briefly mentioned, beginning with culturally contiguous areas such as Lapland and Siberia, Friuli and Dalmatia, and so on. It is not, of course, necessary to postulate a unique source of diffusion.

From all that is said above, it is clear that the diffusion hypothesis is based on numerous facts but an equally large number of conjectures. The alternative hypothesis of a common genetic source is certainly more economical, but involves a linguistic base that is also more evidently conjectural. Linguists have long argued as to the possibility of proving, by a comparison between Indo-European and Uralian languages, the prior existence of an Indo-Uralian linguistic community.[17] But this hypothesis, even in such prudent versions as that of B. Collinder,[18] has aroused much criticism and is far from being generally accepted. Even if it were proved, this would not be proof of the origin of the myths of shamanist inspiration, with regard to which we spoke of a cultural stratum antedating the differentiation of the languages of Eurasia, though such origin would then at least be historically plausible. Like all simple hypotheses this one is extremely attractive, but it is at present a hypothesis and no more.

The divergence between the two hypotheses relates only to the manner and time of the process of transmission, which, on the diffusion hypothesis, might have continued until relatively recent times. But whether we opt for diffusion or a common source, the origin of these myths must in all probability be referred to a very distant, proto-historic period. This antiquity seems to be confirmed by the fact that they coincide with the central core of the fairy-tale genre.

Vladimir Propp, at the end of his *Morphology of the Folktale* (1928), posed the question whether the unexpected discovery of an underlying structure common to all fairy-tales would imply that they derived from a single source. He commented that: 'The morphologist is not entitled to reply to this question. He must pass on his conclusions to the historian, or else become a historian himself.' Propp, as we know, was to adopt the second course. But in the last pages of the *Morphology* he already anticipated the direction his research would take: the 'single source' of fairy-tales was not to be sought in a geographical or psychological domain, but in a central core of religious representa-

---

[17] Aulí Johannes Joki, *Uralier und Indogermanen* (Helsinki, 1973).
[18] Björn Collinder, *Sprachverwandtschaft und Wahrscheinlichkeit*, ed. B. Wickman (Uppsala, 1964).

tions. He added a 'small example of a parallel between fairy-tale and belief':

> In the stories, Ivan [i.e. the hero] is transported through the air by three fundamental types of mount or vehicle: a flying horse, a bird, or a flying ship. But these are precisely the same as those which carry the souls of the dead— the horse being usual with herdsmen and farmers, the eagle with hunters, and the ship with dwellers on sea-coasts.

This in fact was neither a small example nor a random one, for, very soon afterwards, Propp was to formulate—though still necessarily in a conjectural manner—the central thesis of his work on *The Historical Roots of the Fairy-tale* (1946): 'It may thus be accepted that one of the primary elements in fairy-tales, that of a miraculous voyage, is a reflection of the religious concept of souls travelling to the next world.'[19] The fundamental historical nucleus of the structure found in fairy-tales is to be sought here. But in the *Morphology* Propp discovers that this structure implies the presence of two functions that are almost always mutually exclusive: (1) the fight with an antagonist and the victory over him; (2) the difficult task and its accomplishment. In the few cases where both are present, (1) always precedes (2). Hence a further hypothesis: 'It is very possible that historically both types existed, that each had its own history, and that in a distant past two traditions met and fused together.'[20] In *Roots*, however, Propp dwells almost exclusively on the relation between fairy-tales and initiation rites (function (2)). The research on the sabbath, the conclusions of which are summarized here, also throws light on the mythic-religious core of the past (battles fought in a state of trance against the souls of the dead) elaborated in function (1). More generally, this research illustrates the decisive importance, traceable over a very large cultural area, of the image of the traveller, male or female, in a trance in the world of the dead, in relation to the genesis and transmission of the narrative structure—perhaps more ancient and certainly more durable—elaborated by the human species. All this makes it possible to supplement with strictly historical data the too rigorously evolutionist typology indicated by Propp in *Roots*. But the tribute paid by Propp—whether sincerely or not is hard to say—to the then dominant Stalinist orthodoxy does not detract from the genius of his luminous work, indissolubly linked with the *Morphology* written twenty years

[19] Propp, *Morphologie du conte*, pp. 178ff.
[20] Ibid., p. 173.

earlier in the atmosphere of formalist research. The link between morphology and history that Propp specifically proposes in these two works is an example of incalculable fruitfulness.

Thus the stereotype of the sabbath represents a fusion of two distinct images. The first, a product of the learned culture (judges, inquisitors, demonologists), centred on the supposed existence of a hostile sect, inspired by the devil, members of which had to renounce their faith and profane the Cross and sacraments. The second image, rooted in folk-culture, was based on belief in the extraordinary powers of particular men and women who—in a state of trance, and often in animal form or riding upon animals—travelled to the realm of the dead in order to bring prosperity to the community. As we have seen, this second image was much older than the first, and infinitely more widespread. Both took shape in the Western Alps shortly after 1350. It is very possible that the convergence between these widely different cultural complexes was facilitated by the presence of heretical Vaudois (Waldensian) groups in the same area at the same time. The original doctrines of these groups had long been mingled with local folk traditions and dualistic beliefs of the Catharist type from East Central Europe, which lent themselves to being interpreted as devil-worship.[21] The intervention of inquisitors brought all these scattered elements to the point of fusion, and so the sabbath myth was born.

After fusion, diffusion. Besides inquisitors, judges, and demon-ologists, the process was aided by preachers, especially S. Bernardino da Siena. The latter's sermons on 'enchantment, witches and spells' at first met with incredulity in Rome: as he said later on, 'my words made them think I was dreaming.' But trials and burnings of witches were to follow without delay. The records of the Roman trials have not survived; but the trial of Matteuccia di Francesco at Todi in 1428, two years after S. Bernardino's sermons in that town, shows clearly how the idea of the sabbath, which had already crystallized despite its novelty, had merged with an old system of magic beliefs. After a long enumeration of curative and amatory spells, Matteuccia confessed that she had turned herself into a fly by means of an ointment made from the blood of newborn infants, and had been carried to the walnut-tree at Benevento by a demon in the form of a he-goat.[22]

---

[21] Cf. Grado G. Merlo's fine work, *Eretici e inquisitori nella società piemontese del '300* (Turin, 1977).

[22] Giovanni Miccoli, 'La storia religiosa', in *Storia d'Italia*, ii. 1 (Turin, 1974), 815–16; Domenico Mammoli, *Processo alla strega Matteuccia di Francesco, 20 marzo 1428* (Todi, 1983).

Probably the Todi magistrates had obtained, by violence and pressure, a full confirmation of what S. Bernardino's preaching led them to expect. He himself, as he tells us, gained his information from other Franciscans who had been at work in Piedmont: this explains how the idea of the sabbath developed simultaneously in the Western Alps and at Todi.[23]

For the next two and a half centuries the trials for sorcery that took place all over Europe were full of confessions similar to that of Matteuccia and basically stereotyped, though often embellished with details from local tradition. But it must not be thought that the sabbath idea developed with the same rapidity everywhere. At the end of the fifteenth century, the authors of the famous *Malleus maleficarum* had no more to relate on the subject of diabolical assemblies than what Nider had learnt from his informants at Evian and Berne:[24] they were, that is to say, unable to add anything to a dossier already fifty years old. At the end of the sixteenth century, resistance to the inquisitors' pressure by the *benandanti* shows that the image of the sabbath which had come into existence about two centuries earlier at the other extremity of the Alpine chain had still not made its mark on Friulian folklore. In general the European geography of the diffusion of the sabbath idea is extremely variable, with many gaps and time-differences: among the former we may notice (save for a few exceptions) the case of England.

We have seen that the stereotype of the sabbath included elements, such as flight through the air and the assumption of animal form, which, although re-elaborated in a symbolic context different from the original one, clearly originate from a stratum of folk-culture. In some cases the modification to which they are subjected is very slight or completely absent, so that we may discern more or less extensive fragments of this stratum, otherwise totally covered.

But if the stereotype of the sabbath cannot be wholly ascribed to the fears and obsessions of judges and inquisitors, may not the descriptions of witches' meetings contain at least some traces of real events? Murray answered this question in the affirmative, while silently eliminating from the descriptions those elements which most evidently belonged to folklore, particularly flying and the transformation

---

[23] Cf. S. Bernardino da Siena, *Le Prediche volgare . . . dette nella piazza del Campo l'anno MCCCCXXVIII*, ed. L. Banchi, ii (Siena, 1884), 356–7.

[24] J. Sprenger, *Malleus maleficarum* (Venice, 1574), 174 ff.

into an animal.[25] This unscholarly procedure was justly rebuked by subsequent critics. But from the point of view we have adopted here, endeavouring to reconstruct an element of pure folklore underlying the inquisitors' schema, the aspects ignored by Murray are precisely the most interesting. They relate, for instance, to the typically pre-sabbath theme of the procession of the dead (the 'wild hunt' or 'furious horde'). The very full dossier produced by a century of research on this subject includes extracts from penitentials of the high Middle Ages, records of trials, sagas, and even descriptions of rites still surviving in contemporary folklore, in which individuals disguised as animals run about village streets, generally during the 'twelve days'. It has been held with some reason that these rites are closely connected with the myth of the 'wild army', with the disguised individuals personifying, or having personified, the assemblage of the errant dead. But clearly this does not permit us to interpret retrospectively *all* the accounts which speak of processions of the dead, as descriptions of real events indicating the persistence of a very ancient ritual, performed by groups of young people in cultic associations with a warlike background. This was nevertheless maintained by Otto Höfler in his *Kultische Geheimbünde der Germanen* (1934), a work which, unlike Murray's, continues to be accepted as a standard authority, even by scholars of the first rank. (Murray's work is today discredited, but Höfler cited it with significant approval.)[26]

Höfler's view is rather open to the same objection as Murray's, namely, that it rests on a gross confusion between myths and rites. In Höfler's case the implications are far from innocent: the ritual continuity between the *Harii* described by Tacitus, the Icelandic *berserkir*, and the processions of groups of young men disguised as animals fits in with the exaltation of the 'ecstatic cult of the German religion of the

---

[25] Margaret Alice Murray, *The Witch-cult in Western Europe* (London, 1921).

[26] A very favourable review was published by Karl Meuli in *Archives suisses de traditions populaires*, 34 (1935), 77 (followed, some years later, by a more cautious critical judgement in his *Gesammelte Schriften*, i. 227 n. 3). See also Stig Wikander, *Der arische Männerbund* (Lund, 1938); Georges Dumézil, *Mythes et dieux des Germains* (Paris, 1939). Among the few dissenting voices was that of Friedrich Ranke, who suggested that the medieval and post-medieval evidence concerning the assembly of the dead was merely an expression of morbid psychological states (Ranke, 'Das Wilde Heer und die Kultbünde der Germanen', (1940), now in his *Kleine Schriften*, ed. H. Rupp and E. Studer (Berne, 1971), 380–408). This is clearly absurd, no less unacceptable than Höfler's theory, though for quite different reasons. Höfler confirmed his former view in *Verwandlungskulte, Volkssagen und Mythen* (Oesterreichische Akademie der Wissenschaften, Phil.-Hist. Kl., Sitzungsberichte, vol. cclxxix, treatise 2; Vienna, 1973).

dead', and communion with the dead as a unique source of social and tribal energy.[27] This theory, with its unmistakably Nazi overtones, so dominated Höfler's research that it led him to depreciate the connotations of fertility that were part of this mythic complex, and to exalt those which related to warfare.[28] But this distortion is part of a more general methodological error: that of reducing to pure coincidence the complicated relationship between myths and rites. This is the more grave since, as we have said, it is only in the case of the shamans (which Höfler more or less ignores) that the journey to the world of the dead is preceded by a genuine public rite. The ecstatic trance into which the disciplines of Diana, the *benandanti* and others claimed to fall was, as far as we know, a purely private event.

All this does not exclude the possibility of proving the existence of ritual practices linked to the mythic complex of which we have spoken. It is certain, however, that research in this direction will have to make use of less rudimentary means of interpretation and analytical categories than those so far employed.

The conclusions summarized here relate only to the composite mythical structure which can be discerned in descriptions of the sabbath. I am of course well aware that my capacity, linguistic and otherwise, is inadequate to the extent and complexity of the subject-matter. But the chronological and geographical diffusion of accounts of the sabbath, and their stereotyped character, poses questions which one can only attempt to answer by means of a global interpretation. One must sometimes take one's eyes off the trees in order to view the forest.

---

[27] Höfler, *Kultische Geheimbünde*, pp. 323 and 341. A similar passage is recalled by Herman Bausinger in 'Volksideologie und Volksforschung', *Zeitschrift für Volkskunde*, ii (1965), 189 (an excellent essay, worth consulting in full: ibid., pp. 177–204).

[28] See the confused analysis of the old Livonian werewolf reprinted by Höfler as an appendix to *Kultische Geheimbünde* (pp. 345 ff.); a quite different interpretation is given in Ginzburg, *I benandanti*, p. 47 (*The Night Battles*, pp. 28 ff.). After the bloody liquidation of the *Sturmabteilungen* in June 1934, the exaltation of the warlike fury of the ancient Germans came to seem excessive and politically dangerous: a critic in the review *Rasse* was at pains to recall that 'the pagan of Germanic race, especially on German soil, was above all a peasant' (Harald Spehr, 'Waren die Germanen "Ekstatiker"?', *Rasse*, 3 (1936), 394–400).

ENDNOTE

A. The discovery of this relationship has been a slow process. Here I shall only refer to some basic contributions which have often been reached independently. It is not surprising that the analogy between the transformation of witches, Baltic werewolves, Lappish magicians (shamans), and the women mentioned in the *Canon episcopi*—an analogy pointed out by the judge Pierre de Lancre on the basis of trials conducted by him in the Labourd (*Tableau de l'inconstance des mauvais anges et démons* (2nd edn. Paris, 1613), 253ff., esp. 268)—should have escaped the notice of later researchers. But the brilliant hypothesis expressed by Jacob Grimm in an interrogative sentence (*Deutsche Mythologie*, (4th edn. by E. H. Meyer, Berlin, 1876), ii. 906), suggesting that stories in which the soul in an animal form leaves the sleeper's body inanimate are connected with the metamorphoses of witches and with legendary journeys of the soul to the next world, provides sustenance, often indirectly, for lines of research that are initially connected but diverge more and more as they develop:

1. The interpretation of the werewolf myth as a journey into the beyond, formulated by Wilhelm H. Roscher in a basic essay, 'Das von der "Kynanthropie" handelnde Fragment des Marcellus von Side', *Abhandlungen der philologisch-historischen Classe der königlich sächsischen Gesellschaft der Wissenschaften*, 17 (1897), 44–5, 57, in which, following Grimm, the parallel with the witches was taken up, and also that with the Siberian shamans through the work of the psychiatrist R. Leubuscher, who, in turn, made use of G. H. von Schubert's *Geschichte der Seele* (2 vols; Stuttgart, 1830). Commenting on Roscher's essay, Erwin Rohde recalls *inter alia* the story that Aristeas of Proconnesus was transformed into a raven (*Berliner Philologische Wochenschrift*, 18 (1898), cols. 270–6).

2. The research on shamanism in the Indo-European area, begun by Karl Meuli in a celebrated essay ('Scythica', 1935, republ. and suppl. in his *Gesammelte Schriften* (Basle and Stuttgart, 1975), ii. 817–79; cf. also the recapitulation by August Closs, 'Der Shamanismus bei den Indoeuropäern', *Innsbrucker Beiträge zur Kulturwissenschaft*, 14 (1968), 289–302) where Aristeas of Proconnesus is recognized as a shaman and the Scythian ceremonies described by Herodotus are regarded as trances similar to those of the shamans of Siberia. Meuli mentions his debt to a passage in Rohde (*Psyche* (1894; Italian trans. Bari, 1968), ii. 352–3), apparently overlooking the ethnographical interpretation of Herodotus, bk. iv, proposed by J. Potocki (*Voyages dans les steps d'Astrakhan et du Caucase: Histoire primitive des peuples qui ont habité anciennement ces contrées...* (2nd edn., Paris, 1829), ii. 171; I have not been able to consult the 1st edn., St Petersburg, 1802) which mentions the Siberian shamans apropos of the Enareis (Hdt. iv. 68; cf. *Voyages*, loc. cit.).

3. The identification, here also following Rohde, of the journey into the beyond as the central theme of the fairy-tale, proposed with increasing emphasis by L. Radermacher (*Das Jenseits im Mythos der Hellenen* (Bonn, 1903)), H. Siuts (*Jenseitsmotiven im deutschen Volksmärchen* (Leipzig, 1911)), and Vladimir Propp (*Morfologiya skazki* (Leningrad, 1928; English trans. *Morphology of the Folktale*, Austin, 1968; French trans. *Morphologie du conte*, Paris, 1970); and *Istoricheskie korni volshebnoi skazki* (Leningrad, 1946; French trans. *Les Racines historiques du conte merveilleux*, Paris, 1983)). In this line of thought the stories previously pointed out by Grimm (see above) were all interpreted by Ronald Grambo in the light of shamanism ('Sleep as a Means of Ecstasy and Divination', *Acta Ethnographica Academiae Scientiarum Hungaricae*, 33 (1973), 417–25).

4. Research on ritual associations of young men, also mentioned in contemporary folklore and involving animal-skin disguises: cf. Karl Meuli, 'Bettelumzüge im Totenkult, Opferritual und Volksbrauch' (1927–8), in his *Gesammelte Schriften*, i. 33–68; Lily Weiser (afterwards Weiser-Aall), 'Zur Geschichte der altgermanischen Todesstrafe und Friedlosigkeit', *Archiv für Religionswissenschaft*, 30 (1933), 210–27; Otto Höfler, *Kultische Geheimbünde der Germanen* (Frankfurt-am-Main, 1934), cf. n. 29 above. This line of research became connected with the previous ones, esp. through the werewolf theme. But there has been a failure to provide a global interpretation, even on the part of someone like Meuli, whose researches touched successively on the themes of processions symbolizing those of the dead, the shamans' journeys to the beyond, and the mortuary identity recognizable in masks and witches (or *masche*; cf. Meuli, 'Die deutschen Masken', in *Gesammelte Schriften*, i. 84–5).

5
Satanic Myths and Cultural Reality
ROBERT MUCHEMBLED

WITCH-HUNTING is a liturgy of fear. It spreads obsessions that are essentially those of the learned, but which inspire real dread and anxiety among the peasant masses. Holding up to the latter a mirror of Satanism and sorcery, magistrates and demonologists exacerbate the social rifts innate in rural society by conferring on them a cultural, moral, and religious justification. Every villager can recognize his own beliefs and practices, real enough to him, but diabolical in the eyes of his betters; each man must then decide in what fashion to present his own image. The intensity and continuity of persecutions depend on the good pleasure of those in authority, but also on the receptivity of some peasants to the message offered them. It is thus possible to define communities that are 'open' or 'closed' to persecution, and more generally to propose an overall explanatory model, valid for several European countries in the sixteenth and seventeenth centuries. Is not witch-hunting, despite its spectacular appearance, simply one episode in the conquest of the West European countryside by the forces of law and order? In other words, is it not the universal story of the advance of public authority against particularism, against the rural custom of settling disputes between man and man with the least possible recourse to outside tribunals? In this way the myth of diabolism opens the way to a sociology of authority.

I. SATANIC MYTHS AND GENUINE FEARS

In my opinion the sabbath—a nocturnal, demoniac meeting of witches and warlocks—is simply and solely a figment created by theologians, whose ideas governed the imagination of the élite classes of Europe in the late Middle Ages. Drawing on the composite tradition of persecutions of the Jews, the early Christians, and various heretical sects—as Norman Cohn has brilliantly described[1]—the theologians revived

[1] Norman Cohn, *Europe's Inner Demons* (London, 1975).

stereotypes that had no popular basis, in order to demonstrate the existence and progress of a huge satanic plot designed to make the powers of evil triumph upon earth. Such ideas unquestionably reflected the disarray of authority and especially of churchmen, confronted with the fissures that portended the disruption of Christian unity in the sixteenth century. Persecutors and heirs of the Inquisition, the new fraternity of demonologists imagined that they were themselves persecuted, that the world was given up to diabolism, and that secret devil-worshippers were plotting to frustrate their purposes. Their imaginary sabbath was a reversal of the Christian liturgy, a copy of the Mass in which each separate feature was given a negative coefficient—a dark, morbid parody of the original.

However, this construction of the mind did not become fully effective until later, more especially in states strongly influenced by the Tridentine Counter-Reformation, such as the Spanish Netherlands. There, witch-hunting became most intense and widespread between 1590 and 1620 as a result of princely edicts issued in 1592 and 1606, which let loose a fearsome campaign of repression by courts composed of laymen.

It does not seem necessary in the present article to repeat the arguments that I have developed at length elsewhere.[2] The main point to bear in mind is that the sabbath is an alien notion to the peasant actors in these dramas. The witnesses who depose against women accused of witchcraft never mention it. The accused themselves do so only in confessions extracted by torture and generally dictated by very precise questions from their judges, who supply the necessary demonological details as the basis for a verdict on the standard model. As we know, these include a record of initiation, symbolized by a bodily mark insensible to pain and confirmed by copulation with the demon; then comes a description of the sabbath and a list of the wrongs and wicked actions committed by the accused in everyday life with the aid of the powders and unguents furnished during the nocturnal ceremony.

The fact that satanism is a direct product of demonology and of the judicial practice based upon it is confirmed by the experience of certain countries where, exceptionally, the procedure in trials for

---

[2] Robert Muchembled, *Sorcières, justice et société aux 16ᵉ et 17ᵉ siècles* (Paris, 1987), esp. 89–205; Muchembled, *Les Derniers Bûchers: Un village de Flandre et ses sorcières sous Louis XIV* (Paris, 1981).

witchcraft does not centre on proof of dealings with the devil. This applies to England,[3] or to Denmark as described by J. C. V. Johansen.[4] This being so, few authors at the present day maintain that the sabbath was a reality in any shape or form. Some indeed, like Pierre Chaunu in France, still believe in the devil and in diabolic agency, and consequently still defend a hypothesis that has never been proved by concrete evidence. Others see the sabbath as containing an element of folk culture. But lest they be charged with seeking to revive Margaret Murray's unacceptable theory of the 'cult' practised by European witches, these authors are either obliged, like Mircea Eliade, to speak of imaginary orgiastic practices reflecting the longed-for return to an ancient phase of culture, or else, like Carlo Ginzburg,[5] they postulate the existence of a ritual based on a highly composite mythical structure inferred from various descriptions of the sabbath. This latter procedure is the most subtle, but is methodologically flawed, depending as it does on arbitrary associations, with no reference to chronology or, above all, to the social structure of the groups who are supposed to preserve this ritual in the myths of which they inform the judges. When the history of ideas is studied in this completely abstract fashion there is a grave risk that the investigator will describe his own mental processes rather than the subject of his research, by imposing an arbitrary significance on his collection of brief, out-of-context citations, thus in effect applying the structuralist method to his own unconscious. Taking into account, moreover, the number of exceptions, from Holland to Denmark and England, would it not be much better to fasten on a genuine stratum of folklore—the procession of the dead, for instance—in the two latter countries, where the culture of the learned has not succeeded in complicating the problem for us by imposing the concept of the demonic sabbath? In Denmark it is easy to identify popular beliefs, or such as represent a recombining of learned culture and that of the masses, for example, the belief in wizards entering a church by the keyhole. It is all the more striking that there is no mention whatever of a ritual form comparable to the sabbath. But, basically, Carlo Ginzburg's reduction of the nocturnal

---

[3] Alan Macfarlane, *Witchcraft in Tudor and Stuart England* (London, 1970).

[4] Jens Christian V. Johansen in ch. 13, below.

[5] Pierre Chaunu, 'Sur la fin des sorciers au xviiᵉ siècle', *Annales ESC* 24. 4 (1969), 895–911; Mircea Éliade, 'Some Observations on European Witchcraft', *History of Religions*, 14 (1974), 149–72; Margaret Alice Murray, *The Witch-cult in Western Europe* (London, 1921); Carlo Ginzburg, ch. 4, above.

assembly to certain structures leads him to describe universal human practices, including the cult of the dead, without regard to their essential feature, the cultural forms specific to a particular group at a particular time.

Any myth, in fact, is subject to precise sociological forms and does not exist as a mere category of the mind. This is true of the sabbath myth, which creates realities and chains of events which may affect its own consequences. Being a liturgy of fear it leads, domino-fashion, to a multiplicity of trials: a witch denounces her fellow-participants in the alleged sabbath, and one after another is burnt at the stake.[6] But more important than this, a wave of fear spreads throughout the countryside, arousing feelings of dread and even panic, with consequences of two kinds: an exterminating fury against witches, expressed within the bounds of law, and an upsurge of social antagonism, brutality, and private vengeance, directed especially against supposed witches, but also against other persons.

The repressive mania can in this way take hold of an entire region. On 7 July 1612 the lieutenant of the castellany of Bouchain in Hainaut wrote to the Privy Council of the Archduke and Archduchess of the Netherlands that

this district is strangely infected by persons abandoned and enthralled to the Devil, of all ages and of either sex, so that in the past two years I have convicted more than eighty in this town and in six villages, besides a great many suspect and banished and fourteen others now prisoners.

One suspect, a woman, had entered a plea for pardon: the castellan advised the Privy Council, the supreme court in such matters, not to grant it, 'to prevent indignation and disturbances among the populace, which is much incensed against persons of this kind'.[7]

The lieutenant's statement is borne out by the financial accounts of the viceregal domain. Trials for witchcraft were rare in the castellany of Bouchain before the end of the sixteenth century, when they were instituted under a royal ordinance of 1592. There was a lull from 1601 to 1608, despite a second edict against sorcery in 1606. A suspect was tried in 1608, and a married couple in 1609. Then came a dramatic increase: 22 cases in 1610, 59 in 1611, 22 in 1612, 21 in 1613, 12 in 1614,

---

[6] H. C. Erik Midelfort, *Witch-hunting in Southwestern Germany, 1562–1684* (Stanford, 1972).

[7] Archives Générales du Royaume (Brussels), Conseil privé espagnol, no. 1098: case of Isabeau Lesaige, letter of 7 July 1612. (Bouchain is now in France, in the Nord department.)

and 15 in 1615. A return to moderation followed: 12 trials between 1616 and 1619 (8 of which were in 1617), only 1 between 1620 and 1647, and 8 more between 1648 and 1652.[8] The 175 who stood trial between 1608 and 1652 consisted of 123 women, 18 men, and 34 children. Thus the castellan's figures of 1612 were correct. He was himself responsible for the wave of persecutions, having applied the edict of 1606 in all its rigour and ensured that those denounced by the first culprits were brought to book in their turn. But such epidemics of persecution only reach their full extent thanks to a veritable phobia taking hold of the population of a region thought to be contaminated, so that the inhabitants come forward in huge numbers to testify against local sorcerers. The trials in the castellany were confined to two towns, Bouchain and Denain, and six villages. We have a record of their sequence: Rieux and Lieu-Saint-Amand began in 1610 with 15 accused; then Bouchain with 43 cases in 1611, and Lieu-Saint-Amand with 20 more in 1612. Neuville-sur-Escaut had 6 cases in 1613, Féchain 15 in 1615, and Villers-en-Cauchie 8 in 1617.

The sentences were as severe as was commonly the case for witch-craft: 45 per cent of the accused were executed, one acquitted, the rest banished for refusing to confess or because they had no fixed abode, or put 'in care' if they were too young to be executed. Out of thirty-four children tried between 1611 and 1619, thirteen were put to death regardless of age: this was before the edict of 30 July 1612, which laid down that boys under 14 and girls under 12 should be imprisoned until puberty. This was done in the case of twelve children, three of whom were subsequently executed. Thus Anne Hauldecoeur was kept in confinement from 1 September 1614 to 11 July 1619, on which day she was put to death, having been barely 7 years old when first imprisoned!

Like their elders, the child sorcerers and sorceresses of Bouchain fell victim to the convergence of three phenomena. Firstly, anti-sabbath legislation; secondly, the zeal of a minor functionary of the Crown—the castellany being the lowest in the hierarchy of princely courts; thirdly, the demand for purification expressed by the communities themselves and directed even against children of tender age, who were merely sons and daughters of those accused of witchcraft.

A comparison with Artois, the province bordering on Bouchain and Hainaut, shows even more clearly how this conjunction of forces

---

[8] Archives Départementales du Nord (Lille), hereinafter cited as AD Nord; in particular B 11219–29 (1608–59).

accounted for the witch-hunting frenzy. In the very large governorship of Arras, which comprised hundreds of villages and belonged to the same state as Bouchain, the same edicts at the same period produced only a few dozen prosecutions. Only one example of a spread of the epidemic type can be discerned: this was in the castellany of Oisy-le-Verger, at the eastern extremity of the governorship and in the immediate vicinity of Bouchain.[9] This conspicuous variation is clearly due to a certain moderation on the part of the Artois judges, and also to a state of mind amongst the population such that the sabbath bogy failed to arouse reactions of panic fear and widespread denunciations of witches. We do not find in Artois the equivalent of documents signed by 'the sounder part of the people' of certain villages in Cambrésis and Hainaut, calling for local witches to be prosecuted, and even offering to help pay the legal costs.[10]

In my opinion, the acceptance or rejection by local communities of the myth of satanism put about by the authorities was the decisive factor accounting for the success or failure of repressive measures. The Danish ordinance of 1617 directed that accomplices of the devil should be put to death and that ordinary practitioners of witchcraft should be exiled. Over 300 trials took place in Jutland from 1617 to 1625, but the bulk of them fell under the second heading, as though the first related to a foreign ideology.[11] On the other hand, the Norwegian decree of 1593 was applied in a manner reminiscent of the Netherlands and other Continental states.[12] In Sweden, the repression in the late 1660s is to be explained by the propagation of the Continental model among the educated middle class and by 'immense pressure on the part of the lower class, an almost unanimous demand for extensive legal action against witches'.[13]

This attitude, however, of appealing to the law for protection against the dangers it has itself conjured up, is not the only possible reaction. Many sought other remedies, more brutal and more traditional, against the witchcraft in their midst. The incessant burnings of witches and the propagation of rumours created an atmosphere of intense anxiety. There were even localized outbreaks of

---

[9] Robert Muchembled, 'Comportements et mentalités populaires en Artois (1400–1600)' (unpublished, 1985), ch. 9 (see esp. table 33).

[10] Muchembled, *Sorcières, justice et société*, pp. 144–9.

[11] Johansen, ch. 13, below.

[12] Hans Eyvind Naess, ch. 14, below.

[13] Bengt Ankarloo, ch. 11, below.

panic, such that children, at Bouchain or in Sweden, would inform against anyone at all; relatives would suspect one another, and neighbours still more so. The era of suspicion was born; it was aggravated, in the Spanish Netherlands for instance, by the authorities' willingness to reward those who denounced the perpetrators of grave crimes. As early as the reign of Charles V, those who informed against Protestants were promised a portion of their confiscated goods. Such practices continued on an increasing scale: police forces were thin on the ground, and rewards to informers were a means of giving some degree of efficacy to the judicial system.

Thus the siege mentality of the time was reinforced by the horrific deeds attributed to witches and warlocks. The official persecution that took place in several provinces of the Spanish Netherlands after 1606 was matched by a wave of private vengeance against the supposed votaries of Satan. A princely pardon, granted by a letter of remission, was a sign that the authorities were not over-scandalized by such behaviour. In 1607 the gatekeeper of a town in Luxembourg beat to death a woman whom he had accused of witchcraft in a civil suit, but who had been acquitted. His act of violence was accounted for on the ground that he had spent all his money on the court case.[14] On 15 October 1607 two brothers at Wissegem, a village in the Franc de Bruges, murdered an innkeeper who had come to their house to demand the settlement of a debt. They pleaded that they had acted from desperation: they had lost three horses shortly before, and 'were firmly convinced that sorcery was at work'. A fortune-teller in Bruges had told them that this was so, and that the guilty man (whom he did not name) lived near their village church and had a 'young, slender wife': the victim answered this description.[15]

Both these incidents are indirectly related to the ordinance of 1606 against witchcraft, and also stem from deep-seated rural beliefs. The connection is still clearer in the case of Claude Ausseau, a farmer in a Hainaut village who was ruined in about 1607 by the mysterious death of all his cattle. Word had got about that a certain widow had been accused of witchcraft and imprisoned at the instance of her own son. On the patronal feast-day of the village, Claude went to visit her with two men who undertook to make her confess, but who beat her to death. Claude, while claiming to be a mere accomplice, went into

[14] AD Nord, B 1796, fos. 220–1 (pardon granted in May 1609).
[15] Ibid., fos. 287–8 (pardon in Dec. 1609). The places mentioned in the document are in present-day Belgium, near Bruges.

voluntary banishment and was pardoned seven years later. There is no evidence that he blamed the dead woman for his misfortunes, but his behaviour illustrates the effect of the official witch-hunt on the peasantry.[16]

The trials coloured the peasants' mentality, stirred up their fears, and allowed them to vent their hatred on enemies by charging them with sorcery. Whether the charge were true or false, the accused was put in danger of his life and had to react vigorously. A villager in the county of Burgandy named Jean Bring sued a fellow villager and personal enemy, Antoine Tournier. Some years later, on 17 January 1614, he insulted Tournier in the local church by calling him a 'wolf', that is to say, a 'sorcerer and malefactor'. As he left the church Tournier killed him, an act for which he was pardoned.[17] In another village in the same county, on 25 March 1615, the *curé*, Pierre Paris, attempted to dissuade one of his parishioners from associating with another:

Why do you want to go about with that sorcerer? If he cast spells on the animals you have had from me, how would you pay me for them? He is bound to harm you in one way or another. Don't you know his mother was burnt?

The argument grew heated, and the priest was finally killed by the man he had sought to warn.[18]

In this episode we find a priest spreading the accusation of sorcery against someone whose mother was burnt at the stake. Certainly the multiplication of such executions in a particular area would make a profound impression and create an epidemic of morbid suspicion. On 17 October 1610 a day-labourer at Vendegies-sur-Écaillon, in the provostry of Le Quesnoy in Hainaut, killed a woman aged 50 whom he suspected of having caused the mysterious death of several of his horses, and who, like her mother and her sister, was under suspicion of witchcraft.[19] Would he have done so but for the example of the witch-hunt that began at Lieu-Saint-Amand in 1610 and continued for more than two years? Lieu-Saint-Amand, in the castellany of Bouchain, was only a few miles to the west of Vendegies.

Such conditions bred mutual distrust and fear, leading peasants to

---

[16] AD Nord, B 1800, fos. 87–8 (pardon in Apr. 1614).
[17] AD Nord, B 1803, fo. 22 (pardon in Feb. 1616). The Franche-Comté was at that time under the Spanish crown, like the Netherlands.
[18] AD Nord, B 1804, fo. 104.
[19] AD Nord, B 1800, fos. 176–7 (pardon in June 1614).

search for evidence of guilt on their own account, using the ordeal by water or other tests. For instance, in December 1618, in a tavern at Saint-Sylvestre-Cappel in the castellany of Cassel in Flanders, after two farmers had been drinking together for some hours, one of them challenged the other to urinate on the ashes of the fire to prove that he was not a sorcerer. The man refused, and stabbed his companion to death.[20]

Sometimes people would accuse one another of atrocious crimes, as in the case of two peasants at Rumegies near Saint-Amand on 18 April 1620. One said to the other: 'Be silent, you Judas, you traitor! Your father says we are casting spells on your dogs, but it is he who is killing ours. And you too have the eyes of a *Vaudois* [i.e. a Waldensian or witch].' The other struck him dead with a hoe.[21]

Mutual suspicion exacerbated the traditional hostility between neighbouring villages, expressed as usual by derogatory nicknames. On 5 January 1626, in a parish near Vesoul, a young man sought a girl's hand from her father, but was refused. A third person offered to take the youth to La Grange du Val, a nearby village, and introduce him to a girl there. The father exclaimed that the women and girls of that village were all witches—whereupon he was struck dead by the man who had offered his services, and whose mother was a native of le Val.[22]

Many similar cases could be cited. They all tend to confirm that the myth of satanism and the sabbath was alien to popular mentality, but that the savage executions to which it gave rise had a specific influence on social conduct. Some countryfolk sought to exorcize their fear and guard against sorcery by informing on their neighbours, so that the trials multiplied; others used traditional methods of private vengeance. Altogether the mental equilibrium of the rural populace was profoundly disturbed: this is shown by the extraordinary increase in murder and mayhem in the Spanish Netherlands during the first three decades of the seventeenth century,[23] which was also the time when the witch-hunt reached its peak.

The malaise in the countryside was the more acute because the mirror held up by the demonologists, with its false picture of sabbath

---

[20] AD Nord, B 1807, fo. 201 (pardon in Dec. 1620).

[21] AD Nord, B 1809, fo. 51 (pardon in June 1623).

[22] AD Nord, B 1812, fo. 42 (pardon in May 1627).

[23] Muchembled, 'Comportements', ch. 2, esp. graphs showing pardons for homicide in Artois.

rites, was a diabolized version of practices, customs, and beliefs which really existed among peasant folk. There is no need to imagine an ancient stratum of folklore, transformed into vague mythic structures: the description of the sabbath is based on observation of a popular culture which was still very much alive, with the difference that every one of its features is given a negative coefficient.

II. THE OTHER SIDE OF THE COIN: LIVING POPULAR CULTURE

The demonological construction is an intimate blend of certain obsessions of the élite classes of Europe, with which Norman Cohn has dealt as they deserve, and elements of the social reality and popular culture of the time. It is only with the latter that I shall be concerned here.

These elements have nothing to do with any organized non-Christian cult, even of a residual or mythic kind. At all events it is impossible, in my opinion, to formulate such delicate questions concerning the origin of the practices and beliefs involved: the problem is manifestly a false one, after a thousand years of Christianity and syncretism, at the very least, between ancient pagan traditions and those of Catholicism. The important thing is to consider the vision of the world and the attitudes current at the time of the witch-hunts; this may help us to understand, through the conflict of cultures and the crisis, what was vital to one part of the community and rejected by others.

The sabbath-myth enables us to list conveniently the various elements in question: the human body (with the devil's mark); the nocturnal ritual; the role of women; wealth, reputation, and human relationships, all of which the spell-casters sought to destroy. Each of these phenomena has a normal aspect of its own, which the demonologists and those who inspired them refused to acknowledge.

Magistrates saw the devil's mark as a presumption of guilt, a tangible sign that Satan had taken possession of a human body. This idea struck a chord in the peasant mind, reflecting as it does a 'magic' conception of the body's powers, which, however, need have nothing to do with demonology. Artois villagers, for instance, regarded the body as a kind of microcosm, directly related to the outside world and equally capable of acting upon it or being acted upon by it. Thus there is a symmetry or interrelation, for example, between rain or mist and a person's tears. Consequently a witch can call up a storm by using a stick to ruffle the waters of a pond, while uttering mysterious words— she is, in fact, extending into the macrocosm her power over her own body. Belief in the efficacy of the forces inherent in every human being was so widespread that people would avoid contact with a stranger, lowering their eyes so as not to meet his; they would even defend themselves, weapon in hand, if such a person tried to touch them or come close enough to be reached by a sword held in the outstretched arm.[24] As we have seen, the evil eye or 'Vaudois eye' of which the Rumegies peasant spoke was supposed to be capable of killing dogs and causing all kinds of diseases. The myth of satanism transposes these beliefs—which are far from being extinct in the twentieth century—into the realm of diabolism: that is to say, it invites super-stitious rustics to cease believing in the power of human beings and concentrate all their fears on the devil, whose counterpart is the no less unique figure of a God able to save mankind. In other words, a monotheistic explanation is offered to people who are in reality both Christian and polytheistic, since they are disposed to believe them-selves surrounded by a plurality of forces.

By a still clearer process, the notion of the sabbath is used to diabolize the hours of night. Darkness is the devil's domain for theologians, but for them only; in the countryside, at our period, it was full of folk and animation. It was at night-time that bands of armed young men roamed about after the day's work, seeking ritual but very real combat with other groups of youths, generally from neighbouring parishes. Unmarried lads would serenade their girls with the aid of musicians, sometimes at a very late hour; sometimes, too, they would enter the house with the father's tacit consent—this was especially the case in Artois and Flanders.[25] On the way home, drunkenness and passion frequently led to nocturnal brawls that were by no means trifling, as we see from hundreds of letters of remission granted to perpetrators of homicide on such occasions. On Sundays and great feasts such as St John's day there was dancing in the villages, as well as in the surrounding country, after nightfall. Processions and pilgrim-ages likewise offered an excuse for jollity. Pieter Aertsen's *Returning Pilgrims*, painted before the last quarter of the sixteenth century,

---

[24] Muchembled, 'Comportements', ch. 5. See also Robert Muchembled, 'Le Corps, la culture populaire et la culture des élites en France (xvᵉ–xviiiᵉ siècles)', in A. E. Imhof (ed.), *Leib und Leben in der Geschichte der Neuzeit* (Berlin, 1983), 141–53.
[25] Muchembled, 'Comportements', esp. chs. 4–6.

depicts a scene of dancing, music, games, and love-making.[26] True, it is by daylight, but in all probability the merriment will continue after dark. This is confirmed by other sources, even at the height of the Counter-Reformation. We read of a party in the Beaune region, returning home from a wedding on 2 October 1622. They halt at a mill, an arquebus-shot away from a certain village, and start dancing at 2 in the morning.[27] Would not a demonologist have been certain to regard this as a witches' sabbath, instead of an ordinary peasant diversion?

Trials for witchcraft include charges that reveal a clear desire to put a stop to such amusements by night, and even by day. The more obstinately the peasants defended their customs, the more diabolic they seemed to the authorities. In 1613 a young man of Récourt in the castellany of Oisy in Artois was accused of frequenting a sabbath 'with a yellow pipe, whereon he whistled'. Need we see in this anything more than a frolicsome band of youths and musicians? The more so as an archducal ordinance forbidding young people to dance in villages was in force from 1609 to 1610 in that region, as in other Netherlands provinces; heavy fines for infringing it were inflicted in the governorship of Arras, to which Récourt belonged.[28] Here we have trials for sorcery buttressing legislation that was much disobeyed, populating the night-time with demons so as to deter young folk and others from what had been their accustomed pleasures.

The link between women and sorcery—an enormous theme, on which I shall only touch in outline—is connected with the same fierce determination to stamp out the 'errors' and 'superstitions' of rural communities. I have described elsewhere the importance of the peasant woman in transmitting and preserving popular culture.[29] In the 'satanic' version of the sabbath she similarly occupies a central place. For women are the exact equivalent, in their own culture, of demonologists and judges in theirs. They bring up children, but in a very different way from that in which theologians and magistrates seek

[26] Pieter Aertsen (b. 1507/8), *Returning Pilgrims*, Musées royaux des Beaux-Arts, Brussels, reproduced in Ankarloo & Henningsen (eds.), *Häxornas Europa* (Stockholm, 1987), facing p. 113.

[27] AD Nord, B 1812, fo. 46 (pardon in May 1627, for a crime of violence committed on this occasion).

[28] Archives Générales du Royaume (Brussels), Conseil privé espagnol, no. 1098: case of Paul Cailleau, letter of May 1613; AD Nord, B 14060 (11609–10), fos. 61–3, for instance, concerning fines imposed on young people for disobeying the edicts against dancing in Artois villages; also B 14061, fos. 65–7, other cases for the fiscal year 1610–11.

[29] Robert Muchembled, *Popular Culture and Elite Culture in France, 1400–1750* (Baton Rouge, 1985), esp. 66–71.

to educate the people. Certainly the élite culture was capable of taking children in hand and exterminating those guilty of evil thoughts: around 1610, this horrible task was performed by the lieutenant of the castellany of Bouchain. But such actions were scarcely acceptable in themselves, and compromised the future of the entire community; accordingly, in 1612, the official's zeal was curbed by archducal order. The rule thus laid down was intended to prevent the depopulation of a region, and was imitated by the authorities in several other states. One effect was to increase the importance of the school system in educating the younger age-groups and above all limiting the pernicious influence of mothers. Thus the ferocity of magistrates towards women was not only a matter of virulent anti-feminism: it was also a way of casting the main responsibility for diabolism on the weaker sex, and avoiding the disastrous results of applying too strictly the terrible notion of hereditary witchcraft. With relatively few exceptions, the *Malleus maleficarum*—the witch hammer—fell on witches but spared their children. Better still, the persecutors relied on children to inform against their mothers, sometimes on a massive scale: thousands of children did so in the epidemic persecution of 1670 around Lake Siljan in Sweden.[30] In such cases the demonologists succeeded in inducing the young generation to reject their unworthy mothers, guilty of witchcraft. Those mothers who were spared received a severe warning not to behave like the rest: in other words, they had henceforth to regard as devilish and unlawful beliefs and customs that they had shared with other peasant women and were imparting to their children.

Among the various 'superstitions' or 'spells' that are described at length in the trial records we find innumerable magic formulae designed to affect the course of events in regard to property, reputation, or social relations. With much variation among different countries and regions, these ideas are the staple of popular witchcraft in the true sense and can be found everywhere, including countries like England and Denmark where the name of the devil is almost absent from the trials and the witches' sabbath plays a minor part. Here we can really point to structures valid throughout Europe, derived from pre-Christian religions and gradually modified by more than a thousand years of Christianity: a syncretism in a state of permanent evolution, in which it is hard to isolate the constituent

---

[30] Ankarloo, ch. 11, below.

elements, but which is different in character from the purified monotheism which supplies a model to the demonologists. One of the main characteristics of this system is that it enables men and women to believe that they can affect their own destiny by means of rites, by the aid of diviners and sorcerers of all kinds, or again by praying to statues, saints' relics, and so on.

For those who have recourse to such intervention, Christian signs and symbols are often simply a reinforcement, so that, as a twentieth-century historian puts it, the sacred and the profane overlap without difficulty. Do not Danish wizards show a preference for casting spells in churches?[31] Similarly, Bénigne Morand, a villager of the district of Gray in Burgundy, is described as knowing the use of

signs and charms, so that on Good Friday of the past year 1634, being in the church of Scey [his village], he did write signs on a laurel leaf during the divine service of the Passion, whereof many were witnesses; and did confess and say that if a hen were to eat of the said leaf she could not be killed even by an arquebus-shot.[32]

Bénigne Morand's method of protection against bodily harm is paralleled, in the Tournaisis region, by the use of 'mighty names' (*hauts noms*) on the part of young men who wished to be proof against wounds incurred in fighting.[33] Long lists of such beliefs could be drawn up, but they were more and more frowned on by the religious reformers of the sixteenth and seventeenth centuries. The authorities had previously tolerated them, but did so no longer: they were an integral part of the sabbath myth, tarred with the brush of diabolism. Those, such as Bénigne Morand, who practised them were an occasion of scandal. A sharp distinction was henceforth drawn between what was sacred in an orthodox sense, supervised by the clergy, and what was profane and secular, belonging to everyday life. The latter, nevertheless, was also subject to moralization, and, for instance, to the eradication of 'superstitions' that were defined in the synodal statutes of French dioceses.[34]

Both in the demonological mirror and in the peasants' mind, the features of the popular culture fade into a blur behind the single figure

[31] Johansen, ch. 13, below.
[32] AD Nord, B 1814, fos. 7–8.
[33] AD Nord, B 1796, fos. 33–4 (a young man at Tournai in 1604 claims to be invincible because he possesses the *hauts noms*). Another case in 1606: B 1798, fo. 68.
[34] An extensive list is given by Abbé J.-B. Thiers, *Traité des superstitions selon l'Écriture sainte* (Paris, 1679).

of Satan. This more or less coincides with the acme of the witch-hunting process, in all those countries where the sabbath myth falls on fertile ground as far as the peasantry is concerned; and it portends the establishment of a new overall relationship between the law and the rural population, between authority and its subjects.

III. FROM PRIVATE VENGEANCE TO PUBLIC ORDER: A EUROPEAN PATTERN?

The persecution of witches is an effect of the acculturation of rural areas by the religious and political élite. However, it only reaches a high degree of intensity when the judicial system is reinforced by agents within the rural community.[35] The readiness of some peasants to help persecute others can only be understood from a socio-political point of view. It is a fundamental error to see witch-burning as a purely religious phenomenon; it was in fact part of a much wider movement, whose object was to make countryfolk respect law and order and discontinue the practice of private vengeance. From this point of view one can compare the different European countries so as to establish a pattern of the sociology of authority which will take account even of those countries where witchcraft was not severely persecuted.

The myth of satanism, conceived by theologians but applied by lay judges, produced condemnations on a massive scale. It is too often forgotten that the actual burnings were the work of the civil power. The Church furnished ideological weapons and continued in the modern era, in the Spanish Netherlands for instance, to counsel rulers in their fight against devilry. But the persecutions were carried out by royal officers, like the lieutenant of Bouchain already mentioned, or by magistrates who were themselves peasants appointed by the local lord. All these were cogs in a judicial system in which demonology played a specific part. Certainly, village aldermen and the lord's lieges had only an imperfect knowledge of the principles they were applying: some could neither read nor write, as was the case in about 1679 with the lieutenant of the barony of Bouvignies in Flanders.[36] But all were agents of the law and were imbued with its ideas of penal repression;

---

[35] Muchembled, *Sorcières, justice et société*, pp. 144–9.
[36] Muchembled, *Les Derniers Bûchers*, table 8, p. 270.

and in several European states these ideas were taking on a different form. Royal justice no longer endeavoured merely to keep the peace, as in the Middle Ages, but established a whole scale of crimes and punishments culminating in the notion of high-treason (*lèse-majesté*):[37] this occurred in the Spanish Netherlands with the ordinances of 1570, and in France in 1670.

Sorcery, of course, headed the catalogue of crimes; being *lèse-majesté* against the Almighty, it was the most frightful misdeed imaginable. But, we must remember, witch-hunters were not solely engaged in persecuting witches. Much more frequently they had to deal with all sorts of other crimes: to these they were either traditionally indulgent, as with crimes of violence, or progressively more severe, as, for instance, towards thieves, vagabonds, and offenders against morals and religion. In absolutist countries, in particular, as a direct result of the evolution of the sovereign power, there was an attempt through the legal machinery to concentrate and watch over the population and to establish a uniform system of penalties, if not of courts.

This political and institutional change is one of the factors which led to the persecution of witches. The criminal law which emanated from the new political structures created a framework for persecution; and the use of torture, which was in no way confined to witch-trials, naturally multiplied convictions. Few witches were burnt in countries that did not use torture, or used it to a limited extent, such as England, Denmark, and Sweden:[38] this is a sign of a different evolution of the penal system, a mutation of political structures in a different direction from the absolutist kingdoms. This no doubt is one explanation of the unique situation in the United Provinces, where witches ceased to be persecuted at the beginning of the seventeenth century.[39] Legal particularism was strong in Dutch territory; the notion of *lèse-majesté* commanded little sympathy after the revolt against the king of Spain, and the ordinances of 1570 were certainly not applied in the independent Netherlands.

Political and legal forms are not the whole story. The absolutist countries did not all persecute witches to an equal extent; on the other

---

[37] M. Sbriccoli, *Crimen laesae maiestatis: Il problemo del reato politico alle soglie della scienza penalistica moderna* (Milan, 1974).

[38] For England, Denmark, and Sweden, see nn. 3, 4, and 13 above.

[39] Jacobus Scheltema, *Gescheidnis der heksenprocessen: Een bijdrage tot den roem des Vaderlands* (Haarlem, 1828).

hand, persecution was strong in Protestant countries, though here in my opinion two opposite types are to be discerned. Those states, such as Geneva or Scotland, where political and religious power was concentrated in a hierarchical form, persecuted more ruthlessly than those in which authority was more diffused.[40] Exceptions can be found, but I believe there is a link between the incidence of executions for witchcraft and the strength of the process whereby the population was brought under political and administrative control. Emulation among states of different religious persuasion also played a part, for instance in south-west Germany.[41]

Persecuting zeal could be more thorough still. Well-known officials such as Pierre de Lancre, or obscure ones like Charles Van der Camere, lieutenant of the Bouchain castellany around 1610, were personally responsible for dozens or hundreds of executions. Their actions had, of course, to appear within the law, to be encouraged by higher authority and sanctioned by the judicial system. This brings us back to our previous theme, as bloodthirsty judges could not last long unless their acts conformed to the needs and standards of the society they lived in. Such was the case in England during its first revolution, when witch-burnings increased in number but reflected a period of crisis. Conversely, it was not easy for sceptics to impose their way of thinking except in areas where witch-hunting had no deep roots in society, such as the United Provinces in the seventeenth century.

All this does no more than account for the existence of the phenomenon. Its intensity and duration depended in part on the efforts of magistrates, but still more on the reactions of the peasantry itself. I have described the effects of the wave of fear that swept the countryside when the myth inculcated by the upper orders of society was given tangible form by incessant executions. Some peasants reacted in a traditional manner by identifying those of their neighbours who practised witchcraft and driving them out of the village or exacting summary justice. Others denounced the supposed malefactors to the courts or, more often, assembled in crowds to bear witness against the objects of popular suspicion.

The key question is: why did peasants in the second category act as they did? How and why was it that one section of rural society

---

[40] E. William Monter, *Witchcraft in France and Switzerland* (Ithaca, 1976); Christina Larner, *Enemies of God: The Witch-hunt in Scotland* (London, 1981).
[41] Midelfort, *Witch-hunting*.

preferred to get rid of sorcerers and witches by invoking the law instead of by private vengeance?

The picture painted by the demonologists was by no means accepted everywhere as a matter of course. In the Netherlands, the satanic myth was very clearly defined by the ordinances of 1592 and 1606, but the ensuing witch-hunt differed greatly in intensity from one province to another. In the county of Artois, at the opposite extreme to Flanders and Hainaut, the persecution was moderate and short-lived: by and large, it ceased in 1620. Artois was three-quarters rural, and very few of the population were avowed Protestants; it was loyal to the Spanish monarchy, and its lawyers upheld the same values as their colleagues in Flanders and Hainaut. Yet its record as regards witch-hunting is similar to that of the United Provinces, with which it had nothing else in common from 1579 onwards.

The only possible explanation in this case is that the peasant communities in Artois were for the most part averse to legal proceedings: they remained firmly attached to the principle of private revenge, which led to innumerable acts of violence. They apparently detected as many witches in their midst as did the peasantry of neighbouring regions, but preferred to deal with them extra-legally. Their deep mistrust of the courts is shown by (1) the absence of 'epidemics' of persecution, except for a few cases in the castellany of Oisy, situated in the eastern part of Artois and in the vicinity of Bouchain; (2) the rarity of denunciations by those accused; and (3) the absence of any request by the village communities for the prosecution of witches by the courts.[42]

Artois, in short, appears to have been 'closed' to the extension of official justice to rural areas, whereas Flanders and Hainaut were much more 'open'. It should be noted here that local custom in Artois generally allowed parents, if they chose, to leave their property to one of their male children only, whereas in Flanders all the heirs, male and female, had to be treated equally. At the beginning of the seventeenth century, with the cessation of hostilities, a demographic upsurge took place in both regions; its effect was to increase tension within families and to widen the gap between well-to-do peasants and the rural masses. We may suppose that the impact of this phenomenon varied according to the firmness of family structures and the ability of parishes to close ranks against the outside world. In both respects the

---

[42] Muchembled, 'Comportements', ch. 9.

consensus appears to have been much more fragile in Flanders than in Artois. Faced with change, the Flemish peasants were, it seems, unable to preserve the equilibrium of their society except by appealing increasingly to the law—against witches and also, still more frequently, against any of their number who might seem to constitute a threat.[43]

In my opinion, witch-hunts were not the outcome of war and grave civil disturbance, but were associated with periods of rapid demographic expansion and economic change. These produced a ferment of social differentiation in the villages, especially if mass pauperization was increased by local custom in matters of inheritance, as was the case in Normandy or Flanders with its egalitarian system. The changes were often favourable to the better-off, but the resulting fissure exacerbated social tension and envy. Those at the bottom reacted by seeking a 'magic' revenge, uttering explicit threats, and probably believing in their efficacy. This state of things gave full weight to accusations that wizards and witches were ruining their neighbours, causing beasts to die and crops to fail. The example of Cambrésis shows that the alleged sorcerers, while not paupers or vagabonds, belonged to the most numerous and least well-off class of peasants, while those who brought charges or informed against them were often somewhat more prosperous and even rich, or else they were clients of local notables.[44]

Some suspects, it is clear, were obsessively determined to bring down their more powerful neighbours. Marguerite Carlier of Oisy-le-Verger in Artois uttered threats against those who appeared too 'high and mighty', such as a woman who, she thought, behaved slightingly to her at Mass. She predicted to another family that the husband would die in poverty and the children would have to beg their bread.[45]

Fears such as these—together with a process whereby the superior class of peasants differentiated themselves from a popular culture that was more and more confined to the poor—brought about a fundamental rift in those villages that were most affected by demographic and economic change. There emerged a dominant, property-owning minority which sought the aid of law and authority in countering the

[43] Ibid.; also chs. 2 and 6.

[44] Muchembled, *Sorcières, justice et société*, pp. 134–44.

[45] Archives Générales du Royaume (Brussels), Conseil privé espagnol, no. 1098, case of Marguerite Carlier, 1613.

real or magic threats of which it was the object, thus breaching the united front of the local community *vis-à-vis* the outside world.

This pattern of development applies to much more than witch-hunting: it concerns the part played by a section of the peasantry in the modernization of the countryside, using this term in a broad sense. It can be perceived in seventeenth-century England:

> In this process a crucial role was played by the 'middling sort', the local notables who were both the principal beneficiaries of change and the brokers who mediated between forces active in the larger society and their polarizing local communities ... allying themselves as willing auxiliaries of the magistrates and ministers whose values they had come to share just as surely as they shared the economic interests of the gentry.[46]

If the process led in England to consequences very different from witch-hunting, it is simply because the practice of English criminal law was not dominated by the sabbath myth. In other respects the same causes produced the same effects as in the witch-hunting countries, namely, the intensive moralization of the countryside through its 'best and most notable inhabitants'.

K. Wrightson's terminology, referring to English villages as 'open' or 'closed' according to regional or local variations of the general process, is—if one adds to it the demonological myth—perfectly applicable to the wide variations observable in the Continental witch-hunting scene. This is the case not only within a single state—where, as we have seen, Flanders was 'open' and Artois 'closed'—but also with reference to different countries and different periods.

In Denmark, for instance, the sabbath myth had little currency, and the law provided safeguards for accused persons. This is probably why there were few executions there, although the seventeenth century witnessed charges of sorcery, and a rapid increase in population. In the United Provinces, trials ceased at an early date: this was probably due to the importance of towns, the earlier integration of the country-side juridical particularism, and above all the fact that demonology was out of tune with the mentality of the élite classes. From this point of view the case of Sweden should be closely considered. We may notice that the use of torture was limited there and that trials failed to develop in the southern provinces, where there was perhaps more socio-economic change than elsewhere. The exact role there of the better-off peasants during the trials remains to be discovered.[47]

---

[46] Keith Wrightson, *English Society, 1580-1680* (London, 1982), 226-7.

[47] For Denmark, Sweden, and the United Provinces, see nn. 4, 13, and 39 above.

In cases where the demonological doctrine, imparted from above, was not applied by zealous officers or welcomed by peasant 'notables' as a legal remedy against the customs and practices of their own society, witch-hunts might occur, but were no more than a straw fire. In some regions, where magical beliefs were no less common than elsewhere, executions might be few because the harmony of the countryside was little disturbed by demographic or economic changes. Right into the nineteenth century the Gévaudan district, as studied by Élisabeth Claverie and Pierre Lamaison, was still a peasant society based on violence. Breaches of equilibrium were corrected by private revenge; secret arrangements were preferred to lawsuits; the community distrusted the outside world and protected itself against it.[48] Artois in the seventeenth century was similarly shut in on itself, and that is why it and other such regions were spared hundreds of witch-burnings.

Thus witches were the victims of the demonological obsession of the Western élite classes, and also of the fact that some of their fellow citizens abandoned the principles of private vengeance, choosing instead to take their place in a world of law and order. The 'treason' of these rural notables, which took different forms elsewhere, consisted in their case of abandoning an archaic and magic culture disseminated by women. Attracted by the 'modern' forces in operation in towns and at the centre of the realm, they sought help from the law in casting off the restrictions that were still upon them, using the fear of penal sanctions to keep the masses in subjection and to thwart the sorcerers who planned their ruin. In a word, they turned to new methods to ensure their social domination.

In this sense the witch-hunt was the sign of a twofold crisis. A crisis, firstly, of the medieval state and the unity of Christendom, giving birth painfully to new solutions: absolutism, the Counter-Reformation, the Protestant Dutch republic, the Calvinist theocracy, and so on. A crisis, secondly, of the rural world, coming to terms willy-nilly with modernity; obliged to submit to powers more instant and imperious than before; called on abruptly to give up its 'superstitions', its violent ways, the whole structure of a delicate internal balance framed over the centuries. After a process of adaptation requiring several generations, the root-causes of witch-hunting disappear and so do the executions. Magistrates cease to believe in the satanic myth, and the élite

---

[48] Elisabeth Claverie and Pierre Lamaison, *L'Impossible Mariage: Violence et parenté en Gévaudan, 17ᵉ, 18ᵉ et 19ᵉ siècles* (Paris, 1982), 260, 265–70, 301.

cease to regard Christianity in its various forms as a citadel besieged by evil. New types of social equilibrium prevail in 'open' communities, while 'closed' parishes and regions, like Gévaudan, continue for a long time to exhibit forms, inherited from the Middle Ages, of internal consensus and mistrust of what lies outside.

Europe as a whole stands ready at this time to confront a tremendous future of economic and colonial development. Its vital force, the peasantry, produces more and better in a situation of demographic expansion. In the eighteenth and nineteenth centuries a new sociology of authority, varying in form, is associated with the relative docility of the peasant masses, itself an indispensable prelude to the rise of capitalism. We must not mistake the part for the whole: witch-hunting is fundamentally not a religious but a political phenomenon, and it is only one aspect of the penetration and opening-up of the countryside. The witch gives way to the priest, and private vengeance to public order; the authorities invade the heart of the village.

6

'Fantasticall and Devilishe Persons': European Witch-beliefs in Comparative Perspective*

ROBERT ROWLAND

I

THE following narrative sequence is typical of most of the witchcraft confessions recorded in Continental Europe between the late fifteenth and the late seventeenth centuries:

1. the witch encounters the devil;
2. she[1] gives herself to him, both physically and spiritually;
3. she is transported to the sabbath by unnatural means;
4. at the sabbath the devil is worshipped and a number of ritual acts are performed which constitute inversions of 'normal' behaviour;
5. a number of persons known to the witch are named as having been present;
6. the witch is returned to her place of residence by unnatural means;
7. she commits, with the aid of the devil, offences against individuals, property, the community, and/or religion;
8. this sequence of events (3–7) is repeated at regular intervals, often over a period of many years;
9. the cyclical narrative is interrupted by the arrest of the witch.

* Many of the ideas in this essay first took shape in the early seventies, when a handful of historians at the University of East Anglia put together a series of courses in European social history inspired by an anthropological perspective. I should like to acknowledge a special debt to those friends and colleagues in Norwich: James Casey, Morley Cooper, Richard Gordon, Roger Price, and Stephen Wilson.

My title has been borrowed from the Elizabethan 'Act agaynst Conjuracions Inchantements and Witchcraftes' of 1563.

[1] Throughout the paper, the feminine stands for both men and women accused of witchcraft.

One relatively early confession will suffice as an illustration of the standard pattern.[2] In September 1477 Antoinette, the wife of Jean Rose of Villars-Chabod in Savoy, was examined by the Vice-Inquisitor General, Father Stephan Hugonod. At first she denied everything, but after having been submitted to torture,

she said that about eleven years previously, on a feast-day in Summer, she was returning from the chapel in Puys, sad and filled with melancholy. And as she went her way she met Masset Garin, to whom tearfully she explained the reason for her sadness. Masset said to her, 'Do not worry, for we shall find a way out, and I shall find a man who will give you the money to redeem your land. I shall do as promised, and more, but you must do as I tell you and come with me this evening to a place where I shall take you.' When evening fell the accused, leaving her husband and family, went with Masset to the place called laz Perroy where the synagogues of the heretics were held. There she found a large number of men and women who were feasting and dancing backwards (*retroverte*). [Masset] showed her a Devil called Robinet, in the guise of a black man, saying, 'Behold your master, to whom you must pay homage if you want to see your desire satisfied.' The accused asked him what she had to do. Masset replied, 'You will renounce God your creator and the Catholic Faith and that whore they call the Virgin Mary, and then you will take the Devil called Robinet as your lord and master and you will be able to do whatsoever you want and will have all you desire and gold and silver in abundance.' She then renounced God her creator saying, 'I renounce God my creator and the Catholic Faith and the Holy Cross, and I take thee, the Devil Robinet, to be my lord and master.' She paid homage to the Devil by kissing his foot, and as annual tribute gave him one *viennensis*. The Devil her master marked her on the little finger of her left hand. She gave him her soul, then trod with her left foot upon a cross and broke it so as to spite God. He also gave her a wand one and a half feet long; and a box of ointment, which she could use to rub the wand in order to go to the synagogue; once she had rubbed the wand she used to place it between her thighs, saying, 'Go by the Devil, Go!', and was immediately carried through the air at high speed to the place of the synagogue. She also confessed that there they ate bread and meat, and they drank wine, then they danced repeatedly and paid honour to the Devil their master, who had changed his appearance from that of a man into a black dog, by kissing him on the anus. Then, with the fire put out (which was lit with a green light to illuminate the synagogue), the Devil cried, '*Meclet! Meclet!*', and

---

[2] Joseph Maine Lavanchy, *Sabbats ou synagogues sur les bords du lac d'Annécy: Procès inquisitorial à St-Jorioz en 1477* (2nd edn. Annecy, 1896), 48ff. (*apud* Joseph Hansen, *Quellen und Untersuchungen zur Geschichte des Hexenwahns und Hexenverfolgungen im Mittelalter* (Bonn, 1901), 467–99). I have compressed the account for readability and to avoid repetitions.

the men and women had intercourse *more brutali*, and she with Masset Garin, and afterwards each went away to his own house. Asked whom she had recognized at the synagogue, she said she had seen and recognized [three people]. But she did not recognize the others, she said, who had paid honour to the Devil their master, kissing him on the anus. She confessed that she went to another synagogue. Asked whom she had recognized, she said she had seen and recognized [another three people]. [A number of synagogues are then referred to, at which she recognized a handful of people.] She also confessed that the Devil gave the heretics an ointment for producing illness, with which she touched the hand of the daughter of Louis Fabre of Fillioz, who was then four years old, and as a result the girl became suddenly ill, languished for fifteen days, then died. She did this because the said Louis had demanded the repayment of a debt. She also confessed that from the bones and innards of children were made powders for bringing harm (*maleficia*) and illness to children and animals. She also confessed that with the powders given to her by the Devil her master she touched one of the cows of Pierre Jacquemod, and the cow died. By the same means she killed three cows belonging to the same Pierre Jacquemod, because he had struck one of her goats. With the powders given to her by her master the Devil she had performed witchcraft upon (*maleficiavisse*) a cow of Pierre Girard, because he had damaged her oats. Their master the Devil taught them at the synagogues to perform all the kinds of harm that can be performed. And the Devil told her to have no fear, because he would preserve her from all harm and she would not be arrested.

It is remarkable how often, at different times and places, the same narrative pattern recurs. A systematic comparison would reveal some regional variations as well as the inevitable differences of detail between individual confessions; and as one approaches the late sixteenth and the seventeenth centuries, confessions tend to become both more elaborate and more stereotyped. But if we remember that the confessions purport to be factual accounts of what the accused did (or thought they had done), the underlying uniformity demands explanation.

Contemporaries thought it was proof that the innumerable army of Satan really did exist; the liberal rationalist historians of the nineteenth century explained it away by assuming that the uniformity was produced through the use of torture, and by adducing the fact that the interrogators referred continually to the same demonological treatises for guidance as to what leading questions to ask; more recently it has been argued that, particularly since at least some of the accused clearly *did* believe they had done what their confessions said they had done,[3] we are faced with a system of belief that cannot be evaluated in terms of present-day standards of rationality.[4] But this appeal to cultural relativism[5] still does not explain the uniformity. Rather than beginning with a search for *external* sources of uniformity (demono-logical orthodoxy or the use of torture), it is perhaps more useful, as a first step, to inquire into the uniformity itself. What is it, exactly, that *does* recur in so many confessions coming from most of the countries in Western Europe[6] over a period of more than two centuries?

Confessions are narratives. This is clearly so in the case of spontaneous confessions. When the confession is obtained through intense questioning, with or without the use of torture, it may not possess, at least initially, the form of a narrative: yet even when the information is obtained bit by bit over a period of time, even when the form is determined by the questions of the interrogator, what is being pieced together—whether true or not—is the narrative of a sequence of events.

One way of penetrating beneath the surface of the text is to enquire in what ways the elements of the narrative are related, apart from the narrative sequence itself and the temporal dimension it implies. If, instead of regarding witch confessions as narratives, as sequences of chronologically ordered events, we consider them as (synchronic) structures, we find that they can nearly always be reduced to three, and no more than three, interdependent elements: the break with society and religion (apostasy), the sabbath, and the witches' evil-doing (malefice).

The conceptual interdependence between the three components, and the way they are combined in confessions to form a narrative sequence, can be represented by means of a simple diagram (see Fig.

---

[3] Cf. Etienne Delcambre, 'La Psychologie des inculpés lorrains de sorcellerie', *Revue historique du droit français et étranger*, 32 (1954), 383–404, 508–26.

[4] Lucien Febvre, 'Sorcellerie: Sottise ou révolution mentale?', *Annales ESC* (1948); English trans. 'Witchcraft: Nonsense or a Mental Revolution?' in his *A New Kind of History* (London, 1973), 185–92.

[5] On the difficulties raised by cultural relativism, cf. Martin Hollis, 'The Limits of Irrationality', in Bryan Wilson (ed.), *Rationality* (Oxford, 1970), 214–20.

[6] England is a well-known exception to this generalization, and I attempt below to assess some of the implications of this peculiarity. Some other areas appear also to have been exceptional (cf. Norman Cohn, *Europe's Inner Demons* (London, 1975), 239–51), but many more regional studies are required before a comprehensive geography of European witchcraft can be attempted. I should, perhaps, insist at this stage that I am primarily concerned with *confessions*, and that *accusations*—in particular, accusations of malefice—pose rather different problems of interpretation. Cf. section V and n. 27, below.

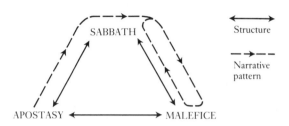

FIG. 6.1. *A standard witchcraft confession*

6.1). The witch's encounter with the devil introduces the first basic element. As a result of this encounter, often preceded by circumstances conducive to turning the witch against her fellow men, she crosses the boundaries of the moral community. The decisive act is nearly always copulation with the devil, whose non-human attributes emphasize both the violation of a basic category distinction and the resultant ambiguity of the witch—still human and (apparently) a member of the community, but intrinsically and sexually compromised with the non-human adversary of that same community.[7]

The motives which prompt the witch to give herself to the devil (lust, avarice, resentment against others) and the nature of the act by means of which she gives herself to him are equally antisocial. This form of 'civil apostasy' is usually accompanied in the existing confessions by actions which constitute apostasy in the narrower, religious, sense. Sometimes the pact with the devil takes the form of a simple ceremony; but sometimes, particularly in later texts, an elaborate and systematic negation of the main elements of Christian belief and practice is involved. The two dimensions—civil and religious—are inextricably intertwined in the consciousness of both accuser and accused: together they reinforce each other and emphasize the fact that by giving herself to the devil, both physically and spiritually, the witch has placed herself outside and against the society—the moral and religious community—to which she belonged.

Apostasy, civil and religious, thus constitutes a *rite de passage* for the witch-to-be. It initiates her into a world different from, and set over against, that of her own society. This other world possesses features

---

[7] The analysis which follows, particularly my emphasis on the ambiguity of the figure of the witch, owes a great deal to Mary Douglas, *Purity and Danger* (London, 1966).

which emphasize the nature and importance of the boundary that the witch has crossed by giving herself to the devil, and is represented in the confessions by the second basic element, the sabbath. Like apostasy the sabbath has two intertwined dimensions. It is essentially a ceremony for worshipping the devil, and as such it represents an inversion of the religious order of society. The other acts which are performed at the sabbath are similarly inversions of normal forms of social intercourse. The prominence given to sexual inversions—copulation from behind or with demons, sodomy, promiscuity, incest, and homosexuality—reflects the prominent role played by sexual rules and conventions in making the family, household, and kinship important principles of social organization in late medieval and early modern Europe. The feasting on human flesh violates the distinction between nature and culture which underlies any society's self-definition. Other common details—food without salt or which does not satisfy the appetite, inverted dancing, etc.—complete the picture of a world different from, and opposed to, that of a 'normal' community.

The sabbath can, in fact, be seen as an elaborate representation of an anti-world and, simultaneously, as an implicit assertion of all the rules which are broken there.[8] This emerges clearly from the systematized descriptions which later demonologists constructed out of earlier confessions and accusations. Guaccio's seventeenth-century account[9] illustrates this dual aspect of the sabbath as a representation.

When the faithful of the Devil are gathered together they light a great bonfire. The Devil presides over the meeting and is seated on a throne, clothed in fearful goat- or dog-skins. They approach him to worship him in a variety of ways, sometimes on bended knee, sometimes with their backs to him, sometimes with their legs in the air and with their heads bent backwards and their chins turned towards heaven. Then they offer him candles black as pitch or children's navels and in sign of homage they kiss his anus. They take their

---

[8] If this is accepted, an exclusive concern with the 'origins' of this or that element in the ever more elaborate representations of the sabbath can be seen to be at least in part misplaced. Attempts like those of Jeffrey Burton Russell (*Witchcraft in the Middle Ages* (Ithaca and London, 1972)) and Norman Cohn (*Europe's Inner Demons*), however suggestive, fail to consider the extent to which the projection on to an imagined 'anti-world' of a systematically inverted representation of 'normal' social behaviour is a sociological commonplace. Cohn does attempt, it is true, to relate the 'fantastical' elements in the sabbath to psychological universals (pp. 258–63), but the exercise depends on assumptions that few social historians would share.

[9] Francesco Maria Guaccio [or Guazzo], *Compendio delle stregonerie* (Milan, 1967), 49–53 (1st edn. 1608). The account has been compressed.

places at the tables which have been laid out and begin to eat the food which the Devil supplies or which each has brought. It is certain that these banquets are so disgusting that even a starving stomach would be revolted by seeing the display or smelling the odour. In a filthy cup the Devil pours out wine for his guests which is like black and rotten blood. There is a great abundance of all kinds of food except bread and salt. Human flesh is also served. And many of the guests say that their hunger and thirst are not satisfied by these foods and beverages. The banquets are followed by dancing in circles, always by the left [i.e. the wrong way]. And whereas our dances have enjoyment as their aim, these dances produce only fatigue, boredom and dreadful torments. When they approach the demons to worship them they turn their backs and retreat backwards like crabs, and to supplicate them they turn their hands backwards. To speak they fix their gaze on the ground, a gesture somewhat different from the customs of men. Sometimes they dance before eating, sometimes afterwards. Usually several tables—three or four—are prepared, at which each takes his place according to his rank and wealth. Each meal is blessed by the Devil with blasphemous words, according to which Beelzebub is declared to be he who creates, gives and conserves all things. And with the same formula they give thanks after the meal. After the banquet each demon takes by the hand the disciple whom he has in his charge—everything takes place according to a senseless ritual—they turn their backs to each other and holding hands in a circle they shake their heads like lunatics and often dance holding the candles which they had previously used to worship the Devil. They sing very obscene chants in honour of the Devil, and the demons and their charges have intercourse in a filthy manner.

The third basic element, evil-doing or malefice, is, like apostasy, characterized by the intrinsic ambiguity of the witch. She is of this world in that she performs concrete actions against individuals, and she does so in the guise of a normal member of the community. But she is also of the anti-world. Through apostasy she has placed herself outside society and the Church, and it is as a result of her apostasy that she has acquired her evil powers. At her regular visits to the sabbath she makes, or is given, the ointments, potions, and powders which enable her to do harm. As if to emphasize the other-worldly nature of her powers, these instruments of malefice are sometimes made from ingredients obtained in this world—the bones of infants the witch has made to die—and transformed, given magical and diabolical potency, in the anti-world.

The three elements are held together by two oppositions. Firstly, there is the clear opposition between the moral community which exists in this world and its abstract negation, projected into an other-world represented by the nocturnal abominations practised on a distant mountain-top or other deserted place. This opposition establishes and reinforces the boundaries of the moral community. Secondly, there is the dual opposition between the witch's *removal* from the *moral community* through her apostasy and her *reinsertion*, transformed by the sabbath, into the *real community* with the power to practise maleficent acts. A real community menaced by the actions of maleficent witches is only possible if individuals have set themselves against the moral community and, through apostasy, become witches. But witches are only possible because there exists, outside and opposed to the moral community, a threatening anti-world to whose members is attributed the power and the will to do harm. The ambiguity of the witch, who remains an apparent member of the community while belonging in reality to an anti-world which threatens and negates it, is underlined by her physical and spiritual apostasy and by her repeated use of supernatural means to harm her neighbours. Her peculiar mode of transport to and from the sabbath is made necessary by the absolute separation and opposition between the moral community and the anti-world. The witch's flight is an expression of the fact that she combines in her person two contradictory and mutually incompatible modes of existence: only by unnatural and extraordinary means can the two worlds be placed in a spatio-temporal relation to one another.

The figure of the witch mediates between the moral community and its abstract negation (the sabbath) and between the same moral community and its concrete negation (the existence of malefice). Her relation to the moral community is defined by apostasy, which is a necessary condition for her participation in the sabbath and for her maleficent practices. At the same time, her relation to the real community is defined by malefice, which is only possible because she has, as a result of her apostasy, participated in the sabbath. The community can only be freed from evil if the real community is made to conform to the moral community; and that implies removing the witch from the community, taking her apostasy to its logical conclusion. Without witches, the anti-world of the sabbath would be severed from the communities of this world, which would no longer be threatened by enemies within.

This mutual dependence between the three elements of the conceptual structure goes part of the way towards explaining the uniformity, over time and space, of European witchcraft confessions.

But unless we assume that these three elements define all witch-beliefs—and in cross-cultural perspective this is clearly not the case—we are still a long way from explaining the particular form taken by West European witch-beliefs, in so far as they are reflected in the confessions, between the fifteenth and the seventeenth centuries.

II

In many primitive societies people hold elaborate beliefs about the nature of witches and are more than willing to expound them to the inquiring anthropologist.[10] The figure of the witch represents super-natural forces of malevolence and causes of misfortune.[11] Belief in the existence and powers of witches is thus part of the wider system of religious belief, in much the same way as belief in the existence and powers of the devil is part of the system of Christian belief. The witches' attributes and behaviour mark them off from normal human society, and the world of the witches often constitutes a systematized structure of negation, an inversion of the world in which people who hold these beliefs live.

The elaborate attributes of witches do not, however, usually serve as a guide for action when an individual thinks he may have been bewitched. The aggrieved person asks, not 'Who has been behaving like a witch?', but 'Who can have been wishing me harm?' He follows established procedures for identifying a suspect (often resorting to 'oracles' or witch-finders), makes an accusation, and sets in motion the society's equally well-established procedures (ordeals, etc.) for dealing with a suspected witch. These procedures are normally such that only if the accusation is socially considered to be plausible will any form of action be taken against the suspect. Ultimately, once an accusation has been made it is the known quality of the suspect's relationships with the victim and other members of the society, and

---

[10] Detailed references to the anthropological literature would be out of place in this brief summary. The best introduction is still undoubtedly Lucy Mair, *Witchcraft* (London, 1969).

[11] Strictly speaking, it would be more correct to define witches as individuals who are considered able to bring evil and/or good by supernatural means. The distinction between the two aspects of their power is an analytical one, and in many witch-believing societies is not clearly recognized. Although particular case-studies must take account of it, in this comparative analysis the potential ambiguity of the supernatural power wielded by the witches will be disregarded.

not the possession or otherwise of witch-like attributes, that will determine what happens to him or to her.

This apparent inconsistency is really a matter of emphasis, and reflects the dual function of witch-beliefs. At one level these beliefs constitute a form of theodicy, an explanation for the existence of evil. Witches are thought of collectively: they are enemies of society and, as such, embody whatever in that society is considered to be anti-social. At the second level, witches are real, antisocial individuals present within society. They are real or potential enemies of individuals, and their socially disruptive malevolence (provided the charge of witch-craft can be made to stick) provides a plausible explanation for individual misfortunes.

Some societies recognize this conceptual distinction by positing the existence of two different kinds of witches: the night-witches, who are elaborate, improbable, the embodiment of antisocial malevolence, and enemies of the community in general; and everyday witches, whose attributes are more 'normal', who exist within society, and whose enemies are individuals. 'Just as the night-witch epitomizes all kinds of unthinkable evils, the everyday witch is the image of what one would not wish one's neighbours to be, and many unpopular people have the qualities ascribed to witches.'[12]

Anthropological studies of witchcraft have tended to concentrate on accusations for the simple reason that they are observable and amenable to sociological analysis; but once the basic groundwork has been done—seeing who accuses whom of what, in what circum-stances, and what happens then—the problem of interpretation reappears. Two lines of analysis have received particular attention. On the one hand, witch-beliefs are analysed in the context of the whole belief-system of the society, and an attempt is made to explain to what extent, and why, witch-beliefs constitute a form of theodicy. On the other hand, students of witchcraft have attempted to establish a sociology of accusations by observing their patterning and its relationship to the social structure. An answer to the question, 'Why did A accuse B?', or 'Why do As tend to accuse Bs?', would be a start towards understanding why in those societies people ever accuse each other of witchcraft at all.[13]

The two approaches, and the two aspects of witch-beliefs, are

[12] Mair, *Witchcraft*, p. 43.
[13] For the sociology of accusations cf. Mary Douglas (ed.), *Witchcraft Confessions and Accusations* (London, 1970), esp. the editor's introduction.

clearly complementary. For an individual to make a meaningful accusation there must exist a collective belief in the existence and powers of witches. It is in this sense that Monica Wilson refers to the witch-beliefs as 'the standardized nightmares of a group'.[14] And witch-beliefs, whatever the relationship in a given society between night-witches and everyday witches, or between the collective representation and the kinds of people actually accused, are kept alive and given meaning by the supposed existence and activities of 'real' or everyday witches within the society.

III

To regard western European witchcraft *confessions* as an accurate reflection of witch-*beliefs*, and to do so in an implicitly cross-cultural perspective, is to beg two orders of questions. Of the two, it would seem in the light of received ideas about the rise of the spirit of rationalism in Europe that the relationship between beliefs (and practices) and confessions is the more important. On it would appear to depend the trust we can place in our sources, for nearly all of these were produced by witch-hunters and not by witches. But it is perhaps more fruitful to leave to one side, for the moment, questions regarding the credibility of our sources and the empirical reality of witchcraft, and to concentrate on the implications of the cross-cultural study of witchcraft.

The legitimacy of cross-cultural comparisons between primitive societies and early modern Europe has been questioned by students of Continental witchcraft. H. C. Erik Midelfort, for example, argues that

sixteenth and seventeenth century Europe can scarcely be compared to today's primitive societies. Early modern Europe already exhibited a series of parallel paths to higher social status, a high literacy rate, an extremely diverse but interlinked religious outlook, a typically "Western" family pattern, and a measure of industrial development that preclude all comparisons with today's primitive societies.[15]

[14] Monica Wilson, 'Witch Beliefs and Social Structure', *American Journal of Sociology*, 56 (1951), 307–13.
[15] H. C. Erik Midelfort, *Witch-hunting in Southwestern Germany, 1562–1684* (Stanford, 1972), 4.

E. William Monter is more incisive:

I do not attempt to reach beyond Europe . . . for comparative material . . . from a conviction that such forays are useless for understanding continental European witchcraft. . . . All things considered, non-Western social anthropology provides keys that do not fit continental European locks.[16]

These comments are, directly or indirectly, prompted by the work of Keith Thomas and Alan Macfarlane, who drew on African anthropological studies for keys to interpret village-level witchcraft in sixteenth- and seventeenth-century England.[17] Working on the Continent, where a simple sociology of accusations proves inadequate to explain the pattern of repression or the content of accusations, confessions, and sentences produced in the context of the organized search for suspected members of the innumerable army of Satan, these scholars conclude that between African and Continental European witchcraft the differences are of kind rather than of scale or degree, and that such attempts at cross-cultural comparison are, as regards the Continent at least, a false start. In particular, such comparisons would appear to preclude taking into account the entire Christian context, and especially the self-imposed struggle of the Church against heresy, the existence of a literate and differentiated theological tradition, and the role of specialized repressive institutions, from the lay courts to the Inquisition. None of these elements are present in the African context; their importance in Continental Europe implies that similarities between African and European witchbeliefs are at best superficial, and in most cases positively misleading.

Thomas and Macfarlane have, it is true, invited criticism by the way they have approached the study of English village-level witchcraft. Both authors concentrate on the available English evidence and attempt to make sense of it by drawing on the studies of anthro-

---

[16] E. William Monter, *Witchcraft in France and Switzerland* (Ithaca and London, 1976), 10–11.

[17] Alan Macfarlane, *Witchcraft in Tudor and Stuart England* (London, 1970); Keith Thomas, *Religion and the Decline of Magic* (London, 1971). Thomas appears to justify his concentration on the similarities between English and African witchcraft by the assertion that 'In the sixteenth and seventeenth centuries England was still a pre-industrial society, and many of its essential features closely resembled those of the "underdeveloped areas" of today' (p. 3). One has only to ask whether Scotland and the Continental countries were any less pre-industrial to realize that the similarity must have other explanations. Macfarlane has since revised his views and attempted to analyse the peculiarities of English social structure in the European context: cf. *The Origins of English Individualism* (Oxford, 1978), 1–2 and *passim*.

pologists. Evan-Pritchard shows them how witchcraft can make sense of misfortune; Malinowski suggests the circumstances under which men resort to magical explanations; and numerous monographs provide a framework for relating accusations to social structure. There is no serious discussion, however, of the *legitimacy* of comparing African witchcraft with witchcraft in England, rather than in Europe as a whole.[18] Both authors appear to have been led astray by the undoubted similarities between what is the general situation in African witch-believing societies and what is, in the European context, a problematic special case.

For English witchcraft was peculiar. English witches did not fly. They did not go to the sabbath. They did not copulate or make pacts with the devil, or make powders and ointments with the bones of murdered infants. They kept 'familiars'—homely, though diabolical, pets. They were accused, not of being heretics, but of harming their neighbours' cows. They were not tortured or burned.

Most of the features which distinguish European from African witchcraft were absent in England. This makes comparison easier, and focuses attention on the sociology of accusations in a village context; but it may induce the student to disregard the fact that English witch-beliefs, and English witch-trials in the sixteenth and seventeenth centuries, were regional variants of phenomena common to all the Christian societies of western Europe. What has to be explained is not why Continental Europe (and Scotland) was so different from England and Africa, but why, within Christian Europe, England and England alone was similar to Africa today.

This requires, in the first place, a comparison between what we call 'witchcraft' in Africa and in Europe. Then, provided we are satisfied that they can legitimately be subsumed under the same general category as *variant forms of witchcraft*, an initial attempt can be made to relate differences in witch-beliefs to differences in the kinds of societies where they are found. Finally—though lack of space precludes doing so here[19]—an attempt could be made to relate

---

[18] Cf. Keith Thomas, 'The Relevance of Social Anthropology to the Historical Study of English Witchcraft', in Douglas (ed.), *Witchcraft Confessions and Accusations*, pp. 47–79.

[19] I hope to return to the problem in a separate paper. In general terms I would suggest that the earlier, and more effective, centralization of the English state, and the remarkable geographical homogeneity of English society, allowed the Crown to dispense with many of the institutional structures which regional disparities and resistances to centralization made into a pre-condition of the establishment of the absolutist state on the Continent. A similar argument underlies Macfarlane's *The Justice*

differences between English and Continental witchcraft to the peculiarities of English society in the context of early modern Europe, and then to examine why, despite the obvious differences between Tudor and Stuart England and Africa today, witchcraft in England appears to have so much in common with the phenomena studied by twentieth-century anthropologists.

A comparison between the general features of African witch-beliefs, as summarized in section II, and the model that underlies European witchcraft confessions (section I), suggests that in both contexts, (1) witches are malevolent individuals present within the community; (2) witches are defined as such by their association with an other-worldly and nightmarish anti-society; and (3) in the context of witch-beliefs, the sabbath is structurally equivalent to the world or attributes of night-witches. These three points of similarity are, to my mind, sufficient to establish African and European witch-beliefs as variant forms of witchcraft.

The most obvious differences between the two derive from the Christian context of European witch-beliefs. The sabbath is presided over by the devil, and the witch is represented as a menace, not only to her fellow men, but also, and especially, to religion, and hence to society in general. She is not only an evil person, but an apostate and devil-worshipper. Although this constitutes a major difference, it is not sufficient to invalidate comparisons, particularly when we remember that among the Lugbara and the Dinka witches are associated, in their nightmarish aspects and in their capacity to do harm, to a 'bad god' or 'black god'.

A second major difference resides in the way malefice is related to the world or attributes of night-witches. In Africa, even when only one kind of witch is thought to exist, accusations are kept distinct from the 'collective nightmare'. Dinka witches are animal-like and have tails, but people who are accused of being witches do not; and accusations relate only to harm done within the community to other people. In Europe, people confessed to *being night-witches*, and an accusation of having been present at the sabbath was enough to set the judicial machinery in motion. The figure of the everyday witch coincided with that of the night-witch; and this identity is reflected in the way malefice and the sabbath are related to one another, in the con-

and the Mare's Ale: Law and Disorder in Seventeenth Century England (Oxford, 1981), esp. 1–16, 173–99.

fessions, by the comings and goings of the witch between the sabbath and the community where she lives.

The third, and last, major difference between Africa and early modern Europe lies in the fact that European confessions displayed a remarkable homogeneity across space and over time, while African beliefs varied from one society to another. When one remembers that European society was much more heterogeneous than its witch-beliefs, the uniformity of the latter—the persistence in confessions of the model analysed in section I—is all the more striking and problematic.

Early modern Europe was a much more complex society than the predominantly African societies where anthropologists have studied witch-beliefs. This has led some students of European witchcraft, as we have seen, to doubt the relevance in a European context of anthropological approaches to the study of witchcraft. But although it is true that the societies where anthropologists have studied witch-beliefs are radically different from those of early modern Europe, this does not imply that anthropological perspectives cannot be brought to bear on European witch-beliefs. In many respects, the central pre-occupations of what has come to be called the social anthropology of complex societies—the forms and consequences of the integration of local communities into higher-level systems like the nation-state, the forms of mediation and articulation between national, regional, and local levels of such systems—are singularly appropriate to some of the problems raised by a sociological analysis of early modern European societies.[20]

Throughout early modern Europe the rise of the absolutist state and of relatively specialized institutions of government interfered with, and modified, both seigneurial jurisdictions and town–country relationships. The Reformation and the Counter-Reformation, despite the religious conflicts they reflected and reinforced, promoted new forms of institutional integration between the parish church, with its localized religious community, and higher-level religious institu-tions.[21] Even though it would be incorrect to speak of 'nations' in the

[20] Cf. Robert Redfield, *The Little Community* (Chicago, 1955), esp. ch. 8, and id., *Peasant Society and Culture* (Chicago, 1956), esp. ch. 3; Eric Wolf, 'Aspects of Group Relations in a Complex Society: Mexico', *American Anthropologist*, 58 (1956), 1065–78; Michael Banton (ed.), *The Social Anthropology of Complex Societies* (London, 1965); and Jeremy Boissevain and John Friedl (eds.), *Beyond the Community* (The Hague, 1975).

[21] Cf. John Bossy, 'The Counter-Reformation and the People of Catholic Europe', *Past and Present*, 47 (1970), 51–71.

modern sense, many of the peculiarities of early modern European society could be approached in terms of the anthropologists' concern, when dealing with complex societies, with forms of community–nation articulation. The appropriate levels for such an analysis would be the local, the regional, the 'national', and—in the religious sphere— the supra-national level, represented by the Catholic church and, over and above the differences brought about by the Reformation, the fundamental doctrinal unity of Christendom.

If early modern Europe is regarded in this sense as a 'complex society', the question of the social context of witch-beliefs has to be redefined to take account of the existence of different levels of integration. On the one hand, we have a supra-national level of religious integration, as expressed in the relatively uniform theology and demonology of western Christendom, whether Catholic or Protestant. On the other hand, as witchcraft accusations arose within local communities and related to malefice committed in a local context, we have the community level of social integration. Between the two, at intermediate levels, we have the Inquisition and various lay courts, and the respective social contexts of their repressive activity; the institutional framework of the Catholic and other churches, providing varying contexts for the emergence or suppression of differences in religious teaching and practice; and the different administrative structures which were being established in different countries. The notion of levels of integration can be enriched by the analogous notion of levels of culture, as used, for example, by some medieval historians to examine the interaction between ecclesiastical, aristocratic, urban, and popular rural cultural universes.[22]

Such a framework of analysis could only be made operative in the context of detailed case-studies. At the very general level of this discussion, it will be sufficient to think in terms of two cultural levels and two levels of integration: the supra-national level of the churches and of the demonological treatises, and the community level to which acts and accusations of malefice relate. European witch-beliefs, in so far as they reflect both Christian demonology and the local contexts of witchcraft accusations, correspond to the complexity of early modern European society. Of the three major peculiarities of European witch-beliefs when compared with their African counterparts, two—their

---

[22] Cf. the papers by Le Goff and Duby in Louis Bergeron (ed.), *Niveaux de culture et groupes sociaux* (Paris and The Hague, 1967).

uniformity across space and over time, and their contamination by Christian demonology—reflect the supra-national integration of western Christendom. The third—the fact that European witches confessed to being night-witches—is less easy to explain directly in terms of the peculiarities of European society.

It does, however, raise a question which was put to one side at the beginning of this section: how far can witch confessions be regarded as an accurate reflection of witch-beliefs? The confessions were, after all, obtained by witch-hunters in the context of the institutionalized repression of witchcraft. To what extent do they reflect not the result, but the process of religious and demonological integration? If integration is regarded not as a state of society, but as a process operating within society,[23] the complexity of early modern Europe gives rise to a further question. The sabbath reflects the demonology of western Christendom, and once religious integration is *assumed*, the constant references to the sabbath in confessions from different times and places would appear simply to reflect that integration. But witchcraft accusations arose within local communities and related to malefice committed in a local context. Why do the confessions not reflect the great diversity of local situations and cultures to be found in western Europe? Can we really assume that western European villagers and townsmen everywhere made sense of malefice by relating it, more or less in the same terms, to the sabbath?

The question is not, as it was for nineteenth-century rationalists, how people came to confess to having done things—flying and copulating with the Devil—they manifestly could not have done, but rather how, all over Europe and regardless of whether witchcraft was a reality or an illusion, people came to produce confessions that all conformed to the tripartite model outlined in section I. How was demonological uniformity produced out of what was, one must suspect, the underlying heterogeneity of regional and local beliefs in Europe regarding good and evil supernatural forces and ways of influencing or controlling them?

Prior to and during at least part of the 'witch-craze' of the sixteenth and seventeenth centuries, local witch-beliefs will have reflected the fragmentation of European society into small pockets of population. Despite their extensive, though mainly short-range, contacts with one

---

[23] Many of the political and cultural dimensions of the process of change from late medieval to early modern Europe could profitably be analysed as aspects of the integration of complex societies.

another, these communities constituted relatively autonomous social universes beyond which the horizons of the majority of the population did not extend. We cannot now reconstitute this patchwork of local 'superstitions', but the evidence which does survive[24] points towards the existence of relatively localized belief-systems,[25] including *both* symbolic representations of evil *and* magical procedures for harnessing or neutralizing supernatural forces of evil in the context of everyday life in the community. If a practical concern with malefice was certainly common to all these belief-systems,[26] there is no reason to suppose that the symbolic representations of evil—the European equivalent of the belief in night-witches—would everywhere have taken the same form. The apparent homogeneity of European witch-beliefs, as reflected in the confessions, can be seen as the result of a process of integration which involved the incorporation of local belief-systems into a wider, uniform system, through the substitution of the sabbath, with all its implications, for the presumably simpler, and possibly quite varied, symbolic representations of evil characteristic of each local or regional belief-system. If we are to understand this process, we shall have to look again at the relationship between the sabbath and malefice in the model underlying the witchcraft confessions.

In African belief, witches are both malevolent persons and the nightmarish embodiment of evil. The world of the night-witches 'explains' the existence of evil, in the abstract, and represents evil as the more or less systematic negation of normal, approved social behaviour. The possibility of attributing misfortune to the malevolence of individuals not only 'explains' the misfortune itself, but relates it concretely to forms of socially disapproved behaviour or to strained social relationships. The everyday witch and the night-witch could be said to stand in a metaphorical relationship to one another, and there is thus no need for the two to be identified.

In late medieval and early modern Europe the existence of distinct

---

[24] Cf., for an attempted reconstitution, Robert Muchembled, *Culture populaire et culture des élites dans la France moderne (XVᵉ–XVIIIᵉ siècles)* (Paris, 1978), pt. 1.

[25] The notion of a belief-*system* has its dangers. Cf. the cautionary note struck by John Davis, 'Honour and Politics in Pisticci', *Proceedings of the Royal Anthropological Institute* (1969), 69–70.

[26] Cf. Jean Delumeau, *La Peur en Occident, XIVᵉ–XVIIIᵉ siècles: Une cité assiégée* (Paris, 1978), and, for parallels in Europe today, Jeanne Favret-Saada, *Deadly Words: Witchcraft in the Bocage* (1977; English trans. Cambridge, 1980), and Carmelo Lisón Tolosana, *Brujería, estructura social y simbolismo en Galicia* (Madrid, 1979).

cultural levels makes the situation more complex. The fear of malefice would appear to have been primarily a feature of popular culture, while the abstract demonological representation of evil, elaborated by the schoolmen, was primarily a concern of ecclesiastical and lay élites. By relating the sabbath to malefice, the model underlying witchcraft confessions was in effect bringing two distinct cultural levels into relation with one another.[27]

The narratives constituted by the confessions of those accused of witchcraft are remarkable not only for their structural uniformity, but also for the extent to which they resemble the standard patterns of magic folk-tales.[28] These folk-tales reflect one form of the popular conceptualization of how the natural and the supernatural are related in terms of a diachronic sequence of concrete events. The theologians' version of the relation between the natural and the supernatural was abstract, and could be represented in terms of a synchronic conceptual structure. But for it to become intelligible to the illiterate mass of the population, such a timeless structure had to be translated into a form which made sense at the popular cultural level, which could be related to everyday experience. Miracle plays and popular lives of saints are translations into readily accessible form of a conceptual relationship between the natural and the supernatural which the mass of the population could not conceptualize in an abstract, synchronic form. The magic folk-tale is a secular variant of the same translation. Witches' confessions display the same formal patterns as folk-tales and popular lives of saints because, within the context of the institutional repression of witchcraft, they performed the same function.

The scholastic conception of evil was an abstract, atemporal conceptual structure. Evil, for the mass of the population, was represented

---

[27] This does not imply that popular culture was not concerned with the nature and origins of the supernatural power wielded by witches. It is probably fair to assume that *any* system of witch-beliefs must by definition, and at least implicitly, include or refer to representations or explanations of such powers and of their potential incidence in everyday life, and I do not share the view (cf. Richard Kieckhefer, *European Witch Trials: Their Foundation in Popular and Learned Culture, 1300–1500* (Berkeley and London, 1976), *passim*; Muchembled, *Culture populaire*, pp. 302–9; and id., *La Sorcière au village (XVIᵉ au XVIIᵉ siècles)*, (Paris, 1979), 144–60) that village-level accusations represent popular—as opposed to learned—conceptions of witchcraft. Such accusations arose in specific contexts, and reflect—in Europe as in Africa—a practical concern with the effects rather than with the essence of witchcraft. The fact that they seldom refer to the origins and nature of the supernatural power supposedly wielded by the accused tells us more about the sociological context of accusations than about the cosmological content of popular witch-beliefs.

[28] Cf. V. Propp, *Morphology of the Folktale* (1928; English trans. Austin, 1968).

by wrongdoing and by misfortune, conceived of as events. Significance was attached to events by their position in a sequence, and supernatural significance derived likewise from the position of an event in a sequence which represented the irruption of the supernatural into everyday life.

In the context of the institutionalized repression of witchcraft, the translation of abstract concepts into significant sequences of events, and the structuring of a series of events, meaningless in isolation, into a narrative sequence with theological significance were both effected by the mechanisms of interrogation. The function of torture was to elicit information which the suspect could not have known if innocent. A single admission made in desperation and derived, perhaps, from local folklore would set in motion an inexorable process whereby, through repeated questioning, suggestion, and torture, the missing links in the damning sequence of events would be elicited one by one. The more confused the suspect the greater the pressures towards providing the information which, in terms of the questioners' élite assumptions, could alone explain and make sense of whatever had already been admitted. In this context, to ask whether the information elicited was true or false is almost beside the point. Given the collective nature of folk-beliefs regarding evil and misfortune, it was to collective representations of the nature and origins of supernatural power to do harm (or, more generally, to popular beliefs regarding the supernatural and its relation to everyday life) that the suspect turned, under close questioning and/or torture, to make sense of his own actions and beliefs.

If we admit that it was through interrogation that the élite and popular cultural levels were brought into relation with one another, and that the élite's abstract representation of evil (the sabbath and devil-worship) was made to explain everyday misfortunes or the chance effectiveness of a malevolent imprecation; and if we admit, further, that the mechanisms of repressive interrogation, and the use of torture in particular, forced suspects to make sense of their actions or malefice *in terms satisfactory to the questioners*, we can see why the outcome of a successful process of interrogation was a confession to being a night-witch. For just as, in the model underlying the confessions, the witch mediates between the sabbath and the real community where malefice is performed, so, in the context of the institutionalized repression of witchcraft, only a confession to being a night-witch could establish the necessary link between the cultural levels of the witch-hunters and the suspected witches, between the accusations of malefice brought by fellow villagers and the demonological significance that the witch-hunters attached to such accusations. As with the other two differences between African and European witch-beliefs, the fact that European witches confessed to being night-witches can also, though less directly, be attributed to the fact that early modern Europe was a complex society, with different levels of cultural integration.

Finally, the mechanisms of interrogation can explain the peculiar effectiveness of the cultural and religious colonization of the European countryside undertaken in the sixteenth and seventeenth centuries by the lay and ecclesiastical authorities,[29] and the remarkable standardization of beliefs it appears to have produced. The outcome of thousands of interrogations was the adoption, by the mass of the rural population, of the sabbath and the night-flying witch as symbolic representations of evil. But at the same time, and as a result of the pressures of interrogation, suspects in different parts of Europe drew on local folklore in an attempt to satisfy their questioners' demands for a complete account of the significance of their actions. Elements of these local and regional belief-systems were incorporated into confessions, and from the confessions and trial reports they passed into the demonological treatises and witch-hunting handbooks. Items of folk-belief were absorbed into the élite's symbolic representation of evil and were made available to judges and interrogators throughout western Europe. Over time, accounts of the sabbath tended as a result to become more elaborate. The difference between the confession of Antoinette Rose and Guaccio's account of the sabbath is, at least in part, the result of over a century of witch-hunting.

IV

The foregoing is, of course, no more than a speculative reconstruction of what might plausibly have been taking place. Nearly all our information regarding European witch-beliefs in the sixteenth and seventeenth centuries was committed to writing as a result and in the

---

[29] This colonization, and its effectiveness, is the subject of Muchembled, *Culture populaire*, pt. II. While not entirely satisfactory as an explanation, this essay does highlight the existence of a real problem.

context of the institutionalized repression of witchcraft. We can have little hope of 'seeing through' the sources and recovering evidence concerning local and regional witch-beliefs in the 'pure' state, and attempts to do so are more likely to reflect the assumptions of the historian regarding the reality of witchcraft than to succeed in separating out the respective beliefs of witch-hunters and suspected witches.

There exists, however, one well-documented case where the beliefs of the suspects and the assumptions of the interrogators were sufficiently distinct from one another to have been preserved in the sources which have survived.

Twenty years ago Carlo Ginzburg discovered in the archives of the Venetian Inquisition a remarkable series of documents.[30] By some historical accident there survived into the seventeenth century in Friuli a nucleus of popular beliefs which appear to constitute a relatively untouched symbolic representation of the nature and origins of evil. Individuals who were born still wrapped ('clothed') in their amniotic membrane were thought to have been born under a special 'planet' and to have been marked off as different from ordinary men. The membrane (called *camiscia*, or 'shirt') was preserved and sometimes worn around the neck. When they reached manhood, these individuals received a 'summons', and from then on, for about twenty years, they were thought to go forth in spirit while asleep, four times a year, to do battle with the witches. These men, called *benandanti*, fought with fennel stalks, the witches with sorghum reeds. The outcome of the battle would determine the success or failure of the crops. The *benandanti* were also believed to have the additional power of detecting the victims of witchcraft, curing them, identifying witches, and discovering the fate of the dead in the other world. They believed that they were doing God's work, and that as a result of championing His cause and preserving the crops against the witches they would go straight to Paradise when they died. They were bound to secrecy regarding the identity of *benandanti*, witches, and any other information they obtained as a result of their nocturnal goings-forth. Revelation of this information to the profane was punished by their being beaten up with cudgels.

From the fragmentary evidence which survives it is impossible to reconstruct the belief-system in its totality, but what remains is

---

[30] Carlo Ginzburg, *I benandanti: Stregoneria e culti agrari tra Cinquecento e Seicento* (Turin, 1966; 2nd edn. 1973).

sufficient for the functions it performed in these isolated communities to be clear. The nocturnal battles of the *benandanti* are structurally analogous to the world of the night-witches in Africa and to the sabbath in European witchcraft confessions. Whereas no explanation is given for the presence of the witches, potential *benandanti* are clearly defined by their special 'planet' and by their 'shirt'.[31] The battle between the *benandanti* and the witches takes place outside society, four times a year. This symbolic battle between good and evil ('We fight for Christ and they fight for the devil') explains good and bad fortune for the community ('And if we win, that year there will be abundance; and if we lose there will be famine that year'). Collective misfortune is the result of the triumph of the witches as agents of the devil and forces of evil.

The *benandanti*, as ambiguous individuals who can mediate between this world and an other-world,[32] can also explain individual misfortune (by witch-finding) and can identify the good or bad fortune of individuals who have left this world. The ambiguity of their role as bridgers of the unbridgeable is emphasized by the rule of secrecy and by their fear of being cudgelled.

Because of the belief-system's function as an explanation of *both* good *and* evil, and because it is built around the image of those who defend the community *against* evil, its main structural oppositions differ from those that can be found in witchcraft confessions. The *benandanti* do not need to place themselves outside and against society, since they have been marked as different due to their exceptional birth, and since they represent the community. Their periodic goings-forth are no more than a parenthesis in their existence in this world. Whereas a witch is a witch even in the intervals between

---

[31] 'All those who are born clothed belong to [the company of the *benandanti*] and when they reach the age of twenty they are summoned with the drum like the one which summons soldiers and we are obliged to go. . . . Everyone goes, provided they were born clothed' (ibid., 2nd edn., p. 217); my translation.

[32] Ginzburg has now (ch. 4, above) quite plausibly argued that the beliefs regarding *benandanti* can be related to shamanistic beliefs in other parts of Europe. His further argument that the origins of the sabbath are to be found in a shamanistic culture-complex is less convincing, and in any case adds little (cf. n. 8, above) to our understanding of the dynamics of witch persecution. A more appropriate question would be the extent to which such beliefs may in some areas have been drawn on by suspects under interrogation and may thus, after incorporation into the stock-in-trade of witch-hunters, have contributed to the ever more elaborate representations of the sabbath to be found in confessions from other parts of Europe where there is no evidence of shamanistic beliefs.

sabbaths, a *benandante* is a *benandante* strictly speaking only when he is 'out there' fighting the witches. Each time the *benandanti* are summoned, and obliged to go; each time they return looking for pure water to drink. Their spirit leaves and returns by the mouth, and if the body is turned over while the spirit is away it cannot return and is condemned to eternal wandering.

Instead of the opposition between this world and its negation, we have the opposition between the other-world (the world of the spirits), where fundamental issues are decided, and this world, where the consequences are felt. Instead of the opposition between the witches' apostasy and their reinsertion into society after the sabbath, we have the opposition between the exceptional birth of the *benandanti* and their exceptional death (when they go—or return?—straight to Paradise). This opposition corresponds to, and is echoed by, those between the original summons (at the age of 20) and the *benandante*'s retirement (at 45), and between the periodic departure and return of the *benandante*'s spirit.

Superimposed upon this structure, and (to my mind) quite distinct from it, we have the role of the *benandanti* as mediators, as purveyors of forbidden knowledge. Their ability to tell the fate of the dead and to identify witches—to answer questions which, as one of them put it, 'should not be asked'—is structurally anomalous. Whereas their role as *benandanti* is that of fighting as exceptional individuals on behalf of the community against collective misfortune, their role as mediators is one where they place their powers at the service of individuals, and one to which the symbolic battle between good and evil is irrelevant. In their role as witch-finders, they are at one and the same time helping the community against individual agents of the devil who are operating *within* the community, and becoming involved in conflicts between individual fellow villagers. Despite the structural anomaly, it is easy to see how the role of mediator grew out of the role of *benandante* in the strict sense. As champions of fertility, endowed with the magical 'shirt', it is natural that they should have been thought able to cure the bewitched; and as adversaries of the witches, it is natural that they should have been thought able to identify individual witches.

Their account of themselves makes it clear, however, that the battle is fought between the *benandanti*, as essentially *anonymous* forces of good, and the witches as *equally anonymous* forces of evil. It is a clash between two 'armies', where all that counts is the cause each is fighting for. Once *benandanti* and witches are conceived as *individual* agents of good and evil, the mythical significance of the battle could become overwhelmed by an obsession with identifying the agents as individuals. When the *benandanti* act collectively on behalf of the community they foster social cohesion; when they divulge what they know they are provoking, or giving supernatural sanction and confirmation to, conflicts between individual members of the community.

These beliefs are interesting in themselves, because they provide what is to date the only clear example known in Europe of a popular belief-system directly comparable to those which anthropologists have studied in Africa. In this remote region, beliefs regarding the nature and origins of evil appear to have been almost entirely unaffected by the plurality of cultural levels which is characteristic of a complex society. Despite the references to Christ and the devil, it is clear that—whether or not Ginzburg is right in believing that they represent the survival of an organized pre-Christian fertility cult—the beliefs relate exclusively to the community level of social integration. It appears, in fact, that at the local level the beliefs were incorporated into religious practice. One of the *benandanti*, born about 1535–40, confessed that 'my mother gave me a "shirt" which I had been born with, saying that she had had it baptized together with me, and that she had had nine Masses said over it, and had had it blessed.'[33] Such practices, which had earlier been condemned by S. Bernardino of Siena as superstitious, probably reflected not only the incorporation of local 'pagan' beliefs and practices, but also the popular, community-based character of pre-Tridentine Catholicism.

It is thus all the more relevant to the argument outlined in the previous section to examine the way the Inquisition reacted, in the century after the Council of Trent, to the existence of these beliefs.

When they first came across the *benandanti* in 1575–80 the inquisitors were puzzled. The *benandanti*'s battles with the witches, their goings-forth at night, their splendid 'captain', all these elements in their story suggested the sabbath. Insistently the inquisitors tried to establish points of contact between the sabbath and the other-worldly battlefield. Under heavy questioning the *benandanti* began to waver. Their own self-definition was fragmentary and, under pressure to produce an account of themselves which would be coherent enough to convince the inquisitors that they really did go forth into battle, but

---

[33] Ginzburg, *I benandanti*, p. 24.

that they were not witches, they appear to have begun improvising and to have drawn on their own confused knowledge of other beliefs.

Q. Who taught you to enter into this company of the *benandanti*?
A. The angel of heaven.
Q. When did he appear? . . . How did he appear?
A. He appeared like an angel, all golden, like those on altars, and he called me, and my spirit went forth. . . .
Q. What did he promise you? Women, food, dancing or what?
A. He promised nothing, *but the others danced*, and I saw because we fought with them. . . .
Q. Does this angel not have you worship him?
A. *We worship him* like we adore Our Lord Jesus Christ in Church . . .
Q. When he appears, does he sit on a throne?
A. We all appear at the same time and he stands near our standard.
Q. Does this angel take you to where the other one sits on his throne?
A. But he does not belong to our league. God preserve us from meddling with that false enemy! (Yielding) *It's the witches who have those fine thrones*.
Q. Have you ever seen the witches by that fine throne?
A. (Agitated) No, all we do is fight!
Q. Which is the most handsome angel, yours or the one on the fine throne?
A. Haven't I told you that I haven't seen those thrones? (Yielding) Our angel is handsome and white, and *their angel is black and and is the Devil*.[34]

Gradually, over the years, as the Inquisition sporadically concerned itself with the *benandanti*, new elements were introduced into their accounts. The inquisitors' incomprehension is properly stressed by Ginzburg. They cannot make sense of what the *benandanti* say, and although some of the latter are made to admit that the angel *may* be of diabolic origin, and are forced to disown their beliefs, the Inquisition fails to establish any real link between the battlefield and the sabbath.

A second line of attack adopted by the Inquisition was to try to get the *benandanti* to name witches. After some hesitation, names were given. But they obstinately insisted that they did not go forth to the sabbath, and their fidelity to what, despite the inquisitors' incredulity, *was* an alternative framework of explanation prevented these interrogations from being transformed into trials for witchcraft.

Nevertheless, under this kind of pressure the beliefs began to lose their coherence. In 1649 the *benandante* Michele Soppe was interrogated. He knew that he went forth at night, but when it came to explaining where he went, instead of the battlefield he described the

---

[34] Ibid., pp. 223–4 (my italics).

sabbath. Although the *benandanti* did not worship the devil, he claimed, it was from their participation in the sabbath that they derived their power to identify witches. This admission was damaging enough, but when he attributed the *benandanti*'s power to cure the bewitched to the same source he had reached the point of no return. This claim was totally incompatible with the original belief-system. Ginzburg considers that the transformation of the *benandanti*'s beliefs was produced by the ideological coercion of the Inquisition.[35] This is obviously true. But his interpretation does not explain *how* the coercion succeeded in transforming the belief-system. The brief structural analysis I sketched out above does, I think, allow for a less one-sided explanation. I argued that the *benandanti*'s role as mediators on behalf of individuals conflicted with their role as champions of the community. Their role as mediators between an other-world (where witches gathered together) and this world was—despite the fact that they were good and the witches evil—structurally equivalent to the role of witches as mediators between the anti-world of the sabbath and this world. If the fear of witches was becoming more of an individual, rather than a collective, concern, the mythical battle would tend to give way, in the minds of members of the community—and hence in the minds of the *benandanti* themselves—before concern with the forbidden knowledge to which they had access and for which there was a perhaps rising demand. This shift of emphasis makes the transition from the battlefield to the sabbath much easier. If, at the same time, the Church's 'model' of witchcraft was becoming more familiar in the area, the definition of a witch as an identifiable sabbath-goer rather than as an anonymous member of the army which fought the *benandanti* with sorghum reeds would have appeared to have greater explanatory power. Internally, then, the *benandanti*'s belief-system had a structural flaw, which could have been accentuated by external factors.

It is possible that changes in the local economy were taking place as a consequence, direct and indirect, of Venice's declining role as a sea-power at the end of the sixteenth century and of her increasing reliance on the *terraferma* as a source of food. If these hypothetical changes had disruptive social effects, then one might expect changes both in the structure of intra-community social relations (increased social differentiation, for example) and an increase in the incidence of individual witchcraft accusations. Ginzburg's material certainly suggests the latter.

It is also possible that belief in the *benandanti*'s goings-forth was no longer widespread in the region by the end of the sixteenth century. The *benandanti*'s confused knowledge about their own supposed activities has already been mentioned. In 1575 a local priest was incredulous when he was told by a *benandante* that forty years earlier his amniotic membrane had been baptized together with him, and that Masses had been said over it. Some of the local people were also clearly muddled, and even spoke of *strigoni benandanti*, missing the whole point of the *collective, anonymous* battle, and seeing the *benandanti* only in their role as witch-finders, curers of witchcraft, perhaps witches themselves—as ambiguous *individuals* who could manipulate occult powers.

Thus when in 1649 Michele Soppe confusedly claimed to have taken part in the sabbath, the only way in which, closely pressed by the inquisitor, he could both make sense of his own story and satisfy the inquisitor's demand that the account be coherent was by admitting a pact with the devil. The individualistic dimension has now clearly come to the surface, the communal dimension has been submerged, and the structural ambiguity of the belief-system has been eliminated. Everything else falls into place. Michele Soppe, having admitted the pact with the devil, produced a full, spontaneous, and thoroughly typical witchcraft confession. The tripartite model underlying European witchcraft confessions had, thanks to its own coherence as a 'structuring structure'[36] and the weaknesses of the rival model, been imposed by the Inquisition.

V

However untypical the case of the *benandanti* may have been, their encounter with the Venetian Inquisition demonstrates very clearly how a concern with the nature and origins of the witch's power to do harm led inevitably, in western Europe, to the view that by placing herself, even implicitly, in the service of the devil she had renounced allegiance to God and to the Church and had placed herself outside

---

[36] Pierre Bourdieu, 'The Thinkable and the Unthinkable', *The Times Literary Supplement*, 3633 (15 Oct. 1971), 1255–6; cf. also the much more developed argument in his *Outline of a Theory of Practice* (Cambridge, 1977).

and against Christian society. This concern was prominent in the definition of the crime of witchcraft that was adopted by those responsible for prosecutions on the Continent. Every time someone was accused of malefice and subsequently prosecuted and convicted of witchcraft, a link was established between the effects and the origins of the witch's power to do harm.

At the level of popular culture people were concerned with the *effects* of the witch's power. They attempted to evade or neutralize it by resorting to forms of counter-witchcraft or by taking informal action against the suspected witch. In this, as in early modern England and in Africa today, they showed little practical concern with the *origins* of the witch's power, and even less concern with the implications of those origins for defining the precise status of the witch. Denouncing a suspected witch to the authorities was a further form of action made possible by the existence of formal institutions empowered to prosecute witches. But these institutions, and their personnel, did not operate with the framework of popular culture. They were representatives of the culture of the élite, concerned with the formal typification of the crime of witchcraft in terms not only of its effects, but of its essence. The courts had to decide whether or not the suspect was a witch before they could take further action. And in attempting to establish this fact through interrogation, they influenced the way people thought about witches.

This does not mean that at the level of popular culture the supernatural power of witches was simply taken for granted. Symbolic representations of the inexplicable, of the boundary between nature and culture, and of the origins of misfortune were widespread and varied. Elements of these representations will have been drawn on, during interrogation, by suspected witches and subsequently incorporated into the standardized model of witchcraft that provided the basis for deciding whether the suspect was or was not a witch. At the same time the standardized model, because of its completeness and coherence, will have been superimposed as a structuring structure on less developed popular conceptions of the nature and origins of the witch's power to do harm.

What distinguishes Continental European witch-beliefs from their counterparts in Africa today is the fact that they derive, in the form in which they have been transmitted to us, from a process of institutional mediation between cultural levels in a complex society. Although traditional anthropology cannot deal with such processes of mediation, comparisons with African witch-beliefs can help specify in what ways European witch-beliefs were different. These differences, and the forms and consequences of institutional mediation in early modern Europe, can quite properly be tackled from the standpoint of social anthropology, as long as it is recognized that we are dealing, in the anthropologists' sense, with complex societies. One of anthropology's contributions to the social history of early modern Europe lies in helping specify the nature of that complexity and in helping us to evaluate the implications of the fact that the sources available to us are themselves a result and a reflection of the institutional mediation that it entails.

7

'The Ladies from Outside': An Archaic Pattern of the Witches' Sabbath *

GUSTAV HENNINGSEN

I. ARCHAIC PATTERNS OF EUROPEAN WITCHCRAFT

IN an article published in 1975 Professor Mircea Eliade, after briefly reviewing the recent historiography of European witchcraft, drew attention to the fact that the phenomenon cannot be properly explained 'as a creation of religious and political persecution'. A satisfactory understanding could not be reached without the help of other disciplines, 'such as folklore, ethnology, sociology, psychology, and the history of religions'. 'Unfortunately,' he went on, 'the few attempts to investigate the phenomenon of European witchcraft in the perspective of the history of religions have been hopelessly inadequate.' This criticism was mainly directed against Margaret Murray's unexpectedly successful and popular book, *The Witch-cult of Western Europe* (Oxford, 1921). The rest of the article was devoted to reflections on a series of popular European belief-complexes: Carlo Ginzburg's important discovery of the North Italian shamans who declared to the inquisitors for the province of Friuli that they were 'good' wizards, *benandanti*, who fought against the witches (*stregoni*); and his own study of the Romanian cathartic dancers and healers (*călușari*), whose speciality is to cure disease caused by the fairies—at the same time as they claim, surprisingly enough, that their secret

* An important part of the research on the theme of the present paper was conducted on study trips to Spain and Italy generously supported by the Svend Grundtvig and Axel Olrik Foundation, the Danish Council of Research in the Humanities, and the Swedish Olin Foundation for the History of Law. The author wishes to express his gratitude to these foundations. Preliminary versions have been published in German ('Die "Frauen von Ausserhalb": Der Zusammenhang von Feenkult, Hexenwahn und Armut in 16. und 17. Jahrhundert auf Sizilien', in Hans Peter Duerr (ed.), *Die Mitte der Welt: Aufsätze zu Mircea Eliade* (Frankfurt am Main, 1984)); Danish ('"Kvinderne udefra": Feer, hekse og fattigdom på Sicilien i det 16. og 17. århundrede', *Norveg*, 27 (1984), 51–67); and Hungarian ('"A kívülről jött hölgyek": Tündérek, boszorkányok és szegénység a korai modern Szicíliában', *Világosság*, 26 (1985), 778–85).

society is patronized by the 'Queen of the Fairies', *Doamna Zînelor*—the Romanian metamorphosis of Diana, also called Irodiada (= Herodias) or Arada (both names having familiar connections with western European beliefs in witchcraft and the Wild Hunt). Eliade also commented upon other archaic beliefs and rituals of Romania, Italy, Austria, Germany, France, and Spain. At the end of his survey the author came to the following conclusion:

The *real or imaginary* [my italics] orgiastic practices of the European witches disclose a certain religious pattern. First and foremost, the sexual orgies reveal a radical protest against the contemporary religious and social situations . . . Secondly, the so-called satanic elements of the witch orgies may have been practically non-existent but forcibly imposed by the trials . . . Thirdly, the [real or imaginary] orgiastic practices witness to a religious nostalgia, a strong desire to return to an archaic phase of culture—the dream-like time of the fabulous 'beginnings'.[1]

Unfortunately this article has been passed over unnoticed by most historians of witchcraft.[2] The reason for the complete lack of discussion of Eliade's views on European witch-belief may be that a superficial reading of his article gives the impression that it is yet another attempt to prove the existence of a European witch cult, and since a whole generation of scholars has dealt so severely with Murray and her dilettante imitators, there is great scepticism of anyone who suggests that any sabbaths took place before the twentieth century. In fact, Eliade's article discusses both real *and* imaginary orgiastic practices, so that he cannot be classified as a Murrayist. I myself have to admit that I did not realize how the considerations in the article might be applied when I made a first superficial reading of it in the late 1970s. But the possibilities became clear to me after a more thorough reading early in 1983, when I went back to it in consequence of a find I had made in the archives of the Spanish Inquisition (Archivo histórico Nacional in Madrid) of about 70 case records of trials held by the

---

[1] Mircea Eliade, 'Some Observations on European Witchcraft', *History of Religions*, 14 (1975), 149–72.

[2] See e.g. Norman Cohn, *Europe's Inner Demons* (London, 1975); Richard Kieckhefer, *European Witch Trials; Their Foundations in Popular and Learned Culture, 1300–1500* (Berkeley and Los Angeles, 1976); Edward Peters, *The Magician, the Witch and the Law* (Philadelphia, 1976); E. William Monter, *Witchcraft in France and Switzerland* (Ithaca and London, 1976); Brian Easlea, *Witch Hunting, Magic and the New Philosophy* (Brighton, 1980); Christina Larner, *Enemies of God: The Witch-hunt in Scotland* (London, 1981)—to mention the most important. And admittedly also Gustav Henningsen, *The Witches' Advocate: Basque Witchcraft and the Spanish Inqisition* (Reno, 1980).

tribunal of the Spanish Inquisition in Palermo of Sicilian witches or 'donas de fuera', as they were called by a slight transcription of the Sicilian donni di fuora (Italian donne di fuori).

II. THE SPANISH INQUISITION AND THE SICILIAN WITCHES

Sicily was part of the Spanish Empire from 1282 to 1713. From 1487 the Spanish Inquisition had a court in Palermo and a network of agents distributed over the whole island. The Inquisition continued to function with a Spanish staff after Spain had relinquished Sicily in 1713, but in 1782, when Sicily came under the government of Naples, it was abolished by a decree from the Spanish viceroy Ferdinando IV, and this occasioned the burning of the tribunal's archives, including the original proceedings, which took place in the courtyard of the palace in Palermo.[3] If it had not been for the bureaucracy of the Inquisition we would thus have been deprived of much knowledge of the activities of the Holy Office in Sicily, but fortunately for us the Council of the Inquisition in Spain (la Suprema) kept strict control over its subordinate courts, which means that in the archives of la Suprema, preserved intact in the Archivo histórico Nacional (Department of Inquisition), we have endless files of correspondence between the inquisitors in Palermo and the Inquisitor-General and his 'Ministry' in Madrid. One particularly important collection is the central register of relaciones de causas, annual reports from all the inquisitions of the Spanish empire with more or less detailed summaries of each heresy trial. Thus five manuscript volumes from the Sicilian tribunal have survived, containing chronologically arranged summaries of completed cases. There is an almost complete series of 115 relaciones de causas for the period from 1547 to 1701, with summaries of a total of 3,188 cases.[4] 456 of these are concerned with superstition: cases of sorcerers, diviners, astrologers, necromantics,

---

[3] Cf. Henry Charles Lea, The Inquisition in the Spanish Dependencies (New York, 1922), 1–44; and for the destruction of the original trial records, my chapter, 'The Archives and the Historiography of the Spanish Inquisition', in Gustav Henningsen and John Tedeschi, in association with Charles Amiel (eds.), The Inquisition in Early Modern Europe: Studies on Sources and Methods (Dekalb, 1986), 58, 126 n. 4.

[4] Archivo histórico Nacional, Sección de Inquisición, libros 898–902; for crimino-logical statistics of the trial summaries contained in this series, see Jaime Contreras, 'Algunas consideraciones sobre las relaciones de causas de Sicilia y Cerdeña', Annuario dell'Istituto Storico Italiana per l'età Moderna e Contemporanea, 37–8 (1985–6), 179–99.

and witches (*donas de fuera*), in all covering about 1,000 pages of manuscript with condensed information extracted from the now lost original proceedings.

By tradition the Spanish Inquisition was extremely sceptical with regard to witchcraft and sorcery. Thus there are no witches amongst the twenty-five people burned for heresy in Sicily in the period in question. *La Suprema* persistently held firm to the *Canon episcopi*'s denunciation of witchcraft as a popular superstition, and only during the renowned mass trial at Logroño did it carry out some few witch-burnings at an *auto-da-fé* in 1610.[5] Both before and after this the Inquisition practised its cautious 'witch policy', and one must look as far back as to the beginning of the sixteenth century to find other examples of witches burned by the Spanish Inquisition. In the period we are concerned with here, the Sicilian witches and sorcerers were sentenced in the main to a few years' banishment or to varying periods of imprisonment. In certain cases the men were condemned to the galleys and the women to whipping, but in numerous other cases the trials were suspended, because the inquisitors found them too trifling, or because the evidence against the accused was not convincing. Torture was applied only to a limited extent, and never at the start of the trial to force a confession from the accused. Invariably, it is clearly stated in the case documents when the accused had been subjected to torture, for this could only be applied after a provisional judgement had been made. Another factor that must be taken into account when assessing the source material left to us by the Inquisition is the duration of the trials: some of the *donas de fuera* spent several years in the cells before the incredible pedantry of the inquisitors enabled them to complete their cases; the effects of this, familiar to us in the twentieth century's brainwashing processes, cannot, therefore, be excluded. (For a discussion of the problems of using sources such as inquisitorial interrogations to shed light on popular ideas, see my analysis of the Basque witch-craze.[6])

---

[5] Henningsen, *The Witches' Advocate*.

[6] Ibid. ch. 3.; see also Jean-Pierre Dedieu, 'The Archives of the Holy Office of Toledo as a Source for Historical Anthropology', in Henningsen and Tedeschi, in association with Amiel (eds.), *Inquisition in Early Modern Europe*, pp. 158–89.

III. FAIRIES AND WITCHES

The Sicilian folklorist Giuseppe Pitrè defined a *donna di fuora* as 'something of a fairy and something of a witch although one cannot really distinguish which is which'.[7] The Spanish Inquisition material clearly reveals that during the sixteenth and seventeenth centuries the Sicilians attached two meanings to the term: it was chiefly used to designate the supernatural, fairy-like creatures (of both sexes) who accompanied the witches on their nocturnal excursions, but several of the accused witches also stated that they themselves were *donas de fuera*. If we take the word *witch* in its ethnological sense, as a person who has rejected the norms of society, and who by virtue of super-natural powers or pacts with demons harms his or her fellow human beings, then to apply the term to the Sicilian 'witches' is totally misleading. It is true that the Spanish inquisitors used the term witch (*bruja*) synonymously with *dona de fuera*, but none of the witnesses in the sixty-five cases brought against male and female *donas*, conducted by the Palermo tribunal between 1579 and 1651, concerned accusa-tions of witchcraft in the true sense of the word. Like southern Spain, Sicily was a region in which sorcery and black magic thrived, but where popular notions of witchcraft were absent. However, in contrast to Spain, Sicily could boast of a particular type of charismatic healer, who was a specialist in curing diseases caused by the fairies: these healers were women, and sometimes men, too, who claimed to possess 'sweet blood' (*sangre dulce*), and who therefore each Tuesday, Thurs-day, and Saturday night were obliged to rush out in spirit (*in espíritu*) and take part in the meetings and nocturnal journeyings of 'the company'.

The picture of the Sicilian fairy cult painted by the Inquisition's trial records displays a flourishing tradition, with variations from district to district. I have not yet made a complete survey of this belief-complex, and what follows can only provide a preliminary sketch of its elements and some of their variations. The fairies are participants in a group of seven (six or five) women, and one of them is 'The Queen of the Fairies' (*Reina de las Hadas*). She is also known as '*La Matrona*', '*La Maestra*', 'The Greek Lady' (*La Señora Griega*), '*Señora Gracia*', '*Doña*

---

[7] Giuseppe Pitrè, *Usi e costumi, credenze e pregiudizi del popolo siciliano* (Palermo, 1889), iv. 153.

Inguanta', 'Mandatta', 'Doña Zabella', or 'The Wise Sybil' (*La Sabia Sibila*). They are described as beautfiul women dressed in black or white, but their supernatural origin is revealed by their feet: cat's paws, horse's hooves, or 'round feet'. In one or two cases it is stated that they have little pig's tails, and that their flesh is 'soft' (*tenían las carnes blandas*). Sometimes one of the group is a male fairy, who plays the lute or guitar to the others when they dance with linked hands.

Fairies and human beings are organized in 'companies', which have different names according to their district: '*Compañía de los Romanos*', '*Compañía de la Matrona*', '*La Compañía de Menzo y Usso*' (The Company for Table and Distaff (?)), '*La Compañía de Palermo*', '*La Compañía de Ragusa*', and so on. A wise woman, Vicencia Rosa from Noto on the south-east coast, related that there were no less than five 'companies' in her town: 'The Company of the Noble', three companies of the ordinary people, and 'the Company of the Poor', to which she herself belonged. The same woman described how 'in the month of March they assembled with many other [companies] from various regions in a wood full of trees, and that their prince did not wish them to do evil things, but to heal [people] (libro 901, fo. 548). There is little information on the size of these companies. In one place twenty-two persons are mentioned, in another thirty, and in another thirty-three, but it is not clear whether the fairies are included in these numbers. In Noto, the Company of the Noble numbered twelve, and each of the others had nine members.

In some places the meetings resemble a sabbath. In 1588 a fisherman's wife from Palermo confessed to the Inquisition that she and her company, with their 'ensign' at their head, rode on billy-goats through the air to

a country called Benevento that belongs to the Pope and lies in the kingdom of Naples. There was a great plain there on which there stood a large tribune with two chairs. On one of them sat a red young man and on the other a beautiful woman; they called her the Queen, and the man was the King. The first time she went there,—when she was eight years old,—the ensign and other women [*sic*] in her company said that she must kneel and worship this king and queen and do everything they told her, because they could help her and give her wealth, beauty and young men to make love with. And they told her that she must not worship God or Our Lady. The ensign made her swear on a book with big letters that she would worship the other two. So she took an oath to worship them, the King as God and the Queen as Our Lady, and promised them her body and soul. . . . And after she had worshipped them like this, they set out tables and ate and drank, and after that the men lay with the women and with her and made love to them many times in a short time.

All this seemed to her to be taking place in a dream, for when she awoke she always found herself in bed, naked as when she had gone to rest. But sometimes they called her out before she had gone to bed so that her husband and children should not find out, and without going to sleep (as far as she can judge) she started out and arrived fully clothed.

She went on to say that she did not know at that time that it was devilment, until her confessor opened her eyes to her errors and told her that it was the Devil and that she must not do it any more. But in spite of this she went on doing it until two months ago. And she went out joyfully because of the pleasure she took in it . . . and because they [the King and the Queen] gave her remedies for curing the sick so that she could earn a little, for she has always been poor . . . (Libro 898, fos. 438ʳ–439ʳ.)

The poor fisherman's wife also told the inquisitors about another witches' assembly, 'which they call "The Seven Fairies". These have the habit of transforming themselves into dogs, cats, and other animals, and into ugly things that they call *aydon*. They go about killing boys and doing other misdeeds. And this is something she has heard somebody say, but she has nothing to do with them' (ibid., fo. 439ʳ). *Aydon* might possibly be interpreted as a distortion of Greek *aidoion*, sexual organs. It should be noted that this is the only time in the Sicilian records that there is mention of 'wicked' witches in the popular tradition.

The year after the hearing of the fisherman's wife, the Inquisition brought a case against a 60-year-old fortune-teller who came from the town of '*la Plaza*'. In her confession she described how she had been made queen at one of her 'fairy sabbaths', and all the others had bowed their heads in obedience to her. She had done the same when one of the others had been elected queen for a night (libro 898, fos. 350ʳ–350ᵛ).

Benevento, the Italian Brocken, appears again in later cases brought against *donas de fuera*. In 1627 a 36-year-old wise woman (married to a journeyman from Alcamo), who was a member of 'the Company of the Romans', related how she was taken by them far and wide, to Rome, Messina, and to 'a vast plain with a big walnut tree in the centre'. Replying to her friends' questions about what kind of folk these 'Romans' were, she had explained on several occasions

that they were the Wise Sybil's people who came from a cave that was in the tower of Babylon, and that the Sybil was King Solomon's sister. She had

instructed the others together with the bliss-crowned Virgin Mary, and had
received the impression that she herself must be the Mother of God. But when
she saw that it was not to be her, but the bliss-crowned Virgin, she threw all
her books on the fire. But Mary kept hers under her arm. (Libro 900, fos. 391ᵛ–
392ʳ.)

The journeyman's wife also entertained her friends (two of whom
were themselves *donas de fuera*) with accounts of the company's tours
around the houses of the town each Tuesday, Thursday, and Saturday
night, when 'the Matron' took the lead carrying a torch to light them
all along, although this was visible only to the members of the
company. When they went into a house with their songs and music
and fine clothes they would say: 'With God's blessing let the dance
increase! (*Dios la bendiga y crezca la danza*)', and when, after taking a look
into people's clothes' chests—and eating some of the food, if there was
a festive gathering in progress—they left to go on somewhere else,
their parting salute was: 'Stop the dance and let prosperity increase!
(*Alto la danza y crezca el bien*).'

Everything considered, we can see that poor Sicilians talked end-
lessly among themselves about the fairies, and that those of them who
were themselves *donas de fuera* gladly described their wonderful
adventures, even when this might be dangerous. The large numbers of
informers and witnesses in the *donas* cases speak for themselves: there
could be ten, twenty, or thirty witnesses against one accused person.
After being informed of the witnesses' statements, a 40-year-old nun
from Ragusa admitted: 'that sometimes to please her listeners she had
told them things that she had neither seen nor had any knowledge of'
(libro 900, fo. 522ʳ). Some of the inquisitors seem to have had a clear
understanding of the real state of affairs. In 1630 they sentenced
30-year-old Vicencia la Rosa from Noto to a brief period of banishment, but strictly enjoined her never in future to speak to anybody of
the things she had been accused of. But alas, Vicencia, or 'La Riciola'
as she was known among friends, could not contain herself. She went
on telling her friends about her familiar spirit, Martinillo, who took
her to the sabbath three times a week, when she consulted her 'Prince'
about people's diseases and bewitchings; and she told them who
belonged to the Company of the Noble, and who to the Company of
the Poor. Six years later the hammer of the Inquisition fell, and this
time she was sentenced to perpetual banishment from her home
district (libro 901, fos. 94ʳ–94ᵛ, 547ᵛ–550ʳ). It can hardly be doubted
that both listeners and story-tellers in the main believed the tales and

took them seriously. The husband and wife from a house where one accused person, a 60-year-old washerwoman from Palermo, had gone to work, stated:

that once when the wife had lost an apron and had said to the accused that she suspected her sister of taking it, the accused replied that she would see to it that she found out if it was true that her sister had taken it or not. Next day she went back and said that it was true: the sister had indeed taken the apron. When the wife asked her how she could know that, the accused replied that she went out at night with 'the women from outside' (i.e the witches) [interpolation by the inquisitors] twice a week and went into some of the houses, and in her sister's house she had seen the witness's apron. And she said this at various times and days. And [she also described] how when they went into the houses it was like a wind, and that they opened the chests and dressed themselves up in the clothes they found, and they played the tambourine and the lute and sang very sweetly. [She went on to say] that she had a son who went out with the witches [that is to say, the *donas*] as well, and [added] that if only she could wander as well as he did—and this made him especially popular.' Her husband and father-in-law had done the same when they were alive.

Another day the washerwoman complained of pain in her arm, and when they asked her what had caused it she answered that the witches demanded that she should be ready to go out, and when she did not want to go—or told someone about it, they beat her with a laurel stick after lifting her up and putting her back to front on an old hack. And [she said] that when they went around to the houses they were invisible, but that she knew everything that went on . . . [The accused had likewise said] that when she went out with the witches they were twelve women and eighteen men. (libro 899, fo. 329ᵛ.)

From the examples I have quoted we might expect to find that there were a number of wealthy and noble persons among the members of the fairy cult, and that there were more men than women in these secret assemblies. But in reality it was not so. Among the 65 'witches' against whom the Palermo inquisitors brought cases during the period from 1579 to 1651 there are no aristocratic persons, and as far as can be judged, no persons of wealth. In every case in which we have an indication of the financial status of the accused, the person involved is poor: four farm-labourers and three farm-labourers' wives, three workmen and two workmen's wives, four fishermen's wives, one tailor, one shoemaker and one shoemaker's wife, one deacon, two Franciscan begging nuns, one *saludador* (charismatic healer), one washerwoman, two prostitutes, two gypsy women, and also seven widows and six women whose poverty is expressly emphasized by the inquisitors (a poor miserable spinning women', 'a married woman in dire straits', 'a poor wife', and so on). The one possible exception is a 30-year-old woman from Alcamo, married to an innkeeper (*mesonero*). In other words, the Sicilian fairy-cult was a daydream religion that allowed poor people to experience in dreams and visions all the splendours denied them in real life. Nor did myth and reality agree in regard to the distribution of sexes: among the sixty-five accused we find only eight male 'witches'. The fairy cult in Sicily was a decidedly feminine phenomenon.

But the Sicilian fairy cult had other functions than dream-compensation for the hopeless poverty of daily life. The majority of the accused were practising wise women and were skilled in various forms of sorcery and magical healing rituals. This was something they had in common with many other cunning folk in Sicily, but in addition to these powers they were known to be able to cure ills brought upon people by the fairies: some of our *donas* seem to have possessed this special talent exclusively. '*Tocadura de brujas*' (witch-touching) is the collective term for these illnesses, that can take every possible form from indisposition to what we must assume to have been attacks of epilepsy. It was invariably caused by the sick person offending a fairy or a *dona*: a young man who suffered an attack of cramp while playing the guitar was told by a wise woman in Noto that he had given a push with his arm to some fairies who had gathered around him to listen to the music; and a nun from Arcara near Messina, who was greatly sought after as a charismatic healer, explained to a woman patient that she was ill as a punishment for having thrown a stone at a snake who was in reality 'a woman of the company', while another patient who had a bad arm was told that, when out in her garden, she had happened to sit down on top of a '*dona de fuera*' who was pregnant, and who therefore in her anger over this had given her the bad arm.

After establishing the cause of the illness, the wise woman would explain to her patient that the fairies can be mollified by an offering, and that she personally will attend the nocturnal meeting in company with her 'Ladies' and persuade them to make the sick person well again. The offering consists almost always of a ritual meal, described in great detail in several of the trial records. In 1600, 40-year-old Antonia Pallalonga from 'Zaragoza of this kingdom', present-day Syracuse, described to the inquisitors how she used to

decorate the sick person's room and set out a table with jugs of water and wine, and with sweetmeats, five loaves, five napkins and a honey-cake, a cup and other eating utensils. [And that she] covered the sick person's bed with a red cloth and perfumed the whole room [sweet-smelling incense] . . . (Libro 899, fo. 6or.)[8]

The fairies come to visit the sick person's home on one of the regular weekdays (Tuesday, Thursday, or Saturday), usually at night while the people of the house are asleep, but one of our *donas* was accustomed to come with her 'Ladies' in the evening, before the family had retired to rest. The following is the account of three witnesses of one of these invisible visits that took place in Santa Ninfa on an occasion in the late 1630s:

[The wise woman] said that the people she had been describing, her 'Ladies', would soon be coming, and every so often she went out into the yard and acted as if she could see them, and waved her hand to them. Shortly after this she said that they had come. And she appeared to be taking them by the hand one by one and leading them to sit down in the chairs. But neither the witnesses nor the others who were present could see anything. Then she walked up and down near the sick person and played on a tambourine, and picking up food from the plates she made as if to put it into the mouths of her friends. She then took ceremonial leave of her friends in the same fashion, and told [the occupants of the house] that they had shown her how the sick [woman] was to be cured, and that now she was well again, for those [Ladies] had touched her with their hands. (Libro 902, fos. 39ʳ–39ᵛ.)

It was not only human beings who fell ill from the '*tocadura de brujas*', it could also strike horses and donkeys; and then the *tabula* ritual would have to be carried out in the stable, as in a detailed description from a trial record of a case brought in 1651 against a very poor wise

---

[8] There are extremely interesting parallels to this *tabula* ritual in Petrus Hispanus, *Practica medicine que Thesaurus pauperum nuncupatur* (Antwerp, 1476): 'Multi in domibus in noctibus praedictis post coenam dimittunt panem et caeseum, lac, carnes, ova, vinum et aquam e huiusmodi super mensas et coclearea, discos, ciphos, cutellos et similia propter visitationem Perhtae cum cohorta sua' (*apud* Arne Runeberg, *Witches, Demons and Fertility Magic* (Helsinki, 1947), 154); for a similar *tabula* ritual devoted to conjuring up German mountain spirits, see ibid., p. 151. The most striking parallel, however, is reported in John Cuthbert Lawson, *Modern Greek Folklore and Ancient Greek Religion* (Cambridge, 1910), 125 f.: 'The occasion on which the Fates have most often been seen . . . is the third (or . . . fifth) night after the birth of a child. Provision for their arrival is then scrupulously made. The dog is chained up. . . . The house-door is left open or at any rate unlatched. Inside a light is kept burning, and in the middle of the room is set a low table with three cushions or low stools round it—. . . On the table are set out such dainties as the Fates love, including always honey; . . . Three white almonds, a loaf of bread, and a glass of water; and ready to hand, as presents from which the goddesses may choose what they will, may be laid all the most costly treasures of the family, such as jewellery and even money.'

woman from Ragusa, 30-year-old Gandolfa Rizo, who, however, told the inquisitors that she was definitely not a *dona de fuera*, but merely carried out the ritual in order to earn money. In one single case we find a wise woman using her fairies to bless the fields: a witness states how he had gone to the accused, 22-year-old Vicenta Pilato from Alcamo, to beg her to ask her fairies whether he would have a good harvest. Vicenta went into an adjoining room and returned a little later to say that 'now she had spoken to them, and he could rejoice, for he was going to have a good harvest, and [she told him] that they had promised her to go out and bless his cornfields three times', after which she sent him away with a request to buy ten loaves of bread for her fairies (libro 901, fo. 255).

The fairies made their mark on Sicilian everyday life in other ways as well. During a journey of visitation to the eastern part of the island undertaken by the inquisitor Lope Varona in the winter of 1588-9, a woman was reported by her neighbours for having said 'she often saw six daintily dressed women in her house who came to help her with her spinning ... They had cats' paws.' The woman was summoned and questioned as to who these women were. But she answered 'that she knew no more than that she had seen them many times' (libro 898, fo. 482). This woman escaped with a warning. But in 1627 the inquisitors found it necessary to imprison an 11-year-old girl in Palermo who had described the fairies at great length to the woman who was teaching her lace-making, and particularly to a girl of the same age who was a fellow apprentice. During her interrogation by the Inquisition, the 11-year-old continued her account:

Likewise she confessed ... that when the two of them were sitting alone working at the lace-pillow, seven women appeared before them; beautifully dressed in red and white they came dancing in through the door of the room with a tambourine in their hand ... and sat down beside the two girls. One of them ... told her that she was called Gracia and was a sister to the Queen of the Fairies. Her dress was of a gold and crimson material and she had on little high shoes (*chapines*) that were round and white. Another of them, who was dressed in white, said her name was Giloca. The others were dressed in bright red, pink, and white, and they all wore their head-dresses wound about their faces as the Greek women do, and had little round high shoes painted red and white. They had very beautiful faces and they said they were 'The Company of Palermo', and that she was to tell the other girl that they were there (for she could not see them)—and that they had come to make her rich. But when she told her friend this the other girl was frightened, which did not happen to the accused, who was not afraid. And they stayed talking to her there for an hour or two, and afterwards they went away, out of the same door that they had come in by . . . without saying anything more than 'Good Morning', when it was early in the day (*mañana*) and 'Good Evening', when it was late in the day (*tarde*). And they came like this five or six times. (Libro 900, fos. 409ᵛ–410ʳ.)

The fairies and the earthly *donas* are particularly fond of small children. On their nightly tour of the houses they take the children out of their cradles and take joy in them, but there is never any question of them harming the children. There is one account of how the fairies and the women who accompanied them went to see a woman who had been confined and had 'given birth to a fine and very well-formed boy, and they heaped blessings upon him so that he should be rich' (libro 900, fo. 519ʳ). The assistance given by the fairies to poor Sicilians in their untiring search for hidden treasure is a whole chapter in itself, but unfortunately lack of space prevents further discussion of this subject here.

But I should like to say something regarding the age of the *donas* complex. It can be traced back in the Spanish Inquisition material only to 1579, when the first case appears, but the Italian historian Guiseppe Bonomo—who, it should be noted, is not acquainted with the comprehensive documentation held in Madrid—with the aid of other source material has established the existence of the belief as far back as the middle of the fifteenth century. In a popular manual for confessors written between 1450 and 1470 by a certain Giovanni Vasallo, the Sicilian priests are advised to question their penitents on 'whether they believe in the women from outside and that they walk by night (*si cridi li donni di fori e ki vayanu la nocti*)'.[9]

If we look outside Sicily we find interesting parallels to the *donas* complex in the fourteenth century, when in the years between 1384 and 1390 the Inquisition in Milan brought cases against two wise women in that city. It appears from the confessions of the two women that they set out every Thursday night with 'Signora Oriente' and her *società*, a secret society for which both living and dead were eligible— although not those who had been hung and beheaded, for they had had their necks broken and therefore were unable to bow their heads

---

[9] Giuseppe Bonomo, *Caccia alle streghe* (Palermo, 1959), 65. The author knows only two Inquisition cases, both from 1640, which he cites from Pitrè, the latter again relying on a published source, not precisely indicated, but apparently some printed or unprinted *auto-da-fé* account (ibid., pp. 68 and 484, nn. 12–13). I have not had the opportunity of seeing the rev. edn. of Bonomo's work (Palermo, forthcoming).

in reverence to 'Madonna Oriente' (which was another name for their leader). Oriente explained to her followers that she ruled in her *società* as Christ ruled in the world, and in order not to offend her it was forbidden to utter the name of Jesus during the meetings. At the nocturnal gatherings they slaughtered all kinds of animals and ate them, but the bones were carefully put into the skins, for at the end of the meal Madonna Oriente went round touching the bundles of bones with a magic stick, after which the animals were restored to life. At least two kinds of animals had to be represented during these ritual meals, otherwise the world would come to an end; but the donkey and the fox were debarred from participation (the donkey because of its close relationship with Christ—no explanation is given for the fox being banned). At the meetings, Madonna Oriente instructed her followers in the uses of medicinal herbs, in foretelling the future, and in exposing evil spells. They were welcome to instruct others in all these arts, but they were forbidden to reveal anything about the *società*. In the same manner as the Sicilian fairies and *donas*, Oriente and her band went on nightly visits to the houses, eating and drinking with the rich, and when they found a home clean and tidy they gave it their blessing. One of the two wise women said that she was 30 years old when she first went to 'Diana's game' (*ad ludum Dianae*)—possibly a paraphrase of the inquisitors—and that her family had obliged her to take part in place of her aunt, who was a member of the 'company', and who was unable to die before she had found a replacement.[10]

IV. FROM DREAM CULT TO WITCHES' SABBATH

The Italian witch-trial records and demonological writings of the fifteenth and sixteenth centuries teem with accounts of orgiastic nocturnal gatherings that people took part in while their bodies remained in their beds. For instance, the Dominican monk Bartholomeo Spina in *Quaestio de strigibus* (Venice, 1525) describes a witches' sabbath in the province of Ferrara that is presided over by a certain 'Domina cursus', whom the witches also call 'The Wise Sybil'. During the nightly meetings that are held twice a week on the bank of the

---

[10] Bonomo, *Caccia alle streghe*, pp. 15, 17; cf. Jeffrey Burton Russell, *Witchcraft in the Middle Ages* (Ithaca and London, 1972), 211–13, based exclusively on Bonomo's account, but with serious errors in the translation: e.g. the Italian *volpe*, 'fox', is translated as 'wolf'.

River Jordan 'The Wise Sybil' tries again and again to fly down and touch the river, striving with all her might; for if she can only get one finger in the water she will have power over the whole world. But she never manages it![11] Here we find again a resemblance to the 'Madonna Oriente' cult from Milan and the fairy cult from Sicily, but a new element has now appeared: 'Domina cursus' demands of her Ferrara witches that they must kill a child once every fortnight, so they run around in the shape of cats and slink into the houses, where they suck the blood from small children, who die a few days later.[12] Everywhere on the Italian mainland there are signs of a similar diabolization of popular idea complexes, like the one so brilliantly documented by Carlo Ginzburg in the case of Friuli. In the first cases brought against *benandanti* from the end of the sixteenth century these popular charismatic healers succeeded in persuading the inquisitors to accept them as specialists in combating witchcraft and consequently to accept that they could not be witches (*stregoni*), but by the beginning of the seventeenth century the inquisitors' 'understanding' had come to an end and the *benandanti* were gradually obliged to confess that they themselves were witches too. As a result, writes Ginzburg, in a *benandante*'s confession from 1634 for the first time anywhere in Friuli we have a coherent description of the witches' sabbath.[13]

In the same way as the Italian inquisitors in Friuli and the other Italian regions succeeded with the diabolizing process, so too did the Spanish inquisitors in Sardinia, aided by the local bishops, meet with success when they conducted dozens of witch-trials.[14] The only place where no witch-hunt took place was Sicily. Inquisition and Church did their utmost to get the people to realize that their 'men and women from outside' were purely and simply witches, but their efforts did not bear the same fruit as in other places, where we must assume that the propaganda started a chain reaction in the population. During confession and inquisitorial interrogation male and female *donas* were naturally obliged to admit that in reality their fairy cult was demonolatry, and a few of them were also encouraged to produce authentic descriptions of sabbaths. However, every time the Inquisition seized

---

[11] Here quoted from Bonomo, *Caccia alle streghe*, pp. 72 ff.

[12] Ibid., p. 73.

[13] Carlo Ginzburg, *I benandanti* (Turin, 1966), 152; cf. Eliade, 'Some Observations ...', p. 156.

[14] See Gustav Henningsen, 'La inquisizione spagnola e le tradizioni popolari della Sardegna', in *Linguaggio musicale e linguaggio poetico in Sardegna* (Cagliari, 1981), 57–60.

upon one of these 'witches', they had to begin all over again. Many of the accused declared under interrogation that they had not known there was anything wrong in these things, until their confessors or the inquisitors had explained to them that there was. In one or two cases the accused even tried to exempt their fairies from the serious accusations by pointing out that they were not, like demons, afraid of the Cross and holy water; indeed, one of the accused went so far as to describe a mass that had been said at her 'fairy sabbath' by some Catholic priests who had been brought by 'Doña Zabella' from Malta (libro 900, fo. 523ʳ). I believe that the reason for the lack of success in diabolizing the Sicilian *donas de fuera* and bringing on them the same fate as that of their charismatic colleagues in Friuli, the lack of success in involving the devil in the poor Sicilians' dream world and giving him a permanent place there, is connected with the fact I have mentioned earlier, that no notions of wicked and mischief-making witches existed in Sicily. In Friuli popular tradition included both 'good' witches (*benandanti*) and 'bad' witches (*stregoni*), while the Sicilians did not hold a similar dualistic system of belief. As we have seen, their *donas de fuera* complex was ambivalent: fairies and 'witches' could exercise both good and ill, although the harm they caused was seldom so bad that it could not be repaired by an expiation ritual. This is the reason for Sicily presumably having retained a particularly archaic form of witch-belief, almost identical with the 'witch-cult' that Margaret Murray attempted to demonstrate on the evidence of north and mid-European material. There is, however, one vital difference: Murray saw the sabbath and the witches' rituals as based on the real, material world, while the Sicilian documentation shows that we must look for the sabbath and most of the rituals in quite another place: in an immaterial world of dream and vision. Once we have recognized this we can perfectly well go along with the grand ambition of Murray and her predecessors: to uncover the popular origins of the sabbath concepts. We no longer need Norman Cohn's complicated explanation of the sabbath as a demonological cocktail of at least four different traditions.[15] The Italian material, and in particular the pure form from Sicily, witness to a popular tradition with

---

[15] Cohn supposes the learned mythology on witches to have originated from four different traditions: (1) ancient slanderous assertions about religious minorities, (2) popular sorcery rituals used when casting spells, (3) learned ritual magic and conjuration of demons, and (4) popular notions of night-flying witches and the traditions concerning women who went out by night to join Diana's train (Cohn, *Europe's Inner Demons, passim*).

all the ingredients. There is an almost total congruence between the popular dream cult and the witch religion that the learned demonologists completed their definition of in about 1600 (see Table 7.1). It is merely that practically all the elements have acquired opposite value: the beautiful fairies have turned into horrible demons, the splendid food into a rotten, stinking mess; the sweet music has become hateful caterwauling, the joyful dance exhausting capering, and the pleasurable love—painful rape.

The prolific monkish fantasies were inexhaustible when it was a matter of diabolizing the popular dream world, a dangerous rival to the joyless society of Christendom. Future research must show whether it is also possible to reconstruct the positive notions of the sabbath for other parts of Europe, or if it is only in Italy that (thanks to especially favourable survivals of sources) we may see the process of diabolization at work.

APPENDIX
The Sicilian Fairy Cult in Comparative Perspective

During the discussion of my paper in Stockholm, Carlo Ginzburg turned the problem upside down and asked whether the fairies' sabbath of Sicily should not be considered as a secondary form. Could the Sicilian folk-imagination have succeeded in creating a 'white sabbath' out of the 'black sabbath'? Two facts point against such a supposition. Firstly, as mentioned already the witches' sabbath was unknown in Sicilian tradition; secondly, the fairy cult which we have described turns out to be a variant of a widely extended and therefore presumably old and deep-rooted Mediterranean and east European complex of shamanistic beliefs. In the folklore of these areas we find a fairy cult very similar to that reflected in the records of the Inquisition of Sicily with special gifted individuals serving as intermediaries between the world of the fairies and the human world, with elaborate rituals for curing people and animals stricken by some illness because they have offended the fairies, and with a complicated linking of events in the two worlds of which one is considered just as real as the other.[16]

---

[16] For Greek and Mediterranean fairy beliefs, see Charles Steward, 'Nymphomania: Sexuality, Insanity and Problems in Folklore Analysis', in M. Alexiou and V. Lambropoulos (eds.), *The Text and its Margins: Post-structuralist Approaches to Twentieth-century Greek Literature* (New York, 1985), 219–52, and Richard and Eva Blum, *The Dangerous*

[*See page 209 for n. 16 cont.*].

TABLE 7.1. *The 'white sabbath' of the Italian fairy cult compared with the 'black sabbath' described in the works of the demonologists, c. 1600*

Aspect/Element	*Donas de Fuera* (Fairies)	Witches
God/goddess/leader	'Queen of the Fairies'; *La Matrona*; *La Maestra*; 'The Greek Lady'; *Señora Gracia*; 'The Wise Sybil'; *Madonna Oriente*	The devil
Instruction of followers	In the uses of medicinal herbs; in discovery of thefts; in exposure of evil spells	In all kinds of evils to be inflicted on the human race
Homage to leader	They bow their heads	They kiss the devil under his tail
Subordinate supernatural beings	Beautiful fairies	Horrible demons
Their characteristics	Clad in white (black); 'soft' flesh	Naked
	Cats' paws (horses' hooves, round feet); animal tails (pigs', horses')	
Relationship of supernatural beings to human world	Ambivalent	Hostile
Examples	Cause disease to offenders, but withdraw it when receiving the *tabula* sacrifice; help people in spinning and other of their daily works	Cause all kinds of mischief; assist witches in their malefic work
Organization	Members militarily organized in local units (of 12, 30, 33) often named by the locality (e.g. 'The Company of Palermo')	

Aspect/Element	*Donas de Fuera* (Fairies)	Witches
Other names	*Compañía de los Romanos*; *Compañía de la Matrona*; 'The Company for Table(?) and Distaff'	
Members' characteristics	'Sweet blood'	e.g. red eyes
Special powers	Can change into animals (toad, snake); can leave the body in spirit form	Can change into animals (cat, hare, bird, toad, snake); can leave the body in spirit form
Weekly nights of meeting	Tuesday, Thursday, Saturday	Various (e.g. Monday, Wednesday, Friday)
Transport to assembly	Suspended in the air 20 inches above ground, or riding on a billy-goat	Flying on a broomstick, or riding on a billy-goat
Meeting activities	Joyful dance Beautiful dresses Sweet music Splendid food	Exhausting capering Nakedness Caterwauling Rotten and stinking mess
	Pleasurable love	Painful rape
Visit to houses	To give prosperity	To cause misfortune
Discipline	Members obliged to appear; to maintain secrecy; and not to mention Jesus during meetings	
Sanctions	Truants and offenders are cruelly beaten	

Hour: The Lore of Crisis and Mystery in Rural Greece (London, 1970), 112–18 (Greek nereids), 358–75 (Mediterranean parrallels). For Balkan beliefs, see Gail Kligman, *Căluş: Symbolic Transformation in Romanian Ritual* (Chicago and London, 1981), esp. ch. 2, 'Historical and Comparative Contexts'; see also Rolf Wilhelm Brednich, *Volkserzählungen und Volksglaube von den Schicksalsfrauen* (Helsinki, 1964), which, although only dealing with one single aspect, the fates, is so far the most extensive comparative study of eastern European fairy beliefs.

How close the parallels are in the Mediterranean and eastern European fairy cults may be demonstrated with a few examples, the first being a case story from rural Greece in the 1960s, where the term for fairies is *exotica*, viz. almost a direct translation of 'women from outside':

> Some years ago my husband was hit by the Bad Hour. One morning he awakened and his mouth was crooked around the cheek and one of his eyes was small and the other too big and his face was swollen. He went to different people for a cure . . . Finally they told him to go to a lady from Asia Minor that knew many things . . . Since he didn't know what had happened she decided to find out . . . So she put three burning coals in an earthenware incense burner and asked her husband to give her some gunpowder . . . Then she took these things and went outside and threw them away. This served to gather the exotica or nereids that had harmed him.
>
> These women . . . know how to gather the nereids and they talk with them just as you and I are chatting now. The nereids tell them what they did and why, and if they are willing to take back the harm they have done or not. Well, this woman talked with the nereids; they told her what had happened and she, in turn, told my husband about it . . .
>
> All this was true. He had gone out with two other people to go hunting and he had his gun in his hands. It was true that he felt something walking on his cheek and he had thought it to be a centipede which he brushed away with his hand.
>
> 'Well,' said the lady, 'it wasn't a centipede. You were standing on the spot where the nereids were having lunch; one of them saw and liked you and she caressed you. There she was being kind and you hit her and brushed her away. No wonder she got mad and hit you back and *that* is why your face is deformed. No matter, in three days you'll be okay.'
>
> And so it happened.[17]

Our second example is from northern Morocco, where the American anthropologist Vincent Crapanzano in the late sixties studied a widespread dream cult centred around the *jnun* (sg. *jinn*), spiritual beings very similar to the Sicilian fairies, and their human followers, a special kind of curers belonging to popular religious brotherhoods where they perform a trance-dance (*hadra*) to a specific musical air (*rih*). They explain their trances in terms of saints and *jnun*, especially in the terms of a female *jinn* called ʿAʾisha Qandisha. She is capable of appearing as a beauty or a hag, but always with the feet of a camel or some other hoofed animal. In her ugly aspect, ʿAʾisha Qandisha is black with long, straggly hair, pendulous breasts, and elongated nipples. She is said to like red and black colours, and the music of the Hamadsha. She is always libidinous and is said to enter into marriage with men by seducing them before they discover her identity. She may require

[17] Blum, *The Dangerous Hour*, pp. 112–13.

them to wear old, dirty clothes and never cut their hair or fingernails.[18] Not only the beliefs but also the rituals indicate that we have to do with variants of a genuine tradition. Thus one of Crapanzano's case stories about a diviner who specializes in dreaming of actions to be taken by those who consult him reveals the same type of diagnosis as described above from Greece and Sicily:

> Moha, who is said to be married to ʿAʾisha Qandisha, lives near a river and is consulted by the sick. Men bring him a thread from their turbans; women a thread from their scarves. He places the thread under his right cheek before going to bed and dreams of ʿAʾisha, who tells him what is wrong with the patients and what cure to follow.[19]

Our third example is from Kacem Ben Hamza's study of the cave dwellers of Matmata in Tunis, a Berber community where many illnesses are explained as possession by the *jnun*.[20] The possessed people are cured by a 'holy' woman (*darwisa*) during an exorcism seance which takes place in the mausoleum of an Islamic saint:

> A l'intérieur de l'enceinte, une séance de musique commence ponctuée par la cadence du *bendir* (instrument à percussion). La cadence est intentionellement modifiée à intervalles successifs, précisément en vue de permettre de diagnostiquer les vrais responsables de la possession. Chaque groupe de *ğnûn* se distingue en effet par une *nûba* (rythme) qui lui est propre. Lorsque le malade commence à réagir en ébauchant des mouvements de danse, la *darwisa* reçoit une première indication sur le groupe auquel appartient le *ğînn* possesseur. Lorsque le malade sort enfin de son inconscience et se lance dans une véritable danse, la musique s'arrête. La *darwisa* entre alors en véritables pourparlers avec le *ğînn* possesseur par le truchement de la bouche du malade. Les raisons de la possession sont alors révélées et les conditions du *ğînn* sont posées. Le malade entre dans une danse rapide et intense et le *ğînn* finit par promettre de quitter le corps dont il avait pris possession en sortant par la bouche du patient.[21]

The last example is taken from Gail Kligman's study of the Romanian *călușari*, the secret brotherhoods of trance dancers who specialize in curing people who have been 'hit' or possessed by the fairies, *iele*. As in the Tunisian case, different tunes are used to diagnose the kind of possession, and the victim is cured during a dancing ritual.[22] We shall not, however, go into a

[18] Vincent Crapanzano, 'Saints, Jnun, and Dreams: An Essay in Moroccan Ethnopsychology', *Psychiatry*, 38 (1975) 145–59, esp. 147 (Jeppe Sinding Jensen, Dept. of Religion, Univ. of Odense, has kindly drawn my attention to this article).

[19] Ibid., p. 149.

[20] Kacem Ben Hamza, 'The Cave Dwellers of Matmata', Ph.D. thesis (Bloomington, 1977), ch. 4; French version in 'Croyances et pratiques en Islam populaire: Le Cas de Matmata', *Revue de l'institute des belles lettres arabes* (June 1980), pp. 87–109 (I am also indebted to Prof. Sinding Jensen for this reference).

[21] Ibid., pp. 104–5.   [22] Kligman, *Căluș*, ch. 3, 'Ritual Healing'.

discussion of these interesting parallels. For our purpose it will suffice to draw attention to the elaborate complex of Romanian beliefs and rituals in connection with the fairies, the structure of which is exposed by the author in a highly elucidating way (see Table 7.2).

The four examples are all taken from regions in the European periphery that never experienced witch-hunts and where the folk religion remained to a great extent undiabolized. But even in areas like southern Italy, where the propaganda of the Church was active for centuries and where witches were persecuted, we may find archaic patterns of European witchcraft. During his fieldwork in some villages south of Naples, the German anthropologist, Thomas Hauschild found that the local cunning men and women on certain nights of the year were believed to transform themselves into animals and fly to the sabbath at Benevento. But this by no means discredited them in public opinion.[23]

In the folk religion of present-day Sicily, too, we may find valuable comparative materials for a better understanding of what is obscure in the records of the Inquisition. In her famous community study of a Sicilian village in the late 1920s, Charlotte Gower Chapman has a vivid description of a 30-year-old woman, married to an innkeeper and the mother of three children. She claimed to be a witch and that she worked in a band with thirteen others: 'Her behavior was ordinary enough, except for rare occasions when she seemed to have attacks of faintness, which she explained on the grounds that her sister-witches were communicating with her.' The witches were supposed to have the power of 'binding' people so that they were unable to move or walk, and our American anthropologist was warned against Tanidda, but no instances were related of her activities.[24] Here we find a modern example of the companies of *donas*—so current at the time of the Inquisition—but unfortunately without any mention of relations to the fairies or of flying. One informant told that 'in times past there were many *donni di notti* (ladies of the night) who were witches who flew about at night and made people powerless.'[25] There is more of a *donna de fuera* in the charismatic healer Marta, portrayed by the ethnologist Elsa Guggino in a recent book on Sicilian magic. The healer, a 50-year-old woman living in a mountain village south of Palermo, claimed to have travelled all over the world in spirit. 'During the

---

[23] In a letter, dated 28 Feb. 1985, Dr Thomas Hauschild (Univ. of Cologne) wrote to me as follows: '. . . reading your essay in the Eliade-Festschrift [see asterisked n., p. 191, above] I felt rather excited by what you write on Benevento. Doing fieldwork in Basilicata last year they told me that the folk healers of Oppido Lucano regularly gather in the form of animals for the sake of flying to Benevento . . . The information given by my informants from Oppido sustains your idea of a quasi ahistorical substratum of folklore: they tell the story "just so", not because they want to blame a witch. On the contrary, they do tell the story full of admiration for these "fattuchieri".'

[24] Charlotte Gower Chapman, *Milocca: A Sicilian Village* (London, 1970), 200.

[25] Ibid., p. 203.

TABLE 7.2. *The Romanian fairy cult: comparison of traits characterizing respectively* iele, *the fairies, and* călușari, *the curers and intermediaries between the human and the supernatural worlds*

	Iele	*Călușari*
Parallel	Most prevalent at the Rusalii (popular Spring festival)	Same
	Patron saint is Diana (Irodeasa)	Same
	Odd number	Same
	Dressed in white	Same
	Live in non-human space	Receive and relinquish power, and cure in same places
	Accompanied by flag-bearer	Same
	Accompanied by bagpipers	Same
	Dance in circle marked by ring that remains	Same (circle is identified by ring drawn in ground)
	Dance as if not touching ground	Same
Opposition	Female	Male
	Active during night	Active during day
	Lunar	Solar
	Act primarily against men	Act primarily against women
Ambivalence	Use herbs to cure	Same, but also for self-protection from harm by *iele*
	Possess people, including *călușari*, and animals— 'anything with a soul'—who are then said to be *luat din iele*	May possess people, who are then said to be *luat din căluș*

Source: Gail Kligman, *Căluș: Symbolic Transformation in Romanian Ritual* (Chicago and London, 1981), p. 540.

flight,' she explained, 'the body remains in its usual place, for it is the spirit that flies (*ciò che vola è lo spirito*).'[26] During a visit to Sicily in 1985 I had the opportunity of interviewing this extraordinary woman, thanks to the kind assistance of Professor Guggino. The three of us sat talking in the (gift and drapery) shop of Signora M. for a couple of hours, frequently interrupted by customers who had to be attended to. I got the impression that on the one hand she had freed herself from the traditional pattern: she did not have any contact with the fairies. On the other hand she claimed to go every autumn to India to a feast given especially in her honour. She also explained to us that her family could hear her snore when she 'was not at home', for 'normally' she never snored, likewise they would take care not to move her, since the spirit then could not find its way back. During her nightly excursions she would meet with other people who travelled in spirit. Among the experiences she told us about was the following event, which is remarkable by beginning in the human world and continuing in the spirit world: Once she quarrelled with a young man in the neighbourhood 'who practised black magic', and the man said to her: 'If I meet you by night at a crossroads, I will kill you!' One night (some time later, when she was out in spirit) she met the same man, together with his mother-in-law, who was a Tunisian, and the man made ready to beat her. But his mother-in-law stopped him: 'Don't you see, that we must be three to go out (there was a third spirit with them), but she is able to do it alone [i.e. she was much stronger than them].'[27]

Whether each of these cases should be classified as shamanism in the traditional sense of the word is highly problematic, and I prefer to leave that discussion to another occasion. To this mosaic of contemporary parallels to the fairy cult reported in the Inquisition records I shall, by way of conclusion, add one more example, night-flying reported in a historical document about a thousand years ago, the famous *Canon episcopi* (*c*.900) by Regino of Prüm, abbot of Treves, later incorporated in the *Corpus Juris Canonici* (*c*.1140) by Gratian of Bologna, and thus part of the Canon Law. In view of all that has been presented above, this old text suddenly becomes transparent, so that we may look through the theological veil and capture a popular cult in its undiabolized form:

> Bishops and their officials must labor with all their strength to uproot thoroughly from their parishes the pernicious art of sorcery and malefice invented by the Devil, . . . It is also to be omitted that *some* wicked *women*, perverted by the Devil, seduced by illusions and phantasms of demons, *believe and profess themselves, in the hours of night, to ride upon certain beasts with Diana, the goddess of pagans, and an innumerable multitude of women, and in the*

[26] Elsa Guggino, *La magia in Sicilia* (Palermo, 1978), 125 ff.
[27] Author's field-notes from Sicily (1985), fo. 56ᵛ. I am indebted to Elsa Guggino for taking notes from the interview with Marta.

silence of the dead of night to traverse great spaces of earth, and to obey her commands as of their mistress, and to be summoned to her service on certain nights. But I wish it were they alone who perished in their faithlessness and did not draw many with them into the destruction of infidelity. *For an innumerable multitude,* deceived by this false opinion, *believe this to be true,* and so believing wander in the error of the pagans when they think that there is anything of divinity and power except God. Wherefore the priests throughout their churches should preach with all insistence to the people that they may know this to be in every way false and that such phantasms are imposed on the minds of infidels and not *by the divine* but the malignant *spirits.* Thus Satan himself, who transfigures himself into an angel of light, when he has captured the mind of a *miserable woman* and has subjugated her to himself by infidelity and incredulity, immediately transforms himself into the *species and similitudes of different personages* and deluding the mind which he holds captive and exhibiting *things, joyful or mournful,* and persons, known or unknown, leads it through devious ways, and while the spirit alone endures this, the faithless mind thinks these things happen not in the spirit but in the body. Who is there that is not lead out of himself in dreams and nocturnal visions, and sees much when sleeping which he had never seen waking? Who is so stupid and foolish as to think that all these things which are only done in spirit happen in the body? . . . Whoever therefore *believes that anything can be made, or that any creature can* be changed to better or to worse or *be transformed into another species or similitude,* except by the Creator himself . . is beyond doubt infidel.[28]

[28] Here quoted from Alan C. Kors and Edward Peters (eds.), *Witchcraft in Europe, 1100–1700: A Documentary History* (Philadelphia, 1972), 29–31 (my italics).

III
WITCH-HUNTING IN
SCANDINAVIA AND
OTHER PERIPHERIES

8

Hungary: The Accusations and the Universe of Popular Magic

GÁBOR KLANICZAY

THE surviving historical records of Hungarian witch persecutions start—as in many other European countries—with a few legal measures against *maleficium* and *veneficium*, to be found in the legislation of the first Hungarian kings: Saint Stephen (1000–38), Saint Ladislaus (1077–95), and Coloman (1095–1116).[1] These laws also mention *strigas*, the existence of which Coloman simply denies, following the tradition of the *Canon episcopi* and the Carolingian capitularies.[2] During the following four centuries, a dozen scattered items of data indicate that witchcraft charges were dealt with at hot-iron ordeal places, at feudal courts, and by town juries.[3] The sentence

---

[1] *Decretum Sancti Stephani*, ii. 33–4; *S. Ladislai Decretum*, i. 34; *Decretum Colomanni Regis*, i. 60 (best edn.: Levente Závodszky. *A Szent István, Szent László és Kálmán korabeli törvények és zsinati határozatok forrásai* (Budapest 1904), 141–56). Cf. their short treatment in Wilhelm Gottlieb Soldan, *Geschichte der Hexenprozesse*, ed. Max Bauer (Berlin–Friedenau, 1911), i. 119.

[2] *Decretum Colomanni*, i. 57: 'De strigis vero que non sunt, ne ulla questio fiat.' For the early medieval distinction between *striga* and *malefica* see Norman Cohn, *Europe's Inner Demons* (London, 1975), 206–19.

[3] There are 14 cases of *maleficium* or *veneficium* in the early 13th-c. register of the hot-ordeal place at Várad, where we have 389 documented cases between 1208–1235. Cf. J. Karácsonyi and S. Borovszky (eds.), *Regestrum Varadinense* (Budapest, 1903). We have traces of trials against 6 female witches in Zagreb between 1360 and 1379: Ivan Tkalčić (ed.), 'Izprave o progonu vješticah u Hrvatskoj', *Starine*, 25 (1892), 1–2; the persecution of witches (*fascinatores et strigas*) is mentioned at the feudal court of Menyhárd Károlyi in 1387: Georgius Fejér (ed.), *Codex diplomaticus Hungariae ecclesiasticus ac civilis* (Budae, 1829–44), vol. x, pt. i, p. 371; in 1408 in the county of Zala 2 witches were condemned: Alajos Degré, *Boszorkányperek Zala megyében* (Witch-trials in Zala County), *A Göcseji Múzeum közleményei*, 15 (Zalaegerszeg, 1960), 227; in 1409 in the county of Vas 3 witches (*fytonissa et incantatrix*) were condemned: Elemér Mályusz (ed.), *Zsigmondkori oklevéltár*, (Documents from the Age of Sigismund) vol. ii, pt. ii (Budapest, 1958), p. 221; in 1429 one witch (*seductrix, incantatrix et fitonissa*) was condemned in the west Hungarian city of Sopron: Jenő Házy, *Sopron középkori egyháztörténete* (Medieval Ecclesiastical History of Sopron) (Sopron, 1939), 313; in 1432 Hermann Cillei, governor of Slovenia, gave a special order about the persecution of witches (*mulieres incantatrices et intoxicatrices*): cf. *Vjesnik*, 6 (1904), 78; in 1435–7 in the NE county of Bereg 3 witches were condemned: Emil Jakubovich, *Adalékok legrégibb nyelvemlékes okleveleink és krónikáink íróinak személyéhez* (Budapest, 1924), 95–6.

of burning witches is to be found in fourteenth- and fifteenth-century compilations of some cities' customs.[4] But a regular persecution only started in the sixteenth century, intensifying towards the end of it, and becoming a mass persecution only a hundred years later, at the end of the seventeenth century. The peak of the witch-hunting came in the first half of the eighteenth century; though it was declining a little towards the 1750s, it had to be stopped from above by various interventions of the Empress Maria Theresa from 1756 on, leading to the definitive prohibition of witch-burning in 1768. The last-known execution *propter magiam* took place in the north Hungarian town of Késmárk (now Kežmarok) in 1777.[5]

I. THREE CENTURIES OF WITCH-HUNTING

To give a general idea of the intensity and the chronological distribution of the persecutions, let me present two tables (Tables 8.1 and 8.2) with some crude calculations based upon the published records of witch-trials in Hungary between 1520 and 1777. These sources consist of legal records (testimony-hearings, acts, and sentences of trials), municipal accounts registering payments to executioners, and cases mentioned in town chronicles and diaries. Due to the collecting work of Andor Komáromy and Ferenc Schram, resulting in the publication

---

[4] For some 13th- and 14th-c. Dalmatian city customs, see Vladimir Bayer, *Ugovor s Đavlom: Procesi protiv čarobnjaka u Evropi a napose u Hrvatskoj* (Conventions with the Devil: Witch-trials in Europe and in Croatia) (3rd edn. Zagreb. 1982), 517–20; for Zagreb 14th-c. customs, see Tkalčić, 'Izprave', p. 2: for the early 15th-c. customs of Buda, see Károly Mollay (ed.), *Das Ofner Stadtrecht* (Budapest, 1959), 169, art. 331. The late 15th-c. customs of the seven greatest Hungarian cities already mention the sentence of burning for witches: M. G. Kovachich (ed.), *Codex authenticus iuris tavernicalis* (Buda, 1803), 185–6.

[5] The few works dealing with a general historical analysis of Hungarian witch-trials are the following: Éva Molnár, *Boszorkányperek Magyarországon a XVII–XVIII. században* (Witch-trials in Hungary in the 17th and 18th c.) (Budapest, 1942): Ákos Szendrey, 'A magyar néphit boszorkánya' (The Witch of Hungarian Folk-beliefs), unpublished (1962): Zsuzsanna Kulcsár, *Inkvizició és boszorkánypörök* (Inquisition and Witch-trials) (3rd edn. Budapest, 1968), 158–77; Tekla Dömötör, *Hungarian Folk Beliefs* (Bloomington and Budapest, 1982), 62–72; András Iklódy, 'A magyarországi boszorkányüldözés történeti alakulása' (The Historical Formation of Witch-hunting in Hungary), *Ethnographia*, 93 (1982), 292–8; Ferenc Schram, *Magyarországi boszorkányperek, 1529–1768* (3 vols.; Budapest, 1970–82; hereafter cited as 'Schram'), iii. 13–110. Important regional studies have been made for Transylvania and for Croatia: Friedrich Müller, *Beiträge zur Geschichte des Hexenglaubens in Siebenbürgen* (Brunswick, 1854); Carl Göllner, *Hexenprozesse in Siebenbürgen* (Cluj–Napoca, 1971); Erzsébet Tarczay, 'Boszorkányüldözés Horvátországban' (Witch-hunting in Croatia), *Századok*, 49 (1915), 162–75; Bayer, *Ugovor s Đavlom*.

of four volumes of witch documentation[6] and a few dozen lesser publications that complete their work,[7] we can consider that the published, or at least registered, material represents about 80 per cent of the existing documents in Hungarian Archives. This does not imply, however, that it is representative for the whole historical period. A very considerable part of these legal sources was lost during the various historical calamities in this region. The loss of complete series of court records is especially frequent for the period before 1690, so the belated peak of persecutions in Hungary, which according to our statistics comes after this date, is to be treated with some caution. The loss or non-existence of written legal sources is particularly grave for the third of Hungary occupied by the Turks between 1541 and 1686.[8] And finally, the incompleteness of documentation should be mentioned for the German- or Hungarian-inhabited towns of north Hungary and Transylvania. These quite well conserved city archives were only partly exploited by Andor Komáromy around the turn of the century, and since the First World War no research on witch-trials has been done in them. The same could be said about department archives of the northern and eastern regions, which have belonged to Czechoslovakia, the Soviet Union, and Romania since 1919, and also the rich Croatian material to be found in the archive of Zagreb.[9] Even given these deficiencies, there is still a representative value in the statistics given in Tables 8.1 and 8.2; they include all the data we at present possess on witch-trials in the territory of Hungary from the sixteenth to the eighteenth century.[10] Considering that the number of

[6] Andor Komáromy, *Magyarországi boszorkányperek oklevéltára* (Documents on Hungarian Witch-trials) (Budapest, 1910; hereafter cited as 'Komáromy'); Schram.

[7] Most of the smaller edns. are registered and documented in the works of Schram and Komáromy, but a few important items are lacking. Tkalčić, 'Izprave'; Friedrich Teutsch, 'Sächsische Hexenprozesse', *Archiv des Vereins für siebenbürgische Landeskunde*, 39 (1915), 709–803; Richard Horna, *Zwei Hexenprozesse in Pressburg zu Beginn des XVII. Jahrhunderts* (Bratislava, 1933); id., *Ein Monstre-Hexenprozess in Samorin gegen Ende des XVII. Jahrhunderts* (Bratislava, 1935).

[8] Only about forty of the 1,642 cases analysed here come from the territory of Turkish occupation, and even these were brought to the Hungarian courts of the unoccupied parts of the country. The Turkish administration seems to have given no attention to the problem of witchcraft. Thus extra-legal proceedings such as lynchings must have been frequent in this area, leaving no documentation behind.

[9] The recent monograph of Bayer, *Ugovor s Đavlom*, is based on the early material published by Tkalčić, 'Izprave', and completes them with some other data. Tkalčić published his work at the beginning of this century, making no use of the archives of Zagreb.

[10] The statistics below were compiled by myself, on the basis of published documentation on Hungarian witch-trials.

TABLE 8.1. *Hungary: Number and sex-distribution of trials and sentences, 1520–1777*

	Women		Men		Total
Death sentences	412	(91.8%)	37	(8.2%)	449
Death in prison or lynching	22		1		23
Lesser punishment (corporal punishment, banishment, monetary fine, etc.)	199	(88.4%)	26	(11.6%)	225
Acquitted	213	(90.6%)	22	(9.4%)	235
Outcome of trial unknown	636		74		710
Total recorded trials	1,482	(90.3%)	160	(9.7%)	1,642

TABLE 8.2. *Chronological distribution of Hungarian witch-trials*

	Death	Lesser fine	Acquitted	Unknown	Total
1520–60	2	1	—	7	10
1560–70	4	—	—	1	5
1570–80	1	1	—	3	5
1580–90	11	—	1	5	17
1590–1600	4	—	1	3	8
1600–10	6	2	2	2	12
1610–20	10	2	—	3	15
1620–30	14	8	3	18	43
1630–40	9	6	2	21	38
1640–50	6	3	3	39	51
1650–60	19	3	3	32	57
1660–70	15	10	9	29	63
1670–80	26	4	3	24	57
1680–90	22	3	2	18	45
1690–1700	39	14	23	27	103
1700–10	46	16	8	36	106
1710–20	62	29	36	90	217
1720–30	64	36	27	100	227
1730–40	36	33	26	85	180
1740–50	51	24	36	74	185
1750–60	21	22	41	59	143
1760–70	1	7	9	30	47
1770–80	3	1	—	4	8
Total	472	225	235	710	1,642

death sentences, deaths in prison, and lynchings (total: 472) practically equals the number of cases where it is recorded that the accused survived the trial (total: 460; that is, 50.6 versus 49.4 per cent), we can risk the supposition that the proportions were the same for the trials where the sentence is unknown to us. So altogether we can speak of more than 800 death sentences during these 250 years.

A short historical comment should be added to these statistics. The 250 years treated here was a very tormented period in Hungarian history. After the fatal defeat suffered from the Turks at Mohács in 1526, where the young king, Louis II, died on the battlefield, there was a double king election. One part of the Hungarian nobility elected Ferdinand Habsburg, the other part elected the most influential leader of the Hungarian nobility, János Szapolyai. Two decades of rivalry and further Turkish attacks (including the occupation of the capital, Buda, in 1541) led to the division of Hungary into three parts. The north-west became the Hungarian Kingdom, ruled by kings of Habsburg origin, which became more and more integrated into the framework of the Central European Habsburg Empire (the Austrian 'Erbländer', the Czech Kingdom, Hungary, and some German and Italian territories). The southern and central part of the country was occupied by the Turks for a century and a half. János Szapolyai died in 1540, and his court fled from Buda to Transylvania, which became, together with the eastern counties of the Hungarian Plain, the Principality of Transylvania, preserving its inner autonomy, but allied to, and sometimes dependent on, the Turkish Empire. During the seventeenth century, while the resistance to and attempts at reconquest from the Turks were going on, there were several uprisings against the Habsburg kings, partly brought about by the nobility and peasants of the northern parts, ruled by the Habsburgs, partly initiated by the princes of Transylvania, who took part in the Thirty Years War on the Protestant side. In the last two decades of the seventeenth century the Turks were driven out of Hungary with the help of Habsburg troops and their allies, but this meant that the whole country, including Transylvania, became a dependent part of the Habsburg monarchy. The increasing resistance to the more and more centralized foreign rule led to the independence war headed by Prince Ferenc Rákóczi (1703–11), which ended in defeat, and—helped by some compromises—in the acceptance of Habsburg rule for more centuries to come.

Now if we take a look again at our statistics (see Table 8.2 and Fig.

8.1), the fluctuations start to make sense: the witch persecutions tended to increase whenever a big war or an uprising came to an end (generally ending in defeat), and there were a few peaceful years to digest the outcome.[11] Witch-hunting, which appears on a considerable scale in the second half of the seventeenth century, first came to a panic in the 1580s, the short peaceful period after the deadly Turkish attacks and the heroic resistance which stopped the further extension of the Turkish occupation. The level of witch persecutions fell back during the Fifteen Years War with the Turks (1591–1606) and the anti-Habsburg uprising of István Bocskai (1604–6). A new intensification of witch-hunting came in the 1620s, and this seems to contradict our thesis of the correlation of peace and witchcraft persecutions (this was the decade when Gábor Bethlen, Prince of Transylvania, directed three campaigns against the Habsburg territories, trying to unite north Hungary and Transylvania). However, a more delicate analysis can explain this contradiction satisfactorily. A more detailed statistical series, taking into account also the geographical distribution of the trials, could prove that in this case, too, the trials were held mostly in peaceful years and regions. On the other hand, there are other specific causes of this sudden increase in the number of trials: Bethlen's law against witches (1614),[12] and the general witch-hunting climate of the Thirty Years War, which brought about unparalleled witch-burning rages in Germany.[13]

Another slight rise in the level of Hungarian witch-hunting can be observed after the end of the Thirty Years War, in the 1650s. But the first dramatic increase came when the country finally got rid of the Turkish occupation, thereby ending the constant warfare against the Turkish troops: after 1690 the number of witches accused in various courts doubled. The second, even more disastrous increase can be

[11] The Hungarian example thus reinforces the argument against Trevor-Roper's assertion that witch-hunting was a direct and immediate consequence of the 16th–17th-c. wars of religion: *The European Witch-craze of the 16th and 17th Centuries* (Harmondsworth, 1969), 67–76. Witch-hunting also tended to coincide with peaceful years and lulls in wars in 17th-c. Franche-Comté: E. William Monter, *Witchcraft in France and Switzerland* (Ithaca and London, 1976), 81; and in late 16th- and 17th-c. Cambrésis: Marie-Sylvie Dupont-Bouchat, Willem Frijhoff, and Robert Muchembled, *Prophétes et sorciers dans les Pays-Bas: XVIᵉ–XVIIIᵉ siècles* (Paris, 1978), 177. Cf. Jean Delumeau, *La Peur en Occident XVIᵉ–XVIIᵉ siècles: Une cité assiégée* (Paris, 1978), 358.

[12] S. Szilágyi (ed.), *Erdélyi országgyűlési emlékek* (Document of Transylvanian Diets) (11 vols.; Budapest, 1876–98), vi. 413.

[13] Cf. Trevor-Roper, *The European Witch-craze*, pp. 83–5; H. C. Eric Midelfort, *Witch-hunting in Southwestern Germany, 1562–1684* (Stanford, 1972).

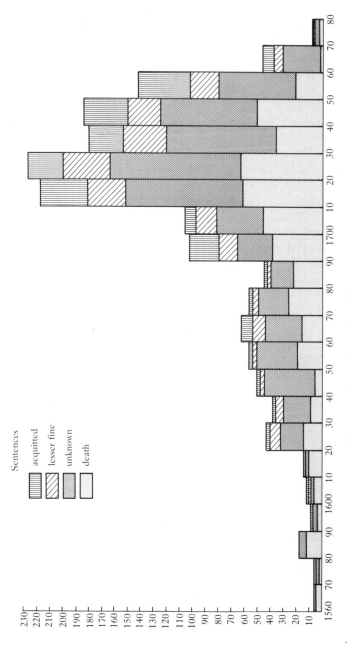

FIG. 8.1. *Hungarian witch-trials by decades, 1560–1780*

observed after the end of the independence war headed by Prince Ferenc Rákóczi. Between 1710 and 1750 the repeated waves of witch-hunting, the interconnected regional panics, show a very similar pattern to the witch epidemics of western European countries in the sixteenth and seventeenth centuries.

This leads us to the second statistical feature to be commented on: the chronological delay in Hungarian witch-hunting, compared to other European countries. For a long time, Hungarian historiography saw in this belatedness the proof that diabolical witch-beliefs and panics leading to mass accusations were alien to the Hungarians; they only imported them in incomplete form after a long resistance, their own original witch-beliefs being concerned only with traditional charges of *maleficium*.[14] An extension of this argument could blame Austrian-German political, legal, and cultural influence for the belated spreading of the persecutions—the peak of their level does indeed coincide with the intensification of Habsburg rule over the whole territory of Hungary. Moreover, there are two important catalysts to be mentioned, which are connected to the new, victorious Habsburg absolutism. The most frequently mentioned legal basis of the witch-hunting was the well-known *Practica Rerum Criminalium* of Benedict Carpzov (1635), codified for Austria by Ferdinand III in 1656, edited (in Latin) in Hungary at the Jesuit-influenced university of Nagyszombat in 1687, and incorporated into the *Corpus iuris* of Hungary in 1696.[15] The other factor, directly connected to the military

---

[14] Komáromy, pp. xvii–xviii; Sándor Eckhardt and Gyula Ortutay, 'Régi magyar varázslóasszonyok' (Hungarian Female Magicians in the Old Times), *Magyarságtudomány*, 1 (1942), 564–80; Molnár, *Boszorkányperek*, pp. 56–9; Schram, iii. 54–68.

[15] Cf. Molnár, *Boszorkányperek*, pp. 33–4; Iklódy in *Ethnographia*, 93 (1982), 296–7. Witchcraft, not being a *crimen exceptum*, was punished with other crimes at feudal, municipal, and county courts. In addition to the medieval laws already mentioned, and the 1614 law of the Transylvanian Diet, there are references in the witch-trials to some articles of the biggest early modern codification of Hungarian law, the *Tripartitum* (i. 15; ii. 72), compiled by István Werbőczy (1st edn. Vienna, 1517); and to the *Carolina* and the Bible (Exod. 22: 18). City customs are referred to in a general way. But in most trials there is no legal reference at all. Use of the water ordeal is frequent, especially in the cities; torture is also general, but in some places it is applied as an aggravation of the punishment (to get the names of the accomplices), and its outcome does not influence the sentence already brought, whereas in other places the burning or the acquittal of the accused depends on his confession during torture; another frequent outcome is the purification oath, to be made with co-jurors (the number of which varies from 2 to 40). The types of sentence are as follows. A capital sentence can be burning alive, or burning after being beheaded, decapitation, stoning to death (in the Calvinist town of Debrecen), or a few other cruel punishments, e.g. being torn into four pieces, buried in a ditch filled with thorns, etc. A non-capital sentence can be banishment, corporal

occupation of Hungarian territories and the presence of imperial military forces in the country, is the frequency of witchcraft accusations originating from Austrian-German soldiers, lodged in Hungarian villages, and bringing to court their hosts or anybody else who gives open expression to hostile feelings against them. Sometimes the German soldiers might even act as real witchfinders.[16]

Before sweeping away these arguments as remnants of the nineteenth-century style of nationalistic historiography, it is worth considering them in the comparative framework supplied by actual witchcraft research. Let us accept Norman Cohn's thesis that one of the reasons leading to mass persecutions was that in the Middle Ages there came to life an amalgam of popular witch-beliefs and learned demonological notions,[17] and one combines this with a consideration of the geographical spreading of this 'innovation' (consisting not only in the inquisitorial image of diabolical witchcraft, but also in the legal machinery willing to extract the proof for it from the accused by torture)—as Trevor-Roper was the first to attempt to do.[18] Thus the claim for Hungary's later involvement in mass-scale witch-hunting because of the later arrival of this innovation and because of the role ascribed to the German mediators seems to retain its validity. One could even give some fresh colour to this argument by pointing to parallels where colonizing, absolutist states released a free flow of uncontrolled witch-hunting at their ethnically, linguistically, perhaps also religiously different peripheral territories.[19]

punishment, or monetary fine. Defence counsels are rare, found mostly in urban or noble trials. There is practically no ecclesiastical participation in the trials, but occasionally the accused are additionally sentenced to religious penitence.

[16] The documents of a typical trial like this, with the soldier not only accusing the host, but also acting as a wise man and a witchfinder, are edited by Göllner, *Hexenprozesse*, pp. 136–63 (Transylvania, Deutschkreuz, 1699). In another case, a lieutenant called Johann Vestmann, whose horse died and who himself fell ill at the same time, started a trial, accusing not only his hosts but nearly the whole village of Füle: Miklós Schneider, *Fejérmegyei boszorkányperek* (Witch-trials in the County of Fejér) (Székesfehérvár, 1934), 7–8; other cases of accusations by German soldiers are given in Schram. i. 111, 113, 265; ii. 28, 50–9, 178, 323, 353, 369, 410, 467, 470, 560, 573, 657.

[17] Cohn, *Europe's Inner Demons*, pp. 164–255.

[18] Trevor-Roper, *The European Witch-craze*, pp. 25–9, with the much-criticized thesis of a 'mountain origin', from where the craze spread to the core of Europe; then, after 1650, the declining witch persecutions changed from 'international to national manias' on the periphery of Europe. See also the Introduction and Burke's Conclusion to this volume. The spread of a witch-panic is described on a regional scale by Gustav Henningsen, *The Witches' Advocate* (Reno, 1980), 107–42; the analogy with 'innovation distribution' is used by Bengt Ankarloo in ch. 11, below.

[19] The most evident of these cases is Pierre de Lancre's persecutions in the Pays de

Without denying the importance of cultural influences, however, I would prefer another explanation for the chronological delay of Hungarian witch-hunting, one which takes into account another paradigm of witchcraft research, the structural one. If we accept that the emergence of witchcraft accusations is a kind of 'social strain-gauge',[20] and points to some inner tensions (not necessarily crises)[21] of the society concerned, then the belatedness of witch-panics in Hungary can be explained by the argument that Hungary—along with other 'peripheral' European countries—was following with at least a century of delay the 'core' countries on the same route of economic, social, and cultural evolution. Three observations can support this argument: one concerning the regional distribution of witch-hunting inside Hungary, one based upon international comparison of the same phenomenon, and one based on more general comparison with the belatedness of other cultural or social features of this same region.

As regards the regional distribution of the trials, the Hungarian case is one of extreme complexity. If we had sufficiently detailed documentation, it could be an extremely useful exercise to decipher the intensity, and resilience of local traditions, the confrontation of ideas and the mixture of different cultural influences within them. With the fragmentary evidence available, however, one can hardly do more than enumerate the problems to be considered. Besides the division of the country into three parts, with different legal and political systems,

Labourd; cf. Henningsen, *The Witches' Advocate*, pp. 23–5. The same peripheral position can be ascribed to the Basque persecutions, described by Henningsen in the same book. Cf. also Ankarloo's description of the Swedish persecutions, starting in the province of Dalarna and stopping when they reached the capital: ch. 11, below; and Hans Eyvind Naess, showing the Norwegian witch-persecutions as being most active in the northernmost county, the half-Lappish Finnmark: ch. 14, below.

[20] The expression is taken from Max Marwick (ed.), *Witchcraft and Sorcery* (Harmondsworth, 1970), 280.

[21] This problem is well analysed in the case of Essex by Alan Macfarlane, *Witchcraft in Tudor and Stuart England* (London, 1970), 147–55, who tests the possible correlations of the number of accusations with a various range of economic and social problems of the time, and arrives at a negative result as far as crises are concerned. The same approach, with similar results, can be found in Jens Christian V. Johansen's contribution to this volume, ch. 13, below, where the Danish persecutions of the 1620s, a period of economic 'splendour', are explained by the competitive tensions between those engaged in the grain trade and those active in the prosperous new trade of raising oxen for export. Another nicely analysed example of witchcraft accusations being the result of competitive tensions in certain spheres of society is the historically distant case studied by Peter Brown in 'Sorcery, Demons and the Rise of Christianity from Late Antiquity into the Middle Ages', in Mary Douglas (ed.), *Witchcraft Confessions and Accusations* (London, 1970), 17–45.

there is variation in religion (Catholic, Lutheran, Calvinist, Orthodox), which combines with ethnic differences (Hungarians, Germans,
Slovaks, Romanians, Serbs, Croats, Gypsies—not to mention Polish
and Italian courtiers or German and Turkish soldiers). Ethnic and
religious differences frequently overlapped with social categories: at
least half of the urban population in Transylvania and North Hungary
was German by origin, while a significant part of the peasantry was
likely to be Slovak in the north, Romanian in the east, Croatian or
Serbian in the south.[22]

We can detect the traces of this regional, ethnical, religious, and
social diversity in the spread of witch-hunting, which did not spread
throughout the country at once, but in various stages, and which did
not arrive in the various regions from the same source. Speaking
about German cultural influence we have to distinguish at least three
different elements in it, from the point of view of witch-beliefs. North
Hungarian and Transylvanian (Saxon) towns started the persecution,
due to the active admonishments of the Lutheran Church, in the
second half of the sixteenth century, following the example of the
Lutheran towns in Germany.[23] West Hungarian cities like Sopron and
Pozsony (Bratislava) or the Croatian Zagreb were influenced at the
same time by the Alpine beliefs of Austrian Catholics. Still in the last
decades of the sixteenth century, Calvinist pastors and preachers of
Debrecen (the big peasant town on the Great Plain) imported witch-
hunting zeal from Switzerland, and later from England. All the same,
the first set of intensive persecutions started neither in Calvinist
Debrecen, nor in the German-inhabited Lutheran or Catholic towns,
but in the religiously mixed and ethnically mainly Hungarian

---

[22] An interesting problem in connection with this ethnic diversity is to what extent
witchcraft accusations were directed against members of socially inferior ethnic
minorities. Among Hungarian witch-trials there are quite a number of cases where
Slovak, Romanian, Serbian, Croatian, and Gypsy women or men are brought to court
and judged by Hungarian judges. However, one should not be too quick to take these
cases as belonging to the prehistory of ethnic hostilities: most of the accused were
practising midwifery, soothsaying, or some other kind of magical activity. So one should
say, rather, that their national difference was one of the useful attributes in their magical
trade; the Gypsies still conserve this role.

[23] The Transylvanian Lutheran synod of 1577 is especially militant against 'die
Zauberei der alten Weiber, und was sonst Teufels-Gespenst ist, als Wahrsagen, von
Krankheiten sagen, und was hieran hanget, soll die Obrigkeit nach dem Gebot Gottes
und kaiserlichen Rechten mit dem Feuer strafen, oder mit dem strengen Edikt der
Obrigkeit wehren und bis solche nicht ablassen, soll man sie zu keinem Sakrament
lassen, denn man muss das Heiligtum nicht vor die Hunde werfen …': *Articuli
Visitationis* (1577), cited by Göllner, *Hexenprozesse*, p. 58; cf. Müller, *Beiträge*, pp. 19–21.

Transylvanian capital, Kolozsvár (Cluj), where we have the record of nineteen witch-trials in the space of twenty-eight years (1565–93), fifteen resulting in burning, while the outcome of four is unknown.[24]

Looking at Map 8.1, one can clearly isolate the nuclei of persecution mentioned above, standing well apart not only religiously, ethnically, and politically, but also geographically. On the other hand, one cannot help being surprised to see witch-hunting starting almost simultaneously in all these different regions, which were subject to different influences but had one thing in common—a considerable number of bigger or smaller towns and boroughs. With a more detailed analysis of the social background of these early persecutions, one could use this argument for explaining witchcraft by certain social tensions. But at present I am more interested in another use of this argument in more urbanized areas: we can see that the same degree of witch-hunting reached the bigger towns and boroughs of the Great Plain (such as Szeged and Hódmezővásárhely[25]) only in the first half of the eighteenth century, a delay accounted for not only by the former Turkish occupation, but also by the belated urbanization of this area, together with the later manifestation of the resultant social tensions— the same tensions that had affected the early witch-hunting regions. This is the first observation to support the idea that the belated witch-hunting of the 'periphery' of Europe could be explained by the belated appearance of the social and cultural causes of these persecutions.

The second observation can be drawn from the precise comparison of the level of witch-hunting on a chronological scale in all European countries. Although there are no all-encompassing statistics in this field, even a few similarities or differences reveal quite a lot. The statistics of Polish witch-hunting, published by Baranowski, reveal the closest resemblance to the Hungarian figures (also peaking in the first quarter of the eighteenth century),[26] just as there are

---

[24] These trials were edited by Komáromy, pp. 1–74.

[25] The famous witch-panic of Szeged in 1728 led to the burning of 13 accused, and to the accusation of a further 28, who were released only after the intervention of Emperor Charles VI. These trials were edited and analysed by János Reizner, *Szeged története* (The History of Szeged) (Szeged, 1900), i. 343 ff., iv. 373–535; cf. Friedrich Möstl, *Ein Szegediner Hexenprozess* (Graz, 1879). Documents from the panics in other boroughs of the Great Plain, following the Szeged one, are mainly edited by Schram, i. 225–348.

[26] Bohdan Baranowski gives percentage statistics for his evaluation of the chronological distribution of Polish witch-trials—unfortunately omitting the actual numbers and a detailed description of the documentary basis of his calculations—in his *Procesy czarownic w Polsce* (Witch-trials in Poland) (Łódź, 1952), 179. It is interesting to observe that the persecution becomes important—with 25% of all trials that occurred between

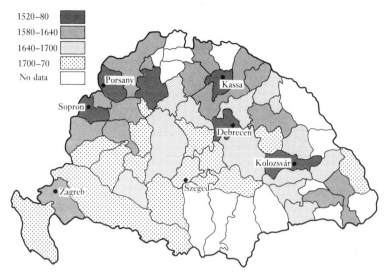

MAP 8.1. *Hungary: Appearance of the first witch-trial, by county. This map is borrowed from András Iklódy, 'A magyarországi boszorkányüldözés történeti alakulása', Ethnographia, 93 (1982), 294. It is slightly corrected, using a larger set of trials for statistical evaluation; Iklódy used only the material in Schram and Komáromy*

resemblances between other social or cultural features of Hungarian and Polish history.[27] Going backwards in time, I think a similar belatedness of social and cultural evolution could account for the late seventeenth-century witch-hunting waves in Mecklenburg (1690), in Salzburg (1677–81), or in Scandinavia (1668–90),[28] and the same social and cultural reasons could be cited to explain the New England crisis of 1692.[29] While aware that a similar chronology of European

1511 and 1775—in the last quarter of the 17th c., just as in Hungary. Similarly, too, there is a further rise in the first quarter of the 18th c., with 32% of all trials, and the level decreases slowly in the second quarter (14%). For more recent analyses of the witch-persecutions in Poland, see Janusz Tazbir, 'Hexenprozesse in Polen', *Archiv für Reformationsgeschichte*, 71 (1980), 280–307.

[27] Two collections of comparative studies can serve as a useful guide here: György Székely and Erik Fügedi (eds.), *La Renaissance et la Réformation en Pologne et en Hongrie (1450–1650)* (Budapest, 1963): Vera Zimányi (ed.), *La Pologne et la Hongrie aux XVI*-*XVIII* *siècles* (Budapest, 1980).

[28] Cf. Trevor-Roper, *The European Witch-craze*, p. 95, and the chapters on Sweden, Finland, and Norway, below.

[29] The New England witchcraft persecutions are well related to their social and cultural causes and surroundings by Paul Boyer and Stephen Nissenbaum, *Salem*

witch-hunting from the beginning would not provide an exact mirror of the rhythm of social and cultural evolution in all the countries and regions concerned, I am still convinced that this argument is valid for the later adoption of the already established models of persecution, and of the legal and cultural patterns solving certain types of crises.

It can be observed, finally, that the rhythm of the diffusion of these waves of witch-hunting is consistent with a more general model of how in European history forms of social organization and cultural patterns have spread to the 'periphery' from the more developed parts of Europe. Let me illustrate this model with a few random examples. The cult of the holy kings, the Christian version of sacral kingship, which first appeared in the Early Middle Ages among Merovingians and the Anglo-Saxon kingdoms, had been adopted by a kind of chain reaction by nearly all the new kingdoms in the ninth to twelfth centuries: Norway, Sweden, Denmark, Russia, Bohemia, Hungary, Serbia—while it had lost its importance in western and Mediter-ranean regions.[30] Courtly culture and chivalry, in full blossom in the twelfth century, could achieve a real social and cultural importance in central Europe only in the fourteenth and fifteenth centuries.[31] The inner tensions of medieval Christianity led to great heretical move-ments in the 'core' as early as the twelfth century, whereas in central and northern Europe this kind of religious popular movement only appears with the fourteenth- to fifteenth-century Hussites and the sixteenth-century Reformation.[32] I think it can be accepted, even without a more detailed analysis of this 'periphery-effect' of European social and cultural evolution, that the belatedness of the witch persecutions fits well into the general cultural position of these northern, central, and eastern regions within Europe.

Having accounted for the general characteristics of Hungarian

Possessed: The Social Origins of Witchcraft (Cambridge, Mass., 1974); and John Putnam Demos, *Entertaining Satan* (New York, 1982).

[30] Cf. Karol Górski, 'Le Roi saint: Un problème d'idéologie féodale', *Annales ESC* 24 (1969), 370–6; Erich Hoffmann, *Die heiligen Könige bei den Angelsachsen und den skandinavischen Völkern* (Neumünster, 1975); František Graus, 'La Sanctification du souverain dans l'Europe centrale des xᵉ et xıᵉ siècles', in *Hagiographie, culture et sociétés* (Paris, 1981), 559–72.

[31] Agnes Kurcz, *Lovagi kultura Magyarországon a XIII–XIV. században* (Hungarian Chivalric Culture in the 13th and 14th Centuries) (Budapest, 1988).

[32] The most recent synthesis of these medieval heretical movements is that of M. D. Lambert, *Medieval Heresy* (London, 1977). The parallel between the role of the Reforma-tion in the countries of the later Christianized periphery and that of the 11th–13th c. heresies in Mediterranean and western Europe remains to be investigated.

witch-hunting, one important peculiarity remains to be mentioned before we can proceed. The learned theoretical foundations of witch-hunting, the demonological-juridical treatises felt to be so essential in (and often responsible for) the explosion of the sixteenth- to seventeenth-century European 'witch-craze' were almost completely lacking in Hungary. Of course, some sixteenth-century Protestant preachers mention witchcraft along with other kinds of magical practices in their polemical works against 'Papist' and 'vulgar' superstitions. Yet however much they stress the devil's collaboration in these matters, they do not even devote a whole page to witchcraft in their writings.[33] There had been a few copies of the *Malleus maleficarum* in Hungary,[34] but they do not seem to have been estimated very highly. 'Fides sit pene ipsos' is what was written about the *Malleus* (and other treatises speaking for the real existence of the witches' devilish practices) by György Komáromi Csipkés, professor at the Puritan school in Debrecen; under his direction two of his students, Joannes C. Mediomontanus and Andreas P. Csehi, compiled the only Hungarian treatise of demonology, a *Disputatio theologica de lamiis veneficiis* (1656), which frequently quotes Johan Wier, and represents a rather sceptical point of view.[35] The only other Hungarian work (and the only one in the Hungarian language) treating the problem of witchcraft in some detail is the sermon by a colleague of Komáromi, Mátyás Nógrádi, the Protestant preacher of Debrecen, on 'Devilish Practices and Sorcery', which was included in his book entitled *Lelki próbakő* (Spiritual touchstone), and appeared a few years before the edition of

[33] The most detailed hints we get come from the militant *Confessio Ecclesiae Debrecinensis*, compiled under the direction of the Hungarian Calvinist leader Péter Méliusz Juhász in 1562, with the help of György Szegedi and György Czeglédi. The passages relating to witches and magical practices are translated and analysed in Dömötör, *Hungarian Folk Beliefs*, pp. 54–6. The Lutheran point of view is represented by Péter Bornemisza, *Ördögi kisértetekről avagy röttenetes utálatosságáról ez megfertéztetett világnak* (About the Temptations of the Devil, or the Loathsomeness of this Wicked World) (Semthe, 1598), ed. Sándor Eckhardt (Budapest, 1955), 129–39.

[34] e.g. we know that Miklós Zrinyi, the greatest poet and writer of the 17th c., had one in his library: S. Kende (ed.), *Die Bibliothek des Dichters Nicolaus Zrinyi* (Wien, 1893), 31; there is an explicit reference to the *Malleus* in the 1691 trials in Somorja (Samorin), cf. Horna, *Ein Monstre-Hexenprozess*, p. 31.

[35] *Disputatio theologica de lamiis veneficiis . . . sub praesidio d. Georgii C. Comarini . . . proponit Joannes C. Mediomontanus* (Varadini, 1656); *Disputatio theologica . . . secunda . . . publico examini subjicit Andreas P. Csehi* (Varadini, 1656). As the authors of these two works did not produce anything else, we might presume that the general conception of the two theses and the fairly wide range of references (from Augustine, Pliny, Horace, to Wier, Agrippa, Voetius, Del Rio, William Perkins, etc.) were suggested to them by their professor, Komáromi, who certainly possessed this level of scholarly erudition.

the *Disputatio*; it argues for the same prudent, sceptical treatment of witchcraft matters.[36] If we add to these two works a few more passages on witchcraft in late seventeenth- and early eighteenth-century religious literature,[37] we seem to have enumerated all that the Hungarians produced in this flourishing branch of early modern scholarship, or imported from other countries. As to the import of foreign demonologies, there is a slight change in the later period: the already-mentioned influence of the *Practica Rerum Criminalium* of Carpzov, which summed up the demonological commonplaces, and also served as a frequently used guide for questioning in torture chambers in eighteenth-century Hungary.

When the mass persecutions of the 1710s and 1720s left some people intellectually perplexed—as was the case with the town magistrates of the Transylvanian Saxon town Nagyszeben (Hermannstadt) in 1718— they had to ask the opinion of the universities of Vienna and Leipzig on whether torture confessions of witches were to be credited, for there was no Hungarian expert or authority in this field.[38] Though in the testimonies and confessions of the trials we can trace back popular doubts about witchcraft as far as the middle of the seventeenth century, and though the defence counsels (when there were any) delivered some eloquent critiques and explanations of these 'silly hearsays',[39] no serious work was written on this subject in Hungary.

[36] Nógrádi's book was printed in Debrecen in 1651. The sermon in question is on pp. 124–93; cf. László Makkai, 'Puritánok és boszorkányok Debrecenben' (Puritans and Witches in Debrecen), *A Hajdú-Bihar Megyei Levéltár évkönyve*, 8 (1981), 113–30.

[37] Imre Pápai Páriz, *Keskeny ut* (The Narrow Road) (Debrecen, 1719); Zsigmond Csuzy, *Evangeliumi Trombita* (1724). Their passages on witchcraft—subscribing to its existence—are reprinted by Zoltán Trócsányi, *A történelem árnyékában* (In the Shadow of History) (Budapest, 1936), 282–6.

[38] The documents of this interesting affair are edited by Heinrich Herbert, 'Die Rechtspflege in Hermannstadt zur Zeit Karls VI.' *Archiv des Vereins für Siebenbürgische Landeskunde*, NF 27 (1896), 118–46. The two opinions sent from Vienna University—and a third one from the 'Generalauditoriat' of the Austrian administration in Transylvania—advised the Nagyszeben jurors to pursue the affair and clear any doubts with the torture of the two accused women. Their opinions were frequently backed by references to Carpzov, Goedelman, Bodin, and other demonologists. The opinion of Leipzig University, on the other hand, made a thorough critique of the inadequacy of the accusations, warned against torture or water ordeal, and advised that the accused be set free. The municipal court adopted this latter solution.

[39] For some examples of defence counsels voicing serious doubts about the authenticity of witchcraft accusations, see Tkalčić, 'Izprave', pp. 19–22 (1657, in Zagreb—a detailed exposition on why dreams and apparitions should not be credited); Endre Varga (ed.), *Uriszék: XVI–XVII. századi perszövegek* (The Feudal Court: Texts of Trials from the 16th and 17th Centuries) (Budapest, 1958), 372–3 (1653: a noble woman, accused by her daughter, denies the charges, her lawyer calling it 'vain gossip of her

However, the lack of defendants or opponents of demonology at the theoretical or theological level did not prevent the multiplication of this element in the eighteenth-century torture confessions. Despite the frequently voiced sceptical view, persecutions went on and on, until the enlightened court doctor of Maria Theresa, Gerard van Swieten (a Dutchman), who wrote an excellent *Mémoire* (1758) on the falsehood of witchcraft accusations, managed to persuade the Empress that witch-hunting should be stopped.[40] In line with the way in which witch-hunting had evolved in Hungary, there was no public debate on the subject (there was no contemporary publication of van Swieten's *Mémoire*, either), just the royal orders, the change of a series of local sentences to acquittals by the royal Appeal Court, the censure by some Hungarian county administrations of this absolutist intrusion into their legal practice, and then the final prohibition of witch-trials in 1768.[41] There are very few sources to reveal what late eighteenth-century Hungarians thought of this whole business, and a quantity of data showing that the persecution must have continued on a local scale for a few more decades still remains to be collected and edited.

daughter', and 'silly hearsays'); Komáromy, p. 148 (1689: a defence counsel in the county of Ugocsa 'totalem actionem domini actoris et magistratus simpliciter negaret et exciperet contra testes tales, si qui essent infantes, incestuosi et non legitimae aetatis existentes vel vero auditu testantes . . .'). The history of popular scepticism and the varieties of defence arguments resorted to by the accused is quite an unexplored subject; a great quantity of data on the trials waits to be analysed. It is interesting that besides simple negation, many accused try to manipulate the specific rationality of witchcraft beliefs: they refuse the charges, saying that the devil must have acted, assuming their physical appearance: Komáromy, p. 93; Schram, i. 338 (1629, in Kolozsvár: here the accused accuses her accuser of doing harm in her shape); cf. also ibid. i. 294; ii. 518; iii. 306.

[40] The *Mémoire* (about the case of a certain Slovenian witch, Heruczina, who was examined by van Swieten personally), written in 1758 to the Empress in French, is edited by Komáromy, pp. 642–59; for the general activity of van Swieten, see Erna Lesky and Adam Wandruszka, *Gerard van Swieten und seine Zeit* (Vienna, Cologne, and Graz, 1973). I have analysed his activity in 'Decline of Witches and Rise of Vampires in the 18th Century Habsburg Monarchy', *Ethnologia Europea*, 17 (1987), 165–80.

[41] For the 1756 order of Maria Theresa, see Komáromy, pp. 600–1; for the intervention of the Royal Court of Appeal, reverting the local sentences, ibid., pp. 606–38, 660–717. Excerpts from the text of the final royal order forbidding witch-trials, written in 1766 and made law two years later, are in Soldan, *Geschichte der Hexenprozesse*, ii. 278–80.

II. FROM THE SOCIOLOGY OF ACCUSATION TO THE PSYCHOLOGY OF SUSPICION AND THE ANTHROPOLOGY OF ENCHANTMENT

In the past decade, mainly owing to the fruitful inspiration of Alan Macfarlane's work, several attempts have been made to investigate witchcraft persecution not on the general, regional, national scale, but in its real, local everyday (or rather nightly) forms.[42] This new approach relies on a hitherto scarcely exploited mass of sources: the many testimonies brought against the witches. It has revealed a new dimension of witch-hunting: besides the fanatic clerical or lay witch-finders, besides the barbarous techniques of early modern justice, besides the problem of a historical short-circuit of Christian human-ism, historians have had to face a whole set of coherent social and intellectual pressures amounting to a witch-persecution from below. And they have tried to explain it with the anthropological theories existing in this field that show how popular witch-hunting provided a way to live out the inner social and moral conflicts of the community, how it could be a kind of reaction to the disturbance of the traditional set of norms. So a broad historical sociology of witchcraft accusations has arisen, in which the generic arguments based upon social and economic history have turned into more concrete investigations of the social roles of the accused and the accusers in their community. The changing structure of the early modern village, the transformation of the traditional set of norms, the conflicts between family members, clans, and village factions have been used to shed more light on the individual and social processes leading to witch-hunting. Without denying the valuable new perspectives gained by this approach (the application of which would certainly elucidate some Hungarian cases, too, though unfortunately nobody has attempted it yet),[43] I should like to formulate some doubts about it.

To reconstruct the entire social network of a community, with all the customs and norms which regulate its life and all the hidden

---

[42] Macfarlane, *Witchcraft in Tudor and Stuart England*; Boyer and Nissenbaum, *Salem Possessed*; Demos, *Entertaining Satan*; Robert Muchembled, *La Sorcière au village (XVᵉ–XVIIᵉ siècles)* (Paris, 1979).

[43] The only attempt to present the problems of Hungarian witch-trials in the light of these studies has been Éva Pócs, 'Gondolatok a magyarországi boszorkányperek néprajzi viszgálatához' (Ideas for an Ethnographic Investigation of Hungarian Witch-trials), *Ethnographia*, 94 (1983), 134–46.

tensions which undermine its existence, is of course a fascinating task. The detailed accounts to be read in the testimonies of the accusers and the witnesses, the vivid descriptions of everyday quarrels, street debates, fears, afflictions might effectively be good starting-points for this reconstruction, if there is sufficient complementary documentation of the persons or communities involved (other legal sources such as inheritance conflicts, and trials for adultery, rape, theft, and murder; tax rolls, parish registers, etc.). But we should not be misled by the precise description of conflicts to be read in witchcraft accusations: they are by no means an adequate representation of contemporary reality.

As the fascinating experiences of Jeanne Favret-Saada have shown, by means of careful observation of contemporary witchcraft cases, and also by exploring the system as a participant in the game, tales of one's bewitching are shaped by a kind of unconscious conforming of one's own misfortune to one of the narrative and mythological stereotypes current in the community. The full witchcraft diagnosis—as well as the strategy with which to make a counter-attack—emerges, if one manages to project this stereotype on to an actual part of one's interpersonal relations, and on to an actual event connected with the selected person, which could be the 'reason' for one's troubles.[44] A conflict named in such a context might be a real one, or might be just a projection of hostility on to somebody who can be a good imaginary substitute for the real enemy and who is a person that can easily be victimized.[45] It can be an important conflict, but it can also be something quite insignificant, just enough to constitute a personal link between the accuser and the accused. In any event, the conflict is just as unsatisfactory as a means of explaining the accuser's motivation as it is in making us believe that the accused has really bewitched his counterpart because of it.

For witchcraft accusations follow the lines of a specific symbolic system, even if they relieve the individuals and communities involved of real social, psychological, and religious tensions. Real characteristics are not only matched by stereotypes (vicious stepmother, quarrelsome wife, neighbour with abusive demands, wicked old woman, suspicious stranger, etc.), but they are fitted into a pattern of two

[44] Jeanne Favret-Saada, *Deadly Words* (Cambridge, 1980); ead., *Corps pour corps: Enquête sur la sorcellerie dans le Bocage* (Paris, 1981).

[45] A convincing analysis of such substitutions in the case of the chief Salem accusers of 1692, the Putnams, is made by Boyer and Nissenbaum, *Salem Possessed*, pp. 143–51.

poles, both having strategic possibilities within the framework of witch-beliefs. These two poles can roughly be summarized as the stronger, the more powerful, the more prosperous person or group on the one side, and the weaker, unsuccessful one on the other. As has frequently been stated,[46] it is generally the former party which accuses the latter one, using the logic that the accused must have taken magical revenge because of their inability to secure by legal means what they had been longing for. This type of accusation can be illustrated with a lot of Hungarian cases, too. It can be as well observed in the dozen witch-trials initiated in the circles of high nobility as in citizens' conflicts or village quarrels. The Transylvanian princes of the sixteenth and seventeenth centuries had a special liability to accuse the families of their defeated political enemies of witchcraft: Sigismund Báthory blamed the mother of Boldizsár Báthory (murdered by him) for his impotence;[47] Gábor Bethlen, after he had taken power from Gábor Báthory, who was murdered (perhaps at his instigation) in 1612, accused Anna Báthory, the sister of the deceased, and two other noblewomen of his entourage with witchcraft;[48] between 1679 and 1686 Prince Mihály Apafy staged a monster witch-trial (with about twenty accused) against the wife of his exiled rival, Pál Béldi, who was accused of causing serious illnesses in the prince's wife, Anna Bornemisza, in revenge for her husband's defeat.[49] Omitting the multiplication of similar examples in city or village trials, I should like to call attention to the opposite type of accusations, more often neglected in the analyses.

The possibility of accusing and denouncing somebody as a witch gave an unprecedented power to *all* members of the community to solve their conflicts and to take revenge for anything—this is in fact the

---

[46] This is the position of Macfarlane, *Witchcraft*, pp. 149–51, and of Johansen and Naess, chs. 13 and 14, below.

[47] Müller, *Beiträge*, p. 25.

[48] The sources of this affair are partly edited by János Szendrei, 'Török Katalin bűnpere', (The Trial of Katalin Török), *Történelmi Tár* (1891), 317–34; for divergent interpretations, see András Komáromy, 'A "bűbájos" Báthory Anna' (Anna Báthory, the 'enchantress'), *Századok*, 28 (1894), 298–314; László Nagy, *Sok dolgot próbála Bethlen Gábor* (The Many Things Tried by Gábor Bethlen) (Budapest, 1981). The trials ended with the exile of the accused and the confiscation of the greater part of their huge estates.

[49] The documents of this trial, filling a whole volume, are published in János Herner (ed.), *Bornemisza Anna megbűvöltetése* (The Bewitchment of Anna Bornemisza) (Szeged, 1989). The accused died in prison in 1686, several of her maids or of the wise women she had consulted were exiled or executed.

underlying mechanism of witch-crazes. In the tension-ridden psychological climate of the witch-craze, the low could as well accuse the high, the poor the rich man, the weak the strong, or the outsider the established members of the community.[50] There was, of course, a suitable explanation in the witch-beliefs for this kind of accusation as well: power and richness could supposedly be gained by illicit, magical means. Let me illustrate this type of accusation, also, with some Hungarian examples. A poor wise woman brought to court during the famous Szeged trials in 1728 accused a highly estimated ex-judge of being the head of the coven, and in the climate of the witch-panic he was soon arrested, tortured, and then condemned to death by burning.[51] Referring to this example—which of course immediately became notorious—a few years later in the nearby borough of Halas, a peasant explained in the local tavern, after a dispute with the municipal jury, that 'all the jurors, and even the judge of Halas, are witches'.[52] The most typical form of this kind of real (and not magical) revenge of the weak is the appearance of young kitchenmaids of 14 to 16 years old, or even children of 9 to 11, as witch-accusers, which can be observed in Hungary in many places where a real witch-panic exploded, just as it can in other countries.[53]

[50] For the general characteristics of a witch-craze see Henningsen, *The Witches' Advocate*, pp. 391–2. The Salem case of 1692—though from the point of view of witch-beliefs an atypical one, since it involves possession beliefs too—could well demonstrate this second kind of accusation. Boyer and Nissenbaum, *Salem Possessed*, have unearthed the documents of the bitter factional struggles within the village, opposing roughly two groups of families. The more prosperous group, headed by the clan of the Porters, possessed the municipal leadership in Salem Village, and their economic position got considerably better in the years preceding the witchcraft crisis through their participation in the new commercial boom of Salem Town. The other group, headed by the clan of the Putnams and including other families with close relations to the village parish (led at the time by the Revd Parris), possessed lands of lesser quality and in an unfavourable geographical position for transport. The development of Salem town had brought about their economic decline, and their interest lay more in the isolation of Salem Village from the town. The witchcraft accusations were nearly all directed by members of this latter faction against members of the former.

[51] The deposition of this woman, Anna Nagy, Mrs Kökény, are edited by Reizner, *Szeged története*, iv. 377–89; the depositions of the accused ex-judge Dániel Rósa, ibid., pp. 407–10; the ex-judge was also accused by a beggar, ibid., p. 430.

[52] The documents of this trial of 1734 are edited by Schram, ii. 433, 436–7.

[53] Child-accusers appear first in Kolozsvár, the city of the biggest 16th-c. persecutions, towards the end of the wave of witch-hunting, in 1615 and 1629: Komáromy, pp. 83–8, 95; grandchildren accusing grandmothers, in 1709: ibid., pp. 233–40; a girl giving a detailed description of the sabbath, in 1718: Schram, iii. 298–300; a young kitchenmaid making accusations, in 1734: ibid. ii. 272; children as professional witch-accusers, in 1683: Herner, *Bornemisza*, p. 21; and a similar case, in 1749: Schram, ii. 440–1. For other child-accusers, cf. the Basque cases analysed by Henningsen, *The Witches'*

This pattern of two poles, with its alternative uses, can of course express or reflect the real sociological dimensions of witchcraft conflicts, but there is more to it than that: it is a symbolic battlefield with its typical actors, scripts, rules, and weapons.[54] To understand it properly, before trying to reach behind the stereotypes, we have to examine in detail what these stereotypes reveal. Witchcraft research can proceed here using the experience of similar historical investigations of other stereotyped historical materials: the long-term transformation of the inner structure of medieval miracles (examined by André Vauchez and others),[55] the learned folklore of medieval *exempla* (studied by Claude Brémond, Jacques Le Goff, and Jean-Claude Schmitt), or the more and more fashionable investigation of medieval and early modern dreams, visions, and prophecies.[56] The innumerable descriptions of *maleficia* and of different kinds of spells and magical apparitions constitute an analogous source to those mentioned.

But there is more to this parallel than a simple juxtaposition effected by the comparative historian. The two poles of the popular

---

Advocate, pp. 209–18; Midelfort, *Witch-hunting*, pp. 139–42 (for the years 1628–42, with an explanation of the special position of children making accusations); Carlo Ginzburg, *I benandanti* (2nd edn. Turin, 1972) (14- and 15-year-old *benandanti* boys as accusers in 1621–2); for Sweden, Bengt Ankarloo, *Trolldomsprocesserna i Sverige* (Lund, 1971), 224–31, 286–99, and ch. 11, below. The problem of child-accusers merits a detailed comparative analysis, for these were the centuries of the great transformation of children's role in society and within the family, as demonstrated by Philippe Ariès, *L'Enfant et la vie familiale sous l'Ancien Régime* (Paris, 1960) and Lawrence Stone, *Family, Sex and Marriage in England, 1500–1800* (London, 1977).

[54] Having exploited the classical anthropological studies in the field, such as Edward Evans-Pritchard, *Witchcraft, Oracles and Magic among the Azande* (Oxford, 1937); Marwick, *Witchcraft and Sorcery*; Victor Turner, 'Witchcraft and Sorcery: Taxonomy versus Dynamics', in his *The Forest of Symbols* (Ithaca and London, 1967); and esp. Mary Douglas, 'Thirty Years after *Witchcraft, Oracles and Magic*', in her *Witchcraft: Confessions and Accusations*, pp. xiii–xxxviii, anthropologists and historians of witchcraft could well use—at least, in my view—the interaction theories of Erving Goffman, or the formulation of Pierre Bourdieu on symbolic power and *champ religieux* (cf. Bourdieu, 'Genèse et structure du champ religieux', *Revue française de sociologie*, 12 (1971), 295–334). The best description of this 'symbolic battlefield' of witchcraft I have found is in the works of Jeanne Favret-Saada.

[55] André Vauchez, *La Sainteté en Occident aux derniers siècles du Moyen Âge* (Rome, 1981), 519–59; Hans Oppel, 'Exemplum und Mirakel', *Archiv für Kulturgeschichte*, 58 (1976), 96–114.

[56] Claude Brémond, Jacques Le Goff, and Jean-Claude Schmitt, *L'"exemplum"* (Turnhout, 1982); William A. Christian, *Apparitions in Late Medieval and Renaissance Spain* (Princeton, 1981). At the École des Hautes Études en Sciences Sociales, in Paris, Jacques Le Goff and Jean-Claude Schmitt have a special course centred on a research project on medieval dreams and visions.

magical universe–the beneficial and the harmful, or the positive and the negative—have in fact always developed in relation to each other. They have borrowed elements from each other, they have reflected changes occurring in the opposite domain. To give just one example: the emergence of female saints in the later Middle Ages, their special access to the sacred field, their prophecies, their eminent political roles, produced such anxiety in the male world that their saintly position became ambiguous. Some eminent representatives of this type, such as Joan of Arc, were on the margin between the categories of the saint and the witch. And this emergence of 'women on top' from the religious point of view definitely contributed to a renewed diabolization of the female sex in the same period. And the relationship is evident not only as regards the persons invested with supernatural power, but also as regards the structure of miracles and *maleficia*, the latter being nothing other than inverted miracles (though a little bit more complicated in their structure). The parallel could be extended to holy visions and sabbath descriptions, to possessions and mystical ecstasies, and to apparitions and nightmares as well—the positive and the negative models are in most ages just different phrasings based on the same code of magical, supernatural beliefs.

The idea outlined above was the starting-point for the research project we have been working on for several years with a small group of historians and folklorists in Budapest.[57] By the meticulous coding of some 20,000 narratives of malefices from the fifteenth to the eighteenth centuries, we hope to detect historical changes, recurrent patterns, and local variants in the seemingly timeless magic world of spells. Let me briefly summarize the aims of this project here, which tries to create a database for a computerized analysis of all Hungarian witch-trials known to us. We abstract from each trial all the data referring to the accused, the conditions of his or her accusation, and the outcome of the trial (this program will enable us to compile the data for the sociology of accusations as precisely as possible). We also abstract from the documents descriptions of witch-beliefs and magical practices, ranging from the stereotypical exterior of the witches and the supernatural abilities ascribed to them, to the stock of mythological elements (metamorphoses, flights, sabbath, etc.), and to the

[57] This work is sponsored by the Ethnographical Institute of the Hungarian Academy of Sciences. The members of the research team are: Éva Pócs, Katalin Benedek, Anna Imreh, Márta Halasi, Monika Lakner, Ildikó Kristóf, István Bacsa, and myself.

magical harming and healing practices. This would mainly be of use in facilitating a detailed morphological analysis of witch-beliefs, and to an exact description of the geographical and chronological variation in different elements. The third aspect of our database, connected directly to our argument here, takes the dramaturgy of a *maleficium* as its basis, trying to encode each account of the witches' misdeeds and spells that can be found in the witnesses' hearings.[58]

We have structured this third aspect according to the following model: (1) The social relations of the accused and the bewitched; (2) The narrative of their conflict; (3) The witch's menace and curses; (4) The narrative about the witch's reappearance in normal conditions or during a nightly apparition, where the bewitched is seriously ill-treated, and sometimes taken to the witches' sabbath; (5) The techniques supposedly used for bewitchment; (6) The harm done; (7) The techniques to identify the harm or illness as bewitchment; (8) The lay or specialist persons (cunning folk, priest, witch-finder) who identify the witch and the techniques used by them; (9) The counter-action against the witch and (if there are any) the magical specialists directing it; (10) Other procedures to get remedy or healing.[59] One of the questions to be answered is whether the time–space structure of *maleficia* underwent similar changes to those undergone by miracles in the later Middle Ages: whether a similar departure from the conception of magic operating only by bodily contact or by physical proximity can be observed throughout the period (for instance, the more prominent role of nightly visions as substitutes for the actual presence of the witch, the belated effect of the witch's curse, greater emphasis on spiritual possession, etc.). Even if it is only a question of relative proportions (which can best be analysed by computer), these histori-cal transformations are worth investigating.

Among other problems to be examined I should like to mention two: the role of healing and of cunning folk in all these dramaturgies of *maleficia* on the one hand, and on the other, the *interchangeability* of the attributes of magical healing and harming in the descriptions. This

---

[58] Out of the 1,500 trials edited so far from the Hungarian materials, we possess for about a thousand the documents of the witnesses' hearings. There are quite a few trials where not just 10–20, but 50–100 witnesses make depositions against the accused, each giving at least one narrative account of his or her bewitchment. Taking 20 *maleficium* cases per trial as average, this would amount to at least 20,000 cases—a quantity that can be handled only by computer.

[59] The structure of the program owes a lot to the work of Jeanne Favret-Saada, *Deadly Words*.

latter aspect, which had a serious historical consequence to which I shall return, is very intriguing also from the structural point of view. It not only reminds us of the previously cited relationship between positive and negative poles of the magical universe, but it also points to the possible mechanisms for the mutual borrowing of each other's elements: magical beliefs could be considered in this respect as morphological elements and transformational rules of a semi-linguistic system, with a lot of flexibility and with only some basic rules of 'generative grammar', which are employed by the individuals for constructing their own account of their misfortune and their attempt at its solution.

While waiting to accomplish these detailed examinations which could lead to a historical anthropology of enchantment and magic, let me sketch a historical view of the transformations and the inner contradictions of the witch-belief system in Hungary with less sophisticated tools. I wish to concentrate upon two key elements: the evolution of sabbath imagery, and the criminalization of popular healers.

III. TRANSFORMATIONS AND BLACKOUTS IN THE UNIVERSE OF POPULAR MAGIC

The recent discovery of a distinct system of popular witchcraft beliefs, as represented in the majority of *maleficium* testimonies,[60] and especially in the witchcraft confessions of some archaic areas untouched so far by the learned demonological propaganda,[61] has led to another branch of witchcraft studies apart from the sociology of popular accusations. Let us call this approach the 'cultural conflict' paradigm.

Viewed from this angle, the witch epidemic of the sixteenth and

---

[60] Besides the already-cited works of Muchembled, *La Sorcière*, and Macfarlane, *Witchcraft in Tudor and Stuart England*, one should mention here above all Keith Thomas, *Religion and the Decline of Magic* (New York, 1971), 502–70; Robert Kieckhefer, *European Witch Trials: Their Foundation in Popular and Learned Culture, 1300–1500* (Berkeley and Los Angeles, 1976); and Richard Horsley, 'Who were the Witches? The Social Roles of the Accused in the European Witch Trials', *Journal of Interdisciplinary History*, 9 (1979), 689–715.

[61] The pioneer study of this aspect is Julio Caro Baroja, *Las brujas y su mundo* (Madrid, 1961).

seventeenth centuries was part of a much wider cultural transformation, where in early modern Europe a new kind of 'élite culture' confronted the popular one. The learned concept of demonological witchcraft, even if it could not any longer be held to be the only cause of persecutions, was now blamed for distorting or perverting the popular belief-systems. One version of these researches considered the witch-hunts as a means of and a pretext for disciplining popular culture, eradicating all its 'superstitions' and ancient customs, and submitting it to a new kind of cultural domination.[62] Another version has tried to unveil the original beliefs and the uncorrupted mythology (or at least, to reconstruct them from the distortions of learned descriptions or torture confessions), and then to illustrate the extent of moral and cultural degradation that occurred with the intervention of learned culture and institutional persecution in this sphere.[63] What could be added to this thesis, using Hungarian sources? The Hungarian witch-trials seem at first glance to give an excellent support to this approach. The lack of innate demonological traditions promises an uncorrupted popular concept of witchcraft; the existence of shamanistic beliefs in the region makes it legitimate to look for local archaic versions of the sabbath.

Let us try to see first whether we can discover traces of this shamanistic background in the historical data on Hungarian witch-beliefs. The Hungarian *táltos* (pl. *táltosok*),[64] a shaman-like sorcerer, does in fact appear in the witch-trials, mainly as accused of witchcraft, and these data are in fact the most archaic ones we can get about these beliefs. We discover that these sorcerers do not learn their abilities (the inquisitors tried to persuade them in vain of the devilish origin of their

---

[62] This is the view represented by Robert Muchembled in his *Culture populaire et culture des élites (XVᵉ–XVIIIᵉ siècles)* (Paris, 1978), 287–340; cf. id. in Dupont-Bouchat et al., *Prophètes et sorciers*, pp. 218–54, and his contribution to this volume, ch. 5, above.

[63] This is the method used by Carlo Ginzburg, *I benandanti*, and also in his essay in this volume, ch. 4, above; cf. also Henningsen, *The Witches' Advocate*, pp. 28–36, 157–60, where he tries to reconstruct the local witch-beliefs of Zugurramurdi and Rentería before the intervention of the authorities.

[64] The historical and folklore data on the Hungarian *táltos* are gathered and analysed in the context of shamanism by Vilmos Diószegi, *A sámánhit emlékei a magyar népi műveltségben* (The Remnants of Shamanism in Hungarian Popular Culture) (Budapest, 1958), partly trans. into German: 'Die Überreste des Schamanismus in der ungarischen Volkskultur', *Acta Ethnographica*, 6 (1959), 97–135; more recently see Mihály Hoppál, 'Traces of Shamanism in Hungarian Folk Beliefs', in Hoppál (ed.), *Shamanism in Eurasia* (Göttingen, 1984), 430–49.

knowledge), but they are 'created to be wise by God', 'God makes them *táltosok* in the womb of their mother', and they are born with teeth.[65] Their knowledge enables them to divine treasure hidden in the ground,[66] to foretell future calamities,[67] to protect from hail or fire,[68] and, of course, to heal. Their most noteworthy activity is the shamanistic soul-journey, when their soul leaves the body in trance and most frequently takes the form of various animals, mainly of a bull, and goes out to fight in the air with other *táltosok*.[69] These fights might take place at regular intervals, they might serve as an initiation rite for young would-be *táltosok*,[70] they might be between *táltosok* of different countries or nationalities,[71] but a more precise aim of the

[65] The first quotation is from the trial of Anna Bácsi, Mrs Szaniszlai, Debrecen, 1711, in Komáromy, p. 253; the second from the confession of Erzsébet Balási, Mrs Bartha, Debrecen, 1725, ibid., p. 360; we hear the same in the trial of Ilona Borsi, Mrs Szabó, Munkács, 1735, in Lehoczky Tivadar, 'Beregmegyei boszorkányperek' (Witch-trials in the County of Bereg), *Hazánk*, 8 (1887), 296–306; a *táltos* called Mihály Szvetics, tried in Pécs in 1752, had his 'secret force' because he was the seventh child in the family: cf. István Szentkirályi, 'Garabonciás-per Pécsett' (Trial of a *garabonciás* in Pécs), *Pécs-Baranyamegyei Múzeum Egyesület értesítője*, 9 (1917), 1–7.

[66] As regards treasure-digging, besides the cases of the three previously mentioned *táltosok*, it is interesting to look at the case of Judit Virág, Mrs Jámbor, Kalocsa, 1764, who was perhaps the only *táltos* executed for her activity, not because of its 'devilish' character, but simply for having committed a fraud and having escaped with the payments: Schram, iii. 220–3.

[67] Anna Bácsi foretells great battles which will destroy the whole city of Debrecen, and attacks by Germans and Turks; she would cook 3 lb. of meat to divine the outcome of the wars between Prince Rákóczi, the Habsburgs, and the Turks at the time of the *kuruc* independence war: Komáromy, pp. 250–2.

[68] Anna Bácsi divines fire in different parts of the city and knows how to divert it: ibid.; the same is said about Ilona, Mrs András Czuppon, Szombathely, 1640 (who is just called *tudós*, wise woman, but her activity resembles very much that of the *táltos*): Tibor Antal Horváth, *Boszorkányok és boszorkányperek Szombathelyen* (Witches and Witch-trials in Szombathely, 1937), 23; Mihály Szvetics chases away hail and fire: Szentkirályi, 'Garabonciás'; the hail-diverting activity, and also the ability to cause hail if not paid, is a historically later evolution of *táltos* beliefs, probably merging here with the Balkan, and also Hungarian, folk-mythological figure of the wandering scholar, the *garabonciás diák*, so it is not by chance that we only hear about it in one of our latest trials, and that in more recent times, it is the dominant motif of *táltos* beliefs; cf. Sándor Szücs, 'Időért viaskodó táltosok' (*Táltosok* Fighting for the Weather), *Ethnographia*, 62 (1951), 403–9.

[69] The animal-form taken by the *táltosok* is identified with their soul with the help of comparative data by Diószegi, *A sámánhit*, pp. 385–94.

[70] The fights are said to take place at harvest-time (Komáromy, pp. 355, 362); or three times a year, on the occasion of the general meeting of the *táltosok* at Pentecost and the feasts of St Jacob and St Michael; or at the third day of Pentecost and at Midsummer; cf. Ferenc Bogdál, 'Egy miskolci "Táltos" 1741-ben' (A *táltos* of Miskolc in 1741), *Néprajzi közlemények* (1960), 308–11.

[71] German and Hungarian *táltosok* are said to be fighting in 1711 (Komáromy, p. 253); they are said to fight in the sky 'for the empire' (ibid., p. 362); men and women are said to

fights, like the *benandanti*'s fight for fertility, is absent from seven-teenth- and eighteenth-century Hungarian *táltos* beliefs.[72] The soul-journey can also take them 'to the other world, to God, where they are accepted with all kinds of pleasures and a great hospitality', before being sent back to the earth to heal.[73] As happened to the Italian *benandanti*, some Hungarian judges tried to persuade these *táltosok* that their visions were in fact of devilish origin and the meeting they were attending was nothing other than the sabbath. Some *táltosok* resisted this charge,[74] some could not. In 1727, near Komárom, a woman, very probably a *táltos*, whose daughter of 8–10 years told that the two of them 'frequently went to the end of the world, and enjoyed a great hospitality, then they went to the bottom of the waters, and again they took part in a big feast', was soon made to confess that she could fly by means of ointments, that she had made a pact with the devil, and that she was in fact attending the sabbath—getting there, however, by means of the shamanistic sieve, used as a ship.[75]

As we can see, the *táltos* mythology did provide a few elements that could be integrated into the witchcraft paradigm, given the historical coexistence of the two belief-systems not only in the popular imagina-tion but also on the bench of the accused. The most obvious merging, and a reinterpretation of the community-protecting function of the *táltos*, can be observed in the cases of the *táltos* healing the bewitched,[76] or acting sometimes as a witch-finder, boasting that he

fight separately (Bogdál, 'Egy miskolci "Tálos"'); their military organization is often mentioned: they are said to have a prince (Komáromy, p. 203); a *táltos* woman boasts that she is the commander of 500 men 'in the same order' (Horváth, *Boszorkányok*, p. 23); they are said to have captains, lieutenants, various officers, shining flags (Komáromy, pp. 250, 362; Bogdál, 'Egy miskolci "Táltos"'; Schram, iii. 220–1).

[72] I have tried to examine the possible analogies and also the Balkan links between *benandanti* and *táltosok*, comparing them also with the Slovenian and Croatian *kersnik*, the Serbian *zduhač*, and other semi-shamanistic sorcerers of Central Europe, in my study 'Shamanistic Elements in Central European Witchcraft', in Hoppál (ed.), *Shamanism in Eurasia*, pp. 404–22. The theoretical possibility of the merging of shamanistic and witchcraft beliefs is discussed there in greater detail.

[73] Trial in 1720 in Eger, where the body of Mrs Antal Mihály, while she is in rapture, lies for nine days as if it were dead, according to the testimonies: Diószegi, *A sámánhit*, p. 77.

[74] Erzsébet Balási saved her life by resisting torture and refusing to accept a diaboli-cal interpretation: Komáromy, pp. 360–3.

[75] Gyula Alapi, *Bűbájosok és boszorkányok Komárom vármegyében* (Witches and Sorcerers in the County of Komárom) (Komárom, 1914), 17–37; quotation from p. 17.

[76] Besides the above-mentioned *táltosok*, who all practise this healing activity, a few more data: (1696) Schram, i. 459–60; (1716) Komáromy, p. 272; (1721) Alapi, *Bűbájosok*, p. 12; a series of data referring to the *táltos* Anók Fejér, put on trial in 1728, but con-

could 'cry out the names of all the witches in town'.[77] Here the *táltosok* simply take the position of the cunning folk, they even borrow one of their common arguments and keep on showing the wounds, scars, and blue spots they have acquired during their nightly confrontation with the witches.[78] Apart from this integration, we can discover traces of shamanistic beliefs in quite a few witch-trials.

The most intriguing of these elements, and not only in a Hungarian context, is the problem of the *soul-journeys* and the *animal metamorphoses* of the witches. As in many European trials, so in Hungary, too, the witch is sometimes said to go to the sabbath only *in spiritu*, leaving the body at home.[79] The most frequent form taken by the soul is a mosquito, a fly, a butterfly, or a bee (eventually returning to the mouth or the nose of the body lying at home as if it were dead)—if these insects cannot be found in the *táltos* beliefs, they can, however, be discovered in the similarly shamanistic Croatian–Dalmatian *kersnik* beliefs.[80] What we do find in the Hungarian sources—even if not with direct reference to a soul-journey but only as one of the possible animal shapes of the witch—is the bull of the *táltos*, with the witch riding on it out of the chimney;[81] witches entering the room of the bewitched through the window in the shape of raging bulls;[82] or midwives fighting each other in the shape of bulls.[83]

Other elements that crop up here or there in the Hungarian witch-trials and show the influence of the *táltos* mythology include the

---

tinuing her healing activities elsewhere: Komáromy, pp. 420, 443, 457; Schram, ii. 333; finally, another *táltos* healer in 1743: Schram, ii. 506–7.

[77] This is what Anna Bácsi said in Debrecen in 1711: Komáromy, p. 250.

[78] Alapi, *Bűbájosok*, p. 10; I omit numerous references to cunning folk saying the same thing.

[79] Cf. Ginzburg, *I benandanti*, pp. 30–3; explicit hints that the witch is leaving her body at home: Gábor Kazinczy, 'Megyaszói boszorkányok 1731-ben' (Witches of Megyaszó in 1731), *Hazánk*, 3 (1885), 374–5.

[80] Let me list the cases of witches transformed into insects. Kolozsvár, 1584: Komáromy, p. 49; Transylvania, 1680: Herner, *Bornemisza*, p. 20; Segesvár, 1670, 1685: Müller, *Beiträge*, p. 58; Deutschkreuz, 1699: Göllner, *Hexenprozesse*, p. 144; Nagyszeben (Hermannstadt), early 18th c.: Herbert, 'Die Rechtspflege in Hermannstadt', p. 113; Szászebes, 1746: Müller, *Beiträge*, p. 58; Slovenia, 1758 (in the *Mémoire* of van Swieten): Komáromy, p. 651. Except for the last one, these cases are near to the similar *kersnik* beliefs (on which see the refs. in my article 'Shamanistic Elements', p. 408). The insect soul journey is a Transylvanian, mainly Saxon, belief.

[81] Heinrich Müller, 'Zur Geschichte des Repser Stuhls', *Archiv des Vereins für siebenbürgische Landeskunde*, NF 37 (1910), 144.

[82] Ugocsa, 1707: Komáromy, p. 212; Békés, 1755: Schram, iii. 135.

[83] Békés, 1755: Schram, iii. 136; Dömötör, *Hungarian Folk Beliefs*, p. 146.

extraction of the bones,[84] a common method of the Hungarian witches for doing harm, which is reminiscent of shamanistic initiation tales.[85] Remotely related to this, we also hear in Hungarian witch-confessions that the witches eat cows and then put the skin and bones together and stuff them with straw.[86] The *magic sieve* used as a ship, which can carry even hundreds of witches, is frequently mentioned.[87] At certain places witches *fight* in groups with each other, armed with sticks, like the Serbian *zduhač*, another semi-shamanistic figure in this region.[88] And finally—though this is not unknown in German territories, either—the *military organization* of witches is described in several dozens of confessions; their flags, drums, and all kinds of officers remind us not only of the constant warfare in sixteenth- and seventeenth-century Hungary, but also of the organization of the *táltosok*.[89]

However, talking about all this 'shamanistic background', we

[84] Beside the cases listed in Schram, iii. 385, let me mention here the interesting case published by Göllner, *Hexenprozesse*, p. 143, where nine holes were to be seen on the hand of the bewitched after the supposed 'extraction'; cf. also Komáromy, pp. 64, 79.

[85] Here the old shamans, according to the beliefs, dismember and take to pieces the initiate, count his bones, and only accept him if he has a *surplus bone*. Cf. Diószegi, *A sámánhit*, pp. 86–148.

[86] Near Sopron, 1743: Schram, ii. 190; Hódmezővásárhely, 1734—the same with a baby eaten, then put together: ibid. i. 247. The medieval and early modern European examples of this belief are nicely analysed by Maurizio Bertolotti, 'Le ossa e la pelle dei buoi: Un mito popolare tra agiografia e stregoneria', *Quaderni storici*, 41 (1979), 470–99.

[87] Pannonhalma, 1629—witches sailing in a sieve on the Danube: László Erdélyi and Pongrác Sörös (eds.), *Pannonhalmi Rendtörténet* (History of the Order of Pannonhalma), iv. 237; Szeged, 1728: Reizner, *Szeged története*, iv. 409; Hódmezővásárhely, 1741: Schram, i. 299; Ugocsa, 1709—nutshell used for sailing: Komáromy, pp. 233, 235, 240; millet-shell for shipping 300 devils: Schram, i. 104.

[88] All these beliefs come from the SE part of the Great Plain, originating probably from Serbs who had fled there from the Turks. Örvénd, Bihar, 1716—a Hungarian sorcerer fights a Turkish one on Mt. Gellért: Schram, ii. 352; Császló, Szatmár, 1745—witches fight each other with sticks, but it does not hurt: Antal Szirmay, *Szathmár vármegye fekvése, történetei és polgári esmérete* (The Situation, History and Exploration of Szathmár County) (Buda, 1809), 82; Nagy-Szerind, Arad, 1755: Komáromy, p. 578. For the *zduhač* beliefs, see my 'Shamanistic Elements', p. 410. From this same region there is a trial echoing another motif of the *zduhač* beliefs, the fight for the fertility of animals and land. In 1723 in Nagydiószeg, Bihar, we hear that on St George's night the witches distribute the cows of the region among themselves, and we also hear that they are active seven times in the spring, at the times of the flowering of the main grain and fruit plants, and that they can steal the best part of it: Schram, i. 104–5.

[89] The data on these organizations are gathered and analysed by Tamás Körner, 'Boszorkányszervezetek Magyarországon' (Witches' Organizations in Hungary), *Ethnographia*, 80 (1969), 196–211. Let me mention here that the widespread myths of the *wütende Heer* and the wild hunt crop up in a few Hungarian witch-trials in connection with the description of witches' armies. All these are from the area round Szeged Mindszent, 1739—a black army of witches rides with laughter at midnight in the sky at Pentecost; also in 1734 and 1750: Schram, i. 258, 260; 247; 285.

should not forget that we are speaking about a small minority of the trials.[90] Though this does not, of course, express the relative weight of the two belief-systems in sixteenth- to eighteenth-century Hungary, it does show that there existed in Hungary, in contrast to sixteenth- and seventeenth-century Friuli or Sicily, a set of popular witchcraft beliefs largely independent of this archaic background. We have to look for other sources if we want to explain the imagery of the witches' sabbath in Hungary, which is represented in about 120 descriptions in the trials, about half of them in witchcraft confessions under torture and the other half in witnesses' accounts and accusations.

The interesting thing about sabbath beliefs in Hungary is the already mentioned lack of learned traditions of demonology—though, of course, the questions put to the witches in torture chambers, on the basis of Carpzov's *Practica Rerum Criminalium*, did have the effect of spreading demonological clichés. One cannot exclude either a certain limited influence on the two demonological treatises in Hungary, compiled under the direction of György Komáromi Csipkés: the most popular meeting-place of the Hungarian witches, Mt. Gellért in Buda, is first mentioned there, after which references start to multiply in the testimonies.[91] But still, the detailed imagery of the sabbath already existed before these vague learned influences arrived, so we have to seek other, popular channels for its diffusion.

The most obvious of these popular channels, the popular spreading of foreign, mainly German, influences, has already been mentioned. The first Hungarian description of the witches' sabbath is from the area around the city of Pozsony, near the Austrian border, from the

---

[90] Apart from the dozen *táltos* trials, witch-trials showing shamanistic traits are fewer than 20 out of 1,500.

[91] Let me briefly quote this description: 'They also believe that during the nightly hours they are carried to certain places, e.g. as the vulgar say (*ut vulgus tenet*) to Mount St Gellért near Buda, to the wine cellars.... They think they ride at the highest speed with a multitude of men and women, raising their flags with their ensigns, beating their drums, blowing their trumpets, then they get seated to have a splendid meal at their royally arranged tables, then they dance most pleasant dances to the sound of all sorts of instruments, and then they return with the same speed to the place where they have been before, just as if they had been lying still in their beds at home ...' (Mediomontanus, *Disputatio theologica de lamiis veneticiis* (1656), p. B2). For the first mention of Mt. Gellért in a trial in Debrecen in 1682 see Komáromy, p. 135; the data referring to Mt. Gellért, which probably acquired its fame because of being named Blocksberg by the local Germans, are analysed by Sándor Dömötör, 'Szent Gellért hegye és a boszorkányok' (Mount St Gellért and the Witches), *Tanulmányok Budapest multjából*, 7 (1939), 92–111, and id., 'A boszorkányok gyűlése a magyar néphitben' (The Meeting of Witches in Hungarian Folk-beliefs), *Ethnographia*, 50 (1939), 210–21.

year 1574.[92] The first confession about the witches' alliance with the devil (1581) is from the German-inhabited north Hungarian mining town of Selmecbánya (Schemnitz; Banská Štiavnica).[93] The first full-fledged account of the diabolical sabbath, of flying on a broomstick, and of copulation with the devil is again from Pozsony from the year 1602, extracted from two Hungarian women.[94] The first (and only) mention of a 13-member coven of witches is also from the western border, from the county of Vas in 1647.[95] And the first bigger series of these sabbath descriptions (mainly torture confessions) is again from this same region, from the area around Sopron in the 1650s and 1660s.[96] The other region where we have a similar early appearance of these diabolical beliefs is the German-inhabited part of Transylvania—we hear of an invocation of the devil in 1582, and we can read a nice prayer to Satan in a confession of 1639.[97]

But there is also another popular route for the evolution of sabbath beliefs: the spontaneous formation of this mythology, based upon the traditional schemas of popular imagination. This aspect is best illustrated by the slow transformation of the witches' nightly appearance and pressure (*Hexendruck*)[98] into a certain kind of sabbath. The witches first start to come together, then make a big feast and party at the home of the bewitched, then drag the person with them to other meetings. Sometimes they transform the victim into a horse, which they ride along on; sometimes they seriously ill-treat the person, carrying out rape and sexual abuse.[99] Here obviously we are con-

---

[92] This description, rather irregular from the point of view of demonology, is given by Péter Bornemisza, *Ördögi kisértetekről*, p. 138. According to this account the witches have a queen; they either go around in the shape of cats or they ride; they make a great frenzy, dance, and fornicate at their meetings, etc.

[93] Komáromy, p. 23.

[94] Horna, *Zwei Hexenprozesse*, pp. 30–42.

[95] Schram, ii. 712.

[96] Körmend, 1653: Schram, ii. 718–21; iii. 260–4. Trausdorf, near Sopron, 1663–5: ibid. ii. 14. Lakompak, near Sopron, 1665: Varga (ed.), *Uriszék*, p. 688.

[97] The text of the prayer, said in Kőhalom, is published by Heinrich Müller, 'Zur Geschichte des Repser Stuhls', p. 144.

[98] The problem of the witches' nightly pressure of the victim is analysed by Akos Szendrey, 'Hexe—Hexendruck', *Acta Ethnographica Academiae Scientiarum Hungaricae*, 4 (1955), 129–69. Let me mention here that this belief, so central to Hungarian witchcraft, appears in the very first trials of Kolozsvár in 1565, where the pressing witches are called *noctuae mulieres*: Komáromy, p. 6. This was the belief that probably gave their name to the Hungarian witches, for *boszorkány* is derived etymologically from the Turkish *basyrkan*, 'to press'.

[99] Some traces of this evolution: Kolozsvár, 1612—somebody is carried at night to the cloister, 'from hole to hole': Komáromy, p. 77; Sempte, near Pozsony, 1618—*night-*

fronted with the mythological enrichment of stereotyped nightmares and sexual phantasies. And we should not forget the influence of the narrative patterns of folklore: some accounts of these nightly tortures develop into real folk-tales or folk-ballads. One person who is carried away by the witches is forced to join them, and because she resists, she is first thrown down the rocks of a mountain, then thrown twice into an oven of bricks;[100] another person, also regularly taken away, finishes the account about her tortures with the following words: 'one red dawn two white doves flew in through her window and a voice was heard, "stand up, for your mouth is thirsty", and she had some icy water at home, first the doves drank from it, then she herself, then she poured out the rest near the well, as she was told, and the nightly visits stopped for ever.'[101]

We can notice the spontaneous formation of sabbath imagery in many details of the descriptions, too. If the witches do not fly to Mt. Gellért, or some other mountain in the surrounding area, the place of the meeting is one of the traditional sites of village feasts: the local tavern, the main street, the village mill (where the witches are sometimes milling flies on the backs of the victims);[102]or the meeting can be a profanation of sacred sites, such as cloister,[103] churchyard,[104] or roadside cross.[105]

---

women enter in groups through the window, and dance around the victim until cock-crow: Schram, iii. 233–4, 245; near Komárom, 1627—a whole witch-family flies into the house of the victim, they dance, take a bath, bewitch the victim, and then fly out: Flóris Rómer, 'Adalék a boszorkányperekhez' (Data on Witch-trials), *Győri történelmi és régészeti füzetek*, 1 (1861), 178, 227–88; Zagreb, 1657—the witches come by night to the victim 'in consortium diabolicae sagarum', and call the woman to go with them. As she does not want to do so, they drag her out of bed, take her out of town to the sabbath, or drag her around into other people's homes: Tkalčić, 'Izprave', pp. 13–14. As for sexual fantasies, we hear of cases where the victim is raped by a witch in the shape of a horse: Schram, iii. 204; a bull; Komáromy, p. 495; or in the shape of her own husband: Schram, ii. 335; or wife: Komáromy, p. 77; they bite and damage the sex organs of men: Schram, ii. 331; and of women: ibid. i. 155.

[100] Schram, ii. 92–3; the deposition of a 16-year-old maid in Csorna, near Sopron, in 1733.

[101] Schram, i. 248: deposition of a 25-year-old woman in Hódmezővásárhely, 1734.

[102] Both previous examples have aspects of village feasts in their descriptions. For the sabbath in a mill, see Schram, i. 490 and ii. 438; in the local tavern: Alapi, *Bűbájosok*, pp. 3–4.

[103] Cf. Komáromy, p. 77 (1612); Horna, *Ein Monstre-Hexenprozess*, p. 43 (1691).

[104] Rómer, 'Adalék a boszorkányperekhez', p. 178—going round the church and having a rest in the churchyard; Schram, i. 74–5—where the witches take people against their will to the churchyard to dance until dawn (is this not a late reflection of medieval prohibitions in this domain? Cf. Louis Gougaud, 'La Danse dans les églises', *Revue*

[*See p. 252 for n. 104 cont. and n. 105*]

The overall image of the Hungarian sabbath does not resemble the pompous court or the blasphemous church of Satan; it is rather like a village feast, with a lot of eating, drinking, music, dancing, and some inconveniences, like food turning into excrement.[106] In 1741, near Sopron, for example, the witches carried off an elderly woman in a miserable peasant cart pulled by six oxen. They drove up the mountain to the vineyard, where they climbed a cherry tree and took delight in obliging the poor old woman to try to pick cherries from branches that they constantly pulled away from her hands. This Pentecost night-adventure might well have taken place in reality, too, with the actors being not witches, but village youth.[107] The sabbath is often called a carnival procession[108] or wedding company.[109] Riding backwards[110] and other customs, ideas based upon symbolic inversion, constitute its basic terms of reference, as Stuart Clark tried to prove, not so long ago, for other countries.[111]

In the Hungarian Sabbath there is rarely a central Satan-figure, just the familiar devil, dressed like a nice lad, even if, sometimes, with negative overtones (in German-inhabited territories he wears Hungarian dress, in Hungarian ones German dress; near Romanian-inhabited regions, Romanian is spoken at the sabbath).[112] Except for one case with horse-legs[113] and a few cases of the devil as he-goat,[114]

---

d'histoire ecclésiastique, 15 (1914), 5–22, 229–43). We even hear of witches dancing on the church tower: Herbert, 'Die Rechtspflege in Hermannstadt', p. 114 (Hermannstadt, 1708–18); or holding a competition to jump over the church: Schram, iii. 298–300 (1717).

[105] Trausdorf, 1663, where witches urinate in the empty vase under the cross: Schram. iii. 263.

[106] e.g. ibid. ii. 484–6 (1741).　　　　　　　　　　　　　　　[107] Ibid. ii. 126.

[108] Near Sopron, 1730: ibid. ii. 58.

[109] Ibid. i. 298–9; Göllner, *Hexenprozesse*, p. 96.

[110] Mád, 1718: Schram, iii. 304.

[111] Stuart Clark, 'Inversion, Misrule and the Meaning of Witchcraft', *Past and Present*, 87 (1980), 98–127.

[112] The devil in Hungarian dress—Sopron, 1663: Schram, iii. 260–4; Kapuvár, near Sopron, 1742: ibid. ii. 171–2; Szombathely, 1877–8: Kálmán Chernel, *Kőszeg szabad királyi város jelene és multja* (Present and Past of Kőszeg) (Szombathely, 1877–8), ii. 232. In German dress—Hermannstadt, 1692; Göllner, *Hexenprozesse*, p. 134; Hódmezővásárhely, 1732: Schramm, i. 239; Kapuvár, near Sopron, 1742: ibid. ii. 148. Speaking *Romanian*—Szirmay, *Szathmár vármegye*, p. 81.

[113] Near Pozsony: Schram, i. 495.

[114] Deutschkreuz, 1700: Teutsch, 'Sächsische Hexenprozesse', pp. 745–6, 761; 1701: Göllner, *Hexenprozesse*, pp. 180–3. Here we can see from the torture confession that this item was suggested very much by the advocate, who happened to be called *generosus dominus Franckenstein*; the he-goat constantly returns in the Szeged trials, which closely adhered to Western demonological models: Reizner, *Szeged története*, iv. 381, 391–3, 409, etc.

the devil takes either the same animal form as the witches, or he appears in human shape, sometimes as a priest,[115] sometimes as a woman,[116] mostly as a young man.[117] Sometimes he is not even the master, but the helpful servant, who can be put in a box or nailed to the wall,[118] according to the well-known patterns of popular demonology.

Does this mean that the Hungarian popular witch-beliefs could remain fairly uncorrupted by learned demonology? To a certain extent only. Because, and this is the last point I should like to develop, the main corrupting feature of learned witchcraft beliefs consisted not in their sophistication, nor in their wide distribution in the form of propagandist pamphlets, but in the very fact of offering an institution to satisfy popular demand to persecute witches.

The main conflict underlying Hungarian witch-hunting (just like witch-hunting in many other places) was that institutionalized, legal persecution was substituted for traditional experts who exercised beneficent magic to cure the bewitched. This did not only mean that for imaginary injuries the sanctions were now no longer imaginary, but a real revenge could be taken, the accused could be burnt at the stake; the legal intervention disturbed the whole inner balance of the universe of popular magic. The hitherto accepted dichotomy of beneficent and maleficent magic started to disappear (this process also being intensified by Church propaganda),[119] and the witchcraft accusations advanced by the popular healers and cunning folk fell back on their own heads. Whereas they were visited from long

---

[115] Kőhalom (Reps), *c.*1700: Friedrich Müller, *Beiträge*, p. 45; near Pest, 1728: Komáromy, pp. 416–17; near Arad, 1756, devil as a black man: ibid., p. 594; Alapi, *Bűbájosok*, p. 45.

[116] Megyaszó, 1731: Kazinczy, 'Megyaszói boszorkányok 1731-ben', p. 372.

[117] Horna, *Zwei Hexenprozesse*, p. 22 (1602), and many other examples. Let me quote a 1741 confession from Madocsa, where the devil was not only a nice young peasant lad, but seems to have been much more tender in love than usual. When asked what the devil said, the accused witch, a midwife, said that he whispered, 'Sweetheart, my dearest, just lie still', while they were making love. She also said she liked to be with him so much that she would 'follow him to Hell'. The joyless sex of the learned demonological imagination got reinterpreted here by popular culture: Schram, ii. 502.

[118] Keresztur, near Sopron, 1743: ibid., pp. 189–90.

[119] On the general outlines of this process in Europe see Thomas, *Religion and the Decline of Magic*, pp. 212–51; Macfarlane, *Witchcraft*, pp. 115–35; Midelfort, *Witch-hunting*, pp. 14–25; Horsley, 'Who were the Witches?', pp. 694–710. For legislation condemning 'good' witches too, see Trevor-Roper, *The European Witch-craze*, pp. 68–9, 129; Thomas, *Religion and the Decline of Magic*, pp. 257–65. The distinction is still made by Mediomontanus and Komáromi Csipkés. On the other hand, in many trials against cunning folk we hear that 'he who sees the Devil is like him'; Komáromy, p. 149 (1689).

distances by people to be cured, in their immediate surroundings they became more and more suspect (harmful magic was supposed to be active in the close environment). If someone asked for a witch-diagnosis from an expert living far away from his home, the easiest solution for the cunning man was to direct suspicion on his or her colleague in the place where his patient lived. A very large number of Hungarian witchcraft accusations, from the earliest periods on, follow this model first described by Robert Muchembled.[120] The competing midwives of different localities often ended up in similar conflicts of mutual accusations—their professional rivalry led them both to the stake.[121] The same thing happened to cunning shepherds, who generally blamed each other for magical misdeeds, and sent wolves to harm each other's animals. Now they were caught, tortured, and made to confess that they were werewolves,[122] or wicked, devil-adoring sorcerers.[123]

The degradation of the position of the cunning folk (called in Hungarian *néző*, seer; *tudományos*, wise man; *javasasszony*, soothsayer; *orvos*, doctor; and so on[124]) was facilitated by another inner contradiction of witch-beliefs. Not only the cunning folk but also the witch was

---

[120] Muchembled, *Culture populaire*, p. 110. The first victims of the trials starting in 1565 in Kolozsvár are nearly all cunning folk mutually accusing each other: Komáromy, pp. 1–12, 27–71. Other good examples of mutual accusations among cunning folk include Debrecen, 1693: ibid., pp. 158–60; Ugocsa, 1707: ibid., p. 216; Komárom, 1727: Alapi, *Bűbájosok*, pp. 28–9; Surd, 1738: Schram, i. 543–8.

[121] Károly Csákabonyi, *Békés megyei boszorkányperek a XVIII. században* (Witch-trials in Békés County in the 18th Century) (Gyula, 1961), 9–17; Schram, ii. 56.

[122] Let me list the Hungarian werewolf cases. Sopron, 1529 and 1531: Házy, *Sopron középkori egyháztörténete*, p. 364; near Sopron, 1651: Ferenc Eckhart, *A földesúri büntetőbíráskodás a XVI–XVII. században* (Feudal Criminal Legislation in the 16th–17th Centuries) (Budapest, 1954), 133; Körmend, 1653: Schram, ii. 721; Szombathely, 1687: Horváth, *Boszorkányok*, p. 32; Halas, 1734: Schram, ii. 430; Otomány, 1735: Komáromy, pp. 475–8; near Sopron, 1743: Schram, ii. 201; Pacsa, Zala, 1743: ibid., p. 615; Nógrád county, 1754: Gábor Török, 'Történeti adatok a küldött farkas mondájához' (Historical Data on Werewolf Legends), *Néprajzi közlemények*, 4 (1959), nos. 1–2, pp. 278–88 (This is the only case where there is a kind of positive aspect of werewolf beliefs, with the werewolf as an ambiguous sorcerer who can also do some positive things, as in the Lithuanian example analysed by Ginzburg, *I benandanti*, pp. 47–9); Köröstarcsa, 1756: Schram, i. 145–6; Békés county, 1757: ibid. iii. 166; near Győr, 1759: Komáromy, pp. 672, 679. For the analysis of these beliefs see Ferenc Gönczi, 'A csordás farkas' (The Werewolf), *Ethnographia*, 16 (1905), 93–6.

[123] An interesting case is that of Gregor Oberman in Körmend, 1653, who confessed to having a devil to serve him for nine years and teach him the power of different animals: Schram, ii. 718–19.

[124] See the only study of Hungarian cunning folk: Tekla Dömötör, 'The Cunning Folk in English and Hungarian Witch Trials', in Venetia Newall (ed.), *Folklore Studies in the Twentieth Century* (Woodbridge and Totowa, 1981), 183–7.

supposed to be able to heal. According to the beliefs expressed in the trials, if the witch is forced to do so (by physical violence or by various menaces), she removes the charm she has cast. So if a *néző* or a *tudományos* undertook the magical healing of the bewitched, they could easily be accused of having been the ones to bewitch the person as well: 'the same devil is healing her who has caused her illness', we hear in 1584 in Kolozsvár.[125] This suspicion was further strengthened by the boasting of some cunning folk that they had the knowledge to heal and to hurt–a necessary sanction to establish their professional prestige and to defend themselves against non-payment, or witchcraft accusation.[126] On the basis of these ambiguities, cunning folk could be accused if healing was unsuccessful (on the argument that they only wanted to increase the effects of bewitchment), but a successful healing could also be brought up in a trial as proof against them. In eighteenth-century torture confessions we can see that the cunning folk were made to furnish 'proofs' for these suspicions, admitting that they were doing a sort of teamwork with the witches, asking them to bewitch people so that they would have clients to heal.[127]

During the explosion of a witch-panic, accusations run along the lines of social or cultural tensions within communities; but in the course of long-term, regular, but not (or rarely) excessive witch-hunting, as was the case in Hungary, the majority of the victims are the people who possess some kind of magical expertise.[128] On the one hand, anybody who knows about magical healing gets suspicious; on the other, everybody resorts to the same techniques, for they have to protect themselves from the magical aggression menacing from all sides. This is the explosive paradox of early modern popular culture, which, once given a helping hand by the legal machinery of the secular power, fell prey to its own inner contradictions. The popular universe of magic could ruin itself in this way, even without the active pressure of an 'élite culture' wishing to reform it.

[125] Komáromy, p. 70. This is the confessed motive why the patients have chosen the accused as a doctor: Csákabonyi, *Békés megyei boszorkányperek*, pp. 9–20.

[126] Already the first Hungarian witch whose trial we have in our documents, Clara Botzi in 1565, in Kolozsvár, claimed that 'si voluero, scientiam, habeo sanandi vel dilacerandi . . .': Komáromy, p. 2.

[127] This argument first as an accusation, in Debrecen, 1725: Komáromy, p. 358; as a confession, in Somogy county, 1737: Schram, i. 540–1; Dunaszentgyörgy, 1741: ibid. ii. 478–9; Kapuvár, 1743: ibid. ii. 203–4.

[128] In connection with this problem, cf. Horsley's analysis, 'Who were the Witches?'

9

Estonia I: Werewolves and Poisoners

MAIA MADAR

ACCORDING to the available redactions of the Livonian Peasant Law, the earliest of which date from the fourteenth century, witches and heretics were to be burnt ('soll man Ketzer und Zauberer verbrennen').[1]

Leonid Arbusow believed that these paragraphs had been added at the beginning of the sixteenth century.[2] The Latvian historian Arveds Švābe at first shared this opinion, but in a later work he argued that the laws against witches and heretics had been enacted in the early thirteenth century during the visitation in Livonia of the papal legate William of Modena. Before arriving in Livonia in 1225 he had been active in suppressing heresy in Lombardy, and presumably he now continued his fight by inserting these paragraphs into the legal code of an as yet unsubmissive nation. He was also guided by the decision of the Lateran Council in 1215 to intensify the battle against heresy.[3]

E. L. Nazarova does not find this evidence convincing, arguing that if the witchcraft paragraphs had been enacted already in the thirteenth century, they should have been inserted in all the Livonian Peasant Codes.[4] But this is not the case in the peasant laws of the Latgallians, the Kurs, the Semgallians, and the Estonians in the Saare-Lääne bishopric. The wording of these paragraphs in the Livonian Peasant Law also differs considerably from that found in analogous German codes from the thirteenth and early fourteenth centuries. In the *Sachsenspiegel* (*c.*1225), a volume of common feudal law compiled by Eike von Repgow, 'a Christian who forsakes his religion, deals with

---

[1] E. L. Nazarova, '"Livonskie Pravdy" kak istoricheskii istochnik', *Drevneishie gosudarstva na territorii SSSR* (Moscow, 1980), 183, 189, 195, 197; Carl J. A. Paucker, *Die Quellen der Ritter-, Lehn- und Land-Rechte Esth- und Livlands* (Dorpat, 1845), 88; Leonid Arbusow, 'Die altlivländischen Bauerrechte', *Mitteilungen aus der livländischen Geschichte*, 23 (1924–6), 60–1.

[2] Arbusow, 'Die altlivländischen Bauerrechte', p. 60.

[3] Arveds Švābe, *Vecākās zemnieku tiesības* (Riga, 1927), 28; id., *Livonijas senākās bruņnieku tiesības* (Riga, 1932), 150f.

[4] Nazarova, '"Livonskie Pravdy" . . .', p. 119.

witchcraft and poisoning and stands convicted thereof, shall be burnt at the stake'.[5] The 'Livonian Mirror', modelled on the *Sachsenspiegel*, incorporates this paragraph nearly word for word. From here it found its way into the so-called 'Middle Livonian Knight Law'.[6] If a corresponding paragraph was added to the peasant laws as early as the thirteenth or early fourteenth century, then it should have resembled the wording of these sources. Instead, the peasant law statute against witchcraft and heresy is an almost literal transcription from the German town laws of the fourteenth century.[7]

At the provincial synod of Riga in 1428 the clergy of Livonia threatened with excommunication all soothsayers, sorcerers, and practitioners of the 'Jewish superstition'.[8] In the visitation orders set up in 1519 by Johannes Kyvel, Bishop of the Saare-Lääne diocese, witchcraft was defined as a capital crime. The visitors were ordered to look for reputed sorcerers, witches, or heretics, who were not true Christians but worshipped sacred groves, stones, and trees; further, those who consulted soothsayers and sorcerers in the event of illness or misfortune and followed their advice in curing cattle; and those worshipping thunderstorms. They were all to be burnt as non-believers and heretics.[9]

The legislation of the sixteenth-century diet forbade blasphemy, witchcraft, and soothsaying, ordering the courts to punish the practitioners of such superstitions. At the 1552 diet of Pärnu it was demanded that 'the poor peasants as well as the Germans should be discouraged from committing the cardinal sin of witchcraft, and similar blasphemies by a just and severe punishment'.[10]

---

[5] *Sachsenspiegel*, II. 13. 7: 'svelk kerstenman ungelovich is unde mit tovere ummegat oder mit vergiftnisse, unde des verwunnen wirt, den sal man upper hort bernen', *apud* Joseph Hansen, *Zauberwahn, Inquisition und Hexenprozess* (Munich and Leipzig, 1900), 367; cf. Wilhelm Gottlieb Soldan, *Geschichte der Hexenprozesse* (1843), ed. Max Bauer, i (Munich, 1912), 180.

[6] *Das Mittele Ritterrecht*, cap. 132. *Sammlung der Gesetze welche das heutige livländische Landrecht enthalten, kritisch bearbeitet*, ed. G. J. von Buddenbrock, i (Mitau, 1802), 178; *Des Herzogthums Ehsten Ritter- und Land-Rechte*, ed. J. Ph. G. Ewers (Dorpat, 1821), 110; H. von Freymann, 'Das Strafrecht der livländischen Ritterrechte', *Zeitschrift für Rechtswissenschaft* (Dorpat), 9 (1889), 211.

[7] Nazarova, '"Livonskie Pravdy" . . .', p. 120.

[8] *Liv-, Est- und Curländisches Urkundenbuch*, ed. F. G. von Bunge and H. Hildebrand, vii (Riga and Moscow, 1881), no. 690; Leonid Arbusow, *Die Einführung der Reformation in Liv-, Est- und Kurland* (Leipzig, 1921), 61.

[9] Arbusow, *Die Einführung der Reformation*, p. 128.

[10] A. W. Hupel, *Neue Nordische Miscellanen*, vii–viii (Riga, 1794), 303, 342.

Thus already in the early legal codes the punishment for witchcraft was burning at the stake, but we have no evidence of its implementation before the sixteenth century. Presumably, less harsh punishments were meted out, such as whipping, fines, and imprisonment.[11]

The records of the Tallinn Advocate's Court (*Vogtsgericht*) for the period 1457–1542 include two cases involving the conviction of magicians. In 1493 two journeymen were released from gaol after promising not to resort to revenge. They had been apprehended at night, dressed as *lustigmachers*, in possession of magic writings which could make people invisible. And in 1526 two women and a male accomplice were whipped for stealing clothes off a hanged man, which they believed would improve their sale of beer.[12]

The total number of witch-trials in Estonia is difficult to ascertain due to the scarcity of the sixteenth-century sources as well as the loss of numerous seventeenth-century court records. In 1527 there is a first brief mention of a witch-burning on the border of the Saha and Maardu estates close to Tallinn. In 1531 a man is recorded as having been burnt a few years previously in the parish of Äksi.[13]

The first trial known to have dealt with a major case of poisoning, *veneficium*, was held in 1542 and culminated in the burning of five Põlula peasants. The owner of the Põlula estate, Johann Meckes, accused his wife of murdering his father with poison and causing his own serious illness. The wife escaped to her brother, Johann Zoyge in Haljala, but only after denouncing a maid, Anna, and an old woman, Margrete, for having mixed the poison. During the interrogation of the two women it became evident that their lady, Anna Zoyge, had wanted to poison both her husband and his father, and with the aid of magic win the heart of a nobleman, Jürgen Maidell. Margrete had cast

---

[11] The agreement of 1241 with the inhabitants of Saaremaa serves as an example of this. It states that anyone attending sacrifices in the pagan manner shall be fined half a silver mark. The sacrificers themselves shall be flogged at the church on three consecutive Sundays (*Liv-, Esth- und Curländisches Urkundenbuch*, ed. F. G. von Bunge, i (Reval, 1853), no. 169); Freymann, 'Das Strafrecht . . .', pp. 232, 262; Artur Vassar, 'Katoliku kiriku reaktsioonilisest osast eesti rahvaa ajaloos 12–16 sajandil', *Religiooni ja ateismi ajaloost Eestis* (Tallinn, 1956), 57.

[12] Eugen von Nottbeck, *Die alte Chriminalchronik Revals* (Reval, 1884), 63, 74; Friedrich Amelung, 'Die frühzeitigen Reformen in der altlivländischen Strafrechtspflege und die hiesigen Hexenprozesse . . .', *Düna Zeitung*, 205 (1907).

[13] *Est- und Livländische Brieflade: Eine Sammlung von Urkunden zur Adels- und Gütergeschichte Est- und Livlands in Uebersetzungen und Auszügen*, ed. von Bunge and von Toll, vol. i, pt. i (Reval, 1856), no. 971, p. 526; *Sitzungsberichte der Gesellschaft für Geschichte und Altertumskunde der Ostseeprovincen Russlands aus dem Jahre 1912* (Riga, 1914), 140–1; Vassar, 'Katoliku kiriku . . .', p. 58.

three spells and sent Anna to deliver the poisoned salt and instructions to the lady. The salt was to be sprinkled under the squire's feet.
The lady had rewarded Margrete with food and drink, a shirt, and two
shillings, and promised her a woollen skirt. The trial ended with
Margrete and Anna, as well as three accomplices—a miller, a
shepherd, and a woman—being condemned to the stake. Anna Zoyge,
the principal culprit, was at first only exiled. But returning two years
later to the parish, she was sentenced to death.[14] There is no information as to whether this sentence was carried out.

No trials are known to have taken place during the Livonian war
(1558–83), but in 1588 five women were burnt in the parish of Juuru.
The accounts of the Kuimetsa estate record the hangman as having
received two sheep and some malt for his work.[15]

It seems that the witch-hunt intensified during the latter part of the
sixteenth century, as in many European countries. Documents concerning a few isolated cases tried in Tallinn and Tartu are preserved,[16]
but the great majority of trials occurred during the seventeenth
century. A total of 140 trials are known, a few of which were held at the
beginning of the eighteenth century, the last in 1725[17] (see Table 9.1).

In the province of Estland, which came under Swedish jurisdiction
in 1561, the persecutions reached their height during the first half of
the seventeenth century. Forty-one trials were held between 1615 and
1652. In Paide, nine witches were burnt in 1615, and a few others were
sentenced to death on the Käravete estate in the parish of Ambla.[18]
The majority of cases were tried at the Tallinn Castellan's Court

---

[14] *Est- und Livländische Brieflade*, vol. i, pt. i, nos. 1190–1200, pp. 656–67; Leonid
Arbusow, 'Zauberer- und Hexenwahn in den baltischen Provinzen', *Rigascher Almanach*
(1911), 102–4.

[15] Rudolf Winkler, 'Über Hexenwahn und Hexenprozesse in Estland während der
Schwedenherrschaft', *Baltische Monatsschrift*, 67 (1909), 323.

[16] Tallinn Central State Archives of the Estonian SSR (hereafter TRKA): c230. f1.
d294 (this reference to documents in the Estonian archival system denotes Collection
no. 230, File no. 1, Document no. 294); Paul Johansen and Heinz von zur Mühlen,
Deutsch und Undeutsch im mittelalterlichen und frühneuzeitlichen Reval (Cologne and Vienna,
1973), 466–9; Central State Archives of History of the Estonian SSR (hereafter RAKA):
c995. f1. d239; F. K. Gadebusch, *Livländische Jahrbücher*, 2. ii 1781), 168; Vello Helk, *Die
Jesuiten in Dorpat (1583–1625)* (Odense University Studies in History and Social
Sciences, 44; Odense, 1977), 84.

[17] RAKA: c915. f1. d498 and d619; c914, f1. d148, d182, and d197; Central State
Archives of History of the Latvian SSR (hereafter CVVA): c109. f3. d755; V. Uuspuu,
Surmaotsused eesti nõiaprotsessides (Tartu, 1938), 22; id., 'Eesti nõiasõnade usulisest
iseloomust', *Usuteadusline Ajakiri*, 1 (1938), 16.

[18] Otto von Riesemann, 'Hexen und Zauberer in Reval (1615–18)', *Beiträge zur Kunde
Est-, Liv- und Kurlands*, 2 (1877), 330.

TABLE 9.1. *Witch-trials in Estonia, 1520–1729*

	Estland	Northern Livland	Total
1520–9	1	—	1
1530–9	—	1	1
1540–9	1	—	1
1550–9	—	—	—
1560–9	—	—	—
1570–9	—	—	—
1580–9	1	2	3
1590–9	3	2	5
1600–9	—	5	5
1610–19	8	2	10
1620–9	7	—	7
1630–9	11	10	21
1640–9	9	18	27
1650–9	6	2	8
1660–9	4	2	6
1670–9	3	3	6
1680–9	2	6	8
1690–9	12	12	24
1700–9	3	1	4
1710–19	—	—	—
1720–9	—	3	3
Total	71	69	140

(*Burggericht*) and at the Harjumaa estates, which lay under its jurisdiction. Some were also tried at the Tallinn and Narva Magistrates' Courts (*Ratsgericht*).[19] Since the crimes committed by the peasants lay under the jurisdiction of the manorial courts, and since no records were kept, there is virtually no information about the trials which

[19] RAKA: c2. f2. d1, d45, and d52; c861. f1. d5a; TRKA: c230. f1. d924; *Ehst- und Livländische Brieflade*, vol. ii, pt. i (Reval, 1861), no. 450, p. 404; Riesemann, 'Hexen und Zauberer', pp. 325–43; Winkler, 'Über Hexenwahn', pp. 325–40; E. Osenbrüggen, 'Ein Hexenprocess in Narva', *Das Inland*, 38 (1848), 818–22; Carl J. A. Paucker, 'Ein Hexenprocess (Werwolf 1617)', *Das Inland*, 22 (1840), 341–4; Antero Heikkinen, *Paholaisen Liittolaiset* (Helsinki, 1969), 44f.

presumably took place there. More source material from the 1630s can be found in the records of a number of Vassals' Courts (*Manngericht*).[20]

Most of the death sentences for witchcraft in the province of Estland occurred during the first three decades of the seventeenth century. By 1636, twenty-seven witches had been executed, while during the period 1637–69 the number dwindled to five. As late as 1694 the famous thief and sorcerer Bertel Thomas Jürgen was given a life sentence by the Vassal's Court of Viru-Järva, but the Higher Provincial Court (*Oberlandgericht*) commuted this to hanging. This is the last-known application of capital punishment for witchcraft in Estland.[21]

After 1650 the number of trials decreased considerably, except for a last sudden increase in the 1690s. The courts continued to collect evidence, but most cases were handed over to the governor or the Higher Provincial Court. As a result the verdict in most of these cases is unknown.

Only a few trials dating from the period of Polish rule in the Estonian (northern) part of Livland, at the beginning of the seventeenth century, are known to us. In 1608 the Magistrates' Court in Tartu sentenced Norrika Cathrin to death for witchcraft. The verdict was based on Exodus 22: 18—and it was carried out the following day. In 1617 a sorcerer named Lauri was burned at the stake. Under torture he had confessed to witchcraft and to a pact with the devil.[22] It is not until the 1630s, after the Swedish conquest of Livland and the consequent reform of the legal system, that the crimes of the peasantry came under the jurisdiction of the Pärnu and Tartu District Courts (*Landgericht*) and more information becomes available concerning the witch-trials in Northern Livland.

The majority of trials during the period 1633–45 were held at the District Court in Pärnu. Of the twenty-two known cases, twelve persons were sentenced to death.[23] The Tartu District Court was

[20] RAKA: c861. f1. d9122–3 and d9138; c862. f1. d257, d2147, d2235, and d2272; c863. f1. d4252–5; G. Hasselblatt, 'Ein Verhör in einem Hexenprocesse', *Das Inland*, 47 (1837), 777–81; Friedrich Toll, 'Zur Geschichte der Hexenprocesse', *Das Inland*, 17 (1839), 257–63; Carl J. A. Paucker, 'Anklage wegen Zauberei in der Mitte des 17. Jahrhunderts', *Das Inland* 43 (1836), 710–15; Friedrich Hunnius, 'Ueber Hexenprocesse', *Baltische Monatsschrift*, 42 (1895), 54–6; Arbusow, 'Zauberer- und Hexenwahn', pp. 115–17; Uuspuu, *Surmaotsused*, pp. 9ff.

[21] RAKA: c862. f1. d2280, pp. 5–6.

[22] Eduard Osenbrüggen, 'Hexenprocesse in Dorpat', *Das Inland*, 7 (1848), 123–9; Heikkinen, *Paholaisen Liittolaiset*, pp. 43f.

[23] RAKA: c915. f1. d1–2 and d4; CVVA: c109, f2. d177; M. Wolffeldt, 'Processe aus auf dem Schlosse vorgefundenen Urkunden', *Mittheilungen aus dem Strafrecht und dem*

more restrained in its prosecution of witches. Only six trials are known to have been held, and none of these resulted in a death sentence. Information regarding witch-trials in Northern Livland during the period 1650–80 is almost non-existent. Only seven are known. During the final decades of the century the Pärnu District Court again tried the majority of cases. In 1684 two peasants, Wakkulepa Jack and Sacke Jürgen, were sentenced to death at the stake. The Tartu Provincial Court (*Hofgericht*) confirmed the sentence of Jack, but Jürgen was to be interrogated again. He was tortured the next year and was ultimately condemned for having taught witchcraft and for *maleficium*. The Tartu Provincial Court suggested that the execution should be held publicly, but the Pärnu town council refused.[24] This is the last-known capital sentence for witchcraft in Pärnu.

The first death sentence in Tartu occurred in 1678, when a peasant wife, Kursi Tenno's Anna, was sentenced to be put to the sword for having caused her lord's illness.[25] Major trials involving thorough interrogations and the application of the death penalty took place at the end of the 1680s, when persecutions were on the decline in the rest of Estonia. By 1699 twelve cases had been tried, and in three of these the death penalty was imposed.[26] The last witch to be executed in Estonia was tried in Tartu in 1699. The defendant, Tattra Santi Michel, had been interrogated at the Räpina estate in the presence of the bailiff, a scribe, and three peasants.[27] As late as 1723 another peasant, Wielo Ado from the Valguta estate in the parish of Rannu, was condemned by the Tartu District Court to be broken and quartered on the wheel for witchcraft, but this cruel punishment was commuted to life imprisonment by the Tartu Provincial Court.[28]

The majority of those sentenced to death were burnt at the stake. Six were executed by the sword. This, being a lighter punishment, was used under extenuating circumstances, for instance, voluntary

[24] RAKA: c915. f1. d140–1, pp. 1–8. 1–17; Uuspuu, *Surmaotsused*, pp. 16f.

[25] RAKA: c914. f1. d65, pp. 1–4; Uuspuu, *Surmaotsused*, p. 18.

[26] RAKA: c914. f1. d18, d24, d66–7, d69, d74–5, and d84–6; J. Kõpp, *Laiuse kihelkonna ajalugu* (Tartu, 1937), 142–8; Uuspuu, *Surmaotsused*, pp. 18–21.

[27] RAKA: c914. f1. d84, pp. 1–7; Karl Heinrich von Busse, 'Der arme Pracher', *Das Inland*, 46–7 (1851), 797–9, 816–20; Uuspuu, *Surmaotsused*, p. 21.

[28] RAKA: c914. f1. d182, pp. 1–53; CVVA: c109. f3. d775, pp. 1–54; Uuspuu, *Surmaotsused*, p. 22.

confession or no evidence of a pact with the devil. In the case of Tattra Santi Michel, the court found

> on the basis of his testimony, that it cannot be positively established that he entered into an agreement with the Devil. However, in his youth, his father gave him to an evil spirit, and he has twice met the Devil in the guise of a dog. He has learned formulas to bewitch and to heal. . . . The hangman is ordered to cut off his head and then burn him to ashes.[29]

The bewitching of one's lord carried a qualified death penalty. Willakasz Jürgen was convicted in 1642 for having murdered the Count of Audru with the devil's assistance. The Pärnu District Court ordered that he be 'repeatedly squeezed with red-hot irons, have his limbs severed at the joints, his heart ripped out, his head chopped off and impaled upon a stake by the roadside, his body burnt'.[30] No other trials are known to have involved such barbaric execution.

The legal basis for the death sentence included the Old Testament, Exodus 22: 18: 'Thou shalt not suffer a witch to live.' A profound influence was also exerted by the German *Constitutio Criminalis Carolina* of 1532, which prescribed death at the stake for those using witchcraft to cause injury and damage (*maleficium*). Livland's Superintendent Hermann Samsonius relied on the *Carolina* for guidance in applying the death sentence for *maleficium*, when editing his 'Nine Sermons against Witchcraft' in 1626.[31] He classified witches in three categories by the severity of their offences: (1) those who in a state of melancholy were blinded by the devil, imagining that they had signed a pact with him without actually doing so. They were not to be punished because they were not evil, but sick in heart and mind; (2) those who had allied themselves with the devil, but had brought no harm to either man or cattle. They were to be admonished to mend their ways, and if this proved of no avail, they were to be expelled from the congregation; and (3) those who had a pact with the devil, served him of their own free will, and had brought harm to man, beast, or harvest. Both God's word and the *Carolina* ordered this third category to be burned alive.

In a collection of 'The Knight- and Land-Laws of the Duchy of Estland' codified in 1650 by the assessor of Tallinn Castellan's Court,

---

[29] RAKA: c914. f1. d84, p. 7; Uuspuu, *Surmaotsused*, p. 21.

[30] RAKA: c915. f1. d1, p. 89; Uuspuu, *Surmaotsused*, p. 15.

[31] Hermann Samsonius, *Neun ausserlessne und wohlbegründete Hexen-Predigten* (Riga, 1626), pages not numbered, sermon 9.

Philipp Crusius (Krusenstjern), the crime of witchcraft was similarly graded into a hierarchy of offences. Those who renounced Christ and allied themselves with the devil, joined him in committing depravities, injured man or beast (with or without poison), and confessed to these crimes, were to be burnt to death. If no pact with the devil had been entered, the accused was to be beheaded with a sword. Those who practised soothsaying, had spoken to the devil out of idle curiosity, cured the sick with spells, and had not harmed anyone, were to be spared. For having abused God's name and for their superstitions they were to be imprisoned and admonished by a pastor to desist. If they erred anew, they were to receive corporal punishment and be sent into exile. Those who had consulted witches and sorcerers had to perform penance, or, depending on the offence, be punished more severely.[32] Crusius's main sources in compiling these laws were the Bible, the *Carolina*, and the German jurist Benedict Carpzov.

Presumably in conjunction with the establishment of Swedish ecclesiastical law in Estland in 1692 and in Livland in 1694, the royal edicts of 1665 and 1687 'Against cursing and swearing as well as the desecration of the sabbath'—initially meant to apply to Sweden alone—were put into use. Anyone having entered a verbal or written agreement with the devil would, as in the case of maleficent witchcraft, be condemned to death. Those merely superstitious persons who sacrificed to trees, lakes, and places, or otherwise made use of forbidden arts, were, depending on the severity of their offence, to be fined, imprisoned on bread and water, forced to run the gauntlet, or were to receive corporal punishment. Age and mental state were to be considered, and if the defendant had relapsed the punishment would be adjusted accordingly.[33] In 1695 a Viimsi peasant, Skytte Jack, was accused of having caused injury to men and beasts with sorcery. He was sentenced in accordance with this edict to 6 pairs of blows.[34]

Sixty-five individuals were condemned to death in the courts of Estland (45) and Northern Livland (20) during the sixteenth and seventeenth centuries. Forty of these executions took place between 1610 and 1650. Twenty-six of the culprits were men, and twenty-nine were women.

The most usual punishment from the middle of the seventeenth century on was flogging at the church pillory (generally 15 to 20 pairs

---

[32] *Des Herzogthums Ehsten Ritter- und Land-Rechte*, pp. 397–9.
[33] *Sammlung der Gesetze*, ed. Buddenbrock, ii (Riga, 1821), 1973–8.
[34] RAKA: c2. f2. d1491, p. 5.

of blows were delivered) followed by exile. The chances of being exonerated and freed from suspicion were quite dismal, but it is known that out of 205 accused at least twenty-four were acquitted.

Many different means of extorting evidence and establishing guilt were used, notably the water ordeal and torture. At the provincial synod of Riga in 1428, the thirteenth-century ban on the ordeal by water or fire was renewed, because 'often he who is innocent is found guilty, being oppressed by his other sins, while he who knows spells and incantations goes free'.[35] Nevertheless, from the end of the sixteenth century the use of the water ordeal was quite common. It is first mentioned in a Tartu witch-trial in 1588. Marzin Gaijnovski had used witchcraft to increase the sale of beer. He was thrown into the water, but 'he swam above the surface'.[36]

There is much evidence of the water ordeal until the 1640s, but it may have been used later as well. In 1698 an ecclesiastical visitation in the parish of Anna indicted a witch, originally from Saaremaa, who on hearsay evidence had there been subjected to the water ordeal. Notwithstanding her strenuous efforts, she had not sunk.[37]

The use of torture was a common practice. The statute of the District Court of Livland in 1632, pertaining to both peasants and townsmen, made it legal 'to subject the accused to torture or imprisonment either before or after interrogation'.[38] Torture was in use throughout the seventeenth century. It was finally prohibited by the Swedish king Charles XI in 1686 in Livland and in 1699 in Estland, but it did not actually disappear from the courts until the eighteenth century.[39]

Witchcraft in western Europe as well as in New England was predominantly a female domain. In Estonia and Finland this general rule is reversed.[40] Of the 193 defendants whose gender is known, 60 per cent were men (see Table 9.2). In general the court records are not very informative, often recording only the names of the defendants, if

---

[35] *Liv-, Est- und Curländisches Urkundenbuch*, vii, no. 690; Arbusow, *Die Einführung der Reformation*, p. 61.

[36] RAKA: c995. f1. d239, p. 12.

[37] Winkler, 'Über Hexenwahn', p. 353; Carl Russwurm, *Eibofolke oder die Schweden an den Küstern Ehstlands und auf Runö*, ii (Reval, 1855), 215 [Anna, 1698].

[38] Friedrich Georg von Bunge, *Geschichte des Gerichtswesens und Gerichtsverfahrens in Liv-, Est- und Curland* (Reval, 1874), 255.

[39] Leo Leesment, 'Piinamise ehk tortuuri kaotamine Eesti- ja Liivimaal', *Ajalooline Ajakiri*, 4 (1931), 189.

[40] Cf. Antero Heikkinen and Timo Kervinen in ch. 12, below.

TABLE 9.2. *Estonia: Numbers indicted and sentenced to death, 1520–1729*

	Indicted			Sentenced to death		
	Men	Women	Total*	Men	Women	Total*
1520–9	—	—	1	—	—	1
1530–9	1	—	1	1	—	1
1540–9	2	3	5	2	3	5
1550–9	—	—	—	—	—	—
1560–9	—	—	—	—	—	—
1570–9	—	—	—	—	—	—
1580–9	2	5	7	—	5	5
1590–9	4	7	11	—	—	—
1600–9	—	6	6	—	1	1
1610–19	4	9	22	2	7	18
1620–9	4	9	14	1	7	8
1630–9	15	10	25	2	2	4
1640–9	27	11	39	9	1	10
1650–9	6	4	10	1	—	1
1660–9	6	4	10	3	1	4
1670–9	7	1	8	—	1	1
1680–9	7	1	8	3	—	3
1690–9	23	5	28	2	1	3
1700–9	5	—	5	—	—	—
1710–19	—	—	—	—	—	—
1720–9	3	2	5	—	—	—
Total	116	77	205	26	29	65

* Including several whose gender is unknown.

even that. It is therefore impossible to ascertain the particulars of their age and social or marital status. Generally, those accused were middle-aged or elderly, married, Estonian peasant men and women. In a few cases it is known that they were of other nationalities—Finns, Swedes, a Lithuanian, a Russian, a Pole.

Accusations were often made against the professional sorcerer of the village, or against those with a generally bad reputation. According to the testimonies given, at least twenty-two men and ten women were healers and were consulted as such. If their cures failed, suspicion came to rest upon them; for it was thought that they might have failed on purpose, using their supernatural powers to cause illness and death rather than to avert it.[41]

In 1632, when the Tartu District Court was on circuit in Kõlleste, the 'well-known' sorcerer Pudell was indicted. He had used various spells and witchcraft paraphernalia, among them a carved stick, a silver shilling, copper wire rings, three pieces of red woollen yarn, and green moss, to help many people, who had paid for these services. In 1636 the squire Frombhold Leps asked the Pärnu District Court to punish Rohttzi Beahtt and Andres for having set a spell on his wife, causing her illness, 'since the peasants respect both doctors (*Arttzer*) as idols (*Abgott*), who have aided many with their craft and blessings'.[42] Pastor Kühn of Nissi filed a complaint with the consistory in 1651, concerning a woman 'who can drive away insanity and paralysis. People like this witch, and even the Germans solicit her help.'[43]

Suspicion of witchcraft ran in families. The art was thought to be inherited. The peasant Trevli Bertel was tried at the Tallinn Castellans' Court in 1694. It was revealed that his entire family had practised witchcraft. His great-grandmother had been burned at the stake, his grandmother had escaped punishment only by fleeing to Hiiumaa, and his mother Wolber had used spells.[44] In many other cases, as well, one finds the trail of guilt by association leading from parent to child or, even more fequently, between spouses.

A typical Estonian trial entailed the prosecution of one, two, or at most three or four defendants. Large-scale witch hunts on the Continental model were unknown. Four out of five accusers were also peasants, who claimed that the defendant had caused injury to them, their families, or their property, through the practice of witchcraft (see Table 9.3). Very few of the accusers belonged to the nobility or the clergy. The most common accusation was poisoning with 'hexed' beer, whereby the victim's body was infested with worms, toads, or vermin. At a Pärnu trial in 1641, the peasant Wilhelm Soerz spoke directly to the defendant Layske Marth, saying: 'you gave my wife frogs (*Poggen*) in the beer you served. You have harmed many and will continue to do so if you remain alive.' Peasant Tõnis's wife placed the curse of snakes on the beer at Kalle Matz's wedding. She had blown

---

[41] Cf. Robert Rowland in ch. 6, above.

[42] RAKA: c914. f1. d1, pp. 31–41; c915. f1. d1, p. 31; Uuspuu, 'Nõiaprotsesse Pärnu', p. 121.   [43] Winkler, 'Über Hexenwahn', p. 347.

[44] RAKA: c2. f2. d1255, p. 2.

TABLE 9.3. *Types of indictments in witch-trials in Estonia*

Accusation	No. of trials
Maleficium resulting in:	
illness or injury to human being	41
homicide	36
death or sickness of cattle	21
causing damage as werewolves	18
bewitching milk, beer, etc.	4
bewitching harvest or fields	4
Diabolism	26
Arson	8
Theft or disclosure of it	11
	169

into the jug of beer and then given it to Matz to drink.[45] At a christening in Hageri, the host had caused madness among the guests with cursed beer. When the witch had been ordered to restore the victims to health, he had advised them to take three pieces of alder-tree, cut them into slivers, place them in the warm beer, and drink it. The plaintiff had brought two pieces of the tree to the trials.[46] At the Lääne Vassal's Court in 1665, Kopso Maie was indicted for having thrown beer in through Sahla Thomas's window, thus bewitching the whole family.[47]

Illness could also be brought on by serving cursed fish (Pärnu, 1637; Harju, 1669), strawberries (Pärnu, 1633), crayfish (Tartu, 1651), and bread (Pärnu, 1633 and 1644).[48] In 1542 a Põlula woman, Margrete, testified that she had thrice blown on to the salt, poisoned it, and ordered it to be strewn under the victim's feet. This had killed him. The judges were unable to find out what she had mixed in with the salt. When asked what effect this concoction would have if eaten, the woman answered that toads and worms would begin to breed in the

[45] RAKA: c915. f1. d1, pp. 6, 58; Wolffeldt, 'Processe aus auf dem Schlosse', p. 202 [Pärnu, 1641, 1633].
[46] Winkler, 'Über Hexenwahn', p. 352.
[47] RAKA: c863. f1. d4253, p. 3; cf. Juhan Kahk in ch. 11, below.
[48] RAKA: c861. f1. d9122, p. 2; c915. f1. d1–2, pp. 6, 30, 180; c914. f1. d6of, p. 3.

victim's body.[49] The sorcerer Lupas Laur had used white herb (*Kraut*), dried bats, wax, salt, and woollen yarn. He had wanted to strew salt under the judge's feet. When casting evil spells he had bound a piece of yarn around his bare right arm, which became slightly shorter with every repetition.[50]

It was believed that witchcraft could cause harm not only to humans, but to domestic animals and property as well. In order to transfer the productivity of someone else's fields to his own, one peasant took two sheaves of rye from the other, threshed them, and mixed the grain with his own. The same peasant taught his farm-hand to take a bag of hay from the neighbour's field on the night of Michaelmas, mix it with his own, and feed it to the cattle. If properly done, the animals would never want for feed and would grow strong. He had also thrown raw meat on a field to bewitch it.[51]

The effects of certain incantations (in the records, generally noted in Estonian) and curses were considered to be profound. Women were especially notorious for their curses. Margareta placed a curse on her sister by saying: 'You shall go around as a millstone, and turn as cold as a stone.' After two weeks Anna fell ill and felt very cold; neither clothing nor fire could warm her.[52]

Belief in werewolves was widespread. At eighteen trials, eighteen women and thirteen men were accused of causing damage while werewolves. At Meremõisa in 1623, the defendant Ann testified that she had been a werewolf for four years, and had killed a horse as well as some smaller animals. She had later hidden the wolf skin under a stone in the fields.[53] Two other women, Anne and Ghert, of Pada estate, had also buried their wolf skins under a large stone.[54] In 1636, a Kurna woman described how she had become a werewolf. An old woman had led her into the woods and fed her sweet roots, then they began hunting together as werewolves.[55]

At Idavere in 1651, 18-year-old Hans confessed that he had hunted as a werewolf for two years and killed small animals. He had received the wolf skin from an old man, dressed in black. It was kept hidden in a

[49] *Est- und Livländische Brieflade*, vol. i, pt. i, nos. 1190–1200, p. 657.

[50] RAKA: c915. f1. d2, p. 142; Uuspuu, 'Nõiaprotsesse Pärnu', p. 125 [Pärnu, 1642].

[51] Winkler, 'Über Hexenwahn', p. 352 [Hageri parish, 1696].

[52] RAKA: c2. f2. d52, p. 2 [Tallinn, 1635].

[53] Ibid. d1, p. 26; Winkler, 'Über Hexenwahn', p. 328.

[54] Hasselblatt, 'Ein Verhör', p. 780; Hunnius, 'Über Hexenprocesse', p. 55 [Viru-Nigula parish, 1640].

[55] Winkler, 'Über Hexenwahn', p. 337.

mouse-hole down by the stream. When asked by the judges if his body took part in the hunt, or if only his soul was transmuted, Hans confirmed that he had found a dog's teeth-marks on his own leg, which he had received while a werewolf. Further asked whether he felt himself to be a man or a beast while transmuted, he told that he felt himself to be a beast.[56] A large pack of werewolves roamed around Vastemõisa in 1696, as testified by Titza Thomas's daughter Greeta. Led by the peasant Libbe Matz, eleven of them operated in the area.[57]

It was acknowledged that people could be transmuted not only into werewolves, but also into bears. According to the sworn testimonies of Gret at Pärnu in 1633, Kanti Hans and his wife roamed as werewolves (*für ein Wolf*), while Simon's wife appeared as a bear (*einen Bähren*).[58]

Accusations of diabolism arose as the result of either leading questions posed by the judge, or confessions elicited under torture. Neither the accusers nor the accused broached the subject of the devil voluntarily. The sources contain no accounts of witches flying through the night to the sabbath. A peasant, Karja Mikk of Kurna, thought that the witches most often met with the devil on Maundy Thursday, Good Friday, and Midsummer's Eve.[59]

The devil generally appeared in the guise of a black dog or cat. Andres, a farm-hand from Saarla, had invoked him in the following way: with his child on his knee he cried 'Kurlitz' two times, and two black dogs appeared.[60] At Pärnu in 1641, Layske Marth confessed that the devil had appeared to him 'as a German', dressed in light blue. Both in Karksi in 1640 and in Tartu in 1692, the defendants described the devil as having been dressed in blue.[61] The devil seen by the peasant Pavel Willapulck had the legs of a rooster and very big eyes. His name was 'Holy Father'.[62]

The court records make it evident that the narrow theological definition of witchcraft—a power arising from a pact with the devil—was not accepted by the Estonian peasantry. For the majority of villagers, witchcraft was a power which could be used for good or evil,

---

[56] RAKA: c862. f1. d257, pp. 163–84; Toll, 'Zur Geschichte der Hexenprocesse', pp. 258–62.
[57] RAKA: c915. f1. d331, p. 6 [Pärnu, 1696].
[58] Ibid., d1, p. 7; Uuspuu, 'Nõiaprotsesse Pärnu', p. 116.
[59] Winkler, 'Über Hexenwahn', p. 338 [Jüri parish, 1636].
[60] Riesemann, 'Hexen und Zauberer', p. 341 [Tallinn, 1616].
[61] RAKA: c915. f1. d1–2, pp. 55, 94; Wolffeldt, 'Processe aus auf dem Schlosse', p. 205; Uuspuu, *Surmaotsused*, p. 20.
[62] RAKA: c915. f1. d2, p. 95; Uuspuu, 'Nõiaprotsesse Pärnu', p. 118 [Pärnu, 1640].

and it was this fear of *maleficium* or *veneficium* which led to most of the accusations.

The end of the seventeenth century was also the end of the era of witch-trials. This is not to say that the peasants no longer believed in supernatural powers, witchcraft, or werewolves. These beliefs lived on in village communities for another couple of centuries. There are court records available for the end of the eighteenth and the beginning of the nineteenth centuries which attest to the fact that peasants still approached the courts with accusations against neighbours suspected of witchcraft.[63] But attitudes had changed and become more sceptical. In most cases the suspects were either acquitted, reprimanded, or given some lighter form of corporal punishment for having dealt with superstitions. In 1808, the Tartu District Court received a letter from a nobleman's wife, Helena von Z., in which she accused her farm-hand Hödere Peep and his wife Mai of having cursed a cow, causing it contagious pleuro-pneumonia. The lady had smoked the lungs, liver, and heart of the dead cow to unmask the witch, and since Peep had fallen ill at this time, he was obviously to blame. Peep and Mai were apprehended, beaten, and tortured on the estate. Presumably, the District Court refused to take up the case, because in her next letter the lady bitterly complained that 'the jabbering council' had protected 'these Hottentots'.[64]

As recently as 1816, the Harju Vassal's Court interrogated the peasant Jacob and a woman Anna from Vana-Harmi for witchcraft. During the inquiry it was ascertained that Jacob had used witchcraft to catch thieves. For having practised 'the deceit which plays on the people's superstitions and ignorance', he was sentenced to 10 pairs of lashes on two consecutive Sundays at the church pillory. Anna, Lülle Hans and his wife, Hinrich's widow, and the innkeeper's wife Marret received a reprimand from the court for having, directly or indirectly, taken part in this deceit and believed in it.[65] This is the last case of witchcraft known to have been tried in any court in Estonia.

---

[63] RAKA: c915. f1. d2158; c861. f1. d9125; 'Ein Hexenprocess im neunzehnten Jh.', *Das Inland*, 49 (1841), 777–82; L. Mark, 'Nõiaprotsessidest Eestis 18. sajandi lõpul ja 19. sajandi alguses', *Ajalooline Ajakiri*, 1 (1938), 20–33.

[64] 'Ein Hexenprocess im neunzehnten Jh.', pp. 777–82.

[65] RAKA: c861. f1. d9125, pp. 90–8; Mark, 'Nõiaprotsessidest Eestis', pp. 28–31.

Estonia II: The Crusade against Idolatry

JUHAN KAHK

DURING the 1650s various disasters befell some families of Vana-Kasti village in western Estonia, all of whom had had dealings with Kopsu Maie or her daughter Ello shortly before the accidents. At a wedding party, for example, Maie had thrown ale on the hearthstone. Within a few years, three children from this family fell into the fireplace, and one was burned to death. The family summoned an exorcist, who blamed Maie's gesture at the wedding as the source of their misfortune.

Kopsu Maie, who liked animals, once stopped to pat some oxen harnessed for a journey, saying that the poor beasts were sure to be beaten on the way. During the journey the oxen became so weak that part of the load could not be delivered. Another time, a neighbour's children played on Maie's barley-field and trampled the grain, provoking her to chase them with sickle in hand. Soon afterwards the children fell ill and their hands were paralysed.

At one farmhouse Maie had praised a newly-born baby boy, who soon sickened and died the day after his christening. In 1648 Nano Jürgen's pigs strayed into Maie's yard, where her dogs attacked them and killed some of them. When Maie's pigs strayed into Jürgen's yard soon afterwards, he captured one, fattened it, and ate it with his family. Learning of this, Kopsu Maie angrily remarked that she wished Jürgen would boil himself as he had boiled the meat—and of course, Jürgen fell ill and bled much.

Other accidents were associated with Maie's daughter Ello, who married Kopsu Hans. Ello's husband had once quarrelled with a neighbour over a patch of field. They finally agreed to divide it, but Ello was not satisfied and blamed her husband. The field was sown with rye. On the morning of Midsummer Day the crop was found trampled, as if by a horse. Suspecting Ello, neighbours scolded Hans, who replied that 'this is the Devil's work; I have not done this, and the Devil take whoever has.'

About the same time, a woman in the neighbourhood was in labour.

'Suddenly everybody in the room noticed a big cat. Although the farmer tried to drive it away, the cat climbed onto the roof. As soon as it reached the spot directly above the woman in labour, she lost consciousness and remained so for several days.' Everyone present was convinced that the mysterious tomcat was really Kopsu Ello.

When Ello moved from one farm to another, a bag full of human hair, animal hair, and cornflowers was found at her former residence, which everyone assumed had been used for witchcraft. From then on her nickname was Hairbag Ello.

She had borrowed butter from a peasant woman and wrapped it in a kerchief. When the kerchief was returned, the owner found five holes in it. From then on she could not make butter from her cows' milk, because it would not curdle.

One evening in 1665, Liiva Jaan saw Ello in his rye-field. Ello later explained that she had been looking for herbs that she needed for dyeing. Since Liiva Jaan had often called her a witch, she was frightened, hid from him, and ran home. But the infuriated Liiva Jaan would not leave the matter alone, and declared at the manor that both Kopsu Ello and her mother Maie were witches. Both women were imprisoned or, as it was called, 'put in a box'. Judges were requested and a thorough investigation begun. On 3 June 1665, on the basis of the evidence summarized above, Kopsu Maie was sentenced to be burned at the stake and her daughter Ello to be whipped in the pillory.[1]

These events at Vana-Kasti have a strong local colour. But even a cursory investigation reveals analogous situations and comparable events in different parts of seventeenth-century Europe. Here as elsewhere, witchcraft accusations emerged from social strains within the village. Old women like Kopsu Maie were often thought to be witches. It was much the same everywhere; one can say in this respect that the Aksi parish of Estonia resembled the county of Essex in England. Across many different parts of Europe one can find similar styles of divination, exorcisms, evil spells, curses, herbal cures, love potions, or the use of witches and wizards to recover stolen property. As Richard Horsely correctly stresses, 'There is a great deal of similarity in the magical practices and formulas used by the wise women or *devins-guérisseurs* from area to area in Europe.' And, he adds, 'Each study

---

[1] Central State Archives of History of the Estonian SSR (hereafter RAKA): c863. f1. d4253. For the reference system of the Estonian archives, see ch. 9, n. 16, above.

confirms the now-familiar generalization that the vast majority of witches were poor, elderly women.'[2]

However, the witch-hunts that caught Kopsu Maie and Ello in 1665 required much more than village tensions and suspicions to produce such tragic results. As Horsley has also summarized, 'Left to themselves, the peasants may well have lynched a few suspects—such as the two Austrian women burned for causing a hailstorm in 1675—but they would never have produced the great witch-hunts in which hundreds of thousands were burned.'[3] In order to comprehend these hunts, we must examine the relationship between popular magic and church ideology.

Early Catholic theoreticians were characterized by willingness to incorporate elements of heathenism into their church practices, instead of forcing the newly-baptized into open conflict between their old and new beliefs. The ancient worship of springs, trees, and stones was not abolished but modified, by turning heathen shrines into Christian ones and associating them with saints instead of pagan gods. As Keith Thomas has stressed, the medieval Church smoothed out many fundamental differences between prayer texts and magic formulas, and supported the notion that mere repetition of sacred words was itself a holy occupation. Church dogmas even implied that prayers could be used to harm other people; prayer texts read in reverse became magic formulas.[4] When peasant 'magic formulas' were being recorded for the first time in seventeenth- and eighteenth-century Estonia, they often included prayer texts and names of Catholic saints—apparently the fruit of many centuries' work by Catholic priests.[5] The Church also encouraged saying prayers to cure sickness. Catholic priests used to bless water and salt, which may explain the Estonian term used to describe procedures of fortune-telling: *soolapuhumine*—'blowing on salt'.[6]

However, we must not overestimate the readiness of the Catholic Church to adapt its ideology to popular magical beliefs. Church ideology developed autonomously, and had a strong influence on the ideas and images dominant in Estonia as well as in many other

[2] Richard Horsley, 'Who were the Witches? The Social Roles of the Accused in European Witch Trials', *Journal of Interdisciplinary History*, 9 (1979), 697, 689.

[3] Ibid., p. 694.

[4] Keith Thomas, *Religion and the Decline of Magic* (London, 1971), 42–7.

[5] Juhan Kahk, 'Nõidumisest ja nõiasõnadest Eestis XVII sajandil', *Keel ja Kirjandus*, 11 (1980), 673–81.

[6] Thomas, *Religion*, p. 29.

regions of Catholic Europe. And although Catholic ideology could find some common ground with popular beliefs in its fight against harmful 'black' magic, it ultimately became a bitter enemy of beneficial or 'white' magic in its popular forms. By the time that Pope Innocent VIII issued his famous bull, *Summis desiderantes*, authorizing the search for and destruction of witches in 1484, Church ideology had become actively involved in the struggle against 'bad' popular magic.

Europe had been officially Christian for many centuries by 1484. Scholars have recently argued that the sixteenth- and seventeenth-century witch-hunts were provoked by the Church striving to enforce orthodoxy on areas which were officially Christian, but in fact were still dominated by pre-Christian magic beliefs. Witch-hunting meant the often forcible subjection of remote, outlying regions to Christianity, where previously the Church's power had been recognized only formally. In Trevor-Roper's phrase, the Church was carrying the Gospel of European 'feudal' Christianity to the incompletely Christianized communes of the mountains, where the ancient superstitions of village society became more menacing when they were discovered in an alien and exaggerated form among 'heretics'.[7] Perhaps a similar situation occurred in 'frontier' regions such as Spain or the Baltic, which had been conquered by relatively recent crusades. Here the struggle was intensified by national and racial antagonism.

Witch-hunting began relatively late in the eastern Baltic, following not the 'crusading' imperialism of the Teutonic Knights, but the conquests of Lutheran Sweden in the early seventeenth century. In both parts of Sweden's eastern Baltic empire, Finland and Estonia, the newly-founded university at Tartu was extremely important in disseminating the official ideology about witchcraft. As Heikkinen has noted, the Swedish magistrate (Nils Psilander) who directed the witch-trials in the Åland islands in 1665–70 had attended Tartu University in 1638, and he also relied on a handbook written by a Tallinn theologian in 1632.[8] Even more important was the Bishop of Turku (Åbo) and Vice-Chancellor of Turku Academy, Johan Gezelius, who once accused a colleague's widow of poisoning him in 1667; Gezelius had earned his Master's degree at Tartu in 1641, where

---

[7] Hugh R. Trevor-Roper, *Religion, the Reformation and Social Change* (London, 1967), 108, 110.

[8] Antero Heikkinen, 'Ahvenanmaa noitoprosessin synty', *Historiallina Aikakauskirja*, 1 (1967), 42–4.

he had served as Professor of Greek and Hebrew and also as Super-intendent-General of the Livonian Church before coming to Finland.[9]

Tartu University had been founded in 1632, while Sweden was still completing the subjugation of Estonia, in order to train the ruling élite, especially the clergy, who had been decimated by the recent wars. The Swedish regent, Johan Skytte, found only seventeen churches on his arrival in Livonia, and complained of the spread of 'repellent idolatry'. Skytte saw the mission of the new Academia Gustaviana as first and foremost to produce 'clergymen who ought to be capable of influencing the peasantry'.[10] And that was exactly what it did. Over the period 1625–1720 a total of 242 pastors were educated at Tartu (the whole of Estonia only contained about 100 parishes). On the other hand, only fourteen of the 305 magistrates serving in the three main Estonian towns (Tartu, Pärnu, and Tallinn) and Riga between 1631 and 1710 had been educated as the Academia Gustaviana.[11]

The Swedish government's church policies were originally carried out in Livonia by Hermann Samson (1579–1643), a Lutheran theologian and preacher at Riga since 1608, who became Superintendent-General of the Livonian Church in 1622. Samson also composed the most important witchcraft treatise in the eastern Baltic: his *Nine Selected and Well-grounded Witch-Sermons, wherein the terms 'Magic' and 'Witchcraft' are explained logically and briefly on the basis of the Word of God and other authors and historians, and which were delivered publically in Riga cathedral* was printed at Riga in 1626.[12]

Samson's Preface explained that during his visitation of Livonian churches, he had 'encountered horrible superstitions and heard complaints of sorcery'. He had therefore delivered and published these sermons in order to inspire his 'poor clergy' in their struggle against the devil and the 'blind Papal faith'. His text repeats the orthodox commonplaces of witch-hunting ideology in their Lutheran

---

[9] A. Heikkinen, *Paholaisen Liittolaiset* (Helsinki, 1969), 166–74; see also the 3-vol. *History of Tartu University, 1632–1982*, in Estonian, i (Tallinn, 1982), 200f., on Gezelius's work there as a publisher and translator of Greek authors into Latin and compiler of a Greek grammar; in all, he was credited with more than 150 works, mostly theological.

[10] Michael Roberts, *Gustavus Adolphus*, i (London, 1953), 420.

[11] A. Terling, *Album Academicum der Universität Dorpat (Tartu) 1632–1710* (Tallinn, 1984), 103, 111.

[12] Hermann Samsonius, *Neun ausserlesen und wohlgegründete Hexenpredigt* ... (Riga, 1626), pages not numbered; cf. pp. 56, 264, and 289 in this volume (Clark, Madar, and Ankarloo).

variants. His first sermon affirmed that witches really do exist ('in this respect we can have no doubts . . .') and defined sorcery as a compact with the devil to give support in harming people. An inclination towards sorcery can be detected even in people who superstitiously believe that a four-leafed clover brings good luck; already in such cases, 'if not openly, then at least secretly the witch-Devil is aroused'. Although his Bible said that sorceresses (*Zauberinnen*) must not be left alive, Samson, citing several authors, believed that men could also be witches: the devil had found many helpers among the Jesuits!

Samson's second sermon asked why, even after the Lutheran Reformation, sorcery could still be found 'in all countries, towns, settlements, villages and remote places'. He explained that God used the scourge of sorcery in order to test and to punish people. He further denied that witches simply had melancholy dispositions, or were mentally deficient: the devil is very ingenious, and his helpers can imitate melancholy or other illnesses as required. Samson's fourth sermon similarly argued that, although witches themselves cannot change weather, God allows the devil to move air masses and clouds in order to harm people through storms. Witches' flights, he admitted, are often the result of morbid fancies or dreams—but genuine instances of witches' flight have occurred, and he cites several examples. Witches can and do harm people, Samson concluded, and he told a horrifying story about witches boiling small children for food recently near Berlin.

The only other seventeenth-century Livonian author to discuss witchcraft was Ludvig Dunte, a pastor in Tallinn, who mentioned it briefly in his *Short and Correct Explanation of a Thousand and Six Questions of Conscience* (1636).[13] Slightly milder than Samson, he warned that some melancholics mistakenly thought they were witches—but otherwise he agreed with his Riga colleague.

As Superintendent of the Livonian Church, Samson required the Livonian Consistory to 'abolish heathen idolatry, sorcery and superstition'.[14] The Consistory in turn urged clergymen in 1637 to discover 'whether the peasants still organized idol-worship and . . . assembled on hillocks or in valleys, near chapels or chapel ruins to worship idols and sacrifice'.[15] Progress, however, was excruciatingly slow. When the

---

[13] L. Dunte, *Decisiones Mille et Sex Casuum . . . Das ist Kurz und richtige Erörterung Ein Tausen und Sechs Gewissens Fragen* (Lübeck, 1636), 296f.
[14] Swedish State Archives, Stockholm, *Livonica*, ii. 643 (Kyrkan och Scholan, Consistorial och Visitationsordning, 1633).   [15] *Livonica*, ii. 442.

Estonian bishop made a visitation to Saaremaa in 1647, he learned that 'almost at every church some impudent elderly people knew nothing of Christianity and did not wish to learn it' and would not obey when ordered to take communion.[16]

The first truly serious attempt by Swedish officials to investigate the full depth of this problem and strengthen the authority of the Lutheran Church over Estonia occurred with the major visitation of southern Estonia in 1667–8.[17] When the Visitors set out in the late summer of 1667, they encountered a depressing situation: almost every parish reported examples of worship at sacred groves and stones where peasants customarily sacrificed; and they also learned the names of several witches. For example, in Torma, a cottar's wife accepted sacrifices on Midsummer Day (St John's Day). Almost at the outset, the Visitors acquired a full description of the Midsummer Night ritual in Maarja-Magdaleena parish, where peasants met at the country manor of Colonel Greifenspeer in order to cure illnesses; because of its ethnographic richness, this account merits extensive quotation.

The undersigned [whose signatures, however, are missing] went to the site of idolatry at nine o'clock on Midsummer Eve [23 June] where the peasants hold their usual sessions of idolatry and had already gathered, and for some time viewed the proceedings, how they built a fire and near the fire there was a stone with three women sitting around it; one of them is the most venerable and something like their priest, who receives the sick and their offerings and conducts the sacrificing. In the meantime the other two widows prepare the wax. Then the sick come, who have internal ailments, and must take bandages with wax and tie one around their bodies and also pick up a dipper of ale, go around the fire three times and while doing this they must bow to certain places of the stone while saying 'O help us, St John.' Having done this, they remove their bandages and hand them to the same old woman who holds it before the patient's mouth to be kissed. Then the bandage will be burned on the stone, the sick will drink from the dipper and pass it to the woman who will make the sign of the cross three times on the dipper and say, 'Help, dear St John, through these healing drugs this person', saying the sick person's name and ailment; afterwards she drank from the dipper and let the two widows drink also. For those with headaches, the wax bandages were tied around the head and the same ceremonies were performed. . . . Also, the old women said that anyone who had some internal illness should sacrifice in the manner

---

[16] *Livonica*, ii. 32 (Memorial of the Bishop of Tallinn on shortcomings discovered during the brief visitation to Saaremaa in 1647).

[17] *Livonica*, ii. 442, from which the next four paragraphs have been drawn.

mentioned above; but if they had some external trouble, like something wrong with their eyes or some injury to their hand or foot [with an axe], they should only make a wax candle, bare the sore place, and hold the candle to it while saying a special prayer. Someone who is cured after such a sacrifice must come to the same place each year at the same time, namely on St John's Eve, bringing a thank-offering made of wax, either a small human figure or else a wax candle, as the women have ordered, and it will then be burned on the stone.

Southern Estonia sacrificed on other days than Midsummer Day in 1668. In Vastseliina, peasants 'put up a wooden picture where they sacrifice on St Lawrence's Day and practice idolatry'. At Palamuse, peasants adorned their church with wreaths of leaves on St Bartholomew's Day. At least two parishes reported sacrifices during the feast of the Assumption. The pastor of Helme reported that some of his congregation sacrificed at his church on that day, while others used a hill on a neighbouring manor; at Räpina, peasants gathered on Ascension Day at a private chapel in order to make sacrifices and 'perform idolatry'. Sometimes the visitation records identify the sites of 'idolatry', as at Tarvastu, Karula, or the Risti chapel, but do not specify when the ceremonies were performed.

In a few parishes, witches were identified by name. In Urvaste, Kulli Jürgen of Antsla was reputed to be a witch; in Pühajärve, a peasant named Tautse Peeter; at Räpina, several people were named. More often the Visitors learned the names of peasants who organized the sacrifices, or who were vehement anti-Christians. In 1668 the authorities were told about an old peasant on a farm near Kalkus who 'offers bread and milk to the Sacrament, worships idols, keeps people away from church, and tells them to blame their calamities and illnesses on the church'. Other peasants, also identified by name, urged their neighbours to avoid attending church. 'It is no use going there— what do you get anyway?' asked one; while another denied the resurrection of Christ, cursed the pastors, and said that pastors 'entice people to receive the sacrament only in hopes of getting money from them—otherwise it is useless'. Apparently at least some peasants in seventeenth-century Estonia still regarded Christianity as an alien form of magic and opposed it vigorously. A traveller (Adam Olearius) who visited Estonia about this time reported that a peasant, upon learning that his neighbour had taken communion, 'jeered at him with very disgraceful, dirty, and blasphemous words'.

We possess nothing comparable to the 1667–8 visitation for

northern Estonia, although the church visitations for the Estonian *guberniya* for 1695–9 are fairly well preserved and provide a kind of religious survey for the north after two generations of Swedish rule. The extent of 'idolatry' can be seen in Table 10.1. Geographically, these visitation records reveal two zones where 'idolatry' persisted into the eighteenth century in northern Estonia. One was located close to the north-western coast, running north from Lihula through Martna and Lääne-Nigula to the parish of Risti and extending east to Keila. A second zone existed in eastern Estonia, from Ambla through Viru-Jaagupi and Viru-Nigula to the parish of Jõhvi.

The same Visitors asked whether heathen burial mounds were still in use. Pastors in only five of thirty-two parishes (the predominantly Swedish-speaking Reigi, Käina, and Noarootsi, plus Harju-Madise and Keila) said they knew nothing abut such mounds. One pastor indicated the precise locations of thirteen burial mounds, and added that when he admonished the peasants about this practice, they answered him that 'Maria's earth is everywhere.' Most pastors reported that there were 'more than enough' burial mounds in their parishes; a few mentioned the 1697 famine as an excuse.

During these visitations in the late 1690s, authorities learned about 'idolatry' on the hill of Vaike-Lihula in Martna parish, where sacrifices were offered on St Olaf's Day (29 July) at a small, tumbledown chapel, and also at some houses along the shore. At another well-known ruined chapel on a hill near Jõhvi, the peasants sacrificed on the Assumption and on St Lawrence's Day (10 August). The pastor of Mihkli mentioned a stone where peasants gathered to sacrifice on St Anthony's Day (17 January).[18]

Once again, visitation records give the names of some well-known local wizards. The pastor at Lääne-Nigula named several exorcists (*Besprecher*) to whom 'godless people turn for help, advice and comfort in cases of illness and distress'. Other pastors also identified notorious local *Zauberer*, *Segensprecher*, and *Wahrsager*.[19]

The Estonian parish clergy were expected not only to name prominent witches but also to see that they were punished. Some of them seem to have carried out this assignment zealously. According to Maia Madar, Estonia had about 140 trials for witchcraft (more than

---

[18] RAKA: c1187. f1. d5169; c1231. f2. d25; c1245. f1. d64; c1187. f1. d5169; c1226. f1. d25; c1187. f2. d5166.

[19] RAKA: c1187. f1. d5169; c1275. f1. d89; c1245. f1. d64; c1240. f1. d14.

TABLE 10.1. *The extent of idolatry in northern Estonia, 1695–1699*

	Districts			
	Läänemaa	Harjumaa	Järvamaa	Virumaa
Total parishes	19	12	8	11
Parishes with visitation records	11	11	1	10
Parishes with data on 'idolatry'	4	4	1	3

one per parish) during the seventeenth century.[20] From 1600 to 1624 there were 22; from 1630 to 1659 the total rose to 56; from 1660 to 1679, there were only 12; and from 1680 to 1699, there were 32 trials. The sex distribution of accused witches seems unusual in Estonia. According to Madar, men were accused almost twice as often as women.

In their fight against sorcery, the Swedish-trained pastors and judges who goverened seventeenth-century Estonia followed the official European witch-doctrines, much as they had been spelled out by Samson in 1626. Nevertheless, some images from the great witch-hunts—pacts with the devil, flying to sabbaths—rarely appear in Estonian witch-trials. Even under torture, peasants seldom (and even then, vaguely) spoke of pacts with the devil. Sometimes a confession began with the devil and then deviated to pre-Christian fairies and wizards, who are described vividly and in detail. Estonian trial records contain no detailed descriptions of flying or sabbaths; on the other hand, the popular belief in werewolves is well represented, although it formed a very minor part of the official witch-ideology.

Witch-hunting was part of Swedish 'imperialism', which oppressed the Estonian population through the imposition of serfdom as well as enforcing an increasingly strict Lutheran discipline on them. At the same time, Sweden—a nation which executed its last witch in 1711—shared fully in the great witch-hunt that covered all of Europe. However, Swedish administration also inadvertently furnished a comprehensive and coherent picture of Estonian religious practices through its great visitation of 1667–8 which demonstrated the extent of

[20] Table 9.1, p. 261, above.

popular resistance to the official state religion. In parish after parish the Visitors recorded information about public meetings of unafraid peasants at sacrificial sites—hills, sacred groves, old chapels—in order to perpetrate 'idolatry'. What was being practised was not a revival of Catholicism, but a continuation of pre-Christian rituals; sacrificial sites included many chapels and chapel ruins only because they had been erected at former 'heathen' sacred places. The organizers and leaders of these rites were usually well-known people—as were the *devins-guérisseurs* who could be found in every parish. Moreover, some peasants openly made caustic remarks about the Christian faith and about the local clergy.

The Swedish authorities, backed up by the Baltic nobility, launched a zealous attack against this opposition. During this campaign torture and stakes spread over Estonia, and dozens of innocent people were executed. Estonia resembled the non-Swedish parts of Finland in so far as most of the accused witches were men. But what made Estonia unique was that its witch-hunt coincided with the first massive offensive against the traditional religion of Estonia—and with the imposition of serfdom.

Despite strenuous efforts, Swedish officials and clergy failed to uproot these pre-Christian beliefs and practices. A decade after the 1667 visitation, the Livonian Church Commission wrote to the King of Sweden that Livonia still contained 'terrible idolatry and heathen blindness that has power over thousands of miserable souls in this country'. The Commission believed that this 'idolatry' represented a serious threat to the Swedish state, since such lost souls could easily 'lean towards the Papal faith and foreign powers' (that is, Poland).[21]

Although persecuted by both state and church—exorcists were brought to trial, witches burned at the stake—Estonian peasants continued to meet openly at their sacred places to sacrifice, right up to the end of the seventeenth century. Apparently the authorities dared not prohibit them from doing so. As late as 1698, the peasants of Lääne-Nigula were warned that if they continued to sacrifice on their traditional hill, such gatherings would be dispersed by cavalry.[22] That same year, the pastor at Jõhvi complained that although the peasants who gathered on Kuremägi (Kurra Meggi) had been 'ordered by the administration of the *guberniya* to be driven off with soldiers, they have

---

[21] *Livonica*, ii. 492 (correspondence of Livonian Church Commission, 1677, to the King of Sweden).

[22] RAKA: c1245. f1. d64; c1187. f2. d5169.

not given up the tradition'.[23] The Risti chapel near Viljandi was widely known as a centre of 'idolatry' during the great visitation of 1667–8; but more than a century passed before the authorities dared to destroy it—and then the local landlord had to start cutting the trees of the sacred grove himself, since the peasants refused to do it.[24]

[23] RAKA: c1226. f1. d25.
[24] A. W. Hupel, *Topographische Nachrichten von Lief- und Estland*, iii (Riga, 1782), 318.

11

Sweden: The Mass Burnings (1668–1676)

BENGT ANKARLOO

I. THE MEDIEVAL BACKGROUND

THE oldest recorded Swedish laws were written down in the thirteenth century. A comprehensive national code was enacted around 1350. These early legal sources reflect an agrarian society in transition from primitive to feudal forms of production. In the labour force, slavery (thraldom) was still important, but was gradually giving way to newer forms of exploitation such as servitude and tenancy. The social difference between the landowning warlord élite and the productive majority was relatively advanced already in the Viking era (*c*.800–1000), but was to some extent mitigated by the existence of a class of free farmers, the size of which varied over time and from region to region.

In the northern parts, including Finland, where large forested areas were open for colonization, the free farmers were in the overwhelming majority. Land use was extensive, with pastoralism, hunting, and slash-and-burn agriculture on sparsely scattered single farms. This is the area of the violent witch-craze in the 1670s.

Further south the population was much denser, the land was more intensively cultivated, and social relations were more complex. In general Denmark, southern Sweden, and the fjord and valley districts of Norway had a more pronounced feudal structure than the rest of the Nordic area. Agriculture was organized around village communities with small family holdings as in most other parts of western Europe. At the end of the medieval period the percentage of land cultivated by free farmers was roughly: in Denmark, 15 per cent; in Norway, 30; in Sweden, 50; and in Finland, 95.[1]

The provisions in the medieval laws were mostly concerned with

---

[1] Eino Jutikkala, *Bonden, adelsmannen, kronan: Godspolitik och jordegendomsförhållanden i Norden, 1550–1750* (Copenhagen, 1979), 9, 11, 17; Lars-Arne Norborg and Lennart Sjöstedt, *Grannländernas historia* (Lund, 1977), 35; Sten Carlsson and Jerker Rosén, *Svensk historia* (Lund, 1978), i. 298.

conditions within the free, landholding classes. Real estate, farm land, was more or less taken for granted as the main productive resource of the family and the extended kin group. The status of the provincial laws in force up to about 1350 varied widely. Some were enacted by the king, or were at least given royal sanction, whereas others were simply records of local customs. This formal difference, which in the past has been given much attention, should not be exaggerated. In fact, the structural and factual similarities are striking throughout the Nordic area.[2]

An ancient common basis of legal culture probably existed, but such a tradition is hard to single out in the written codes. The attempts in this direction made by the Germanistic school of legal history now come under heavy criticism. Recent research has stressed the influence from Continental laws. Both the provincial and national codes of Sweden have obviously incorporated provisions from abroad. Materials from German (Hanseatic), possibly from Lombard, and certainly from canon law have been freely used.[3]

Swedish law, in line with comparable codes on the Continent, originally appears to have penalized only witchcraft that was physically injurious to human beings (*maleficium*; Sw. 'förgörning'). The punishment was outlawing: the victim's kinsmen were free to take revenge and kill the witch. However, this very old form of penalty was soon replaced throughout the system by a formal death penalty. At the same time the crime was extended so that the killing of cattle by magic was also deemed to be a capital offence. This trend, most evident in the laws of the southern provinces (Götaland), was probably spurred on by the Church, as also was the adoption of statutes in the thirteenth century against superstitious practices of a less harmful nature. Cases of this type were to be brought before a bishop's court.[4]

In the laws of central Sweden (Svealand), only fatal *maleficium* against human beings was included among capital offences. On the other hand, the restrictive stipulation that a criminal be caught *in flagrante* was missing. Other harmful but not fatal forms were punished by fines. No mention is made of the bishop's court. The influence of the Church seems therefore to be less than in the southern

---

[2] Per Nyström, *Historieskrivningens dilemma* (Stockholm, 1974), 62–78; Elsa Sjöholm, 'Rättshistorisk metod och teoribildning', *Scandia*, 44 (1978), 233–41; Kjell Modéer, 'Rättshistorisk forskning i Sverige', *Rättshistoriska studier*, 6 (1979), 30–1.

[3] Sjöholm, 'Rättshistorisk metod', p. 240.

[4] Bengt Ankarloo, *Trolldomsprocesserna i Sverige* (Lund, 1971), 29–34.

provinces. The Svea laws were to become models for the paragraphs on witchcraft in the National Code (*Magnus Erikssons Landslag*, 1350), which, however, do not mention superstition. Thus the code, which after being revised in the 1440s (*Christoffers Landslag*) was in force right up to the first half of the eighteenth century, legislated only against enrooted, harmful witchcraft.[5]

In legal practice, ecclesiastical law continued to be adapted from the older provincial laws, commonly Uppland law. This also contained regulations against superstition. Towards the end of the fourteenth century the crimes were defined in closer detail. The forbidden practices are condemned as the devil's arts (*ars dyabolica*). In devotional literature (*exempla*), compacts, exorcism, defilement of the host, and other heretical acts are described directly after similar phenomena in Continental texts (for example, Vincent de Beauvais). The very sparse court material from the fifteenth century contains examples of people being condemned to death in a secular court for making a compact with the devil. The Church also brands magical activities (*incantationes, sortilegia*) as crimes against the Faith comparable to heresy and usury.[6] It has not, however, been possible to find any traces of the systematic concept of the witch that was emerging in Continental doctrine during the fifteenth century. As a rule the ecclesiastical courts dealt with the simple popular customs associated with everyday problems and conflicts.

A few hints about the popular beliefs concerning witches and *maleficium* are given already in the oldest provincial laws from the thirteenth century. Harmful magic is brought about with the aid of certain paraphernalia such as horns and hair. This is the same kind of dangerous stuff as that constantly referred to in the court rolls of the sixteenth and early seventeenth centuries. The night-riding witch is also mentioned in a statute from the early thirteenth century. If someone says about a woman that she was seen riding on a fence with flying hair in the shape of a troll at the time of the equinox, this shall be considered an unlawful insult.[7] It is assumed that accusations of this kind are directed against women only. In the oldest statutes, legal

[5] Ibid., pp. 35–7.
[6] Ibid., pp. 37–42. In canonical doctrine witchcraft was regarded as a *causa mixti fori*, a case for both ecclesiastical and secular courts. Cf. Joseph Hansen, *Zauberwahn, Inquisition und Hexenprozess* (Munich and Leipzig, 1900), 299, 321; *Malleus maleficarum*, pt. iii, q. 1, intro.
[7] *Äldre Västgötalagen*, Rättslösabalken, ch. 5, para. 5.

responsibility for the criminal acts of a woman is normally taken by her father or husband, but cases of witchcraft are specifically cited as exceptions to this rule. 'A woman . . . cannot be hanged or beheaded except for witchcraft.'[8]

Night-riding and harmful magic with the aid of bones and hair are thus offences associated with women at an early stage. To judge from later court rolls, this was well founded in popular beliefs. Similar ideas can also be found all over Europe at this period. The interpretation of such activities within the framework of a Christian demonology had only just begun at the end of the Middle Ages. For another century or more the concept of *maleficium* would remain the basis for both legal and popular actions against people suspected of witchcraft.[9]

II. FROM *MALEFICIUM* TO SABBATH

The Protestant Reformation in the sixteenth century did not change the belief in the forms and effects of witchcraft. If anything, the popular magical activities increased when official exorcisms and benedictions disappeared from approved usage. One important institutional change was that the secular state presumed to be the highest instance also in religious cases. The Crown was, as Melanchton put it, custodian of both the tablets of law (*custos utriusque tabulae*).[10]

There are still relatively few court rolls preserved. However, from what is left it seems evident that the intensity of persecutions increased towards the end of the century. In the three towns of Stockholm, Jönköping, and Vadstena during the period 1490–1614 the trials are found to be about seven times as frequent after 1580 as before.[11]

Maleficium trials arising from the stipulations of the National Code were in the overwhelming majority. The magical methods were similar to those of the medieval era. Public opinion was clearly aroused and hostile to such activities. In most cases there was active peasant involvement in the accusations. But during the decades around 1600 we begin to find isolated but specific references to the witches' sabbath. From the very beginning it is connected with Blåkulla ('Blue Hill'), the north-Scandinavian equivalent to the

[8] *Äldre Västgötalagen*, Tjuvabalken, 33.

[9] Ankarloo, *Trolldomsprocesserna*, pp. 46–7.

[10] Ibid., pp. 54, 90–100; Sven Kjöllerström, *Guds och Sveriges lag under reformationstiden* (Lund, 1957), 15–17.

[11] Ankarloo, *Trolldomsprocesserna*, pp. 43–6.

German Brocken. The name occurs already in the fifteenth century. It is then (as also later in the south) identified with Jungfrun, a desolate and forbidding rock island in the southern Baltic. Further north, Blåkulla is in the later trials the name of any nearby hill or mountain. In his great book about the Nordic people (1555), Olaus Magnus remarks that Blåkulla

is used at certain times of the year by Nordic witches for their meetings. They compete in magic and superstitious arts. Those who are late for this devil's service are terribly punished. But in this matter everyone should trust his own judgement rather than relying on others.[12]

When first occurring in court, the Blåkulla myth is met with similar scepticism. In Stockholm in 1596 a woman confessed to be 'of the bad sort riding to Blåkulla. Not long ago she had intercourse with the devil. But she was admonished to tell the truth and to refrain from lies and deceptions.'[13]

So opinion was divided. The courts were in doubt how to treat such confessions. If *maleficium* was part of the offence, the case was clear. The death sentence against the evil Björn, who had bewitched two men, was confirmed by the king. But was night-riding to the sabbath and intercourse with demons a capital offence? During the first decades of the seventeenth century, the bishops' council and other church authorities were asked to give their opinion on witch cases brought before the Royal Court of Appeal. As late as 1619 the bishops held the view that according to Swedish law and Christian statutes it was necessary to prove *maleficium* in order to invoke the death penalty.[14] Reference was made to conservative German opinion based on the *Carolina* (section 109). Hermann Samsonius, the Bishop of Riga, took the same position in his collection of witch sermons (*Hexen Predigt*) dedicated to the Swedish chancellor Axel Oxenstierna and published in 1626.[15]

---

[12] Olaus Magnus, *De Gentibus Septentrionalibus*, ii. 23. Olaus was widely read in 16th-c. Europe and contributed to giving Scandinavia a solid reputation for witchcraft and sorcery. See e.g. Jean Bodin, *De la démonomanie des sorciers* (Paris, 1581), 91: 'Il y a plus de Sorciers en Noruege, et Liuonie et autres parties Septentrionales, qu'il n'y a en tout le reste du monde, comme dit Olaus le grand.'

[13] *Stockholms stads tänkeböcker från 1592*, ii (Stockholm, 1951), 70, 165; Ankarloo, *Trolldomsprocesserna*, pp. 49–50.

[14] The Royal Library, Stockholm, MS A. 945: 'Episcoporum, capitularium et variorum literae et responsa', fos. 12 ff.; Ankarloo, *Trolldomsprocesserna*, pp. 92–3.

[15] Ibid., p. 97: Hermann Samsonius, *Ausserlessne und wohlbegründete Hexen-Predigten* (Riga, 1626).

As in other parts of the North, the first decades of the seventeenth century were crucial for the introduction in Sweden of modern demonological and legal concepts of witchcraft. The witches' sabbath was easily accepted in popular tradition, since it was perceived merely as an extension or elaboration of local beliefs, going back at least to the late Middle Ages, in night-flying women and a witches' gathering at Blåkulla. If anything, the élite tradition was slower to absorb the new ideas.

From the end of the sixteenth century the secular courts had begun to take action against the religiously shaded forms of witchcraft: the witches' sabbath, journeys to Blåkulla, and compacts with the devil. At the same time, Continental ideas and legal practices can be distinguished. Interrogations were accompanied by water ordeals, shaving, and formal torture. However, with a few notable exceptions, these modern trials were restricted to Götaland in the south.[16]

Torture was explicitly forbidden in Swedish legal proceedings. It is therefore significant that coercive methods were openly and regularly employed in witchcraft cases, often by direct royal decree. In 1614 a bailiff in Småland who used torture was brought before the Court of Appeal. The local court in a defence petition pointed out that torture had been used only in a witchcraft interrogation. The suspect had been questioned about *maleficium* 'and nothing else'. Other cases indicate that both the Court of Appeal and the king himself regarded torture as justifiable and suitable in witchcraft cases. The advent of such terms as *crimen exceptum* and *crimen laesae Divinae Maiestatis* applied to witchcraft indicates the connection with Continental doctrine.[17]

Later on, other methods became more common against suspects who refused to confess their crime. They were condemned to death, and led out to the place of execution 'in the firm belief that they were about to die'. A priest reminded them of the conditions for the salvation of the soul, and urged them finally to confess. Those who then submitted were executed on the spot, those who refused to comply were returned to prison.[18]

With the institution in 1614 of the Royal Court of Appeal in Stockholm, the central authorities took a more firm control of legal practice, particularly in the treatment of capital cases. With the exception of

[16] Ankarloo, *Trolldomsprocesserna*, pp. 67–72.
[17] Ibid., pp. 70–6.
[18] Ibid., pp. 73–4.

simple and clear cases such as confessed murders, all death sentences in the local courts were to be brought to Stockholm for final approval.[19] The precedences in witchcraft cases established by the Royal Court in co-operation with the Church during the first two decades were upheld until the 1650s. Executions were rare, probably below a hundred. Proven *maleficium* or open and definite rejection of God was required for capital punishment.[20]

Up to and even during the great witch-craze in the 1670s, several members of the ruling élite expressed their doubts about the realities of the witch confessions and urged the courts to go cautiously about these matters. The Swedish regime in northern Germany earned a certain reputation for its careful handling of witchcraft in the occupied areas. Queen Christina, speaking of the trials in Verden, boasted that during her reign she expressly forbade the death penalty for witches, as long as they could not clearly be proved guilty of murder. She was convinced, she said, that the crimes which women confessed were often illusions, caused either by disturbances in their female functions of by the frauds of the devil.[21]

In fact, the royal rescript to Verden makes no such distinction between fatal witchcraft and other forms, nor can this distinction be seen in the Swedish cases from the queen's period of sovereignty. On the contrary, there are at least three death sentences with the queen's confirmation in which fatal *maleficium* against a person is not found among the charges. It is probable that Christina's statement was a rationalization made after the cessation of the great trials in Sweden and France in the 1670s.[22]

It was also during Christina's reign that the church authorities began to advocate sterner practice in witchcraft cases. In a number of reports from the 1650s, several offences against the Decalogue, each of

---

[19] Sture Petrén, 'Hovrättens uppbyggnad 1614–1654', in Sture Petrén, Stig Jägerskiöld, and Tord Nordberg (eds.), *Svea Hovrätt* (Stockholm, 1964), 36.

[20] Ankarloo, *Trolldomsprocesserna*, 72–4, 90–8.

[21] Ibid., p. 99. The royal rescript in B. Hauber, *Bibliotheca, Acta et Scripta Magica*, iii (Lemgo, 1745), 250; National Archive, Stockholm, MS: 'Riksregistraturet' (16 Feb. 1649): cf. Dietrich Mahnke, 'Das Hexenunwesen in Verden und sein Ende'. *Stader Archiv*, 13 (1923), 1; H. Schwarzwälder, 'Die Geschichte des Zauber- und Hexenglaubens in Bremen', *Bremisches Jahrbuch*, 46 (1959), 220–2; Kjell Modéer, *Gerichtsbarkeiten der schwedischen Krone im deutschen Reichsterritorium*, i (Lund, 1975), 404.

[22] Ankarloo, *Trolldomsprocesserna*, pp. 99–100. Christina's claim first appears in Cardinal Albizzi's book *De inconstantia in Iure* (1683). For the position of Albizzi and the Roman Inquisition in cases of witchcraft, see John Tedeschi's essay in this volume, ch. 3, above.

which is worthy of death, are lumped together under the heading Witchcraft. In accordance with the current theocratic doctrine of punishment, the Old Testament (Exodus 22) is cited as the single most important legal source.

The influence from Continental theory and practice is most clearly visible in the theological and academic literature produced in the chapters and at the universities. It deals at special length with the problem of delimiting the power of the devil in relation to God and man. The journey to Blåkulla and the sabbath are described in roughly the same way as in the great trials later on. The aspect of witchcraft as religious transgression is given prominence, to justify demands for stricter application of the law. In the decades around 1650, the clergy and the local state bureaucracy of the countryside were theoretically and ideologically prepared for what was to come.[23]

Peasant witch-beliefs were elements of a peripheral cosmology, explaining evil in a context of society and nature which was only partially Christian and diabolic in the orthodox sense. But now this cosmology was gradually transformed. In the interpretation of Robert Rowland, this was the result of an integration process incorporating local (peripheral) belief-systems into a wider, uniform system. 'Items of folk belief were absorbed into the elite's symbolic representation of evil and were made available to judges and interrogators throughout western Europe.'[24]

A more ominous side of this integration was the growing emphasis on witchcraft as a threat to communal order rather than as inter-personal conflict. Both in its religious and political sense this inter-pretation was clearly in line with the general doctrinal trend in criminal law. The procedure of the courts was moving away from an accusatorial and highly formalized type of conflict-resolution towards a ruthless public prosecution and inquisitorial methods.

This interventionist trend applies not only to popular magic, but to the whole field of peasant culture. In seventeenth-century Sweden there was a growing sensibility in leading circles, that the population at large had to be educated. The chancellor Axel Oxenstierna described in 1640 a province in Finland as hopelessly backward, 'there is no culture, the inhabitants are beasts.' And a few years later he told the Mayor of Stockholm that the main task of the government was to

---

[23] Ankarloo, *Trolldomsprocesserna*, pp. 100–12.
[24] Rowland, ch. 6, above.

'civilize our nation'. In this educational work the protestant clergy was assigned a specially important role.[25]

Travelling through the Netherlands in 1685, the future Bishop of Scara, Jesper Swedberg, remarked in his diary:

> Order and discipline is—like everything else among these people—excellent. And they hold a strong hand over it. Not so, alas, among us. We have good ordinances in full measure, but those responsible for upholding them are doing nothing. As the saying goes: *Sveci ordinant, et reordinant, et semper sine ordine vivunt.*[26]

The good ordinances included a series of sumptuary, vestiary, and disciplinary regulations enacted in 1664, only five years before the great witch-hunt. They were not the first of their sort in the country, but for the first time they were ordered in a comprehensive system. The local élite, both civil and ecclesiastical, was held responsible for the implementation of this civilizing programme.[27]

Sweden's imperial growth in the seventeenth century had created a new middle class in the provincial towns, and even in the countryside. These middle-class groups—priests, petty bureaucrats, judges, and officers—were, through their educational background and socio-economic position, on the whole inclined to support the system. They often shared the view of their superiors that the peasantry, especially in remote areas, was boorish, dull, and potentially dangerous. Foreign travellers like the French ambassador d'Avaux in the 1630s and the English Whitelocke twenty years later were often met in the provincial towns by a local élite apologizing for the poor accommodation and the churlishness of the people in the countryside. Swedberg's criticism of those supervising the law was directed not only at the polity, but against his own colleagues. But being an ambitious man he probably underestimated the contribution of the members of his profession as educators of the common people.[28]

The moral programme of 1664 was beginning to be implemented in

---

[25] Bengt Ankarloo, 'Europe and the Glory of Sweden: The Emergence of a Swedish Self-image in the Early 17th Century', in Göran Rystad (ed.), *Europe and Scandinavia: Aspects of the Process of Integration in the 17th Century* (Lund, 1983), 241–8; Ankarloo, 'Domstolarnas arbetsformer', in Ulf Teleman (ed.), *Det offentliga språkbruket och dess villkor i Sverige under 1700-talet* (Småskrifter från institutionen för nordiska språk i Lund, 7; Nordlund, 1985), 129–37.

[26] Jesper Svedberg, *Levernes Beskrifning* (Skr. utg. av Vetenskaps-Societeten i Lund, 25/1; 1941), 110; Ankarloo, 'Domstolarna', p. 131.

[27] Ankarloo, 'Domstolarnas arbetsformer', p. 131.

[28] Ankarloo, 'Europe and the Glory of Sweden', p. 242.

several areas. For sexual offences, a transition from fines to corporal or even capital punishment can be discerned (but was often mitigated by extensive use of royal pardon). Premarital sex as a regular prelude to marriage was actively fought throughout the period, seemingly with very little effect. Popular feasts, ceremonies, and processions in connection with life-cycle transitions such as baptism, marriage, and funerals often had a quasi-religious character, which may account for their suppression. Others were clearly contrary to a growing sensibility of the dignity and sanctity of the church space. Wedding processions, including the traditional singers and musicians, were forbidden to enter the church. Feasting and drinking immediately before the church ceremony was prohibited, since it gave rise to indecent behaviour. Singing and dancing and other more colourful aspects of public life were suppressed. Beggars and vagrants were often popular actors: in fact, singing, jesting, and dancing were in a sense forms of begging. So the cultural aspects of destitution were considered as revolting as its social aspects. When discussing the laws of 1664 in parliament, the speaker of the clergy remarked:

Jesters and market fools, as well as new-year beggars, booksellers and print hawkers should be prohibited. There are many ways of begging: some do it for themselves, some for others, for prisoners, for churches; likewise makers of maypoles, school singers and other such nonsense like prints for invitations, New Year, funerals and weddings.

And finally, as in the rest of Europe, folk-beliefs and magical practices were reinterpreted. What previously was condemned and punished as mere superstition was now given a more sinister meaning, implying diabolic assistance or outright witchcraft. In the great witch-hunt of the 1670s, local clergymen and civil servants took a very active part, sometimes in aggressive opposition to a more reluctant or even sceptical attitude on the part of high-ranking officials sent out by the government to handle the unrest.

III. THE GREAT CRAZE

The great trials began in northern Dalarna in the summer of 1668. From the very beginning, the confessions and evidence display most of the peculiarities and special characteristics which were to become typical for future cases in Norrland, Uppland, and Stockholm. The

extensive and detailed cosmology of Blåkulla is immediately dealt
with at considerable length by all involved. The creative fantasy of the
children and young women acting as witnesses gives minor individual
variations on a given theme, apparently well known by all.[29]

The inquiries were conducted by the local court, assisted by the
parish priest and the sheriff. In all, eighteen death sentences were
passed, four of which were for minors aged below 15. These sentences
were submitted in the prescribed manner to the Court of Appeal in
Stockholm, which made considerable changes. Only seven adults, all
of whom had confessed, had their penalties confirmed. Their confessions had in some cases been extracted under torture, evidence of
which was removed from the court rolls before they were sent to
Stockholm. Even apart from this, the convictions rested largely upon
the evidence of children and accomplices. Thus, the Royal Court took
a step away from established, cautious practice. The government of
Regents was informed.

The executions took place at the end of May 1669. The seven condemned persons were first beheaded and their bodies were then
burnt, the normal form of execution for witches in Sweden. By then
new interrogations had shown that the craze was far more widespread
than had been anticipated. The centre was the parish of Mora by lake
Siljan. The people of the district had sent a representative to Stockholm to ask for more energetic measures to protect the children
involved.

The government appointed a royal commission with full powers to
carry out its death sentences. The commission completed its assignment in Mora in a fortnight in August 1669. Sixty suspects were
interrogated, and several hundred children came forward with charges
and tales of journeys to Blåkulla. Twenty-three persons, mostly
women, were sentenced to death. Of these, the fifteen who had confessed were executed immediately. They went 'on Bartholomew's day,
seven on the first pyre, five on the second and three on the third, a
horrifying spectacle'. A further six persons from Älvdalen, the first
parish to be affected, also went to the block. (See Endnote A.)

During 1670 the craze spread through the parishes around Siljan.
Reports of at least 300 suspected witches and thousands of possessed
children poured in to the government and the Court of Appeal. The
bishops of Strängnäs and Västerås, together with a delegation of

---

[29] The following account of the great craze is based on my dissertation, Ankarloo,
Trolldomsprocesserna, pp. 113–214.

farmers from the stricken parishes, went to Stockholm to demand that new measures be taken. The government had to yield to this impressive manifestation of public opinion. In early 1671 a new royal commission went to the Siljan district to carry out its arduous task. Considering the large number of suspects, its verdicts of death were relatively few. This was largely due to the current legal principle that only those who had confessed of their own accord could be executed. These amounted to no more than fifteen. Among the remainder, those who had particularly damaging evidence against them from the accomplices and the possessed children were picked out. They were sentenced to be led out to the place of execution in the hope that they would confess in face of death. This failed in every case, and they were all brought back.

In Continental practice, torture would of course have been resorted to in such instances. The disadvantage with the Swedish method was that the secret on which it depended for success became general knowledge. As a consequence, only those who confessed were seriously in danger of losing their lives. This reluctance to kill an impenitent person was due to religious considerations for her immortal soul. During 1672, when new cases of witchcraft began to appear in the neighbouring provinces, the Court of Appeal began to depart from this inefficient practice. In at least three cases, unconditional death sentence was passed against witches who stubbornly refused to confess.

These problems were to crop up again in the trials in Hälsingland, the province to the east of Dalarna. The first cases had been dealt with by the local authorities. The Court of Appeal had confirmed eight death sentences. When in the autumn of 1672 a large number of new cases were brought before the court, the government decided to appoint a commission for Hälsingland. The president of the court was Gustav Rosenhane, a member of the aristocratic bureaucracy with a modern and wide education. At his side he had two legal experts from the Court of Appeal and the Faculty of Law at Uppsala. The remainder of the commission were local clergymen, judges, and farmers. Right from the start, the three gentlemen objected strongly to the way the trials were conducted. Their criticism was both formal and rational. To base a verdict, particularly when it concerned a death penalty, on evidence from accomplices and small children was downright illegal. Moreover, the factual content of the stories about Blåkulla was of such a nature that it left grave doubts as to their verity and substance. The majority held a different opinion. Both the priests and the local representatives demanded harsh, effective, legal measures, and ten death sentences were enforced at the first place of investigation. The commission's tour promised to be a bloody one.

At this moment Rosenhane wrote a letter of appeal directly to King Karl XI, who had just come of age. By picturing the coming trials and exaggerating the number of death sentences, he was able to suggest the error of such extravagant loss of life. He requested more precise instructions as to those who could be spared. The king took Rosenhane's advice and ordered that only those who had confessed and who were in addition 'the root and source' of the craze were to be executed. The old order was thereby, at least temporarily, restored. In practice it was left to the three gentlemen to decide who should die. Out of a total of twenty death sentences, a maximum of eight were executed, all of whom had confessed.

The king's orders to Rosenhane also appear to have influenced the future practice of the Court of Appeal. After the termination of the Hälsingland commission in February 1673, and during the remainder of the year, a large number of fresh investigations were remitted from the local courts to the Court of Appeal, which, as far as can be seen, followed Rosenhane's prescriptions. In a report from the end of the year, the Court states that only in such cases where 'there have been clear grounds and self-confession have the old, incorrigible witches, admitting their guilt, been condemned to death'.

But the same report also made it clear that the craze was rampant throughout the entire coastal provinces of northern Sweden, and that the journeys to Blåkulla and the transvection of children 'daily increase so that one district after another becomes subject to the tyranny of Satan'. Only in exceptional cases had the Court itself been able to pass judgement. Most of the cases were incompletely reported, and the evidence was so confused that only the resident judge was able to form some fair idea as to where guilt lay. The hint was sufficient. The government set up a new commission, the fourth in order. The instruction prescribed that the first task of the new court was to single out and punish the old, hardened witches who had led others astray. This reflected the king's directive to Rosenhane, with one important omission: voluntary self-confession. The remainder, who without malice or intent had been persuaded or forced into complicity, were to be led back on the right path.

The province of Ångermanland was first on the list. The investigations started here in September 1674 and were continued right up to Christmas. Probably due to misunderstandings, the priests and local representatives had the majority in court. Nor was there, as in Hälsingland, anyone among the officials who was able, clearly and with authority, to criticize the formal and factual shortcomings of the proceedings. With the consent of the authorities, the priests in the affected parishes had actively taken part in tracing suspected witches. They furnished the court with endless lists of accused women and possessed children. The local courts were also set to work conducting preliminary investigations in order to alleviate the long and arduous task of the commission. At least 400 witches and thousands of children were interviewed and recorded.

All these circumstances, combined with the vagueness of the instructions, helped to sharpen praxis. Forty-eight suspects, many of whom denied the charges against them, were executed. By then only four of the affected parishes had been visited. The commission, and in particular its president, Governor Sparre, felt somewhat uneasy about continuing the work during 1675.

The great number of suspects in other provinces of the north and the slowness of the proceedings made the government decide to split the commission into two parts. The use of torture against strongly suspected but stubborn witches was now officially sanctioned. Sparre's fears of an intolerably large number of executions were rejected. 'The honour of God and the liberation and purging of the country from such a grave sin must be our prime concern. One cannot relax a rule in the face of mere quantity.'

The year 1675 was to mark the zenith of the trials. Over a hundred death sentences were executed. In addition to Ångermanland, the divided commission also worked in Gästrikland further south. Both divisions of the court passed sentence without consulting Sparre, president of the commission and governor in the province. This led to a struggle over competence. Sparre began to give stronger voice to his hitherto vague distaste for the turn which the trials had taken. The evidence of the children, the most important proof against the stubborn, was conflicting and uncertain. Before this and other legal and practical problems had been solved he refused to participate in any further executions. He got the king's approval to terminate the commission.

After four years of witch-hunt in the northern provinces the craze was now on its way south. In Uppland, immediately north of Stockholm, isolated cases had occurred by the beginning of 1675. Their number increased during the year, clearly influenced from the north. In October, at the coronation Riksdag in Uppsala, peasants from the vicinity presented the king with a petition 'to receive a commission against witchcraft'. It was not granted. After Sparre's intervention in · the north the government had decided to postpone all further investigations until the legal problems had been discussed and new directives for the trials had been formulated.

Only in the summer of 1676, when Stockholm was also involved, were new commissions appointed, one each for Uppland and the capital. President of the former was Anders Stiernhöök, who had supported Rosenhane's critical views in Hälsingland in 1673 (see above). In consequence, the investigations in Uppland proceeded with such caution that only a couple of death sentences had been carried out by the time decisive events in Stockholm put an end to the great persecutions once and for all.

For it was in Stockholm that the end was to come. For the first time the leading politicians and judges saw the craze at close quarters. Gradually they were able to assess the criticism which had for a long time been voiced in the provinces. But it took a long while, almost two years, before the change definitely took place. In spring 1676 matters started in earnest. The Court of Appeal began for the first time to employ direct interrogations. Up until then, all its proceedings had been based on the records sent from the lower courts in the provinces. After a month's work, a prominent member of the Court, Councillor Johan Gyllenstierna, summed up his experiences with surprise and doubt: 'This matter must be approached with great caution, for the longer I look at it the more necessary I find it to have more light from outside.' The Court of Appeal soon asked to be freed from its unpleasant assignment. It was at this point, summer 1676, that the two last commissions were appointed.

In the beginning the Stockholm commission conducted its investigations along the lines of its predecessors. Several death sentences were passed and a few were executed. One woman was burnt alive—the only instance during the whole craze. And then, all of a sudden, the children began to confess that their stories were pure make-believe and that the accused witches were innocent. The court thereupon sifted all previous evidence, which was now rejected. The most recently condemned women were set free.

This volte-face has traditionally been associated with the scientist Urban Hiärne, a member of the commission. A careful study of the source-material, however, shows that this view must be modified. During the three weeks prior to the disclosures, during which some of the children were put under pressure, other members of the court were active, not least the young priests. Hiärne was not even present at this stage. His contribution came later, when, by brilliantly summarizing the experiences gained, he succeeded in convincing those who were still in doubt.[30]

And so the craze came to an abrupt end. Official proceedings were launched against a handful of the most active witnesses. Four of them, including a 13-year-old boy, were sentenced to death and executed. A prayer of thanksgiving was printed and distributed throughout the country: God had finally subdued the ragings of Satan.

In the following decades, scattered individual cases of witchcraft were still sent to the Court of Appeal. Even a few executions took place. The experiences from Stockholm were seriously repeated only once again, in the 1720s, when tales of Blåkulla and transvected children were told in Värmland in the west. In the lower courts, nothing seemed to have been learnt. Minors were admitted as witnesses, torture was resorted to, and several women were sentenced to death. All the verdicts were, however, reversed in the Court of Appeal, and the most active persecutors were punished.[31]

In the new National Code of 1734, *maleficium* (*förgörning*) was still a capital offence. The statute was never used and it was finally taken off the book in 1779.

IV. THE DYNAMICS OF THE CRAZE

The spatial and temporal distribution of the craze is a matter of great interest. From the nucleus area around lake Siljan in Dalarna the trials spread north and north-east. The mining district in the southern parts of the province was completely spared, as was southern Sweden as a whole. Until 1675, when Uppland and Stockholm were also affected, the whole craze was restricted to the northern parts of the country (including Finland). Cases do not pop up randomly, or occur

---

[30] Ankarloo, *Trolldomsprocesserna*, pp. 210–11.

[31] Bengt Ankarloo, 'Häxprocesserna på Värmlandsnäs', *Värmland förr och nu* (Meddelanden från Värmlands museum; Karlstad, 1977), 65–8.

everywhere over the whole area. On the contrary they can be followed from province to province, at times even from farm to farm, in a clearly visible time/space pattern. Map 11.1 shows two cases of distribution in Dalarna during the early years. Judging from the rate and direction of the spread, it seems clear that the close communication between neighbours and villages played a decisive role.[32]

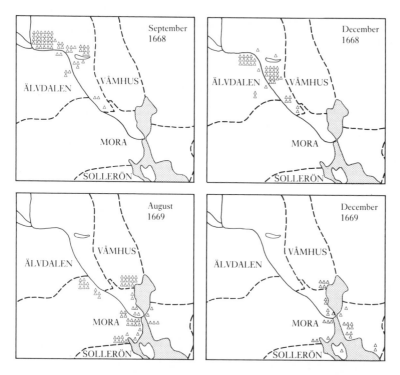

MAP 11.1. *Sweden: The spread of indictments north of Lake Siljan, 1668–9*

The spread of the craze has been compared to the epidemiology of the Black Death. This is clearly misleading. The plague took only a year to reach even the remotest areas. The witch-craze was still on the move after eight years. Another theoretical construct which comes to mind is that of an innovation process. But the message, whatever it

[32] Ankarloo, *Trolldomsprocesserna*, pp. 300–6.

contained, was not transmitted along the regular and most frequented highways, those leading southwards to the mining district and towards Stockholm. Instead, it went east and north through sparsely settled regions with few and small villages and with large forested areas between settlements. There did exist, however, a trade-route between southern Dalarna and the valley of Ljusnan in Häsingland, the first area outside Dalarna to be affected.[33] Why the craze should have followed a secondary rather than a primary channel of communication is hard to explain. But the routes of gossip are not necessarily those of trade and politics. And the messengers were not travelling merchants or bureaucrats, but the marginal members of the local communities, young people in search of work, poor children on the run, soldiers and their families on the move to and from the armies.

Later, there were professional witch-finders, mostly children, who could 'see', who travelled to Blåkulla and were paid for their services out of the parish coffers. Some bold lads exacted food and drink from people in return for not defaming them. This combination of begging and blackmail was mostly carried on by poor orphans. The authorities tried to stop this traffic, but it was kept going by the priests and the public. Like the general mobility among the poor, this mobility was enhanced by a succession of crop failures during the 1670s. The destitute made their way to the towns or headed south. Parents sent their children to relatives in Stockholm, or quite simply travelled there and abandoned them in the streets.

From autumn 1675, Sweden was at war with Denmark. The preparations, particularly for a naval expedition, attracted many people to Stockholm, where they helped to spread rumours. When the craze reached Finland and the Baltic provinces, Swedish soldiers and their families were most prominently involved.[34] It is impossible to say what could have followed further south if the disclosures in Stockholm had not put an end to the whole thing. Uppland, a southern-type, 'feudal' province, seemed prepared, in 1675, to take part in the craze. But whatever the reason, most of the south and central provinces remained unaffected during the eight years the craze lasted.

From the very beginning the children's tales and testimonies played an important, sometimes decisive, role in the court proceedings.[35] In

[33] Nils and Inga Friberg, *Om Dalarnas kommunikationer och handelsförbindelser i äldre tid* (Stockholm, 1975), 49–52.
[34] Ankarloo, *Trolldomsprocesserna*, pp. 309–10. See also the essay on Finland in this volume, ch. 12, below.   [35] Ankarloo, *Trolldomsprocesserna*, pp. 286–95.

Swedish legal tradition, persons below the age of 15 were not admitted as witnesses in court. Only by systematically disregarding this established practice was it possible to convict a large number of unrepentant suspects during the craze. This relaxation of important procedural rules mostly took place in the local courts, but it was silently accepted by the Court of Appeal and even by the government. There were some influential participants—a few priests and several jurists—who were opposed to the method, but they were long ignored.

The child witnesses were counted as fractions of adult, legitimate ones. A 5-year-old child may have been considered as one-tenth of a witness, a 14-year-old as at least half. By adding the fractions, the stipulated two whole witnesses were soon arrived at. It was not unusual for twenty, thirty, or forty children to give testimony against the same witch. By this mechanical method the burden of proof became heavy indeed. Many of the most active children successively transferred their charges to new suspects as the trials proceeded. A relatively small, but busy, group of children were responsible for most of the accusations. The others only followed suit. In one parish the 20 per cent of the child witnesses who were most active were responsible for about half of all charges. These boys and girls were the leaders and organizers among their peers, and they decided what suggestive details were to be given in the following day's proceedings ('we rode on a black cow', 'a brown horse', and so on). Those in favour of this procedure maintained that the innocent children were incapable of fraud and bad faith (*doli incapaces*). In fact, the proofs of veritable conspiracies are numerous.[36]

The co-ordination of the child testimonies was made possible in the wake-houses set up to protect the children. All those children who confessed to having been brought to Blåkulla by one or several witches were gathered here under the supervision of adults, and were kept awake with prayers and sermons. Only too late the courts became aware of the psychological pressure brought to bear on the witnesses through this dangerous practice. It explains the striking, but also very mechanical, similarities between the testimonies. Those who did not conform with the established pattern were excluded as 'liars'. There was no external control mechanism. The legal and ideological elements tended to confirm each other.

The children could, with relative impunity, give voice to what

[36] Ibid., pp. 249–56.

others could not or dared not say in the open. Since they were legally under age, they could not be punished for being in league with the devil. They were only victims, seduced by others. But also, in a social sense, they acted as proxies for the adult: they could take the risk of telling the almost impossible, the barely credible tales from Blåkulla. They were admitted in court merely to confirm all the suspicions of their elders. This role they shared with other marginal, 'irresponsible' elements—maidservants, soldiers, immigrant Finns.

Who, then, were the victims? Were they the enemies and adversaries of the accusers? An observer of the Stockholm trials called them 'a revolt of the maidservants' directed against their employers. This and other similar theories postulate a conflict between the parties involved. Indeed, the European witch-hunt as a whole has sometimes been interpreted as arising out of social tensions, more specifically, as an expression of inter-class conflict. If by this it is simply meant that the persecutions took place in a society where feudal exploitation led to antagonistic class relations, the statement is trivial. If, on the other hand, it is qualified to mean that the persecutions were a direct expression of such a conflict, it is indeed worth discussing and testing.

The presence of conflict is of course evident in the court records from the very beginning. Evil deeds are performed in secret, damage is inflicted on man and nature, and the culprit is eventually put to death in a justly harsh and painful way. But the question remains: who is in conflict with whom?

The evidence is ambiguous. Alan Macfarlane found the witchcraft accusations in Tudor England to be more often directed downwards in the social order. In a period of population increase and social differentiation, the better-off families could escape from their communal obligations towards the poor by accusing them of magical practices. The witches may, according to this view, be recognized with the aid of socio-economic criteria as poor, aggressive beggars or as unattached, unprotected vagrants. The accusations were used to get rid of these unwanted and potentially dangerous elements.[37]

Historians have been extremely careful when discussing the relative importance of the judiciary, the witnesses, and the accused themselves in the shaping of the records. The existence of interrogation manuals and torture chambers, and of a legal doctrine to justify their use, have on the whole made people tend to place not only the initiative but also

---

[37] Alan Macfarlane, *Witchcraft in Tudor and Stuart England* (London, 1970), 151.

all further proceedings in the hands of the judge. The persecutions were directed from the top down the social ladder. The inquisitorial process in itself leaves little room for intrusion from outside into the terrifying dialogue between the bench and the culprit. It is often hard to tell from the records if the witch was hated by the whole community, by only a few, or by nobody.

It has been demonstrated in several cases how inquisitors and court officials imposed their interpretations on the depositions of both witnesses and the accused. Carlo Ginzburg's *benandanti* were in the course of long inquisitions finally persuaded that their shamanistic travels to the realm of the dead had a quite different significance: they were looked upon as the equivalent of the witches' sabbath.[38] This is clearly a case of acculturation. But the shaping of the sabbath myth in itself has to be explicated. What conflicts and what anxieties did it give voice to? Robert Rowland interprets it, as we have seen, as 'the élite's symbolic representation of evil', that is, the diabolized theodicy of kings, nobles, and churchmen. The fierce struggle for power within the aristocracy during the late Middle Ages makes this hypothesis eminently plausible. It is also supported by the high incidence of aristocratic and even royal witch-trials in the fifteenth and sixteenth centuries.[39] This sabbath myth, created in the fourteenth and fifteenth centuries on one cultural level as an expression of intra-class tensions, was a century later imposed upon or transferred to another level, that of the common people. But does it even then have to be seen as a weapon in the class struggle?

To decide whether the conflicts behind the witch persecutions were primarily to be found between or within classes, some scholars have tried to sort out the popular from the learned elements in witchcraft ideology.[40] Was the whole thing a conspiracy between a reactionary church and a corrupted state? Were the ideas of theologians and jurists imposed upon an ignorant but innocent peasantry? This was the interpretation of the Enlightenment philosophers. Or was the European demonology of the early modern era the result of a dialectic interaction between different cultural levels, a syncretist fusion of folklore and learned ideas? The latter would probably be a more acceptable explanation today. It means, however, that the content of

---

[38] Ginzburg, ch. 4, above.
[39] Rowland, ch. 6, above; Richard Kieckhefer, *European Witch Trials* (Berkeley and Los Angeles, 1976), 1–26.
[40] Kieckhefer, *European Witch Trials*.

the accusations will be hard to interpret in class terms. A way of getting around this problem would be to look, instead, for the participation of the common people in the trials, as witnesses, as members of the jury or the audience, as a crowd outside the court-house, and, of course, at the place of execution.[41]

The penal procedure in Swedish courts of law was still in the early seventeenth century relatively free from the harsh inquisitorial elements of Continental law, at least at the local level. A relatively passive attitude from the bench left room for a more extensive inter-action between commoners. In other words, there were fewer institu-tional obstacles to a public display of intra-class conflict, if such should happen to arise. And it did. The Swedish evidence is fairly extensive. I shall confine myself to presenting only a few cases from each of three categories: the scattered, single trials in the countryside from the last third of the sixteenth century up to about 1650; the great witch-hunt in the 1670s; evidence from members of the ruling class about their awareness of aggressive attitudes among the common people.

To start with, let us try to establish the incidence of active peasant involvement in the accusations. The depositions of the jury in some cases confirmed the opinion of the plaintiffs. This jury, selected for a year at a time from among the local farmers of some repute, clearly represented local sentiments. A typical case of this kind would involve a peasant accusing his neighbour's wife of causing his cows to run dry. His allegations are supported by a number of other villagers with similar experiences. Sometimes the accused can persaude eleven other persons to join him in a formal oath of non-guilt. Then he is duly acquitted. At other times he cannot, and is convicted. The outcome in such cases is almost totally dependent on local opinion about the suspect. The whole situation is similar to that of a conflict in a simple society in the anthropological sense. And such cases constitute in fact the great majority in this early phase.

A step further from this pattern is the case where a few accusations are combined with the silent withdrawal of local support from kin and neighbours, and when a majority of the community takes an active part in demanding legal reprisals. In 1611 a sheriff from a southern province reported on a trial in his district, stating that 'since at that

---

[41] Bengt Ankarloo, 'Das Geschrei der ungebildeten Masse. Zur Analyse der schwedischen Hexenprozesse', in Christian Degn, Hartmut Lehmann, and Dagmar Unverhau (eds.), *Hexenprozesse* (Neumünster, 1983), 172–8.

time we were at war [the Calmar war 1611–13 with Denmark] nobody was willing to vouch for her, nor could she be kept in the county jail. But I could not let her go without punishment, since the whole county called for revenge upon her.' Instead, and with some support from the district governor, he resorted, quite illegally, to torture. There is no direct evidence of local support for this drastic step, but twelve farmers' wives were present as witnesses during the search for the devil's mark and the torture. As the sheriff was afterwards obliged to defend his actions, he did so by referring to local pressure: 'and all, the vicars as well as the jurymen and the whole county have cried in unison, demanding that such an evil body should be put to death'. In a similar case, where an extended jury of twenty-four farmers had sentenced a male witch to death, the court record adds that 'every man in the parish stood up and demanded with one voice that he should be put to death.'

It may be useful here to introduce a distinction made in social theory between realistic and non-realistic conflicts. The former type of conflict is a means to an end, for example, to make cows give milk again. The methods of conflict-resolution are optional, ranging from peaceful negotiation to naked violence. The object of the conflict and the person of the adversary cannot be substituted. In non-realistic conflicts there is no discernible end but the conflict itself. It is expressive rather than instrumental. It cannot be solved in non-violent terms, but both the object of conflict and the enemy can be replaced. Any witch, or any Jew, will do.

These concepts as historical categories clearly present some problems. What to us seems to be a highly unrealistic perception of physical causation, for instance, the role of magic in crop-failure or disease, was to most people of the sixteenth century quite realistic. They acted on the reasonable assumption that the litigation they entered into would solve the problem. Bringing a witch to court after a crisis must be considered a culturally realistic way of conflict-resolution. This ambiguity in the contemporary and historical perception of reality and its importance for the interpretation of antagonism at different times cannot be ignored.

Again, nothing is as simple as the theoretical categories lead us to believe. Quite obviously the accusations during the great persecutions in the 1670s, especially those coming from the children, had several non-realistic traits, even for their times. The victims were to a great extent interchangeable, the methods and content of the accusations were not. But even here, realistic elements enter the conflict, especially when the parents act on behalf of their allegedly or visibly tormented children. At the very beginning of the troubles in Dalarna, the local bailiff reported that 'he had been asked by the elders of the parish as well as the vicar and the county sheriff to start the procedures, since the county judge could not come', and in the summer of 1669, when the same bailiff was collecting taxes from the Mora farmers, he was approached 'by the parents of the transvected children, who were in great anxiety and lamentation, humbly and sadly complaining that their tender, helpless and simple children are being seduced by the old witches to submit to the power of Satan . . . and that they want all this to come to the attention of the authorities, and with all due respect they demand, that if the old ones are not exterminated, it is to be feared, that all this will go further than anyone can believe'. Later, numerous equally humble but very specific demands reached the government in Stockholm from the parishes in newly infested areas further north.

In fact, the commissioners sent out to pass royal sentence on the witches can be seen as the very reluctant response of the authorities to urgent demands from below. This was clearly perceived by the parish men of Mora, as they convened a few weeks after the execution of sixteen witches in their midst. Many of those who were spared on that occasion were still riding to the sabbath bringing children with them. The parish could do nothing 'except arresting them, hoping that they mend their ways, or else that the authorities again will lend us their hand . . . We must have patience and rest content with the actions and sentences of the royal commission.'

The reluctance of the government was based both on intellectual doubts and previous experience, both in Sweden and abroad. This cautious attitude from members of the ruling class also led to criticism from below. One commissioner, who was more willing than some of his colleagues to meet the demands of local opinion, remarked after a sentence where some witches had been spared, that 'here is going to be much quarrels and complaints after us, since we have been far too lenient and indulgent.' The sceptical parson of Gävle, a lone and despised figure, was said to have 'bragged about having in his sermons somewhat coolled down the common opinion held by the *vulgus*, so that they now are less credulous of the rumours'. And when Johan Stiernhöök, the leading jurist of his times, gave some fatherly advice to his son, who had been appointed president of the Uppland com-

mission, he warned him about the difficulties in 'finding a tempera-
ment between your own conscience and the cries of the rude
multitude: take away, crucify!'

The physical and spiritual well-being of the many transvected
children seems to have been the main concern of the excited public
opinion. In this sense the craze was but a continuation of the conflicts
of the earlier trials. The emergence of strong inquisitorial elements in
the procedure during the great hunt in the 1670s meant, from our point
of view, that the common people were deprived, to some extent, of
their traditional rights to use the legal system as a means of intra-class
conflict-resolution, regardless of whether such conflicts were realistic
or not. This in turn may have had an influence on the ideology of
witchcraft, encouraging a transition from physical manipulations
centred around the concept of *maleficium* to spiritual transgressions as
defined by Christian demonologists.

How can we explain these observations of strong pressure from
below in the Swedish witch persecutions up to, and including, the
great craze in the 1670s? In his elaboration and reformulation of
George Simmel's interesting work on the nature of human conflict,
Der Kampf, Lewis Coser points out that antagonism is usually an
element in intimate relations. Since these involve much interaction
and the whole personality of the participants, such relations can be
said to contain a strong element of ambivalence in their motivational
structure. A conflict arising out of such deep and deeply felt similarities between the parties tends to be stronger and more violent than
conflicts between strangers. 'Aggression like charity begins at home',
as Malinowski has remarked. In a closely knit group, one party will
hate the other so much more intensely as the conflict is perceived to
constitute a threat to the unity and identity of the group. In this sense
intensive conflict and group loyalty are sides of the same coin.[42]

To say this is not to underestimate the role of class conflict, even in
the history of witchcraft. But it is structural rather than associated with
action. Obviously the legal system worked to the disadvantage of the
poor and the outcast. The learned concepts of theology and law were
imposed on the people so that their conflicts were reinterpreted in
more dangerous categories. But this reinterpretation was hardly used,
as it were, to terrorize the peasantry and prevent them from realizing
where the real issues lay. At most the sceptical aristocrats can be

[42] Ankarloo, 'Das Geschrei der ungebildeten Masse . . .', p. 178.

criticized for their cruel indifference. In 1675 the Counts de la Gardie took the French ambassador de Feuquières to one of the wake-houses set up in Stockholm for the supervision of the transvected children. Having seen the little girls falling in trance, he reported coolly in a letter to his king that 'j'ai vu quelquefois cette petite comédie, que j'ai trouvée au moins fort bien jouée.'[43] He was moving in circles where people had grave doubts or were open disbelievers. Still they did not bother to stop the court procedures, but looked upon them as an amusing spectacle.

Very little in the behaviour of the children during the craze indicates that they were involved in realistic conflicts of any kind. The objects of their accusations seem interchangeable. Only the content is always and monotonously the same. But even if there is scant evidence of individual conflicts between the children and the witches, aggression may in this way be expressed against the latter as a group: of mother-figures, of sexual rivals, of old hags, or of demanding employers, whatever it may be. We shall probably never know. It is, however, possible to ascertain some of the social characteristics of the accused witches.[44]

Men comprised in all less than 15 per cent, with locally significant variations. Almost half of these belonged to the youngest age-group (15–24). Many were members of the youthful gangs of accusers, but since they were over 15 they ran the risk of being convicted. Old male witches often belonged to families with a bad reputation. Their wives, sisters, or daughters were also accused. Out of 116 men brought to trial during the craze, only six (or about 5 per cent) were executed. Among the women, almost 15 per cent went to the block. This bias was strong already in the testimonies, but it was further enhanced in the courts: the judges were more reluctant to pass a sentence of capital punishment against a man. In Mora, an old man, pointed out by a great number of children as the most prominent leader in Blåkulla, was lashed and then released.

The age distribution and family status of the accused and convicted women is shown in Table 11.1. The accusations are more often directed against older women. They are also more severely treated in court. Family status seems to be a rather weak index, but in court married women were better protected than widows. The overall impression is that age was the strongest single factor among those

[43] [Jean de Feuquières], *Lettres inédites de Feuquières*, iii (Paris, 1846), 475.
[44] Ankarloo, *Trolldomsprocesserna*, pp. 263–86.

TABLE 11.1. *Age distribution and family status of Swedish witches, 1668–1676* *(%) (N = 740)*

	Total female population	Accused witches	Executed witches
Age 15–44	62	36	31
45–	38	53	57
unknown	—	11	12
Unmarried	35	32	32
Married	50	49	43
Widowed	15	19	25

accused and convicted of witchcraft, and secondly, that widowed women ran a somewhat greater risk, but that otherwise the witches represented a fairly normal cross-section of the female community as far as family status is concerned.

An assumption made by those who have tried to interpret the persecutions in conflict terms has been that the witches could be recognized, with the aid of socio-economic criteria, as poor, aggressive beggars, or as unattached and unprotected vagrants. In both cases accusations and trials were the methods used by the stable, more affluent population to get rid of unwanted and potentially dangerous elements. This may very will have been true in Essex, England or in Rogaland, Norway, where observations have been made to support such a view.[45] However, in Mora, out of sixty persons brought before the Royal witch court in August 1669, all but one, a 70-year-old widow, can be found in the parish registers and the church records as regular members of the community. Most had probably lived there all their lives. Only one, a 60-year-old, unmarried women, lived by herself. All the others were members of households ranging in size from 2 to 13 persons (average household size was 6.3 and median size 6). All these witch households can also be found in the tax records, where the area under cultivation, the harvest, and the tithe is assessed. The poverty or relative affluence of the accused witches can be compared to the general level in Mora, as shown in Table 11.2.

[45] Macfarlane, *Witchcraft*, pp. 172–6; Naess's essay on Norway, ch. 14, below.

TABLE 11.2. *Mora witches: Distribution of households by acreage under cultivation and units of tithe (%)*

	All households (N = 777)	Witch households (N = 59)
Acres		
1–10	65	45
11–20	28	46
21–30	4	5
31–	3	4
Tithe		
1–25	71	62
26–50	21	28
51–75	6	7
76–	2	3

Source: Bengt Ankarloo, *Trolldomsprocesserna i Sverige* (Lund, 1971), 285.

Again, all but one witch lived in households with landed property and which paid tithe from out of the harvest. A majority belonged in fact to the middling or more affluent groups. Of course, that does not mean much in a society where all but a few lived under hard pressures. But there is no support whatever for the theory that the witches were living on the margin of or even outside the community. They were right in the middle of it.

So the hard facts from church and tax records refuse to give evidence on particular or well-defined groups of witches. On the contrary, the witches seem average on most counts. And yet, some were singled out, accused, and convicted. In the early trials in Älvdalen and Mora more than half of those accused, but also many of the child witnesses, belonged to a limited group of families. The judge was quite conscious of this and illustrated his records with a number of family trees of the kind commonly used in connection with intestate succession and other cases of family law. Clan feuds may naturally have contributed to this. But in fact accusations within families were just as common as between them. Numerous little girls gave evidence against their grandmothers, mothers, and older sisters.

Another way to reveal the secrets of the witches has recently been tried by scholars devoting themselves to a close and careful reading of the confessions and accusations. The hermeneutics of the court records have become the domain of social anthropologists and ethnologists with an interest in the past. Their contributions are thought-provoking and, indeed, promising. Historians and jurists on the other hand have long taken a rather sceptical position in their assessment of the legal source-material as expressing popular beliefs. What is handed down in court rolls, official reports, and learned books by distinguished lawyers and theologians can at best be popular beliefs in a highly distorted and misleading form. Much was confessed under torture and with the aid of prefabricated lists of interrogations.

There is often an implicit assumption behind this kind of careful criticism: the cultural gap between the ruling classes and the peasant majority was great and growing in the seventeenth century. In its most extreme form, this school of thought interpreted the witch persecutions as a uniquely European conspiracy between the Church and greedy bureaucrats, with no ideological foundation whatsoever in the popular mind. That, of course, is a highly unreasonable position.

On the other hand, some students of witchcraft have tended to over-emphasize the universal character of it. There is no basic difference between Blind Anna in Mora in 1668, a Sioux witch in Dakota in 1868, another in Trobriand Islands in the 1920s, or in east Africa in 1955. True, in all cases there may be people who are subjectively convinced that they themselves are witches and go through the motions of being one: mixing herbs and bones, chanting curses, and making secret signs. In all cases too, the societies around these witches may be convinced that their activities are real and dangerous, and therefore apprehend and punish them for it. But Blind Anna in Mora was executed by the servants of a highly centralized, bureaucratic government. The legal and ideological justification for her fate was formulated not only by her angry neighbours, but by a universal church and an international community of scholars.

The children's tales about Blåkulla, as recorded in the court rolls, are as close to the source as we can reasonably expect. Even they contain legal expressions and traces from a learned terminology indicating that their information has immediately been interpreted by the judge or the scribe. In the comprehensive accounts in official reports this distortion has been brought a step further. The interpretation of witchcraft as a crime, not only against an individual, but against the whole social and spiritual order, is another contribution from above.

Compacts with the devil and transvection of children are the most common charges. *Maleficium*, so important in earlier trials, is edged into the background or given new implications. The witches take the children in Blåkulla riding on brooms, animals, or even people.[46] The idea of mounting a naked sheriff or reverend was of course amusing to most villagers. In Blåkulla the broom, goat, or sheriff is placed outside the house, head-down against the wall. Blåkulla, as described by the children, is a reflection of the surrounding reality. It is built up with the aid of bits and pieces from the everyday life of the village. Most of the features are not only reflections, they are truly mirror images, dichotomous transformations: one eats with the back of the neck; holds things with the left hand; copulates back to back; and gives birth from the anus, 'but it does not hurt'.

The meaning of these everyday but back-to-front activities is scarcely evil. On the contrary. Blåkulla is depicted at this stage as pleasant, a light, decorated dining-hall, a marriage feast with lots of food: milk, porridge, and sweet white bread. It is only the religious customs there which, when transformed, acquire sinister implications. The dichotomy becomes a perversion: rejection of God, compact with Satan, baptism and being entered in the black book, prayers of damnation ('Our Father which art in Hell'). But apart from this intrusion from the holy sphere, Blåkulla left to itself functions in a pleasant, friendly manner. However, she who breaks the agreement with the devil (for instance, by confessing in court) is subjected to mistreatment: her food is turned into toads and mire, the dining-hall becomes cold, dark, and painful. Satan, who first appeared as a friendly, bearded man, suddenly becomes hairy, with horns and tail, nakedly diabolical. Snakes are woven into lashes to be used on those who confess and denounce. Some witches appear as crows, ravens, or other black birds. The traitors are flayed alive and their hides are put on spikes on the wall, or filled with air and light, so that they can be seen occupying the top seat at the banquet like empty ghosts, 'luminescent'.

The social distinctions are very strong. Beginners are not even admitted to the feast, but must remain in the doorway. The old hags openly compete for the favours of Satan. When they start fighting he is

---

[46] Ankarloo, *Trolldomsprocesserna*, pp. 217–31.

pleased and laughs. The rank order along the table is a matter of dispute. Among the humans there are leaders, sometimes called king and queen, sometimes priest. Most people play their ordinary roles: making shoes, cooking, milking, and churning. Some, especially the older, are given strange and degrading tasks. The old women are placed upside-down on the table and burning candles are inserted into their orifices. The records refer to this in discreet Latin 'fuit candelabrum'. But horror, too, has it bounds. Blåkulla is not Hell. Hell lies in the nether regions. The evil, menacing devil is sometimes chained under the table. White angels step in to protect the tormented children. They are, in fact, living next door, in the Angels' Chamber.

All these things appear simultaneously. Good and evil are mixed together, to be experienced differently by different witnesses. And in this unstable, chaotic universe the struggle between Good and Evil is manifested by the white angels coming to defend the children, the innocents. Clearly eschatological concepts are connected with this graphic confrontation between light and dark.

Traditional *maleficium* plays a minor role. There is, however, a tendency to interpret the transvection or seduction of children as a dangerous *maleficium*. It is not so much the tender body as the immortal soul which is endangered by the journeys. This terminological confusion would appear to be intentional on the part of the courts, as is also the case for the variety of *maleficium* called *taciturnitas*. It usually meant a witch's ability to withstand torture without confessing. The devil helped his adherents at their own request. Denial in the Swedish trials is compulsory: the devil silences the victim by gripping her throat or blocking her mouth. She is irretrievably in his power. This is why towards the end the old condition of personal confession before being put to death is reversed: she who confesses, there is still hope for. She can be spared. She who denies is forever lost, and should be removed.

The Blåkulla lore thus gives voice to aggression in several contexts: against the Church and the Christian order, against the adult world with its social distinctions, against competition especially among women, against sexuality. But the conflict of the witch-hunt is not easily described as one between high and low, between poor and affluent, not even on the local level. It still remains to be proved that the majority of accusations were directed from the top down. On the other hand, it is beyond any doubt that in Sweden, as in most other European countries, the great majority of those accused of witchcraft were women rather than men. The proportions were approximately 5 to 1.[47] The stereotype witch of medieval laws, learned tracts, and popular lore was always a woman. An interpretation in terms of a conflict between the sexes seems therefore highly appropriate. To serve such a purpose, the picture of the witch must be other than that of the class-conflict school: she was not an old, poor, outcast hag, but a younger, brighter, and more active woman, a real threat to male supremacy in the peasant community. It goes almost without saying that for this generalization it is even harder to find support in the source-material. But it raises the interesting and relevant question, whether there were in the early modern centuries any significant changes in the status and cultural role of European women.

In a thoughtful essay, Christina Larner has suggested a number of interlocking processes that converged to create a picture of women as disorderly and threatening to patriarchal order.[48] In the legal and criminal context, woman gained more independence after the Middle Ages: she was more and more held personally responsible for her actions and therefore for her crimes, and at the same time a number of specific female actions such as prostitution and infanticide were criminalized. She could gradually resort to conflict-behaviour, and cursing and bewitching was the female equivalent of the direct physical violence prevalent among males. In addition there may have been a surplus female population in an era when men led more dangerous lives. This hypothesis is strongly substantiated by the conditions in Dalarna during the great hunt. The moral independence of women, as expressed in the religious sphere, was linked to a greater female responsibility for the transmission of cosmological and other transcendental elements of popular culture. During the great hunt in Dalarna, a public school system was suggested as a substitute for the demoralizing influence by women on the children. Furthermore, the sex ratio was highly unbalanced. The Continental wars had greatly reduced the number of adult men. In Mora in 1668 there were 2,100 women per 1,000 men in the age-range 15–45; so more than half of them went unmarried.[49]

The world of God and men was thus set in opposition to a realm

[47] Ankarloo, *Trolldomsprocesserna*, p. 269; Naess, ch. 14, below; Christina Larner, 'Witchcraft Past and Present', in *Witchcraft and Religion: The Politics of Popular Belief* (Oxford, 1984), 85.

[48] Larner, *Witchcraft and Religion*, pp. 84–8.

[49] Ankarloo, *Trolldomsprocesserna*, p. 270: Nils Friberg, 'Dalarnas befolkning på 1600-talet', *Geografiska annaler*, 35 (1953), 388–9.

where Satan and women ruled.[50] Some of the old hags who had confessed, and who were asked if they did not realize the enormity of their crimes, replied that they did not think much of it. The men in the farm community were ambiguous. They had little to do with the women's dreams of free feasts, a free sexuality, and the superhuman freedom of flying through the air. Their concern was for the children. Were they to be brought up according to the rules of God and a Christian lord, or by the devil and flying women? When freedom and constraint were expressed in female terms, the men joined forces with the authorities, secular and ecclesiastical. And the women were the rivals of each other.

[50] Cf. the interpretation of Stuart Clark, 'Inversion, Misrule and the Meaning of Witchcraft', *Past and Present*, 87 (1980), 98–127.

ENDNOTE

A. A report of the Mora trials written by the parish vicar Elaus Skragge was printed in Dutch in the following year: *Translaet uyt het Sweets; Zijnde getrocken uyt het Prothocol...over de examinatie de ontdeckte Toveryen in het Dorp Mohra ...* (s'-Gravenhage, 1670); from the Dutch version it was translated into German: *Ausfürliche Bericht von dem entdeckten grausamen Zauberei in dem Dorffe Mohra und umbliegenden Plätzen in Schweden* (1670); it was reprinted in *Diarium Europaeum*, xx (Frankfurt am Main, 1670), *Theatrum Europaeum*, x (1677), and in Heppel's *Relationes Curiosae*, v (Hamburg, 1691). An English translation, also from the Dutch version, was made by E. Horneck, *An Account of what happened in Sweden*. It was printed with the 1683 and numerous later editions of Glanvil's famous *Sadducismus Triumphatus*. In Scotland, George Sinclair used it in his *Satan's Invisible World Discovered* (Edinburgh, 1685), and in America, Cotton Mather included it in his *Memorable Providences Related to Witchcraft and Possessions* (Boston, 1689). The English version was used by Balthazar Bekker in his celebrated *De Betoverde Weereld* (Amsterdam, 1691), (the Account is in pt. iv, ch. 29). With Bekker's book it was again translated into several languages, German in 1693, French in 1694, and English in 1695.

Already in the first Dutch edition the facts about the Mora trials were distorted and grossly exaggerated. The number of those burnt alive was said to be 84 adults and 15 children (rather than 17 adults beheaded and then burnt). Even in modern, 'scholarly' works the Account in quoted as the plain truth, e.g. Rossell Hope Robbins, *The Encyclopaedia of Witchcraft and Demonology* (London, 1959), 348.

12

*Finland: The Male Domination**

ANTERO HEIKKINEN AND TIMO KERVINEN

IN the sixteenth and seventeenth centuries Finland made up the eastern part of the kingdom of Sweden. Its population of about 300,000 to 400,000 persons was concentrated in southern and south-western Finland and along the coast. Farming was the main means of living. In the south and along the coast corn was cultivated in fields, elsewhere slash-and-burn agriculture predominated. With the exception of Turku and Viipuri, Finnish towns remained very small, partly due to strict mercantilist legislation which limited the activities of most towns, especially from the beginning of the seventeenth century. Only a few, such as Turku, were allowed to engage in foreign trade. Other towns had to export their products through them, or through Stockholm.

The staple export commodity was tar. In the seventeenth century, Finland became the most important tar-producing region in the Baltic. Tar was burnt primarily in Ostrobothnia, which traded with Stockholm and south-eastern Finland. In the seventeenth century, the south had lively trade connections with the other Swedish provinces around the Baltic.[1]

I. PERIODS OF WITCH-TRIALS[2]

From 1520 to 1699, 710 cases of people being accused of sorcery and witchcraft are known in Finland.[3] Since the archives of the Turku

---

* Sections I–IV were written by Timo Kervinen, the rest by Antero Heikkinen.

[1] Eino Jutikkala and Kauko Pirinen, *A History of Finland* (New York, 1962).

[2] This section is a summary of Timo Kervinen, 'Noituus—aikansa rikos' (Witchcraft as the Crime of the Time), unpublished MS (Faculty of Law, Helsinki University, 1983), produced as part of a larger project, 'Aikansa rikos' (The Crime of the Time).

[3] It is hard to make a sharp distinction between witchcraft, sorcery, fortune-telling, and healing in Finland. The courts were not interested in such categories, but rather in the difference between 'natural' and 'unnatural' healing.

Court of Appeal were destroyed in a fire, research in Finland must
necessarily be based on the records of the lower courts. Considering
that some of these records also are lost, the number of people charged
with witchcraft in the secular courts during the period can be
estimated to be over a thousand. Table 12.1, which gives the number of
those accused and of death sentences passed, provides therefore at
best only the minimum number for each period.

From the available sources, we can estimate that from the middle of
the sixteenth century up to 1640 Finnish courts dealt with two or three
accusations for witchcraft per year. In the 1640s more attention was
paid to the crime, and the number of accused persons began to rise.
The first to be brought before the court were professional sorcerers
and their customers. Sentences became increasingly severe and the
number of death sentences rose. The courts passed most of their
sentences in accordance with the National Code (*c*.1350), in which
only fatal *maleficium* was considered a capital offence. In the 1650s,
however, this policy changed. The Court of Appeal sometimes
reversed the sentences passed by lower courts and made them more
severe, even if no deaths by witchcraft were involved. A similar trend
has been observed also in Sweden during the 1650s.[4]

In the next decade the number of accused per trial increased even
more, and death sentences became fairly common. This indicates that
the lower courts had learnt to conform to the harsher practice introduced by the Court of Appeal: in clear-cut cases they passed their
sentences according to God's law rather than the lenient National
Code. In addition, the power to mitigate death sentences belonged
exclusively to the Court of Appeal or the king himself. Charges of
diabolism became more common, which also contributed towards
increasing the number of death sentences.

In the 1670s Finland experienced a witch-hunt which reached its
peak in 1675–6. During the decade, at least 157 witches were accused
in the lower courts, forty-one of which were sentenced to death. In
fact, the number of accused must have exceeded 200, and so the difference when compared to previous decades becomes even more
pronounced than that indicated in Table 12.1.

By the 1680s the hunt had started to subside. Even if the number of
accused was still high by Finnish standards, the decline is seen from
the fact that the number of death sentences dropped sharply.

---

[4] See Bengt Ankarloo, ch. 11, above.

TABLE 12.1. *Number of people accused of sorcery and witchcraft in Finnish Courts and number of death sentences passed, 1520–1699*

Decade	Accused	Death sentences
1520–9	1	—
1530–9	—	—
1540–9	8	—
1550–9	12	1
1560–9	16	4
1570–9	22	3
1580–9	15	2
1590–9	8	1
1600–9	7	2
1610–19	6	—
1620–9	22	3
1630–9	27	2
1640–9	66	11
1650–9	73	10
1660–9	87	25
1670–9	157	41
1680–9	121	9
1690–9	62	1
Total	710	115

During the last decade of the seventeenth century the number of charges decreased considerably, and the accused were usually no longer found guilty of harmful witchcraft but only of sorcery and superstition.

II. THE ACCUSED

Contrary to the west European rule, witchcraft in Finland was not primarily associated with the female sex. Out of 641 known people accused, only 325, or 50.7 per cent, were women. Out of the 277 convicted whose sex is known, 133, or 48 per cent, were male.

Considerable variations in time and locality existed in the sex distribution of the accused and convicted. As late as the sixteenth century, 60 per cent of the accused and 75 per cent of those found guilty were men, but as soon as the number of trials went up, the percentage of women started to increase, surpassing that of men in the 1650s.

In the 1660s, 53 per cent of the accused and nearly 58 per cent of the condemned were women, and when persecutions reached their peak in the 1670s, 59 per cent of the accused and almost 64 per cent of the convicted were female. As soon as the culmination of the witch-hunt had passed, the percentage of women began to decrease, and in the 1690s men dominated again in both categories.

When comparing the different parts of the country we see that the percentage of women was highest in Österbotten (Ostrobothnia), whereas those brought to trial in Karelen were nearly always men. Not even in Österbotten was witchcraft originally associated with women. In the sixteenth century, those sentenced to death in this area were almost without exception men.

There is a pattern in the way the incidence of female witchcraft fluctuated. The number of women tends to increase the longer the witch-hunt in a given area lasts. The longer the traditions of persecution, the higher the percentage of women. By the 1670s, Österbotten had almost a century of tradition in witch-hunting, whereas in Karelen trials had been conducted for only twenty years. The impact of the witch-doctrine on the sex of the accused was also clear. In cases where diabolism was among the charges, the number of women was consistently higher than in trials concerning traditional magic. In Österbotten there were diabolic trials and female witches, whereas in Karelen the accused were local professional sorcerers.

In sixteenth-century Finland, the stereotype sorcerer was a man. This is probably due to Finnish folk traditions and the ancient Finnish religion, in which supernatural powers were not associated with women but with men. It is probable that the modern European witch-doctrine broke down this stereotype, and people in Finland finally accepted the idea that witches were women. This learning process started on the west coast and began to work its way slowly inland. In Karelen, however, the female witch never replaced the male sorcerer.

III. THE TRIALS

The majority of the charges were for traditional magic, less frequently for diabolism. In fact, the first genuine witch persecutions were conducted as late as the 1650s, although indications of the influence of the witch-doctrine can be found in some earlier trials where professional sorcerers stood accused.

In a typical trial there was only one, at the most two or three accused, and mass trials involving dozens of accused never took place. The procedure was mainly accusatorial. The plaintiff was normally a private person, who claimed that the defendant had caused him or his property some harm. However, certain inquisitorial elements were also present. Denunciations made by accomplices were admitted, and charges could also be made on the basis of a rumour or the bad reputation of the accused. On the other hand, in every third case the trial was initiated by the alleged witch in an attempt to clear himself. The Church may have refused to admit the suspect to the Communion, he may have been called a witch, or a rumour to that effect may have spread so much that it damaged his reputation—a matter then of great importance to people.

The plaintiff and the defendant were on the whole equal parties in the process, and the former was required to prove his case or be condemned to fines. This cooled down people's eagerness to start accusing each other too easily. There were no professional witch-hunters, except for a few self-made amateurs, and accusations made by children, as in Sweden, were not significant.

It seems that everywhere the first people to be accused were professional sorcerers and those who had a reputation for magical activities. The accusations were often preceded by a conflict between the accuser and the accused, and its disclosure played an important role in the actual trial. After all, a motive for an act of *maleficium* had to be established.

A study of the objectives of the acts of witchcraft performed between 1600 and 1649 indicates that most were associated with foodstuff and cattle. By contrast, witchcraft rarely had anything to do with traditional agriculture or hunting. Black magic was used as an explanation for individual bad luck, whereas white magic was used for improving one's lot. Accidents that affected the whole community were not understood as witchcraft, but rather as the result of divine providence.

The second largest category of maleficent objectives were concerned with health. A victim of witchcraft or his relative accused the witch of having caused his illness. If the parties to a conflict did not possess the powers to bewitch the enemy, these services were bought from a travelling professional. Often those from whom things had been stolen turned to a sorcerer in order to find the stolen goods and to revenge themselves upon the thief.

Not all the accused were found guilty. In the lower courts, at least 283 out of 710, or 40 per cent, were released. Taking into account the trials whose final outcome is not known, we can estimate that more than half of those examined were released at any given time. Although the punishments, as we have seen, tended to be harsher after the mid-seventeenth century, the overall percentage of acquittals did not decrease as the persecutions were intensified.

During the period under review, at least 115 death sentences for witchcraft were passed in Finland. More than half of these belong to the 1660s and 1670s. The death sentences for witchcraft were normally not mitigated in the sixteenth century, even though at the time this was not uncommon for other acts of homicide. After the foundation, in the 1620s, of the Turku Court of Appeal, the reduction of punishment was the privilege of this court. Due to the destruction of the archives in Turku, it has not been possible to determine the extent of these reductions, but we know that about sixty death sentences were carried out.

At least 20 per cent of the defendants were condemned to pay fines, but if the condemned person lacked money he was flogged instead. Imprisonment became more common in the late seventeenth century, but the Court of Appeal seems to have favoured flogging. Some witches appear to have got away with only church penitence, which was also regularly added to other non-capital punishments.

IV. THE REGIONAL INCIDENCE

In the sixteenth century the witch-trials in Finland were concentrated on the west coast, in northern Österbotten, Satakunta, and Varsinais-Suomi (Map 12.1). Some accusations were also brought up along the trade-route from Satakunta to Savo. The incidence of charges decreased considerably further inland. On the coast the greatest number of trials took place in the vicinity of the ports.

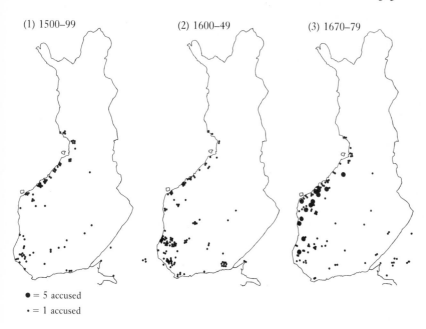

(1) 1500–99   (2) 1600–49   (3) 1670–79

● = 5 accused
• = 1 accused

MAP 12.1. *Number of accused in the known trials in Finland, 1500–1679*

The number of trials was not proportionate to the size of population. Österbotten in particular was clearly over-represented, even more so when considering the number of death sentences. Charges of witchcraft were made in the prosperous areas where cattle were abundant and the farmers were involved in a flourishing export trade. Economic specialization had already started here, and the relative differences in wealth were more pronounced than elsewhere in Finland. In the inland settlements, where people had a subsistence economy and the community had not undergone the same kind of changes, very few charges of witchcraft were made.

In the period between 1600 and 1649, most accusations were still made in the same districts as in the previous century, but the incidence of charges is higher, especially in Varsinais-Suomi and Satakunta. This is partly due to a sharp increase in accusations made against professional sorcerers, particularly in the areas where the new kinds of economic activities flourished. Regionally, accusations turn out to be a very stable phenomenon. The main areas of persecutions did not change in the 1650s and 1660s, except for a slight movement to the east in the southern parts of Finland.

Not even a marked growth in intensity during the 1670s could cause any significant change in this regional pattern. The organized witch-hunt took place primarily in the old areas, where persecutions had century-old traditions.

V. THE GREAT PERSECUTIONS

The seventeenth-century witch persecutions in Finland may be divided into three fairly distinct periods. Demonic magic (involving a compact with the devil to obtain wealth) clearly dominates the trials from the 1640s to the 1660s. For the next decade and a half the trials were mainly for witchcraft proper. Witch-hunts are limited to this period. At the end of the century, attitudes towards witchcraft had become very sceptical.

VI. THE TURKU TRIALS

The spread of Continental ideas about witchcraft was furthered by the founding, in 1640, of Finland's first university, the Turku Academy. Although it remained very small, it brought the Finnish educated classes, for better and for worse, into closer touch with Europe's spiritual life. As early as the 1640s two dissertations were published at the Turku Academy dealing with natural magic, and also discussing compacts with the devil.[5]

There was also a trial at the Academy in the 1640s, during which the consistory actually passed a death sentence for a compact with the devil. The main figures in this trial were professors and students, among them Martin Stodius, professor of Greek and Hebrew in 1640 and of theology in 1654. Stodius, who was born in Turku, had studied at Wittenberg in the 1620s and was interested in the literature of magic. He was denounced in 1644 for having taught diabolic acts to a

---

[5] Antero Heikkinen, *Paholaisen Liittolaiset: Noita- ja magiakäsityksiä ja -oikeudenkäyntejä Suomessa 1600-luvun jälkipuolella (n. 1640–1712)* (Allies of the Devil: Notions and Trials of Witchcraft and Demonic Magic in late Seventeenth-century Finland, *c.*1640–1712) (Helsinki, 1969), 78–9.

student, who went mad. Stodius denied the charge and was acquitted
by the consistory. But rumours firmly stuck to him, and in 1658 he was
forced to leave the Academy. To placate the Chancellor his departure
was camouflaged as a voluntary transfer to the position of vicar in
Naantali. Stodius's exile was instigated by J. E. Terserus, bishop of
Turku and Vice-Chancellor of the Academy. Terserus was a steadfast
theologian who had no intention of tolerating the practice of demonic
magic at the Turku Academy.

In 1661 rumours were spread that Henricus Eolenius, a student and
the son of a burgher in Turku, had practised diabolic arts. He had with
suspicious ease and speed learnt the Arabic and Syrian languages. He
was suspected of being Stodius's pupil. Terserus and the consistory
sentenced Eolenius to death for his 'pactum cum Diabolo'. However,
the Chancellor, Count Per Brahe, ordered the sentence to be submitted to the Court of Appeal at Turku, where Eolenius was
sentenced to church penitence and was expelled from the Academy.

In 1665 the bishop and Vice-Chancellor Johan Gezelius charged
Elisabeth Nilsdotter, the widow of a professor, with having prepared a
magic potion to poison his wife. The case was tried, but the widow was
finally acquitted and Gezelius was forced to pay heavy damages.

Finally, in 1670, Isacus Gunnerus, a student and the son of a vicar,
was suspected of having committed diabolic acts. He was also
Stodius's pupil. The consistory expelled him from the Academy.

The main reason for this very severe attitude towards rumours of
magic was the desire to protect the reputation of the Academy. Otherwise the professors did not take much interest in witchcraft, and
before the great trials in the 1660s and 1670s the allies of the devil were
not much discussed in Finland.

VII. THE ÅLAND TRIALS

The particular nature of the Åland cases is underlined by the fact that
up until then, only a few witch-trials had been held in the islands.
During the years 1655–64 there were nine, and only one of these gives
an indication of future events. From 1662 to 1664, a peasant, Olof
Hanson in Lemland, and his mother-in-law, Kirstin Hansdotter, were
tried. Kirstin was accused of having used magic spells to harm cattle.
The records give the impression that the judge seriously contem-
plated using capital punishment. But the jury did not find the death

sentence justified, and proposed exile from the country. Olof and Kirstin were fined. The verdict was, however, based on the theory of implicit pact. There was no evidence that the two accused had made an agreement with the devil to learn soothsaying, incantation, and the practice of witchcraft. They were merely sorcerers and performers of magic tricks.[6]

The judge in Åland was Nils Psilander, a Swede from an educated family. His father, Petrus, had studied at the University of Wittenberg in 1607, and was later a clergyman in Sweden. The son, Nils, born in the 1620s, was matriculated at the Tartu Academy in 1637 and later served the future king of Sweden, Karl X Gustav. In 1655 Psilander had been appointed judge for Åland. In Sweden and Finland it was at the time still usual for judges to employ a deputy, using the office only as a source of income and prestige. But Psilander carried out his official duties himself until his death in 1682.

Psilander had studied at the Tartu Academy, where the influence of German thought was very strong. He had the habit, when pronouncing judgement, of referring to the views of jurists and theologians on the subject concerned. From these references it is obvious that he was familiar with the best-known Swedish jurists (for instance, Johannes Loccenius and Johan Stiernhöök) and many influential German jurists, such as Benedict Carpzov. It is certain that he was also well versed in the literature of witchcraft.[7]

Psilander obviously suspected that allies of the devil were to be found in Åland. In 1665 the ailing wife of a peasant, Karin Persdotter, was indicted for having practised soothsaying. She had, for instance, tried to solve cases of theft. She explained that she had been sick as a child, which turned out to be the work of Satan, who appeared to her and helped her to find thieves.

From the beginning of the trial Psilander was convinced that Karin had made an open pact with the devil. The woman was led to believe that her explanation regarding her sickness was accepted. She then replied readily to all questions asked by the court. Already as a child

---

[6] Heikkinen, *Paholaisen Liittolaiset*, pp. 204–7.

[7] Ibid., pp. 208–19. Among the authors quoted by Psilander are Benedict Carpzov, *Practica Nova Imperialis Saxonicae Rerum Criminalium* (1635); Ludovicus Dunte, *Decisiones Mille et Sex Casuum Conscientiae* (1636); Michael Freude, *Prozesse wider die Hexen* (1667); Arnold Mengering, *Informatorium Conscientium Evangelicum* (1644); Balthazar Menzerus, *De Conjugio Tractatus* (1612); Johan Stiernhöök, *De Jure Sveonum et Gothorum Vetusto* (1672); Bernhard Waldschmidt, *Pythonissa Endorea* (1660); Gottfried Voigt, *Deliciani Physicae* (1671).

she had been regarded as different, and her uncle, too, had been clairvoyant. A couple of years previously a black man had come to her, mocking her poverty, promising to end it if she would serve him. Karin had accepted his offer, and had been taken to Blåkulla, after which she had been quite bloody: the black man had bitten her on both breasts, where marks of teeth could still be seen. Karin often visited Blåkulla and received from the man supernatural skills.[8]

Later, when the court informed Karin that it did not believe her story of illness, she was apparently ready to disavow it. This was ignored, and the court succeeded in obtaining a full confession that she had made a compact with the devil. She was also accused of *maleficium*. No torture was used. Karin firmly believed herself to be unusual. It is obvious from her story that her fantasies of Satan were connected with attacks of illness causing unconsciousness. She was sentenced to death on the basis of Exodus 22: 18.[9]

During the trial, Karin had not denounced anyone as an accomplice. Before the execution she spent four months in Kastelholm prison where she was free to receive visitors and talk to people. Psilander and the clergy from Åland visited her and succeeded in obtaining denunciations of thirteen women from her. Karin had no longer anything to lose. She explained that the denounced women had practised magic, mainly on their neighbours' cattle. She had seen one of the women at the sabbath in Blåkulla, but the court was convinced that all of them were allies of the devil.

Karin Persdotter's confession thus was important for the future course of the Åland witch-trials. Her denunciations were not entirely spontaneous, but no torture was used. Apart from Karin considering herself an exceptional person, another factor may also explain her readiness. She was a beggar, and her only skill was her alleged power to foretell the future, which caused people to consider her wise and to be afraid of her. When the interrogation started, she suddenly found herself the centre of attention, an important person, whom the judge

[8] Heikkinen, *Paholaisen Liittolaiset*, pp. 219 ff.

[9] Carlo Ginzburg has called my attention to the shamanistic features in the case of Karin Persdotter. They are to be found in other cases, too. A well-known example is the professional sorcerer Antti Lieroinen, born in Savolaks and sentenced to death in 1643. He was charged with killing people and burning houses. He confessed that in his sleep he could predict when people were coming to consult him, what kind of questions they would have, and what they had lost. He had a spirit helping him to see and to do what people asked him for. His death sentence was confirmed by the Turku Court of Appeal. His father had also been charged with sorcery, and in the 1660s another professional sorcerer advertised himself as Antti's son: Heikkinen, *Paholaisen Liittolaiset*, pp. 103–5.

and the spectators listened to intently. She knew that she would be sentenced to death. In this situation there was no reason for her to cease talking. The pronouncement of the death sentence and continued pressure made her ready to act as an informer, which she had not been at all prepared to do originally.

Up to the beginning of the year 1668, the witch-trials continued in a chain, and by March six women denounced by Karin had been sentenced to death. The pattern was always the same. Those convicted were interrogated in Kastelholm prison. Psilander was helped by the clergy, in particular by the vicar of Sund, Bryniel Kjellinus, who was praised by Psilander as 'an excellent handler of witches'.

The most serious charge was to have been seen in Blåkulla. The body of each woman was examined, and in every case a scar was found, which was interpreted as the devil's mark. This was considered a justification for torture, which was carried out with thumbscrews, and under that pressure all the women confessed. Maria Nilsdotter was the first to be tortured, but it was not until the interrogation of a second suspect, Lisbeta, Per Skarp's wife, that the Court of Appeal in Turku was asked to give its permission for torture. In that connection the value of the denunciations from accomplices was questioned. This was the first sign of doubts concerning the trials in Åland, but there was no immediate effect. A widow, Ebba, was sentenced to death as a result of two denunciations, a witch's mark, and her own confession under torture. She was not charged with *maleficium* of any kind.[10]

The case of Margeta Mårtinsdotter, who was sentenced to death in 1670, is different, because none of the accused had clearly denounced her. However, it was said that Karin Persdotter had regarded her as a witch. *Maleficium* was the main issue in Margeta's case: all those present at her trial stamped her as 'the most terrifying malefica' of all in Åland. Margeta was too ill to be tortured. She confessed to *maleficium*, but not even at the place of execution would she admit to having made a compact with the devil.

The end of the trials in Åland is as interesting as their beginning. Not all women denounced by Karin Persdotter had been questioned, and Margeta Mårtinsdotter had denounced many more. But Margeta was the last to be convicted.

The court records show that Psilander had apparently not changed his opinion, and still suspected that allies of the devil were to be found

---

[10] The records of the Åland trials have been published in Reinh. Hausen (ed.), *Bidrag till Finlands Historia*, i. (Helsinki, 1894–8), 257–364.

in the islands. But he had become more careful. In February 1667 it had become obvious that the convicted and suspected had been able to talk freely together in Kastelholm prison. Bryniel Kjellinus had ordered them to give him their witch-ointment, since flights were only possible with the aid of a certain salve received from the devil, and thus they were bound to possess it. With threats he had induced Lisbeta and Ebba to hand over some kind of fat, which he at once burned in the prison stove. Now it was discovered that a deception had taken place: when the vicar had threatened to burn down Lisbeta's house if the witch-salve was not found, she had stolen some shoe grease from the prison guard, hidden it in her bodice, and given some of it to Ebba.

This was a blow, and the court recognized that the confessions might be fabricated to avoid torture. In interrogating Ingeborg Olsdotter, Psilander was already more cautious. Previously a devil's mark had been considered a justification for torture. Now the mark was tested: following the advice in Michael Freude's work *Prozesse wider die Hexen*, a servant of the court was ordered to pierce the mark with a needle, unnoticed by Ingeborg. It was concluded that the accused had felt no pain, and torture was started. The use of Freude's work is a proof of the energy with which Psilander conducted the trials. It had been published only in 1667 and was obtained specifically for the trial.

Ingeborg Olsdotter did not confess to being an ally of the devil. Her denunciation by Karin Persdotter and the witch's mark would obviously have convinced Psilander, but the jury was in doubt. It considered Ingeborg guilty, but asked the Court of Appeal whether a sentence less severe than death could be considered, since the case remained obscure. The woman was sentenced to death, but on other grounds than those on which she had previously been accused: she had misled people with her magic, and had misused the holy name of God when practising her secret soothsaying talent. But she was not directly accused of being in league with the devil.

Later, the role of the jury became clearer. It considered Margeta Mårtinsdotter a witch because of *maleficium* committed by her. When in May 1670 another Margeta, the wife of Lars Hansson, who had been denounced by Karin Persdotter, was heard, the jury was again critical. It was proved that Margeta had been taught magic by Karin, and an insensitive devil's mark was found on her, but the jury was not at all convinced, and said that the Church should investigate the charge.

Since the vicar saw no reason to accuse Margeta, the jury decided to 'leave to God to decide this secret matter'.

Psilander was not satisfied with the jury's decision and expressed this clearly in the records. The Court of Appeal ordered a new hearing, but expressly forbade the use of torture. The jury was still not convinced and refused to continue investigations, if torture could not be used. Although Psilander was satisfied, the hearings had to be abandoned. In a letter to the authorities he stated that the devil could sometimes deceive the investigator by making such marks and then removing them. Margeta was not sentenced to death.

The last examination in the great witch-trial in Åland was held in 1678, when Margeta, the wife of Göran Michelsson, was examined. She had been denounced already in 1670. Many witnesses had explained that she practised magic, and now new evidence was presented. Margeta's niece told that she had seen a woman of her aunt's appearance walking about dressed in a fur coat. Suddenly the woman disappeared, and the girl's cows completely lost their strength. Psilander confirmed that witches were able to disappear in this sudden manner, but the hearing proceeded no further in this respect. In the verdict the Court of Appeal was requested to exile Margeta from Åland, just as Kirstin Hansdotter had been exiled in 1664.

The specific nature of the Åland trials is due to the prominent part played by learned theories of witchcraft in the court's decisions. The most important charge was that of having a pact with the devil. Accusations of *maleficium* played only a supporting role. The suspects were interrogated after conviction in order to obtain denunciations of others. Torture was used to obtain confessions. The devil's mark and witch-ointment were searched for.

The theories of witchcraft were a very important part of Psilander's thinking, but one would also like to know about the personal background to his actions. All the sources concerning him are, however, official, and in this respect inadequate. Perhaps he wanted to see himself as an expert on the subject. It must be born in mind that Psilander's theoretical interests were not limited to witchcraft alone, and it must also be considered that he did not try to condemn the accused at any price. As we have seen, the jury often had a different opinion, and their views were taken into consideration when sentences were passed.

VIII. THE TRIALS IN ÖSTERBOTTEN

The other area of major witch-trials in Finland was Österbotten, where at least twenty women and two men were sentenced to death between 1674 and 1678. As far as we know, fifteen of these sentences were carried out. The cases here are clearly different from those in Åland.[11]

Traditionally there had been many more witch-trials in Österbotten than in any other province of Finland (see Map 12.1 above). Those from 1665 to 1684 will be more closely examined here (see Table 12.2).

The second half of the 1670s was an exceptional period in two respects. First, the number of accusations in both rural and urban areas was much higher than before and after. Secondly, charges of being an ally of the devil are concentrated in this period. Further, it is noteworthy that these accusations were relatively more numerous in the towns than in the rural districts.

Österbotten was a very large province. As far as witch-trials are concerned, the main area was the coast of southern Österbotten: Pedersöre (town and parish), Nykarleby (town and parish), Vörå (parish), Vasa (town), Mustasaari (parish), Närpes (parish), Kristinestad (town), Lappfjärd (parish). Almost half (48.6 per cent) of the accusations came from this area.

TABLE 12.2. *Number of accused in the witch-trials in Österbotten (Finland), 1665–1684*

	1665–9	1670–4	1675–9	1680–4
Rural areas				
Suspected allies of the devil	—	2	21	2
Other accused	18	13	32	24
Towns				
Suspected allies of the devil	—	4	17	—
Other accused	4	2	13	2
Total	22	21	83	28

[11] Heikkinen, *Paholaisen Liittolaiset*, pp. 244 ff.

It used often to be thought that the witch-trials in Österbotten were mostly directed against beggar-women with a bad reputation, but the overall picture is different (see Table 12.3). We can see in the accusations and denunciations the basic elements of the community in Österbotten: peasants and burghers. Among the accused, 81.5 per cent were from these groups. Moreover, it is obvious that the trials were not primarily persecutions from above, because only about one-fifth of the accused were brought to trial following indictments from civil servants and clergymen. Accomplices were responsible for another fifth of the denunciations, which shows that most of the trials were individual ones, but the denunciations increased with the sabbath trials during the 1670s, as might be expected.

TABLE 12.3. *Social status of denouncers* (D) *and of the accused* (A) *in the witch-trials in Österbotten, 1665–1684*

	1665–9		1670–4		1675–9		1680–4		Total	
	D	A	D	A	D	A	D	A	D	A
Peasants	9	16	4	13	5	36	—	20	18	85
Propertyless	—	4	—	—	1	9	—	5	1	18
Burghers	1	2	—	7	5	29	1	1	6	39
Soldiers with families	—	—	—	—	1	5	—	1	1	6
Civil servants, clergymen	4	—	4	—	10	1	10	—	28	1
Accomplices	1	—	4	—	21	—	1	—	27	—
People under 20 years	—	—	—	—	11	—	—	—	11	—
Libel suits	7	—	7	—	9	—	15	—	38	—
Others	—	—	—	—	7	—	1	—	8	—
Unknown	—	—	2	1	12	2	—	—	14	3
Total	22	22	21	21	82	82	27	27	152	152
Women		16		15		65		22		118

Maleficium is very prominent among the charges (see Table 12.4), comprising about 70 per cent (because the group 'other' includes such charges, too). On the other hand, one can see that the use of healing magic could also lead to indictment, mainly through libel suit.

TABLE 12.4. *Content of accusations in the witch-trials in Österbotten, 1665–1684*

Charge	No.	%
Maleficium, man	44	27.5
Maleficium, animal	47	29.4
Maleficium, property	7	4.4
Healing, man	26	16.3
Healing, animal	5	3.1
Other	31	19.3
Total	160	100.0

The number acquitted (see Table 12.5) is very large, since the group 'unknown' obviously includes acquitted persons, too. The latter half of the 1670s was, as we have seen, a period of greater activity: almost all death sentences were given then.

The trials in Österbotten, where accusations of visits to Blåkulla played an important role, were concentrated in a rather small area, but they did not form such a coherent whole as those in Åland. Underlying these trials was no doubt widespread belief—especially among people on the Swedish coast[12]—in the existence of allies of the devil. For a

TABLE 12.5. *Verdicts in the witch-trials in Österbotten, 1665–1685*

Verdict	No.	%
Death	20	13.2
Prison	5	3.3
Fines	12	7.9
Church penitence	8	5.2
Acquittal	87	57.2
Unknown	20	13.2
Total	152	100.0

[12] In Finland most of the population on the Baltic coast was of Swedish origin, speaking Swedish, as opposed to the indigenous Finnish population further inland and in the east.

long time the most important contacts of this area had been with the mother country, especially with Stockholm. Southern Österbotten was the main region of tar production, and the towns sold their tar in Stockholm. Information about major witch-trials in northern Sweden could, then, easily cross the Baltic.

Belief in the existence of allies of the devil is clearly seen in Pedersöre. As early as the beginning of the 1670s there were rumours about them, spread by a confused peasant, Martti Laukus, who eagerly told about flying witches he had seen. When the first witch in the area was denounced—the beginning of the case is unknown—these rumours were taken seriously and the clergymen held their own hearings.

The connection with the Swedish trials is also clear in Mustasaari in 1675. Agneta Kristoffersdotter, one of the first to be accused, had come from northern Sweden. This trial provoked another in nearby Nykarleby. There a soldier, Mats Simonsson, said that his wife had confessed after a visit to the hangman who had executed Agneta. But his wife strongly denied the charge. It is probable that Mats had invented the story to get rid of her.

The great trials in nothern Sweden clearly had influence in Kristinestad in 1676, in Nykarleby in 1677, and in Uleåborg in 1678. Everywhere children and young people played an important role as witnesess, just as they had done in Sweden.

The basic content of the children's stories was the same as in Sweden: a witch had taken them for a ride to Blåkulla. For instance, Brita Stål's 14-year-old daughter Margeta said that her mother had taken her three times to Blåkulla. The first time a couple of years previously the trip had been made with a white cow. Another time they had travelled on a red horse which was upside-down: the mother and all three daughters sat on the horse's belly. On the third trip they rode on a white horse. The mother transvected her daughters when they were asleep.

Maria Jönsdotter, the 9-year-old daughter of a burgher in Nykarleby, confessed in 1677 that she had visited the sabbath twice, at Easter and at Christmas. One of the women she had recognized had been sitting at a table and had given food to Maria, who was standing on the floor. Another woman had stirred a pot, and a third had cut bread and served it to the others.

The wave of witch-trials in Österbotten was undoubtedly connected with the events in Sweden, but naturally this connection was not automatic. There must have been something in the society in Österbotten to bring this wave about.

The towns of northern Finland were small, with only a few hundred inhabitants, but their business life was relatively lively because of the tar trade. As compared to the rest of Finland, the southern coast of Österbotten was a wealthy region. The suspicions voiced in the trials are partly connected with misfortune in business, reasons for which were sought in witchcraft. This connection is to be seen very clearly in Kristinestad, where the bad luck and illness of the mayor's family nourished strong suspicions. The rumours also brought to light many long-standing quarrels between people.

Since there were so many rumours dealing with witchcraft, a great persecution could easily have taken place in Österbotten. As we have seen, there were plenty of denunciations, and those condemned were willing to denounce still others. The reason why this did not happen is to be found in the court procedures:

1. the denunciations by the accused were seldom regarded as sufficient in themselves;
2. formal torture was not used, although both mental and physical pressures were severe;
3. no devil's marks were looked for;
4. in the confessions of the accused the most important thing was proven *maleficium*; the accusations were more easily believed, if the accused had a bad reputation.

In short, the procedure of the courts mostly preserved its traditional character, even in the latter half of the 1670s.

Outside Österbotten, charges of compacts with the devil were rare in the 1670s. It is symptomatic that the few cases elsewhere were concentrated on the coast, especially in Satakunda south of Österbotten, where there had been many witch-trials earlier.

In the early 1680s plenty of denunciations were still made in Österbotten. From 1685 to 1689 fourteen people were accused, and from 1693 to 1697 the number was twenty-two. There were also many rumours about the allies of the devil, but the denunciations were not sufficient for conviction. The final outcome of the great trials in Sweden had obviously made the courts very cautious. A voluntary confession of having visited Blåkulla could now be taken as a sign of insanity.

Only if *maleficium* could be clearly proved did the charges become serious. This is what happened in the town of Pedersöre in 1680, when a burgher's wife, Beata Pitarintytär, was denounced. There were twenty witnesses against her, and the whole community was afraid of her. The clergyman also questioned her. Beata confessed nothing, and the court ordered a woman to search her clothes to see if there were any magic instruments hidden in them. On her skin was found 'a big sack', and this was taken to be the devil's mark. Beata was sentenced to death, but the court of Appeal at Turku released her in 1701. The days of the allies of the devil were already over in Finland.

13
Denmark: The Sociology of Accusations

JENS CHRISTIAN V. JOHANSEN

I. THE LEGAL FOUNDATIONS

THE earliest cases of Danish witchcraft legislation are found in Section 7 of the Scanian Church Law and Section 11 of the Sealandian Church Law,[1] promulgated about 1170; both mention sorcery, although only in connection with homicide. The secular Jutlandic law of 1241,[2] on the other hand, contains no mention of sorcery in its original version, whereas a manuscript from the fifteenth century includes a section (book III, chapter 69) providing a detailed description of procedures to be adopted in cases of witchcraft and sorcery.

There is, however, a significant distinction between the Jutlandic statute and the trials of the sixteenth and seventeenth centuries; it is personal possessions that are subjected to bewitchment, and not the persons themselves. On the other hand, one should take into account the phrasing of town statutes from Scania, from the early fourteenth century, which mention bewitchment of persons only;[3] but there are parallels for this in contemporary Swedish legislation.[4] Whatever the relationship between the legislation of the two countries may have been, we are left with the fact that, as far as Denmark is concerned, we do not know, owing to the lack of sources, how the courts dealt with the crime before the sixteenth century. We can assume that witchcraft was regarded as a threat to the existence of society, since laws and statutes concerning witchcraft were promulgated.

The risk that Denmark would become one of 'the heartlands of the

---

[1] Scania was a Danish possession until it was ceded to Sweden after the peace treaty of Roskilde in 1658.

[2] Jutland Law was one of a number of provincial laws that were in force in medieval Denmark.

[3] *Danmarks gamle købstadlovgivning* (Denmark's Ancient Town Legislation), ed. Erik Kroman, iv (Copenhagen, 1961), 338. I am obliged to Dr Grethe Jacobsen for drawing my attention to this legislation.

[4] Bengt Ankarloo, *Trolldomsprocesserna i Sverige* (Lund, 1971), 35f.

witchcraze'[5] was partially eliminated in 1522 by the revolt against the Danish king, Christian II. After the insurgents had installed Frederik I (Christian II's paternal uncle) on the throne, all the laws of the dethroned king were annulled. These included the ecclesiastical law of 1521, which contained the outline for an inquisitorial procedure, although the substance of the crime remained unchanged in relation to Jutlandic law and the Scanian town statutes.

Despite the fact that witches and sorcerers had allegedly made strenuous efforts to prevent King Christian III's fleet from leaving Elsinore harbour at the beginning of the 1540s,[6] two extremely important clauses affecting the Danish witchcraft trials were adopted in the Copenhagen Articles of 1547. One clause established that no statement of evidence from a dishonest person (witches and sorcerers were included in this category) could form the basis of the conviction of a third party, while the other clause ensured that no torture was permissible until after the final sentence. Throughout the seventeenth century the Jutland courts adhered to these two clauses: no accused person was convicted on the sole grounds of a denunciation. When damage had been proved by witnesses, the judges might possibly add that the accused had also been denounced; but the denunciation was regarded as merely a rounding-off of the case. 'Legal' torture was not applied before the final sentence, which tallies with the surprisingly small number of confessions (here designating statements that were made 'spontaneously' by the accused before the verdict of the jurors) in the Jutland trial records.

The two clauses in question were not solely directed at the crime of sorcery. They were part of the overall effort made throughout the sixteenth century by the Danish authorities to regulate and control legal procedure. The same is true of another piece of witchcraft legislation: Article 8 in the Kallundborg Articles of 1576. We shall discuss this witchcraft legislation in more detail.

In spite of the wishes of the authorities to proceed with witchcraft cases in accordance with the law, excesses inevitably occurred. At the beginning of the 1570s a death sentence was issued by a district court in Funen. When appealed to the County Court, the judges rejected the

---

[5] H. C. Erik Midelfort, 'Heartland of the Witchcraze: Central and Northern Europe', *History Today*, 31 (1981), 27–31.

[6] Niels M. Pedersen, 'Dokumenter til en Troldomssag under Christian III' (Proceedings from a Sorcery Trial during the Reign of Christian III), *Danske Magazin*, 3 R., 1 (1843), 52–67.

verdict of the lower court. This evidently took place *after* the accused woman had been burned, and this unfortunate incident brought about the adoption of the clause in the articles of 1576. This stipulated that no person found guilty by the jurors was to be executed before the case had been appealed to the County Court and a final sentence had been pronounced. It must be strongly emphasized that the use of jurors at the lowest court caused at least 90 per cent of the Danish witchcraft cases to be appealed.[7] The jurors came from the same parish as the accused and had, therefore, a strong and understandable desire to do away with the assumed witches. Viewed against a European background, the 1576 article was unique, as it is the first example of automatic appeal in witchcraft cases heard at secular courts; about fifty years later the Parlement of Paris passed similar measures. On the other hand, the Spanish Inquisition had adopted the procedure as early as 1526.[8]

The number of cases seems to have decreased after the promulgation of the 1576 article.[9] This must mean that the authorities had obtained a measure of success in controlling the work of the courts. In any case, forty years went by before Denmark brought in new witchcraft legislation. This was the ordinance of 12 October 1617, in which the nature of the crime was defined for the first time and the corresponding penalties specified: only those who had entered into a pact with the devil were to be burned; 'cunning men' and 'wise women', on the other hand, were to be fined and exiled (which in Denmark meant that the people concerned were banished from Jutland to Funen, or vice versa). The theological aspect of the crime was brought into the forefront for the first time in the legislation: witches and sorcerers were those who had entered into a pact with the devil.

This ordinance remained in force for the next sixty-five years, until 1683, when the Danish Law Code (Christian V's new Statute Book, valid throughout the kingdom) made its appearance. In this law, a distinction was made between witches and sorcerers in accordance with the 1617 ordinance, and witches and sorcerers who made use of

---

[7] Since *c*.10% of all known witchcraft trials at the County Court of Jutland had at the lower courts resulted in a verdict of not guilty, I presume that it had become a rule in that century to appeal every case of witchcraft.

[8] Cf. Bengt Ankarloo, ch. 11, above, and Gustav Henningsen, *The Witches' Advocate: Basque Witchcraft and the Spanish Inquisition* (Reno, 1980), 23, 371 ff.

[9] Karsten Sejr Jensen, *Trolddom i Danmark, 1500–88* (Witchcraft in Denmark, 1500-88) (Copenhagen, 1982); Merethe Birkelund, 'En analyse af danske trolddomsprocesser' (An Analysis of Danish Witchcraft Trials), thesis (Århus University, 1981).

'mad, imaginary arts with which to bewitch and harm others'; thus the authorities were now of the opinion that it was possible to harm others without seeking the aid of the devil. Without suggesting any influence from the French edict of 1682, it is none the less remarkable to observe the similarities of phrasing (the 1682 edict speaks of 'pretendue magie'). Yves Castan has pointed out that as time went on it became more difficult to hand down a sentence for witchcraft in France.[10] This was not so in Denmark. Here the cases were reduced in number, but death sentences formed the same proportion as earlier.

In 1686, Denmark carried though its final witchcraft legislation, an ordinance which stipulated that all death sentences pronounced by the County Courts had to be appealed to the Supreme Court. This provision had no far-reaching consequences for the severity of the penalties, as the Supreme Court in one single instance only modified a sentence. Instead of being burned alive, the convicted witch was to be beheaded, after which the body was to be burned.[11]

Legislation is one thing, the courts' application of this legislation, another. (Since the theological view of witchcraft had gained its influential position with the ordinance of 1617, the considerations that follow are concerned only with the period after 1617.) The fact that the central authorities in Copenhagen had focused on the pact with the devil did not necessarily mean that the courts followed in their footsteps. The most significant element in this connection is the practice of the *Landsting*, the County Courts—in particular when seen against the backgroud of the French investigators' emphasis on the fact that peasants who gave evidence at the lower court displayed an almost total indifference to the question of the pact with the devil.[12] They were solely interested in specific damages, in sorcery. The same holds true for Jutland: the peasants were completely uninterested in the fact that the devil might or might not have played a part. What mattered was the harm brought about by evil people. And the County Court judges went along with the peasants' point of view. To a great extent this was a result of the legislation: the 1547 articles remained valid after the introduction of the 1617 ordinance, and without the use of

[10] Yves Castan, *Magie et sorcellerie à l'époque moderne* (Paris, 1979), 192.

[11] Jørgen C. Jacobsen, *Den sidste Hexebränding i Danmark 1693* (The Last Execution for Witchcraft in Denmark, 1693) (Copenhagen, 1971), 105.

[12] Robert Muchembled, 'Sorcières du Cambrésis', in Marie-Sylvie Dupont-Bouchat, Willem Frijhoff, and Robert Muchembled, *Prophètes et sorciers dans les Pays-Bas* (Paris, 1978), 192ff.

torture it was extremely difficult to obtain proof of a pact. Torture was still forbidden until after the pronouncement of the final sentence.

On the whole, the County Court judges merely had to adopt the peasants' opinion in order to convict witches and sorcerers. If they had abided by the wording of the 1617 ordinance they would have been obliged to acquit about 95 per cent of all the accused, which would have been totally unacceptable. By sentencing as they did, the judges showed that on the whole they held the same view of the nature of the crime as did the general public. To make it absolutely clear: in Denmark the conflict between a popular and a learned culture took place at a far higher level than, for instance, Peter Burke maintains when, in order to exemplify his views, he makes frequent use of material from witchcraft trials.[13] Eradicating the crime of witchcraft did not come into conflict with the desire for criminal cases to be tried in a correct manner. One example will suffice as illustration: a woman confessed that she and three other women had had the devil among them in the figure of a cat, while they hit 'him' with a rod to get 'him' to bewitch a man. Despite this, the jurors brought in a verdict of not guilty, and at the County Court the judges did not find any reason for changing this verdict, since the jurors had not been convinced that sorcery had played any part in the affair, and because the woman had not promised anything evil.[14] Thus the pact with the devil played a limited part in the crime of witchcraft in Denmark.

The procedure was accusatory, and unless the accused could find bail, they were imprisoned, either in the house of the accuser, or in a prison. In this connection the remarkable fact should be noted that those few confessions that were made before the verdict of the jurors and the final sentence were in practically every case made by accused who had been imprisoned with their accuser. In court the accuser, with the aid of witnesses, had to prove that the accused was guilty of the damage in question, and at least one of the accusers (there might be several) had to place his hand on the head of the accused and charge him or her with causing the damage. Because of the legalistic attitude of the judges, this action was significant: in actual fact the County Court judges sent a number of cases back to the lower court for a new trial because the accused had not been charged in accordance with the law. On the basis of the evidence given, the jurors

---

[13] Peter Burke, *Popular Culture in Early Modern Europe* (London, 1978), 241 f. and 274 f.
[14] Landsarkivet for Nörrejylland, Viborg Landstings Dombog, B. 24–514, fos. 402ʳ–403ʳ.

pronounced their verdict: guilty or not guilty. At the County Court the judges gave the case a further hearing; the accused, at least one of the accusers, and members of the jury were present; they brought with them the documents from the trial at the local court, and based on these papers, along with, for the most part, a very brief statement from the parties involved, the judges decided on the case. None of the County Court judges, who before 1660 were appointed from among the nobility, had any legal training; but this deficiency was counterbalanced by the long periods for which they held the office of judge, most of them for about twenty years.

About 50 per cent of the accused were acquitted by the County Court, and two major factors can be discerned. Firstly, the details of the charge had to be attested by at least two impartial witnesses; this prevented an individual from sending his or her arch-enemy to the stake solely on the basis of his or her evidence. In addition, the judges did not attach enough weight to evidence from members of his or her family to bring in a death sentence; the family's confirmation of a witness's evidence was considered part of the accuser's own testimony. Secondly, the judges did not take evidence based on hearsay into account; the judges rejected evidence that described what the witness had heard others say about the accused. Without this caution, the percentage of death sentences could easily have risen to the same amount as in 'the heart lands of the witchcraze'.

II. NUMBER AND CONTENT OF THE TRIALS

Before discussing the number of Danish witchcraft trials, it will be necessary to make a few comments regarding the source-material. Generally, the number of trials in an area is calculated by one of two methods: either with the aid of accounts containing information on the financing of the executions,[15] or by a search of the legal material. The first method is impossible to apply in Denmark because the accusers risked being saddled with all the expenses of the trial, so that in these cases public accounts give no information on these trials. The other possibility exists for certain parts of Denmark only, and then only for the seventeenth century. After 1576, however, it becomes evident that

---

[15] Rainer Decker, 'Die Hexenverfolgungen in Herzogtum Westfalen', *Westfälische Zeitschrift*, 131–2 (1981–2), 340.

the County Court records can give us a figure at least for those cases in which the lower courts had reached a verdict of guilty. Thus before 1576 it is clear that we can obtain only a very uncertain picture of the total number of trials. But even after 1576 the situation for large parts of Denmark is uncertain. Only in Jutland and only after 1609, can we evaluate the extent of witchcraft trials. From that year and until the end of the century series with insignificant lacunae can be reconstructed. For the rest of the country the position as regards source-material resembles that of the sixteenth century. Continuing series of court records are available for the last thirty to forty years of the seventeenth century only, and judging from the conditions in Jutland, this was a period when the number of cases fell drastically. Taking these conditions into account, I have made use only of legal records from the Jutland County Court in this paper, and limited the statistical investigations solely to the seventeenth century. I must therefore emphasize that I find an interpolation of the total number of cases in Denmark to be impossible.[16]

As the witchcraft ordinance was issued in 1617, this is a suitable starting-point for a discussion of events. But at once one must ask, why 1617? What had been happening in the period leading up to that year that made legislation against witchcraft necessary? I feel that several factors contributed to create conditions that were ripe for new legislation. First, while the Norwegian parts of the kingdom had obtained new witchcraft legislation in 1593, Denmark was still in need of a similar law. Secondly, King Christian IV (1588–1648) was greatly concerned personally with this crime and was probably alarmed by certain happenings that took place in 1612–13 in the town of Køge, in Sealand, in which eleven women were executed. Thirdly, the most important diocese in the country (that of Sealand) was occupied in 1615 by a theologian who was far more othodox than his predecessor, which resulted in a policy of strict Lutheranism. Fourthly and finally, the witchcraft ordinance must be seen in the context of other laws which were enacted on the same day, 12 October 1617: one a sumptuary law, and one a ruling with harsher repression of adultery and fornication than in previous decrees. It would be too hasty to regard this complex of laws as part of a conscious policy of acculturation; on

[16] Gustav Henningsen, 'Witch Hunting in Denmark', *Folklore*, 93 (1982), 131–7. [Henningsen estimates that the total number of witches tried in Denmark during the persecutions of 1536–1693 was less than two thousand, and that a maximum of one thousand were burned: ibid., p. 135. Editor's note.]

the other hand, the obvious attempts of this legislation to discipline the Danish people must not be overlooked. The laws of 1617 were an attempt to tighten the hold on Danish society.

In Jutland the effects of the publication of the ordinance were immediate. In 1616 seven trials were held in Jutland, in 1617 the number rose to eighteen, and the increase continued in 1618 to forty-one. The sequence from 1609 to 1618 is noteworthy (see Fig. 13.1), for in itself it indicates that the level had been relatively stable and low during the years preceding 1617.

This indication is confirmed by the distribution of examples of the 'settlement-out-of-court' phenomenon, in which a suspect escaped further charges when the suspicion did not lead to a court case. The Jutland records contain seven mentions of 'settlement out of court', and in six of these cases reference is made to events that took place before 1618. This indicates that before this date the parties involved

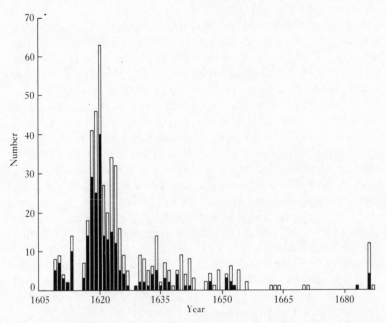

FIG. 13.1. *Witch-trials at the Jutland County Court at Viborg (Denmark), 1609–87. Documents are not available for the years 1614–15, 1628, 1644, 1650, 1658–9, 1665, 1668, and 1676–81. Shading represents the number of trials that resulted in capital punishment*

were more inclined to let off the suspect if he or she promised not to do any more of their evil deeds. It was characteristic that the suspect promised not to behave in such a way again, thus pouring oil on troubled waters. In a case from 1613 in the south Jutland town of Ribe, three men testified that a woman had been apprehended by a man because she had bewitched his wife, but when the woman promised to remove the spell and make the wife better, the man had let her go.

The picture did change after the ordinance was issued. However, the result was not an even, albeit higher, level, corresponding to the intensity in the years preceding 1618; instead we find a very jagged curve, with peaks during the period 1617 to 1625 when persecutions reached Continental dimensions. If we look at the graph marking the 494 trials from 1609 to 1687, when the last actual witchcraft trial was held in Jutland, we notice a surprisingly pronounced grouping: in the eight years from 1617 to 1625, 297 trials were held, which makes up 60 per cent of all those in Jutland between 1609 and 1687. A similar concentration of *maleficium* trials has to my knowledge not been documented from any other European country.

The graph of the Jutland trials can be divided into four phases: (1) before 1617, (2) 1617–25, (3) 1626–56, and (4) 1657–87. Phases (1) and (3) are characterized by a relatively stable and low total of trials, phase (2) by the dramatic increase we have noted, and phase (4) by a very low number of trials. To begin with we shall concentrate on phase (2).

International research into witchcraft beliefs has discussed manifold conditions that may have influenced the fluctuations in the number of trials. Here we shall consider one of them, which may probably have had a greater influence on the *maleficium* trials than on the sabbath trials, namely, economic development. To begin with it must be emphasized that previous discussion has placed too much emphasis on economic conditions as a whole, rather than making selective observations. In Professor E. Ladewig Petersen's words, 'the period from the 1550s to the end of the 1620s ... [was] far from an unbroken period of economic splendour, but as a whole the booming state of the market and rapid market changes gave Denmark ... enormous economic growth.'[17] Denmark's main export was grain, but it is open to discussion whether the peasant farmers themselves had any grain at all to sell and, if so, to what market. In any event, it must be

[17] E. Ladewig Petersen, *Dansk socialhistorie* (Social History of Denmark), iii (Copenhagen, 1980), 252.

asserted that it was the grain from the estates of the nobility that was sold on the export market, while any saleable crops from the small farms went to the towns. An export crisis for Danish grain hit the whole country in 1618–19, and prices fell, while in contrast oxen export reached its absolute high point in the years 1610–20. Certainly, the Jutland peasants had a large share of this export, and if the grain crisis meant loss of income for some farmers, this was no doubt retrieved through the oxen export; although possibly not for the same persons. It would therefore be incorrect to talk of crisis years in general for the rural sector; but the growth, or at least the stability, probably had a corresponding effect in the towns, where every price rise would be felt as an additional pressure on the poorest sections of society. In line with this we might expect a variation of development in the trial-pattern of town and country respectively, but on the contrary, the statistics of the Jutland trials show parallel development: in the period from 1617 to 1625 the number of trials *both* in country *and* town increased.[18] In other words, witch-trials were not solely a function of general economic conditions; the causes must be sought elsewhere.

Although peasants and citizens had accepted 'settlement out of court' in the preceding period, fear must have lurked very close to the surface, and the moment it became clear that the authorities not only sanctioned, but positively encouraged witchcraft trials, fear would break out and lead to a catharsis involving a purge of those individuals about whose evil-doing there was general agreement. Naturally this observation applies to the overall picture, and does not imply that it is not possible to discover in the individual case specific causes that at a certain point in time provoked the trial. But whatever the reasons might be in concrete cases, there was always the consistent aim of removing destructive elements: persons who, according to popular opinion, threatened society with their harmful actions.

During the eight years from 1617 to 1625, most of the witches and sorcerers on whom there was a consensus of opinion were apparently got rid of. One obvious conclusion arises from the outlined course of events: for Jutland these eight years were extraordinary. A wave of persecution of such size had never previously occurred, nor did it recur. This evaluation rests on a particular feature of *maleficium* trials: a witch was not created in a day. It took the community many years to

[18] Jens Christian V. Johansen, 'Als die Fischer den Teufel ins Netz bekamen . . .', in Christian Degn, Hartmut Lehmann, and Dagmar Unverhau (eds.), *Hexenprozesse* (Neumünster, 1983), 159–66.

build up this reputation of an individual, and this is one reason why there was no recurrence of a persecution of dimensions corresponding to this one.

The stable and low number of trials in phase (3) was thus to a great extent the result of the explosion in the preceding period. Other factors also played a part. In the course of the second half of the seventeenth century we find that a certain scepticism appears concerning the reality of the witch phenomenon. This is seen, for instance, in a statement by the Jutland County Court judge Villum Lange, who in 1662 said that he could not sentence a person to the stake on the evidence produced. On the other hand, it must be emphasized that with an accusatory procedure in which cases were brought 'from below', a condition for the cessation of witchcraft charges was that a view corresponding to that of Villum Lange should come to be accepted among the rural population. It is doubtful if this happened. The relative proportions of guilty and not guilty verdicts remained unchanged throughout the period studied: in slightly less than 90 per cent of the cases a verdict of guilty was pronounced at the lower courts, and as mentioned earlier, these verdicts were pronounced by jurymen who were ordinary peasants. So when determining the causes of the cessation of trials, we should not look for a scepticism concerning witchcraft among the general public, but we may find doubts on the effectiveness of taking witchcraft cases to court when the accused were in any case acquitted. From 1656 to 1686 only one single death sentence is known to have been pronounced in Jutland, and in the 1670s it was said in Copenhagen that the County Court judges sided with the witches.[19] Then in 1686 there was a final flare-up before burnings at the stake died out. That year twelve trials were held in Jutland, in the course of which at least four persons were sentenced to the stake; but for the zealous witch-hunter Jørgen Arenfeld of Rugård in Djursland it was a Pyrrhic victory. He was involved with eight of the twelve cases, which far more than the usual Jutland trials took on the characteristics of Continental persectuions. At Rugård both 'swimming' and 'pricking' were employed.

What led Arenfeld to become infected with the witch-craze is not known, but the reason for his being stopped—and with him, in fact, the Jutland trials as well—was similar to what had occurred in

---

[19] Leonora Christina, *Jammers Minde* (Memoir of Woe), ed. Johannes Brøndum Nielsen and C. O. Bøggild-Andersen (Copenhagen, 1949), written 1673-4.

Germany: when Arenfeld pressed for still more accusations, the system collapsed from within. In May 1686 Anne Sørensdatter was sentenced at Rugård district court, and a month later this sentence was confirmed by the County Court judges. She had, however, involved several prominent citizens in Århus and Grenå as a result of Arenfeld's threats, and only five days after the County Court sentence she retracted these statements in the presence of Arenfeld, a councillor and an assessor from Århus, and the minister from Tvilum, saying that she was not acquainted with the people concerned at all. It was unfortunate for Arenfeld that he had not succeeded in having Anne Sørensdatter burned straight away, for now the case was brought before the Supreme Court, who in September of the same year reprieved her from the stake, but on account of her false statements condemned her to be whipped at the whipping-post and then banished. Moreover, it was revealed at the Supreme Court that Arenfeld had overstepped his authority when he arrested Anne Sørensdatter and her mother, as they both lived outside the bounds of his jurisdiction. A man who had also been sentenced by Arenfeld managed to escape, and later he had his case brought before the king; and in November 1686 these cases resulted in an order that all cases of witchcraft be appealed to the Supreme Court before execution took place. Arenfeld himself was suspended from his district court.

As to the decisions of the County Court, it should be noted that the acquittal percentage for the whole period was slightly under 50, and that no marked changes can be ascertained in the various phases: but for the years 1626 to 1656 the percentage rose to upwards of 70. Comparison with the rest of Europe is not easy. One needs to find areas with a similar legal system, including automatic appeal, and here only the Parlement of Paris offers an adequate basis for comparison. But one definite conclusion can be drawn: in Jutland, as in most other parts of Europe, lower courts were more severe than the appeal courts.

The difficulties immediately become greater when we turn to the socio-economic realities underlying the witchcraft trials. It has already been indicated that the development in economic conditions exhibited variant tendenceis in country and town; these must now be subjected to closer analysis.

In the rural areas, one problem is that 80 per cent of those accused were women, and as such appear only in the legal records and hardly ever in quantitative sources. The determination of the socio-economic status of these women must, therefore, be based on the status of their husbands. However, the statistics reveal that the marital status of one-third of the accused cannot be traced, and that slightly more than one-sixth were widows. Furthermore, the Scandinavian custom of women retaining their maiden name when they married makes it difficult to determine precisely who their husbands were. Unless the husband's name is stated, it is almost impossible to place the accused person accurately on the socio-economic scale. Material for evaluation is found in three groups of sources: inventories from tenant registers of the Lord-Lieutenant, tax censuses, and rent rolls. None of these groups can provide definitive answers, due to their limited function and in-built conservatism. The use of the rent rolls is unsatisfactory because naturally only the copy-holder is listed.[20] The tax censuses have their own internal problems, so that it is only possible to set up a relative socio-economic gradation from them: copy-holders—small-holders—farm hands.[21] For these reasons, and not least because inventories from the early part of the seventeenth century are extremely scarce, it must be emphasized that an evaluation of the socio-economic position of the parties involved will be tenuous; and I would merely suggest that it is noteworthy that copy-holders as accusers seem to confront smallholders' wives as accused.

There are much better possibilities for estimating the socio-economic conditions when we turn from the country to the town. Wills and inventories from several towns have been preserved, in which the parties involved can be traced. But above all the urban taxes were assessed individually. Tax-payments were based on trade as well as on property, and during the first half of the seventeenth century at least, trade was the most important factor. It is possible, therefore, to place accused, accusers, and witnesses on an economic scale. With that one is obliged to be satisfied, in spite of the fact that reality is thereby distorted. Society was dominated by the concept of social status, and this dimension is lost. A moderately well-to-do guild artisan might possess a higher social status than a rich mercer. Based on these considerations I have made analyses of two towns: Elsinore in Sealand and Ribe in southern Jutland. In both places clear patterns emerge. It is the moderately poor who accuse the absolute poor. It may be

[20] In addition, the rent (manorial due) was a sum paid for the right to use the soil, which did not rise or fall with increase or decline in income, and so could only be altered through change of tenancy; however, throughout the 17th c. this tax was relatively stable.

[21] The head-tax (*kopskat*) was assigned to individuals in advance as a fixed sum according to their category.

significant that some of the accusers and witnesses had experienced financial setbacks in the years preceding the witchcraft trials, during a period characterized by hard times for the poorer groups of the urban population. I believe that the trials can be seen as an expression of a desperate struggle for survival by the people involved, a struggle to avert the slide from moderate poverty into absolute poverty from which there could be no escape. One example may be appended to show the role played by social status: during the years immediately preceding the witchcraft trials, a woman in Elsinore had twice been involved in lawsuits concerning attacks on life and limb, but in both cases one testimony counterbalanced the other, and the woman emerged triumphantly from the suit. But when a couple of years later she was involved in a witchcraft trial, the tables were turned. Her social status had fallen drastically, the authorities no longer believed her, and she was convicted.

When these considerations are summed up we get no coherent picture of the basic causes of the outbreak of the trials. Economic realities had specific consequences for rural and urban people respectively. In the towns the lower social classes in particular went through hard economic times, while in the country people at least enjoyed economic stability. Consequently, socio-economic conditions are only part of the explanation for the trials. Additional factors must be considered in order to produce satisfactory explanations.

III. FROM REPUTATION TO CHARGE OF WITCHCRAFT

I have stressed that a witch in a *maleficium* trial was not created over-night. I shall now attempt to prove that the fact that no outbreak similar to that in the period between 1617 and 1625 occurred in Jutland later in the century was due in part to the length of time it took to build up a reputation for witchcraft.

Before a certain person was charged, it was a prerequisite that this person had already acquired the reputation of being a witch. This reputation could arise in various ways; but the important point is that in a very large number of the trials recorded it is possible to define the date and the cause of the reputation. In the majority of cases it can be traced back either to one event or to a series of occurrences within the space of only a few years. In a case from 1620, a witness in a village related that her brother had come to her in 1614 describing how the

witch had threatened him with evil because he had chased her heifer
from his oat-field. Shortly afterwards he had fallen ill and died. The
collective testimony of the parish shows us that the witch had been
suspected of sorcery since the man's death in 1614.

In a few cases it is possible to put an exact date to the origin of the
reputation for witchcraft. In a case in 1625, three people testified that
on 28 October 1607 they had heard a man and the witch arguing after
he had broken her windows, and she had then threatened him with
mischief. When she was brought to trial, evidence was produced
stating that on 7 November 1607 the woman had testified that a
fortnight before, the man in question had gone to her house around
midnight and had called her a whore, after which he had smashed her
windows and shouted for her to come out with his brother-in-law and
fight; but the brother-in-law was not at her house. In 1621 the same
man went to the parish vicar and accused the woman of having
bewitched his cattle, and when shortly afterwards he himself fell ill, he
told the vicar that she was also to blame for his illness. Twenty-three
people testified that she had been suspected of the man's death. But
the County Court judges acquitted her, particularly because her son
pointed out, referring right back to the first incident, that it was
remarkable that the man in question, who was said to have been
threatened by his mother, had lived in good health for more than ten
years afterwards.

While on the Continent denunciations often proved the deciding
factor in the development of trials, they played a less important part in
Jutland. For the most part they merely had the function of prompting
witnesses to appear in court. But a considerable time could elapse
between the denunciation and the sworn testimony: a condemned
witch denounced another woman in March 1618, but at least two and a
half months passed before the people of the parish could make up
their minds to testify against her, and even then it seems to have been
without any great conviction, for no one accused her, whereupon the
County Court judges suspended the case. It is obvious, however, that
she was held in ill repute in the parish, for she made no attempt to
defend herself—on the contrary, eight men witnessed that she fell on
her knees in the churchyard and begged people not to blame her.

The process could take even longer, as when a woman was
denounced three times before finally being charged. She was first
denounced in November 1622, next in December of the same year,
and the third time in June 1623, after which she was finally charged in

January 1624. It seems strange that so much time was necessary in this case, for when details of the charge and statements of evidence finally came to light, the witnesses' memories stretched right back to the end of the previous century, and none of them gave testimony about events occurring during the period between the first denunciation and the charge.

We have seen how the cause of a reputation for witchcraft might have arisen many years earlier, in some few cases between forty and fifty years previously. In the years between this initial point and the day when the reputed witch or warlock was charged, various bewitchments were ascribed to him or her. In one man's case the allegations covered thirty years. In 1590 he had bought a cow which had just calved, but he was unable to get the calf included in the bargain, and it died shortly afterwards. In 1605 and also in 1608 he was suspected of having bewitched someone's milk yield, in 1611 he was blamed for a man losing his horses, in 1617 for another losing cattle and horses after he had quarrelled with the sorcerer about the wages of the latter's daughter, and in 1619 he was suspected of being responsible for a similar loss when a man had told the daughter that her father was a warlock. In 1620 he was finally accused. It is important to note how the recollections of individuals about a particular bewitching come together in a collective memory which at a given point in time leads to an accusation of witchcraft. As Alan Macfarlane has shown to be the case in Essex, a charge in Jutland is not the immediate result of a quarrel or of one inexplicable happening; the suspicion smoulders, while the suspect slowly but surely builds up a reputation leading to the eventual charge. On the other hand, as far as Jutland is concerned one must agree with Christina Larner's complaint that it is often impossible to decide why the charge is made at one particular time and not another. To return to the example given, it is not at all clear why this warlock was not taken to court until 1620, three years after the witchcraft ordinance of Christian IV.

I shall not pursue further the situations that led to accusations of witchcraft, as they so closely resemble the situations that Macfarlane found in Essex. Only one more illustration will be included here. One of the few female vagrants to be charged had arrived at a baptismal party, but had been thrown out; she had then threatened the 'offender' with mischief. Although the latter maintained in court that he had merely asked her to leave when she entered the room, he believed nevertheless that she was to blame for his falling ill after the episode. It seems that in fact the woman had been treated with scant sympathy at the party, as the new father testified that she had begged for a quart of mead, but 'as they had hardly any left' his wife had said that she could not have any, to which the witch (understandably, but unwisely) had replied that they would not get any more mead from their bees, and shortly afterwards all the bees died.

I shall now look more closely at the objects of bewitchment, since these provide very precise information on popular perceptions and notions of witchcraft. The bewitchings ascribed to the Jutland witches were not merely different from those for which the Essex witches were blamed, they had also on the whole a completely different character from, for instance, those of the French witches. A demonstration of the actual differences will therefore aid in a definition of the witchcraft belief common to the whole of Europe, a belief that was homogeneous in its foundation—bewitchment—but which displayed various manifestations. Such a demonstration can make possible a more exact understanding of the demand made by the general public for the elimination of the witches. Three major objects of bewitchment account for more than two-thirds of the total number of 1,715 statements of evidence produced in the Jutland trials: human death (16 per cent), human sickness (30 per cent), and the death of cattle (22 per cent) (see Fig. 13.2).

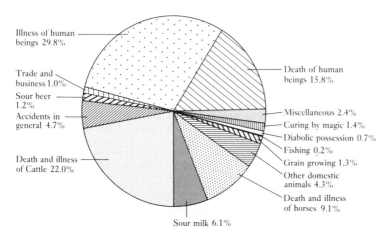

FIG. 13.2. *Types and objects of* maleficium *in Danish witch-trials*

As a basis for comparison, I have arbitrarily chosen research on witchcraft in an area extending from southern Belgium to southern France. Here we find not merely bewitchment patterns but also bewitchment methods of a different nature. Perhaps the most striking difference is that the witches were blamed for stillbirths and for killing the newborn in their cradles. This is seen, for instance, in one of the southern Belgian provinces, Namur,[22] and in the French department of Ariège, where the witches, with the aid of magic, asphyxiated slightly older children. 'Both of them went by night to Guilhem Caus's house, where they found a little girl of two or three called Marie in her bed. They pulled her out of bed and suffocated her by pressing down on her chest; she died two or three days later.'[23] It is important to note here that J. F. Le Nail emphasizes the popular nature of the belief, as the judges in this region had no knowledge of the works on demonology, but nourished the same ideas as the accused.[24] In the region neighbouring Ariège, Emmanuel Le Roy Ladurie emphasizes the popular notions underlying attacks on newborn babies in their cradles, although here the attacks took a slightly different form.[25] Included in the same complex of ideas must be the widespread fear of the 'aiguillette', whose predominant feature was masculine impotence. Against Ladurie's emphasis on the popular origin of this type of bewitchment,[26] I believe, following the opinion of Jean Delumeau, that the notion derives from a learned tradition.[27] In any case, stillbirths and the bewitching of small children were a predominant feature in this large area; if we now return to Jutland, we are struck by the small part these accusations played there.

271 testimonies relating to deaths can be enumerated for Jutland, but only 6 per cent applied to children; there was a still lower percentage of testimonies concerning children's illness (only 3 per cent). This distinction is so remarkable that we must ask whether the statis-

[22] Jacques Beckman, 'Une épidémie de sorcellerie à Novilles-Bois au début du xviiᵉ siècle', *Annales de la société archéologique de Namur*, 54 (1968), 442; see also Alfred Soman, 'La Sorcellerie vue du Parlement de Paris au début du xviiᵉ siècle', *Actes du 104ᵉ congrès national des sociétés savantes*, Bordeaux, 1979, Section d'histoire moderne et contemporaine (Paris, 1981), ii. 394; Muchembled, 'Sorcières du Cambrésis', p. 193.

[23] Jean-François Le Nail, 'Procédures contre des sorcières de Seix en 1562', *Bulletin de la société ariégeoise*, 31 (1976), 201.

[24] Ibid., p. 186.

[25] Emmanuel Le Roy Ladurie, *La Sorcière de Jasmin* (Paris, 1983), 42.

[26] Ibid., p. 29.

[27] Jean Delumeau, *La Peur én Occident, XIVᵉ–XVIIIᵉ siècles: Une cité assiégée* (Paris, 1978), 58.

tics reflect actual circumstances. If they do, it follows that the anxieties weighing on individual communities can be perceived in the witchcraft accusations. Demographic analysis should make it possible to verify such a view. The fact that the accusations were expressed through collective memory, however, makes them indicative of situations that must have existed for generations.

If we look more closely at the accusations regarding impotence in Jutland, we find a picture corresponding to that involving child deaths; the percentage is 3.5, and we must conclude that Jutlanders did not fear witches being able to cause impotence. This state of affairs is more understandable if we assume, as above, that the role of impotence in witchcraft was impotence derived from the learned tradition.

To note one further example from Belgium and France: it could happen in Namur that witches bewitched each other,[28] and in Gascogne they were so dangerous that they bewitched their husbands.[29] In Jutland, on the other hand, the witches behaved very well towards their husbands and towards each other, and only in 0.5 per cent of cases do we hear of any mutual abuse. However, I am unable to account for this divergence in the professed behaviour of the witches.

To make a further comparison with Essex, Macfarlane found that the English witches were blamed in particular for causing people's deaths. A glance at the statistics for Jutland reveals a marked difference: the Jutland witches were accused of causing sickness among their fellow-villagers twice as frequently as death. Unfortunately, my lack of knowledge of the situation in England precludes me from venturing on an explanation for this significant difference.

What I have demonstrated elsewhere is that the charges levelled against the Danish witches in town and country corresponded to varying 'occupational structures'. In the towns the witches were often accused of bewitching trade and business, but these accusations were never made in the country; conversely, accusations of causing death and illness to cattle occur two and a half times as often in the country as in the towns. The rural witches were charged with having turned the milk sour three times as often as the urban witches.[30] Similar

---

[28] Beckman, 'Un épidémie de sorcellerie', p. 447.

[29] Ladurie, *La Sorcière de Jasmin*, p. 41; cf. Alfred Soman, 'Les Procès de sorcellerie au Parlement de Paris (1565–1640)', *Annales ESC* 32 (1977), 801.

[30] See Johansen, 'Als die Fischer den Teufel . . .', p. 163. Cf. Robert Higgins, 'Popular Beliefs about Witches: The Evidence from East London, 1645–60', *East London Record*, 4 (1981), 40.

investigations should reveal corresponding differences in other countries.

IV. A POPULAR MYTHOLOGY

Although the indictments against the Jutland witches concentrated on *maleficium*, it appears from the confessions made by sentenced witches that a popular mythology also existed about the witches. This is most evident in the confessions produced 'spontaneously' by the accused before the jury had pronounced their verdict (and thus not evoked during the application of 'legal' torture). In general, these confessions show that certain beliefs existed among the population as to how the witches and sorcerers were organized in order to perform their magic, how they met together on certain days, first and foremost at churches, how they underwent an initiation ritual, and how they had certain supernatural assistants at their disposal (in the Jutland records these usually appear under the designation of 'lads').

A woman from north-west Jutland confessed the week after she had been imprisoned that twelve years before, another woman had made her dance three times widdershins around Ydby church, after which she had blown through the keyhole of the church door, committed her soul to the devil, and renounced her baptism and Christianity. When she had done this the devil appeared to them in the form of a big, black, hairless dog without a tail. Another north Jutland woman made a pact with the devil in Lodbjerg churchyard, where she blew in through the keyhole and renounced God; with her in the churchyard were thirteen or fourteen people who were in the same coven. The feature of blowing through the keyhole must have been part of a popular belief, but it is impossible to discover how it made its way into the witch mythology.

Other details, however, seem to be explainable as elements of ideas stemming from pre-Reformation times. While the learned witch-tradition was first fully developed during the second half of the sixteenth century in Central Europe, it is reasonable to assume that at least some elements had a popular origin. An old woman from the Randers district confessed that her 'lad' had come to her forty-three years earlier and said that she would never lack anything if she followed him. They rode together to Vammen church and walked round the church three times, whereupon the 'lad' kicked open the church door with his foot and went up to the high altar with her. Here he told her to renounce her baptism and Christianity, and forswear God the Father and God the Mother; then he disappeared in a fog. Later on he appeared before her in Fastruplund and was as lovely as a maiden, and he told her to take the chalice, the paten, and the altar-cloth in the church and forswear them. Parts of this confession (high altar, God the Mother) obviously originate in pre-Reformation ideas.

A new feature of the initiation ritual emerges during the early 1620s, the 'mark of Satan'. One may partially trace the development of this feature, while the trials in Jutland were at their height. The first time that the 'mark of Satan' appears in the Jutland material is in 1621, and then not in connection with the performance in church, which some years later came to be the central feature in the complex of ideas. A woman confessed that when she bound herself to the Evil One he came to her bed as a dun colt; later he turned into a little naked 'lad'. She promised to serve him, whereupon he gave her a mark on her right arm. The woman continued by confessing that afterwards she had gone with him to Gudbjerg church, where she danced round the church numerous times. After this she blew in through the keyhole and went into the church, where she danced around the altar with blue candles in her hands. The uneven reception during the 1620s of the idea of the 'mark of Satan' can be demonstrated in confessions from 1623 and 1624. In the latter year a woman told how her 'lad' tried to scratch a hole above her eyes, and when she put up her arms to protect them, he tore a big scratch in her left arm. In the former year, however, we find in three confessions from Vendsyssel a complete fusion of the 'mark of Satan' motif and the initiation in church. A woman confessed that she had taught her own son witchcraft, and that he forswore his Christianity at Bjergby church. He often went with the witches to Troms church in Norway, where he acted as their 'parish clerk'. Their coven leader preached in Latin and German, so they were unable to understand what he said. Her 'lad' was called Plett, and he had placed his mark on her stomach (the woman may have thought this was somewhat indecent, so in the County Court she changed it to a mark on her nose). About three weeks later another woman from the same district confessed that five years previously she had been threatened by two women and forced to accompany them to St Hans Church in Hjørring, where she blew in through the keyhole and renounced her Christianity. Then a black dog came out through the door of the church and pricked her on the forehead so that it bled. The witches gathered every year on Walpurgis Night, Midsummer Night, and St Lucia's Eve (12 December). Finally, three months later a third woman confessed that earlier in the year she had gone to a house where twelve people were gathered together. They went to Hørby church, and when they arrived at the church porch they found a beautiful 'lad', whom the others wanted to give to the woman. They asked her to blow through the key-hole and renounce her Christianity, which she did. When she turned round the beautiful 'lad' had turned into a hairless black dog; the devil struck her on the forehead and made a hole, the scar of which could still be seen at the trial. Three years later, yet another woman from the same district confessed that she had been to Ulsted churchyard in the company of three other women, where she blew through the keyhole and renounced her Christianity. Then a little black shaggy dog appeared which scratched her on the nose so that it bled, and since then the dog had stayed with her.

In trial records from 1632 and 1653 we can trace the development of the devil's mark idea in other parts of Jutland; in Fasterlund the mark was set on the witch's forehead, and in Mors under her chin. There can thus be no doubt that here we have an idea that had spread until it was common knowledge among the populace. Oral tradition had fused the devil's mark and the initiation in church into a unified concept. The notion first spread in a relatively short space of time over a limited area, from which it extended to larger portions of Jutland.

Although I consider these concepts to originate largely in popular beliefs, careful consideration must also be given to the fact that theological thought can also be traced in the Jutland records. But only sporadically, and in quite specific circumstances.

The most notorious witch in Denmark came from Ribe and was called Maren Splids. Although hers is a gripping story we shall not include it here, except for one particular point: it was extraordinarily difficult for the authorities to get this woman condemned to the stake, owing to opposition from certain influential circles in the Ribe community. Her case therefore made its way to the very top of the appeal system: to the King's Court. When she had been taken to Copenhagen she apparently lost courage and confessed. But consider-ing the furore her case had aroused, her confession is remarkably short on detail: she had become a member of the coven after one of the other witches had come to her with a red dog. Maren Splids called it Andreas, and the dog touched her clothes, which had the effect of making her his servant. The witches gathered three times a year, on

Walpurgis Day, Midsummer Day, and Michaelmas Day, either in the home of one of the women or at Fardrup churchyard. There was one single international feature in her confession, and this can probably be ascribed to the fact that she was first interrogated in Copenhagen, where the theologians present were able to make use of their Continental expertise in demonology. Maren Splids was the only Danish witch to confess that when she went to holy communion she took the bread and hid it in her apron, and that afterwards she trampled and spat on it. The names of the theologians who interrogated her are not known, but such testimony leads one to surmise that it was inspired by the bishop of Sealand, Jesper Brochmand (in office from 1639 to 1652), who in his chief dogmatic work *Universae theologiae systema* (1633) described how witches could travel through the air at wondrous speed to their gatherings, dances, and so on.[31]

Brochmand presumed a far more sophisticated and intellectual concept of witches than the Danish representatives were able to provide in their confessions. This is clearly apparent in a trial record from 1632, when a witch described in her confession something most nearly approaching a sabbath. It is almost exaggeration to call it a description of a sabbath, but nevertheless, it is typical of the Jutland witches. Ten years earlier three women had instructed the accused in witchcraft when she had met all twelve of the coven at Borris churchyard. They made her walk backwards three times around the church and renounce her Christianity, after which she blew three times through the keyhole in the name of the devil. After this the devil came to her in the figure of a black dog and set his mark on her forehead. Jørgen Simensen was the leader of their coven, Las Krag their drummer, and Chresten Pedersen their piper. They had danced at Faster churchyard in the autumn, when they took beer and mead with them. Jørgen Simensen fornicated with the wealthiest women in the coven. When the coven went to Faster churchyard to dance and enjoy themselves they first went into the church, where their 'lads' were counted. Here the members repeated their promise to continue to live as witches, and Jørgen Simensen preached, now and again lifting the alb over his head. He committed fornication with one of the women, which was his custom when they were out on their wicked business.

As in the confessions described earlier, the absence of a personified devil is a distinctive feature; and when he does occasionally appear, he

---

[31] Jens Glebe Møller, 'Det teologiske fakultet, 1597–1732', in *Københavns Universitet, 1479–1979*, V (1979), 137.

usually turns out to be one of the so-called assistant devils, in most instances in the form of a dog. Indeed, it is most often the witches who dominate 'the devil', as in the case recounted earlier of the three women who had the devil with them in the figure of a cat that they beat with a rod to make 'him' bewitch a man. (Several examples of this type could be given.) The sabbath notion *can* be glimpsed, but only to a rudimentary degree, and the night-flying witch is hardly traceable at all.

Thus in Denmark one can find three levels of witch- and sorcery-belief: (1) a popular belief in witchcraft which is dominated by *maleficium*: (2) a learned witch-belief which in reality can be documented only by the work of Bishop Jesper Brochmand (and forty years later, by the vicar Johan Brunsmand's book on the Køge 'Vixens'), where the concept is a practically verbatim copy of the Continental demonologists. It is noteworthy in this connection that after 1633 Brochmand's *Systema* was *the* textbook in dogmatics at the theological faculty in Copenhagen. (3) Somewhere between these two positions can be placed a third and hitherto unnoticed form: a popular witch-belief.

My definition of this belief as popular must be regarded in the light of the fact that the most renowned Danish theologian of the time, Niels Hemmingsen, in the second half of the sixteenth century certainly accepted the existence of witches and sorcerers who were able to harm people and animals, but only vaguely admitted that they could fly through the air.[32] The influence Hemmingsen exercised on the next generation of Danish clergy was decisive.[33] Considering Hemmingsen's status, it is reasonable to assume that the Danish parish vicars took him as their guide on the question of what they were to believe and think about witchcraft. However, Hemmingsen categorically declared the notion of the sabbath an illusion.[34] As there

---

[32] Niels Hemmingsen, *Admonitio de superstitionibus magicis vitandis* (Copenhagen, 1575), sig. Liiᵛ: 'Specialiter enim hic malefici dicuntur propter facinorum detestandam abominationem, qui arte magica hominibus, animalibus aut fructibus maligne … nocent, aut eas de loco in locum transferunt.'

[33] Poul G. Lindhardt, 'Til belysning af Niels Hemmingsens indflydelse på dansk prædiken omkring 1600' (For the Elucidation of Niels Hemmingsen on Danish Preaching around 1600), in *Festskrift til Jens Nørregaard* (Copenhagen, 1947), 131–3.

[34] Hemmingsen, *Admonitio de superstitionibus*, sig. Kiiiiʳ: 'Proinde cum quaeri solet, num Sagae et veneficae mulieres noctu ad certa loca conveniant, transformatis corporibus et conviventur, certo statuendum est illusionem Diabolorum esse, qui et illarum et eorum quibus occurrere videtur, oculus praestringunt, ut putent se videre quod nusquam est. Videtur quidem hoc sagis ipsis, sed revera est Diabolorum illusio. Imponunt enim isti callidi hostes miserorum sensibus, ut credant omnia revera agi, quae nihil sunt nisi spectra quaedam et praestigiae.'

was no other Danish source[35] where the vicars could read about these subjects, it must be regarded unlikely that they would have described the organizational side of the witch-system from the pulpit.

Nevertheless, we learn from the confessions that the witches were admitted to the coven in the churchyard, and that the devil stood at the open door of the church when the aspirant witches had blown through the keyhole. This was indeed the oddest place of all for the witches to meet the devil—in the church itself! The clergy would hardly have told their congregations that the devil was at work in this holy place—but there is no doubt that he had a very firm footing there in the popular consciousness. The explanation is that the church wall-paintings were teeming with devils, and more than one vicar may very likely have added weight to his sermon by pointing to these devils[36] in order to warn his congregation against the horrors that awaited them if they did not follow the straight and narrow way of orthodox Lutheranism.[37]

If we study the wall-paintings, we see the devil performing various functions: he tempts the proud and unchaste, he incites gossip during divine service, he lures people into leaving the church early, he makes people over-indulgent with food and drink, he helps the witches meddle with the milk, he drives the damned to Hell.[38] The devil was indeed in the church, and through these scenes on its walls popular consciousness created its own mythology, which could maintain deeply rooted convictions, as when a woman confessed that the devil led her up to the high altar.

The wall-paintings may also offer an explanation of why the assistant devils often appear as dogs, a more probable reason than the one recently promoted: that the accused were often kind to animals.[39]

[35] As stressed above, Bishop Jesper Brochmand obviously exhibited other opinions on the subject. That he was well versed in demonology is apparent from the catalogue of his library: it contained not only supporters but also opponents of the demonological theory, thus on the one hand for instance Delrio, Binsfeld, Remy, as well as the *Malleus maleficarum*, and on the other hand Weyer, Scot, and Spee (The Arnamagnaean Collection, University of Copenhagen, MS 'Bibliotheca Brochmanniana', AM 901, 4to).

[36] *Peder Palladius' Visitatsbog* (Peder Palladius's Book of Visitation), ed. Lis Jacobsen (Copenhagen, 1925), 36: 'tafflerne eller billeder kunne de sla paa veggen, at dj kunde verre goede eenfoldigis spegel' (they could hang the paintings and pictures on the walls as a mirror for good and simple-minded people).

[37] Cf. Robert Scribner, 'Cosmic Order and Daily Life: Sacred and Secular in Pre-industrial German Society', in Kaspar von Greyerz (ed.), *Religion and Society in Early Modern Europe* (London, 1984), 25: 'the demonic was not regarded by the laity with the same abhorrence as it was by the clergy or theologian.'

[38] Ebbe Nyborg, *Fanden på væggen* (The Devil on the Wall) (Århus, 1978).

[39] Merete Birkelund, *Troldkvinden og hendes anklagere* (The Witch and her Accusers) (Århus, 1983), 81.

In Ejsing church, Christ is tempted in the desert by the devil—in the shape of a ferocious-looking dog! Popular imagination was so vivid that on given occasions the devil came to take this form.

The notion of the witches beating the devil with a rod was clearly also a popular belief, originating from the wall-paintings. The idea was strongly contested by the first superintendent of Sealand. Peder Palladius, who wrote at the beginning of the 1540s, 'it is nothing but lies to say that the Devil himself is afraid of her [i.e. the witch], he is only afraid of God.'[40] Considering the high esteem enjoyed by Palladius long after his death, it is unlikely that the parish vicars would have disagreed with his views.[41] Even taking into account a medieval tradition concerning the whipped devil,[42] we can exclude the idea of a Danish vicar after the Reformation teaching that the devil was subject to the witches. At that time fear of the devil was so strong that there can have been no doubts among our native theologians as to who wielded the power. But the congregation could see in the wall-paintings that the devil was beaten. There were representations of this in at least six churches. Four in Jutland: at Gjerrild in Djursland, Voldby also in Djursland, Vejlby near Århus, and Estruplund near Randers,[43] and two in Falster: Brarup and Åstrup, painted by the same artist[44]—in the latter case the painting was on the women's side, above the church door. The idea was there in popular consciousness, and was so strong that it was expressed in the confessions. This is the more surprising since in the seventeenth century it was not a matter of the somewhat ridiculous devil-figure of the late Middle Ages, but of an almost equal opponent. Even if we assume that the devils of the wall-paintings were transformed in the collective consciousness into 'assistant devils', it must not be forgotten that it was frequently the 'assistant devils' who carried out the various bewitchings. They were certainly opponents to be reckoned with.

[40] Peder Palladius was superintendent from 1537 to 1560. *Peder Palladius' Visitatsbog*, p. 111.

[41] Cf. Hemmingsen, *Admonitio de superstitionibus*, sig. Biiiᵛ: 'Ex quo sit, ut interdum sequatur cum ea, ut nunc sub hac, nunc sub illa forma, se videndum exhibeat, adeo ut interdum se ab ea flagellari, quod imperata non fecerit, simulet, atque ita ex parvis initiis detestada a Deo ad Diabolu sit defectio.'

[42] This behaviour bears some resemblance to the beating of statues of saints when the saints did not respond to the prayers directed to them; cf. Robert Muchembled, *Culture populaire et culture des élites* (Paris, 1978), 85.

[43] Nyborg, *Fanden på væggen*, pp. 82, 84, and 89.

[44] Lektor Niels Saxtorph's picture collection, Department of History, University of Copenhagen; cf. reproductions in Ankarloo and Henningsen, *Häxornas Europa*, facing p. 194.

It is impossible to say how the idea of the devil's mark took shape; it appears so relatively late in the Jutland confessions that one might assume that some vicars may have suggested that the witches were marked by the devil. On the other hand, this idea took form in popular consciousness comparatively slowly, and was connected with the notion that the witches gathered in and by churches.

In conclusion, it must be maintained that in Denmark three levels of belief in witchcraft and sorcery are observable, of which one only was dominant: the belief in *maleficium*. Another level comprised a popular witch-belief that was obviously contrary to the theologial stance on the problem. The witches' presence in church, their power over the devil, and other motifs belong to this folk-tradition, which may very possibly have originated in a learned tradition, but which in the course of the sixteenth century was transformed in popular consciousness, fed by the presence of painted devils in the churches.

There are relatively few references to this folk-belief in the trial records; it did not have the intrinsic power to dominate the subject-matter of the trials, but it lived a life of its own, and must have been regarded with great displeasure by the clergy.

14
Norway: The Criminological Context
HANS EYVIND NAESS

I. THE ADMINISTRATION OF JUSTICE

FROM the late fourteenth century, Norway was joined with Denmark in a personal union, that is, the two countries had their king in common, but otherwise their political and legal administrations were kept apart. This system was changed in 1536. The war of succession (1534–6) had discredited the noblemen and prelates of the Norwegian council, who supported the losing cause. All political power was now vested in the king's person and in a council without Norwegian representation. The king in council decided that from now on Norway was to be considered a province of the Danish kingdom like Jutland, Sjælland, and Fyn. This real union lasted until 1814.

As a result, the king's council ruling Norway after 1536 consisted mostly of Danish noblemen. Gradually the High Court of Justice, the *Herredag*, was staffed with Danes, even when in session in Norway. The district governors, the *lensherrer*, were noblemen appointed by the king. Soon they too were all Danes. Even the local bailiffs were mostly recruited from Denmark, having started their careers as servants in the household of the governors. These bailiffs were responsible for the day-to-day administration of most local affairs, their superiors often being away on their manors in Denmark.

Also the district judges, the *lagmenn*, were slowly being replaced by men of foreign origin. From 1591 on the king's governors appointed councillors, *sorenskrivere*, to the local courts. In most cases they were from the southern provinces. After legal reforms in 1634 these councillors controlled the local courts.

After the Reformation, the old Norwegian Catholic clergy were in due course replaced by Lutheran pastors, many of whom were Danish students who had studied theology in Wittenberg and other German universities as well as in Copenhagen.

II. THE LEGISLATION

The thirteenth-century national law of Norway, the *Landsloven*, stated that *maleficium*, killing or injuring by supernatural means, was a capital offence. This statute, however, does not seem to have been in much use until after the Reformation. As far as we know some time went by until the death penalty in cases of witchcraft was generally accepted. The burning or decapitation of witches probably started earlier in Denmark, with quite a few executions already in the 1530s, and many more in the following decades.

The king and his council had tried to intervene in the procedures adopted in these trials, enacting that denunciations by witches should not be accepted as proof in any trial. Furthermore, the new statutes emphasized that the use of torture was forbidden until after a sentence had been passed. These acts date from 1547, 1558, and 1576.[1]

It is noteworthy that already in the 1520s King Christian II had introduced new and harsher rules for procedures in criminal cases. They were, however, never put into effect. The procedure in witch-trials in mid-sixteenth-century Denmark nevertheless seems to have been influenced by the harsher practice on the European Continent. In 1584 the king agreed to the necessity of introducing the full learned concept of demonology into the criminal code of Norway, when his Lutheran bishop in Stavanger demanded it. The king's attention was drawn to the fact that the habit of consulting wise men and women was widespread in the Norwegian countryside. In his letter to the king the bishop described this practice as a deadly sin against God. One of the cases brought before the bishop involved a district judge, a *lagmann*, who had consulted several wise men and women to cure his wife. The king immediately responded by making white magic a capital offence in the diocese of Stavanger. In 1593 this local criminal law was extended over all of Norway.[2]

The statutes of 1584/93 make it clear that the government paid attention to the prevailing demonological concepts. At the same time a new criminal code in progress was heavily influenced by the Mosaic law of the Old Testament. The king enacted severer laws against homicide and theft. White magic was criminalized in Denmark too,

---

[1] Cf. Jens Christian V. Johansen, ch. 13, above.
[2] Hans Eyvind Naess, *Trolldomsprosessene i Norge på 1500–1600-tallet* (The Witch-trials in Norway in the 16th and 17th Centuries) (Oslo, 1982), 78–80.

punishable by banishment from the province. Infanticide, incest, blasphemy, and *crimen bestialis* were included in the penal code as indisputable capital crimes alongside rape, repeated adultery, treason, and secret murder.[3] The use of reprieve was restricted. The new severe laws were in most cases based upon the Mosaic code. This was also the case when a new witchcraft act was put into effect in 1617. Its distinction between demoniacal and white magic meant, however, that the latter ceased to be a capital crime, as it had been in the statutes of 1584/93. Nevertheless, from the court records we know that wise women in several cases after 1617 were put to death without being accused of *maleficium* or a pact with the devil.[4]

III. WITCHCRAFT AND CRIME

In the medieval Norwegian (and Danish) laws the crime of witchcraft was defined as *maleficium*. Only when leading to death or injuries in people or animals was it considered a capital crime. White magic, such as healing practices, was not considered a crime to be punished. It is important to remember that witchcraft, in spite of all the attention given to it in modern research, does not emerge as the main or out-standing capital crime in the laws of the sixteenth and seventeenth centuries. It was one of a number of capital offences, such as murder and manslaughter, theft, adultery, incest, infanticide, *crimen bestialis*, treason, and blasphemy. Numerous minor sexual and moral offences, as well as fighting and swearing, were frequently brought before the local courts.

In order to illustrate the relative importance of the crime of witch-craft I have examined the records of the county of Rogaland. During the 1620s, 1650s, and 1690s, only 2 out of 40 death sentences in two rural jurisdictions of the county were passed for witchcraft. The rest were for incest (12), theft (10), homicide (9), infanticide (4), and adultery (3). From another preliminary examination of all capital crimes in Rogaland in 1610–60, it turns out that out of 223 death sentences in the rural jurisdictions, only 116 were executed. The difference was due to the fact that 63 persons escaped and another 44 had their sentences reduced. The offences committed were theft (33 executions), incest (21), homicide (15), witchcraft (14), vagabondage in

---

[3] Ibid., pp. 40–63.
[4] Ibid., Appendix, pp. 502–67, cases no. 570 (1618), 267 (1633), and 206a (1667).

combination with theft or adultery (13), infanticide (10), and the use of false weight, measures, and passports (2).

Thus the number of death sentences for witchcraft account for 5 per cent and the executions for about 12 per cent of the total in the period 1610–60, when the persecutions were at their height. Considerably more people were executed for infanticide or incest, even during the great witch-hunt. The relative importance of witchcraft was of course even less both before and after that period.[5]

IV. THE NUMBER OF TRIALS

The rather distinct difference in numbers of trials in the various counties must not lead to the conclusion—at least, not until the problem has been further examined—that the distribution of witch persecutions in Norway was due to large regional differences in popular beliefs and in the practice of criminal justice. The variation in numbers is mainly explained by the fact that the primary sources are better preserved in some areas. The highest number of trials are, not surprisingly, to be found where the court records are more fully preserved.

In other areas we have to rely on information from other types of material. Apart from the court records, the main sources for the study of crime are the bailiffs' accounts, where expenditure on custody in prison, torture, water ordeals, and executions was entered. Useful information is also to be found on the credit side of the accounts, where the revenues from the trials—that is, fines and the confiscation of the estate of convicted witches—were minutely recorded. The best and most complete records, both court rolls and bailiffs' accounts, have been preserved in the counties of Rogaland, Finnmark, and Hordaland.

The bulk of the trials took place between 1570 and 1700, with a few minor and scattered cases before and after that period. One single trial is known from the Middle Ages. In 1325 a woman was summoned to the ecclesiastical court in Bergen accused of having performed love magic. From the brief document we know that she had to do penance and was sent on a pilgrimage.[6] The first-known capital convictions are

---

[5] Alfred Soman, 'Deviance and Criminal Justice in Western Europe, 1300–1800', *Criminal Justice History*, 1 (1980), 1–28.

[6] Naess, *Trolldomsprosessene*, p. 14. The source in *Diplomatarium Norvegicum*, ix (Christiania, 1876), 112–15.

from the 1560s. The total number of persons known to have been summoned to court under the laws against witchcraft is 863 (Table 14.1). This figure includes 95 defamation cases, where a stigmatized person initiated a lawsuit to rid himself of the dishonour resulting from the rumours. If we subtract these 95 defamation trials, and an additional 35 where the indictment was directed against persons who had consulted, or were considered accomplices of wise women, a total of 730 cases of witchcraft proper emerge.

The accusations were based on abusive remarks or the suspicion of *maleficium*, a pact with the devil, or sorcery. 280 executions are recorded. This indicates a capital conviction rate as high as 38 per cent. However, such a rate is obviously too high. Quite a number of less serious cases are probably missing from the court records, and

TABLE 14.1. *Norwegian witch-trials, 1551–1760*

	Trials	Capital convictions
1551–60	—	—
1561–70	4	—
1571–80	25	3
1581–90	17	5
1591–1600	16	7
1601–10	21	11
1611–20	73	33
1621–30	134	69
1631–40	80	31
1641–50	97	41
1651–60	80	26
1661–70	157	47
1671–80	56	5
1681–90	64	1
1691–1700	26	1
1701–10	2	—
1711–20	2	—
1721–30	1	—
1731–40	6	—
1741–50	1	—
1751–60	1	—
Total	863	280

since they did not lead to execution, fines, or confiscation they have left no traces in the bailiffs' accounts either.

It is therefore somewhat difficult to estimate the total number of witch-trials in Norway. The archives from the sixteenth century are incomplete. The bailiffs' accounts are preserved from the 1590s onwards, and they are relatively complete in most counties throughout the following century. Consequently one must suppose that the majority of the witch executions are known to us. Taking into account those who were sentenced before the 1590s, an estimate of about 350 persons executed as witches in Norway may be considered reasonable. Roughly guessed, the total number of trials may have been around 1,400. The Norwegian persecutions, as measured in numbers as well as in a capital conviction rate estimated at 25 per cent, do not seem to have surpassed those in other comparable European countries.

V. THE TYPOLOGY OF WITCHCRAFT

One can reasonably assume that all the many stories of magic and witchcraft told in the courts during the witch-hunt by the plaintiffs, witnesses, bailiffs, pastors, and judges give a fairly comprehensive picture of contemporary concepts in this field. The accusation of diabolism, that is, of pacts with the devil and participation in the sabbath, were invariably put forward by bailiffs and pastors. The private accusers, the neighbours and the other members of the local community, never brought into court accusations of this kind; neither did the accused witches and sorcerers willingly confess to such allegations. On the other hand, the accusations covered a wide range of beliefs in magic and sorcery, as can be seen from Table 14.2.

As other studies have observed, the step from white to maleficent magic was sometimes short. Men and women at first accepted as members of the local community because of their healing abilities often turned out to be feared and hated persons when doubts arose as to whether they were good or evil neighbours. The rumours accumulated over many years. Suspicions on the part of individuals changed to collective fear and subsequently to formal accusations of witchcraft.

Much information comes from the witches' own confessions. They indicate that there existed various beliefs running counter to the dogmas of the Church. These included healing practices using herb mixtures and substances such as teeth, toes, and animal tails, and

TABLE 14.2. *Norway: Types of accusation*

Type	Subtotal	Total
White magic		263
Maleficium resulting in:		398
homicide	90	
human sickness or injuries	129	
death of cattle	13	
sickness or injuries in cattle	37	
sinking of ships, killing of crew	63	
destruction of crops	19	
arson	6	
storms, tidal waves	9	
loss of fortune	8	
loss of love, impotence	14	
other	10	
Diabolism		128
Grand total		789

resting upon pre-Christian, supernatural beliefs. Furthermore, the magical formulas often contained stories of Jesus and Mary or other holy persons, or distorted elements from biblical texts and prayers heard during sermons in the church. Wise women charged with witchcraft were naturally rather astonished and made very anxious by the alleged connection with the devil; more often than not, they considered their activity to be directed towards helping their neighbours rather than committing a deadly sin. Their practices, however, made it possible for the authorities, both lay and clerical, to raise charges of witchcraft with reference to the prevailing demonology.

In many cases the accused turned the balance in their own disfavour. They often scorned their neighbours, and the result of their activities, for which they were rather well paid, often turned out to be deadly rather than curative. Traditional popular rites were also in use, such as walking around the church thrice or performing various acts a specific number of times. The plaintiffs representing the solid part of the local community, together with the bailiffs and pastors, shared a common fear of the accused witches. For the pastors responsible for

the examinations the guilt was beyond question. For them the important issue was to make the witches confess in order to save their
immortal souls before they were burnt or beheaded.

I fully share the view that prior to the period of witch persecutions
there existed a popular belief in the supernatural alongside a traditional clerical teaching about the devil and his impact upon mankind,
to which the systematic learned concept of witchcraft as formulated in
the manuals of the demonologists was added.[7] Beginning in the
second half of the sixteenth century, the clergy in Denmark–Norway
were educated in the orthodox Lutheran theology, including
demonology and the learned concept of witchcraft. They would
preach this concept from the pulpit and warn their congregations
against witches and sorcerers.

The early Lutheran bishops had been quite outspoken to this end.
In Denmark, Peder Palladius and several of his colleagues had since
the 1530s demanded that witches be brought to trial and executed.
This firm attitude from the leading authorities in the Danish Lutheran
Church reached its climax in Jørgen Erikssøn, who had studied in
Copenhagen and Wittenberg. As bishop in the diocese of Stavanger he
succeeded, as we have seen, in obtaining a new local law in 1584,
according to which all forms of witchcraft should be punishable by
death. During the first decades of the seventeenth century the death
penalty became more often used, alongside harsh procedural means,
the water ordeal and torture.

The clergy made practical use of their demonological education.
The records show that they were responsible for the examinations
both before and during torture.[8] Their interrogations seem to have
been in accordance with the series of questions recorded in manuals of
demonology. And the most zealous pastors were not content until the
confessions satisfied the demands laid down in these manuals. At the
height of the witch persecutions in Norway, the pastors were no doubt
as active as were their colleagues on the Continent.

As a matter of course, the learned concept of witchcraft spread all
over Norway, enhancing people's traditional fears of *maleficium*. In the
same period there was a rather marked migration of people in search
of farm land. Many were constantly on the move, and the number of
vagrants and beggars increased in the wake of population increase.

---

[7] Johansen, ch. 13, above.
[8] Naess, *Trolldomsprosessene*, p. 197.

The stories of the pact with the devil and the sabbath were spread from the pulpits and the torture chambers. They soon became common knowledge. It is no surprise, then, that persons wishing to avoid cruel treatment by their bailiff knew what to confess even before the examination had begun.

VI. THE LEGAL PROCEDURES

Criminal cases were conducted according to accusatorial procedures. The offended party indicted the aggressor. Where public safety and order was considered endangered, the bailiff or his sheriff acted as prosecutor. This was often the case when thieves, killers, rapists, and traitors were brought before the court. Public prosecution was also resorted to when rumours of witchcraft were at hand. According to the *landslov* such rumours must, however, have come from at least three independent quarters, or 'houses'.

When the indictment was based on a private accusation, at least two independent witnesses would have to swear to the guilt of the accused. In most cases the indictments were presented to the local court by the bailiff or his sheriff on behalf of the plaintiff.

The bailiff had an enormous influence on the trial. Besides being the public prosecutor, he administered the court. He imprisoned the defendants and was responsible for the examinations out of court. He decided when torture, threats, or water ordeals were to be used. He co-operated in his examinations with the local pastor, who advised on the administration of the moral code and God's will. He had the condemned persons tortured, and he executed all sentences. He could even come to terms with the delinquent out of court, thus adding a special authority to his office, combining the role of prosecutor and judge.

We know that torture was applied in forty Norwegian witch-trials. In ten of these cases it was resorted to before sentence had been passed, although this was against the mid-sixteenth-century laws already mentioned. Great pain was inflicted on the accused witches and sorcerers. The pastors were present and asked the prisoners to confess to diabolism. Naturally they did in the end. Trials starting as *maleficium* cases often ended in convictions for a pact with the devil or participation in the witches' sabbath.

To further strengthen the evidence, suspects were submitted to the water ordeal, known to have been in use in Norway since 1606.[9] 23 cases are known. In the 1660s the ordeal was prohibited, but several bailiffs continued to make use of it for some time.

Not a single man or woman may be said to have confessed voluntarily to *maleficium* or diabolism in the Norwegian trials. On the contrary, we have a large number of incidents where the accused lamented their situation, complaining that the bailiffs and pastors had forced them to confess. In the end they also gave in and acquiesced to all questions asked.

Thus the authorities did not always try to conduct a fair trial in accordance with the law, but circumvented it to extract the largest possible number of confessions. One witch gave another sound advice: 'Should you choose not to confess at once, they will try you on the water and next you will be put on the rack. After having extended your limbs they will increase your pains by pinching you with redhot iron tongs.'[10]

The rack was in common use. In some cases, burning sulphur was poured on the prisoner's breasts. The pains of prison and torture led to several deaths before trial. Some froze to death. In another case, 'the witch having committed suicide was thrown into the fire with the other witches that were burnt that day.'[11] In several trials the accused were persuaded to confess, erroneously believing that their co-operation would get them acquitted.[12] But as long as they could stand the pain, most accused pleaded not guilty, maintaining that they knew nothing about witchcraft. One woman swore to God 'that she was completely innocent; she had not committed any of the evil deeds of which she was accused'.[13] A judge who was about to acquit several women previously sentenced to death, asked one of them why she had confessed to all the unbelievable things like the sabbath and diabolism. She answered that she 'would rather lay this crime upon [herself] and shorten [her] life than suffer more torture than strictly necessary'.[14]

The convicted were forced to denounce accomplices. These were promptly indicted and in many cases sentenced to death without any further proof. This was also in contravention of the laws of 1547 and 1558. From ninety well-documented trials we know the names of 353 persons who were denounced in this way.[15] In fact, the majority of

---

[9] Naess, *Trolldomsprosessene*, p. 199.   [10] Ibid., p. 219.
[11] Ibid., p. 558 (trial no. 753).   [12] Ibid., p. 218.
[13] Ibid., p. 242.   [14] Ibid., p. 220.   [15] Ibid., p. 224.

death sentences for witchcraft in Norway were passed in such denunciation cases.

The population of Norway increased from about 100,000 to 440,000 in the period 1500–1650. The annual rate of increase was rather drastically reduced in the late seventeenth century, due to various demographic crises, but the growth continued, although on a somewhat lower scale, reaching 600,000 by about 1750.

Some 30 per cent of the Norwegian farms had been abandoned subsequent to the Black Death. As the number of inhabitants increased, nearly all the old farms were taken up anew and were eventually subdivided into smaller units. In the sixteenth and seventeenth centuries a new social group came into existence, a poor class of crofters renting small fields on the outskirts of farms. At the same time the number of beggars, vagrants, and poor increased, as in many other European countries. Calculations have shown that around 1600, in several areas these poor classes reached 10 per cent of the population.[16] They represented, of course, a grave social problem. They were no longer able to pay their taxes. The beggars became a burden to their communities and were more often involved in various kinds of criminal activities than their more well-to-do neighbours. My research in the source-material from the county of Rogaland indicates that there was a connection between the circumstances leading to indictments for witchcraft and the social standing of the suspects. In 160 of the 196 trials containing documentation on the economic situation of those accused, they were characterized as extremely poor.

One could argue that the 196 cases add up to no more than about 20 per cent of the total number of recorded trials. On the other hand, they were mostly trials ending in serious punishment, execution, or banishment. In these cases, then, we know that the large majority of victims were in fact very poor. The convicted witches and sorcerers were beggars, vagrants, or both. They lived in miserable dwellings. One witch owned a single cow, another three sheep. Their estate was normally too small to cover the cost of the trial and the execution. They left nothing for their kith and kin when they expired. Once,

---

[16] Carlo M. Cipolla, *Before the Industrial Revolution* (London, 1976), 14–19.

when a district judge demanded that he himself examine a woman imprisoned for witchcraft, the bailiff had to buy her a fur coat because she was lying completely naked in the dungeon in the middle of the winter. Several witches owned nothing but their old torn clothes, which barely hid their naked bodies.[17]

About 80 per cent of the accused were women. In 279 out of 313 trials containing matrimonial information, the accused was married or widowed.[18] Only a small number were young people or unmarried men or women. It is noteworthy that in about forty cases we know that the person indicted for witchcraft (including white magic) had earlier been brought before local courts for other crimes.[19] In several parishes the bailiff laid before the court proofs that the person accused had had a reputation for witchcraft for many years.

The witches, then, were very often already social outcasts when they were brought to trial. They were feared by their neighbours as bad and dangerous members of the community, whom the better-off would like to see rooted out. In conclusion, the person most likely to be accused of witchcraft in Norway was the oldish, poor, married woman. Being turned away when asking for the simplest form of help or support, such as milk, food, beer, clothes, money, or a night's sleep, she threatened her neighbours and thereby slowly made them fear her and want to get rid of her. It was sometimes told in court that the neighbours feared the witch so much that they fled the farm when they saw her approaching.

This connection between the characteristics of the persons being accused of witchcraft and the trends in contemporary demographic, social, and criminal history is interesting. Admittedly, neither the Norwegian trials nor the European witch persecutions may be fully explained by such correlations. However, it is difficult to see how the trials could have started off in communities where the economic as well as the social and cultural conditions were progressing. The ruthless trials against burdensome members of society must be explained by the coincidence of the depressed social situation in the local communities and the prevailing theology, criminal policy, and mental attitudes in society at large.

---

[17] Naess, *Trolldomsprosessene*, pp. 304–7.
[18] Ibid., p. 304.
[19] Ibid., pp. 302–3.

VIII. THE CESSATION OF THE WITCH-TRIALS

The rather abrupt halt to the witch-trials—or at least, to the executions—that took place in most European countries in the second half of the seventeenth century has long puzzled scholars. Norway is in this respect to be found in the European mainstream, the executions being rather numerous until almost totally coming to an end at about 1670.

In his essay on the Danish trials, Jens Christian Johansen argues that because the old witches were mostly accused before the 1630s, no more suspects with a long record of *maleficium* activities were to be found in that and later decades—and consequently, there were fewer trials.[20] The trials in Norway followed a different pattern, as they continued at an even pace until a sudden change took place in the 1660s.

Obviously, the situations that created rumours and suspicions in the villages had not disappeared, and the popular fear of witches and sorcerers continued, as manifested in later accusations and trials. But in Norway the judges of the Court of Appeal, the *lagmenn*, began shortly after 1650 to influence the course of witch-trials by taking a more critical view of the procedures in the lower courts.

When presiding in Finnmark in 1653, the district judge of the northern counties, Mandrup Schönneböl, found several women accused of witchcraft in the castle dungeon, locally known as the 'witches' hole'.[21] He had them brought before him and examined them personally, but found no valid proof against them. Accordingly they were all released. The members of the local court and the bailiff were criticized for having treated the women illegally. The judge, however, only visited this outpost of his enormous district every three years. The persecutions and burnings of witches in Finnmark had taken place regularly since the beginning of the century. Nearly always several among the small population were suspected of witchcraft. After the judge had left for his triennial absence, the local bailiff and his sheriffs renewed the indictments, and several women were burnt in spite of the ruling of the *lagmann*. Schönneböl, however, returned three years later. The whole performance at court was repeated. The

---

[20] Johansen, ch. 13, above.
[21] Naess, *Trolldomsprosessene*, pp. 268–72.

new suspects were again acquitted. Not until 1663 did the judge finally succeed in stopping the trials for good.

Almost simultaneously, during the 1660s, similar steps were taken by district judges in Trondheim, and by several judges in the southern provinces.[22]

At this moment private persons for the first time appeared in courts as defence counsel for the accused witches. The district judges as well as the defenders found that illegal procedures, including the use of forced examinations, torture, swimming, false denunciations, illegal use of confessions from accomplices, and so on, were in general practice. An end was put to all this. Several local judges, pastors, and bailiffs were heavily fined for their actions. The accused witches were acquitted and the local authorities were forced to compensate them for their expenses and inconvenience. In the course of a few years this was sufficient to discredit the trials for witchcraft altogether.

When force against suspects was no longer used, when the pastors were no longer allowed to take part in examinations, when the statutes of 1547 and 1558 were finally upheld, this in sum contributed to the breakdown of the mechanisms that had kept the trials going.

IX. CONCLUSIONS

For more than a century the townsmen and villagers of Norway had acted in close co-operation with the authorities in their endeavour to get rid of the performers of *maleficium*. The suspects were squeezed between their neighbours and the court system, the regular court procedures being set aside in these cases of *crimen exceptum*.

The result was that several hundred individuals, mostly poor, old women, were sentenced to the stake or the sword. The proof against them might consist solely of one or two denunciations. The law required that at least two independent accusers took full responsibility for the indictment. It also forbade the words of any witch or sorcerer or any other criminal to be used as evidence in court. These rules were frequently ignored. Death sentences were passed in cases of white magic, despite this also being forbidden according to the law modified in 1617.

When interpreting these actions by the local officers responsible for the administration of justice, we must take into consideration that they

[22] Naess, *Trolldomsprosessene*, pp. 269–74.

themselves believed in witchcraft, and that they had the support of popular opinion. In addition, the clergy warned their congregations against the servants of the devil, and the law required in no uncertain terms that measures be taken against witches. The procedures in common use on the Continent in such trials were brought to Norway by pastors, judges, and bailiffs born or educated in Denmark and Germany.

Hans Petter Graver has recently emphasized that the adverse re-actions to the procedures were not the result of one single man's rational conclusions in one court in one particular year.[23] One must surely allow for the change of opinion in certain quarters of the civil service and among the well-bred and well-read part of society to have taken place gradually up to the middle of the seventeenth century. The reaction against the illegal procedures came from the *lagmenn*, the ten district judges personally responsible for the judgements passed in the Courts of Appeal.

We still have no studies of the general administration of justice by the *lagmenn*. Research on their influence upon the history of criminal justice has been advocated by Sölvi Sogner. She accepts as an interesting hypothesis my contention that the measures taken by these leading judges against the illegal procedures in witch cases may have been crucial for the reduction of the number of trials.[24] She is, however, inclined to place more weight on the change of mental attitude in governments generally in the mid-seventeenth century, and chooses to see the reduction of trials as the result of a more relaxed attitude to dangers from outside, from the devil, invasions, wars, and devastations of various kinds. The situation had been brought under control. The weak culture of the early sixteenth century had stood its test. It had grown strong and safe, thanks to the spread of educational institutions. A Protestant Christianity which had felt itself under siege could now demobilize; earlier militant doctrines began to be ques-tioned.[25]

We know for certain that such changes in mental attitudes had taken place in high quarters. At the Danish court the king's physician, Thomas Bartholin, had already expressed scepticism as to the reality of witchcraft before the radical reduction in executions. The largest

---

[23] Hans Petter Graver, 'Rett under sosialt trykk: Rettssosiologiske aspekter ved troll-domsprosessene i Norge', *Lov og ret*, 1 (1984), 54–5.
[24] Sölvi Sogner, 'Trolldomsprosessene i Norge på 1500–1600-tallet', *Norveg* (1982), 174–6. [25] Ibid., p. 180.

number of examples of this new attitude come from the court records, where they are articulated by the judges and the defenders.

Even after a new criminal code had been issued in 1687, the law continued to use the terms of demonology: a man or woman making a pact with the devil should be burnt at the stake. In the local communities people continued for several years to demand that witches, sorcerers, and wise men and women should be punished according to the law. Even the old procedures and the swimmings continued.

Graver's conclusions are as follows. From one angle it may be maintained that the judicial system lent itself to fulfil religious, ideological, and social needs. Central authorities did not take any independent and decisive steps, but they did not do much to stop the process, either. This use of the legal system was tolerated even when it ran counter to those rules for criminal procedures which represented a safeguard against irregularities. This way of conducting criminal cases, however, was stopped from high quarters under the influence of a new ideology incompatible with the established procedures. Thus rules of fair and safe treatment and common safety for the defendants protected by law were of little use for suspects until new ideological considerations on the part of the authorities made it convenient to stop the witch-hunt.[26]

At the local level, prosecutions of witches continued, even when the use of death sentences was brought to a halt in the courtrooms. But it did not take long before the number of indictments was reduced as well. This was, I believe, the result of an accelerating process of change of mental attitudes spreading from above down to the rank and file of society, first reaching the judges, then the local administrators, the prosecutors, and at last the pastors and the common people. The general fear of impoverished neighbours tended to weaken as social responsibility for the poor increased both within the local bureaucracy and the Church. These changes in ideology and in social life help to explain the ultimate end of witch-beliefs, long after the courts of justice had ceased to deal with such cases.

[26] Graver, 'Ret under sosialt trykk', pp. 56–7.

15
Iceland: Sorcerers and Paganism
KIRSTEN HASTRUP

ICELAND is situated on the geographical margins of Europe, and the links of communication across the North Atlantic were not always intensive. Yet historically Iceland was always embedded in the wider Nordic and European context, a fact which is reflected also in the seventeenth-century witch-trials.

The present paper is concerned with these trials under the double perspective of the witch-craze in Early Modern Europe, in relation to which Iceland is but a peripheral instance, and the local cultural categories of witchcraft, defined from the core of a distinctive Icelandic culture. As elsewhere, the local shaping of the witch-hunt owed as much to pre-existing notions of supernatural powers as to the new ideas of satanic influence. Since the Viking Age and the first settlements on Iceland, a whole range of popular notions of magic intervention in nature and history had been central to the world-view of the Icelanders, and even the conversion to Christianity in AD 1000 had not estranged these notions.[1] In many ways the Catholic times represented a continuation of the heathen traditions, at least in practice, if not in theological doctrine. It is beyond the scope of this paper to discuss the implication of the alleged continuity between heathenism and Catholicism in Iceland; for the present purpose it suffices to note that the seventeenth-century witch-trials were post-Reformation, and that 'traditional' concepts of witchcraft were viewed from this post-Reformation perspective. From the point of view of the implantation of the European witch-hunt into Icelandic reality, the Reformation seems to have presented a much more significant event than the introduction of Christianity in general. One single court-case of witchcraft is known from Catholic times in the Norse colony in Greenland. There in 1407 a man was burnt after being found guilty of having practised 'black art' (svartakonst) to get his will with a woman.[2] It is an

---

[1] For an analysis of this original society I refer to Kirsten Hastrup, *Culture and History in Medieval Iceland* (Oxford, 1985).

[2] G. Storm (ed.), *Islandske Annaler indtil 1578* (Christiania, 1888), 288.

open question whether this should be regarded as an instance of Icelandic witchcraft at all. In any case, the remaining records of witch *prosecutions* in Iceland are post-Reformation, even though witchcraft as such was a recurrent theme also in pre-Reformation culture. This is the reason why I shall not dwell on the distinction between pre-Christian and Catholic times, but deal with 'traditional' concepts of witchcraft as pre-Reformation in general. Before the Reformation even the Church, which may have had theological misgivings, accepted magic in practice.

The paper is organized in four parts. I start with a general overview of the trials and their social setting. Next, the cultural categories of witchcraft and magic are discussed in their traditional form. This discussion serves as a necessary background for the presentation of a number of actual cases of witchcraft. Finally, I analyse the particular Icelandic realization of the witch-craze in a general European perspective. This brings us to a position where we can identify both similarities and differences between Iceland and other parts of Europe. Further, it illustrates the historical dynamism inherent in any conjunction between traditional cultural categories and new times.

I. THE SETTING

In the seventeenth century the Icelandic population consisted of some 50,000 individuals living in scattered farmsteads that nowhere clustered into villages; towns were entirely absent.[3] In this far northern island, living conditions were hard, the yields of nature were scarce, and the Danish rulers seemed more interested in gains on trade than in expenditure on the welfare of their remote subjects.[4] A trade monopoly from 1602 to 1789 had severe consequences for the Icelandic economy.[5] In addition, the climate worsened during the seventeenth century, hitting the rock bottom of the Little Ice Age in the last decade.[6] In conjunction with internal social and economic

---

[3] The first census in Iceland was made in 1703, when 50,358 inhabitants were counted. Possibly the number was higher in the 17th c. but only marginally so.

[4] Iceland was under Danish rule from 1380, when Norway and Denmark were united. Iceland had come under Norwegian supremacy in 1262–4. This political dependence accounts for the similarities between Icelandic and Scandinavian history.

[5] See Jón J. Aðils, *Einokunarverzlun Dana á Íslandi, 1602–1787* (2nd edn. Reykjavik, 1971) and Gisli Gunnarsson, *Monopoly Trade and Economic Stagnation: Studies in the Foreign Trade of Iceland, 1602–1787* (Lund, 1983).

[6] Þorvaldur Thoroddsen, *Árferði á Íslandi í þusund ár* (Copenhagen, 1916–17).

measures, these external factors resulted in a general impoverishment of the Icelanders and in recurrent famines and deaths from starvation.[7] Catastrophe was an ever-present accompaniment to life; misfortune was everyone's experience. Under these circumstances it is not surprising that the Icelanders should have looked for devilish causes of their ill-luck and should have engaged in the general witch-craze. It is more surprising, perhaps, that they should have done it to such a limited extent. Some 120 witch-processes are known from the period.[8] The numbers are slightly uncertain, mainly because the vocabulary of the witch-trials predominantly derived from an age-old language of black magic and only secondarily from the international demonology. Thus a case reported from 1554, when a priest was defrocked and exiled for having beguiled a young girl to intercourse by means of magic spells contained in *galdrabækur* ('books of magic'), may or may not be classified as a witch-trial.[9] In this case as in later trials the accusation is one of *galdur* ('witchcraft'). Apart from such doubtful cases we have reports, however meagre, of some 120 witch-trials from 1604 to 1720. Of these, twenty-two sent the witch to the stake. The first person to suffer this fate was sentenced in 1625, the last one in 1685.

Even within this short span of time, the trials were not evenly distributed. From 1625 many years were to lapse until the next fire was lit in 1654. From 1654 to 1656 five persons were burnt as witches. Again, there is a lapse of time until 1667 when one more person succumbs in the flames. Then from 1669 to 1685 fifteen individuals were sentenced to the stake. The uneven distribution in time is matched by an uneven distribution in space. There is a remarkable concentration of cases in the Westfjords (north-west Iceland). Both of these factors are related to the rulings of particular local sheriffs (*sýslumenn*), and they give us a first hint of the accidental nature of witchcraft accusations.

Iceland was part of the Danish kingdom, and in judicial matters a double standard existed. In internal matters of social organization Iceland had autonomy, and the annual *Alþingi* ('people's assembly')

---

[7] Hannes Finnsson, *Mannfækkun af hallærum*, ed. Jón Eyþórsson and Jóhannes Nordal (Reykjavik, 1970).

[8] General surveys of witchcraft are: Siglaugur Brynleifsson, *Galdrar og brennudómar* (Reykjavik, 1976); Ólafur Daviðsson, *Galdur og galdramál á Islandi* (Reykjavik, 1940–3); Páll E. Ólason, *Saga Íslendinga* (Reykjavik, 1942); Þorvaldur Thoroddsen, *Landfræðissaga Íslands* (4 vols.; Copenhagen, 1892–1904). The primary sources are annals, court records from the *Alþingi* (the 'national' court), contemporary treatises on evil, books of magic, legends, and folk-tales, and also one autobiographical account of witchcraft made by a victim.

[9] *Diplomatarium Islandicum (Íslenzk Fornbréfasafn)*, xii. 750–2.

was a centre of legislation and jurisdiction. Other matters were
decided externally. Thus the Reformation was forced upon the
Icelanders by the Danish king, certainly not without resistance. The
Reformation had certain consequences for the administration of daily
life; the Icelanders no longer had the right to define their own ways of
dealing with sexuality and religion. After the *stóridómur* (1564), local
sheriffs, who were appointed by the Danish rulers, had to take action
in all cases of 'heresy' and bring them to court.[10] This provided the
governmental precondition for the dealings with witchcraft of any
particular *sýslumaður* ('sheriff'). Some of these were more zealous
than others and took immediate local action against witchcraft. Until
1686 Icelandic courts could of themselves sentence people to death
and execute them, but in 1686 it was decreed that all death sentences
had to be referred to the High Court in Copenhagen. This was
probably instrumental in the disappearance of the witch-stakes in
Iceland.

One remarkable feature of Icelandic witchcraft has still to be
mentioned in this general overview. Of the 120 trials, only ten
concerned women, and among the twenty-two burnt witches, only one
was a woman. One other woman was smothered and thrown in the
river for witchcraft in this period (and one more man was hanged, and
another decapitated, allegedly also for witchcraft). Given the nature of
such 'atypical' sentences it is uncertain whether the latter cases should
be regarded as proper witch-trials. This is not only a matter of
definition for the analyst; for the persons living in seventeenth-century
Iceland it may also have posed a serious problem, how to deal with
'traditional' instances of magic without contaminating the cases with
European-derived notions about witchcraft. In this connection we
should also note that death sentences in general were rather common
in Iceland in the seventeenth century. These considerations do not
have much relevance for the number of female witches. In contrast to
other countries, including England and Scandinavia, the typical witch
in Iceland was male.

In another respect, however, Iceland was like England and
Scandinavia. The root of the charge was always found in *maleficium*.[11]
Concrete harm done to people or animals was the trigger for the
accusation, while association with the devil was secondary, and mainly

[10] *Lovsamling for Island* (21 vols.; Copenhagen, 1853–89), i. 84–9.
[11] E. William Monter, *Ritual, Myth and Magic in Early Modern Europe* (Brighton,
1983), 29.

entered the proceedings as part of the judges' general vocabulary of evil and heresy. The idea of the sabbath was entirely absent in Iceland.

II. THE CULTURAL CATEGORIES OF MAGIC AND WITCHCRAFT

Two categories were predominant in this field: *galdur* and *fjölkyngi*. *Galdur* may best be translated as 'magic', and as elsewhere there was a distinction between white and black magic. Historically, *svartagaldur* ('black magic') came to dominate over *hvítagaldur* ('white magic') in the post-Reformation period. Thus, in the seventeenth century *galdur* was more or less unanimously associated with wickedness and the powers of darkness. A *galdramaður* ('magic-man') was anyone possessing such powers; the concept equally covers sorcerers, warlocks, and those 'witches' who were accused and judged according to European standards, as established by the *Malleus maleficarum*.[12] *Galdrakona* ('magic-woman') was a little-used term, correlating with the scarce representation of women in the *galdramál* ('witch-trials'). The best-known female witches were referred to by derivations of their first name, like Galdra-Manga (Margrét Þorðardóttir), who was the woman smothered for witchcraft. Her story has been transmitted orally in a popular folk-tale.[13] It seems, then, that the generic term for witch in Iceland was masculine.

In Old Icelandic, *galdr* referred to a song mainly in the sense of 'charm' or 'spell'. The corresponding verb was *gala*, to 'chant' or to 'cast spells'. This linguistic derivation of the seventeenth-century concept of *galdur* (sg.) or *galdrar* (pl.) is important for the understanding of the semantics of witchcraft. It also points directly to the most important instrument of supernatural power in Iceland, that is, *words*. Words were the main vehicles of magic influence, whether expressed in love-poetry, defamatory prose, or in secret codes. In this respect there is a remarkable continuity in Icelandic culture over the centuries, even though the actual forms of expression chosen and the powers attributed to different kinds of words changes from one period to the next.

The other category used for witchcraft was *fjölkyngi*. Literally this means 'much (magical) knowledge'. The term is derived from the

---

[12] *Malleus maleficarum* was probably unknown in Iceland until *c*.1625.

[13] Jón Árnason, *Íslenzkar þjóðsögur og ævintyri* (6 vols.; Leipzig, 1860; repr. Reykjavik, 1980), i. 517–20.

adjective *fjölkunnugur*, 'much knowing'. A man who 'knew a thing or
two' was also referred to as *kunnáttumaður* ('man of knowledge'). The
boundary between wisdom and magical power was not easily drawn in
practice and was totally absent in the category of 'knowledge'. The
historical reality of this confusion of general learning and occult
knowledge in seventeenth-century Iceland is abundantly attested by
the many instances of *galdrar* and *kukl* (another term for magic) in the
Cathedral-schools, which functioned as centres of learning.[14]

If words were the principal instrument of magical practice, knowledge was its ultimate source. In principle everyone could utter words,
and in medieval Icelandic literature and legislation clearly everyone
was a potential spell-maker. Of course, not all Icelanders had the
necessary knowledge, but they could learn. Theoretically, at least, this
meant that it was within the reach of every Icelander to become a
magician, that is, to affect the natural course of history. This is an
important cultural precondition for the historical 'oddity' of the
seventeenth-century accusations of *maleficium* against individual Icelanders. It also serves as a primary indication of why the typical
Icelandic witch was male. Knowledge or wisdom (*fræði*, *fróðleikur*) was
associated with the men, at least after the introduction of Christianity
and the emergence of a new kind of literati or *kennimenn*.[15]

The words used for magical purposes could be either spoken or
written. Spoken forms of magical practice included particular forms of
skáldskapur ('poetry'). In the early medieval laws there were extensive
rules about which kinds of poetry were defamatory and hence subject
to legal punishment.[16] In *Jónsbók*, the law of 1281 which was in force
until the nineteenth century, the rules are less elaborate. Here it is
simply stated that *skáldskapur* is illegal when used for derision.[17] The
passages about *skáldskapur* in both of these sources demonstrate how
verses could violate the integrity of man. While we cannot conclude
from this or other evidence that *skáldkapur* was originally inherently
magical, we may point to the power that was latent in metric forms of
various kinds. In *Hávamál* it is recounted how Oðinn himself had
learnt magical verses (*fimbullióð*), and in the early Icelandic literature
several instances of magic chanting are recorded from pre-Christian

---

[14] Brynleifsson, *Galdrar*, pp. 162ff.

[15] Cf. Kirsten Hastrup, '"Text and Context": Continuity and Change in Medieval
Icelandic History as "Said" and "Laid down"', in *Continuity and Change* (Odense, 1986).

[16] *Grágás*, ed. Vilhjálmur Finsen (3 vols.; Copenhagen, 1852–83), ib. 183ff.

[17] *Jónsbók*, ed. Ólafur Halldórsson (Copenhagen, 1904), 66.

times. In this early period the notion of *galdrar* referred to such verses of magical power,[18] which again testifies to the 'origin' of witchcraft in chants, and to the power in metric forms.

The distinction between real and symbolical influence upon the course of history at any level, from life histories of individuals to natural catastrophes, is not easily drawn. The Icelander who directed *níð* ('defamation') against his contemporary, and thus induced him to action, essentially performed a magical act. In this respect, the performer is like the spell-maker or the man who chants *galdrar* to achieve a particular goal. Both appropriate the ideas of the community and put them to work on their own behalf and by means of individual imagination. The social anthropologist Marcel Mauss formulated a general theory of magic in 1950 in which he concluded: 'Magic is the domain of pure production, *ex nihilo*. With words and gestures it does what techniques achieve by labour.'[19] From this perspective the chants of *galdrar* are no more magical than the *níð*-verses, even if loss of honour may appear more 'symbolical' to us than calming the sea.

By the seventeenth century, the magical poet had obtained a proper name. The *kraptaskáld* ('power-scald') emerged in the fifteenth century, and was to remain an important feature in popular tradition until the nineteenth century.[20] The conceptual roots of this category must be sought in the Viking Age tradition of binding power in verse form and directing it towards a particular purpose, even if these links cannot be established inductively. A very famous *kraptaskáld* was Jón *lærði* ('the learned') Guðmundsson (*c*.1574–1658), who was among the first persons to be accused of witchcraft according to the new European standards set by *Malleus maleficarum*. Among the deeds of Jón *lærði* was his successful averting of a 'Turkish' slave-raider ship by means of a powerful poem.[21] Jón escaped the stake, but his case illustrates the point that the *kraptaskáld* was a potential 'witch' in the seventeenth-century discourse on witchcraft, even if earlier he had just been a poet of particular gifts.

Apart from powerful poems, magical force was also found in spells of different kinds, including Christian prayers. In Latin these were little more than magic formulas, and in some of the *galdrabœkur*

---

[18] Bo Almquist, *Norrön Niddiktning* (Stockholm, 1965), 26.
[19] Marcel Mauss, *A General Theory of Magic* (1950; English trans. London, 1972), 141.
[20] Árnason, *Þjóðsögur*, i. 447–57; iii. 470–82; Almquist, *Norrön Niddiktning*, pp. 15 ff.
[21] The poem is published in Sigfús Sigfússon (ed.), *Íslenzkar Þjóðsögur og -sagnir* 16 vols. (Reykjavik, 1922–58), viii. 41–2; cf. also Árnason, *Þjóðsögur*, iii. 554, 611.

('books of magic') that have been handed down, Christian prayers are
mixed up with spells of different origins. A notorious example is the
very popular *brynjubæn*, designed for protection.[22]

This brings me to the written word as a source of magical power.
The oldest form of this was the runes, which had been used as
formulas of incantation or exorcism in Scandinavia since the late Iron
Age.[23] *Rún* or *rúna* in Old Scandinavian referred to something 'secret'
or 'occult', and still in seventeenth-century Iceland, *rúnir* ('runes')
were used to conceal curses which could not be spoken openly. The
first witch burnt at the stake in Iceland (1625) was convicted for having
in his house a sheet full of runes. By then, these could be read as proof
of devilish undertakings.

In addition to runes, *galdrastafir* ('magic staves') were used in
combination with formulas. As elements in a largely 'oral' tradition,
the staves and the formulas were generally transmitted from one
generation to the next without mediation. However, some of them
were collected in *galdrabækur* used by learned magicians.[24] Such books
were often located at the See-schools, which were inundated by occult
knowledge in the seventeenth century.[25]

To possess *galdrabækur* was to have direct access to magical powers,
and after the Reformation they were strictly banned. I have already
mentioned the case of 1554, when a priest was defrocked and exiled for
possessing *galdrabækur* and using some of the spells for private
purposes.

Words and knowledge were means of magical intervention in history.
They had to be directed by man, who was attributed with certain
natural characteristics that made him a potent mediator between the
material world and other worlds. The old Nordic concept of *hugr*
('mind') referred to an immaterial aspect of man which was believed to
be able to liberate itself from the body. When it left the body it could

---

[22] *Brynjubæn* (the coat-of-mail prayer) has been published by Ivar Lindquist, *En
isländsk svartkonstbok från 1500-talet* (Uppsala, 1921).

[23] Emanuel Linderholm, *Nordisk magi: Studier i nordisk relgions- och kyrkohistoria*
(Stockholm, 1918); Folke Ström, *Nordisk hedendom* (Lund, 1961), 230–3.

[24] Lindquist, *En isländsk svartkonstbok*, pp. 8–9; Davíðsson, *Galdur*, pp. 61 ff.

[25] In Icelandic tradition and imagination the most famous *galdrabók* of all times was
Rauðskinna, compiled by Bishop Gottskálkur Nikolásson (in Hólar, 1498–1520). The
book was written in runic staves of extreme power. The bishop took the book with him
to his grave, and in the 17th c. the famous magician Galdra-Loftur (an apprentice at
Hólar) attempted to reclaim it by conjuring up the bishop from his grave. He almost
succeeded: Árnason, *Þjóðsögur*, i. 572–5.

materialize in a new form, thereby enabling the individual to change shape (*hamr*). A person who could change shape at will was *hamrammr*.[26] Other cultural categories are related to the same semantic field, but suffice it to note here that in Iceland there was always an element of shamanism present in popular belief.[27]

This shamanistic element was an important precondition for various notions of divination, soothsaying, bewitching, or invocation of spirit, because it made of every individual a potential transgressor of the boundary between this world and the supernatural realm. In *Jónsbók* it is stated that one has forfeited one's life if one has engaged in *fordæðuskap ok spáfarar allar ok útisetur at vekja tröll upp ok fremja heiðni* ('. . . sorcery and all soothsaying and out-sitting to wake up trolls and promoting heathenism').[28] No one was to get killed for these practices until after the Reformation, but when in 1625 the first witch was sentenced to death at the stake, it was because he had woken up a ghost and caused malignity through him. Perhaps the most interesting notion in the passage quoted from *Jónsbók* is that of *útiseta* ('sitting out'). By the act of sitting out, which was a metaphor for leaving the ordinary social space, it was possible to invoke supernatural beings. In legal terminology as well as in popular tradition the practice was generally referred to as *seta úti til fróðleiks* ('sitting out for wisdom').[29] Again, wisdom or knowledge was a token of extraordinary powers. As already hinted at, all of these cultural categories were important elements in the seventeenth-century Icelandic context of witchcraft.

III. THE WITCHES

In 1589 an Icelandic observer noted that delusions of Satan were probably of less moment in Iceland than in various other countries,

---

[26] Ström, *Nordisk hedendom*, p. 205.

[27] Peter Buchholz, 'Shamanism: 'The Testimony of Old Icelandic Literary Tradition', *Medieval Scandinavia*, 4 (1971), 7–20; Hastrup, *Culture and History*, pp. 152–4.

[28] *Jónsbók*, p. 38.

[29] An example from the legal discourse is found in *Diplomatarium Islandicum*, i. 243. In popular tradition it is notable in e.g. *Skíðaríma*: Finnur Jónsson (ed.), *Rimnasafn: Samling af de ældste islandske rimer*, i (Copenhagen, 1905–22), 19. The rich semantic connotations of *útiseta* and *útilega* (lying out) and of the 'outside' in general have been dealt with in Kirsten Hastrup, 'Cosmology and Society in Medieval Iceland', *Ethnologia Scandinavica* (1981); ead., *Culture and Society*, ch. 5; ead., 'Tracing Tradition: An Anthropological Perspective on *Grettis saga Ásmundarsonar*,' in John Lindow, Lars Lönnroth, and Gerd Wolfgang Weber (eds.), *Structure and Meaning: New Approaches to Old Norse Literature* (Odense, 1986), 281–313.

where Hell also had a more prominent position.[30] After the Reformation a lot of traditional practices, including bewitching, adultery, and incest, were deemed heretical by official legislation, and more or less explicitly linked to the doings of Satan. This was a result of the previously mentioned *stóridómur* ('big verdict') of 1564. Still, in 1589 Satan seems to have had little grip on the popular imagination of the Icelanders, if we are to believe Oddur Einarsson.

In 1625 things changed. The year had been full of misfortune; the winter had been cold and there had been great losses of livestock, on top of which there was an outbreak of plague costing many lives.[31] At Munkaþverá the *sýslumaður* ('sheriff') Magnús Björnsson learned that ghosts had caused a boy to fall ill and horses to die. He had been educated in Copenhagen and Hamburg, and had become acquainted with *Malleus maleficium*. The *malificium* was beyond question, but the *galdramaður* still had to be identified under the tacit assumption that such ghosts worked on behalf of men 'of much knowledge'. We do not know why, but the bewitched boy pointed to a certain Jón Rögnvaldsson as the offender; he took God as his witness.[32] The sheriff seized Jón and searched his house. There a sheet of runes was found, which Jón admitted he had made. The general opinion was then that Jón was *fjölkunnugur*.[33] Now Jón's brother, Þorvaldr, was a well-known scald, but even his testimonial about Jón's simple-mindedness could not prevent Jón from being accused of *fjölkyngi*. The sheriff needed no further proof than the runes and the boy's oath, and he was convinced that Jón worked with Satan himself. Since he was familiar with *Malleus* he knew that such doings had to be dealt with properly and without further ado. Normally, all cases of any gravity had to be put before the court at the Althing, but Jón Rögnvaldsson was locally condemned to the stake. What is more, the case never seems to have been published at the Althing. At least, it is absent from the records. The most detailed record is found in the annal written by Björn *á* Skarðsá. He notes succinctly: 'Jón Rögnvaldsson from Svafaðardalur was burnt to death in Eyafjörður after conviction for witchcraft. He had woken up a dead person who had attacked a boy at Urður and killed horses and played other malevolent tricks.'[34]

---

[30] Oddur Einarsson, *Íslandslýsing: Qualiscunque descriptio Islandiae* (1589, Reykjavik, 1971), 48–9.   [31] Thoroddsen, *Árferði á Íslandi*, pp. 67–8.
[32] Daviðsson, *Galdur*, p. 109; Þorsteinn M. Jónsson, *Brennan á Melaeyrum, 1625* (Akureyri, 1957), 9–10.   [33] Jón Espolín, *Árbækur*, vi (Reykjavik, 1943), 27–8.
[34] *Annálar 1400–1800. (Annales Islandici. Posteriorum saeculorum)* (4 vols.; Reykjavik, 1922–42), i. 221: 'Brenndur til dauðs i Eyrafirði eptir dómi Jón Rögnvaldsson ur

We note that the annalist takes the accusation for witchcraft at face-value. Jón's scald brother was less sure of the case. In a poem he laments the loss, and says that even if Jón had practised *galdur* it was hardly deliberate. Jón did not have the necessary power (*vald*); he was much too simple-minded (*einfaldur*).[35] He sensed a paradox there, but apparently the officials did not.

In Iceland there was a legal institution of *tylftareiður* ('judgement by twelve lay persons') which in most cases could be used for acquittal. If twelve men were prepared to swear to one's innocence, the accusation could be dropped. When the next witch-process after Jón Rögnvaldsson's came up in 1629, the accused witch was given the possibility of acquittal by *tylftareiður*. He was unable to find twelve people in his home district who were prepared to swear to his innocence, but finally he succeeded in his paternal home district.[36] Others were later to have similar luck.

In 1630 a royal decree about witchcraft (passed in Denmark in 1617) was enforced in Iceland, and we gain an impression of increasing tension in these matters.[37] It is not until 1654 that the next fire was made, however. Three men were burnt for witchcraft within a few days at the same place. They were victims of another zealous *sýslumaður*, Þorleifur Kortsson in Strandasýsli.[38] The composer of *Sjávarborgarannáll* explains the burnings by noting that the entire area was haunted by 'ghost-devils'.[39] The author of *Seiluannáll* corroborates this in his own way by mentioning atrocious devil's attacks; he adds that only one of the men had shown remorse.[40] The important thing here is to note that apparently the devil had become a more 'popular' figure than before. This may be due to the fact that a couple of writings about the devil's workings had emerged and gradually become known. The first Icelandic demonology was written in 1627 by Guðmundur Einarsson, who was prompted to do so by the occult practices of Jón *lærði* Guðmundsson, the *kraptaskáld* and wise men to whom I referred earlier. This work has an elaborate title, part of which is *litil hugrásyfir svik og vélræði djöfulsins* ('some reflections on the deceit and contrivance

---

Svarfaðardal fyrir fjölkyngishátt. Hann hafði uppvakið einn dauðan, hver að sótti að einum pilti á Urðum, drap þar hesta og gerði aðra skráveifur.'

[35] This poem is quoted in Espolín, *Árbækur*, vi. 28.
[36] *Annálar*, iv. 256.
[37] *Alþingsbækur Islands. (Acta comitorum generalium Islandiae)* (Reykjavik, 1912–82), v. 188–9.
[38] Sigfús H. Andrésson, 'Þorleifur Lögmaður Kortsson,' *Skirnir*, 131 (1957), 152–71.
[39] *Annálar*, iv. 293.   [40] Ibid. i. 305.

of the devil'), and it is best characterized as a linking of Lutheran demonology with ancient practices of *galdrar* in Iceland.[41]

Character Bestiae, written by Páll Björnsson in about 1630, is a truly international piece of scholarship. Páll Björnsson refers extensively to *Malleus maleficarum* among other works, and *galdrar* is directly defined as satanic learning (*djöflalærdómur*).[42] Other writings appeared in the 1650s and 1670s corresponding in time with the two most serious waves of witch-hunts.[43] Generally speaking, demonology was élitist and little referred to in the court-cases, even if the devil was spoken of with increasing frequency. The witches rarely admitted association with the devil, even though they were often accused of it. Also, there is no trace of the witches having thought of themselves as a coven or a satanic community, as elsewhere in Europe.[44]

Among the more spectacular witch-processes, I shall mention the one that resulted in two burnings in 1656. The case is famous because the afflicted person, Jón Magnússon, wrote an elaborate account of his adversities in a *pislarsaga* ('passion story'). *Pislarsaga síra Jóns Magnússonar* is autobiographical, but it is also an important cultural document about witchcraft in general.[45]

In 1655 *síra* Jón was stricken by a strange (mental) illness. The devil haunted him while he was carrying out some of his priestly functions at Kirkjuból.[46] His household began to experience strange incidents; one of the farm-hands was struck dumb by the devil's spirit once, when he was out fishing.[47] Such devilry continued, and *síra* Jón fulminated against it from the pulpit. After a while he formed the opinion that his illness and the general evil were caused by two of his parishioners bewitching him. He had first seen the devil at their farm-stead. He then went to the *sýslumaður* and convinced him about the charges, after which the case was brought before the local court.

The two parishioners, father and son, were charged of *fjölkyngi og galdragjörningi* ('witchcraft and magic work'). In the proceedings of the court the offences are listed point by point. They fall roughly into three categories, and apply more or less equally to both Jón Jónsson *eldri* (the father) and Jón Jónsson *yngri* (the son). First, they had both incarnated the devil; he had haunted *síra* Jón in both of their shapes.

---

[41] Thoroddssen, *Landfræðissaga*, pp. 43–6.
[42] Ibid., pp. 49–50.   [43] Ibid., pp. 50–1.
[44] Norman Cohn, *Europe's Inner Demons* (London, 1975), 102.
[45] *Pislarsaga síra Jóns Magnússonar*, ed. Sigurður Nordal (ed.) (Reykjavik, 1967).
[46] Ibid., pp. 40ff.   [47] Ibid., pp. 63–4.

Second, they possessed *galdrabækur* and *galdrastafir*, both of which were found in their houses. Third, the father had inflicted harm on livestock, while the son had attempted to beguile an unwilling girl by means of love-magic (*rúnir*). They were found guilty of association with devil, of possession of Books of the Black Art, and of the offensive application of this art. In the first place, the father admitted having possessed a *galdrabók*, and the son acknowledged the presence of *galdrablöð* ('magic-sheets'); upon further probing the father admitted having cast spells upon a cow and having willed the priest's weakness. He did not directly testify to the association with the devil. The son did, however. In his attempt to cure a calf of his, which the devil had pestered, he had used an old magical device, *Solomons insigli*. The devil had made his appearance before him the following night and had asked Jón why he had done that. To this Jón answered, 'Fye upon you, you shall not deceive me.' Later the same night the devil had drawn a cow from the mountains to demonstrate his power. The son also admitted the lesser charges.

To decide on the sentence all possible legal documents were consulted. It was generally argued that the Lord had urged people to fight against witchcraft; several passages from the Bible were quoted to this effect. Second, *Jónsbók* (of 1281) was quoted for its prohibition of witchcraft, soothsaying, and 'sitting out'. Third, the royal degree of 1617 (instituted in Iceland in 1630) was invoked; this decree introduced death penalty for witchcraft. Fourth, it was said that all Christian laws, including old Icelandic ones, enforced burning as the only proper penalty for this ungodly crime. The conclusion was clear; father and son were sentenced to the stake. The sentence was executed in 1656, after which it was published at the Althing, where 'all the God-fearing and justice-loving judges thought it right'.[48]

For father and son this was the end, but the sufferings of *síra* Jón continued. The devil reappeared, and Jón was soon convinced that Þuríður Jónsdóttir (daughter and sister of the two witches already disposed of) was bewitching him. This suspicion once raised, Jón produced endless evidence of her evils. The girl, however, was allowed to clear herself by *tylftereiður*. Þuríður and her family sued *síra* Jón for damages, which he had to pay. He had forfeited all his property.[49] After this, Jón sat down to write his *píslarsaga* with the

---

[48] *Annálar*, vi. 384.
[49] Loc. cit.

double aim of justifying himself and of accusing the administrators of inadequate rule and lenient practice.

Lenience certainly seems to have governed the witch-processes in Iceland. In the Westfjords they continued, but only a limited number of cases ended with fire, most of which were concentrated in the 1670s. I shall relate only one more case, namely that of 1679 with the only woman to suffer the stake.

The most comprehensive source on the matter is the contemporary *Mælifellsannáll*, in which the annalist states:

Þuriður Olafsdóttir and her son Jón were burnt in the Westfjords; they were accused of witchcraft (*galdur*); the woman had spent all her life in Skagafjörður [in the Northland], and never been involved in *galdur*. Like other poor people she had gone westwards in spring 1677 together with her son Jón, of whom little is known except that he was also without any reputation for *galdur*. Her son is reported for saying that she had traversed all the waterfalls of the Northlands without horse or ferry, by means of *galdur*, and she must then have been in possession of magical powers. His lie was believed and later they were both arrested and burnt, what he thought would not happen.[50]

In another annal (*Eyraannáll*) it is said, 'two relatives from the Northlands, Þuriður and her son Jón Þorðarson, were burnt for having caused illness to Helga Halldórsdóttir in Selárdal.'[51] The said Helga was the wife of the rural dean, and she fell ill shortly after the arrival of the two foreigners. On the basis of no evidence but some coincidence, including perhaps a general suspicion of strangers, Þuriður and Jón were burnt without ever having admitted anything at all.

Although a woman this time succumbed in the flames, we are a long way from the idea of the sabbath and of a possible sexual relationship with the devil, even if the rumour of her flying over the waters is worth noting.

IV. ICELANDIC WITCHCRAFT IN EUROPEAN PERSPECTIVE

The Icelandic witch-trials of the seventeenth century have a number of features in common with witch-trials elsewhere in Europe. They

---

[50] *Annálar*, i. 550.
[51] Ibid. iii. 310.

show signs of 'a temporary syncretism of the witch-beliefs of the common people with those of the more specialized or educated classes', like Basque witchcraft, so extensively documented by Gustav Henningsen.[52] Like English witchcraft, the Icelandic cases demonstrate a 'solitary pattern'.[53] The witches are lone figures, caught in a web of suspicion arising out of age-old categories and translated by local governors into modern satanic notions. This interpretation of popular belief as Satan-worship is a widespread feature of the European witch-craze.[54]

The root of the accusations was always found in a concrete instance of *maleficium*. In this respect Iceland is truly akin to other Northern European Protestant nations.[55] The common people were concerned about individual damage or misfortune, while the ruler waged war against Evil at a much more abstract level. Satan was an apt metaphor for Evil in this sense. Generally, he belonged in a learned discourse— learning here refers to Latin or international schooling. The *sýslumaður* or the priest who had been educated abroad was more likely to refer to Satan than local 'men of knowledge'. The popular notions of *galdur* and *maleficium* merge with foreign learning in the case of Jón Magnússon, whose *píslarsaga* documents the syncretism at the autobiographical level.

The similarities between Icelandic and other manifestations of the witch-craze are not surprising, given the overall integration of Iceland into a European religious community. Also, the political status of the island as part of the Danish kingdom made Iceland an immediate object for new moral standards and legislation in the political centre of Copenhagen. With the Reformation, which more or less had to be forced upon the Icelanders, a single moral standard replaced the double standard of Catholic times, when clerical and secular judgement were rarely consistent with one another.[56]

Just as monotheism is a prerequisite for the unequivocal identification of Evil,[57] one single moral standard is a precondition for the

[52] Gustav Henningsen, *The Witches' Advocate: Basque Witchcraft and the Spanish Inquisition* (Reno, 1980), 391.

[53] Alan Macfarlane, *Witchcraft in Tudor and Stuart England* (London, 1970).

[54] Norman Cohn, 'The Myth of Satan and his Human Servants', in Mary Douglas (ed.), *Witchcraft Confessions and Accusations* (London, 1970), 71.

[55] Monter, *Ritual, Myth and Magic*, p. 29; Keith Thomas, *Religion and the Decline of Magic* (London, 1971), 531.

[56] For a discussion of the shift from a double to a single standard in Iceland, see Kirsten Hastrup, 'Entropisk elegi', *Stofskifte*, 12 (1985), 45–60.

[57] Cohn, 'The Myth of Satan', p. 4.

identification of 'heresy' in the broad sense of the term used in the *stóridómur* (1564), for instance. Thus the Reformation in Iceland entailed a sharpening of moral and social categories. This meant that everything falling outside or between these categories was a potential (conceptual) danger to the social order.[58] This was the historical precondition for witchcraft in seventeenth-century Iceland. *Galdur* and *fjölkyngi* were no longer tolerated.

Fjölkyngi was not only knowledge that was occult and un-Christian, it was also associated with the forces reigning beyond society. 'Outside' the boundaries of the social sphere, ghosts, trolls, and spirits could be invoked to harm people by men who possessed knowledge. From an internal perspective, this equation between *galdur* and the 'outside' made *galdur* a prominent target for rulers who wanted to purge the categories of the social sphere of 'wild' elements.[59] This, then, is part of the structural explanation for the witch-trials in seventeenth-century Iceland.

There is no ready functional explanation, it seems. While perhaps providing some relief of tension at the individual level, there are no indications that witch-beliefs upheld old conventions of village life, as reported from England.[60] The clash between old ideas of neighbourliness and mutual support within the village and new social necessities and public responsibility may have spurred a number of witchcraft accusations in England,[61] but there is no such evidence from Iceland. In England, two essential features were a necessary background to allegations of witchcraft, the occurrence of a personal misfortune, and an awareness on the victim's part of having neglected or refused a traditional social obligation.[62] Here, the victim of the misfortune came to play the active part in witchcraft; the suspect needed to give no evidence of her malevolence. Most witches in England were elderly women of low social status; from the point of view of the local community they were more-or-less anomalous social persons. Here, the functional explanation is ready at hand.

In Iceland things were different, because the social historical circumstances were of a particular kind. There were no local com-

[58] Mary Douglas, *Purity and Danger* (London, 1966).
[59] See n. 29, above.
[60] Thomas, *Religion*, p. 68.
[61] Alan Macfarlane, 'Witchcraft in Tudor and Stuart Essex', in Douglas (ed.), *Witchcraft Confessions*. See also Thomas, *Religion*.
[62] Keith Thomas, 'The Relevance of Social Anthropology to the Historical Study of English Witchcraft', in Douglas (ed.), *Witchcraft Confessions*, p. 63.

munities of the village type, and partly because of the generally very poor living conditions, there was little or no idea of neighbourliness.[63] Families barely managed to survive on their own on the scattered farmsteads. The *hreppur*, which was the smallest administrative unit since the Middle Ages, had the collective responsibility for the paupers (*ómagir*), and taxes were levied on individual farmers to meet this demand.[64] Thus poor relief was always public in Iceland. What is more, with the scattered habitation it was difficult to locate 'outsiders' in relation to a geographical centre. We know that poor Þuriður, who was burnt at stake in 1679 together with her son, came from the Northlands and was conceived of as a stranger. But generally the Icelandic witches were neither outcasts nor strangers. They were ordinary men; some of them well-to-do.

They were *men*, yes. This leads me to a consideration of the specific features of Icelandic witchcraft. I have already argued that the generic term for witch in Iceland was masculine, and this, I think, is one reason why women were so few in the trials. They were less 'visible' than men, when seen through the cultural filter of 'witchcraft' and 'knowledge'. The *kunnáttumaður*, 'wise man', had no immediate female counterpart.[65] Men were the wise ones, and the ones in touch with the 'outside'.[66] Jón *lærði* Guðmundsson epitomized this conjunction of wisdom and magic. What is more, he was sufficiently learned to be a match for his prosecutors. Unlike the simple-minded Jón Rögnvaldsson, burnt for *fjölkyngi* in 1625, the truly wise Jón Guðmundsson, who was brought before the court for *galdur* several times in the 1630s, survived, albeit in exile for a brief period.[67] Also, Jón *lærði* had the good fortune of being prosecuted at the *alþingi*, while the other Jón was entirely at the mercy of local zeal. (In turn, this also ensured far better records on Jón *lærði*'s case.)

Although the Icelandic witches themselves are rather silent in the sources, with the exception of Jón Magnússon and Jón *lærði*

---

[63] According to the census of 1703, more than 15% of the population were paupers. In the Eastfjords, up to 23% were registered as such, while in Westfjords only 5–10% were dependent on poor relief. (It will be recalled how Þuriður and Jón went westwards in search of a living.)

[64] Lýður Björnsson, *Saga sveitarstjórnar á Íslandi* (2 vols.; Reykjavik, 1972–9).

[65] In the Viking age, women were the ones who practised *seiðr* (magic): Dag Strömbeck, *Sejd* (Stockholm, 1935); but generally they seem to have lost touch with the 'external' powers after the Middle Ages.

[66] Kirsten Hastrup, 'Male and Female in Icelandic Culture', *Folk*, 27 (1985), 49–54.

[67] *Annálar*, v. 482–5.

Guðmundsson, we have enough information to make substantiated guesses as to how the modern European idea of witchcraft could be accepted by the ordinary Icelander. Demonology as such was élitist, but there was a latent shamanistic imagery which made the idea of a change of shape familiar to the populace. Thus of the two Jóns burnt in 1656 the younger accepted the charge that they had assaulted Jón Magnússon in the devil's shape. I argue that the ancient shamanistic notions, including the notion of possible contact with the evil forces of the uncontrolled 'outside', provided the cultural precondition for the collective acknowledgement of witchcraft in the European, demonized, sense.

Similarly, the traditional concept of *galdur* was very easily translated into new ideas of *maleficium*. By the standard of local cultural categories, *galdur* was a means to inflict harm upon persons at your will. The main vehicle of *maleficium* was words, spoken or written, incanted or engraved. Everyone had access to words, and many formulas and magical staves were in popular possession for various purposes of healing and protection. Potentially, words might wage war, and there was no safe place outside discourse, given the nature of magical power. As a historical consequence, anyone could become accused of witchcraft. Misfortune was explained by retrospective reference to malevolent acts, which had not been so interpreted when they had occurred. 'Proof' was then found in a sheet of runes, or in a tale about having flown over water. Finally, the court-procedures and the sentence itself firmly classified the alleged *maleficium* as Satan's work.

In the conjunction between particular Icelandic categories of supernatural forces and the general European (Christian) notions of witchcraft and evil, we note a two-way translational process. Age-old notions of *galdur* and *fjölkyngi* were translated into new categories of *maleficium* and devil-worship that were of foreign extraction. The process of translation may have started well back in Catholic times, but it was not until the Reformation that 'witches' could readily be identified and prosecuted. Conversely, European ideas were translated into a specific cultural discourse on magical influence. This double process of translation accounts for both similarities and differences between Icelandic and other forms of witchcraft in Early Modern Europe.

From a European perspective, Iceland was on the periphery; the witch-craze struck rather late, and the number of trials was small.

From an internal Icelandic perspective, seventeenth-century notions about witchcraft were not insignificant. The Icelanders lived in the centre of their own world, and although they were marginalized in a whole set of ways, we should not treat their culture as peripheral or otherwise inferior to European Christendom. Icelandic culture was distinctive, and it generated its own reality. While objectified 'cultures' by definition materialize as bounded entities in contrast to one another,[68] perceived realities are not easily measured against external standards, let alone such 'unrealities' as witchcraft.[69]

The reality-generating process involves two kinds of structuring mechanisms: one forms, another builds.[70] The form derives from cultural 'templates', expressing the persistence of certain themes of belief.[71] In Iceland the idea of witchcraft as based in words and knowledge was such a template and a token of continuity. However, as we have seen for seventeenth-century Icelandic witchcraft, such structures are not just replicated. First, 'replication' only occurs when other elements in the social environment combine to permit this;[72] misfortune was every man's experience, but personal malevolence was not the general explanation. Second, the actual details of the realization of the basic structure, that is, the event through which replication takes place, may be different on every occasion.[73] As time passes and history continues, the media of realization change. In Iceland, 'knowledge' was conceptually transformed from wisdom to Satan-worship. Like the *bricoleur* in the writings of Lévi-Strauss,[74] people generate realities out of a more or less accidental assembling of current features of the environment, through which old categories (or structures of *la longue durée*) are 'replicated'. This is the truly dynamic point in history. Old forms are built into new times, whereby categories may be reformulated and new eras inaugurated.

Whether the result is negative or positive by some external standard of judgement, the historical dynamism inherent in the clash between culture and history points to a singular feature of humanity. It is immensely creative.

---

[68] James A. Boon, *Other Tribes, Other Scribes* (Cambridge, 1982); Kirsten Hastrup, 'Anthropology and the Exaggeration of Culture', *Ethnos*, 50: 3–4 (1985), 311–24.

[69] For a discussion of the 'unreal' as part of the reality we have to deal with, see Kirsten Hastrup, 'The Challenge of the Unreal', *Culture and History*, 1 (1986), 50–62.

[70] Edwin Ardener, 'Some Outstanding Problems in the Analysis of Events', *Yearbook of Symbolic Anthropology*, 1 (1978), 103–21.

[71] Edwin Ardener, 'Witchcraft', Economics and the Continuity of Belief', in Douglas (ed.), *Witchcraft Confessions*, p. 156.   [72] Ibid.

[73] Ibid.   [74] Claude Lévi-Strauss, *La Pensée sauvage* (Paris, 1962).

16
Portugal: A Scrupulous Inquisition
FRANCISCO BETHENCOURT

THE European witch myth, which we can characterize very briefly by five main elements—pacts with the devil, night flights, participation in collective assemblies (sabbaths), ability to metamorphose, and ability to produce malefice against persons and property[1]—emerged fragmented (and even reinterpreted) in most of the statements by witnesses and accused persons as recorded in the Portuguese Inquisition files. The pact often had no connection with night flights and sabbaths; supernatural flight was not the exclusive province of witches and magicians and could involve others under their influence; the image of the witch was not clearly distinguished from that of the sorcerer; witches' powers were often considered innate rather than granted by the devil; their action was not viewed as exclusively malefic, for considerable ambiguity can be observed in the moral assessment of their acts.[2]

The complexity of the witch myth in Portugal can be clarified in two ways. First, one can analyse the distorting effect of the repression exercised by ecclesiastical and inquisitorial élites on the statements of agents of magic, whose practices and beliefs were reduced to a dichotomy between the power of God and the power of the devil, thus giving the notion of a pact a central role in the trials. Secondly, one can study the diffuse characteristics of the mythical universe within which the various social orders and strata of Portuguese *ancien régime* society operated (with their different modes of production, appropriation, and reproduction of images, ideas, and myths).

---

[1] On the characterization of this myth, see the contributions of Carlo Ginzburg and Robert Rowland, above (chs. 4 and 6).

[2] This and other statements are further developed in Francisco Bethencourt, *O imaginário da magia: Feiticeiras, saludadores e nigromantes no século XVI* (Lisbon, 1987).

I. REPRESSION OF WITCHCRAFT

The witch-craze which affected most central and western European countries from the middle of the sixteenth century to the middle of the seventeenth century did not occur in Portugal.[3] The overwhelming majority of denunciations occurred within the institutional framework established by the Church, that is, during pastoral visits to the dioceses. There was no great pressure of accusations coming from rural or urban communities to justify waves of repression; the Inquisition did not particularly engage itself in the production of denunciations—in so far as this branch of activity was concerned, the Inquisition fed on information or trials transferred from ecclesiastical tribunals, denunciations obtained from prisoners, and occasional official inquiries into public crimes.

Witchcraft was considered in confessors' manuals (one of the types of religious literature with greatest impact on the population in the fifteenth and sixteenth centuries) to be a sin against the First Commandment.[4] The reasoning behind almost all the moral and catechetic theological works consulted for this study is structured on the following antitheses: worship of God v. worship of the devil; appeal to divine protection v. appeal to the devil's protection; resort to God's agents on earth (clergymen) v. resort to the devil's agents on earth (witches and sorcerers). Despite this tradition, witchcraft was classified by both civil and ecclesiastical law as a public crime, like sorcery and superstition.[5] This fact is revealing as to the secondary role that the élite of jurists assigned to this type of deviant practice: witchcraft was considered to be related to illicit magic (sorcery, divination of the occult, exerting control over the feelings and will of others), with its profane and sacrilegious (ab)use of Catholic rites (in particular, the use of altar-stone fragments for benevolent sorcery, the use in charms of the words applied to bless the Host and the use of the clerical habit to gather herbs of virtue on the dawn of St John's day).

---

[3] Besides the fundamental studies by Alan Macfarlane, Keith Thomas, William Monter, Erik Midelfort, and Robert Muchembled, see the outline by Jean Delumeau, *La Peur en Occident, XIVe–XVIIIe siècles: Une cité assiegée* (Paris, 1978), 450–506.

[4] In particular Martin de Azpilcueta Navarro, *Manual de confessores e penitentes* (Coimbra, 1560), 68–72.

[5] Among civil legislation, see the *Ordenaçoes do Senhor Rey D. Manuel* (reprint), vol. iii, bk. v (Coimbra, 1797), 92–6; among ecclesiastical legislation, the *Constituiçoens do Arcebispado de Lisboa* (Lisbon, 1537), fos. lxx^v–lxxi^v.

The pattern of repression confirms the low standing of witchcraft within the formal hierarchy of heresies (dominated by Judaism, in the Portuguese case):

1. The only known death sentences applied to witches during the sixteenth century were passed by civil courts (five witches from Aveiro were burned at the stake in Lisbon's Rossio square in 1559; this was followed by an official inquiry in the Lisbon area, ordered by Queen Regent Catarina, which resulted in another execution), and seem to have represented an exceptional situation.[6]

2. During most of the period of its activity (1536–1821), the Inquisition maintained jurisdiction over the crime of witchcraft (except for the cases already mentioned), and there was only one case of execution,[7] in Évora in 1626 (it should, however, be noted that our information on the Lisbon and Coimbra courts is not as complete as that on the Évora court).

3. The number of trials involving witchcraft, sorcery, clairvoyance, and superstition is clearly a small proportion of inquisitorial activity as a whole (in the Évora court, with jurisdiction over the south of the country, they accounted for 291 trials out of 11,743, that is, 2.5 per cent, and there are indications of a similar or even lower percentage in the Lisbon and Coimbra courts, which covered the centre and north of the country, respectively).

4. Torture was seldom used in cases of illicit magic during the sixteenth century, although an increase in its use was recorded in the seventeenth century and first half of the eighteenth century (this did not imply a substantial change in the kinds of sentences passed).

Although the number of trials for illicit magic was very small in the Évora Holy Office Tribunal, it is interesting to analyse their chronology and the prisoners' geographical origin. First of all, one should note that the pace of inquisitorial activity in this field did not keep up with the pace of European repression, for we notice two main high periods, one during the 1550s and the other from 1710 to 1760 (see Fig. 16.1). The first peak can be partly accounted for by the fact that it occurred in the period during which the Holy Office was set up, and

[6] Biblioteca Nacional de Lisboa, Reservados, Colecção Moreira, MS 861, fos. 8–13.
[7] Arquivo Nacional da Torre de Tombo (hereafter ANTT), Inquisição, Processos Apartados, *Pasta* 17, no. 8176.

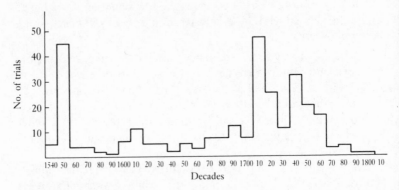

FIG. 16.1. *Portugal: Witchcraft, sorcery, and superstition trials in the Évora inquisition,*
1540–1810

by the political goal of ascertaining the extent of all types of crimes falling within the Faith Tribunal's jurisdiction. This was followed by a long period in which illicit magic played a very minor role among the activities persecuted by the Inquisition. There is no doubt, however, that the influence of the European witch-craze was nipped in the bud in a clear attitude of cultural rejection on the part of the religious élite (repressive strategy was directed elsewhere: collective fears were traditionally embodied in other social agents). The wave of repression during the first half of the eighteenth century is harder to explain: besides being an attempt by the Inquisition to extend the scope of its activity in a situation of social assimilation of people converted from Judaism, the New Christians, there is evidence of greater public sensitivity towards magic during the reign of João V, which has yet to be studied.

Lastly, one should note that the geographical origin of prisoners in the Évora trials does not reflect the actual spatial distribution of cunning men and women. Although the most important of them were caught in the meshes of the Inquisition net, there is no doubt as to the dominant effect of the Holy Office's bureaucratic structure: most of these arrested lived in cities and townships, and one can note an excessive concentration of detainees in towns with district courts.

The relative 'mildness' of inquisitorial repression of witchcraft does not mean that there was no knowledge of the demonological model established by various medieval inquisitors (such as Bernard Gui, Jacob Sprenger, and Heinrich Institoris), based on witness statements gathered during their many long journeys seeking to establish spiritual control, the main manuals are quoted by the prosecutors, and the concept (both legal and mythical) of the pact with the devil, which defines the boundaries of heresy—that is, of Inquisition jurisdiction— guides all interrogation of prisoners. The fact is that inquisitors soon began to exhibit a certain scepticism towards the confessions of the accused and the witnesses' statements,[8] which were sometimes not taken into consideration for the final verdict, due to 'lack of proof'. On the other hand, there was considerable vigilance and punishment as regards witchcraft: there was simply a subtle strategy of public punishments (whippings; banishment from township, city, municipality, or diocese; humiliating exposure at the parish church door during a Sunday or holiday; abjuration in an *auto-da-fé*; temporary imprisonment; and wearing of a penitential garment in daily life), by means of which the deviation was exposed and the norm inculcated.

The policy of 'mild' repression of deviant practices and beliefs on the part of Old Christians (for instance, illicit magic, blasphemy, heretical propositions, and Lutheranism) contrasted with the policy of violent repression against vestiges of Jewish rites detected among New Christians. In the case of Old Christians, there was a strong but prudent long-term strategy of social control through punishment, example, and persuasion, where the clergy's day-to-day actions, sacraments, preaching, and pastoral visits played a fundamental role in captivating and recovering souls. In the case of New Christians, however, there was a deliberate strategy of spectacular exclusion of the active Judaizing minority (who comprised over 80 per cent of those prosecuted in the seventeenth and eighteenth centuries, accounting for almost all the trials transferred to secular justice after judgement for execution), tending to increase the social integration of Old Christians. This strategy had contradictory results among the New Christians: on the one hand, brutal external pressure led to greater cohesiveness within the *converso* community, strengthening its ties of solidarity in the face of a hostile society; while on the other hand, this same pressure made it difficult to pass on Jewish religious knowledge, which was thus gradually eroded. The inversion of Catholic rites and

---

[8] The same thing happened in the other Iberian Peninsula kingdoms and has been studied in depth by Gustav Henningsen, *The Witches' Advocate; Basque Witchcraft and the Spanish Inquisition* (Reno, 1980).

the reproduction of practices publicly condemned as Judaizing constituted a grotesque effort to recover a lost religion: acculturation was
achieved by the eighteenth century, thus completing the process of
forced social assimilation of a major religious and national community.[9]

II. AGENTS OF MAGIC

Differences in repressive strategies were based on criteria such as
limpeza de sangue (literally, 'clean blood') and 'religious purity', which
in a very particular way constituted the framework of the then central
system of values in the Iberian Peninsula (together with the notions of
order, lineage, and honour). In a certain sense these criteria protected
those Old Christians who practised illicit magic, sparing them from
capital punishment, but it did not prevent their activity from being
subjected to systematic control aimed at reducing its social effects.
What was basically at stake was the maintenance of the legitimate
religious agents' monopoly of spiritual power over the population.
The Catholic Church had a unique position in the religious field: it
was a state within the state, with an autonomous organization whose
network covered all of the nation's territory; it owned land, had
income and taxation privileges; and it enjoyed institutional support
from the Crown. The higher-order role assigned to it constituted
public recognition of its function as a legitimizer of the social
hierarchy. This recognition extended to belief in its state of grace as an
institution of mediation with holiness. Its monopoly on the religious
supply of means of salvation, which was established over Islamism and
Judaism during the Christian Reconquest of the Iberian Peninsula
(eleventh to fifteenth centuries), was later upheld through the creation
of the Holy Office Tribunal in 1536: the integration of the converted
Jewish community was achieved by systematic and continuing
repression; the purge of deviant practices and beliefs on the part of
Old Christians (that is, the re-Christianization of town and country)
gained new momentum; the penetration of religious ideas coming
from Protestant Europe was blocked; the efforts towards a Tridentine
reform of the clergy were supported by the Inquisition bureaucracy
(an élite body which controlled both oral and written expression).

[9] Preliminary conclusion of my research into the Inquisition in Portugal (1536–1821).

The religious field was polarized, as we can see, by the Catholic Church and the Inquisition. Together they held a monopoly on the means of reproduction of the population's religious *habitus*, that is, on the means of control over collective beliefs and behaviours, relegating religious self-consumption and alternative practices of manipulation of supernatural powers to a minor and peripheral position. Under these circumstances, agents of magic could not establish a truly competitive relationship with legitimate religious agents: whilst the former had no institutional support, and worked as 'small independent entrepreneurs'[10] who established among themselves an informal hierarchy of competence based on personal charisma and voluntary exchange of information, the latter were expert members of a complex salvation-enterprise with a specific institutional charisma and a clearly established internal organization. Furthermore, the moral community of believers of the same faith, which characterizes any church,[11] adjusting religious supply to its corresponding demand, was absent from the magician's day-to-day activity. The magician established a relationship with his client similar to that of a physician with his patient. Lastly, priests guided their activity by dogmas and rites described in the written tradition of the church authorities, a fact which gave greater solidity to doctrine and ceremonies of faith, whilst, in most cases, magicians worked with rites which were established by oral tradition and which, due to their flexibility, could be adapted to new circumstances but could hardly resist confrontation with symbolic systems supported by the written word.

The preferential scope of action is one of the fundamental factors that differentiated magicians and priests, although there were some overlapping areas. Agents of magic moved within a utilitarian level of religious belief, characterized by the formula *do ut des*, where issues such as health, love, money, and social promotion were the main concern, whereas clergymen were situated on a higher level of belief based on aloofness from the most immediate material interests, on distance from bodily needs, and on the search for salvation of the soul by means of acts of faith. In fact, the whole ethical system of Christianity

[10] Notions underlying this analysis can be found in Max Weber, 'Religious Groups (the Sociology of Religion)', in his *Economy and Society* (1921; English trans. Berkeley, 1978), i. 399–634; in Pierre Bourdieu, 'Une interprétation de la théorie de la religion selon Max Weber', *Archives européennes de sociologie*, 12 (1972), 3–21; and in id., 'Genèse et structure du champ religieux', *Revue française de sociologie*, 12 (1971), 295–334.

[11] Cf. Émile Durkheim, *Les Formes élementaires de la vie religieuse* (1912; 6th edn. Paris, 1979), 60–3.

rests on this last assumption, and tries to model collective behaviour according to the utopia of achievement of Heaven after physical death, thus considering spiritual rescue from the devil's rule on earth to be a central task. This eschatological ethic was absent from the magicians' practical sense. They used God and the devil indiscriminately in their daily procedures.

Cunning men were one of the main types of agents of magic. Their work was originally directed at sick livestock, whose loss was deeply felt by the rural population, and then slowly extended to human patients. This strategy was connected with the fact that medical assistance to livestock breeding was non-existent: veterinarians have only appeared in the contemporary period, and their predecessors, the *alveitares* and blacksmiths, did not have the level of training demanded by royal examiners from physicians and surgeons. That is why the work of the *saludadores* in this sphere was sought by the population and tolerated by the civil and ecclesiastical authorities. Their procedure was usually based on the miraculous blessing of water in a bowl with a cross of salt, together with an invocation of the Holy Trinity or, sometimes, of demons; this water was then sprinkled over the 'damned livestock' with a branch of spurge-laurel. The mime of Catholic rites is noticeable in the blessing of the water and the aspersion of holy water over the livestock using a kind of aspergillum (although some of the elements used, such as salt and the branch of spurge-laurel, belong to a symbolism of popular origin).

The extension of the cunning men's activities to humans elicited close vigilance by the authorities. First, because to attend to the human body there were university-trained experts, who had the necessary authorization to practise their profession and were not willing to give up such a privilege. Secondly, because the king controlled the whole procedure for granting special licences to practise healing in well-defined conditions (such as wounds, sores, buboes, scrofulae), so any attempt to avoid undergoing the compulsory official examinations by the royal doctor or royal surgeon was suspicious (it should be pointed out that the answer to any application depended on the payment of a large sum of money). Thirdly, and this is the main reason, because the body was the prime target for demoniacal action— it was by tempting the flesh with bodily delights and vices that the soul was perverted and became prey to the kingdom of darkness. This explains the demand for a greater 'scientific' and, above all, religious control over those dealing with the human body.

In attending to human illnesses, the agents of magic, usually cunning men, although we do have information on the existence of 'wise women', used the legacy of traditional medicine, based on knowledge of the healing effects of certain plants, fruits, and nectars. There was also thaumaturgical healing (a hand touching the patient's head, frequently backed up with prayers), which implied recognition of the *saludador*'s supernatural powers, as well as magico-religious cures (exorcism, unbewitching, invocation of saints or demons, devotion, *ex voto*, ordering of masses or of pilgrimage to a sanctuary). Diagnosis of the illness, prior to any healing process, was attained by clairvoyance (in this case, observation of the affected body's interior), divination on a flat surface (on still water or the earth itself), dreams, or testing the patient's urine (a redundant imitation of the procedure used by physicians).

The regional and sometimes inter-regional impact of a well-known *saludador*'s activity usually raised strong suspicions of heresy in the ecclesiastical or inquisitorial courts (to which the case was eventually transferred). The problem for a learned judge's mentality was the following: how can an illiterate person who has no specific training to attend to and cure an illness be successful in his activity? From this question arises a whole chain of different ones: how did that person know that he had the healing virtue? How did the first cures take place? What is the origin of that virtue, is it divine or diabolical? How can a notorious sinner be gifted by the grace of God with an extraordinary power?

The *saludador*'s personal charisma was built, on the one hand, through public recognition of his virtue by an older cunning man, and on the other hand, by frequent successful cures. More-or-less veiled references to the direct intervention of the supernatural had the effect of enhancing his prestige among the population: this explains the fabulous narration of premonitory dreams and apparitions of the Virgin diagnosing the illness and suggesting the way to neutralize it. The reproduction of these accounts before the inquisitors was a clear act of recklessness, because the confession by a sinner of having had contacts with the other world gave a clue as to the existence of diabolical intervention, even when using images consecrated by the Church.

Sorcerers (almost always women) were another major type of agents of magic. Their activity was preferentially in the area of feelings and will: it was directed at making love possible or impossible, at reconciling or breaking up marriages, at obtaining favours or grace from others, at attaining a good social position for the client, friend, or kin. At a secondary level there was the divination of past and future, and the practice of abortion and poisoning. The means used for benevolent and malevolent magic included: devotions, conjuration, *cartas de tocar* (touching with magical cards), *fervedouros* (brews), invocations of demons by circles or *signa Salomonis* drawn on the ground, formulas for charms, *lançamento de sortes* (casting of lots), and communication with souls. The sorcerer, contrary to the *saludador*, was not an individual with innate powers: he was an individual who mastered a group of well-defined magical techniques and rites.

The population's attitude towards sorcerers was ambiguous, using their services when in need (as happened in 1578 in the collective wave of consultation to diviners as soon as news spread of the disaster of Alcacer Quibir[12]), but keeping a fearful and respectful distance from them. In effect, sorcerers operated in very sensitive areas, and their activity could be beneficial to their client but damaging to another person—as in the case of the *rito de ligamento* (binding rite), which aimed to produce selective impotence. Furthermore, control over a technique of supernatural manipulation of the feelings and will of others constituted a constant threat to the population, because a knowledge of the positive rite meant a knowledge of the negative rite (due to the reversibility of symbols). The somewhat unfavourable light in which sorcerers were viewed by the population is confirmed by the large number of denunciations and Inquisition trials against them (a large majority of the trials for illicit magic were against sorcerers).

The activity of sorcerers extended to areas which should, in principle, have been under clergymen's control. Communication with souls through lengthy fasts and devotions was the clearest example of a direct relationship with the other world. The aim of these rites, which placed souls under the rule of conjurers, forcing them to a painful return to the world of the living, consisted in obtaining information on the occult (more specifically, on the future). Besides this, the destiny of souls could itself be subjected to divinatory practices: if the sorcerer concluded that the questioned soul was in purgatory, he could suggest that his client undertake a series of devotions (not very orthodox ones) so as to help relieve its suffering. The syncretism of

[12] A battle in N. Africa in which King D. Sebastião died and thousands of Portuguese soldiers died or were taken prisoner.

these practices and the boldness of the inquiry into matters forbidden to laymen were more than sufficient reason for inquisitorial action.

There are very few references to *magi*—in the traditional sense of manipulators of the normal course of nature—in connection with control of storms or of river-flooding. On the other hand, learned diviners did gain fame in Portugal, as is noticeable from at least the fifteenth century. Chiromancers above all, but also physiognomists, necromancers, and those who practised the *ars notoria*, left signs of their presence in handwritten books, usually copies of foreign texts; and there are records of some bolder individual cases (clergymen, students, and professional diviners) which were caught by the Holy Office.

This typology may give too schematic and clear-cut an idea of magical activity in Portugal. In fact, there was considerable overlap, with divination being practised by cunning men, sorcerers, or learned magicians, and communication with the world of the dead not being the exclusive province of necromancers. The difference between written-tradition magic and oral-tradition magic is also not clear: we have found several cases of illiterate sorcerers who included written formulas (such as the *cartas de tocar*) in their procedures, or began their divination by asking someone to read magic words, and we have also detected cases of written records of their practices. Lastly, we have detected efforts at convergence made by magicians with different training and yet facing common problems, such as the search for enchanted Arab treasures, which was an activity specific to the Iberian Peninsula.

The informal networks of magicians were primarily established according to specialty criteria (defined by common problems and identical rites) and life-patterns (geographical proximity and social kinship). The most closely knit group were undoubtedly the sorcerers, who lived in urban areas. Since they were an illiterate group, the technical side of their rites called for a considerable amount of personal exchange of information; furthermore, the environment surrounding them (the towns and cities) still had a strong influence of neighbourhood relationships and a community atmosphere where the spirit of mutual aid prevailed. The characteristics of the cunning men's activity—in which personal virtues were of the utmost importance—favoured greater individualism, and this tendency was even more noticeable amongst learned magicians, whose preferential relationship with written works freed them from reliance on any interpersonal relationships.

The clientele of the various types of agents of magic showed a certain social stratification, in terms of background, cultural level, and kinds of problem posed. This explains the frequent presence of astrologers and chiromancers at the royal court, for their activity included scientific calculations and a mastery of writing, which enabled them to acquire credibility amongst the learned élite (the determinism of their predictions was considered a heretical deviation, and was closely watched by both Church and Inquisition). However, resort to illiterate sorcerers and cunning men on the part of noblemen, clergymen, and Crown officials was not rare, and there were periods when the royal family itself regularly employed the services of well-known seers.

III. WITCHES

'Witches are born, sorcerers are made'—this saying, which can still be heard in Portugal today, summarizes the difference between the two types of agents of magic in popular imagery: the former endowed with powers (innate, or obtained by transfer of power from a dying witch), the latter having powers acquired through long apprenticeship. The different sources of their powers imply completely different modes of procedure: while the sorcerer has acquired knowledge and operates through technical mastery of magical rites, the witch is prescient and operates directly and spontaneously.

Curses are, among witch's crafts, the one most feared by common people. This simple form of magical aggression through the spoken word makes it possible to achieve surprising results over the victim. The victim incorporates the curse, and allows himself to be gradually overcome by the image of an irreversible destiny built up around him. In effect, the common belief in the power of curses plays an essential role in the whole process of the victim's psychological and social erosion. The victim is rendered defenceless and isolated, awaiting the ineluctable outcome.[13]

The evil eye is an even more subtle form of magical aggression, for it is not overt. The invisible evil spirit which exudes from the witch's eyes penetrates the most vulnerable bodies, in particular the tender and porous bodies of children, causing illness and sometimes death.

---

[13] This process was studied by Claude Lévi-Strauss, 'Le Sorcier et sa magie', in his *Anthropologie structurale* (2nd edn. Paris, 1974), 183–226.

The evil eye is also called *quebranto* ('breakdown') in Portugal, because feeling ill without fever, loss of strength without obvious cause, or the inexplicable paralysis of arms or legs are all physical events attributed to supernatural causes, that is, to the witch's craft. The sole Portuguese medical treatise on the evil eye, published in 1680 and again in 1705, attributes a material base to this whole process: foul, fetid, and malignant fluids, accumulated in the witch's body—the witch usually being a 'mal menstruada' (irregularly menstruating) old woman or old maid—are stirred and aroused by envy, becoming a thin spirit that emanates from the eyes like a fleeting arrow and pierces the victim's body.[14]

Although bad harvests and losses of livestock may in certain specific cases have been attributed to witches, it is an indisputable fact that these agents of magic were not viewed simply in terms of malefice, and that there was a certain ambiguity in the attitudes towards them and in the moral assessment of their procedure. In effect, the witch could play the role of seer, unveiling the future and advising her clients, or the role of 'cunning woman', diagnosing illness, exorcising evil spirits, and effecting thaumaturgical cures. Her connection with occult powers was itself ambiguous, for it could be used both for good and for evil. That is why the local community feared the wise woman or sorceress that lived in its midst, because unchecked communication with the supernatural could cause collective disasters. However, consulting a wise woman in a faraway place was common practice.

This ambiguity does not imply that there were no fragments (and even complete narratives) of the European night-witch myth, in which the witch is identified solely with the forces of evil, with which she establishes a connection (a pact with the devil) which is periodically renewed in ritual ceremonies (sabbaths). This connection was not decisive, however, in characterizing the witch, at least not among the people, given the belief in her innate powers. Furthermore, any other agent of magic could make a pact with the devil in order to increase his powers—an explicit or tacit (consented) pact. The former could take the notarial form of a 'dressed' pact (one set out in writing) or a 'naked' pact (verbal). In certain cases the pact could be sealed without the Evil One's presence: according to a rite common in Alcácer do Sal in the sixteenth century, it sufficed to slash a finger, introduce it into the

---

[14] Fr. Manuel de Azevedo, *Correcção de abusos introduzidos contra o verdadeiro methodo de medicina* (Lisbon, 1680), 9–12, 31.

earth, dedicate the blood to the devil, and renegue God, to have your request granted.[15]

The core of the European witch myth was the sabbath. It was designed as a night ceremony of devil-worship, involving prior supernatural flight by participants, a banquet, ritual dance, and group copulation. However, there are accounts of magical flight without the sabbath, for supernatural long-distance travel (for oneself or for others) was one of the main goals of magical practices in Portugal. The belief that the soul of the living was a double that could be detached from the body and travel elsewhere was a prerequisite for these practices—a prerequisite of shamanistic inspiration,[16] juxtaposed with beliefs about the devil's powers. The banquet and feast are part of the land of Cockaigne imagery, and its function is obvious in a society marked by chronic undernourishment and ravaged by cyclical famines.[17] In this case the banquet and dance were connected with a sexual orgy, symbolizing a climax of bodily licence and excitement of the senses, in a Judaeo-Christian context of satanized desire. Ritual nudity and ceremonial free copulation constituted powerful magico-religious forces, for they re-created the paradisaical state that preceded the fall of the first men, a state where there were no sex taboos or moral rules.[18] Devil-worship bestowed meaning upon the ceremony, for the effectiveness of the forces produced depended upon ritual obeisance to the Prince of Darkness.

From among the descriptions of sabbaths recorded in Portuguese Inquisition files, one may single out, for its originality, the 1585 confession of Margarida Lourenço—born in Sarzedas and residing in the town of Tomar—which can be summarized as follows:

1. When the defendant became an orphan at the age of 15 or 16, she was employed as a servant in the household of Mécia Afonso, a widow residing in Sarzedas. This woman had three unmarried sisters who used to meet at night. One day they proposed to the defendant that if

[15] ANTT, Inquisição de Évora, Processo no. 5089, fos. 15ᵛ–16ʳ.
[16] See Carlo Ginzburg, *I benandanti* (Turin, 1966), 52; and also Ginzburg, ch. 4, above, *passim*.
[17] On the imagery of hunger see Piero Camporesi, *Il paese della fame* (Bologna, 1978), and id., *Il pane selvaggio* (Bologna, 1981).
[18] I am following the interpretation given by Claude Gilbert Dubois, *Le Baroque: Profondeurs de l'apparence* (Paris, 1973), 108, and by Mircea Eliade, 'Quelques observations sur la sorcelleries européenne', in his *Occultisme, sorcellerie et modes culturelles* (French trans. Paris, 1978), 119.

she did not expose them, 'they would take her to a place where she could eat and drink and be merry to her heart's content'.

2. They then took from a chest an unused pan with a certain ointment, which they used to anoint themselves, becoming 'huge black birds and saying that they would rather fly above the tree tops and not below them'. Then they would leave the house through any orifice and travel by air to Vale de Cavalinhos, near Lisbon.

3. In Vale de Cavalinhos sat Beelzebub in a chair, wielding an iron bar, and they all went to pay their respects to him. Beside him was a basin where they went to offer themselves and leave money, pledging before the devil *Mazagão* that they belonged to Beelzebub and that they would return. Then the devil *Mazagão* would extract blood from their left arm with a lancet and use it to enter their names in a book. In the case of the accused the devil is purported to have changed her name from Domingas to Margarida.

4. Having recovered their human appearance, they moved a little further on to a place where there were 600 women at table with devils, eating bread and meat and drinking wine. The place was all brightly lighted with burning torches. Then they danced, the women with torches—one in front and one behind—and with a pan on their heads, while timbrels and tambourines were played. Then the devil *Mazagão* had sexual intercourse with her, from behind and from the front, as many times as he pleased.

5. There were many devils. They were black men, with ugly faces, and wore friars' apparel, with cowls woven out of goats' hair.

6. When any woman missed the 'gathering' (this was checked through the log-book) and later returned, she was beaten as punishment. The gatherings took place on either Mondays, Wednesdays, or Fridays, between midnight and 1 a.m. When it was 1 o'clock, the devils would give the women ointments with which they would anoint themselves, become big birds again, and return home. The defendant had personally attended five gatherings.

7. The defendant and the other women mentioned would go to certain crossroads to talk with the devils, who would inform them of the dates and times of the gatherings at Vale de Cavalinhos. The gatherings included married, widowed, single, and New Christian women from many parts, including Lisbon, Castelo Branco, Sobreiro, Sarzedas, and Oleiros.[19]

[19] ANTT, Inquisição de Lisboa, Processo no. 11642, fos 9ᵛ–12ᵛ.

The metamorphosis of witches into 'huge black birds' is one of the most interesting elements in this narrative, for it corresponds to an adaptation of the Roman myth of the *strix* (a night bird which sucks children's blood) to the demonological context.[20] There are also vestiges of the *lamia* myth (a human-faced and animal-bodied figure, commonly described as a goat-footed woman) in Portuguese medieval tales. The witch's animal metamorphosis, denounced by the population within a context of malefice against children, may be viewed in the light of the inversion principle that marked the thinking of the time[21] as symbolizing the replacement of reason by instinct and virtue by brutality.

The prior use of ointments appears in all descriptions of sabbaths. This fact seems to indicate the use of hallucinogenic plants in the ointments' production. Indeed, we know that there was mandrake root in Portugal, and that it was traded among sorcerers. This plant has a certain amount of atropin, which can be absorbed through contact with the skin and which causes hallucinations similar to those described by the witches—travelling through the air, erotic assemblies, and animal metamorphoses.[22] However, while this line of research suggests the possibility of a strong sensory experience of the supernatural, it does not provide an answer to the essential question of which myths and cultural complexes shaped the account we have just summarized.

The figure of Beelzebub presiding over the sabbath sitting in a chair wielding a staff might have been inspired by the image of a king wielding the sceptre as a symbol of sovereignty, but this symbol was not common in the Portuguese monarchy. The guiding image is very probably that of a court judge, all the more so in that he has a kind of clerk by his side to mark the witches and record their names in a book. These symbols appear in other accounts of communication with the devil. Ana Rodrigues, a resident of Montemoro-Novo, confessed in 1609 to the inquisitors that she had once been ordered by a witch to anoint herself, and that they had both flown on female ducks to a 'kind of tribunal' where there were six horse-bodied and human-faced

[20] Alex Scobie points out the scarcity of literary references in Europe to the metamorphosis of witches into bird-women ('Strigiform Witches in Roman and other Cultures', *Fabula*, 1–2 (1978), 74–101).

[21] On inversion rites, see the now classic study of Giuseppe Cocchiara, *Il mondo alla rovescia* (Turin, 1963), and Stuart Clark, 'Inversion, Misrule and the Meaning of Witchcraft', *Past and Present*, 87 (1980), 98–127.

[22] Cf. Michael J. Harner, *Hallucinogens and Shamanism* (New York and London, 1973).

devils, which she had worshipped on her knees, reneguing the Christian faith and giving blood from her arm as a seal.[23]

Descriptions of devils as black, ugly-faced men dressed like friars and with cowls woven out of goats' hair are quite frequent, particularly the detail about skin colour. Black is the opposite of white, and it symbolizes darkness as opposed to light, night as opposed to day, death as opposed to life. Ugly faces are not always mentioned in other accounts, for the devil can put on many appearances, all designed to seduce mortals. Friars' clothes signify that there was social disapproval of the clergy's moral behaviour, and that the religious orders' decadence was blamed on the influence of the Evil One. In fact, representation of the devil as a friar is a recurrent theme in Portuguese literature during the first half of the sixteenth century (before censorship was fully enforced by the Inquisition). The use of goats' hair to make cowls and hoods follows the traditional image of goats as symbols of lust, perversion of instinct, and impurity.

Communication with devils at crossroads—the last significant element in Margarida Lourenço's account—is common in many descriptions of sorcerers, who used to draw circles or *signa Salomonis* there in order to control the forces that had been invoked. Crossroads were also used for the ritual gathering of stones or herbs to be used in sorceries. Their symbolic importance as a passage from the world of the living to the world of the dead is derived from the fact that they are a crossing of roads, a kind of centre of the world.

IV. CENTRE AND PERIPHERY

The problem of centre and periphery[24] can be posed on several levels. First, it is important to identify the Portuguese learned élite's position in the European scene, seeking to detect different internal views and practices of repression. Secondly, it would be interesting to follow the various popular views of witchcraft in Portugal, seeking to establish any possible spatial and temporal variations. Thirdly, it is important

---

[23] ANTT, Inquisição de Évora, Processo no. 9124.

[24] I am following in part the notion of Edward Shils (*Centre and Periphery* (Chicago 1975)), which has the merit of shifting the problem from geographical space to social space. I disagree, however, with the passivity that the author assigns to the periphery, an issue already brought up by Enrico Castelnuovo and Carlo Ginzburg, 'Domination symbolique et géographie artistique', *Actes de la recherche en sciences sociales*, 40 (1981), 51–72.

to locate the various types of agents of magic, seeking to identify their forms of establishment in the country. Some indications on these problems have already been given. We will now seek to systematize and be more thorough.

The Portuguese ecclesiastical élite participated actively in sixteenth-century Catholic reorganization:

1. They implemented a pre-Reformation policy from the 1530s onwards; this policy was adopted and enlarged at the Council of Trent, where some Portuguese bishops and theologians came to play an important role;
2. They promptly implemented the Tridentine directives, benefiting from Crown support (Cardinal D. Henrique held both the post of Inquisitor-General and that of Regent between 1562 and 1568, and in 1564 he enacted the Tridentine resolutions as Laws of the Kingdom);
3. Some of Portugal's major theologians and religious thinkers of the second half of the sixteenth century, such as Jerónimo de Azambuja (Oleastro), Francisco Foreiro, Diogo Paiva de Andrade, Gaspar do Casal, Jerónimo Osório, and Heitor Pinto, had books published abroad;
4. The missionary effort in the East—which was one of the Roman Church's directions of expansion—was organized with Portugal as its base.

The Portuguese ecclesiastical élite's relatively central position in the sixteenth-century Catholic world (a position which was lost in the seventeenth and eighteenth centuries) does not account for the 'mildness' of repression against agents of magic, if we consider the diversity of situations that existed in Europe. Apart from factors relating to cultural area (the Mediterranean did not, as a rule, suffer such violent repression of witches as did Central Europe between 1550 and 1650), there are endogenous factors of a social, religious, and political nature—whose outline we have tried to establish—that led to a model of Christianization based on gradual control over Old Christians' deviant beliefs and behaviours, without violent eradication. In fact, the only radical attitudes in the sixteenth century came from the élite of lay judges (as happened in other countries), for they were not involved with any specific policy concerning the religiosity of Old Christians. Lastly, it is not possible to identify a regional differentiation in repressive practices: the available information indicates the existence of a certain homogeneity throughout mainland Portugal.

This same problem of dimension appears when we seek to detect spatial variations in popular beliefs concerning witchcraft. Descriptions of pacts with the devil, flying by night, and sabbaths (particularly the latter) are not very abundant, but they did occur both in the south and the north of the country. It is not possible to identify cultural areas in this respect. While the Inquisition trials are not very representative as a 'sample', the vestiges gathered in this past century by ethnographers do not provide any reliable indication either. It remains to be said that the sixteenth century was a time of great social and geographical mobility, with considerable migrational flows, both internal and cross-border, and that therefore there must have been a lively exchange of ideas and cultural models within mainland Portugal. The originality of Portuguese witchcraft with respect to the European model lies in the occasional metamorphosis of witches into birds (clearly a remnant of the *strix* myth) and in the generally zoomorphic depiction of the devil.

Popular views of witchcraft exhibit surprising stability throughout the centuries: in the second half of the eighteenth and the first decades of the nineteenth centuries—the final period of dismantlement of the Faith Tribunal—we can find many denunciations of malefices which the inquisitors did not follow up. While in the sixteenth and seventeenth centuries the inquisitors displayed a certain 'practical scepticism'—for they organized their interrogations on the demonological model, but did not pass sentences proportional to the confessions' seriousness—from the middle of the eighteenth century this scepticism became 'theoretical' too, for the inquisitors explicitly considered statements on communication and pacts with the devil to be fantasy.

The various types of agents of magic appeared all over the country. There was a great dispersion of *saludadores* and witches, while on the contrary there was a certain concentration of sorcerers. In fact, the *saludadores* exercised their profession in the countryside, for their healing practices began with sick livestock—although individual success could provide access to an urban milieu, or even to the royal court. Witches were similarly dispersed, for accusations of malefice normally arose within a village, where neighbourhood conflicts and personal antagonisms always played a considerable role. Sorcerers preferred to operate in cities, where they set up large informal networks (we detected twenty-three sorcerers in Alcácer do Sal, and sixty-two in Évora during the 1550s), even though there were frequent denunciations of love-related sorcery in small towns and villages, due to the importance of matrimonial strategies in all sections of *ancien régime* society.

As we have seen, the relation between centre and periphery cannot be precisely identified within the strategies of repression, nor even within the magical practices and beliefs. This notion displays all its usefulness in the social space of powers, enabling us to understand the relationship between legitimate religious agents and outcast agents of magic, the relationship between the central system of values (modelled by religious thinking in the period under consideration) and outcast attitudes, feelings, and religious experiences. This explains the gradual assimilation of urban and rural peripheries, a slow process of cultural and religious assimilation (consider the model of Christianization that was adopted) that permitted the survival of considerable remnants, which are still visible today.

IV
CONCLUSIONS

17

Scandinavian Witchcraft in Anglo-American Perspective

E. WILLIAM MONTER

ATTEMPTING to assess the significance of Scandinavian witch-trials both through similarities with and direct influences on witch-trials in the English-speaking world requires at least three separate tasks. First, one must try to isolate the most important distinctive features of these trials within the various parts of this large region: what was peculiarly interesting about witch-hunting in Scandinavia? Second, one must search for any common features which may help distinguish witch-trials in northern Europe (Scandinavia plus the British Isles) from those on the Continent. Finally, given both the distinctive features of Scandinavian witch-hunting *vis-à-vis* Continental Europe and its common features with the British Isles, one can see how two of the unusual Scandinavian features played important roles in the two most famous witch-hunts of the English-speaking world.

For an outsider, the best way to seek the important peculiarities in Scandinavian witch-trials is to start with the region itself. During the great age of witch-hunting, Scandinavia maintained one important cultural uniformity; it was the largest bloc of solidly Lutheran lands anywhere in Europe. But ever since the 1520s it had been split into two major polities: the 'parent' kingdom of Denmark administered Norway and Iceland in the west, while the 'parent' kingdom of Sweden governed Finland and Estonia in the east. Numerous conflicts between Denmark and Sweden eventually resulted in the shift in control of the southernmost province in the major peninsula, Skane, from Danish to Swedish sovereignty around the middle of the seventeenth century—in other words, at a very important time in the history of their witch-trials. However, it does not seem that this territorial change had any effect whatsoever on the pattern of these trials in either Sweden or Denmark; we may safely ignore it. The geography of early modern Scandinavia, with its two parent kingdoms and several 'colonial' districts, does not appear so very different from that of the British Isles, where the parent kingdom of England administered several colonial regions, including Ireland and Wales, while sharing the main island with a second kingdom, Scotland, which spoke an almost identical language but followed a different political destiny—at least until 1707, when the witch-trials had virtually ended.

Bearing its political geography in mind, let us quickly try to see what unusual features seem to distinguish witch-trials in the various parts of Scandinavia. Probably the most remarkable development in the region was the great Swedish panic from 1668 to 1676, affecting at least four separate provinces plus Stockholm, and resulting in more trials, and probably in more deaths, than during the rest of Sweden's history combined. But even more significant is the fact that this panic was both begun and maintained by means of accusations from children and adolescents, who had been forcibly transported to sabbaths by adult witches. This feature reminds one forcefully of the accusations from Basque children that dominated the greatest witch-hunt in Spanish history in 1610, studied by Gustav Henningsen;[1] Protestant Europe could offer nothing remotely comparable to these events until the outbreak in Dalarna fifty-eight years later. Sweden therefore has the sad distinction of having experienced not just the first witch-panic started by children in Scandinavia, but the first important panic of this type anywhere in Protestant Europe. As we shall see, Sweden provided an important example for another great Protestant kingdom of northern Europe, England, before the end of the seventeenth century.

In Finland, the most important of the Swedish dependencies, the most significant peculiarity of the witch-trials seems to lie in the sex of those accused: apart from the special circumstances of the 1670s, when the great Swedish panic spilled over onto the nearby western coast of Finland, in the largely Swedish-speaking parts of Ostrobothnia, the accused witches of Finland were more often than not men—apparently something like shamans. And they were very rarely condemned to death, unlike the women of Ostrobothnia in the 1670s.[2] In the other colonial district of seventeenth-century Sweden, Estonia, the accused witches were also more often men than women.[3]

---

[1] G. Henningsen, *The Witches' Advocate: Basque Witchcraft and the Spanish Inquisition* (Reno, 1980).

[2] Antero Heikkinen and Timo Kervinen, ch. 12, p. 322, above.

[3] Juhan Kahk, ch. 10, p. 282, above. Apparently the only people ever put to death in Iceland were men.

Within the boundaries of Scandinavia's other major kingdom, I must confess that I can find few remarkable or distinctive features in the history of witch-trials in Denmark proper. Here were perhaps the greatest number of trials and of executions anywhere in Scandinavia: the peninsula of Jutland, which contains about half of Denmark's population today, shows around 500 witch-trials and 250 deaths during the seventeenth century. Danish witch-hunts had begun relatively soon by Scandinavian standards. The earliest important set of regulations governing Danish witch-trials came in 1547, well ahead of other parts of Scandinavia. And here was the earliest legislation requiring automatic appeals to a superior court on witchcraft convictions that we know of anywhere in Europe, in 1576. Finally, Denmark appears to be the only part of Scandinavia to have largely ceased hunting witches by the mid-1650s. Precocity throughout, certainly on a Scandinavian scale and sometimes on a European scale.

Within Denmark's most important 'colonial' region, Norway, two peculiarities stand out. First, as Dr Naess has stressed, the witch-trials were conducted and managed by Danish officials, but not in accordance with Danish law (torture was illegally applied before sentence was pronounced, there was illegal use of the water ordeal, and so on); and the accused witches seem to have included an unusually high percentage of vagrants and beggars (apparently more than in such places as Elsinore, Mora, or Ostrobothnia). It seems to me that these peculiarities are tightly connected: the legal nonchalance of Danish bailiffs and pastors and judges makes more sense if they were dealing with a landless proletariat in Rogaland, and even more when dealing with the transient fishermen of Finnmark. Christian IV's recommendation to Finnmark's governor in 1609 to 'exercise a crude control with such devilish people'[4] was cruelly followed; this terribly remote region, holding only 1.5 per cent of Norway's population, saw close to one-third of its recorded executions for witchcraft. But there was another and even more remarkable peculiarity within Norwegian witchcraft accusations: Dr Naess's list of Norwegian *maleficia* includes considerably more instances of spells against ships than spells against livestock—unlike agricultural Jutland.[5] The important point is that

---

[4] Hans Eyvind Naess, ch. 14, p. 377, above (on the social status of accused witches, cf. the remarks of Jens Christian V. Johansen, ch. 13, pp. 350–2; Bengt Ankarloo, ch. 11, pp. 311–12; Heikkinen and Kervinen, ch. 12, p. 334, all above).

[5] Heikkinen and Kervinen, ch. 12, p. 335, above (they were primarily concentrated in the county of Finnmark); cf. esp. Johansen, ch. 13, p. 355, above, on the relative insignificance of nautical *maleficia* in Jutland.

nautical *maleficia* appear to be a Norwegian, and to a lesser extent a Danish, speciality; and the bewitched ship proves to be an important motif when we examine the impact of Scandinavian witchcraft upon the British Isles.

It is now time to attempt to set out a few of the common features that serve to differentiate Scandinavian witch-trials from those held on the Continent in the early modern centuries, but which also distinguished British from Continental trials. Any search for such shared peculiarities must begin with Scandinavian law. When one begins reading about accusatory procedure rather than inquisitorial procedure, about the use of juries presided over by judges whose social position was often greater than their legal training, about the general reluctance to use torture, one senses the same absence of Roman law as in England. All these features made the ordinary operation of the law very much a community enterprise, balancing the individual responsibility of the accuser against the collective involvement of many of his peers: as compurgators in the earliest (Swedish) laws; as witnesses, because a case required 'valid' testimony from at least two separate families (the city of Stockholm in 1593 required six 'reliable' witnesses to convict a witch);[6] and as jurors. Scandinavian reliance on local initiative and community judgement meant that 'popular culture' would be more important that 'élite culture' in determining the outcome of a witch-craft accusation. In other words, witch-trials would ordinarily revolve around the proof of specific, concrete *maleficia* rather than the degree or extent of pacts with the devil. We are told that the sabbath came to Jutland only in attenuated form in about 1632, even later than it first arrived in England.[7] In Sweden, witches' gatherings seem much more traditional, and the Sabbath appeared around 1600, but here too it was *maleficium* rather than night-riding to Blåkulla that formed the core of any witchcraft accusation, as the Swedish clergy acknowledged even in the 1620s. Accusatory procedure inhibited the formation of witch-panics except under extraordinary circumstances (as apparently happened at Koge in Denmark in 1612–13 and of course in the Swedish province of Dalarna in 1668).

It is important to realize that Scandinavian legal procedures

---

[6] Ankarloo, ch. 11, p. 289, above.

[7] Johansen, ch. 13, p. 360, above; Keith Thomas, *Religion and the Decline of Magic* (London, 1971), 445, who dates the first traces of the Sabbath in England to 1612. Cf. Ankarloo, ch. 11, p. 289, above, for Sweden, and note that Klaniczay, ch. 8, p. 250, above, dates the introduction of the sabbath into Hungary to 1602.

encouraged many reputed witches to retaliate against their accusers through defamation suits. In Norway, every eighth 'witch-trial' was actually a defamation suit, while in Finland every third such case was actually brought by the slandered 'witch'. In Sweden, where the thirteenth-century laws of Västergötland described female witches in the context of an 'unlawful insult', a substantial number of the recorded 'witch-trials' at local or county level during the sixteenth and seventeenth centuries were actually defamation suits of this type— probably the highest percentage of such suits anywhere in Europe. In England, where such defamation suits seem to have been relatively common in the late Middle Ages, legal historians have so far found few traces of them after the criminalization of witchcraft in 1563.[8]

Scandinavian legal systems found ways to supplement the homely procedures that regulated their ordinary witch-trials by overlaying them with provisions for legal review in a more professional court. As we have seen, Denmark—perhaps recognizing that trials by local juries produced extremely high conviction rates—led the way in 1576 by automatically transferring all such local witchcraft convictions to the royal appellate court; Sweden followed suit in 1615, extending the system to Finland via the appellate court in Turku (Åbo) a decade later.[9] Using an appellate court, staffed by more prestigious judges, did something to alter the conviction rates of accused witches—in Denmark, about half of all lower-court convictions were upheld, though the judges' reasons are often difficult to grasp. Although no British appellate court ever got automatic cognizance of witchcraft convictions, King James VI of Scotland came close to copying the Danish method in 1597, when he required his Privy Council to approve any application for a local court to try a witch, and otherwise reserved all cases of witchcraft for Scotland's appellate tribunal, the Court of Justiciary. Like the Danish appellate judges, Scotland's high court convicted close to half of the witches whose cases it tried during the 1600s.[10]

---

[8] Naess, ch. 14, p. 371, Heikkinen and Kervinen, ch. 12, p. 323, Ankarloo, ch. 11, p. 287. The only surviving original depositions in English witchcraft trials before 1500 occur in defamation suits: see Richard Kieckhefer, *European Witch Trials: Their Foundations in Popular and Learned Culture, 1300–1500* (Berkeley and Los Angeles, 1976), 28–9.

[9] Johansen, ch. 14, p. 341; Ankarloo, ch. 12, p. 290; Heikkinen and Kervinen, ch. 13, p. 324, all above.

[10] Johansen, ch. 13, p. 350, above; Christina Larner, *Enemies of God: The Witch-hunt in Scotland* (London, 1981), 36, 63. My own work on the appellate judges in the 17th-c. Habsburg province of Franche-Comté also showed slightly under half of all convictions

The age when Scandinavia's appellate courts oversaw witch-trials coincided with the time when its clergy were probably most active in indoctrinating their flocks. Both groups contributed to the slow and gradual diabolization of Scandinavian witchcraft that culminated in the great Swedish panic of 1668–76. Here I can only subscribe to the schema of Peter Burke and Jean Delumeau, the 'triumph of Lent' or the belated Christianization of Europe—a schema that seems peculiarly vivid when Sweden's scandalized clergy encountered the rampant paganism of seventeenth-century Estonia. Such remote corners of a nominally-Protestant region of northern Europe remind one of contemporary developments in the Highlands of Scotland, whose supposedly Calvinist inhabitants were still worshipping saints by sacrificing bulls, honouring sacred stones, and leaving milk outside to placate the spirits. Such places were natural fields for Protestant missionary work—backed up by cavalry, in the case of Estonia.[11] However, in such remote regions very few witches were ever put on trial, despite—or more likely, because of—the pervasiveness of sorcery. Finnmark, at the northernmost tip of Norway, provides an excellent illustration: it was peopled largely by Lapps, who have always been famous sorcerers, and it saw prodigious numbers of witch-trials in the seventeenth century—all of them, however, directed against coastal fishermen rather than the inland Lapps.

It is time to leave the general structural similarities within Scandinavian witch-hunting and between Scandinavia and the British Isles, and turn to two very specific and very important points at which the latter was decisively influenced by the former. Neither instance occurred in England proper. One had a decisive effect on the first great witch-panic in the British Isles; the other played a significant role, as example and as justification, in the final important witch-panic in the English-speaking world.

The first 'Scandinavian witchcraft connection' resulted from the marriage of James VI of Scotland to the Danish Princess Anna in 1589. King James travelled in person to Norway and then Denmark in order to meet her—a rare custom in the annals of royalty—and spent six months at his father-in-law's court. There he probably met the greatest Danish theologian of the time, Niels Hemmingsen, whose

by lower courts for witchcraft upheld (E. William Monter, *Witchcraft in France and Switzerland* (Ithaca and London, 1976), 73–8, 216–20).

[11] Kahk, ch. 10, p. 283, above.

views on witchcraft and diabolism were cited approvingly by King James in his well-known *Demonology* of 1597. Perhaps more importantly, James's return voyage to Scotland with his wife was marked by terrible storms; Peder Munk, the admiral of the Danish fleet carrying them to Scotland, blamed the weather on witchcraft by the wife of a Danish official whom he had insulted. (He was following a Danish tradition, dating back to the 1540s and repeated in 1567, of blaming disasters to Denmark's war-fleet on witches in the pay of foreign powers.) King James soon became convinced that his stormy voyage was due to witchcraft, but was doubtful whether the witches who had caused it were exclusively Danish.[12] A few months later the great cluster of trials began at North Berwick under James's direct leadership, ending with the indictment of one of Scotland's most important nobles; these events were of course known in Denmark, and parallel witch-trials were held in both countries. (To the best of my knowledge, this is a unique development in the history of European witchcraft, far surpassing the Franco-Spanish co-operation at the time of the great Basque witch-trials a quarter-century later; these trials were also unusual in that both sets of them involved politically prominent defendants). King James seems to have paid very little attention to witchcraft before 1590, and was introduced to the dangers of witchcraft at sea—the nautical *maleficia* which, as we have seen, were a Norwegian and Danish peculiarity, and which were otherwise virtually unknown in the British Isles. By the time he wrote his *demonology* six years later, King James no longer saw nautical *maleficia* as a central dimension of witchcraft, but he had not forgotten Hemmingsen and Denmark.

My second and final 'Scandinavian witchcraft connection' leads from the Swedish panic of 1668–76 (more precisely, from the events at Mora in the autumn of 1669) to the panic at Salem Village in New England in 1692. Historians of old and new England have always been uncomfortably aware that these events were unprecedented in British history: large numbers of deaths in a single village in a single year, and worst of all, condemnations based on 'spectral evidence' mostly offered by way of demonically possessed children and young un-

<hr>

[12] Christina Larner, 'James VI and Witchcraft', in Alan G. R. Smith (ed.), *The Reign of James VI and I* (London, 1973), 80–1; for the Danish accusations and trials, see esp. Bering Liisberg, *Vesten for Sø og østen for Hav: Trolddom i København og i Edinburgh 1590* (Copenhagen, 1909). [Cf. Thomas Riis, *Should Auld Acquaintance Be Forgot . . . Scottish and Danish Connections c.1450–1707* (Copenhagen, 1988), ch. 11, 'Queen Anne'—editor's note.]

married women. No recent historian has paid much attention to the fact that the developments at Salem Village were not unparalleled in the world of European Protestantism, although New England's well-educated clergy knew this in 1692. Both before and after the Salem panic, the most famous clergyman of New England, Cotton Mather, used the example of the Swedish panic in order to explain the dangers of witchcraft and to defend the use of spectral evidence in convicting accused witches. 'It is hardly twenty years ago,' he remarked in his *Discourse on Witchcraft* (1689), 'that a whole kingdom in Europe was alarmed by such potent witchcrafts, that some hundreds of poor children were invaded with them'.[13] He was far more explicit about Swedish parallels in his major statement about witchcraft written after the Salem trials, *The Wonders of the Invisible World* (1693): on its title-page, fourth among a group of five accompanying pieces, his readers could find 'A short Narrative of a late Outrage committed by a knot of Witches in Swedeland. Very much Resembling, and so far Explaining, that under which our parts of America have labored!'[14] Of course, the Salem Village panic was no carbon copy of events in Dalarna, and Mather had to downplay such elements of the Swedish accounts as the children's trips to Blåkulla, which had no direct parallel in New England. But the structural similarities were real.

Where did Cotton Mather learn about the bewitched children of 'Swedeland'? Quite likely, he looked no further than the most famous recent English work in defence of traditional opinions about witch-craft, Joseph Glanvil's *Sadducismus Triumphatus*, first published in 1668. Later editions of Glanvil's book contained not only some additional material by the famous Cambridge Platonist Henry More, but also, 'two Authentick, but wonderful Stories of certain Swedish Witches, done into English by A. Horneck, D.D.', translated from a Dutch pamphlet of 1670. By 1683 this had become a 34-page appendix at the end of the work, now entitled 'An Account of what happen'd in the Kingdom of Sweden in the Years 1669, 1670, and upwards in Relation to some Persons that were accused for witches; and Tryed and Executed by the King's Command. Together with the Particulars

[13] C. Mather, *Discourse on Witchcraft* (1689), repr. in D. Levin (ed.), *Witchcraft in Salem* (New York, 1967), 100.

[14] The full title of Mather's *Wonders of the Invisible World* (Boston and London, 1693) is reprinted in G. L. Burr (ed.), *Narratives of Witchcraft Cases, 1648–1706* (New York, 1914), 209. Note that James VI's old Danish mentor Niels Hemmingsen reappears in Mather's text as 'Pious Hemingius' (ibid., p. 247).

of a very sad Accident that befel a Boy at Malmoe in Schonen [Skåne], in the Year 1678, by the means of Witchcraft.'[15]

Probably the 1683 edition of Glanvil was the one used by Mather; it was also apparently the one used by Francis Hutchinson, the first sceptic who dared to compose *An Historical Essay Concerning Witchcraft* (histories being generally studies of subjects that are no longer alive) in 1718. His essay contains a brief chapter, the sixth, devoted to 'The pretended Witchcrafts at Mohra in Sweden'.[16] It follows a chapter on the New England panic of 1692, which of course followed it chronologically. Hutchinson included his Swedish material in order to compare it (unfavourably) with the New England panic, which had ended happily with a partial apology by some of the judges involved. Hutchinson's fictional Scottish advocate asks in the chapter on Sweden, 'Were there only some odd diseases amongst the Children; and did superstitious Principles and Prosecutions blow it up into such a sad calamity? In a word, Do you think, this Case was like that in New England?' And his partner in dialogue, a British clergyman, immediately answers, 'I make not the least Question but it was.' (Unknown to Hutchinson, the governor of Massachusetts had written a letter in October 1692, after the trials had ended, explaining that 'It [the Salem panic] hath been represented to mee much like that of Sweden thirty years ago.')[17] Subsequent pages serve to point out the similarities, especially at the end of the Swedish panic: 'I have heard', says the clergyman, that 'these judges did not go on accusing and burning more . . . for the same reason for which they stopped in New England, because it came to the wealthy, and because they could see no end to executions.'

Cotton Mather, both before and after the Salem Village panic, cited Swedish evidence—and only Swedish evidence—apart from British cases of witchcraft. Francis Hutchinson, a quarter-century later, used entirely British evidence in his major chapters, apart from his section on Mora. Glanvil collected other foreign items, but advertised only the Swedish material on his title-page. The Swedish panic of 1668–76 thus occupies a very special niche in the search for justification (or, in

---

[15] Joseph Glanvil, *Sadducismus Triumphatus* (1681), ed. C. O. Parsons (Gainesville, Fla., 1966), 563–97. Cf. Ankarloo, ch. 11, p. 317.

[16] Francis Hutchinson, *An Historical Essay Concerning Witchcraft* (1718; 2nd edn. London, 1720), 122–30.

[17] Hutchinson, *Historical Essay*, pp. 123–4; cf. Governor Phips's letter in Burr, *Narratives*, p. 196.

Hutchinson's case, for refutation) of late seventeenth-century British witch-trials; and the parallels with Salem's famous panic were obvious both to contemporary and subsequent observers, for only a respectable Protestant country like Sweden could give a respectable precedent to earnest clerics trying to use the shabby legal evidence of afflicted children to convict witches.

In summary, I think that a 'Scandinavian connection' was operating in both the first and last major witch-panics in the English-speaking world, a full century apart. Denmark at the beginning: an international conspiracy of nautical witchcraft afflicting an erudite Scottish king and his Danish bride. Sweden at the end: afflicted children used by a serious Protestant government to start a witch-hunt that rapidly grew to huge dimensions, offering the best and handiest example to the embattled clergymen of New England as they confronted their own afflicted children. Such special features overcame the common-law conservatism that dominated most witch-trials both in Scandinavia and in the British Isles, and that generally prevented such panics from developing in either region.

18
The Comparative Approach to European Witchcraft

PETER BURKE

In the last twenty years or so, witchcraft has moved from the periphery of historical attention to a place near the centre. When, in the later 1960s, Professor Trevor-Roper published his lively essay on what he called, following nineteenth-century German scholars, the European 'Witch-craze', he can hardly have guessed that he was summarizing and synthesizing the conventional historical wisdom on the subject at the very time when this conventional view was being undermined. Trevor-Roper took Europe for his province, ranging from Scotland to Transylvania, but he deliberately limited himself to the beliefs of clerical and lay élites. A sturdy rationalist, he expressed a firm lack of interest in what he called 'those elementary village credulities which anthropologists discover in all times and at all places', and his account of the 'craze' attempted to relate its rise and subsequent decline to such major intellectual movements such as Aristotelianism and Platonism, Reformation, and Scientific Revolution.[1]

It was at just this point, in the sixties, however, that conventional views of historical writing were being turned upside-down by the movement to write history 'from below'. Witchcraft was one of the first topics to be studied in the new way, by Ginzburg, Macfarlane, Thomas, Ankarloo, Midelfort, Boyer and Nissenbaum, Monter, Muchembled, and others.[2] All these scholars began with the village

---

[1] Hugh R. Trevor-Roper, *Religion, the Reformation and Social Change* (London, 1967); id., *The European Witch-craze of the 16th and 17th Centuries* (Harmondsworth, 1969).
[2] Carlo Ginzburg, *The Night Battles: Witchcraft and Agrarian Cults in the Sixteenth and Seventeenth Centuries* (1966; English trans. London, 1983); Alan Macfarlane, *Witchcraft in Tudor and Stuart England* (London, 1970); Keith Thomas, *Religion and the Decline of Magic* (London, 1971); Bengt Ankarloo, *Trolldomsprocesserna i Sverige* (Lund, 1971); H. C. Erik Midelfort, *Witch-hunting in Southwestern Germany, 1562–1684* (Stanford, 1972); Paul Boyer and Stephen Nissenbaum, *Salem Possessed: The Social Origins of Witchcraft* (Cambridge, Mass., 1974); E. William Monter, *Witchcraft in France and Switzerland* (Ithaca and London, 1976); Robert Muchembled, 'Sorcières du Cambrésis: L'Acculturation du monde rural aux XVIᵉ et XVIIᵉ siècles', in Marie-Sylvie Dupont-Bouchat,

and emphasized the relevance of all problems and fears of the villagers
to the sharp rise in the number of trials and executions for witchcraft
in different parts of Europe and America in the sixteenth and seventeenth centuries. They employed quantitative methods and attempted
to map the distribution of trials in space and time. Where Trevor-
Roper painted with a broad brush on a European canvas, these
historians concentrated—like social anthropologists—on regional
variation and local context, rejecting the traditional account of witch-
hunting as too monolithic, and asking instead what kinds of people
accused what other kinds of people of witchcraft, and in what
situations. They tended—again like anthropologists—to put rationalism in brackets, if not to reject it altogether, to write about witches and
their accusers without using words like 'craze', 'credulity', or
'hysteria', and even to suggest that accusations of witchcraft served a
social function.[3]

What substantive results emerged from this group of studies?
Thomas and Macfarlane came to two major conclusions. In the first
place, that accusations of witchcraft in early modern England were 'a
normal part of village life, widespread and regular', endemic rather
than epidemic. 'For the most part the story is of steady and un-
spectacular annual prosecution.'[4] In the second place, Thomas and
Macfarlane noted that the accusers, or victims, were generally neighbours of the so-called witches, somewhat more prosperous than they
were, and that the accusations tended to follow quarrels which centred
on the refusal of charity to the witch, usually a poor woman living
alone. They concluded that the rise of witch-trials was related to the
crisis of charity, though they formulated this relationship in opposite
ways. Thomas made the functionalist point that 'witch-beliefs helped
to uphold the traditional obligations of charity and neighbourliness at
a time when other social and economic forces were conspiring to
weaken them.'[5] In other words, their fear of witchcraft made the
neighbours less stingy than they would otherwise have been. Macfarlane, on the other hand, argued that witchcraft was 'a means of
effecting a deep social change; a change from a "neighbourly", highly
integrated and mutually interdependent village society to a more

Willem Frijhoff, and Robert Muchembled, *Prophétes et sorciers dans les Pays-Bas* (Paris,
1978); id., *La Sorciére au village (XVF au XVIF siècles)* (Paris, 1979).

[3] More especially Macfarlane, *Witchcraft* and Thomas, *Religion*.
[4] Macfarlane, *Witchcraft*, p. 30; Thomas, *Religion*, p. 451.
[5] Thomas, *Religion*, p. 564.

individualistic one'; that is, the imputation of witchcraft was a rationalization for the refusal to give charity.[6]

These studies were deliberately confined to England. Thomas indeed contrasted the English situation with that obtaining on the Continent; preoccupation with *maleficium* versus preoccupation with pact and sabbath; persecution from above versus persecution from below; extraordinary witch hunts versus ordinary litigation. However, new interpretations of the great witch-hunts and the timing of their rise and decline in different regions have also been put forward. Erik Midelfort focused on what he called the 'large panic trials' of South West Germany, and argued that their sudden end in the seventeenth century owed nothing to the new science but was the result of an internally generated 'crisis of confidence', a reaction against accusations which became more and more indiscriminate. Christina Larner's work on Scotland concentrated on the rise of what she called a 'moral panic', an 'attack on deviance' which she went on to explain in terms of the government's need for 'legitimacy'.[7]

Midway between the two approaches to witchcraft, the Thomas-Macfarlane approach via ordinary villages and the Midelfort-Larner approaches via large hunts, lies a third body of recent work. Paul Boyer and Stephen Nissenbaum took the most notorious witch-hunt of the seventeenth century, in Salem, Massachusetts in 1692, and showed that the split between supporters and opponents of the trials followed the lines of established factions in Salem Village.[8] William Monter's work on 'small panics' in France and Switzerland steered between Thomas and Midelfort. Robert Muchembled's study of the Cambrésis offered what the author called an 'acculturation model' emphasizing the role in the witch-trials of the village élite, the mediators between the community and the outside world of Counter-Reformation and absolute monarchy.[9] Although it was published earlier than any of the studies cited so far, Carlo Ginzburg's book on the *benandanti* also belongs to this cluster, since it deals with an

[6] Macfarlane, *Witchcraft*, p. 107. On the other hand Macfarlane takes English 'individualism' back to the 13th c. (id., *The Origins of English Individualism* (Oxford, 1978)).

[7] Christina Larner, *Enemies of God: The Witch-hunt in Scotland* (London, 1981), a study as much inspired by sociological theory as Thomas and Macfarlane have been by social anthropology.

[8] Boyer and Nissenbaum, *Salem Possessed*, pp. 65, 185.

[9] Muchembled, 'Sorcières du Cambrésis', extended to France in id., *Popular Culture and Elite Culture in Early Modern France* (1978; English trans. Baton Rouge, 1985).

encounter between inquisitors and villagers in Friuli in which the latter disconcerted their interrogators by claiming to fight witches 'in the spirit', at night, four times a year, in order to defend their crops. However, Ginzburg's work also points in another direction. The author drew attention to a trial of a so-called werewolf in Livonia in 1692, in which the accused claimed that he fought witches three nights a year, in hell, in order to bring back to earth the animals and crops the witches had stolen.[10] Ginzburg's comparison suggested that archaic practices had survived into the seventeenth century in regions such as Livonia and Friuli, on the European periphery.

After some twenty years of intense research on witch-trials in their local context, it is perhaps time to return to a more global approach. After all, the European witch-hunts of the early modern period did not respect regional boundaries.[11] Even the distinction between England and the rest of Europe does not look as sharp as it did in the early 1970s. The next wave of research showed that what might be called the Thomas–Macfarlane model was far from irrelevant to other parts of Europe. Norman Cohn pointed out that in the Lucerne area around 1500, villagers brought accusations of *maleficium* without any mention of the devil.[12] William Monter discussed 'endemic' as well as 'epidemic' witchcraft in France and Switzerland, and noted that the accused were generally women, poor, and isolated.[13] Robert Muchembled gave French and Flemish examples of refusals of charity leading to accusations of witchcraft.[14]

If local studies are too limited, while the traditional view of early modern witchcraft was too monolithic, there remains a third possibility: systematic comparison. The value of comparative history is that it allows us to test explanations more rigorously, just as it allows us to 'see' the significance of what is not there—the relative lack of witch-trials in the Netherlands, for example.[15] It is worth asking whether

---

[10] Ginzburg, *Night Battles*, ch. 1, section 16.

[11] Two essays in synthesis on a European scale have just appeared, too late to be taken into account by contributors to this volume, Brian Levack, *The Witch-hunt in Early Modern Europe* (London 1987), and G. R. Quaife, *Godly Zeal and Furious Rage: The Witch in Early Modern Europe* (London, 1987).

[12] Norman Cohn, *Europe's Inner Demons* (London, 1975), 239.

[13] Monter, *Witchcraft*, pp. 46, 118, 120.

[14] Muchembled, *Sorcière au village*, pp. 35, 106, 159.

[15] Ivo Schöffer, 'Heksengeloof', *Tijdschrift voor Geschiedenis*, 86 (1973), 215–35; Willem de Blécourt and Marijke Gijswijt-Hofstra (eds.), 'Kwade Mensen: Toverij in Nederland', *Volkskundig Bulletin*, 12 (1986), 1–263.

regional variations are structured, whether they form what the Swiss linguist Ferdinand de Saussure called 'systems of differences'.

Commenting on the importance of Roman law in the pattern of witch-hunts in Scotland, Christina Larner remarked that 'Areas on the periphery of this system, such as England, Russia, Denmark and Finland, experienced milder hunts with less reference to diabolism and conspiracy.'[16] The desire to test this hypothesis, as well as to ensure that generalizations about Europe were supported by data from all over the Continent, led to the conference which in turn gave rise to the present book. The book contains a number of essays on regions, from Iceland to Hungary and from Portugal to Livonia, which have never before been seriously discussed in English. However, its major contribution to studies of witchcraft resides in the systematic use of the model of 'centre and periphery'.

This model, developed in the 1960s by economists and sociologists, has begun to attract the attention of a number of historians, with interests ranging from the spread of the Renaissance to the rise of capitalism.[17] For example, cultural historians want to explain what is sometimes called 'cultural lag', the time taken by the diffusion of innovations. If they ever thought that this lag was uniform, with the provinces thirty years behind the metropolis, but accepting more or less enthusiastically whatever was sent, this certainty has dissolved in the face of studies which distinguish political or economic centres from geographical ones, and emphasize the active role of the periphery in resisting as well as in adapting innovations.[18] The 'acculturation' model employed by a number of French historians (Muchembled among them) is a special case of the centre-periphery model, used to analyse situations where cultural changes are unusually rapid and deep.[19]

---

[16] Larner, *Enemies of God*, p. 197.

[17] Immanuel Wallerstein, *The Modern World System* (New York, 1974); Johan Galtung, 'Sosial posisjon og sosial adferd', in Galtung (ed.), *Periferi og sentrum i historien* (Oslo, 1975), a general discussion; Enrico Castelnuovo and Carlo Ginzburg, 'Domination symbolique et géographie artistique', *Actes de la recherche en sciences sociales*, 40 (1981), 51–72. Let us hope that the time-lag in the model's perception by historians does not imply that we are on the periphery of social studies.

[18] Edward Shils, *Centre and Periphery* (Chicago, 1975) distinguishes types of centre but offers, typically, a consensus model, which is criticized in Nigel Mckenzie, 'Centre and Periphery', *Acta Sociologica*, 20 (1977), 55–74.

[19] The model is discussed in Peter Burke, 'A Question of Acculturation?', in Paola Zambelli (ed.), *Scienze, credenze oculte, livelli di cultura* (Florence, 1982), 197–204, and Jean Wirth, 'Against the Acculturation Thesis', in Kaspar von Greyerz (ed.), *Religion and Society in Early Modern Europe* (London, 1984), 66–78.

In the case of the great witch-hunts of the early modern period, the time-lag between their rise and decline in Italy (say) and Poland (where the peak of death sentences was reached only in the early eighteenth century) is well known.[20] On the other hand, general studies of European witchcraft, from Hansen to Trevor-Roper, have concentrated on the centre, or centres (adding Wittenberg and Geneva to Rome after the Reformation). This volume redresses the balance by concentrating on Europe's geographical peripheries, mainly north-eastern (but including Portugal and Sicily as well). In a number of these cases, 'periphery' can also be understood in a political sense, with Finland and Sicily, for example, forming part of the Swedish and Spanish Empires respectively. The term may also be understood in a cultural sense, and be associated with what is generally called 'popular', or sometimes 'unofficial', culture.

In this volume, Bengt Ankarloo explicitly concerns himself with the diffusion of new ideas about witchcraft within Sweden, but a similar diffusion model is implicit in many of the studies collected here. The way in which the ideas of the theologians, Catholic and Protestant, were interpreted and received by the laity varied according to the local context, as these essays show. All the same, the concentration on the periphery does suggest some more general conclusions. Because the great witch-hunts came to these regions relatively late, and because the Scandinavian legal system allowed witnesses more initiative than elsewhere, it is somewhat easier than usual to discover what ordinary people believed about witches before pastors or inquisitors arrived to put them right. What we get is a view of the supernatural before its 'diabolization', with little reference to pacts with the devil or to witches' sabbaths (except in the intriguing case of Sicily, where we see a 'white sabbath'). What people fear is *maleficium*, and the way they defend themselves against it is to go to a cunning man or wise woman. The English pattern charted by Thomas and Macfarlane turns out to be not uniquely English at all, but the traditional pattern which survived best on other parts of the geographical and legal periphery (defining the legal 'centre' with reference to Roman law). The references to 'endemic' witchcraft in France, Switzerland, and elsewhere now fit into place.

On the other hand, the Thomas–Macfarlane model of the witch as a poor and elderly woman, a model which seems to be applicable to

---

[20] Bohdan Baranowski, *Procesy czarownic w Polsce* (Łodź, 1952).

much of Europe, does not work for Finland or for Iceland, as Heikkinen, Kervinen, and Hastrup show. In these cases, the men accused of witchcraft seem to have not a little in common with shamans. Shamanistic elements can also be found further to the south, in Sicily, Romania, Hungary, and Croatia, as Klaniczay and Henningsen suggest. The analogy noted by Carlo Ginzburg between shamans and *benandanti* now seems to fit into a much larger pattern. It is as if we are looking at the tip of an iceberg, the shape and size of which is still unknown.

Behind the diabolical witchcraft of the witch-hunters has been discovered a more traditional, neighbourly witchcraft. Behind this in turn we are seeing glimpses of a still more archaic, shamanistic witchcraft. It would be unwise to take this three-stage model as representing any kind of norm. The studies collected into this volume illustrate as well as urge the importance of regional variation and local context, and the reconstruction of popular beliefs in the early Middle Ages or even earlier is necessarily speculative and uncertain. All the same, the comparative approach has produced important conclusions. In any study of witchcraft over the long term, the evidence from the European periphery is absolutely central.

NOTES ON CONTRIBUTORS

BENGT ANKARLOO is Lecturer in History at Lund University. His speciality is Swedish and American social and legal history; his publications include *Trolldomsprocesserna i Sverige* (1971) and *At stilla herrevrede: Trolldomsdåden på Vegeholm 1653–54* (1988).

FRANCISCO BETHENCOURT, currently at the European University Institute in Florence, is a lecturer at the Faculty of Social and Human Sciences in the Universidade Nova, Lisbon. He is the author of *O imaginário da magia: Feiticeiras, saludadores e nigromantes no séc. 16* (1987).

PETER BURKE is Lecturer in History at Emmanuel College, Cambridge. His publications include *Popular Culture in Early Modern Europe* (1978) and most recently *The Historical Anthropology of Early Modern Italy: Essays on Perception and Communication* (1987).

JULIO CARO BAROJA is one of the leading scholars of our time in Spanish studies. In 1961 he published his pioneering analysis of European witchcraft, *The World of the Witches*. Since then over a dozen works have followed on folklore, ethnography, and history.

STUART CLARK, currently at the Institute of Advanced Studies, Princeton, is Lecturer in History at the University of Wales, Swansea. He has published articles in *Past and Present*, vols. 87 and 100, and in S. Anglo (ed.), *The Damnèd Art: Essays in the Literature of Witchcraft*; B. Vickers (ed.), *Occult and Scientific Mentalities in the Renaissance*; and Q. Skinner (ed.), *The Return of Grand Theory in the Human Sciences*. He is now completing a work on the ideological history of early belief in witchcraft.

CARLO GINZBURG is Franklin D. Murphy professor of Italian studies at University of California, Los Angeles. He has written several books, including *I benandanti*, *The Cheese and the Worms*, and *The Enigma of Piero della Francesca*.

KIRSTEN HASTRUP, currently research professor of the Danish Research Council for the Humanities, is Professor of Social Anthropology at Århus University. She has written several books and articles on anthropological theory and method and on the Icelandic past and present, including *Culture and History in Medieval Iceland: An Anthropological Analysis of Structure and Change* (1985).

ANTERO HEIKKINEN is Assistant Professor of Finnish History at Joensuu University. His treatise (in Finnish) *Allies of the Devil: Notions of Witchcraft and Demonic Magic in Late Seventeenth-Century Finland* was published in 1969.

GUSTAV HENNINGSEN is Research Leader at the Danish Folklore Archives, Copenhagen. He undertook anthropological field-work and archival research in Spain from 1965 to 1972. He has written *The Witches' Advocate: Basque Witchcraft and the Spanish Inquisition* (1980; Spanish translation 1983) and a popular work *Fra heksejagt til heksekult 1484–1984* (1984), and (together with John Tedeschi) edited *The Inquisition in Early Modern Europe: Studies on Sources and Methods* (1986).

JENS CHRISTIAN V. JOHANSEN is a researcher at the Historical Institute, Copenhagen University. He has published several essays on Danish witchcraft, which is also the topic of a larger treatise to appear shortly.

JUHAN KAHK is a professor at the Estonian Academy of Sciences and leader of its Social Science section. Among his most recent publications are *Peasant and Lord in the Process of Transition from Feudalism to Capitalism in the Baltics* (1982) and several articles on historical demography.

TIMO KERVINEN is a lawyer in Helsinki. During his studies at Helsinki University he took part in Professor Heikki Ylikanga's project on legal history, *Aikansa rikos*, 'The Crime of the Time'.

GÁBOR KLANICZAY is Assistant Professor of History at the Eötvös Lóránd University, Budapest. He has published a number of historical articles on the medieval cult of saints, popular culture, and witchcraft in the early modern period.

MAIA MADAR is a researcher at the Historical Institute at the Estonian Academy of Sciences.

E. WILLIAM MONTER is Professor of History at Northwestern University, Evanston, Ill. Among his books may be mentioned *Witchcraft in France and Switzerland* (1976), *Ritual, Myth and Magic in Early Modern Europe* (1983), and *The Spanish Inquisition from the Basque Land to Sicily* (1989).

ROBERT MUCHEMBLED is Professor of History at the Université de Paris XIII (Paris-Nord), Villetaneuse. He is the author of *Popular Culture and Elite Culture in France, 1400–1750* and *Sorcières, justice et société aux 16e et 17e siècles* (1987). He is also the editor of a new journal first appearing in 1988: *Mentalités: Les mentalités dans l'histoire* (Paris, Imago).

Hans Eyvind Naess is a State Archivist in Stavanger. He has published *Trolldomsprosessene i Norge på 1500–1600-tallet* (1982)—in a popular version as *Med bål og brann* (1984)—and several articles on local administration and the courts in Norway.

Robert Rowland is Professor of Social History at the European University Institute, Florence. He has published essays and articles chiefly on the anthropology, historical demography, and social history of the Mediterranean area.

John Tedeschi is Curator of Rare Books and Special Collections at the University of Wisconsin, Madison. Among his most recent works may be mentioned 'Preliminary Observations on Writing a History of the Roman Inquisition', in F. F. Church and T. George (eds.), *Continuity and Discontinuity in Church History* (1979). Together with Gustav Henningsen he edited *The Inquisition in Early Modern Europe: Studies on Sources and Methods* (1986).

BIBLIOGRAPHY OF SECONDARY WORKS

Aðils, Jón, *Einokunarverzlun Dana á Íslandi, 1602–1787* (2nd edn. Reykjavik, 1971).

Alapi, Gyula, *Bubájosok és boszorkányok Komárom vármegyében* (Komárom, 1914).

Almquist, Bo, *Norrön Niddiktning: Traditionshistoriska studier i versmagi*, in *Nid mot furstar* (Stockholm, 1965).

Alsheimer, Rainer, 'Katalog protestantischer Teufelserzählungen des 16. Jhts', in *Volkserzählung und Reformation* (Berlin, Wolfgang Bruckner (ed.), 1974), 417–519.

Amelung, Friedrich, 'Die frühzeitigen Reformen in der altlivländischen Strafrechtspflege und die hiesigen Hexenprozesse', *Düna Zeitung*, 205 (1907).

Anchel, Robert, *Les Juifs en France* (Paris, 1946).

Andrésson, Sigfús H., (Þorleifur Lögmaður Kortsson', *Skírnir*, 131 (1957), 152–71.

Anglo, Sydney (ed.), *The Damnèd Art: Essays in the Literature of Witchcraft* (London, 1977).

Ankarloo, Bengt, *Trolldomsprocesserna i Sverige* (Lund, 1971).

——, 'Häxprocesserna på Värmlandsnäs', in *Värmland förr och nu* (Meddelanden från Värmlands museum; Karlstad, 1977), 65–8.

——, 'Das Geschrei der ungebildeten Masse: Zur Analyse der schwedischen Hexenprozesse', in Christian Degn, Hartmut Lehmann, and Dagmar Unverhau (eds.), *Hexenprozesse* (Neumünster, 1983), 172–8.

——, 'Europe and the Glory of Sweden: The Emergence of a Swedish Self-image in the Early 17th Century', in Göran Rystad (ed.), *Europe and Scandinavia: Aspects of the Process of Integration in the 17th Century* (Lund, 1983), 241–8.

——, 'Domstolarnas arbetsformer', in Ulf Teleman (ed.), *Det offentliga språkbruket och dess villkor i Sverige under 1700-talet* (Småskrifter från institutionen för nordiska språk i Lund, 7; Nordlund, 1985), 129–37.

——, and Henningsen, Gustav (eds.), *Häxornas Europa 1400–1700: Historiska och antropologiska studier* (Stockholm, 1987).

Arbusow, Leonid, 'Zauberer- und Hexenwahn in den baltischen Provinzen', *Rigascher Almanach* (1911), 102–4.

——, *Die Einführung der Reformation in Liv-, Est- und Kurland*, iii (Leipzig, 1921).

——, 'Die altlivländischen Bauerrechte', *Mitteilungen aus der livländischen Geschichte*, 23 (1924–6), 1–144, 634–45.

Ardener, Edwin, 'Witchcraft, Economics and the Continuity of Belief', in

Mary Douglas (ed.), *Witchcraft Confessions and Accusations* (London, 1970), 141–60.

——, 'Some Outstanding Problems in the Analysis of Events', *Yearbook of Symbolic Anthropology*, 1 (1978), 103–21.

Ariès, Philippe, *Centuries of Childhood* (1960; English trans. London, 1962).

Augé, Marc, *Génie du paganisme* (Paris, 1982).

Aureggi, Olimpia, 'Stregoneria retica e tortura giudiziaria', *Bollettino della società storica valtellinese*, 17 (1963–4), 46–90.

Bamford, Paul, *Fighting Ships and Prisons: The Mediterranean Galleys of France in the Age of Louis XIV* (Minneapolis, 1973).

Banton, Michael (ed.), *The Social Anthropology of Complex Societies* (London, 1965).

Baranowski, Bohdan, *Procesy czarownic w Polsce w XVII i XVIII wieku* (Łódź, 1952).

Barber, Malcolm, 'The Plot to overthrow Christendom in 1321', *History*, 66 (1981), 1–17.

Battistella, Antonio, *Il S. Officio e la riforma religiosa in Bologna* (Bologna, 1905).

Bausinger, Herman, 'Volksideologie und Volksforschung', *Zeitschrift für Volkskunde*, 2 (1965), 177–204.

Bayer, Vladimir, *Ugovor s Đavlom: Procesi protiv čarobnjaka u Evropi a napose u Hrvatskoj* (3rd edn. Zagreb, 1982).

Beckman, Jacques, 'Une épidémie de sorcellerie à Novilles-Bois au début du XVII\ue\ siècle', *Annales de la société archéologique de Namur*, 54 (1968).

Belmot, Nicole, *Les Signes de la naissance*, (Paris, 1971).

Bendiscioli, Mario, 'Penetrazione protestante e repressione controriformistica in Lombardia all'epoca di Carlo e Federico Borromeo', in E. Iserloh and P. Manns (eds.), *Festgabe Joseph Lortz* (2 vols.; Baden-Baden, 1958), 369–404.

Ben Hamza, Kacem, 'The Cave Dwellers of Matmata', Ph.D. thesis (Bloomington, 1977).

——, 'Croyances et pratiques en Islam populaire: Le Cas de Matmata', *Revue de l'institute des belles lettres arabes* (1980), 87–109.

Bergeron, Louis (ed.), *Niveaux de culture et groupes sociaux* (Paris and The Hague, 1967). Bertolotti, Antonio, 'La schiavitù in Roma dal secolo 16 al 19', *Rivista di discipline carcerarie*, 17 (1887), 3–41.

——, *Le prigioni di Roma nei secoli XVI, XVII e XVIII* (Rome, 1890).

Bertolotti, Maurizio, 'Le ossa e la pelle dei buoi: Un mito popolare tra agiografia e stregoneria', *Quaderni storici*, 41 (1979), 470–99.

Bethencourt, Francisco, *O imaginário da magia: Feiticeiras, saludadores e nigromantes no século 16* (Lisbon, 1987).

Binz, Carl (ed.), *Augustin Lerchheimer und seine Schrift wider den Hexenwahn* (Strasbourg, 1888).

Biondi, Albano, 'Lunga durata e microarticolazione nel territorio di un

Ufficio dell'Inquisizione: Il sacro tribunale a Modena (1292–1785)', *Annali dell'istituto storico italo-germanico in Trento*, 8 (1982), 73–90.

——, 'Gianfrancesco Pico e la repressione della stregoneria: Qualche novità sui processi mirandolesi del 1522–23', in *Mirandola e le terre del basso corso del Secchia della Deputazione di storia patria per le antiche provincie modenesi, Biblioteca*, n.s. 76 (1984), 331–49.

Birkelund, Merete, 'En analyse af danske trolddomsprocesser', thesis (Århus University, 1981).

——, *Troldkvinden og hendes anklagere* (Århus, 1983).

Björnsson, Lyður, *Saga sveitarstjórnar á Íslandi* (2 vols.; Reykjavik, 1972–9).

Blécourt, Willem de, and Gijswijt-Hofstra, Marijke (eds.), 'Kwade Mensen: Toverij in Nederland', *Volkskundig Bulletin*, 12 (1986), 1–263.

Blum, Richard and Eva, *The Dangerous Hour: The Lore of Crisis and Mystery in Rural Greece* (London, 1970).

Bogdál, Ferenc, 'Egy miskolci "Táltos" 1741-ben', *Néprajzi közlemények* (1960), 308–11.

Boissevain, Jeremy, and Friedl, John (eds.), *Beyond the Community: Social Process in Europe* (The Hague, 1975).

Bonomo, Giuseppe, *Caccia alle streghe: La credenza nelle streghe dal sec. XIII al XIX con particolare riferimento all'Italia* (Palermo, 1959).

Boon, James A., *Other Tribes, Other Scribes: Symbolic Anthropology in the Comparative Study of Cultures, Histories, Religions, and Texts* (Cambridge, 1982).

Borromeo, Agostino, 'Spanische und römische Inquisition: Identitäten und Verschiedenheiten der beiden Institutionen im 16. Jahrhundert', forthcoming in the *Vorträge* of the Institut für Europäische Geschichte, Mainz.

Bossy, John, 'The Counter-Reformation and the People of Catholic Europe', *Past and Present*, 47 (1970), 51–71.

Bourdieu, Pierre, 'Genèse et structure du champ religieux', *Revue française de sociologie*, 12 (1971), 295–334.

——, 'Une interprétation de la théorie de la religion selon Max Weber', *Archives européennes de sociologie*, 12 (1972), 3–21.

——, *Outline of a Theory of Practice* (Cambridge, 1977).

Boyer, Paul, and Nissenbaum, Stephen, *Salem Possessed: The Social Origins of Witchcraft* (Cambridge, Mass., 1974).

Braudel, Fernand, *The Mediterranean and the Mediterranean World in the Age of Philip II* (1949; English trans. 2 vols., London, 1972–3).

Brednich, Rolf Wilhelm, *Volkserzählungen und Volksglaube von den Schicksalsfrauen* (Helsinki, 1964).

Brémond, Claude, Le Goff, Jacques, and Schmitt, Jean-Claude, *L"exemplum'* (Turnhout, 1982).

Briggs, Robin, 'Witchcraft and Popular Mentality in Lorraine, 1580–1630', in Brian Vickers (ed.), *Occult and Scientific Mentalities in the Renaissance* (Cambridge, 1984), 337–49.

Brough, John, 'The Tripartite Ideology of the Indo-Europeans: An Experiment in Method', *Bulletin of the School of Oriental and African Studies*, 23 (1959), 69–85.

Brown, Peter, 'Sorcery, Demons and the Rise of Christianity from Late Antiquity into the Middle Ages', Mary Douglas (ed.), *Witchcraft Confessions and Accusations* (London, 1970), 17–45.

Brückner, Wolfgang (ed.), *Volkserzählung und Reformation* (Berlin, 1974).

Brynleifsson, Siglaugur, *Galdrar og brennudómar* (Reykjavik, 1976).

Buchholz, Peter, 'Shamanism: The Testimony of Old Icelandic Literary Tradition', *Medieval Scandinavia*, 4 (1971), 7–20.

Bunge, Friedrich Georg von, *Geschichte des Gerichtswesens und Gerichtsverfahrens in Liv-, Est- und Kurland* (Reval, 1874).

Burke, Peter, *Popular Culture in Early Modern Europe* (London, 1978).

——, 'A Question of Acculturation?', in Paola Zambelli (ed.), *Scienze, credenze, oculte, Livelli di cultura* (Florence, 1982), 197–204.

——, 'Centres and Peripheries of European Witchcraft', conference paper (Stockholm, 1984).

Busse, Karl Heinrich von, 'Der Arme Pracher', *Das Inland*, 46–7 (1851), 797–9, 816–20.

Caeneghem, Raoul Charles van, 'La preuve dans le droit du moyen âge occidental', *Recueils de la société Jean Bodin pour l'histoire comparative des institutions*, 17 (1965), 691–753.

Camporesi, Piero, *Il paese della fame* (Bologna, 1978).

——, *Il pane selvaggio* (Bologna, 1981; English trans. forthcoming).

Carlsson, Sten, and Rosén, Jerker, *Svensk historia*, i (Lund, 1978).

Caro Baroja, Julio, *Las brujas y su mundo* (Madrid, 1961; English trans., *The World of the Witches*, Chicago and London, 1964).

——, *Vidas mágicas e Inquisición* (2 vols.; Madrid, 1967).

——, 'Martín del Rio y sus *Disquisiciones mágicas*', in *El señor inquisidor y otras vidas por oficio* (Madrid, 1968), 171–96.

——, 'Arquetipos y modelos en la historia de la brujería', in *Ritos y mitos equívocos* (Madrid, 1974), 215–58.

——, *Las formas complejas de la vida religiosa: Religión Sociedad y carácter en la España de los siglos XVI y XVII* (Madrid, 1978).

Castan, Yves, *Magie et sorcellerie à l'époque moderne* (Paris, 1979).

Castelnuovo, Enrico, and Ginzburg, Carlo, 'Domination symbolique et géographie artistique', *Actes de la recherche en sciences sociales*, 40 (1981), 51–72.

Chapman, Charlotte Gower, *Milocca: A Sicilian Village* (London, 1970).

Chaunu, Pierre, 'Sur la fin des sorciers au XVIIᵉ siècle', *Annales ESC* 24. 4 (1969), 895–911.

Chernel, Kálmán, *Kőszeg szabad királyi város jelene és multja* (Szombathely, 1877–8).

Christian, William A. *Apparitions in Late Medieval and Renaissance Spain* (Princeton, 1981).

Cipolla, Carlo M., *Before the Industrial Revolution* (London, 1976).

Clark, Stuart, 'King James's *Daemonologie*: Witchcraft and Kingship', in Sydney Anglo (ed.), *The Damnèd Art* (London, 1977), 167–73.

——, 'Inversion, Misrule and the Meaning of Witchcraft', *Past and Present*, 87 (1980), 98–127.

——, 'The Scientific Status of Demonology', in Brian Vickers (ed.), *Occult and Scientific Mentalities in the Renaissance* (Cambridge, 1984), 351–74.

——, and Morgan, Prys, 'Religion and Magic in Elizabethan Wales: Robert Holland's Dialogue on Witchcraft', *Journal of Ecclesiastical History*, 27 (1976), 31–46.

Claverie, Elisabeth, and Lamaison, Pierre, *L'Impossible Mariage: Violence et parenté en Gévaudan, 17ᵉ, 18ᵉ et 19ᵉ siècles* (Paris, 1982).

Closs, August, 'Der Schamanismus bei den Indoeuropäern', *Innsbrucker Beiträge zur Kulturwissenschaft*, 14 (1968), 289–302.

Cocchiara, Giuseppe, *Il mondo alla rovescia* (Turin, 1963).

Cohn, Norman, 'The Myth of Satan and his Human Servants', in Mary Douglas (ed.), *Witchcraft Confessions and Accusations* (London, 1970), 3–16.

——, *Europe's Inner Demons: An Enquiry Inspired by the Great Witch-hunt* (London, 1975; 2nd edn. St Albans, 1976).

Collinder, Björn, *Sprachverwandtschaft und Wahrscheinlichkeit*, ed. B. Wickman (Uppsala, 1964).

Constant, A., *Relation sur une épidémie d'hystéro-demonopathie en 1861* (Paris, 1863).

Contreras, Jaime, 'Algunas consideraciones sobre las relaciones de causas de Sicilia y Cerdeña', *Annuario dell'Istituto Storico Italiana per l'età Moderna e Contemporanea*, 37–8 (1985–6), 179–99.

Crapanzano, Vincent, 'Saints, Jnun, and Dreams: An Essay in Moroccan Ethnopsychology', *Psychiatry*, 38 (1975), 145–59.

Crick, Malcolm, *Explorations in Language and Meaning* (London, 1976).

Csákabonyi, Károly, *Békés megyei boszorkányperek a XVIII. században* (Gyula, 1961).

Damaska, Mirjan, 'The Death of Legal Torture', *Yale Law Journal*, 87 (1978), 860–84.

Dansk Social Historie (7 vols.; Copenhagen, 1979–82).

Daviðsson, Ólafur, *Galdur og galdramál á Islandi* (Reykjavik, 1940–3).

Davis, John, 'Honour and Politics in Pisticci', *Proceedings of the Royal Anthropological Institute* (1969), 69–70.

Davis, Natalie, Z. *The Return of Martin Guerre* (Cambridge, Mass., 1983).

Decker, Rainer, 'Die Hexenverfolgungen in Herzogtum Westfalen', *Westfälische Zeitschrift*, 131–2 (1981–2).

Dedieu, Jean-Pierre, 'The Archives of the Holy Office of Toledo as a Source for Historical Anthropology', in Gustav Henningsen and John Tedeschi, in association with Charles Amiel (eds.), *The Inquisition in Early Modern Europe* (Dekalb, 1986), 158–89.

Degré, Alajos, *Boszorkányperek Zala megyében* (Zalaegerszeg, 1960).

Delcambre, Etienne, 'La Psychologie des inculpés lorrains de sorcellerie', *Revue historique du droit français et étranger*, 32 (1954), 383–404, 508–26.

Del Col, Andrea, 'L'abiura trasformata in propaganda ereticale nel duomo di Udine', *Metodi e ricerche*, 2 (1981), 57–72.

Delumeau, Jean, 'Les Progrès de la centralisation dans l'état pontifical au xvie siècle', *Revue historique*, 226 (1961), 399–410.

——, *Catholicism between Luther and Voltaire* (1971; English trans. London, 1977).

——, 'Les Réformateurs et la superstition', *Actes du colloque sur l'Amiral Coligny et son temps* (Paris, 1974), 451–87.

——, *La Peur en Occident XIVe–XVIIIe siècles: Une cité assiégée* (Paris, 1978).

Demos, John Putnam, *Entertaining Satan* (New York, 1982).

Diefenbach, Johann, *Der Hexenwahn vor und nach der Glaubensspaltung in Deutschland* (Mainz, 1886).

Diószegi, Vilmos, *A sámánhit emlékei a magyar népi műveltségben* (Budapest, 1958).

——, 'Die Überreste des Schamanismus in der ungarischen Volkskultur', *Acta Ethnographica*, 6 (1959), 97–135.

Dömötör, Sándor, 'Szent Gellért hegye és a boszorkányok', *Tanulmányok Budapest multjából*, 7 (1939), 92–111.

——, 'A boszorkányok gyűlése a magyar néphitben', *Ethnographia*, 50 (1939), 210–21.

Dömötör, Tekla, 'The Cunning Folk in English and Hungarian Witch Trials', in Venetia Newall (ed.), *Folklore Studies in the Twentieth Century* (Woodbridge, and Totowa, 1981), 183–7.

——, *Hungarian Folk Beliefs* (Bloomington and Budapest, 1982).

Dondaine, Antoine, 'Le Manuel de l'inquisiteur (1230–1330)', *Archivum Fratrum Praedicatorum*, 17 (1947), 85–194.

Douglas, Mary, *Purity and Danger: An Analysis of the Concepts of Pollution and Taboo* (London, 1966).

—— (ed.), *Witchcraft Confessions and Accusations* (London, 1970).

——, 'Thirty Years after *Witchcraft, Oracles and Magic*', ibid. pp. xiii–xxxviii.

Dubois, Claude Gilbert, *Le Baroque: Profondeurs de l'apparence* (Paris, 1973).

Dumézil, Georges, *Le Problème des centaures* (Paris, 1929).

——, *Mythes et dieux des Germains* (Paris, 1939).

——, *Leçon inaugurale* (Nogent-le-Rotrou, 1950).

——, *Mythe et épopée* (3 vols.; Paris, 1973).

Dupont-Bouchat, Marie-Sylvie, Frijhoff, Willem, and Muchembled, Robert, *Prophètes et sorciers dans les Pays-Bas: XVIe–XVIIIe siècles* (Paris, 1978).

Durkheim, Emile, *Elementary Forms of the Religious Life* (1912; English trans. New York, 1965).

Easlea, Brian, *Witch Hunting, Magic and the New Philosophy*, (Brighton, 1980).

Eckhardt, Sándor, and Ortutay, Gyula, 'Régi magyar varázslóasszonyok', *Magyarságtudomány*, 1 (1942), 564–80.

Eckhart, Ferenc, *A földesúri büntetőkíráskodás a XVI–XVII században* (Budapest, 1954).

Eliade, Mircea, 'Some Observations on European Witchcraft', *History of Religions*, 14 (1974), 149–72.

Evans, Robert, *The Making of the Habsburg Monarchy, 1550–1700* (Oxford, 1979).

Evans-Pritchard, Edward, *Witchcraft, Oracles and Magic among the Azande* (Oxford, 1937).

Favret-Saada, Jeanne, *Deadly Words: Witchcraft in the Bocage* (1977; English trans. Cambridge and Paris, 1980).

——, *Corps pour corps: Enquête sur la sorcellerie dans la Bocage* (Paris, 1981).

Febvre, Lucien, 'La Sorcellerie: Sottise ou révolution mentale?', *Annales ESC* (1948; English trans., 'Witchcraft: Nonsense or a Mental Revolution?' in his *A New Kind of History*, London, 1973 185–92).

Fiorelli, Pietro, *La tortura giudiziaria nel diritto comune* (2 vols.; Milan, 1953).

Firpo, Luigi, 'Il processo di Giordano Bruno', *Rivista storica italiana*, 60 (1948), 542–97; 61 (1949), 5–59.

—— 'Una relazione inedita su l'inquisizione romana', *Rinascimento*, 9 (1958), 97–102.

—— 'Esecuzioni capitali in Roma (1567–1671)', in *Eresia e riforma nell'Italia del '500, Miscellanea*, i (Florence and Chicago, 1974), 307–42.

Fogelström, Per Anders, 'Häxorna i Katarina', *Historia kring Stockholm: Vasatid och stormaktstid* (Stockholm, 1966), 87–115.

Fontana, Bartolomeo, 'Documenti vaticani contro l'eresia luterana in Italia', *Archivio della società romana di storia patria*, 15 (1892), 71–165, 365–474.

Freymann, H. von, 'Das Strafrecht der livländischen Ritterrechte', *Zeitschrift für Rechtswissenschaft* (Dorpat), 9 (1889).

Friberg, Nils, 'Dalarnas befolkning på 1600-talet', *Geografiska annaler*, 35 (1953), 145–414.

——, and Friberg, Inga, *Om Dalarnas kommunikationer och handelsförbindelser i äldre tid* (Stockholm, 1975).

Fumi, Luigi, 'L'inquisizione romana e lo stato di Milano', *Archivio storico lombardo*, ser. 4, 13 (1910), 5–124, 285–414, and 14 (1910), 145–220.

Galtung, Johan, 'Sosial posisjon og sosial adferd', in *Periferi og sentrum i historien* (Studier i historisk metode, 1; Oslo, 1975).

Garrett, Clarke, 'Witches and Cunning Folk in the Old Regime', in Jacques Beauroy *et al.* (eds.), *The Wolf and the Lamb* (Saratoga, Calif., 1976), 53–64.

Gauthier, Philippe, 'Le "De daemonibus" du Pseudo-Psellos', *Revue des études byzantines*, 38 (1980), 105–94.

Gijswijt-Hofstra, Marijke, and Frijhoff, Willem (eds.), *Nederland Betoverd* (Amsterdam, 1987).

Ginzburg, Carlo, *I benandanti: Stregoneria e culti agrari tra Cinquecento e Seicento* (Turin, 1966; 2nd edn. 1973; *The Night Battles: Witchcraft and Agrarian Cults in the Sixteenth and Seventeenth Centuries*, Baltimore and London, 1983).

——, *Storia notturna: Una decifrazione del sabba* (Torino, 1989).

Göllner, Carl, *Hexenprozesse in Siebenbürgen*, (Cluj–Napoca, 1971).

Gönczi, Ferenc, 'A csordás farkas', *Ethnographia*, 16 (1905), 93–6.

Górski, Karol, 'Le Roi saint: Un problème d'idéologie féodale', *Annales ESC* 24 (1969), 370–6.

Gougaud, Louis, 'La Danse dans les églises', *Revue d'histoire ecclésiastique* 15 (1914), 5–22, 229–43.

Grambo, Ronald, 'Sleep as a Means of Ecstasy and Divination', *Acta Ethnographica Academiae Scientiarum Hungaricae*, 33 (1973), 417–25.

Graus, Frantisek, 'La Sanctification du souverain dans l'Europe centrale des 10e et 11e siècles', in *Hagiographie, culture et sociétés (IVe–XIIe siècles)* (Études Augustiniennes, Paris, 1981), 559–72.

Graver, Hans Petter, 'Rett under sosialt trykk: Rettssosiologiske aspekter ved trolldomsprosessene i Norge', *Lov og ret*, 1 (1984), 50–5.

Grendler, Paul F., *The Roman Inquisition and the Venetian Press, 1540–1605* (Princeton, 1977).

Greyerz, Kaspar von (ed.), *Religion and Society in Early Modern Europe 1500–1800*, (London, 1984).

Grimm, Heinrich, 'Die deutschen Teufelbücher des 16. Jhts', *Archiv für Geschichte des Buchwesens*, 16 (1959), 513–70.

Grimm, Jacob, *Deutsche Mythologie*, (1835; new edn. Berlin and Vienna, 1981; English trans. 4 vols., London, 1900).

Guerchberg, S., 'La Controverse sur les prétendus semeurs de la peste noire d'après les traités de peste de l'époque', *Revue des études juives*, 108 (1948), 3–40.

Guggino, Elsa, *La magia in Sicilia* (Palermo, 1978).

Guglielmotti, Alberto, *Storia della marina pontificia* (10 vols.; Rome, 1886).

Gunnarsson, Gisli, *Monopoly Trade and Economic Stagnation: Studies in the Foreign Trade of Iceland, 1602–1787* (Lund, 1983).

Hägerstrand, Torsten, *Innovationsförloppet ur korologisk synpunkt* (Lund, 1953; English trans. as *Innovation Diffusion as a Spatial Process*, Chicago and London, 1967).

Hallier, Christian, *Johann Matthäus Meyfart* (Neumünster, 1982).

Hansen, Joseph, *Zauberwahn, Inquisition und Hexenprozess im Mittelatter und die Entstehung der grossen Hexenverfolgung* (Munich and Leipzig, 1900).

—, *Quellen und Untersuchungen zur Geschichte des Hexenwahns und Hexenver-folgungen im Mittelalter* (Bonn, 1901).

Harner, Michael J., *Hallucinogens and Shamanism* (New York and London, 1973).

Hasselblatt, G., 'Ein Verhör in einem Hexenprocesse', *Das Inland*, 47 (1837), 777–81.

Hastrup, Kirsten 'Cosmology and Society in Medieval Iceland', *Ethnologia Scandinavica* (1981), 63–78.

—, 'Anthropology and the Exaggeration of Culture', *Ethnos*, 50: 3–4 (1985), 311–24.

—, 'Entropisk elegi: Kristendommen og den sociale uorden på Island efter år 1000', *Stofskifte*, 12 (1985), 45–60.

—, 'Male and Female in Icelandic Culture', *Folk*, 27 (1985), 49–54.

—, *Culture and History in Medieval Iceland: An Anthropological Analysis of Structure and Change* (Oxford, 1985).

—, 'The Challenge of the Unreal', *Culture and History*, 1 (1986), 50–62.

—, '"Text and Context": Continuity and Change in Medieval Icelandic History as "Said" and "Laid Down"' in *Continuity and Change* (Odense, 1986), 9–25.

—, 'Tracing Tradition: An Anthropological Perspective on *Gretti's saga Ásmundersonar*', in *Structure and Meaning: New Approaches to Old Norse Literature* John Lindow, Lars Lönnroth, and Gerd Wolfgang Weber (eds.), (Odense, 1986), 281–313.

Házy, Jenő, *Sopron középkori egyháztörténete* (Sopron, 1939).

Heikkinen, Antero, 'Ahvenanmaa noitoprosessin synty', *Historiallina Aikakaus-kirja*, 1 (1967), 42–4.

—, *Paholaisen Liittolaiset Noita-ja magiakäsityksiä ja -oikeudenkäyntejä Suomessa 1600-luvun jälkipuolella (n. 1640–1712)* (Helsinki, 1969).

Helk, Vello, *Die Jesuiten in Dorpat (1583–1625)* (Odense, 1977).

Henningsen, Gustav, *The European Witch-persecution* (Copenhagen, 1973).

—, *The Witches' Advocate: Basque Witchcraft and the Spanish Inquisition* (Reno, 1980).

—, 'L'inquisizione spagnola e la tradizioni popolari della Sardegna', in *Linguaggio musicale e linguaggio poetico in Sardegna: Atti del convegno di studi coreutico musicali sardi svoltosi a Nuoro ... 1975* (Cagliari, 1981), 57–60.

—, 'Witch Hunting in Denmark', *Folklore*, 93 (1982), 131–7.

—, and Tedeschi, John, in association with Amiel, Charles (eds.), *The Inquisition in Early Modern Europe: Studies on Sources and Methods* (Dekalb, 1986).

Herbert Heinrich, 'Die Rechtspflege in Hermannstadt zur Zeit Karls VI.', *Archiv des Vereins für siebenbürgische Landeskunde*. NF 27 (1896), 118–46.

Hermannsson, Halldór, 'Jón Gudmundsson and his Natural History of Iceland', *Islandica*, 15 (1924).

Higgins, Robert, 'Popular Beliefs about Witches: The Evidence from East London, 1645–60', *East London Record*, 4 (1981), 36–41.

Hoffmann, Erich, *Die heiligen Könige bei den Angelsachsen und den skandinavischen Völkern* (Neumünster, 1975).

Höfler, Otto, *Kultische Geheimbünde der Germanen* (Frankfurt-am-Main, 1934).

——, *Verwandlungskulte, Volkssagen und Mythen* (Österreichische Akademie der Wissenschaften, Phil.-Hist. Kl., Sitzungsberichte, vol. cclxxix, treatise 2; Vienna, 1973).

Hollis, Martin, 'The Limits of Irrationality', in Bryan Wilson (ed.), *Rationality* (Oxford, 1970), 214–20.

Holmes, Clive, 'Popular Culture? Witches, Magistrates and Divines in Early Modern England', in Steven L. Kaplan (ed.), *Understanding Popular Culture* (Berlin, 1984), 85–111.

Hoppál, Mihály, 'Traces of Shamanism in Hungarian Folk Beliefs', in Hoppál (ed.), *Shamanism in Eurasia* (Göttingen, 1984).

Horna, Richard, *Zwei Hexenprozesse in Pressburg zu Beginn des XVII. Jahrhunderts* (Bratislava, 1933).

——, *Ein Monstre-Hexenprozess in Samorin gegen Ende des XVII. Jahrhunderts* (Bratislava, 1935).

Horsley, Richard, 'Who were the Witches? The Social Roles of the Accused in the European Witch Trials', *Journal of Interdisciplinary History*, 9 (1979), 689–715.

——, 'Further Reflections on Witchcraft and European Folk Religion', *History of Religions*, 19 (1979), 71–95.

Horváth, Tibor Antal, *Boszorkányok és boszorkányperek Szombathelyen* (Szombathely, 1937).

Huerga Criado, Pilar, 'Los agentes de la inquisición española en Roma durante el siglo 17', in Joaquín Pérez Villaneuva (ed.), *La inquisición española* (Madrid, 1980), 243–56.

Hunnius, Friedrich, 'Über Hexenprocesse', *Baltische Monatsschrift*, 42 (1895), 54–6.

Iklódy, András, 'A magyarországi boszorkányüldözés történeti alakulása', *Ethnographia*, 93 (1982), 292–8.

Inger, Göran, *Svensk rättshistoria* (Lund, 1983).

Itkonen, T. I., 'Der Zweikampf der lappischen Zauberer', *Journal de la société finno-ougrienne*, 62 (1960), fasc. 3, pp. 3–76.

Jacobsen, Jørgen C., *Den sidste Hexebränding i Danmark 1693* (Copenhagen, 1971).

Jakobson, Roman, and Ruzicic, G., The Serbian *Zmaj Ognjeni Vuk* and the Russian Vseslav Epos', *Annuaire de l'institut de philologie et d'histoire orientale et slave*, 10 (1950), 343–55.

——, and Szeftel, Marc, 'The Vseslav Epos', *Memoirs of the American Folklore Society*, 42 (1947), 13–86.

Jakubovich, Emil, *Adalékok legrégibb nyelvemlékes okleveleink és krónikáink íróinak személyéhez* (Budapest, 1924).

Janssen, Johannes, *History of the German People at the Close of the Middle Ages*, English trans. (17 vols.; London, 1896–1910).

Jensen, Karsten Sejr, *Trolddom i Danmark, 1500–88* (Copenhagen, 1982).

Jobe, Patricia, 'Inquisitorial Manuscripts in the Bibliotheca Apostolica Vaticana: A Preliminary Handlist', in Gustav Henningsen and John Tedeschi, in association with Charles Amiel (eds.), *The Inquisition in Early Modern Europe* (Dekalb, 1986), 33–53.

Johansen, Jens Christian V., 'Als die Fischer den Teufel ins Netz bekamen', in Christian Degn, Hartmut Lehmann, and Dagmar Unverhau (eds.), *Hexenprozesse* (Neumünster, 1983).

——, 'Witchcraft in Elsinore, 1625–6', *Mentalities*, 3 (1985), 7–8.

Johansen, Paul, and von zur Mühlen, Heinz, *Deutsch und Undeutsch im mittelalterlichen und frühneuzeitlichen Reval* (Cologne and Vienna, 1973).

Joki, Aulí Johannes, *Uralier und Indogermanen* (Helsinki, 1973).

Jónsson, Þorsteinn M., *Brennan á Melaeyrum, 1625* (Akureyri, 1957).

Jutikkala, Eino, *Bonden, adelsmannen, kronan: Godspolitik och jordegendomsförhållanden i Norden, 1550–1750* (Copenhagen, 1979).

——, and Pirinen, Kauko, *A History of Finland* (New York, 1962).

Kahk, Juhan, 'Nõidumisest ja nõiasõnadest Eestis XVII sajandil', *Keel ja Kirjandus*, 11 (1980), 677–80.

Kaplan, Steven, (ed.), *Understanding Popular Culture: Europe from the Middle Ages to the Nineteenth Century* (Berlin, New York, and Amsterdam, 1984).

Kazinczy, Gábor, 'Megyaszói boszorkányok 1731-ben', *Hazánk*, 3 (1885), 374–5.

Kervinen, Timo, 'Noituus—aikansa rikos', unpublished (1983).

Kieckhefer, Richard, *European Witch Trials: Their Foundations in Popular and Learned Culture, 1300–1500* (Berkeley and Los Angeles, 1976).

Kiehl, Robert Walinski, 'Catholicism, Cultural Conflict and Witch-Hunting in 17th-Century Bamberg', unpublished conference paper (May 1985).

Kittelson, James M., 'Successes and Failures in the German Reformation: The Report from Strasbourg', *Archive for Reformation History*, 73 (1982), 153–75.

Kjöllerström, Sven, *Guds och Sveriges lag under reformationstiden* (Lund, 1957).

Klaniczay, Gábor, 'Benandante–kresnik–zduhač–táltos', *Ethnographia*, 94 (1983), 116–33.

——, 'Shamanistic Elements in Central European Witchcraft', in Mihály Hoppál (ed.), *Shamanism in Eurasia* (Göttingen, 1984), 404–22.

——, 'Decline of Witches and Rise of Vampires in the 18th Century Habsburg Monarchy', *Ethnologia Europea*, 17 (1987), 165–80.

Kligman, Gail, *Căluş: Symbolic Transformation in Romanian Ritual* (Chicago and London, 1981).

Komáromy, Andor, *Magyarországi boszorkányperek oklevéltára* (Budapest, 1910).

Komáromy, András, 'A "bűbájos" Báthory Anna', *Századok*, 28 (1894), 298–314.

Kõpp, J., *Laiuse kihelkonna ajalugu* (Tartu, 1937).

Körner, Tamás, 'Boszorkányszervezetek Magyarországon', *Ethnographia*, 80 (1969), 196–211.

Kors, Alan C., and Peters, Edward (eds.), *Witchcraft in Europe, 1100–1700: A Documentary History* (Philadelphia, 1972).

Kroman, Erik (ed.), *Danmarks gamle købstadslovgivning*, iv (Copenhagen, 1961).

Kulcsár, Zsuzsanna, *Inkvizíció és boszorkánypörök* (3rd edn. Budapest, 1968).

Kunstmann, Hartmut, *Zauberwahn und Hexenprozess in der Reichsstadt Nürnberg* (Nuremberg, 1970).

Kurcz, Agnes, *A magyarországi lovagi kultura a XIII–XIV. században* (Budapest, forthcoming).

Labrousse, Elisabeth, 'Le Démon de Maçon', in Paola Zambelli (ed.), *Scienze, credenze oculte, Livelli di cultura* (Florence, 1982), 249–75.

Lambert, M. D., *Medieval Heresy* (London, 1977).

Langbein, John, *Prosecuting Crime in the Renaissance: England, Germany, France* (Cambridge, Mass., 1974).

——, 'The Historical Origins of the Sanction of Imprisonment for Serious Crime', *Journal of Legal Studies*, 5 (1976), 35–60.

——, *Torture and the Law of Proof: Europe and England in the Ancien Régime* (Chicago and London, 1977).

Längin, Georg, *Religion und Hexenprozess* (Leipzig, 1888).

Larner, Christina, 'James VI and I and Witchcraft', in Alan G. R. Smith (ed.), *The Reign of James VI and I* (London, 1973), repr. in Larner, *Witchcraft and Religion: The Politics of Popular Belief* (London, 1984).

——, *Enemies of God: The Witch-hunt in Scotland*, (London, 1981).

——, 'Witchcraft Past and Present', in *Witchcraft and Religion* (London, 1984).

Lavanchy, Joseph Maine, *Sabbats ou synagogues sur les bords du lac d'Annecyz: Procès inquisitorial à St.-Joroiz en 1477* (2nd edn. Annecy, 1896).

Lawson, John Cuthbert, *Modern Greek Folklore and Ancient Greek Religion: A Study in Survival* (Cambridge, 1910).

Lea, Henry Charles, *A History of the Inquisition of Spain* (New York, 1906–7).

——, *The Inquisition in the Spanish Dependencies* (New York, 1922).

——, *Materials toward a History of Witchcraft* (3 vols.; Philadelphia, 1939; repr. New York, 1957).

Lebrun, François, 'Le *Traité des superstitions* de Jean-Baptiste Thiers', *Annales de Bretagne*, 83 (1976), 443–65.

Leesment, Leo, 'Piinamise ehk tortuuri kaotamine Eesti- ja Liivimaal', *Ajaloo-line Ajakiri*, 4 (1931).

Lehtisalo, Toivo, *Entwurf einer Mythologie der Jurak-Samojeden* (Helsinki, 1924).

Le Nail, Jean-François, 'Procédures contre des sorcières de Seix en 1562', *Bulletin de la société ariégeoise*, 31 (1976).

Le Roy Ladurie, Emmanuel, *La Sorcière de Jasmin* (Paris, 1983).

Lesky, Erna, and Wandruszka, Adam, *Gerard van Swieten und seine Zeit* (Vienna, Cologne, and Graz, 1973).

Levack, Brian, *The Witch-hunt in Early Modern Europe* (London, 1987).

Lévi-Strauss, Claude, 'The Sorcerer and his Magic', in his *Structural Anthropology*, English trans. (New York, 1965).

Levron, Jacques, *Le Diable dans l'art* (Paris, 1935).

Liisberg, Bering, *Vesten for Sø og østen for Hav: Trolddom i København og i Edinburgh 1590: Et Bidrag til Hekseprocessenes Historie* (Copenhagen, 1909).

Linderholm, Emanuel, *Nordisk magi: Studier, i nordisk religions- och kyrkohistoria* (Svenska landsmål och svenskt folkliv, 20; Stockholm, 1918).

Lindhardt, Poul G., 'Til belysning af Niels Hemmingsens inflydelse på dansk prædiken omkring 1600', in *Festskrift til Jens N'rregaard* (Copenhagen, 1947), 131–45.

Lisón Tolosana, Carmelo, *Brujería estructura social y simbolismo en Galicia* (Madrid, 1979).

Lorenz, Sönke, 'Johann Georg Godelmann—Ein Gegner des Hexenwahns?', in Roderich Schmidt (ed.), *Beiträge zur pommerschen und mecklenburgischen Geschichte* (Marburg, 1981), 61–105.

Lottes, Günther, 'Popular Culture and the Early Modern State in 16th Century Germany', in Steven Kaplan (ed.), *Understanding Popular Culture* (Berlin, 1984), 173–9.

Macfarlane, Alan, *Witchcraft in Tudor and Stuart England: A Regional and Comparative Study* (London, 1970).

——, 'Witchcraft—Tudor and Stuart Essex', in Mary Douglas (ed.), *Witchcraft Confessions and Accusations* (London, 1970).

——, 'A Tudor Anthropologist: George Gifford's *Discourse* and *Dialogue*', in Sydney Anglo (ed.), *The Damnèd Art* (London, 1977), 140–55.

——, *The Origins of English Individualism: The Family, Property and Social Transition* (Oxford, 1978).

——, *The Justice and the Mare's Ale: Law and Disorder in Seventeenth Century England* (Oxford, 1981).

Mahnke, Dietrich, 'Das Hexenunwesen in Verden und sein Ende', *Stader Archiv*, 13 (1923).

Mair, Lucy, *Witchcraft* (London, 1969).

Maisonneuve, Henri, *Etudes sur les origines de l'inquisition* (2nd edn. Paris, 1960).

McKenzie, Nigel, 'Centre and Periphery', *Acta Sociologica*, 20 (1977), 55–74.

Makkai László, 'Puritánok és boszorkányok Debrecenben', *A Hajdú-Bihar Megyei Levéltár Évkönyve*, 8 (1981), 113–30.

Mammoli, Domenico, *Processo alla strega Matteuccia di Francesco, 20 marzo 1428* (Todi, 1983).

Mark, L., 'Nõiaprotsessidest Eestis 18. sajandi lõpul ja 19. sajandi alguses', *Ajalooline Ajakiri*, 1 (1938), 20–33.

Marwick, Max (ed.), *Witchcraft and Sorcery* (Harmondsworth, 1970).

Mathieux, Jean, 'Trafic et prix de l'homme en Méditerranée aux 17ᵉ et 18ᵉ siècles', *Annales ESC* 9 (1954), 157–64.

Mauss, Marcel, *A General Theory of Magic* (1950; English trans. London, 1972).

Mellinkoff, David, 'Right to Counsel: The Message from America', in Fredi Chiappelli (ed.), *First Images of America* (2 vols.; Berkeley, 1976), i. 405–13.

Mercati, Angelo, *Il sommario del processo di Giordano Bruno* (Vatican City, 1942).

Merlo, Grado G., *Eretici e inquisitori nella società piemontese del '300* (Turin, 1977).

Meuli, Karl, 'Bettelumzüge im Totenkult, Opferritual und Volksbrauch', in his *Gesammelte Schriften* (Basle and Stuttgart, 1975), i. 33–68.

——, 'Die deutschen Masken', ibid. i. 84–5.

——, 'Scythica', ibid. ii. 817–79.

Miccoli, Giovanni, 'La storia religiosa', *Storia d'Italia*, ii. 1 (Turin, 1974), 431–1079.

Michelet, Jules, *La Sorcière* (Paris, 1862).

Midelfort, H. C. Erik, *Witch-hunting in Southwestern Germany, 1562–1684, The Social and Intellectual Foundations* (Stanford, 1972).

——, 'Were there really Witches?', in Robert Kingdon (ed.), *Transition and Revolution* (Minneapolis, 1974), 189–205.

——, 'Heartland of the Witchcraze: Central and Northern Europe', *History Today*, 31 (1981), 27–31.

——, 'Sin, Melancholy, Obsession: Insanity and Culture in 16th-Century Germany', in Steven Kaplan (ed.), *Understanding Popular Culture* (Berlin, 1984), 134–42.

Modéer, Kjell, *Gerichtsbarkeiten der schwedischen Krone im deutschen Reichsterritorium*, i (Lund, 1975).

——, 'Rättshistorisk forskning in Sverige', *Rättshistoriska studier*, 6 (1979), 25–45.

Møller, Jens Glebe, 'Det teologiske fakultet, 1597–1732', in *Københavns Universitet, 1479–1979*, v (1979), 93–208.

Möstl, Friedrich, *Ein Szegediner Hexenprozess* (Graz, 1879).

Molnár, Éva, *Boszorkányperek Magyarországon a XVII–XVIII században* (Budapest, 1942).

Monter, E. William, *Witchcraft in France and Switzerland: The Borderlands during the Reformation* (Ithaca and London, 1976).

——, *Ritual, Myth and Magic in Early Modern Europe* (Brighton, 1983).

Muchembled, Robert, 'Sorcières du Cambrésis: L'Acculturation du monde rural aux XVIᵉ et XVIIᵉ siècles', in Marie-Sylvie Dupont-Bouchat, Willem Frijhoff, and Robert Muchembled, *Prophètes et sorciers dans les Pays-Bas* (Paris, 1978), 155–261.

——, *Culture populaire et culture des élites* (Paris, 1978; English trans., *Popular Culture and Elite Culture in France, 1400–1750*, Baton Rouge, 1985).

——, *La Sorcière au village (XVIᵉ au XVIIᵉ siècle)* (Paris, 1979).

——, *Les Derniers Bûchers: Un village de Flandre et ses sorcières sous Louis XIV* (Paris, 1981).

——, 'Witchcraft, Popular Culture, and Christianity in the Sixteenth Century with Emphasis upon Flanders and Artois', in Robert Forster and Patricia Ranum (ed.), *Ritual, Religion, and the Sacred*, (London, 1982), 213–36.

——, 'Le Corps, la culture populaire et la culture des élites en France xvᵉ– xviiiᵉ siècles)', in A. E. Imhof (ed.), *Leib und Leben in der Geschichte der Neuzeit* (Berlin, 1983), 141–53.

——, 'Comportements et mentalités populaires en Artois 1400–1660)' (unpublished, 1985; first 2 parts to be published as *La Violence au village, XVᵉ– XVIIᵉ siècles* (Turnhout, Belgium).

——, *Sorcières, justice et société aux 16ᵉ et 17ᵉ siècles* (Paris, 1987).

Müller, Friedrich, *Beiträge zur Geschichte des Hexenglaubens in Siebenbürgen* (Brunswick, 1854).

Müller, Heinrich, 'Zur Geschichte des Repser Stuhls', *Archiv des Vereins für siebenbürgische Landeskunde*, 37 (1910).

Murray, Margaret Alice, *The Witch-cult in Western Europe* (London, 1921).

Naess, Hans Eyvind, *Trolldomsprosessene i Norge på 1500–1600-tallet* (Oslo, 1982).

Nagy, László, *Sok dolgot próbála Bethlen Gábor* (Budapest, 1981).

Nazarova, E. L., '"Livonskie Pravdy" kak istoricheskii istochnik', *Drevneishie gosudarstva na territorii SSSR* (Moscow, 1980).

Norborg, Lars-Arne, and Sjöstedt, Lennart, *Grannländernas historia* (Lund, 1977).

Nottbeck, Eugen von, *Die alte Chriminalchronik Revals* (Reval, 1884).

Nyborg, Ebbe, *Fanden på væggen* (Århus, 1978).

Nyström, Per, *Historieskrivningens dilemma* (Stockholm, 1974).

Oberman, Heiko, *Masters of the Reformation* (Cambridge, 1981).

Olason, Páll, E., *Saga Islendinga: Seytjánda öld* (Reykjavik, 1942).

Oppel, Hans, 'Exemplum und Mirakel', *Archiv für Kulturgeschichte*, 58 (1976), 96–114.

Orano, Domenico, *Liberi pensatori bruciati in Roma del XVI al XVIII secolo* (Rome, 1904; repr. Livorno, 1971).

Osenbrüggen, Eduard, 'Hexenprocesse in Dorpat', *Das Inland* 7 (1848), 123–9.

——, 'Ein Hexenprocess in Narva', *Das Inland*, 38 (1848), 818–22.

Paglia, Vincenzo, *'La pietà dei carcerati': Confraternite e società a Roma nei secoli 16– 18* (Rome, 1980).

——, *La morte confortata: Riti della paura e mentalità religiosa a Roma nell'età moderna* (Rome, 1982).

Paschini, Pio, 'Episodi dell'inquisizione a Roma nei suoi primi decenni', *Studi romani*, 5 (1957).

Pastor, Ludwig von, *History of the Popes from the Close of the Middle Ages*, English trans. (40 vols.; St Louis, 1898–1953).

——, 'Allgemeine Dekrete der Römischen Inquisition aus den Jahren 1555–1597. Nach dem Notariatsprotokoll des S. Uffizio zum erstenmale veröffentlicht', *Historisches, Jahrbuch der Görres-Gesellschaft*, 33 (1912), 479–549.

Paucker, Carl J. A., 'Anklage wegen Vergiftung durst Zauberei in der Mitte des 17. Jahrhunderts', *Das Inland*, 43 (1836), 710–15.

——, 'Ein Hexenprocess (Werwolf 1617)', *Das Inland*, 22 (1840), 341–4.

——, *Die Quellen der Ritter-, Lehn- und Landrechte Esth- und Livlands* (Dorpat, 1845).

Paulus, Nikolaus, *Hexenwahn und Hexenprozess vornehmlich im 16. Jahrhundert* (Freiburg im Breisgau, 1910).

Pedersen, Niels M., 'Dokumenter til en Troldomssag under Christian III', *Danske Magazin*, ser. 3, vol. 1 (1843), 52–67.

Peters, Edward, *The Magician, the Witch and the Law* (Philadelphia, 1976).

Petrén, Sture, 'Hovrättens uppbygnad 1614–1654', in Sture Petrén, Stig Jägerskiöld, and Tord Nordberg (eds.), *Svea Hovrätt* (Stockholm, 1964), 1–117.

Pike, Ruth, 'Penal Servitude in Early Modern Spain: The Galleys', *Journal of European Economic History*, 2 (1982), 197–217.

——, *Penal Servitude in Early Modern Spain* (Madison, 1983).

Pitrè, Giuseppe, *Usi e costumi, credenze e pregiudizi del popolo siciliano* (4 vols.; Palermo, 1889).

Pócs, Éva, 'Gondolatok a magyarországi boszorkányperek néprajzi vizsgálatához', *Ethnographia*, 94 (1983), 134–46.

Prodi, Paolo, *La crisi religiosa del XVI secolo* (Bologna, 1964).

——, *Il sovrano pontefice: Un corpo e due anime: La monarchia papale nella prima età moderna* (Bologna, 1982; English trans. forthcoming).

Propp, Vladimir, *Morphology of the Folktale* (1928; English trans. Austin, 1968).

——, *The Historical Roots of the Fairy-tale* (Moscow, 1946).

Prosperi, Adriano, 'Il sangue e l'anima: Ricerche sulle compagnie di giustizia in Italia', *Quaderni storici*, 17 (1982), 959–99.

Quaife, G. R., *Godly Zeal and Furious Rage: The Witch in Early Modern Europe* (London, 1987).

Radermacher, L., *Das Jenseits im Mythos der Hellenen* (Bonn, 1903).

Ranke, Friedrich, 'Das Wilde Heer und die Kultbünde der Germanen', in his *Kleine Schriften*, ed. H. Rupp and E. Studer (Bern, 1971), 380–408.

Ravis-Giordani, Georges, 'Signes, figures et conduites de l'entre-vie et mort: *Finzione, mazzeri et streie* corses', *Études corses*, 12–13 (1979), 361 f.

Re, Niccolò del, *La curia romana* (3rd edn. Rome, 1970).

Redfield, Robert, *The Little Community* (Chicago, 1955).

——, *Peasant Society and Culture* (Chicago, 1956).

Reizner, János, *Szeged története* (Szeged, 1900).

Reviglio della Veneria, Carlo, *L'inquisizione medioevale* (2nd edn. Turin, 1951).

Reyes, Antonio, 'La confesión y la tortura en la historia de la iglesia', *Revista española del derecho canonico*, 24 (1968), 595–624.

Riesemann, Otto von, 'Hexen und Zauberer in Reval (1615–18)', *Beiträge zur Kunde Est-, Liv- und Kurlands*, 2 (1877).

Rivière-Chalan, V. R., *La Marque infâme des lépreux et des christians sous l'ancien régime* (Paris, 1978).

Robbins, Rossell Hope, *The Encyclopaedia of Witchcraft and Demonology* (London, 1959).

Roberts, Michael, *Gustavus Adolphus*, i (London, 1953).

Rohde, Erwin, review of Roscher, op. cit., in *Berliner Philologische Wochenschrift*, 18 (1898), cols. 270–6.

Rohde, Ewin, *Psyche* (1894; Italian trans. Bari, 1968).

Rokkan, Stein, 'Dimensions of State Formation and Nation-building: A Possible Paradigm for Research on Variations within Europe', in Charles Tilly (ed.), *The Formation of National States in Western Europe* (Princeton, 1975), 562–600.

Rómer, Flóris, 'Adalék a boszorkányperekhez', *Győri történelmi és régészeti füzetek*, 1 (1861).

Roscher, Wilhelm H., 'Das von der "Kynanthropie" handelnde Fragment des Marcellus von Side', *Abhandlungen der philologisch-historischen Classe der königlich sächsischen Gesellschaft der Wissenschaften*, 17 (1897).

Runeberg, Arne, *Witches, Demons and Fertility Magic* (Helsinki, 1947).

Russell, Jeffrey Burton, *Witchcraft in the Middle Ages* (Ithaca and London, 1972).

Russwurm, Carl, *Eibofolke oder die Schweden an den Küstern Ehstlands und auf Runö*, ii (Reval, 1855).

Sala-Molins, Louis, 'Utilisation d'Aristote en droit inquisitorial', in *XVI Colloque International de Tours: Platon et Aristote à la Renaissance* (Paris, 1976), 191–9.

Sarti, Nicoletta, 'Appunti su carcere-custodia e carcere-pena nella dottrina civilistica dei secoli 12–16', *Rivista di storia del diritto italiano*, 53–4 (1980–1), 67–110.

Sbriccoli, M., *Crimen laesae maiestatis* (Milan, 1974).

Scaduto, Mario, 'Tra inquisitori e riformati', *Archivum historicum Societatis Jesu*, 15 (1946), 1–76.

Scarabello, Giovanni, 'La pena del carcere: Aspetti della condizione carceraria a Venezia nei secoli XVI–XVIII: L'assistenza e l'associazionismo', in Gaetano Cozzi (ed.), *Stato, società e giustizia nella repubblica veneta* (sec. XV–XVIII) (Rome, 1980), 317–76.

Schneider, Miklós, *Fejérmegyei boszorkányperek* (Székesfehérvár, 1934).

Schöffer, Ivo, 'Heksengeloof', *Tijdschrift voor Geschiedenis*, 86 (1973).

Schram, Ferenc, *Magyarországi boszorkányperek, 1529–1768* (3 vols.; Budapest, 1970–82).

Schulte, J. Friedrich, von, *Die Geschichte der Quellen und Literatur des canonischen Rechts* (3 vols.; Stuttgart, 1875; repr. Graz, 1956).

Schwarzwälder, H., 'Die Geschichte des Zauber- und Hexenglaubens in Bremen', *Bremisches Jahrbuch*, 46 (1959), 156–233.

Scobie, Alex, 'Strigiform Witches in Roman and other Cultures', *Fabula*, 1–2 (1978), 74–101.

Scribner, Robert, 'Ritual and Popular Religion in Catholic Germany at the Time of the Reformation', *Journal of Ecclesiastical History*, 35 (1984), 47–77.

——, 'Cosmic Order and Daily Life: Sacred and Secular in Pre-industrial German Society', in Kaspar von Greyerz (ed.), *Religion and Society in Early Modern Europe* (London, 1984), 17–32.

Shannon, Albert C., 'The Secrecy of Witnesses in Inquisitorial Tribunals and in Contemporary Secular Trials', in John Mundy (ed.), *Essays in Medieval Life and Thought, Presented in Honor of Austin Patterson Evans* (New York, 1955), 59–69.

Shatzmiller, J., 'Les Juifs de Provence pendant la peste noire', *Revue des études juives*, 133 (1974), 457–80.

Shils, Edward, *Centre and Periphery: Essays in Macrosociology* (Chicago, 1975).

Siuts, H., *Jenseitsmotiven im deutschen Volksmärchen* (Leipzig, 1911).

Sogner, Sölvi, 'Trolldomsprosessene i Norge på 1500–1600-tallet', *Norveg* (1982), 155–82.

Soldan, Wilhelm Gottlieb, *Geschichte der Hexenprozesse* (1843), ed. Max Bauer (2 vols., Munich, 1912).

Soman, Alfred, 'Les Procès de sorcellerie au Parlement de Paris (1565–1640)', *Annales ESC* 32 (1977), 790–812.

——, 'La Sorcellerie vue du Parlement de Paris au début du xviie siècle', *Actes du 104e congrès national des sociétés savantes*, Bordeaux, 1979, Section d'histoire moderne et contemporaine (Paris, 1981).

——, 'Deviance and Criminal Justice in Western Europe, 1300–1800: An Essay in Structure', *Criminal Justice History*, 1 (1980), 1–28.

——, 'La Décriminalisation de la sorcellerie en France', *Histoire, économie et société*, 4 (1985), 179–223.

Spehr, Harald, 'Waren die Germanen "Ekstatiker"?', *Rasse*, 3 (1936), 394–400.

Steward, Charles, 'Nymphomania: Sexuality, Insanity and Problems in Folklore Analysis', in M. Alexiou and V. Lambropoulos (eds.), *The Text and its Margins* (New York, 1985), 219–52.

Stone, Lawrence, *Family, Sex and Marriage in England, 1500–1800* (London, 1977).

Storm, G. (ed.), *Islandske Annaler indtil 1578* (Christiania, 1888).

Strauss, Gerald, 'Success and Failure in the German Reformation', *Past and Present*, 67 (1975), 30–63.

——, *Luther's House of Learning: Indoctrination of the Young in the German Reformation* (London, 1978).

Ström, Folke, *Nordisk hedendom: Tro och sed i förkristen tid* (Lund, 1961).

Švābe, Arveds, *Vecākās zemnieku tiesības* (Riga, 1927).

——, *Livonijas senākās bruņnieku tiesības* (Riga, 1932).

Svedberg, Jesper, *Levernes Beskrifning* (Skr. utg. av Vetenskaps-Societeten i Lund, 25/1; 1941), 110.

Szczucki, Lech, *Philippus Camerarius* (Warsaw, 1984).

Szendrei, János, 'Török Katalin bűnpere', *Történelmi Tár* (1891), 317–34.

Szendrey, Akos, 'Hexe—Hexendruck', *Acta Ethnographica Academiae Scientiarum Hungaricae*, 4 (1955), 129–69.

——, 'A magyar néphit boszorkánya', unpublished (1962).

Szentkirályi, István, 'Garabonciás-per Pécsett', *Pécs-Baranyamegyei Múzeum Egyesület értesítője*, 9 (1917), 1–7.

Szücs, Sándor, 'Időért viaskodó táltosok', *Ethnographia*, 62 (1951), 403–9.

Tarczay, Erzsébet, 'Boszorkányüldözés Horvátországban', *Századok*, 49 (1915), 162–75.

Tazbir, Janusz, 'Hexenprozesse in Polen', *Archiv für Reformationsgeschichte*, 71 (1980), 280–307.

Teall, John, 'Witchcraft and Calvinism in Elizabethan England: Divine Power and Human Agency', *Journal of the History of Ideas*, 23 (1962), 21–36.

Tedeschi, John, 'Preliminary Observations on Writing a History of the Roman Inquisition', in F. Forrester Church and Timothy George (eds.), *Continuity and Discontinuity in Church History* (Leiden, 1979).

——, 'The Roman Inquisition and Witchcraft: An Early 17th-Century "Instruction" on Correct Trial Procedure', *Revue de l'histoire des religions*, 200 (1983), 163–88.

——, 'The Dispersed Archives of the Roman Inquisition', in Gustav Henningsen and John Tedeschi, in association with Charles Amiel (eds.), *The Inquisition in Early Modern Europe* (Dekalb, 1986), 13–32.

Tenenti, Alberto, 'Gli schiavi di Venezia alla fine del '500', *Rivista storica italiana*, 67 (1955), 52–69.

——, *Cristoforo da Canal: La Marine vénitienne avant Lépante* (Paris, 1962).

Teutsch, Friedrich, 'Sächsische Hexenprozesse', *Archiv des Vereins für siebenbürgische Landeskunde*, 39 (1915), 709–803.

Thomas, Keith, 'The Relevance of Social Anthropology to the Historical Study of English Witchcraft', in Mary Douglas (ed.), *Witchcraft Confessions and Accusations* (London, 1970), 47–79.

——, *Religion and the Decline of Magic* (London, 1971; paperback edn. Harmondsworth, 1973).

Thorndike, Lynn, *A History of Magic and Experimental Science* (6 vols.; New York, 1934–58).

Thoroddsen, Þorvaldur, *Landfrœðissaga Islands* (4 vols.; Copenhagen, 1892–1904).

——, *Árferði á Íslandi i þusund ár* (Copenhagen, 1916–17).

Tivadar, Lehoczky, 'Beregmegyei boszorkányperek', *Hazánk*, 8 (1887), 296–306.

Toll, Friedrich, 'Zur Geschichte der Hexenprocesse', *Das Inland*, 17 (1839), 257–63.

Török, Gábor, 'Történeti adatok a küldött farkas mondájához', *Néprajzi közlemények*, 4 (1959), nos. 1–2, pp. 278–88.

Trevor-Roper, Hugh, R., 'The European Witch-craze of the Sixteenth and Seventeenth Centuries', in his *Religion, the Reformation and Other Essays* (London, 1967); also as separate edn., *The European Witch-craze of the 16th and 17th Centuries* (Harmondsworth, 1969).

Trócsányi, Zoltán, *A történelem árnyékában* (Budapest, 1936).

Turner, Victor, 'Witchcraft and Sorcery: Taxonomy versus Dynamics', in his *The Forest of Symbols* (Ithaca and London, 1967), 112–27.

Uuspuu, V., 'Nõiaprotsesse Pärnu Maakohtu arhiivist kuni 1642-ni', *Usuteadusline Ajakiri*, 3–4 (1937), 115–26.

——, *Surmaotsused eesti nõiaprotsessides* (Tartu, 1938).

——, 'Eesti nõiasõnade usulisest iseloomust', *Usuteadusline Ajakiri*, 1 (1938).

Vajda, László, 'Zur phaseologischen Stellung der Schamanismus', *Ural-Altaische Jahrbücher*, 31 (1959), 456–85.

Vassar, Artur, 'Kaltoliku kiriku reaktsioonilisest osast eesti rahvaa ajaloos 12–16 sajandil', *Religiooni ja ateismi ajaloost Eestis* (Tallinn, 1956).

Vauchez, André, *La Sainteté en Occident aux derniers siècles du Moyen Âge* (Rome, 1981).

Vekene, Emil van der, *Bibliotheca bibliographica historiae Sanctae Inquisitionis* (2 vols.; Vaduz, 1982–3).

Viario, Andrea, 'La pena della galera: La condizione dei condannati a bordo delle galere Veneziano', in Gaetano Cozzi (ed.), *Stato, società e giustizia nella repubblica veneta (sec. XV–XVIII)* (Rome, 1980), 377–480.

Vickers, Brian (ed.), *Occult and Scientific Mentalities in the Renaissance* (Cambridge, 1984).

Wallace, D., 'George Gifford, Puritan Propaganda and Popular Religion in Elizabethan England', *Sixteenth-century Journal*, 9 (1978), 27–49.

Weber, Max, *Economy and Society* (1921; English trans. Berkeley, 1978).

Weiser, Lily, 'Zur Geschichte der altgermanischen Todesstrafe und Friedlosigkeit', *Archiv für Religionswissenschaft*, 30 (1933), 210–27.

Wikander, Stig, *Der arische Männerbund: Studien zur inde-iranischen Sprach- und Religionsgeschichte* (Lund, 1938).

Wilson, Monica, 'Witch Beliefs and Social Structure', *American Journal of Sociology* 56 (1951), 307–13.

Winkler, Rudolf, 'Über Hexenwahn und Hexenprozesse in Estland während der Schwedenherrschaft', *Baltische Monatschrift*, 67 (1909).

Wirth, Jean, 'Against the Acculturation Thesis', in Kaspar von Greyerz (ed.), *Religion and Society in Early Modern Europe* (London, 1984), 66–78.

Wittgenstein, Ludwig, *Remarks on Frazer's 'Golden Bough'*, (London, 1979).

Wolf, Eric, 'Aspects of Group Relations in a Complex Society: Mexico', *American Anthropologist*, 58 (1956), 1065–78.

Wolffeldt, M., 'Processe aus auf dem Schlosse vorgefundenen Urkunden', *Mittheilungen aus dem Strafrecht und dem Strafprocess in Livland, Ehstland u. Kurland*, 2 (1848), 199–207.

Wrightson, Keith, *English Society, 1580–1680* (London, 1982).

Zambelli, Paola (ed.), *Scienze, credenze oculte, livelli, di cultura* (Florence, 1982).

Index